Culture
and Values

reproduced on the cover and title page:
Gian Paolo Panini. *View of the Colosseum and the Arch of Constantine.* 1747. Oil on canvas,
2′8¼″ × 4′4½″ (.82 × 1.33 m). Walters Art Gallery, Baltimore. (Cover: detail; title page:
entire work.)

Holt, Rinehart and Winston
New York Chicago San Francisco Philadelphia
Montreal Toronto London Sydney Tokyo
Mexico City Rio de Janeiro Madrid

Culture and Values
A Survey of the Western Humanities

Lawrence Cunningham
The Florida State University

John Reich
The Florida State University

VOLUME I

Publisher Robert Rainier
Editor Karen Dubno
Special Projects Editor Pamela Forcey
Picture Editor Joan Scafarello
Picture Research Marion Geisinger
Picture Research Assistant Andrea Aronson
Copy Editor H. L. Kirk
Editorial Assistant Barbara Curialle
Production Manager Nancy Myers
Art Director Louis Scardino
Book and Cover Design Caliber Design Planning

Composition and camera work York Graphic Services
Color separations The Lehigh Press, Inc.
Printing and binding R. R. Donnelley & Sons Co.

Library of Congress Cataloging in Publication Data

Cunningham, Lawrence.
  Culture and values.

  Includes bibliographies and indexes.
  1. Civilization, Occidental. 2. Europe—Intellectual life.
I. Reich, John. II. Title.
CB245.C86   909′.09821   81-7053

ISBN 0-03-054001-1 (v. 1)   AACR2

 3 4 5 6 039 9 8 7 6 5 4 3

CBS COLLEGE PUBLISHING
Holt, Rinehart and Winston
The Dryden Press
Saunders College Publishing

Literary acknowledgments **13** Reprinted from "The Song of the Harper," translated by Miriam Lichtheim, in *Journal of Near Eastern Studies*, IV (1945), 192–193, by permission of The University of Chicago Press. Copyright © 1945 by The University of Chicago Press. **15–16** Excerpts from "Egyptian Hymns and Prayers," translated by John A. Wilson, in *Ancient Near Eastern Texts Relating to the Old Testament*, ed. James B. Pritchard, 3rd ed. with Supplement (copyright © 1969 by Princeton University Press), pp. 370–371. Reprinted by permission of Princeton University Press. **23, 24–25** From *The Epic of Gilgamesh*, translated by N. K. Sandars (Penguin Classics, rev. ed., 1972), pp. 110–111, 90–93, 114–117. Copyright © 1960, 1964, 1972 by N. K. Sandars. Reprinted by permission of Penguin Books, Ltd. **29** Reprinted from *The Origin and History of Hebrew Law* by J. M. Powis Smith (1931), pp. 183–217, by permission of The University of Chicago Press. Copyright © 1931 by The University of Chicago Press. **44–75** All Bible selections from the Revised Standard Version of the Bible, copyright 1946, 1952, © 1971, 1973. Reprinted by permission of the National Council of the Churches of Christ. **76–77** From pp. 77–79 ("My Dear Fellow Clergymen: . . . within its bounds") in "Letter from Birmingham Jail—April 16, 1963" from *Why We Can't Wait* by Martin Luther King, Jr. Copyright © 1963 by Martin Luther King, Jr. Reprinted by permission of Harper & Row, Publishers, Inc. **98** Excerpt (38 lines) from pp. 260–261 in *The Odyssey of Homer*, translated by Richmond Lattimore. Copyright © 1965, 1967 by Richmond Lattimore. Reprinted by permission of Harper & Row, Publishers, Inc. **100–101, 101–105** Reprinted from the *Iliad* by Homer, translated by Richmond Lattimore (1951), pp. 341–342, 487–493, by permission of The University of Chicago Press. Copyright © 1951 by The University of Chicago Press. **115** From Archilochus, "My Goodly Shield," translated by W. R. Castle, in *Classics in Translation*, Vol. I, p. 94. Madison: The University of Wisconsin Press; copyright © 1952 by the Regents of the University of Wisconsin. **116, 117** Five poems reprinted by permission of Schocken Books, Inc., from *Greek Lyric Poetry*, translated by Willis Barnstone. Copyright © 1962, 1967 by Willis Barnstone. **123–127** From Herodotus, *The Histories*, translated by Aubrey de Selincourt (Penguin Classics, 1954), pp. 419–420, 486–494. Copyright © 1954 by the Estate of Aubrey de Selincourt. Reprinted by permission of Penguin Books, Ltd. **132** From Thucydides, *The Peloponnesian War*, translated by Rex Warner (Penguin Classics, 1954), pp. 24–25. Copyright © 1954 by Rex Warner. Reprinted by permission of Penguin Books, Ltd. **134, 136–137** From *Aeschylus One: Oresteia, Agamemnon, The Libation Bearers, The Eumenides,* translated by Richmond Lattimore, from *The Complete Greek Tragedies,* ed. by Richmond Lattimore and David Grene, pp. 44, 115–120, by permission of The University of Chicago Press. Copyright © 1953 by The University of Chicago Press. **138** From Sophocles, *Antigone,* translated by Shaemus O'Sheel, from *Ten Greek Plays in Contemporary Translations,* ed. with an intro. by L. R. Lind. Riverside Edition No. C19. Copyright © 1957 by L. R. Lind. Reprinted by permission of Houghton Mifflin Company. **140–161** *Oedipus Rex,* translated by Albert Cook. Reprinted by permission of the translator. **162, 162–163** From Euripides, *The Suppliant Women,* translated by L. R. Lind, from *Ten Greek Plays in Contemporary Translations,* ed. with an intro. by L. R. Lind. Riverside Edition No. C19. Copyright © 1957 by L. R. Lind. Reprinted by permission of Houghton Mifflin Company. **174–177, 177–178, 179–181** From *Great Dialogues of Plato,* translated by W. H. D. Rouse, ed. by Eric H. Warmington and Philip G. Rouse. Copyright © 1956 by John Clive Graves Rouse. Reprinted by arrangement with The New American Library, Inc., New York, N.Y. **197** From the *Aeneid* by Vergil, translated by C. Day Lewis. Copyright © 1952 by C. Day Lewis. Reprinted by permission of Literistic, Ltd. **204–207** From Plautus, *Mostellaria,* translated by Harry J. Leon, in *Classics in Translation,* Vol. II, pp. 21–24. Madison: The University of Wisconsin Press; copyright © 1952 by the Regents of the University of Wisconsin. **207–208** From *The Lyric Genius of Catullus,* translated by Eric Alfred Havelock. Oxford, England, Basil Blackwell, 1939; reissued New York, Russell & Russell, 1967. **215–216, 217–223** From the *Aeneid* by Vergil, translated by C. Day Lewis. Copyright © 1952 by C. Day Lewis. Reprinted by permission of Literistic, Ltd.

(continued on page 483)

Photographic credits appear on page 484.

Preface

Our aim when we started to write *Culture and Values* was very simple: to create a readable and reliable textbook for college and university courses in the integrated humanities that would satisfy the standards of instructors and engage the interest of students. We planned to describe, as clearly as we could, the most important landmarks in the Western cultural tradition; we also planned to describe, as enthusiastically as we could, our own reactions to these works. We hoped that the excellence of the works and the passion of their creators would inspire the minds and hearts of students, just as they inspired our own minds and hearts when we first encountered them.

It was one thing to set forth the goal and another to achieve it in a practical way. Early in the project, therefore, we made certain basic decisions derived from our own teaching experience. Those decisions shaped the final character of the work. First, we decided to write the book in a chronological manner. After an Introduction in which we describe the nature and importance of the study of the humanities, we begin with the ancient Near East in Volume I and trace our cultural roots through the Greek, Roman, and Hebrew experience and the subsequent rise of medieval culture as exemplified in the Byzantine and Carolingian periods and the High Middle Ages. A final chapter in Volume I sketches the character of the 14th century, a century that prepares for the Renaissance.

After an Introduction similar to that in Volume I, we begin Volume II with the Florentine Renaissance, trace it to both Rome and the North, and deal with the interaction of the Renaissance and the Reformation, both Protestant and Catholic. The next chapters treat the Baroque, neoclassical, and revolutionary-romantic periods of Europe and America. The final chapters describe the cultural environment between the two world wars and after 1945. In an Epilogue we present three artists from three different fields who epitomize the contemporary spirit but whose work draws heavily on the cultural tradition of the past. The Epilogue brings our work full circle (though each volume has been structured to stand on its own without reference to the other).

We chose the chronological approach because we feel very strongly that students need a better sense of historical perspective. We thought it important to tell our story as an unfolding one, with constant references back to the past and pointers to future developments. This approach is supported by illustrated cultural chronologies, one at the beginning of each chapter, that enable the student to see at a glance what historical and cultural events were occurring at a particular time. The chronological approach is also reinforced by maps that reflect the changing face of the world.

To personalize the history we have included in each volume three "Interludes." Each of these focuses on a particular couple who were emblematic of their own age and whose influence has inspired later periods of art and culture. Antony and Cleopatra, for example, not only help us understand late Republican Rome but also permit us to approach the imaginative genius of Shakespeare and Shaw. We hope, in addition, that the Interludes will help redress the too frequent neglect of women in history and culture.

A second decision we made was to integrate art, philosophy, history, literature, and music as closely as we could in each chapter. In culture, after all, the humanities do interact. We wanted to eliminate any possibility of seeming to give a glimpse of art, a dab of music, a peek at literature. Thus we have tried to show the various humanities working together, mutually touching each other, not flowing in separate currents. In the chapter on the High Middle Ages, for example, we have focused not on art, architecture, and theology as separate disciplines (though of course they are), but on how these disciplines were brought to bear on the construction of the Gothic cathedral.

A third decision we made was to create a textbook self-contained enough to stand as the single text for an integrated humanities course. Accordingly, we have included primary readings in each chapter ranging from entire plays, short stories, essays, and poems to significant excerpts from such works. We have included enough of these readings so that supplementary paperbacks are not necessary. The illustrations, almost 700 in black and white and color, have analytical captions that supplement information in the text. Each chapter also has an annotated bibliography, a selected discography that offers advice on developing one's own record library, and study questions that can be used for classroom discussion or for term papers. Each volume has a glossary of important terms, identified in the text by italics.

Another decision we made was to be selective in what we chose to discuss. Any survey of the humanities runs the risk of becoming an encyclopedia. We have tried to cover those indispensable works and persons that throw light on their own period and provide relevance and illumination for ours. One of the recurring joys of studying the humanities is the shock of recognition when a poem or painting leaps across the centuries and speaks directly about an experience which we had thought uniquely our own.

In deciding what to include we had both an easy time (one *must* speak of the Parthenon and of Shakespeare) and a difficult time: once the masterpieces had been chosen we had to decide what to leave out. No final selection in any of the disciplines will please everyone. Nevertheless, even though others would have come up with a different final list, we are comforted by the thought that instructors may be inspired to fill in where we have been silent.

We have set forth what we consider the very finest that human genius has accomplished, with the hope that people will wish to emulate or better those achievements. A study of human accomplishment in the humanities can well give us criteria to assess and critique the present with some sense of historical and informed perspective. We are a notoriously non-historical-minded people. That is a perilous condition. It was a wise person who said that those who marry only today's fads and customs soon find themselves widowed.

A final word. We have described a few of our decisions and some of our problems in writing this book. We know where our shortcomings are, and our readers will soon find out. Our consolation is that this book is not meant to replace instructors but to serve as an adjunct and an aid as they go about the task of teaching. We trust that they will qualify where we generalize and elaborate where we have been brief.

An Instructor's Manual that covers both volumes is available. It includes useful information on how to use the text, supplementary bibliographies, and suggestions for testing.

In the course of a project this large we were helped by many people who deserve our thanks. Leon Golden, director of the Humanities Program at The Florida State University, initially recommended us to Holt, Rinehart and Winston as authors; Rita Gilbert had the courage to sign us and helped shape the project. To both of them we owe a great debt. We acknowledge the aid and advice of Walter E. Wehrle and David Levenson and the secretarial and clerical help of Kay V. Stops, Dianne Weinstein, Caroline Rowe, and Alberto Vannini. Karen Bickley handled the extensive literary permissions work with efficiency and extreme good will.

Colleagues throughout the country provided helpful criticism. The following read portions of the manuscript: Thomas Cooper, Monroe Community College, New York; Charles Davis, Boise State University, Idaho; Mary Giles, California State University, Sacramento; Peter S. Hoff, University of Wisconsin, Parkside; Doris A. Smith, El Reno Junior College, Oklahoma. The following read the entire manuscript through several drafts and were helpful at every step of the way: Janice L. Allen, Seminole Community College, Florida; Dorothy Corsberg, Northeastern Community College, Colorado; Sister Andrée DuCharme, Silver Lake College, Wisconsin; David McKillop, Grove City College, Pennsylvania; Ethel Quickle, Central State University, Oklahoma. We thank all of these people for their fine work.

The staff at Holt, Rinehart and Winston have been exemplary in their professionalism and concern for this project. Our thanks go to Nancy Myers and Louis Scardino, who, respectively, choreographed the intricate production and design programs. Every author's work should be as professionally cared for from final manuscript to bound book as was ours by Pamela Forcey. Joan Scafarello supervised the massive task of picture research with great care and dedication. H. L. Kirk was unfailingly helpful as copy editor. Special thanks go to Joan Curtis for her work on the chronologies and for help on the initial stages of the picture program. We are particularly grateful to Karen Dubno, who was, at the same time, tough editor, constant supporter, mother confessor, and unfailing friend.

Lastly, we would like to thank Barbara Reich and Cecilia Cunningham, both trained art historians, for their professional help and for being tolerant spouses as this book was being written.

L.C.
J.R.

Contents

2

JERUSALEM AND THE BIBLICAL TRADITION 41

3

EARLY GREECE 91

4

5

8

THE HIGH MIDDLE AGES: THE SEARCH FOR SYNTHESIS 345

9

THE 14TH CENTURY: A TIME OF TRANSITION 427

INTRODUCTION

"History is bunk," said the industrialist Henry Ford. "Those who do not learn the lessons of history are condemned to relive them," wrote the philosopher George Santayana. These judgments are two extremes; yet we often hear variations of them. Some students insist that dates, wars, and reigns are unimportant. Other students—and many professors—maintain that past events give us essential perspective on our own times.

The study of the poetry, music, and arts of bygone ages also brings out strong opinions. This is a complex world of microprocessors, bottom-line economics, and the scramble for entrance into professional school. There are those who ask: Who can afford to spend (some say waste) time on subjects that seem frivolous, or at least distant from the real concerns of this world?

Four centuries ago, there were no conflicting opinions. During the Renaissance and even earlier, the path to prestigious employment in government or the church was through systematic study of the ancient classics—then considered to be the humanities. The tools of diplomacy, government service, and the law were believed to be knowledge of the philosophical and historical achievements of the Greeks and Romans, along with clear and elegant use of the spoken and written language.

In our own time the idea of the humanities as the mastery of classical culture has given way to a much broader understanding. Indeed, what we mean by the humanities today is so broad that once-sharp divisions between academic disciplines seem to blend and blur. For instance, some psychologists, anthropologists, and sociologists like to use the adjective "humanistic," as in "humanistic psychologist," to distinguish themselves from those social scientists who are interested only in rigorous research conducted according to the scientific method. These humanistic social scientists, on the other hand, do not strain to keep their research or writing "value-free," that is, free of judgment. In this text, however, we use the term "humanities" to describe the expression of certain enduring human values in our culture through the medium of the literary, artistic, and musical arts.

The word "value" is important in any discussion of the humanities. It denotes a principle or a quality generally considered to be good, beautiful, valuable, or desirable. "Culture" is another basic word in the humanities. Culture, broadly understood, is the human manipulation of nature. A forest is nature; a garden is culture. Many aspects of culture are utilitarian. People make gardens for food; they build structures for shelter; they cut roads to facilitate movement; they clothe themselves for warmth and health. Beyond this, there is also an almost innate tendency to create gardens with a certain symmetry, to embellish buildings with ornament, to make clothes that look attractive. In short, people invest even their most commonplace activities with certain expressions of their sense of beauty, ego, longing, and power. We all recognize this human tendency. We describe everything from people to music as having class or style or as being cool or hip—expressions that indicate certain values beyond mere utility.

When we study the humanities as a historical tradition we look at examples of the most significant and enduring values in artistic culture. We are interested in those people who have used language with the most intensity; we want to understand how others have expressed the human impulse toward beauty with brush, chisel, pen, or musical notes. Certain superficial reasons for this perspective quickly spring to mind. We need to understand our past; we can be "enriched" by the best experiences of human culture; we must possess certain qualities beyond those needed for merely existing (or even thriving) in the economic sphere. But there are other less cliché-ridden reasons that are more worthy of consideration.

First, there is immense if often unrecognized power in cultural achievement. We tend to think that the humanities are to be found only in museums, libraries, concert halls, or the stage or screen. Worse, we often tacitly assume that the humanities are a highbrow or elitist pastime. Yet, when a society wishes to consolidate total power over its citizens it first tries to silence poets, writers, and artists and then tries to create a culture of its own. There are many examples of this recognition of the power of the humanities: Hitler expelled the prominent writers and artists of his country and replaced them with an official "Nazi culture." In the Soviet Union today the leading dissidents are, by and large, the cultural intelligentsia. It is said that Aleksandr Solzhenitsyn's short novel *One Day in the Life of Ivan Denisovich* revolutionized Russian society in the post-Stalinist period.

In other words, those who create can wield great power. When they feel profound emotion or wish to express an overwhelming idea that boils within them, they search mind and heart for the sharpest word or the most precise image in order to convey that emotion to the consciousness of others. When they succeed, others share the emotion. Obviously, not all who try do succeed. Much bad poetry and atrocious music has been written. But every once in a while someone says it just right or expresses it just so. A survey of the humanities is really a study of some of those who have said it just right—those who have deeply influenced and even inspired others.

At first glance, the humanities seem like a bewildering catalogue of unrelated material. What, for example, do the pyramids of ancient Egypt, the poetry of Catullus, the music of Mozart, and the films of Ingmar Bergman have in common? What could they all say to us here and now? At second glance, the answer is evident. The various landmarks of the humanities reflect a few basic themes that endure even if they are manifested at different times in very different ways. The ancient pyramids reflect a preoccupation with death, as do Bergman's modern films. The nature of the preoccupation is different, but the ancient Egyptian and the modern European both feel impelled to face the basic question of mortality.

A bare familiarity with the "facts" of our cultural tradition (when was this painted? why was that written? where did a certain person live?) will not unlock the power of the humanities or answer the basic questions that they pose. This book cannot do that, either. It can give you some of the "raw materials" and a few hints that will help you listen, look, and read. In the last analysis, however, only the sympathetic aid of your instructor and your own willingness to take the time to think will enable you to get what you really want to get—and should get—from this course.

The point about taking the time needs emphasis. We live in an age that encourages instant intellectual gratification. We are surrounded by millions of television images; we are assaulted by multicolored advertisements; we are encouraged to consume the enormous numbers of instant books, records, and posters that are constantly rolling off presses. All of this becomes "old" in a very short time, only to be replaced by the "new." Inevitably, words, images, and notes are cheapened by such speed. Our eyes and ears become calloused. The "classics" of our cultural tradition, however, cannot be absorbed rapidly. These words, images, and notes are different enough, complex enough, rich enough that we must take the time to look intensely, to listen without distraction, to read with reflection.

Taking time is a difficult and somewhat alien task, but it is worth the effort. A willingness to slow down and reflect—to become a contemplative, if you will—might help all of us to savor once again the power of language and image. That would be a great boon for ordinary life. It would enrich us and, most important, it would help us to be warily skeptical of the almost universal abuse of language and the shallowness of much of our artificial environment.

A study of the humanities will not save your country, your soul, or your bank account. It will, however, give you a whole set of attitudes that support a "better life": a sense of proportion; a feeling for the right word, the correct image, the true note; a certain quizzical skepticism; a thirst for what is striking; a pace in looking and listening; perhaps even the habit of thought and reflection. These attitudes may not sound vitally important, but when you have them you will wonder how you got along without them.

Successful completion of this course with this book as a guide will not give you a complete education in the humanities. It will not even acquaint you with every significant part of the Western cultural tradition. Indeed, one of the agonizing aspects of writing such a book is deciding what to leave out—not what to put in! Nevertheless, there are certain outcomes that we can reasonably expect from this introduction to the humanities.

First, we hope that you will acquire a basic literacy in the humanities. That is, we hope that the main lines of our cultural past, as it derives from its Greek and Judaic sources, will become visible in its historical unfolding. We also hope that you will acquire a beginning vocabulary of technical terms to discuss the various arts.

Second, we emphasize in the text and in the illustrations that the landmarks of the past—musical, artistic, and literary—are not curious relics but the embodiment of enduring values and ideas. These ideas and values may be expressed differently today, but they themselves persist. By a historical study of our cultural tradition you should acquire a sense of the continuity and inventiveness of the human creative spirit. We point out that each particular creative landmark is a reflection of a certain culture and its values; at the same time we try to show that later generations have absorbed the meaning of that landmark and used it in new and pertinent ways. As a student of the humanities you will be concerned not only with the interrelation of the arts at a given period but also with the persistence of specific artistic ideas or insights over the long run of history. The cowboy film, for instance, may seem to be a typically American phenomenon, but tales of rugged individuals subduing nature and the animal world and battling evil are, in fact, as old as literature itself. The humanities student learns to recognize those threads that link us to the common heritage of the human experience.

Finally, we very much hope you will develop a genuine love for the humanities. We recognize that many of you will devote very little of your academic career to the study of the humanities and that not everyone is tempted to enter a career as a professional critic or student of the arts. Yet we strongly feel that every student should have the opportunity to acquire enough knowledge of and taste for the arts to reap the many nonacademic rewards the humanities can bring to a person's life. Furthermore, the cultivation of such interests is beneficial for us not only as individuals but also as members of a society. A lifelong interest in the humanities helps us to a better use of leisure time for personal enrichment. It also makes us impatient with the shoddy and second-rate aspects of the society we have in common. It is not an exaggeration to say that the humanities reflect the best that we as a people have accomplished and, further, that they provide the ideas, experiences, and insights that enrich us as both individuals and citizens. There is no way to measure these rewards. They are often personal and private. Incalculable satisfaction by its very nature cannot be measured. And yet it is what those who have permitted themselves the richness of an encounter with the humanities receive. The humanities give us the simple pleasure of wonder at the manifold gifts of humanity. Wonder, as Aristotle observed long ago, is the beginning of wisdom.

PREHISTORY

2,000,000 B.C. ——————————

c. 100,000 First ritual
burying of dead

c. 15,000–10,000 Cave art at
Lascaux and Altamira

c. 15,000–10,000 *Venus of
Willendorf;* worship of female
creative power

Hunting predominates

Stone weapons

**PALEOLITHIC PERIOD
(OLD STONE AGE)**

8000 ——————————

Domestication of animals;
cultivation of food

Villages formed

First wars

c. 5000 Pottery invented

First large-scale
architecture; bronze tools

**NEOLITHIC PERIOD
(LATE STONE AGE)**

3000 ——————————

Most dates are approximate

EGYPT

8000 B.C. ——————————

3200–2700 PREDYNASTIC PERIOD

c. 3100 Development of hieroglyphic writing

3000 ——————————

2700–2250 OLD KINGDOM: development of
mummification ritual; art reflects confidence and certainty

c. 2650 Imhotep constructs first pyramid for King Zoser
at Saqqara

2650–2514 Great Pyramids
and Sphinx built at Giza

c. 2470 *Seated Scribe,* from Saqqara

2250–1990 FIRST INTERMEDIATE PERIOD

1990–1790 MIDDLE KINGDOM: art reflects new
uncertainty

c. 1900 "Song of the Harper"

c. 1878–1841 Reign of Sesostris III; Portrait: *Sesostris III*

1790–1570 SECOND INTERMEDIATE PERIOD

1570–1185 NEW KINGDOM

1379–1362 Reign of Amenhotep IV (Akhenaton);
religious and political reform; worship of single god
Aton; capital moved from Thebes to Tel el-Amarna;
naturalism in art

BRONZE AGE

c. 1370 Portrait: *Nefertiti;* Akhenaton,
"Hymn to Aton"

1361–1352 Reign of Tutankhamen;
return to conservatism

1298–1232 Reign of Ramses II;
colossal buildings constructed at
Luxor, Karnak, Abu Simbel

1185–500 LATE PERIOD: Egypt's
power declines; artists revert to
Old Kingdom styles

1000 ——————————

**IRON AGE
(1000 B.C.–)**

671–663 Assyrian occupation of Egypt

600 ——————————

**NEOLITHIC
PERIOD**

The Beginnings of Civilization

c. 6000 Introduction of new
agricultural techniques from the East

3500–2350 SUMERIAN
PERIOD: development of
pictographic writing;
construction of first ziggurats;
cult of mother goddess

c. 3000 *Lady
of Warka*

c. 2700 Reign
of Gilgamesh

c. 2600–2400 *Ram in a
Thicket,* from Royal Cemetery
at Ur

2350–2150 AKKADIAN
PERIOD: rule of Sargon and
descendants; ended by
invasion of Gutians from Iran

2330–2320 *Head of Akkadian
king,* probably Sargon

c. 2300 *Stele of Naram-Sin*

2150–1900 NEO-SUMERIAN
PERIOD

2100–2000 Construction of
ziggurat at Ur

c. 2100 Gudea, governor of
Lagash

c. 2000 Earliest version of *The
Epic of Gilgamesh*

1900–1600 BABYLONIAN
PERIOD

1792–1750 *The Law Code of
Hammurabi*

c. 1760 *Stele of
Hammurabi*

1600–1150 KASSITE
PERIOD

1150–612 ASSYRIAN
PERIOD

883–859 Reign of
Assurnasirpal II; palace at
Nimrud

668–626 Reign of
Assurbanipal; palace at
Nineveh

612 Fall of Nineveh

2800–2000 Early Minoan Period on
Crete; growth of Cycladic culture

c. 2500 Cycladic idol

2000–1600 Middle
Minoan Period on
Crete; construction of
palace complexes;
development of linear
writing

c. 1700 Knossos Palace destroyed by
earthquake and rebuilt on grander scale;
Wasp Pendant, from Mallia

1600–1400 Late Minoan Period on Crete

c. 1600 First Mycenaean palace constructed;
Royal Grave Circle at Mycenae

c. 1600 *Snake Goddess,* from Knossos

c. 1550 Gold death
mask, from
Mycenae

1500 Frescoes from House Delta, Thera

1400 Fall of Knossos and decline of
Minoan civilization

1400–1200 Mycenaean empire
flourishes

1250 Mycenaean war against Troy

100 Final collapse of Mycenaean
power

1100–1000 DARK AGE

1000–750 HEROIC AGE

c. 900–700 Evolution of Homeric
epics *Iliad* and *Odyssey*

750–600 AGE OF COLONIZATION

The Western Cultural Tradition

The Western cultural tradition first began almost three thousand years ago with the Greeks. This tradition spread from the Mediterranean basin throughout all of Europe and, in due course, to the New World. From age to age and place to place, though the tradition has taken on new forms and faced new problems, a basic unity has always linked the many diverse stages in its development. It is this unity that justifies us in thinking of our cultural tradition as a continuous one.

The unity is twofold: intellectual and historical. From the time of the Greeks, artists, writers, and thinkers in the Western tradition have all shared many of the same intellectual concerns. One of the principal areas they have explored is the relationship of individual human beings to the world around them and, in particular, to each other. Their approach has been recognizably different from that of other cultures. For example, the concept of romantic love, although by no means unique to the Western tradition, has played a stronger part in it than in other cultural traditions. Another example of a recurring theme in Western thought has been the importance of social justice—though all too often practice has not lived up to the ideal.

Most striking of all in the West has been the continuing attempt to discover a purpose for existence and to relate that purpose to the universal fact of death. With the rise of Christianity, the two great streams of Western thought, the classical and the Judeo-Christian, merged to provide new and complex answers to these questions—answers that often have in turn raised new, equally complex questions.

As we move now into a world where Western culture no longer dominates but takes its place among equals, it becomes increasingly clear that the problems that challenged the earlier formers of our tradition are no nearer solutions. We may have little chance of solving them ourselves, but there is some comfort in at least identifying them and seeing how others have tried to deal with them.

The purpose for existence—a central problem—has been questioned in all cultures throughout history. In the Western cultural tradition, however, there has been a continuous attempt to come to grips with it by approaching it intellectually. Such an approach is certainly not to be considered superior. In fact, Western culture has paid a price for its obsessive drive to understand. It is notably deficient in faith. It tends always to search for rational solutions to problems, ignoring the very real possibilities offered by instinctive solutions. But, for better or worse, Western culture has produced this continuous tradition of intellectual inquiry of which we are the heirs.

Tradition depends on history—the sense of historical continuity that is the other part of the basic unity in Western culture. The Western cultural tradition has evolved through a continual building on the past. Some achievements and events of the past have been deliberately imitated; others have been deliberately disregarded. But whether the reaction to past events has been positive or negative, the Western tradition has always been firmly aware of their existence. This sense of history is not, of course, unique to our tradition. All cultures have their own history. But our history is in a real sense ours. Greek philosophers like Aristotle or Renaissance artists like Michelangelo

1 *Venus of Willendorf.* Lower Austria, c. 15,000–10,000 B.C. Limestone, height 4⅜″ (11 cm). Natural History Museum, Vienna. This tiny statuette is one of a series of female figurines from the Upper Paleolithic period that are known as Venus figures. The statuette, which has no facial features, is evidently a fertility symbol.

have permanently changed the way we think and see; Confucius or Chinese artists have not. Only in the last hundred years or so has contact with non-Western cultures enriched our own.

Our art and civilization did not begin in Greece. Long before the Greeks other peoples had already constructed societies and created works of art. In fact, the basic advances that made possible the growth of Western civilization were first achieved by the earlier civilizations of the ancient Middle East.

These ancient peoples were the first who systematically produced food, mined and processed metals, organized themselves into cities, and devised legal and moral codes of behavior, together with systems of government and religion. In all these areas they had a profound influence on later peoples. At the same time they produced a major artistic tradition which, quite apart from its high intrinsic interest, was to have a number of effects on the development of Western art.

To discover the origins of Western civilization, therefore, we must look at cultures that at first seem remote in both time and place. Yet these peoples produced the achievements described in this chapter—achievements that form the background to the history of our own culture.

The Earliest People and Their Art

Even the earliest civilizations appeared relatively late in human history, at the beginning of the period known as the Neolithic or Late Stone Age (c. 8000 B.C.). The process of human evolution is long and confusing, and many aspects of it remain uncertain. Our first ancestors probably appeared between a million and half a million years ago, in the Paleolithic period or Old Stone Age. For most of the succeeding millennia, people were dominated by the physical forces of geography and climate, able to keep themselves alive only by a persistent search for food and shelter. Those who chose the wrong places or the wrong methods did not survive, while others were preserved by their instincts or good fortune.

Primitive conditions hardly encouraged the growth of civilization, yet there is some evidence of a kind of intellectual development. Archaeological evidence has shown that about one hundred thousand years ago the ancestors of *Homo sapiens* belonging to the type known as Neanderthal people were the first to bury their dead carefully and place funerary offerings in the graves—the earliest indication of the existence of religious beliefs.

Toward the end of the Paleolithic period, around 15,000 B.C., there was a major breakthrough. The human desire for self-expression resulted in the invention of visual art. The cave paintings of Lascaux and Altamira and statuettes like the *Venus of Willendorf* are among the earliest products of the human creative urge. Although the art of this remote age would be valuable for its historical significance alone, many of the paintings and statues can stand as masterpieces in their own right. The lines are concentrated but immensely expressive. In some cases artists used the surface on which they were painting to create an added sense of realism—a bulge on a cave wall suggested the hump of a bull [Plate 1, page 21]. The combination of naturalistic observation and abstraction can only be described as sophisticated. It is not at all surprising that since their discovery in our own century the paintings have served as a powerful inspiration to modern eyes.

The choice of subjects tells us something about the world view of Paleolithic people. The earliest cave paintings show animals and hunting, not surprising as these played a vital part in providing food and clothing. More significant, perhaps, is the fact that all the oldest known statuettes of human figures represent women, who are shown with their sexual characteristics emphasized or enlarged [1]. The Paleolithic world perhaps saw woman's practical role—the source of birth and life—as symbolic of a more profound feminine life force that underlay the masculine world of the hunt. Worship of female creative power was also to play an important part in the religion of the ancient Middle East and of Bronze Age Greece. Even though the Greeks of a later period emphasized other aspects of human power, reverence for a mother goddess or Earth Mother was to live on.

The Neolithic period (c. 8000 B.C.) represents in all aspects a major break with the past. After a million years of hunting, ways to domesticate animals and cultivate food were discovered. People began to gather together in villages where they could lead a settled existence. The development of improved farming techniques made it possible for a community to accumulate stores of grain and thereby become less dependent for their survival on a good harvest each year. But these stores provided a motive for raids by neighboring communities. Thus war, for the first time in human history, became profitable. Other more constructive changes followed at a rapid pace. Pottery was invented around 5000 B.C. and not long afterward metal began to replace stone as the principal material for tools and weapons. The first metal used was copper, but it was soon discovered that an alloy of copper and tin would produce a much stronger metal, bronze. The use of bronze became widespread, giving its name to the Bronze Age, which lasted from around 3000 B.C. to the introduction of iron around 1000 B.C.

At the beginning of the Bronze Age, large-scale architecture began to appear. The fortified settlements which had been established in Egypt and Mesopotamia now were able to develop those aspects of existence which entitle them to be called the first true civilizations.

Egypt and Mesopotamia have much in common. Their climates are similar, and both are dominated by great rivers, Egypt by the Nile and Mesopotamia by the Tigris and Euphrates (see map below). Yet each was to develop its own distinct culture and make its own contribution to the history of civilization.

Ancient Egypt

One major determinant in the development of ancient Egyptian culture was geography. In total area, ancient Egypt was only a little larger than the State of Maryland. At the delta of the Nile was Lower Egypt, broad and flat, within easy reach of neighboring parts of the Mediterranean. Upper Egypt, more isolated from foreign contacts, consisted of a long narrow strip of fertile soil, hemmed in by high cliffs and desert, running on either side of the Nile for most of its 1250 miles (2000 kilometers). Since rainfall was very sparse along the Nile, agriculture depended on the yearly flooding of the river.

The immensely long span of Egyptian history was divided into 31 dynasties by an Egyptian priest, Manetho, who wrote a *History of Egypt* in Greek around 280 B.C. Modern scholars still follow his system, putting the dynasties into four groups and calling the period that preceded them the Predynastic. The four main divisions, with their approximate dates, are: the Old Kingdom, c. 2700 B.C., the Middle

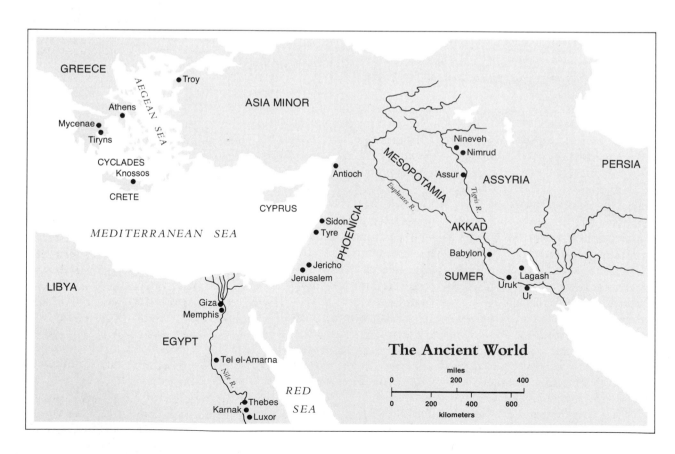

The Ancient World

Kingdom, c. 1990 B.C., the New Kingdom, c. 1570 B.C., and the Late Period, c. 1185 B.C. until Egypt was absorbed into the Persian empire around 500 B.C. The periods were separated from one another by intermediate times of disturbances and confusion.

In spite of its long history, the most striking feature of Egyptian culture is its unity and consistency. Nothing is in stronger contrast to the process of dynamic change initiated by the Greeks and still characteristic of our own culture than the relative absence of change of Egyptian art, religion, language, and political structure over thousands of years. Naturally, even the Egyptians were subject to outside influences, and events at home and abroad affected their world view. It is possible to trace a mood of increasing pessimism from the vital, life-affirming spirit of the Old Kingdom to the New Kingdom vision of death as an escape from the grim realities of life. Nevertheless, the Egyptians maintained a strong resistance to change. Their art, in particular, remained conservative and rooted in the past.

In a land where regional independence already existed in the natural separation of Upper from Lower Egypt, national unity was maintained by a strong central government firmly controlled by a single ruler, the pharaoh. He was regarded as a living god, the equal of any other deity. He had absolute power, although the execution of his orders depended on a large official bureaucracy whose influence tended to increase in time.

Beneath the pharaoh were the priests, who saw as their responsibility the preservation of traditional religious beliefs. One of the most fundamental of these was the concept of divine kingship involving the pharaoh himself, a concept that reflected the Egyptian view of creation. The first great god of Egyptian religion, the Sun god Aton-Ra, had created the world by imposing order on the primeval chaos of the universe; in the same way, the pharaoh ordered and controlled the visible world.

The most striking aspect of Egyptian religious thought, however, is its obsession with immortality and the possibilities of life after death. All Egyptians, not only the ruling class, were offered the hope of survival in the next world as a reward for a good life, a survival that was thought of in literal, physical terms. Elaborate funeral rituals began to develop at which the dead would be judged and passed as worthy to move on to the next life. The god who presided over these ceremonies was Osiris [2]. The worship of Osiris, his wife Isis, and their son, the falcon

2 Painted relief from the funerary temple of Sethos I at Abydos. c. 1300 B.C. Sethos in the guise of the god Osiris, standing at left, is conversing with Thoth, the ibis-headed god of writing.

god Horus, which came in time to symbolize a sense of spiritual afterlife, as opposed to simple material survival, represented the mystical side of Egyptian religion.

At the same time the Egyptians worshiped a host of other deities, subdeities, and nature spirits, whose names were often confused and sometimes interchangeable. These deities, responsible for all aspects of existence, inspired mythology and ritual that affected the daily life of every Egyptian. The deities included Hathor, the goddess of beauty and love, often represented as a cow; Bes, the god of war; and Hapi, the god of the Nile. A number of animals, like the jackal and the cat, also had special sacred significance.

Traditional Egyptian religion involved, then, a bewildering confusion of deities whose rights and privileges were jealously guarded by their priests. One of the ways to worship them was to give them visible form in works of art—a principal function of

3 Great Pyramids at Giza. Right: Pyramid of Cheops, the largest of the three. c. 2650 B.C. Height 449′ (136.86 m), original height 482′ (146.91 m), base 755′ (230.12 m) square. Center: Pyramid of Chefren. c. 2600 B.C. Left: Pyramid of Mycerinus. c. 2575 B.C. The small pyramids of three of Mycerinus' queens are in front of his pyramid.

Egyptian artists. Egyptian art as a whole, in fact, like every aspect of Egyptian life, was conditioned by religion. In addition to producing images of deities, artists were required to provide temples and shrines where they could be worshiped. Even the buildings that commemorated the names and deeds of real people served religious purposes. Thus the same central authority that controlled religion affected the development of the arts. The pharaoh's court laid down the standards applied throughout Egypt. Individual artists had little opportunity to exercise their own ingenuity by deviating from them.

Art and Literature in the Old and Middle Kingdoms

The huge scale of many Egyptian works of art is at least in part the result of the easy availability of stone, the most frequently used material from the early Old Kingdom to the Late Period. In the Third Dynasty,

the architect Imhotep used stone to construct the earliest pyramid as a tomb for his master, the pharaoh Zoser. This began the tradition of building massive funerary monuments which would serve to guarantee immortality for their occupants. At the same time, the practice of mummification developed. The body was embalmed to preserve its physical form, since Egyptian religious belief held that preservation of the body was necessary for the survival of the soul. Imhotep himself, who is, incidentally, the first architect known to history, was in later ages regarded as the epitome of wisdom and was deified.

The great age of the pyramid came in the Fourth Dynasty with the construction of the three colossal pyramids at Giza for the pharaohs Cheops, Chefren, and Mycerinus [3]. In size and abstract simplicity, these pyramids show Egyptian skill in design and engineering on a massive scale—a scale made possible only by slave labor. The pyramids and almost all other Egyptian works of art perpetuate the memories

4 Sphinx at Giza. c. 2540–2514 B.C. Limestone; length 240′ (73.2 m), height 65′ (19.83 m). The lion's body symbolizes immortality. The pharaohs were often buried in lion skins. About 500 yards (457 meters) away are the Pyramids of Chefren, right, and Mycerinus.

of members of the upper classes, but their life style would not have been possible without slaves. There were also many poor Egyptians who were farmers. We still know little about the farmers and slaves.

The construction of the pyramids was an elaborate and complex affair. Stone quarried on the spot formed the core of each structure, but the fine limestone blocks used for facing came from across the Nile. These were quarried in the dry season; then when the floods came they were ferried across the river, cut into shape, and dragged into place. At the center of each pyramid was a chamber in which was placed the mummified body of the pharaoh, surrounded by the treasures which were to follow him into the next life. These massive constructions the pharaohs planned as their resting places for eternity and as monuments that would perpetuate their names. Their success was partial. Four and a half thousand years later, their names are remembered— their pyramids, still dominating the flat landscape,

symbolize the enduring character of ancient Egypt. As shelters for their occupants and their treasures, however, they were vulnerable. The very size of the pyramids drew attention to the riches hidden within them, and robbers were quick to tunnel through and plunder them, sometimes only shortly after the burial chamber had been sealed.

Chefren, who commissioned the second of the three pyramids at Giza, was also responsible for perhaps the most famous of all Egyptian images, the colossal Sphinx [4], a guardian for his tomb. The aloof tranquility of the human face, perhaps a portrait of the pharaoh, set on a lion's body made an especially strong impression fifteen hundred years later on the Classical Greeks, who saw it as a divine symbol of the mysterious and enigmatic. Greek art makes frequent use of the sphinx as a motif, and it also appears in Greek mythology, most typically in the story of how Oedipus solved its riddle and thereby saved the Greek city of Thebes from disaster.

The appearance of Chefren himself is preserved for us in a number of statues that are typical of Old Kingdom art [5]. The sculptor's approach to anatomy and drapery is realistic, and details are shown with great precision. But the features of the pharaoh are idealized; it is a portrait not of an individual but of the concept of divine power, power symbolized by the falcon god Horus perched behind the pharaoh's head. The calmness, even indifference, of the expression is particularly striking. In other works of the same period there are sometimes more expressiveness and individuality, as in a limestone statuette of a seated scribe [6], but the general spirit remains one of calm certainty in the face of both life and death.

left: 5 *Chefren.* Giza, c. 2560 B.C. Dark green diorite, height 5′ (1.52 m). Egyptian Museum, Cairo.

left below: 6 *Seated Scribe.* Saqqara, c. 2470 B.C. Painted limestone, height 21″ (53 cm). Louvre, Paris.

below: 7 *Sesostris III.* c. 1878–1841 B.C. Black granite, height 4′10½″ (1.5 m). Egyptian Museum, Cairo.

The art of the Old Kingdom reflects a mood of confidence and certainty which was brought to an abrupt end around 2200 B.C. by a period of violent disturbance. Divisions between the regions began to strengthen the power of local governors. By the time of the Middle Kingdom, it was no longer possible for pharaoh, priests, or nobles to face the future with complete trust in divine providence. Middle Kingdom art reflects this new uncertainty in two ways. On the one hand, the Old Kingdom came to represent a kind of Golden Age; artists tried to recapture its lofty serenity in their own works. At the same time, the more troubled spirit of the new period is reflected in the massive weight and somber expressions of some of the official portraits. The furrowed brow and grim look of Sesostris III convey the impression that to be a Middle Kingdom pharaoh was hardly a very relaxing occupation [7].

The pharaoh's more humble subjects, however, could find ways to escape from the uncertainties of life not open to one still regarded as divine. A remarkable song of this period still exists; it expresses the disillusion with which some of Sesostris' contemporaries looked back to past glories, but it also gives a recipe for present happiness. In its cynical advice to forget both the past and the future and live only for today it strikes a note that has reverberated through the ages, from Horace's advice to his fellow Romans, *carpe diem* (seize the day), to the great medieval Persian poet Omar Khayyám, best known for Edward Fitzgerald's 19th-century English version of his *Rubáiyát*.

SONG OF THE HARPER

One generation passes away
And others remain in its place
Since the time of the ancestors.
The gods that were aforetime
Rest in their pyramids;
Nobles and glorified likewise
Are buried in their pyramids.
They that built houses,
Their places are no more;
What has been done with them?   10
I have heard the sayings of Imhotep and Djedefhor,
With whose words men still speak so much;
What are their places?
Their walls have crumbled,
Their places are no more,
As if they had never been.
None cometh from thence

That he might tell their circumstances,
That he might tell their needs
And content our heart   20
Until we have reached the place
Whither they have gone.
May thy heart be cheerful
To permit the heart to forget
The making of funerary services for thee.
Follow thy desire while thou livest!
Put myrrh upon thy head,
Clothe thyself in fine linen,
Anoint thee with the genuine wonders
Which are the god's own.   30
Increase yet more thy happiness,
And let not thy heart languish;
Follow thy desire and thy good,
Fashion thine affairs on earth
After the command of thy heart.
That day of lamentation will come to thee,
When the Still of Heart does not hear their lamentation,
And mourning does not deliver a man from the netherworld.
Make holiday!
Do not weary thereof!   40
Lo, none is allowed to take his goods with him,
Lo, none that has gone has come back!

The Art of the New Kingdom

In spite of increasing contacts with foreign cultures, New Kingdom artists continued basically to work within age-old traditions. In the Eighteenth Dynasty, however, there was a remarkable change. The pharaoh Amenhotep IV, who ruled from 1379 to 1362 B.C., single-handedly attempted a total reform of Egyptian religious and political life. He replaced the numberless deities of traditional religion with a single one, the sun god Aton, and changed his own name to Akhenaton, or "the servant of Aton." In order to make these revolutionary changes more effective and to escape from the influence of the priests at the royal court of Thebes, he moved the capital to a new location, known today as Tel el-Amarna.

Here a new kind of art developed. The weight and idealism of the traditional style gave way to a new lightness and naturalism. For the first time, physical characteristics are depicted in detail, and scenes are relaxed and even humorous. A stone relief showing the royal couple and three of their children sitting quietly under the rays of the sun disc is an astonishing departure from the dignified style of the preceding thousand years [8]. Queen Nefertiti herself is the subject of perhaps the most famous of all Egyptian portraits [Plate 2, page 21], a sculpture that shows none of the exaggeration to which Amarna art is sometimes prone, but a grace and elegance very different from earlier official portraits.

All these artistic changes were, of course, the result of Akhenaton's sweeping and revolutionary religious reforms. These reforms did not last long. Akhenaton's belief in a single god who ruled the universe was threatening to the priests, who had a vested interest in preserving the old polytheistic traditions. Not surprisingly, Akhenaton's successors branded him a heretic and fanatic and cut his name out of all the monuments that survived him.

If Akhenaton's monotheism is unique for his culture, so is the profound sincerity with which he expresses his devotion to the sun god in the "Hymn to Aton." Its essential humanity finds a moving counterpart in the surviving portraits of the pharaoh [9].

8 *Akhenaton, Nefertiti, and Three of Their Children.* Amarna, c. 1370–1350 B.C. Limestone relief, height 17" (43 cm). Egyptian Museum, State Museums, West Berlin. The naturalism of this relief, which verges on sentimentality, is typical of late Amarna art.

9 *Akhenaton.* Karnak, c. 1375 B.C. Sandstone, more than twice lifesize. Egyptian Museum, Cairo. This is a fragment of one of more than 30 statues of Akhenaton that were set up in the early years of his reign in the Temple of Aton at Karnak.

14

HYMN TO ATON

Thou appearest beautifully on the horizon of
  heaven,
Thou living Aton, the beginning of life!
When thou art arisen on the eastern horizon,
Thou has filled every land with thy beauty.
Thou art gracious, great, glistening, and high
  over every land;
Thy rays encompass the lands to the limit of all
  that thou hast made:
As thou art Re, thou reachest to the end of
  them;
Thou subduest them for thy beloved son.
Though thou art far away, thy rays are on earth;
Though thou art in their faces, no one knows
  thy going.   10

When thou settest in the western horizon,
The land is in darkness, in the manner of death.
They sleep in a room, with heads wrapped up,
Nor sees one eye the other.
All their goods which are under their heads
  might be stolen,
But they would not perceive it.
Every lion is come forth from his den;
All creeping things, they sting.
Darkness is a shroud, and the earth is in stillness,
For he who made them rests in his horizon.   20

At daybreak, when thou arisest on the horizon,
When thou shinest as the Aton by day,
Thou drivest away the darkness and givest thy
  rays.
The Two Lands are in festivity every day,
Awake and standing upon their feet,
For thou hast raised them up.
Washing their bodies, taking their clothing.
Their arms are raised in praise at thy appear-
  ance.
All the world, they do their work. . . .

Creator of seed in women,   30
Thou who makest fluid into man,
Who maintainest the son in the womb of his
  mother,
Who soothest him with that which stills his
  weeping,
Thou nurse even in the womb,
Who givest breath to sustain all that he has
  made!
When he descends from the womb to breathe
On the day when he is born,
Thou openest his mouth completely,
Thou suppliest his necessities.
When the chick in the egg speaks within the
  shell,   40

Thou givest him breath within it to maintain
  him.
When thou hast made him his fulfillment within
  the egg, to break it,
He comes forth from the egg to speak at his
  completed time;
He walks upon his legs when he comes forth
  from it. . . .

How manifold it is, what thou hast made!
They are hidden from the face of man.
O sole god, like whom there is no other!
Thou didst create the world according to thy
  desire,
Whilst thou wert alone:
All men, cattle, and wild beasts,   50
Whatever is on earth, going upon its feet,
And what is on high, flying with its wings.

The countries of Syria and Nubia, the land of
  Egypt,
Thou settest every man in his place,
Thou suppliest their necessities:
Everyone has his food, and his time of life is
  reckoned.
Their tongues are separate in speech,
And their natures as well;
Their skins are distinguished,
As thou distinguishest the foreign peoples.   60
Thou makest a Nile in the underworld,
Thou bringest it forth as thou desirest
To maintain the people of Egypt
According as thou madest them for thyself,
The lord of all of them, wearying himself with
  them,
The lord of every land, rising for them,
The Aton of the day, great of majesty.

All distant foreign countries, thou makest their
  life also,
For thou hast set a Nile in heaven,
That it may descend for them and make waves
  upon the mountains,   70
Like the great green sea,
To water their fields in their towns.
How effective they are, thy plans, O lord of
  eternity!
The Nile in heaven, it is for the foreign peoples
And for the beasts of every desert that go upon
  their feet;
While the true Nile comes from the underworld
  for Egypt. . . .

Thou art in my heart,
And there is no other that knows thee
Save thy son [Akhenaton],
For thou hast made him well-versed in thy
  plans and in thy strength.   80

10 The first view of the treasures of Tutankhamen: this is what Howard Carter saw when he opened the doorway of the antechamber of the tomb of Tutankhamen on November 26, 1922. The objects include three gilt couches in the form of animals and, at the right in back, the pharaoh's golden throne. The tomb itself was opened three months later.

The world came into being by thy hand,
According as thou hast made them.
When thou hast risen they live,
When thou settest they die.
Thou art lifetime thy own self,
For one lives only through thee.

Eyes are fixed on beauty until thou settest.
All work is laid aside when thou settest in the
    west.
But when thou risest again,
Everything is made to flourish for the king, . . .
Since thou didst found the earth   91
And raise them up for thy son,
Who came forth from thy body:
the King of Upper and Lower Egypt, . . . Akh-
    en-Aton, . . . and the Chief Wife of the King
    . . . Nefert-iti, living and youthful forever
    and ever.

The reaction against Akhenaton's religious reforms and the Amarna style was almost immediate. His successor, Tutankhamen, however, is remembered not for leading the reaction, nor indeed for any event in his short life. He owes his fame to the treasures found intact in his unrobbed tomb. These sumptuous gold objects, enriched with ivory and precious stones, still show something of the liveliness of Amarna art, but a return to conservatism is beginning, and in fact by the Nineteenth and Twentieth Dynasties Akhenaton and his age had been completely forgotten.

In any case, it is not so much for what they reveal about the trends in art that the treasures of Tutankhamen are significant. The discovery of the tomb is important for a different reason. Our knowledge of the cultures of the ancient world is constantly being

11 Temple of Ramses II at Abu Simbel. c. 1257 B.C. Height of statues about 60′ (18.3 m). These four huge statues, erected in commemoration of Ramses' military victories, are all of the pharaoh himself. Between and near the feet are small statues of Ramses' mother, wife, and children. Below are statues of the pharaoh as the god Osiris and the falcon god Horus, to whom the temple was dedicated. (This photograph shows the temple in its original site. In 1968 the whole temple was moved to higher ground to save it from submersion in the new Aswan Dam reservoir.)

revised by the discoveries of archaeologists; many of these finds are minor, but some are major and spectacular. When major finds are made, such as the tomb of Tutankhamen, the process of uncovering the past sometimes becomes as exciting and significant as what is discovered. The long search conducted by Howard Carter in the Valley of the Kings, which culminated in the opening of the inner chamber of the sealed tomb of Tutankhamen on February 17, 1923, and the discovery of the intact sarcophagus of the king, has become part of history [10].

The excavations of Knossos and Mycenae, discussed later in this chapter, and the discovery of Pompeii (Chapter 5) are also major turning points in the growth of our knowledge of the past. But sensational finds like these are exceptions. Understanding

the cultural achievements of past civilizations involves a slow and painstaking series of minor discoveries, each of which adds to the knowledge that thus must be constantly revised and reinterpreted.

By the end of the New Kingdom the taste for monumental building had returned. The temples constructed during the reign of Ramses II (1298–1232 B.C.) at Luxor, Karnak, and Abu Simbel are probably the most colossal of all Egyptian buildings [11]. Within a century, however, internal dissensions and foreign events had produced a sharp decline in Egypt's power. Throughout the Late Period, artists reverted again to the styles of earlier periods. Tombs were once again constructed in the shape of pyramids, as they had been in the Old Kingdom, and sculptors tried to recapture the realism and sense of volume of Old and Middle Kingdom art. Even direct contacts with the Assyrians, Persians, and Greeks—during the period between the Assyrian occupation of 671–663 B.C. and Alexander's conquest of Egypt in 331 B.C.—produced little effect on late Egyptian art.

To the end of their history, the Egyptians remained faithful to their three-thousand-year-old tradition. Probably no other culture in human history has ever demonstrated so strong a conservatism and determination to preserve its separate traditions.

12 *Top:* Picture writing: limestone tablet from Kish. c. 3500 B.C. Ashmolean Museum, Oxford. *Center:* Hieroglyphics: detail of a pillar of a festival building of Sesostris I, Karnak. c. 1940 B.C. Egyptian Museum, Cairo. *Bottom:* Cuneiform: detail of the *Stele of Hammurabi* (see figure 20). c. 1760 B.C. The limestone tablet is the oldest known example of picture writing. Among the signs are several representing parts of the human body, including a head, hand, and foot. This writing system later developed into cuneiform. The Egyptians, however, continued to use hieroglyphics throughout their history.

The Cultures of Mesopotamia

The unity so characteristic of ancient Egyptian culture has no parallel in the history of ancient Mesopotamia. A succession of different races, each with its own language, religion, and customs, produced a wide variety of achievements. This makes it far more difficult to generalize about Mesopotamian culture than about ancient Egyptian. The picture is further complicated by the presence of a series of related peoples on the periphery of the Mesopotamian territory. The Hittites, the Syrians, and the peoples of early Iran all had periods of prosperity and artistic greatness, although in general they were overshadowed by the more powerful nations of Mesopotamia and Egypt. A description of their achievements would be beyond the scope of this book.

Sumer

The history of Mesopotamia can be divided into two major periods, the Sumerian (c. 3500–2350 B.C.) and the Semitic (c. 2350–612 B.C., when Nineveh fell). The earliest Sumerian communities were agricultural settlements on the land between the rivers Tigris and Euphrates. Unlike Upper Egypt, the land here is flat, and so dikes and canals were needed to prevent flooding during the rainy season and to provide water during the rest of the year. When the early settlers found that they had to undertake these large-scale construction projects in order to improve their agriculture, they began to merge their small villages to form towns.

By far the most important event of this stage in the development of Sumerian culture was the invention of the first system of writing. It consisted of a series of simplified picture signs that represented both the objects they showed and, in addition, related ideas. Thus a leg could mean either a leg itself or the concept of walking. The signs were drawn on soft clay tablets which were then baked hard. The Egyptian hieroglyphic system of writing, which was probably derived from this method, retained throughout its history the use of recognizable pictures. The Sumerians, however, evolved their pictorial signs into a series of wedge-shaped marks that were pressed in clay with a split reed. The system was known as cuneiform [12]. The ability to write made it possible to trade and to administer on a wider scale, and with the increasing economic strength this more highly organized society brought, a number of powerful cities began to develop.

The central focus of life in these larger communities was the temple, the dwelling place of the particular god who watched over the town. Religion, in fact, played a central part in all aspects of Sumerian culture. The gods themselves were manifest in natural phenomena, sky and earth, sun and moon, lightning and storm. The chief religious holidays were closely linked to the passage of the seasons. The most important event of the year was the New Year, the crucial moment when the blazing heat of the previous summer and the cold of winter gave way to the possibility of a fertile spring. The fertility of the earth was symbolized by the Great Mother and the sterility of the winter by the death of her partner, Tammuz. Each year his disappearance was mourned at the beginning of the New Year festival. But when his resurrection was celebrated at the end of the festival, hope for the year to come was expressed by the renewal of the sacred marriage of god and goddess.

As in the Paleolithic period, the importance of female creative power is reflected in Sumerian art. Among its finest achievements is the so-called *Lady of Warka* [13], a female head from the city of Uruk (now

13 *Lady of Warka*. Uruk, c. 3000 B.C. White marble, height 7⅞″ (20 cm). Iraq Museum, Baghdad. Originally, the hair was probably gold leaf and the eyes and eyebrows were colored inlays.

called Warka). It is not certain whether the head is of a divine or mortal figure. The face shows an altogether exceptional nobility and sensitivity.

The governing power in cities like Uruk was in the hands of the priests, who controlled and administered both religious and economic affairs. The ruler himself served as the representative on earth of the god of the city, but, unlike the pharaoh, was never thought of as divine and never became the center of a cult. His purpose was to watch over his people's interests by building better temples and digging more canals, rather than acquiring personal wealth or power. Over the centuries rulers began to detach themselves increasingly from the control of the priests, but the immense prestige of the temples assured the religious leaders a lasting power.

The Epic of Gilgamesh

The most famous of all Sumerian rulers was Gilgamesh, who ruled at Uruk around 2700 B.C. [14]. Around his name there grew up a series of legends which developed into one of the first great masterpieces of poetic expression, *The Epic of Gilgamesh.* The epic begins with the adventures of Gilgamesh and his warrior friend Enkidu. Gilgamesh is courted by no less a figure than the goddess Ishtar, the queen of heaven. He rejects her advances, and the two friends kill the divine bull which she sends to punish them. In revenge, the gods kill Enkidu—his death forms the turning point in the mood of the poem. The exuberance of the earlier sections gives way to the tragic realization that even the bravest of lives must end in death, and Gilgamesh sets out in search of the meaning of existence. Toward the end of his journey he meets Utnapishtim, the only mortal to whom the gods have given everlasting life, seeking to learn from him the secret of immortality. In the course of their meeting, Utnapishtim, who is the Babylonian equivalent of Noah, tells him the story of the flood. By the end of the epic, Gilgamesh's search has taken him to the ends of the earth, but all his attempts to achieve immortality fail and he finally comes home to die.

Originally composed in Sumerian about 2000 B.C., the epic was in time written down on clay tablets in their own languages by the Babylonians, the Hittites, and others. It must have been familiar throughout the ancient Middle East. The story of the flood, which appears in the eleventh tablet, shows a striking re-

14 *Gilgamesh,* from the Palace of Sargon II at Khorsabad, Iraq. Assyrian, c. 700 B.C. Gypsum wall relief, height 15'11" (4.85 m). Louvre, Paris. The colossal relief shows the king as a tamer of wild beasts.

above: Plate 1 Hall of Bulls, left wall, Lascaux (Dordogne), France. c. 15,000–10,000 B.C. Paintings like these were not intended to be decorations, since they are not in the inhabited parts of the caves but in the dark inner recesses. They probably had magical significance for their creators, who may have believed that gaining control of an animal in a painting would help to defeat it in the hunt.

left: Plate 2 *Queen Nefertiti*. Tel el-Amarna, c. 1370 B.C. Painted limestone, height 20″ (51 cm). State Museums, West Berlin. Though the portrait is not exaggerated, it is idealized.

Plate 3 Room with landscape frescoes, House Delta, Thera. Minoan, c. 1500 B.C. National Archaeological Museum, Athens. A springtime scene—bright flowers and soaring birds—covers three sides of a small room.

semblance to the later account in Genesis, although the Biblical version is very different in tone. In contrast to the single supreme God of the Hebrews, who acts out of moral disapproval, the Sumerian gods apparently send the flood merely because the noise made by mortals has been disturbing their sleep, and when the waters come, the gods themselves panic. There is a curious combination of respect and humorous contempt in the poet's description.

from THE EPIC OF GILGAMESH
The Flood

With the first light of dawn a black cloud came from the horizon; it thundered within where Adad, lord of the storm, was riding. In front over hill and plain Shullat and Hanish, heralds of the storm, led on. Then the gods of the abyss rose up; Nergal pulled out the dams of the nether waters, Ninurta the war-lord threw down the dykes, and the seven judges of hell, the Annunaki, raised their torches, lighting the land with their livid flame. A stupor of despair went up to heaven when the god of the storm turned daylight to darkness, when he smashed the land like a cup. One whole day the tempest raged gathering fury as it went, it poured over the people like the tides of battle; a man could not see his brother nor the people be seen from heaven. Even the gods were terrified at the flood, they fled to the highest heaven, the firmament of Anu; they crouched against the walls, cowering like curs. Then Ishtar the sweet-voiced Queen of Heaven cried out like a woman in travail: "Alas the days of old are turned to dust because I commanded evil; why did I command this evil in the council of all the gods? I commanded wars to destroy the people, but are they not my people, for I brought them forth? Now like the spawn of fish they float in the ocean." The great gods of heaven and of hell wept, they covered their mouths. ▪

The overall mood of *The Epic of Gilgamesh* is one of profound pessimism. Unlike the Egyptians of the Old Kingdom, the Mesopotamians saw life as a continual struggle against disaster that was nevertheless preferable to death because the next life offered nothing but darkness and dust. The dying Egyptian of any social class was guaranteed, providing his life had been a righteous one, a place in the fields of paradise. Even for the Mesopotamian king himself there was only the bleak prospect described in the following passage by Gilgamesh's friend Enkidu as he lies dying:

from THE EPIC OF GILGAMESH
The Afterlife

Enkidu slept alone in his sickness and he poured out his heart to Gilgamesh, "Last night I dreamed again, my friend. The heavens moaned and the earth replied; I stood alone before an awful being; his face was sombre like the black bird of the storm. He fell upon me with the talons of an eagle and he held me fast, pinioned with his claw, till I smothered; then he transformed me so that my arms became wings covered with feathers. He turned his stare towards me, and he led me away to the palace of Irkalla, the Queen of Darkness, to the house from which none who enters ever returns, down the road from which there is no coming back.

"There is the house whose people sit in darkness; dust is their food and clay their meat. They are clothed like birds with wings for covering, they see no light, they sit in darkness. I entered the house of dust and I saw the kings of the earth, their crowns put away for ever; rulers and princes, all those who once wore kingly crowns and ruled the world in the days of old. They who had stood in the place of the gods, like Anu and Enlil, stood now like servants to fetch baked meats in the house of dust, to carry cooked meat and cold water from the water-skin. In the house of dust which I entered were high-priests and acolytes, priests of the incantation and of ecstasy; there were servers of the temple, and there was Etana, that king of Kish whom the eagle carried to heaven in the days of old. I saw also Samuqan, god of cattle, and there was Ereshkigal the Queen of the Underworld; and Belit-Sheri squatted in front of her, she who is recorder of the gods and keeps the book of death. She held a tablet from which she read. She raised her head, she saw me and spoke: 'Who has brought this one here?' Then I awoke like a man drained of blood who wanders alone in a waste of rushes; like one whom the bailiff has seized and his heart pounds with terror. O my brother, let some great prince, some other, come when I am dead, or let some god stand at your gate, let him obliterate my name and write his own instead." ▪

The story of Gilgamesh rises to a universal level in the section that describes the last stages of his journey. Then the epic touches on questions that still retain their profound significance for us today. Does all human achievement become futile in the face of death? Is there some purpose to human existence? If so, how can it be discovered? The quest of Gilgamesh symbolizes the basic human search for self-understanding. The remote Sumerian king is the ancestor of many others who in the course of the humanistic tradition have faced the same problems. The poet's choice of a journey to symbolize Gilgamesh's spiritual and intellectual search for knowledge is brilliantly effective; many later writers were to choose the same image. Odysseus in Homer's *Odyssey* (see pages 94–98), Aeneas in Vergil's *Aeneid* (see pages 212–223), Dante in his own *Divine Comedy* (see pages 373–416), and Gulliver in Swift's *Gulliver's Travels* are four very different examples of the traveler as symbol of the search for knowledge. In more recent times, James Joyce's *Ulysses* uses the same device.

In the case of Gilgamesh, the results of the search are not comforting. In keeping with its generally pessimistic tone, the epic seems to tell us that human wisdom is severely limited by human capabilities. The tragic irony which this suggests permeates the final stages of Gilgamesh's journey, reproduced below. The futility of his quest is expressed in his failure to pass even the simple tests which the gods set him. He wants to live forever, but he cannot even stay awake for seven nights. He discovers that material objects are more permanent than human existence when the clothes on his back show less signs of wear than he does. Even when he is finally given a magic plant that renews youth, he fails to guard it adequately and lets a serpent steal it.

Only at the very end do we sense that the purpose of the journey may have been the journey itself and that what is important is to have asked the questions. By his return Gilgamesh has seen mysteries and knows secret things. Weary though he is, he is wiser than when he left, and in leaving us an account of his experiences, "engraved on a stone," he communicates them to us, a powerful and moving illustration of the strength of the written word.

from THE EPIC OF GILGAMESH
The Return of Gilgamesh

Utnapishtim said, "As for you, Gilgamesh, who will assemble the gods for your sake, so that you may find that life for which you are searching? But if you wish, come and put it to the test: only prevail against sleep for six days and seven nights." But while Gilgamesh sat there resting on his haunches, a mist of sleep like soft wool teased from the fleece drifted over him, and Utnapishtim said to his wife, "Look at him now, the strong man who would have everlasting life, even now the mists of sleep are drifting over him." His wife replied, "Touch the man to wake him, so that he may return to his own land in peace, going back

through the gate by which he came." Utnapishtim said to his wife, "All men are deceivers, even you he will attempt to deceive; therefore bake loaves of bread, each day one loaf, and put it beside his head; and make a mark on the wall to number the days he has slept."

So she baked loaves of bread, each day one loaf, and put it beside his head, and she marked on the wall the days that he slept; and there came a day when the first loaf was hard, the second loaf was like leather, the third was soggy, the crust of the fourth had mould, the fifth was mildewed, the sixth was fresh, and the seventh was still on the embers. Then Utnapishtim touched him and he woke. Gilgamesh said to Utnapishtim the Faraway, "I hardly slept when you touched and roused me." But Utnapishtim said, "Count these loaves and learn how many days you slept, for your first is hard, your second is like leather, your third is soggy, the crust of your fourth has mould, your fifth is mildewed, your sixth is fresh, and your seventh was still over the glowing embers when I touched and woke you." Gilgamesh said, "What shall I do, O Utnapishtim, where shall I go? Already the thief in the night has hold of my limbs, death inhabits my room; wherever my foot rests, there I find death."

Then Utnapishtim spoke to Urshanabi the ferryman: "Woe to you Urshanabi, now and for ever more you have become hateful to this harbourage; it is not for you, nor for you are the crossings of this sea. Go now, banished from the shore. But this man before whom you walked, bringing him here, whose body is covered with foulness and the grace of whose limbs has been spoiled by wild skins, take him to the washing-place. There he shall wash his long hair clean as snow in the water, he shall throw off his skins and let the sea carry them away, and the beauty of his body shall be shown, the fillet on his forehead shall be renewed, and he shall be given clothes to cover his nakedness. Till he reaches his own city and his journey is accomplished, these clothes will show no sign of age, they will wear like a new garment." So Urshanabi took Gilgamesh and led him to the washing-place, he washed his long hair as clean as snow in the water, he threw off his skins, which the sea carried away, and showed the beauty of his body. He renewed the fillet on his forehead, and to cover his nakedness gave him clothes which would show no sign of age, but would wear like a new garment till he reached his own city, and his journey was accomplished.

Then Gilgamesh and Urshanabi launched the boat on to the water and boarded it, and they made ready to sail away; but the wife of Utnapishtim the Faraway said to him, "Gilgamesh came here wearied out, he is worn out; what will you give him to carry him back to his own country?" So Utnapishtim spoke, and Gilgamesh took a pole and brought the boat in to the bank. "Gilgamesh, you came here, a man wearied out, you have worn yourself out; what shall I give you to carry you back to your own country? Gilgamesh, I shall reveal a secret thing, it is a mystery of the gods that I am telling you. There is a plant that grows under the water, it has a prickle like a thorn, like a rose; it will wound your hands, but if you succeed in taking it, then your hands will hold that which restores his lost youth to a man."

When Gilgamesh heard this he opened the sluices so that a sweet-water current might carry him out to the deepest channel; he tied heavy stones to his feet and they dragged him down to the water-bed. There he saw the plant growing; although it pricked him he took it in his hands; then he cut the heavy stones from his feet, and the sea carried him and threw him on to the shore. Gilgamesh said to Urshanabi the ferryman, "Come here, and see this marvellous plant. By its virtue a man may win back all his former strength. I will take it to Uruk of the strong walls; there I will give it to the old men to eat. Its name shall be 'The Old Men Are Young Again'; and at last I shall eat it myself and have back all my lost youth." So Gilgamesh returned by the gate through which he had come, Gilgamesh and Urshanabi went together. They travelled their twenty leagues and then they broke their fast; after thirty leagues they stopped for the night.

Gilgamesh saw a well of cool water and he went down and bathed; but deep in the pool there was lying a serpent, and the serpent sensed the sweetness of the flower. It rose out of the water and snatched it away, and immediately it sloughed its skin and returned to the well. Then Gilgamesh sat down and wept, the tears ran down his face, and he took the hand of Urshanabi; "O Urshanabi, was it for this that I toiled with my hands, is it for this I have wrung out my heart's blood? For myself I have gained nothing; not I, but the beast of the earth has joy of it now. Already the stream has carried it twenty leagues back to the channels where I found it. I found a sign and now I have lost it. Let us leave the boat on the bank and go."

After twenty leagues they broke their fast, after thirty leagues they stopped for the night; in three days they had walked as much as a journey of a month and fifteen days. When the journey was accomplished they arrived at Uruk, the strong-walled city. Gilgamesh spoke to him, to Urshanabi the ferryman, "Urshanabi, climb up on to the wall of Uruk, inspect its foundation terrace, and examine well the brickwork; see if it is not of burnt bricks; and did not the seven wise men lay these foundations? One third of the whole is city, one third is garden, and one third is field, with the precinct of the goddess Ishtar. These parts and the precinct are all Uruk."

This too was the work of Gilgamesh, the king, who knew the countries of the world. He was wise, he saw mysteries and knew secret things, he brought us a tale of the days before the flood. He went a long journey, was weary, worn out with labour, and returning engraved on a stone the whole story. ◧

The Epic of Gilgamesh is, of course, a work of art, not history. It gives us some incidental information on the way of life in Sumerian times, but there is probably little resemblance between its hero and the actual man, Gilgamesh. More solid evidence on how the Sumerians lived comes from other sources, most notably from the excavation of great cities like Ur. Not only have houses and temples been uncovered, but the greatest of all treasures from the Sumerian period were found in the graves of the Royal Cemetery there [15]. The quantity and quality of the gold-

15 *Ram in a Thicket,* from the Royal Cemetery, Ur. Sumerian, c. 2600 B.C. Wood overlaid with gold and lapis lazuli, height 20″ (51 cm). British Museum, London (reproduced by courtesy of the Trustees). The ram's shoulders originally supported a vessel probably intended for funerary offerings.

work and the richness of the inlaid decoration are certainly a vivid indication of the level of prosperity reached by the leading Sumerian cities of this period.

Akkadian and Babylonian Culture

In the years from 2350 to 2150 B.C. the whole of Mesopotamia fell under the control of the Semitic king Sargon and his descendants. The art of this Akkadian period (named for Sargon's capital city, Akkad) shows a continuation of the trends of the Sumerian age, although total submission to the gods is replaced by a more positive attitude to human achievement. A bronze head from Nineveh [16], perhaps a portrait of Sargon himself, expresses a pride and self-confidence that recur in other works of the period like the famous *Stele of Naram-Sin* (stele: sculpted stone slab), showing a later Akkadian king standing on the bodies of his enemies [17].

When Akkadian rule was brought to an abrupt and violent end by the invasion of the Gutians from Iran, the cities of Mesopotamia reverted to earlier ways. As in the early Sumerian period, the chief buildings constructed were large brick platforms

below: 16 Head of a king (Sargon?), from Nineveh. Akkadian, c. 2330 B.C. Bronze, height 14¼″ (37 cm). Iraq Museum, Baghdad. Originally, the eyes were probably precious stones.

right: 17 *Stele of Naram-Sin,* from Susa, Iran. Akkadian, c. 2300 B.C. Red sandstone, height 6′6″ (2 m). Louvre, Paris. The king, wearing a horned crown, stands beneath symbols of the gods. The diagonal composition is well suited to the triangular shape of the stele.

with superimposed terraces, known as *ziggurats*. These clearly had religious significance; the one built at Ur around 2100 B.C. [18] had huge staircases that led to a shrine at the top. The same return to traditional beliefs is illustrated by the religious inscriptions on the bases of the many surviving statues of

18 Ziggurat at Ur. Neo-Sumerian, c. 2100–2000 B.C. Mudbrick faced with baked brick laid in bitumen. The drawing shows the probable original appearance. The photograph shows the ziggurat now, partially restored. The Akkadian word *ziggurat* means "pinnacle" or "mountain top"—a place where the gods were thought to reveal themselves. These plains dwellers made artificial mountains surmounted by shrines.

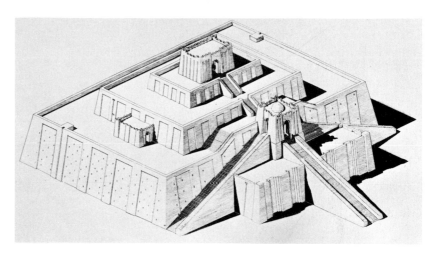

Gudea, the governor of the city of Lagash around 2100 B.C., as well as by his humble attitude [19].

By around 1800 B.C. Mesopotamia had once again been unified, this time under the Babylonians. Their most famous king, Hammurabi, was the author of a law code which was one of the earliest attempts to achieve social justice by legislation—a major devel-opment in the growth of civilization. The laws were carved on a stele, with Hammurabi himself shown at the top in the presence of the sun god Shamash [20]. The following excerpts show how the law code orga-nized human relationships; they also show a rela-tively enlightened attitude toward equal rights in the 18th century B.C.—almost four thousand years ago.

below: 19 *Gudea.* c. 2100 B.C. Diorite, height 41″ (105 cm). Louvre, Paris. Gudea is shown in an attitude of devotion, hands tightly clasped, as he stands before the gods.

right: 20 *Stele of Hammurabi.* c. 1760 B.C. Basalt, height 7′3¾″ (2.25 m). Louvre, Paris. The sun god is dictating the law to the king, who is listening reverently. They are shown on a moun-tain, indicated by the irregular ridges beneath the god's feet. Below is *The Law Code of Hammurabi,* carved in cuneiform.

128. If a man take a wife and do not draw up a contract with her, that woman is not a wife.

129. If the wife of a man be taken in lying with another man, they shall bind them and throw them into the water. If the husband of the woman spare the life of his wife, the king [also] shall spare the life of his servant [the other man].

131. If a man accuse his wife and she have not been taken in lying with another man, she shall take an oath in the name of god and she shall return to her house.

136. If a man desert his city and run away, and afterward his wife enter into another house, if that man return and seize his wife, because he hated his city and fled, the wife of the fugitive shall not return to her husband.

138. If a man put away his wife who has not borne him children, he shall give her money to the amount of her marriage settlement and he shall make good to her the dowry which she brought from her father's house and then he may put her away.

141. If the wife of a man who is living in his house set her face to go out, playing the fool, ruining her house, and belittling her husband, they shall convict her; if her husband announce her divorce, he may put her away. For her journey home no alimony shall be given to her. If her husband do not announce her divorce, her husband may take another woman. That woman [the first wife] shall dwell in the house of her husband as a maidservant.

142. If a woman hate her husband and say, "Thou shalt not have me," her past shall be inquired into for any deficiency of hers; and if she have been careful and be without past sin and her husband have been going out and greatly belittling her, that woman has no blame. She shall take her dowry and go to her father's house.

143. If she have not been careful, have been going out, ruining her house and belittling her husband, they shall throw that woman into the water.

145. If a man take a wife and she do not present him with children, and he set his face to take a concubine, that man may take a concubine and bring her into his house. That concubine shall not take precedence of his wife.

146. If a man take a wife and she give a maidservant to her husband and she bear children and afterward that maidservant would take precedence of her mistress; because she has borne children, her mistress may not sell her for money, but she may reduce her to bondage and count her among the maidservants.

150. If a man make his wife a present of field, garden, house, and goods and deliver to her a sealed deed, after the death of her husband her children may not make any claim against her. The mother after her death may give them to her child whom she loves, but to a brother she may not give them.

159. If a man who has brought a present to the house of his [prospective] father-in-law and has given the marriage settlement look with longing upon another woman and say to his father-in-law, "I will not take thy daughter," the father of the daughter shall take to himself whatever was brought to him.

160. If a man bring a present to the house of his [prospective] father-in-law and give a marriage settlement and the father of the daughter say, "I will not give thee my daughter," he the father-in-law shall double everything which was brought to him and return it.

162. If a man take a wife and she bear him children and that woman die, her father may not lay claim to her dowry. Her dowry belongs to her children.

165. If a man make a present of field, garden, and house to his son who is first in his eyes and write for him a sealed deed; after the father dies, when the brothers divide, he shall take the present which the father gave him, and over and above they shall divide the goods of the father's house equally.

168. If a man set his face to disinherit his son and say to the judges, "I will disinherit my son," the judges shall inquire into his past, and if the son have not committed a crime sufficiently grave to cut him off from sonship, the father may not cut off his son from sonship.

170. If a man's wife bear him children and his maidservant bear him children, and the father during his lifetime say to the children which the maidservant bore him, "My children," and reckon them with the children of his wife; after the father dies the children of the wife and the children of the maidservant shall divide the goods of the father's house equally. The child of the wife shall have the right of choice at the division.

The Assyrians

By 1550 B.C. Babylon had been taken over by the Kassites, a formerly nomadic people who had occupied Babylonia and settled there, but they too were to fall in turn under the domination of the Assyrians, who evolved the last great culture of ancient Mesopotamia. The peak of Assyrian power was between 1000 and 612 B.C.—the time when Greek civilization was developing, as described in Chapter 3. But Assyrian achievements are the culmination of the culture of ancient Mesopotamia.

A huge palace constructed at Nimrud during the reign of Assurnasirpal II (883–859 B.C.) was decorated with an elaborately carved series of relief slabs. The subjects are often religious, but a number of slabs that show the king on hunting expeditions have a vigor and freedom that are unusual in Mesopotamian art. The palaces of later Assyrian kings were decorated with similar reliefs. At Nineveh the palace of Assurbanipal (668–626 B.C.) was filled with scenes of war appropriate to an age of increasing turmoil. The representations of dead and dying soldiers on the battlefields are generally conventional, if highly elaborate. But again the hunting scenes are different—they show a genuine and moving identification with the suffering animals [21].

With the fall of Nineveh in 612 B.C. Assyrian domination ended. The Assyrian empire fell into the hands of two nomadic tribes, first the Medes and then the Persians; the great age of Mesopotamia was over. Lacking the unifying elements provided in Egypt by the pharaoh and a national religion, the

peoples of Mesopotamia perhaps never equaled Egyptian achievements in the arts. However, they formed ordered societies within independent city-states that anticipated the city-states of the Greeks. They also evolved a comparatively enlightened view of human relationships, as shown by *The Law Code of Hammurabi*. And they gave the eternal questions of life, death, and the nature of existence a mature and poetic expression in *The Epic of Gilgamesh*.

Aegean Culture in the Bronze Age

Neither the Egyptians of the Old Kingdom nor the Sumerians seem to have shown any interest in their contemporaries living to the west of them, and with good reason. In Greece and the islands of the Aegean Sea, though the arrival of immigrants from further east in the early Neolithic period (c. 6000 B.C.) had brought new agricultural techniques, in general, life continued there for the next three thousand years almost completely untouched by the rise of organized cultures elsewhere.

Yet, beginning in the early Bronze Age, there developed in the area around the Aegean Sea a level of

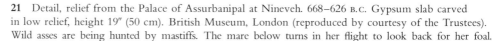

21   Detail, relief from the Palace of Assurbanipal at Nineveh. 668–626 B.C. Gypsum slab carved in low relief, height 19″ (50 cm). British Museum, London (reproduced by courtesy of the Trustees). Wild asses are being hunted by mastiffs. The mare below turns in her flight to look back for her foal.

civilization as brilliant and sophisticated as any other in the ancient world. Then around 1100 B.C., after almost two thousand years of existence, this civilization disappeared as dramatically as it had arisen. The rediscovery in the 20th century of these peoples, the Minoans of Crete and the Mycenaeans of mainland Greece, is perhaps the most splendid achievement in the history of archaeology in the Mediterranean—an achievement that has opened up vast new perspectives in the study of the later Greeks.

What connection is there between later Greek culture and the magnificent achievements of the Bronze Age? Did much of later Greek religion, thought, and art have its origins in this earlier period, even though the Greeks themselves seemed to know nothing about it? Or was the culture of the Minoans and Mycenaeans an isolated phenomenon, destroyed utterly near the end of the Bronze Age, lost until it was found again in our own time? This Aegean culture is important not only for the possible light it throws on later times. Its existence also shows that the ancient world could reach beyond the monumentality and earnestness of the Egyptians and Mesopotamians, that it could attain a way of life that valued grace, beauty, and comfort—a life that could truly be called civilized.

Cycladic Art

During most of the Bronze Age the major centers of Aegean culture were on Crete or the mainland, but in the early phase there were settlements on a group of islands of the central Aegean, the Cyclades. Little is known about these Cycladic people. They used bronze tools. They also produced pottery which, though less finely made than that produced elsewhere in the Aegean at the time, sometimes shows remarkable imagination and even humor [22]. The chief claim to fame of Cycladic art—a considerable one—lies in the marble statues, or idols, that were produced in large quantities and in many cases buried with the dead. The statues range in height from a few inches to almost lifesize; the average is about a foot (30.5 centimeters) high. Most of the figures are female; the most common type shows a naked woman standing or, more probably, lying, with her arms folded and head tilted back [23]. The face is indicated only by a central ridge for the nose. The simplicity of the form and the fine working of the marble—marble of superb quality—often produce an effect of great beauty. Among the rare male figures, the most out-

22 Cycladic vase in the shape of a hedgehog drinking from a bowl. Syros, c. 2500–2200 B.C. Painted clay, height 4¼″ (11 cm). National Archaeological Museum, Athens.

23 Cycladic idol. c. 2500 B.C. Marble, height 19¾″ (50 cm). British Museum, London.

standing are two of musicians, a flute player and a harpist [24], both from the island of Keros.

The purpose of the Cycladic idols remains uncertain. The fact that most of them have been found in graves suggests that they had a religious function in the funeral ritual. The overwhelming preponderance of female figures seems to indicate that they were in some way connected with the cult of the mother goddess, which we have already seen in Mesopotamia and which dominated Aegean Bronze Age religion. Whether the figures actually represent goddesses remains uncertain. In any case, the abstract elegance of the statues has a special appeal for modern eyes. A number of contemporary artists have been influenced by them, most notably the Italian painter Amedeo Modigliani (1884–1920) [25]. Even in the Bronze Age they seem to have been popular—they were exported to Crete and mainland Greece.

We now know that the period of the production of the Cycladic idols was one of increasing development on Crete. Yet for the Classical Greeks of the 5th century B.C. Crete was chiefly famous as the home of the legendary King Minos, who ruled at Knossos. Here, according to the myths, was a Labyrinth that housed the Minotaur, a monstrous creature, half man and half bull, the product of the union of Minos' wife

24 *Harpist,* from Keros. Cycladic, c. 2500 B.C. Marble, height 8¾″ (22 cm). National Archaeological Museum, Athens.

right: 25 Amedeo Modigliani. *Yellow Sweater (Portrait of Mme. Hébuterne).* 1919. Oil on canvas, 39⅜ × 25½″ (100 × 65 cm). Solomon R. Guggenheim Museum, New York.

Pasiphae with a bull. Minos exacted a regular tribute from Athens of seven boys and seven girls, who were sent to be devoured by the Minotaur. According to the myths, after this had been going on for some time, the Athenian hero Theseus volunteered to stop the grisly tribute. He went to Knossos with the new group of intended victims and, with the help of the king's daughter Ariadne, who had fallen in love with him, killed the Minotaur in his lair in the middle of the Labyrinth. He then escaped with Ariadne and the Athenian boys and girls. Theseus later somewhat heartlessly abandoned Ariadne on the island of Naxos, but the god Dionysus discovered her there and comforted her. The story had many more details, and other myths describe other events. The important point is that the later Greeks had a mythological picture of Knossos as a prosperous and thriving community ruled by a powerful and ruthless king from his palace. Nor was Knossos the only center mentioned in Greek stories of Crete. In the *Odyssey* Homer even refers to "Crete of a hundred cities."

But these were legends. By the time of Classical Greece no evidence whatever for the existence of the Palace of Minos or the other cities could be seen. It is not surprising that the Greeks themselves showed no inclination to try to find any hidden traces. Archaeology, after all, is a relatively modern pursuit, and there is little indication of any serious enthusiasm in Classical antiquity for the material remains of the past. Later ages continued to accept the Greeks' own judgment. For many centuries the story of Minos and the Labyrinth was thought to be a good tale with no foundation in fact.

The Excavation of Knossos

By the end of the 19th century, however, things had changed. Heinrich Schliemann had proved that the stories of the war against Troy and the Mycenaeans who had waged it were far from mere legends (see page 36). Was it possible that the mythical palace of King Minos at Knossos also really existed?

In 1894 the English archaeologist Arthur Evans first went to Crete to see if he could discover something of its history in the Bronze Age. At Knossos he found evidence of ancient remains, some of them already uncovered by amateur enthusiasts. He returned in 1899 and again in 1900, this time with a permit to excavate. On March 23, 1900, serious work began at Knossos, and within days it became apparent that the

finds represented a civilization even older than that of the Mycenaeans. The quantity was staggering: pottery, frescoes, inscribed tablets, and, on April 13, a room with elaborate paintings and a raised seat with high back—the throne room of King Minos. Evans' discoveries at Knossos (and finds later made elsewhere on Crete by other archaeologists) did much to confirm legendary accounts of Cretan prosperity and power. But these discoveries did far more than merely give a true historical background to the myth of the Minotaur.

Evans had in fact found an entire civilization, which he called Minoan after the legendary king. Evans himself is said to have remarked modestly once: "Any success as an archaeologist I owe to two things: very short sight, so I look at everything closely, and being slow on the uptake, so I never leap to conclusions." Actually, the magnitude of his achievement cannot be exaggerated. All study of the Minoans has been strongly influenced by his initial classification of the finds, especially the pottery. He divided the history of the Bronze Age in Crete into three main periods, Early Minoan, Middle Minoan, and Late Minoan and further subdivided each of these into three. The precise dates of each period can be disputed, but all the excavations of the years following Evans have confirmed his initial description of the main sequence of events.

Life and Art
in the Minoan Palaces

The Early Minoan period was one of increasing growth. Small towns began to appear in the south and east of Crete, and the first contacts were established with Egypt and Mesopotamia. Around 2000 B.C., however, came the first major development in Minoan civilization, marking the beginning of the Middle Minoan period. The earlier scattered towns were abandoned, and large urban centers evolved. These centers were generally called palaces, although their function was far more than just to provide homes for ruling families.

The best known of these centers is Knossos (other important ones have been excavated at Phaistos, Mallia, and Zakro). The main palace building, which was constructed around an open rectangular courtyard, contained rooms for banquets, public receptions, religious ceremonies, and administrative work. In addition, there were living quarters for the royal family and working areas for slaves and craftsmen [26, 27]. Around the palace were the private houses of the aristocrats and chief religious leaders. The technical sophistication of these great centers was remarkable. There were elaborate drainage systems, and the palaces were designed and constructed to remain cool in summer and be heated easily in winter.

Middle Minoan art shows great liveliness and color. The brilliantly painted pottery, superb jewelry such as the famous *Wasp Pendant* from Mallia [28], and the many exquisitely carved seal stones all attest to the Minoans' love of beauty and artistic skill. Unlike their contemporaries in Egypt and Mesopotamia, the Minoans showed little interest in monumental art. Their greatest works are on a small, even miniature, scale. At the same time they invented a writing system of hieroglyphic signs that was used in the archives of the palace for administrative purposes.

Toward the end of the Middle Minoan period (c. 1700 B.C.) the palaces were destroyed, probably by an earthquake, and then rebuilt on an even grander scale.

right above: 26 Throne Room, Palace of Minos at Knossos. The room was reconstructed about 1450 B.C., shortly before the final destruction of the palace. The frescoes around the throne show sacred flowers and griffins—mythological beasts with lion bodies and bird heads.

right: 27 Plan of the Palace of Minos at Knossos. c. 1600–1400 B.C. Each Cretan palace had a central court oriented north-south, state apartments to the west, and royal living apartments to the east.

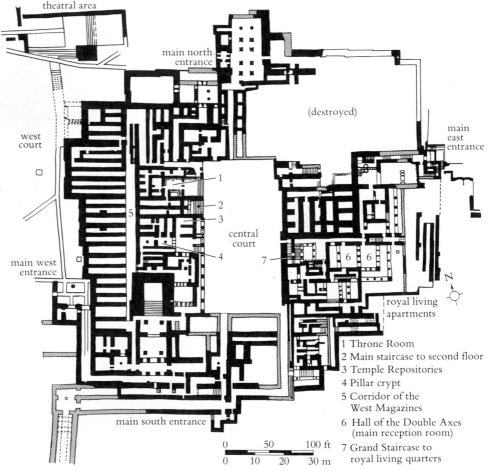

theatral area

main north entrance

(destroyed)

main east entrance

west court

central court

main west entrance

royal living apartments

main south entrance

1 Throne Room
2 Main staircase to second floor
3 Temple Repositories
4 Pillar crypt
5 Corridor of the West Magazines
6 Hall of the Double Axes (main reception room)
7 Grand Staircase to royal living quarters

0   50   100 ft
0 10 20 30 m

There was further rebuilding about a century later, perhaps because of another eathquake. These palaces of the Late Minoan period represent the high point of Minoan culture. The wall paintings of this period are among the greatest treasures of all. Their spontaneity and freedom create a mood very different from Egyptian and Mesopotamian art, and they show a love of nature expressed with brilliant colors and vivid observation. Most of the best examples of these later paintings are from Knossos, but some particularly enchanting scenes have been found in the recent excavation of a Minoan colony on the island of Thera [Plate 3, page 22].

Although the rulers of the palaces seem to have been male, the central figure of Minoan religion was a mother goddess who, like the Great Mother of Mesopotamian religion, was connected with fertility. She seems to have taken on different forms, or rather the function of female divinity was divided among several separate deities. Sometimes when she is shown flanked by animals, the Mistress of the Beasts, she seems to be the ancestor of the Greek goddess Artemis. Other depictions show goddesses of vegetation. The most famous of all Minoan figurines is the so-called *Snake Goddess* [29].

Throughout the last great age of the palaces, the influence of Minoan artistic styles began to spread to the mainland. But Minoan political and military power was on the wane, and Knossos seems to have been invaded and occupied by mainlanders around 1450 B.C. Shortly afterwards, both at Knossos and elsewhere, there is evidence of widespread destruction. By 1400 B.C., Minoan culture had come to an abrupt end. The causes are mysterious and have been much argued; we shall probably never know exactly what happened. The eruption of a volcano on Thera a century earlier, about 1500 B.C., may have played some part in changing the balance of power in the Aegean. In any case, there is no doubt that throughout the last period of the palaces a new power was growing, the Mycenaeans. These people may well have played a part in the destruction of Knossos.

29 *Snake Goddess,* from the Temple Repository at Knossos. c. 1600 B.C. Faience, height 11½″ (30 cm). Archaeological Museum, Heraklion. The bare breasts are typical for Minoan court ladies, but the apron indicates a religious function. The figure probably represents a priestess serving the goddess, not the goddess herself.

28 *Wasp Pendant,* from Mallia. c. 1700 B.C. Gold, width 1⅞″ (5 cm). Archaeological Museum, Heraklion. This enlarged view shows the exquisite craftsmanship, using the techniques of granulation and wire-working. Two wasps (or perhaps hornets) are curved around a honeycomb.

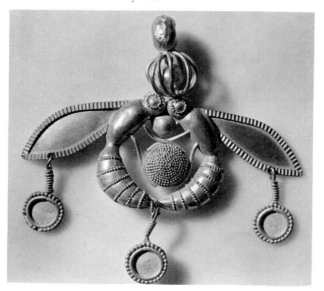

Schliemann and the Discovery of Mycenae

The Mycenaeans, the people of mainland Greece in the Bronze Age, are named after the largest of their settlements, Mycenae. Most of the Mycenaean centers were in the southern part of Greece known as the Peloponnesus, although there were also some settlements farther north, of which the two most important were Athens and Thebes. Like the Minoans, the Mycenaeans were familiar from Greek myths long before their material remains were excavated. They were famous in legend mainly for launching an expedition against Troy, across the Aegean Sea. The Trojan War (c. 1250 B.C.) and its aftermath provided the material for many later Greek works, most notably the *Iliad* and the *Odyssey,* the two great epic poems of Homer, but for a long time it was believed that the war and even the very existence of Troy were myths.

Heinrich Schliemann dedicated his life and work to proving that the legends were founded on reality. Schliemann, who was born in Germany in 1822, was introduced to the Homeric poems as a child by his father and was overwhelmed by their incomparable vividness. He became determined to discover Homer's Troy and prove the poet right. Excavation has always been expensive, and Schliemann therefore decided to make his fortune in business, retire early, and devote his profits to the pursuit of his goal. By 1863, this remarkable man had accumulated a considerable amount of money from trading in, among other things, tea and was ready to devote himself to this second career. After a period of study and travel, in 1870 he finally began excavations on the site where he had decided the remains of Homer's Troy lay buried underneath the Roman city of Ilium. By 1873 he had found not only walls and the gate of the city but quantities of gold, silver, and bronze objects, as well as the jewelry in which his wife Sophia was photographed [30].

Inspired by the success of his Trojan campaign, Schliemann moved on to the second part of his task: to discover the Mycenaeans who had made war on Troy. In 1876 he began to excavate within the walls of Mycenae itself, and there he almost immediately came upon the Royal Grave Circle with its stupendous quantities of gold treasures [31]. Homer had described Mycenae as "rich in gold," and Schliemann was always convinced that the royal family whose graves he had unearthed was that of Agamemnon, leader of the Mycenaean expedition against Troy. We

30 Heinrich Schliemann and his wife. Engraving made from a photograph taken in 1877.

now know that the finds date to an even earlier period, and later excavations both at Mycenae and at other mainland sites have provided a much more exact picture of Mycenaean history. This does not diminish Schliemann's achievement. However unscientific his methods, he had proved the existence of a civilization in Bronze Age Greece which surpassed in splendor even the legends; he had opened a new era in the study of the past.

31 "Mask of Agamemnon," from Shaft Grave V, Mycenae. c. 1550 B.C. Beaten gold, height 10⅛" (26 cm). National Archaeological Museum, Athens. This death mask is actually a portrait of a Mycenaean ruler of three centuries earlier than Agamemnon.

32 Reconstruction of the Citadel of Mycenae as it would have looked around 1300 B.C. The very thick walls are visible. The palace has a commanding position at the summit.

Mycenaean Art and Architecture

Like the Minoans, the Mycenaeans centered their life around great palace complexes. In Mycenae itself, the palace probably was first built around 1600 B.C., and the graves found by Schliemann date to shortly thereafter. Until the fall of Knossos in 1400 B.C., the Mycenaeans were strongly under the influence of Minoan culture, but with the end of Minoan power they became the natural leaders in the Aegean area. From 1400 to 1200 B.C., Mycenaean traders traveled throughout the Mediterranean, from Egypt and the Near East as far west as Italy. The Mycenaean empire grew in power and prosperity. Toward the end of this period, around 1250 B.C., the successful expedition was launched against Troy, perhaps for reasons of trade rivalry. A short time later, around 1200 B.C., the Mycenaean empire itself fell, its major centers destroyed and most of them abandoned. Invasion by enemies, internal strife, and natural causes have all been suggested, but the fall of the Mycenaeans still remains mysterious.

Their collapse is made even more incomprehensible by the massive fortifications that protected most of the palaces. At Mycenae itself, the walls are 15 feet (4.6 meters) thick and probably were 50 feet (15.3 meters) high. As in the case of other Mycenaean centers, the actual location was chosen for its defensibility [32]. The somber character of these fortress-palaces is reflected in the general tone of Mycenaean civilization. Unlike the relaxed culture of the Minoans, Mycenaean culture as reflected in its art was pre-

occupied with death and war. It is no coincidence that many of the richest finds came from tombs. Even when the style, and in some cases the actual craftsman, is Minoan, the subject is often Mycenaean in taste, as in the scene of violent combat on a seal ring from the Royal Grave Circle [33]. Like the Minoans, the Mycenaeans decorated their palaces with frescoes, although the Mycenaean paintings are more solemn and dignified than their Minoan counterparts.

The disaster of 1200 B.C. brought a violent end to the Mycenaeans' political and economic domination of the Mediterranean, but their culture lingered on for another hundred years. A few of the palaces were

33 Seal ring, from Shaft Grave IV, Mycenae. c. 1500 B.C. Gold, 1⅜ × 1⅛″ (3.5 × 3 cm). National Archaeological Museum, Athens. This enlarged view shows how ferocious the combat is. Although the craftsmanship is probably Minoan, the violent subject would have appealed to Mycenaean taste.

inhabited again, and some Mycenaeans fled eastwards, where they settled on the islands of Rhodes and Cyprus. By 1100 B.C., however, renewed violence had extinguished the last traces of Bronze Age culture in Greece. A century later, after a period which our lack of information forces us to call the Dark Age, the story of Western culture truly begins with the dawning of the Iron Age.

Before leaving the rich achievements of the Bronze Age world, both in Greece and farther afield, it is worth asking how much survived to be handed down to our own civilization. For the Greeks themselves, the Iron Age brought a new beginning in most material respects. At the same time, however, there are links with the earlier era in less tangible areas. In particular, although Greek religion never placed as strong an emphasis on worship of the mother goddess as the Bronze Age did, she remained a potent force in traditional beliefs. Behind the official reverence for Zeus, father of the gods and mortals, there lay a profound respect for goddesses like Hera, patroness of the family, Artemis, Mistress of the Beasts and goddess of childbirth, and Demeter, the goddess of fertility and agriculture. The continued worship of these goddesses, which was to last under different guises for centuries, represents a reverence for female creative power which is one of the oldest legacies from the period before our culture began—we saw it as far back as the Paleolithic period—and perhaps one of the most significant.

As for Egypt and Mesopotamia, much of their impact on later culture was secondhand. In the course of their growth and development, the Greeks were brought into contact with the later Egypt and Mesopotamia of their own times, and Greek art and architecture were decisively influenced by them. Although the Greeks retained their artistic independence, the style they developed under the inspiration of eastern models has conditioned the entire history of Western art. The cultures of ancient Egypt and the Middle East had very little direct influence on the formation of our civilization, partly because Greek culture had a vitality which was by this time lacking in the older peoples and at least partly because of historical accident. Egypt and Assyria, powerful though they were, fell to the Persians, while Greece managed not only to survive but even to inflict an ignominious defeat on her Persian invaders.

Yet even if ancient Egypt and Mesopotamia lie outside the mainstream of our cultural tradition, they continue to exert a powerful influence on the Western imagination, as the Tutankhamen exhibitions and their accompanying "Tut mania" showed in the 1970s. In part their fascination lies in their exoticism and in the excitement of their rediscovery in our own day. The pharaoh who can curse his excavator from beyond the grave is certainly a dramatic, if fictional, representative of his age. At the same time the artistic achievements of those distant times—the buildings and sculptures, *The Epic of Gilgamesh,* the "Hymn to Aton"—need no historical justification. Created in a world very remote from our own, they serve as a reminder of the innate human urge to give expression to the eternal problems of existence.

Further Reading

Aldred, C. *The Egyptians*. New York: Praeger, 1961. A short but comprehensive account of Egyptian culture by one of the leading Egyptologists of the century.

Childe, V. Gordon. *What Happened in History*. Baltimore: Penguin, 1942. One of the most important of all books on the early development of civilization. The author's account is strongly influenced by his political views but is fundamental to an understanding of modern research on early Mesopotamia.

Daniel, G. *The First Civilizations*. New York: Crowell, 1968. An excellent account, both of early civilization and of modern scholarship, which succeeds in making difficult material easy to read.

Frankfort, H. *The Art and Architecture of the Ancient Orient*. Baltimore: Penguin, 1970. The best single-volume guide to its subject. Technical in places but written with immense breadth of knowledge and fully illustrated.

———, et al. *Before Philosophy*. Baltimore: Penguin, 1949. Subtitled "The Intellectual Adventure of Ancient Man," this book discusses Egyptian and Mesopotamian views on life, death, the function of the state, and the nature of the world. Not easy to read, but well worth the effort.

Hood, S. *The Arts in Prehistoric Greece*. Baltimore: Penguin, 1978. An up-to-date introduction to Minoan and Mycenaean art. The author, who has himself dug both in Crete and at Mycenae, includes evidence from the most recent excavations.

Lange, K., and M. Hirmer. *Egypt*. London: Phaidon, 1956. A superb collection of photographs of Egypt and Egyptian art, with a good introduction.

Marinatos, S., and M. Hirmer. *Crete and Mycenae*. New York: Abrams, 1960. Chiefly valuable for its pictures, although Marinatos' commentary is authoritative and informative.

Renault, Mary. *The King Must Die*. New York: Pantheon, 1958. An engrossing novel that retells the Theseus legend, with particularly interesting emphasis on the civilization of ancient Greece.

———. *The Bull from the Sea*. New York: Pantheon, 1962. A companion novel to *The King Must Die*, this describes the parts of the Theseus legend that are set in Athens and gives a vivid, if hypothetical, picture of Bronze Age religious customs.

Strommenger, E., and M. Hirmer. *The Art of Mesopotamia*. New York: Abrams, 1964. Highly recommended.

Warren, P. *The Aegean Civilizations*. Oxford: Elsevier-Phaidon, 1975. A good general account of Bronze Age Aegean culture, especially well illustrated. The author includes an interesting account of his own excavations in Crete.

Woolley, Charles L. *Ur of the Chaldees*. Baltimore: Penguin. 1954. An engrossing account of the excavations at Ur by one of the greatest of modern archaeologists.

Suggestions for Listening

There is little doubt that music played a role in the lives of all the peoples discussed in this chapter, but what instruments were used in the earliest periods, or what they actually sounded like, can now only be conjectured. We do know that a musical culture existed in Egypt as early as the 4th millennium B.C. and that chiefly small harps and flutes were used to produce quiet and reserved music in the Old Kingdom (before the 18th century B.C.). The introduction of Asiatic instruments and music at the beginning of the New Kingdom (16th century B.C.) brought a complete change and an orchestra that included large harps, lutes, oboes, and assorted percussion instruments such as drum and sistrum. The musical pendulum swung back around 600 B.C. with the reinstitution of ancient sacred rites—with the result that Plato, Herodotus, and other Greek writers reported the highly restrained character of Egyptian music. Egyptian music, in any event, doubtless influenced the development of Greek music (see Chapters 3 and 4). And in the early Christian era, Alexandria was an important center of psalm-singing as part of Christian worship.

Ancient Mesopotamia and Egypt nevertheless served as subject matter for later composers, as two examples show. The 20th-century Czech composer Bohuslav Martinů wrote his *The Epic of Gilgamesh* for orchestra, chorus, and soloists in 1955, a dignified and sometimes moving setting of extracts from the epic, including the death of Enkidu (available on Supraphon 1121808).

Much more familiar is Giuseppe Verdi's late-19th-century version of ancient Egypt in his opera *Aida*, commissioned by the Khedive of Egypt for the new Opera House in Cairo and produced there in 1871 (many recordings available). Verdi did inspect some old Egyptian musical instruments in the Archaeological Museum in Florence and said that he used a few Egyptian musical themes. The splendid result is scarcely the Egypt of any of the pharaohs but is surely romantic Italian opera at its grandest.

Questions for Further Discussion

1. All the civilizations described in this chapter eventually declined and collapsed. Did they share certain characteristics which made them unlikely to survive? Are any of these present in our own world?

2. Our picture of the past is inevitably conditioned by the nature of the evidence which has survived, and in the case of ancient Egypt and Mesopotamia most of it casts light only on the lives of the upper classes. Why is this, and what kind of discoveries would need to be made for us to reconstruct the lives of the average Egyptian or Sumerian?

3. It is often said that the art of the Egyptians was strongly influenced by their natural environment. The rectangles formed by the line of the flat desert meeting the vertical cliffs at its edge have been compared to the cubic forms that Egyptian sculptors preferred, and the sense of being enclosed which the landscape produces perhaps finds a parallel in the burial chambers of the pyramids and other tombs. Does it seem probable that the natural landscape exerted a strong influence on artists? Is there any evidence of this in the art of today?

4. The worship of the mother goddess played an important part in the religious life of many early peoples. Why did it disappear? Are there any traces of its survival in later times?

5. The excavations at Knossos, Mycenae, and Troy proved that stories which were thought to be only legends had a strong factual basis. What aspects of the myths have been confirmed by archaeological discoveries? Are there other examples of apparently mythical events which have subsequently been found to be true?

		GENERAL EVENTS	LITERATURE & PHILOSOPHY	ART

3000 B.C. ——

BRONZE AGE

Before 1260 B.C.

1800–1600 Age of the Hebrew Patriarchs: Abraham, Isaac, Jacob

1600 Israelite tribes in Egypt

1280 Exodus of Israelites from Egypt under leadership of Moses

1260 ——

Period of the Judges

1260 Israelites begin to penetrate land of Canaan

1040 ——

1040–1000 Reign of Saul, first king of Israel

1000 ——

Age of the Monarchy

1000–961 Reign of King David

961–922 Reign of Solomon; use of iron-tipped plow and iron war chariots; height of ancient Israel's cultural power: achievements form basis of Judaic, Christian, and Islamic religions

c. 1000 Formation of the Scriptures in written form

c. 950 Book of Psalms

10th–9th cent. Book of Kings

c. 961–c. 922 Hiram of Tyre constructs bronze "sea" in courtyard of Solomon's Temple

922 ——

Age of the Two Kingdoms

922 Civil war after death of Solomon; split of Northern Kingdom (Israel) and Southern Kingdom (Judah); classical prophetic period begins

721 Northern Kingdom destroyed by Assyria

8th–6th cent. Old Testament books of Isaiah, Jeremiah, and Ezekiel

Depiction of divinity in art prohibited in Jewish religion

734 Oxen from bronze "sea" given to King of Assyria by King Achaz

587 ——

IRON AGE (1000–)

Age of Exile, Return, and Occupations

587 Southern Kingdom defeated; Jews driven into captivity in Babylonia

539 Cyrus the Persian permits Jews to return to Jerusalem

516 Dedication of Second Temple in Jerusalem

332 Conquest of Jerusalem by Alexander the Great

after 5th cent. Book of Job

end of 2d cent. Apocryphal Book of Judith

63 ——

Roman Period

63 Conquest of Jerusalem by Romans under Pompey

37 B.C.–A.D. 4 Reign of Herod the Great under Roman tutelage

c. 6 B.C. Birth of Jesus

B.C. -
A.D.

c. A.D. 30 Death of Jesus; beginnings of Christianity in Palestine

45–49 First missionary journeys of Saint Paul

66–70 Jewish rebellions against Romans

c. 70 Titus destroys Jerusalem and razes the Temple; Jews sent into exile

c. A.D. 70 "Sermon on the Mount" in Gospel of Saint Matthew, New Testament

c. A.D. 81 Reliefs from Arch of Titus, Rome, commemorate Roman victory in Jerusalem

324 A.D. ——

Dates before the 10th cent. B.C. are approximate and remain controversial

2
Jerusalem and the Biblical Tradition

c. 961–c. 922 Building of Temple of Solomon; city of Megiddo rebuilt by Solomon

Music often accompanied the Psalms; musical instruments in use: drums, reed instruments, lyre, harp, horns

587 Solomon's Temple destroyed by Babylonians

c. 536–515 Second Temple of Solomon constructed

19 Herod the Great begins rebuilding Third Temple of Solomon

A.D. 70 Herod's Temple destroyed by the armies of Titus under Emperor Vespasian

c. 81 Arch of Titus, Rome, commemorates victory of Roman army in Jerusalem

Solomon as King and Hero

Nearly a thousand years after his death, the magnificence of Solomon [34] was so proverbial among the Jewish people that Jesus could allude to it and expect that the audience would immediately recognize the point of his comparison: "Consider the lilies of the field, how they grow; they neither toil nor spin; yet I tell you, even Solomon in all his glory was not arrayed like one of these" (Matthew 6:28–29). The reign of Solomon the King (from about 961 to 922 B.C.) marked the high point of Israelite power and achievement, as well as a turning point in the history of Israel. The Israelites had come out of Egypt (the Exodus) some three centuries before, about 1280 B.C., and, after their wanderings in the Sinai, penetrated and slowly conquered the land of Palestine. An essentially tribal people became a monarchy in the time of Saul (c. 1040–1000 B.C.), who was succeeded by the great King David. Solomon ascended the throne after the death of David, his father. He was to be the last king of the the United Kingdom, since civil war split the country after his death.

When Solomon became king of Israel in 961 B.C., the times were auspicious for a brilliant reign. The traditional "superpowers," neighboring Egypt and Assyria, were relatively weak; their internal problems dampened their taste for external conquest. To consolidate his position, Solomon entered into alliance with the always potentially dangerous Egyptians by marrying the daughter of the pharaoh.

Solomon was a decisive ruler who took advantage of this tranquil period both to consolidate and extend his power. He expanded foreign trade and equipped his armies with iron war chariots (a relatively new innovation of the times); he also was a renowned trader of horses, used for farming and war. It was probably during Solomon's reign that the iron-tipped plow came into general agricultural use, thus increasing food output. Solomon reorganized Israel's administrative districts to make the country more responsive to the demands of the royal administration in Jerusalem, which he kept as his capital, following David's decision. Archaeological excavations in this century have revealed the far-ranging projects of Solomon outside Jerusalem. The fortified city of Megiddo (I Kings 10:26) had elaborate stables that testify to the use of the war chariot and the horse [35, 36]. Excavations at the Red Sea port city of Ezion-geber (conducted in 1940 by the American scholar Nelson Glueck) revealed a huge smelting operation for refining copper, a metal that was of the utmost importance for Solomon's other projects.

In addition to his economic and administrative ability, Solomon is remembered in the biblical tradition as a man of wisdom; indeed, the "wisdom of Solomon" has not only become proverbial in our language but has long been a revered subject for the

34 *Solomon,* from the *Pala d'Oro* (gold altarpiece), Saint Mark's, Venice. This panel: c. 1100; entire altarpiece completed: 14th century. Enamel and gold. Solomon was often shown in Christian art because he was regarded as a forerunner of Christ, as indicated by the Greek words at upper left and upper right, which mean "The Prophet Solomon." The words on the scroll Solomon is holding mean "Wisdom built for herself a house." These, the first words of Proverbs 9:1, link the concepts of Solomon as a wise man and as builder of the Temple (see page 46).

35 Megiddo. c. 950 B.C. This aerial view was taken in 1932 by a balloon-carried camera from a height of 820′ (250 m). It is one of the first photographs of an archaeological site taken from a balloon. (Photography from tethered balloons is essential in much archaeological work because airplanes cannot fly low enough to record details and helicopters vibrate, raise dust, and ruffle water surfaces over submerged sites. Sophisticated radio-controlled cameras and infrared and color films are now used.)

36 Excavated stables at Megiddo. This ancient city was rebuilt by Solomon. Archaeological work has uncovered fortified gates, palaces, and these stables from his time. It is thought that 450–480 horses were stabled here. Stone mangers can be seen at center.

artist [37]. The Bible attributes Solomon's wisdom to a gift from God. The famous story deserves to be read in the language of the Scriptures:

I Kings 3:1–28
THE WISDOM OF SOLOMON

Solomon made a marriage alliance with Pharaoh king of Egypt; he took Pharaoh's daughter, and brought her into the city of David, until he had finished building his own house and the house of the Lord and the wall around Jerusalem. The people were sacrificing at the high places, however, because no house had yet been built for the name of the Lord.

Solomon loved the Lord, walking in the statutes of David his father; only, he sacrificed and burnt incense at the high places. And the king went to Gibeon to sacrifice there, for that was the great high place; Solomon used to offer a thousand burnt offerings upon that altar. At Gibeon the Lord appeared to Solomon in a dream by night; and God said, "Ask what I shall give you." And

37 *Solomon as the Symbol of Wisdom,* from the *Hours of Catherine of Cleves.* c. 1440. Manuscript illumination, 2½ × 2⅝" (6 × 7 cm). Pierpont Morgan Library, New York. Solomon is distributing bread to three supplicants—an obvious reference to Proverbs 9:5, where Wisdom invites everyone to share her bread and wine. In the corners above, the apostles Andrew and Paul unfurl banners inscribed with quotations from the Bible referring to the bread of the Eucharist. The bread of Wisdom was an antetype of the Eucharist for the Christian church.

Solomon said, "Thou hast shown great and steadfast love to thy servant David my father, because he walked before thee in faithfulness, in righteousness, and in uprightness of heart toward thee; and thou hast kept for him this great and steadfast love, and hast given him a son to sit on his throne this day. And now, O Lord my God, thou hast made thy servant king in place of David my father, although I am but a little child; I do not know how to go out or come in. And thy servant is in the midst of thy people whom thou hast chosen, a great people, that cannot be numbered or counted for multitude. Give thy servant therefore an understanding mind to govern thy people, that I may discern between good and evil; for who is able to govern this thy great people?"

It pleased the Lord that Solomon had asked this. And God said to him "Because you have asked this, and have not asked for yourself long life or riches or the life of your enemies, but have asked for yourself understanding to discern what is right, behold, I now do according to your word. Behold, I give you a wise and discerning mind, so that none like you has been before you and none like you shall arise after you. I give you also what you have not asked, both riches and honor, so that no other king shall compare with you, all your days. And if you will walk in my ways, keeping my statutes and my commandments, as your father David walked, then I will lengthen your days."

And Solomon awoke, and behold, it was a dream. Then he came to Jerusalem, and stood before the ark of the covenant of the Lord, and offered up burnt offerings and peace offerings, and made a feast for all his servants.

Then two harlots came to the king, and stood before him. The one woman said, "Oh, my lord, this woman and I dwell in the same house; and I gave birth to a child while she was in the house. Then on the third day after I was delivered, this woman also gave birth; and we were alone; there was no one else with us in the house, only we two were in the house. And this woman's son died in the night, because she lay on it. And she arose at midnight, and took my son from beside me, while your maidservant slept, and laid it in her bosom, and laid her dead son in my bosom. When I rose in the morning to nurse my child, behold, it was dead; but when I looked at it closely in the morning, behold, it was not the child that I had borne." But the other woman said, "No, the living child is mine, and the dead child is yours." The first said, "No, the dead child is yours, and the living child is mine." Thus they spoke before the king.

38 Giorgione. *The Judgment of Solomon.* c. 1500. Oil on canvas, 35 × 28⅜" (89 × 72 cm). Uffizi, Florence. The real mother is pleading for the life of her baby. The opulent landscape and costumes are of Giorgione's own time. The judgment of Solomon was often depicted in that period as a symbol of the just and wise ruler.

Then the king said, "The one says, 'This is my son that is alive, and your son is dead'; and the other says, 'No; but your son is dead, and my son is the living one.'" And the king said, "Bring me a sword." So a sword was brought before the king. And the king said, "Divide the living child in two, and give half to the one, and half to the other." Then the woman whose son was alive said to the king, because her heart yearned for her son, "Oh, my lord, give her the living child, and by no means slay it." [38] But the other said, "It shall be neither mine nor yours; divide it." Then the king answered and said, "Give the living child to the first woman, and by no means slay it; she is its mother." And all Israel heard of the judgment which the king had rendered; and they stood in awe of the king, because they perceived that the wisdom of God was in him, to render justice. ◗

The Bible contains another anecdote that emphasizes the wisdom of Solomon and his immense wealth: the visit of the Queen of Sheba (modern Yemen) to the court of Solomon [Plate 4, page 55]. The opulent character of the biblical description and the romantic nature of the theme have inspired any number of other artists to try and capture its lushness on canvas.

I Kings 10:1–13
SOLOMON AND THE QUEEN OF SHEBA

Now when the queen of Sheba heard of the fame of Solomon concerning the name of the Lord, she came to test him with hard questions. She came to Jerusalem with a very great retinue, with camels bearing spices, and very much gold, and precious stones; and when she came to Solomon, she told him all that was on her mind. And Solomon answered all her questions; there was nothing hidden from the king which he could not explain to her. And when the queen of Sheba had seen all the wisdom of Solomon, the house that he had built, the food of his table, the seating of his officials, and the attendance of his servants, their clothing, his cupbearers, and his burnt offerings which he offered at the house of the Lord, there was no more spirit in her.

And she said to the king, "The report was true which I heard in my own land of your affairs and of your wisdom, but I did not believe the reports until I came and my own eyes had seen it; and, behold, the half was not told me; your wisdom and prosperity surpass the report which I heard. Happy are your wives! Happy are these your servants, who continually stand before you and hear your wisdom! Blessed be the Lord your God, who has delighted in you and set you on the throne of Israel! Because the Lord loved Israel for ever, he has made you king, that you may execute justice and righteousness." Then she gave the king a hundred and twenty talents of gold, and a very great quantity of spices, and precious stones; never again came such an abundance of spices as these which the queen of Sheba gave to King Solomon.

Moreover the fleet of Hiram, which brought gold from Ophir, brought from Ophir a very great amount of almug wood and precious stones. And the king made of the almug wood supports for the house of the Lord, and for the king's house, lyres also and harps for the singers; no such almug wood has come or been seen, to this day.

And King Solomon gave to the queen of Sheba all that she desired, whatever she asked besides what was given her by the bounty of King Solomon. So she turned and went back to her own land, with her servants. ◼

Had Solomon only presided wisely over a wealthy and successful kingdom we would pay little attention to him. The history of humanity is studded with such monarchs. Solomon remains important, in both culture and religion, because he centered the Israelite cult of God at Jerusalem and built the first magnificent temple there.

Solomon's Temple as Monument and Myth

Solomon's Temple was not merely an architectural or artistic triumph; it marked a symbolic moment in the history of Western values, a moment that has had immense ramifications for both our history and our cultural consciousness down to the present time.

Chapters 5 through 9 of the First Book of Kings describe the building of the Temple of Solomon in Jerusalem. None of that Temple is now extant, so we must reconstruct its main outlines from the information in the Bible and what little evidence we have from the archaeological remains of pagan temple-building in Israel.

A temple, unlike a church or a synagogue, was not designed primarily for the worshiper. A temple housed a divinity. That distinction is important, since it determines, to a large extent, why temple architecture is so different from church architecture. At the very core of the temple was a space that was the dwelling place of the god. In another space, the priests ministered to the needs of the god and conducted the rites that honored the presence of the divinity. The worshipers generally held their services and offered their prayers outside the temple proper in a courtyard. They might go into the temple to "visit" the god in prayer or homage, but that is not where they usually worshiped.

The temple was the "sacred space" of the god; indeed, our word "profane" etymologically means "outside the sacred place." The ancients had a clear distinction in mind between sacred and profane space. The difference becomes clear if we compare the functions of the temple and the synagogue. Synagogues (from the Greek meaning "to gather together") were developed by the Jews outside the land of Israel in a much later period as places for prayer, study, and assembly (indeed, Yiddish-speaking Jews call the synagogue a *shul*—a school or a place of study). The temple, by contrast, was the house of God; it was in the temple that the *Shekinah* (The Presence) uniquely dwelt.

In a vast courtyard in front of Solomon's Temple was a great bronze altar for burnt offerings [39]. The altar was about 15 feet (4.6 meters) high and 30 feet (9.2 meters) square at its base. Next to this huge altar was perhaps the most spectacular object commissioned by Solomon for his Temple: the large bronze bowl known as the "sea."

39 Reconstruction drawing of the altar of Solomon's Temple. The three levels may have symbolized a mountain. The altar is similar in style to Babylonian temple towers, ziggurats (see figure **18,** page 27).

40 Reconstruction drawing of the "sea" outside Solomon's Temple. The Bible also mentions ten mobile bronze lavers—large basins used for carrying water. The symbolism of this great bowl is not clear, but some scholars think it may have represented the primordial sea of chaos overcome by God at the time of the creation (see page 58).

This great "sea" was a huge bowl about 7½ feet (2.29 meters) high and 15 feet (4.6 meters) in diameter [40]. It rested on twelve bronze oxen who, in groups of three, indicated the four cardinal points of the compass. Cast in bronze, it was "the thickness of a handbreadth; its rim was made like that of a cup, shaped like the calyx of a lily" (I Kings 7:26), Archaeologists have estimated its weight at about 25 tons (22.7 metric tons). The design and execution of the bronze "sea" were done by Hiram of Tyre, an artisan brought to Jerusalem by Solomon. No piece of this great "sea" has survived. The oxen were given as tribute to the King of Assyria by King Achaz in 734 B.C., while the bowl itself was broken up and carried off as spoils of war when the Babylonians herded the Jews into exile in 587 B.C.

Two huge bronze pillars flanked the entrance of the temple [41]. About 18 feet (5.5 meters) high, they were called *Jakin* (it shall stand) and *Boaz* (in strength), presumably from the first words of inscriptions carved on them. The temple vestibule measured about 15 feet (4.6 meters) by 30 feet (9.2 meters). Great wooden doors leading to the temple itself were carved with palms, flowers, and cherubim, which were winged beasts that symbolized guardianship of sacred places.

The first room of the temple proper was the *Hekal*, the Holy Place, about 45 feet (13.7 meters) high, 60 feet (18.3 meters) long, and 30 feet (9.2 meters) wide. Light entered through windows at the top of the walls, which were paneled in cedarwood (the famous cedars of Lebanon) richly carved in floral motifs. This main room contained sacred furnishings appropriate for the cult of God. There were ten large lampstands, five on each side of the hall. To one side was an inlaid table for the priestly offerings of bread

41 Reconstruction drawing of Solomon's Temple. The significance of the two bronze pillars is uncertain, but some scholars suggest that they may have represented the twin pillars of fire and smoke that guided the Israelites during their wanderings in the desert after the Exodus.

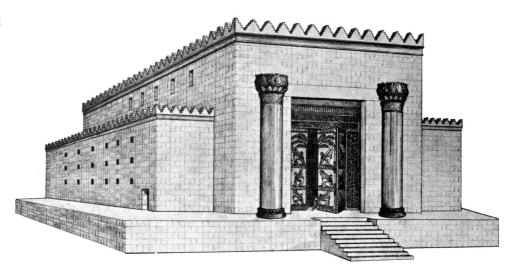

42 Reconstruction cutaway drawing of Solomon's Temple. Used with permission from Bernhard W. Anderson, *Understanding the Old Testament* (3rd ed., 1975). The Temple had a court with gates for public worshipers and another court that connected with Solomon's palace next to the Temple.

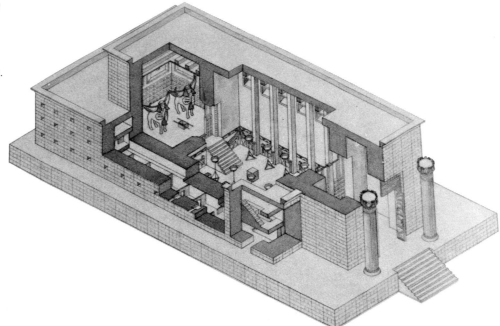

43 Cherubim guarding a citadel gate, Khorsabad, Iraq. Assyrian, c. 725 B.C. Winged animals with human faces are often found in the art of the Canaanites, Hittites, Mesopotamians, Assyrians, and Egyptians. For scale, note the man standing at right.

(the "shewbread" of the Bible), and at the far end of the room, directly in front of a small set of steps, was a cedarwood altar covered with gold for the offering of incense. The room as a whole—with its rich odors of incense and cedarwood, its filtered light and flickering lamplight, its soft burnished gold furnishings—was designed to give a sense of the sacredness of the place befitting the presence of God [42].

Steps directly in front of the incense altar led to the most sacred spot of the Temple; the Holy of Holies. This windowless cubicle, 30 feet (9.2 meters) square,

contained the ancient Ark of the Covenant, which the Jews had carried during their sojourn in the wilderness as a sign of God's presence among them. The Ark rested on the floor flanked by two great carved cherubim made from olivewood covered with gold. The cherubim took up nearly all the space in the Holy of Holies, since each wing was about 7½ feet (2.29 meters) long. Cherubim, common in the art of the time, were variously shown with human or animal faces. They were guardians not only of sacred places but even of cities [13].

The Temple of Solomon, though it was the crowning achievement of his reign, was also a costly one—economically, socially, and politically. The forced levies of workers who were either sent to Lebanon to quarry the stone (the Book of Kings mentions about thirty thousand workers involved in this project alone) or who labored on the construction site in Jerusalem demoralized the nation. Solomon spent such vast sums on this and other building projects that he was forced to cede whole villages to his creditors. These huge expenditures, of both manpower and money, split the nation after his death, and a civil war between north and south followed.

Furthermore, Solomon's activities endangered the purity of the Israelite religion. When he built the Temple, Solomon had to import artists and materials from the lands to the north. He also imported, inevitably, ideas. To a greater or lesser degree, the cult of God at the Temple thus became set in the context of Canaanite and Phoenician symbolism. Some scholars have argued that several of the Temple appurtenances, including the great "sea" and the bronze altar in the courtyard, echoed pagan symbolic motifs. The Bible itself says that in his old age Solomon was led astray and away from God, influenced by some of his foreign wives. Solomon, then, symbolized both the highest cultural achievement of Israel and the dangers prestige and cosmopolitanism could bring to it. In the centuries after Solomon, the prophets would fiercely warn against these dangers.

The civil war after Solomon's death eventually led to the establishment of the Kingdom of Israel in the north and the Kingdom of Judah (with the capital at Jerusalem) in the south. This weakened political and social situation invited outside intervention. The Kingdom of Assyria invaded and eventually destroyed the Kingdom of Israel in 721 B.C. [44]. The Kingdom of Judah, along with the holy city of Jerusalem, lasted until 587 B.C., when Jerusalem was destroyed by the Babylonians and the Jews were herded into exile. The intense sorrow at this catastrophe is poignantly recorded in the Book of Psalms:

44 Attack on a walled city. Assyrian, c. 700 B.C. Gypsum bas relief, 3′7″ (1.09 m) square. British Museum, London (reproduced by courtesy of the Trustees). Note the armored archers and the covered battering ram. At upper left are naked prisoners impaled on stakes to frighten those in the city. Near them a city-dweller on a turret pleads for mercy.

PSALM 79

O God, the heathen have come into thy
  inheritance;
    they have defiled thy holy temple;
    they have laid Jerusalem in ruins.
They have given the bodies of thy servants
    to the birds of the air for food,
    the flesh of thy saints to the beasts of the
      earth.
They have poured out their blood like water
    round about Jerusalem,
    and there was none to bury them.
We have become a taunt to our neighbors,
    mocked and derided by those round about
      us.

How long, O Lord? Wilt thou be angry for
    ever?
    Will thy jealous wrath burn like fire?
Pour out thy anger on the nations
    that do not know thee,
and on the kingdoms
    that do not call on thy name!
For they have devoured Jacob,
    and laid waste his habitation.

Do not remember against us the iniquities of
    our forefathers;
    let thy compassion come speedily to
      meet us,
    for we are brought very low.
Help us, O God of our salvation,
    for the glory of thy name;
deliver us, and forgive our sins,
    for thy name's sake!
Why should the nations say,
    "Where is their God?"
Let the avenging of the outpoured blood of thy
    servants
    be known among the nations before
      our eyes!

Let the groans of the prisoners come before
    thee;
    according to thy great power preserve those
      doomed to die!
Return sevenfold into the bosom of our
    neighbors
    the taunts with which they have taunted thee,
      O Lord!
Then we thy people, the flock of thy
    pasture,
    will give thanks to thee for ever;
    from generation to generation we will
      recount thy praise.

PSALM 137

By the waters of Babylon, there we sat down
    and wept,
    when we remembered Zion.
On the willows there
    we hung up our lyres.
For there our captors
    required of us songs,
and our tormentors, mirth, saying,
    "Sing us one of the songs of Zion!"

How shall we sing the Lord's song
    in a foreign land?
If I forget you, O Jerusalem,
    let my right hand wither!
Let my tongue cleave to the roof of my
    mouth,
    if I do not remember you,
if I do not set Jerusalem
    above my highest joy!

Remember, O Lord, against the Edomites
    the day of Jerusalem,
how they said, "Raze it, raze it!
    Down to its foundations!"
O daughter of Babylon, you devastator!
    Happy shall he be who requites you
    with what you have done to us!
Happy shall he be who takes your
    little ones
    and dashes them against the rock!

The Jews were permitted to return to their homeland by the Persians who had conquered Babylonia.
The returnees began to rebuild the Temple of Solomon sometime after 537 B.C.; it was dedicated in 515
B.C. For the next four centuries the restored Temple
was in use despite repeated invasions and occupations
of the country.

In 19 B.C., Herod the Great decided to rebuild the
Temple again in a project that was to be lengthy. It
was Herod's Temple that Jesus knew and to which
the Gospels make constant reference. In fact, this
Temple, one of the focal points of the Gospel narra-
tives, assumes a deeply symbolic significance in the
New Testament.

In A.D. 70, only six years after the final completion
of Herod's Temple, the armies of the Emperor Vespasian, led by his son Titus, marched into Jerusalem,
destroyed the city, burned down the Temple, and
dispersed its inhabitants. The triumphal Arch of
Titus near the Colosseum in Rome—which visitors
can still see—has sculptured reliefs showing Roman

soldiers marching off with the booty of victory [45]. On one relief soldiers are shown carrying away the massive seven-branch candelabrum, the *menorah* [46]. The modern state of Israel uses a stylized version of the *menorah* for its official seal [47].

The Temple was never rebuilt, but it was never forgotten. To this day, pious Jews pray at the Western Wall of Herod's Temple—the Wailing Wall—the only part of the Temple left standing [48]. Observant Jews remember the destruction of the Temple in other ways in their religious life. Homes and synagogues maintain a *mizrah*—usually a plaque or framed print—to show the direction toward which the faithful should pray—toward Jerusalem and its Temple [49]. The destruction of Jerusalem and the Temple are recalled in other ways. The Jewish litur-

below: 45 *The Triumph of Titus,* from Arch of Titus, Rome. c. A.D. 81. Passageway relief. The relief, now marred by the ravages of time, is one of those that commemorated Titus' triumphal return to Rome after the destruction of Jerusalem. (The whole arch is shown in figure **151,** page 231.)

bottom: 46 *The Spoils of Jerusalem,* from Arch of Titus, Rome. c. A.D. 81. Passageway relief. The *menorah* is prominent in the scene.

below: 47 Official emblem of the State of Israel. The *menorah* is modeled on the one on the Arch of Titus. The Hebrew word is "Israel."

bottom: 48 The Wailing Wall in Jerusalem. Observant Jews pray at this wall daily and leave petitions and prayers written on papers that they push into the crevices of the wall.

right: 49 *Mizrah.* Safed, Palestine, 1887. Lithograph on paper, 29 ½ × 21 ½" (75 × 55 cm). Jewish Museum, New York (gift of Harry G. Friedman). The Hebrew word *mizrah* (The East) is at the top, crowned between two lions. Below is a *menorah,* symbol of the Temple. The lower part is a stylized representation of the Temple.

gical year includes a day of fasting and prayer, the feast of *Tishah b'Av*; appropriately, the scriptural readings are taken from the Lamentations of the prophet Jeremiah. Jewish tradition advises observant Jews to leave a bit of their home unfinished, such as an unplastered section of wall, also in memory of Jerusalem and its Temple. Each year, at the Passover meal, Jews pray that the Passover next year will be in Jerusalem.

The destruction of Jerusalem and the Temple by the Romans had a profound impact on the later development of Judaism. Judaism did not have a geographical center after A.D. 70. The synagogue, not the Temple, became the focal point of Jewish worship. The priesthood went into decline, and the rabbis (teachers) became central to Jewish life. Jewish religious energies, under the leadership of the rabbis, became centered around the study of the biblical writings and the oral tradition that grew up around them. It was the rabbis who maintained Jewish culture and preserved the Hebrew language as a living language. They jealously guarded the integrity of the sacred text of the Bible and systematized the daily and festival liturgy, thus preventing Judaism from becoming regionalized. They also interpreted the meaning of the Law in terms of new needs and new cultural challenges. This devotion to the traditions of Israel kept Judaism alive during centuries of segregation, persecution, and dispersal. The memory of the Temple became a powerful symbol for maintaining a people as a people during their long period of exile.

The God of the Bible

When the Roman soldiers first broke into the Temple in Jerusalem, they were surprised to find that the Holy of Holies contained no cult figure. A thousand years earlier, in Solomon's Temple, the room contained only the Ark of the Covenant guarded by the cherubim. The Ark was destroyed during the Babylonian siege of Jerusalem; there is no mention of it in the historical books of the Bible after the period of the Babylonian exile. The Holy of Holies was, in fact, an empty room. The Israelites were unique among the ancient peoples of the world in maintaining a strict monotheism and a divinely sanctioned prohibition against the depiction of divinity in any art form: "You shall have no other gods before me. You shall not make yourself a graven image, or any likeness of anything that is in heaven above, or that is in the earth beneath, or that is in the water under the earth; you shall not bow down to them or serve them; for I the Lord your God am a jealous God" (Exodus 20:3–5).

The prohibition against the making of images in the Jewish religion was a clear indication of how different culturally the Jews were from their neighbors. This prohibition was a very effective way of saying that the God of Israel was different from any other god, that he was one God. God was, in fact, unknowable except as he revealed himself. Even in those revelations, he is well hidden. This was not a speculative form of monotheism. The Israelites had not come to the idea of a single God on the basis of metaphysical reason. In fact, they had no Hebrew word for philosophy. Their belief in one God was experiential. That is, their faith was certain because God had done "mighty things" for them. The reality of the one God was to be found, not in philosophy, but in history.

Who was this God? What were his characteristics? How did the Israelite concept of divinity eventually become the starting point for the great theologies of the Western religions of Judaism, Christianity, and Islam?

When Solomon dedicated his Temple on its completion, he offered a dedicatory prayer. A close examination of that sacred oration provides some clues about the nature of the biblical God:

I Kings 8:22–61
SOLOMON'S PRAYER

Then Solomon stood before the altar of the Lord in the presence of all the assembly of Israel, and spread forth his hands toward heaven; said, "O Lord, God of Israel, there is no God like thee, in heaven above or on earth beneath, keeping covenant and showing steadfast love to thy servants who walk before thee with all their heart; who hast kept with thy servant David my father what thou didst declare to him; yea, thou didst speak with thy mouth, and with thy hand hast fulfilled it this day. Now therefore, O Lord, God of Israel, keep with thy servant David my father what thou hast promised him, saying, 'There shall never fail you a man before me to sit upon the throne of Israel, if only your sons take heed to their way, to walk before me as you have walked before me.' Now therefore, O God of Israel, let thy word be confirmed, which thou hast spoken to thy servant David my father.

Plate 4 Lorenzo Ghiberti. *The Meeting of Solomon and the Queen of Sheba,* from the East Doors of the Baptistery, Florence. 1425–1452. Gilt bronze, 31″ (79 cm) square. Note the highly idealized Temple of Solomon in the background. This panel shows a fine Renaissance sense of proportion and dimensionality.

Plate 5 *David Composing the Psalms,* from the Paris Psalter. c. 900. Manuscript illumination, 14⅛ × 10¼″ (36 × 26 cm). Bibliothèque Nationale, Paris. This is an allegorical picture that mixes biblical and pagan motifs. The female figure next to David is Melody, while Echo peers from behind a column. The figure in the foreground may be a symbol of the River Jordan. Note that David plays a lyre. David is described in the Bible as a musician, but the artist here clearly was inspired by Orpheus, a mythical Greek hero who was supremely skilled in music.

"But will God indeed dwell on the earth? Behold, heaven and the highest heaven cannot contain thee; how much less this house which I have built! Yet have regard to the prayer of thy servant and to his supplication, O Lord my God, hearkening to the cry and to the prayer which thy servant prays before thee this day; that thy eyes may be open night and day toward this house, the place of which thou hast said, 'My name shall be there,' that thou mayest hearken to the prayer which thy servant offers toward this place. And hearken thou to the supplication of thy servant and of thy people Israel, when they pray toward this place; yea, hear thou in heaven thy dwelling place; and when thou hearest, forgive.

"If a man sins against his neighbor and is made to take an oath, and comes and swears his oath before thine altar in this house, then hear thou in heaven, and act, and judge thy servants, condemning the guilty by bringing his conduct upon his own head, and vindicating the righteous by rewarding him according to his righteousness.

"When thy people Israel are defeated before the enemy because they have sinned against thee, if they turn again to thee, and acknowledge thy name, and pray and make supplication to thee in this house; then hear thou in heaven, and forgive the sin of thy people Israel, and bring them again to the land which thou gavest to their fathers.

"When heaven is shut up and there is no rain because they have sinned against thee, if they pray toward this place, and acknowledge thy name, and turn from their sin, when thou dost afflict them, then hear thou in heaven, and forgive the sin of thy servants, thy people Israel, when thou dost teach them the good way in which they should walk; and grant rain upon thy land, which thou hast given to thy people as an inheritance.

"If there is famine in the land, if there is pestilence or blight or mildew or locust or caterpillar; if their enemy besieges them in any of their cities; whatever plague, whatever sickness there is; whatever prayer, whatever supplication is made by any man or by all thy people Israel, each knowing the affliction of his own heart and stretching out his hands toward this house; then hear thou in heaven thy dwelling place, and forgive, and act, and render to each whose heart thou knowest, according to all his ways (for thou, thou only, knowest the hearts of all the children of men); that they may fear thee all the days that they live in the land which thou gavest to our fathers.

"Likewise when a foreigner, who is not of thy people Israel, comes from a far country for thy name's sake (for they shall hear of thy great name, and thy mighty hand, and of thy outstretched arm), when he comes and prays toward this house, hear thou in heaven thy dwelling place, and do according to all for which the foreigner calls to thee; in order that all the peoples of the earth may know thy name and fear thee, as do thy people Israel, and that they may know that this house which I have built is called by thy name.

"If thy people go out to battle against their enemy, by whatever way thou shalt send them, and they pray to the Lord toward the city which thou hast chosen and the house which I have built for thy name, then hear thou in heaven their prayer and their supplication, and maintain their cause.

"If they sin against thee—for there is no man who does not sin—and thou art angry with them, and dost give them to an enemy, so that they are carried away captive to the land of the enemy, far off or near; yet if they lay it to heart in the land to which they have been carried captive, and repent, and make supplication to thee in the land of their captors, saying, 'We have sinned, and have acted perversely and wickedly'; if they repent with all their mind and with all their heart in the land of their enemies, who carried them captive, and pray to thee toward their land, which thou gavest to their fathers, the city which thou hast chosen, and the house which I have built for thy name; then hear thou in heaven thy dwelling place their prayer and their supplication, and maintain their cause and forgive thy people who have sinned against thee, and all their transgressions which they have committed against thee; and grant them compassion in the sight of those who carried them captive, that they may have compassion on them (for they are thy people, and thy heritage, which thou didst bring out of Egypt, from the midst of the iron furnace). Let thy eyes be open to the supplication of thy servant, and to the supplication of thy people Israel, giving ear to them whenever they call to thee. For thou didst separate them from among all the peoples of the earth, to be thy heritage, as thou didst declare through Moses, thy servant, when thou didst bring our fathers out of Egypt, O Lord God."

Now as Solomon finished offering all this prayer and supplication to the Lord, he arose from before the altar of the Lord, where he had knelt with hands outstretched toward heaven; and he stood, and blessed all the assembly of Israel with a loud voice, saying, "Blessed be the Lord who has given rest to his people Israel, according to all that he promised; not one word has failed of all his good promise, which he uttered by Moses his servant. The Lord our God be with us, as he was with our fathers; may he not leave us or forsake us; that he may incline our hearts to him, to walk in all his ways, and to keep his commandments, his statutes, and his ordinances, which he commanded our fathers. Let these words of mine, wherewith I have made supplication before the Lord, be near to the Lord our God day and night, and may he maintain the cause of his servant, and the cause of his people Israel, as each day requires; that all the peoples of the earth may know that the Lord is God; there is no other. Let your heart therefore be wholly true to the Lord our God, walking in his statutes and keeping his commandments, as at this day." 📖

There are some noteworthy points here. First, Solomon recognizes that the Temple is a pale attempt to represent God's presence among the people of Israel, for "will God indeed dwell on the earth?" God is beyond the confines and precincts of the Temple. That might seem like a commonplace to us (we are, after all, heirs of this tradition), but many ancient peoples believed their temples contained the very presence of the divinity—the presence that guaranteed the health and well-being of the political and social order. God's presence for the ancient Israelites was far beyond the confines of a particular people or a physical structure. The second point to note is that God is passionately involved in the history of the people of Israel. He led them out of Egypt; he chose them as a special people and entered into a covenant with them; he guided them into the Promised Land.

The prayer of Solomon, then, contains two concepts that might seem at first to be paradoxical or even contradictory: God is above all human affairs and somewhat removed from the reality of the world; in other words, God is transcendent. God is, at the same time, intimately involved with the history and the destiny of his people; indeed, as some prophets would later insist, God is concerned with the destiny of all people while maintaining a special relationship with Israel.

The relationship of God to the world and its relationship to him is further clarified by one of the most familiar passages from the Bible—the creation story that opens the Book of Genesis:

Genesis 1:1–2:4
THE CREATION STORY

In the beginning God created the heavens and the earth. The earth was without form and void, and darkness was upon the face of the deep; and the Spirit of God was moving over the face of the waters.

And God said, "Let there be light"; and there was light. And God saw that the light was good; and God separated the light from the darkness.

God called the light Day, and the darkness he called Night. And there was evening and there was morning, one day.

And God said, "Let there be a firmament in the midst of the waters, and let it separate the waters from the waters." And God made the firmament and separated the waters which were under the firmament from the waters which were above the firmament. And it was so. And God called the firmament Heaven. And there was evening and there was morning, a second day.

And God said, "Let the waters under the heavens be gathered together into one place, and let the dry land appear." And it was so. God called the dry land Earth, and the waters that were gathered together he called Seas. And God saw that it was good. And God said, "Let the earth put forth vegetation, plants yielding seed, and fruit trees bearing fruit in which is their seed, each according to its kind, upon the earth." And it was so. The earth brought forth vegetation, plants yielding seed according to their own kinds, and trees bearing fruit in which is their seed, each according to its kind. And God saw that it was good. And there was evening and there was morning, a third day.

And God said, "Let there be lights in the firmament of the heavens to separate the day from the night; and let them be for signs and for seasons and for days and years, and let them be lights in the firmament of the heavens to give light upon the earth." And it was so. And God made the two great lights, the greater light to rule the day, and the lesser light to rule the night; he made the stars also. And God set them in the firmament of the heavens to give light upon the earth, to rule over the day and over the night, and to separate the light from the darkness. And God saw that it was good. And there was evening and there was morning, a fourth day.

And God said, "Let the waters bring forth swarms of living creatures, and let birds fly above the earth across the firmament of the heavens." So God created the great sea monsters and every living creature that moves, with which the waters swarm, according to their kinds, and every winged bird according to its kind. And God saw that it was good. And God blessed them, saying, "Be fruitful and multiply and fill the waters in the seas, and let birds multiply on the earth." And there was evening and there was morning, a fifth day.

And God said, "Let the earth bring forth living creatures according to their kinds: cattle and creeping things and beasts of the earth according to their kinds." And it was so. And God made the beasts of the earth according to their kinds and the cattle according to their kinds, and everything that creeps upon the ground according to its kind. And God saw that it was good.

Then God said, "Let us make man in our image, after our likeness; and let them have dominion over the fish of the sea, and over the birds of the air, and over the cattle, and over all the earth, and over every creeping thing that creeps upon the earth." So God created man in his own image, in the image of God he created him; male and female he created them. And God blessed them, and God said to them, "Be fruitful and multiply, and fill the earth and subdue it; and have dominion over the fish of the sea and over the birds of the air and over every living thing that moves upon the earth." And God said, "Behold, I have given you every plant yielding seed which is upon the face of all the earth, and every tree with seed in its fruit; you shall have them for food. And to every beast of the earth, and to every bird of the air, and to everything that creeps on the earth, everything that has the breath of life, I have given every green plant for food." And it was so. And God saw everything that he had made, and behold, it was very good. And there was evening and there was morning, a sixth day.

Thus the heavens and the earth were finished, and all the host of them. And on the seventh day God finished his work which he had done, and he rested on the seventh day from all his work which he had done. So God blessed the seventh day and hallowed it, because on it God rested from all his work which he had done in creation.

These are the generations of the heavens and the earth when they were created.

First, God creates the world effortlessly by simply speaking his word over the chaos of the earth [50]. In the creation accounts of the peoples neighboring Israel, the world is created only after a fierce battle between the gods and the forces of chaos. In the famous Babylonian creation myth, the *Enuma Elish,* Marduk defeats the goddess Ti'amat and from her dismembered carcass creates the earth and the heavens. Humanity is created by mixing the blood of another semidivinity with the clay of the earth.

Second, there is a distance between God and His creation. God existed before the creation; he was not born out of the chaos before creation, as in many Middle Eastern creation myths. Nor is any part of the creation divine. This account of creation in the Bible is careful to describe the sun and the moon as mere creations of the power of God. There is a hidden po-

50 *The Architect of the Universe,* from the *Bible Moralisée.* Paris, 13th century. Manuscript illumination, 10 × 7″ (26 × 18 cm). Austrian National Library, Vienna. Implicit in this conception was the medieval belief that God viewed creation much as an architect does. That idea probably derives from the Book of Job, chapter 38 (see page 64).

lemic in this statement, since the *Enuma Elish* depicted the heavenly bodies as images of various divinities. In the Genesis account, only God is divine. The universe of the Bible is not a divine universe; it is a created universe which comes from the power of the Divine.

Finally, God pronounces the world to be good. The Bible sees the world as neither evil nor divine. In that sense the biblical view of the world is radically different from the Hindu or Buddhist view of the material world as illusion (*maya*) to be penetrated. Nor is it the world view of many primal religions like that of the American Indian, which sees the world as divine or animated by divinity. Finally, the world view of the Bible must be distinguished from those that consider the created physical world as essentially evil.

Some scholars have suggested that one of the reasons why technology and science have been so successful in the Western world is that we are cultural heirs to a biblical tradition which has never mystified the world by considering it divine or by avoiding it as illusory. More recent writers considering ecological problems have also pointed out that the biblical view of the world has made it easier for the West to think of nature only in terms of domination and exploitation.

The Psalms

Another fruitful source in the Bible for our understanding of the image of God is "Israel's Prayer Book"—the Book of Psalms. The psalms are in our common culture not only because they are part of the Bible but also because so much of their language has entered our heritage in our hymns, our prayer books, and our music. The psalms have provided much of our common terminology used to describe God: our refuge (Psalm 7); our strength (Psalm 18); a shepherd (Psalm 23); our light and salvation (Psalm 27); our shelter (Psalm 46); our judge (Psalm 82.)

The 150 psalms in the Bible are Hebrew poems composed, for the most part, to be sung at religious services, and many were probably used in the Temple services in Solomon's time [Plate 5, page 56]. This ancient Hebrew poetry has a rather distinctive style, characterized by *parallelism*. Parallelism means that a thought expressed in a line (or series of lines) is reexpressed in the following lines in different words. *Antithetical parallelism* means that an idea expressed in a line is contrasted in a following line with the statement of an opposite idea. The first psalm in the Book of Psalms illustrates both types of parallelism quite graphically:

PSALM 1

Blessed is the man
   who walks not in the counsel of the wicked,
nor stands in the way of sinners,
   nor sits in the seat of scoffers.

But his delight is in the law of the Lord,
   and on his law he meditates day and night.

He is like a tree
   planted by streams of water,
that yields its fruit in its season,
   and its leaf does not wither.
In all that he does, he prospers.

The wicked are not so,
   but are like chaff which the wind drives
     away.

Therefore the wicked will not stand in the
    judgment,
   nor sinners in the congregation of the
    righteous.

For the Lord knows the way of the
    righteous,
   but the way of the wicked will perish.

The first verse of the psalm contrasts the good and wicked man; verses 2 and 3 spell out what the good man is like by antithetical parallelism. Verse 4 provides another contrast with the evil man; verse 5 (by the use of parallelism) states that the evil man will not stand, while verse 6 contrasts the fate of both the good and the evil person.

Many of the psalms were sung to musical accompaniment. We have no accurate knowledge about the musical notation of the ancient Near East. Indeed, even the musical instruments mentioned in the Bible are only imperfectly understood by comparing biblical descriptions with contemporary illustrations from neighboring cultures such as that of Egypt [51]. The Bible mentions drums, reed instruments, stringed instruments such as the lyre and harp, and horns of various kinds. In the Book of Psalms there are some tantalizing, but fragmentary, notations in the text about musical usage. Some psalms (for example, 4, 6, 54, 55) are to be accompanied by strings, Psalm 5 by the flute, and Psalm 8 "with the harp of Gath." Other psalms have notations that seem to indicate that they were to be sung to a certain melody (for example, 57, 58, 59), but those melodies are lost to us. The word *selah* at the head of a number of psalms may have indicated a musical mode, but its meaning is total conjecture. A large number of the psalms seem to have been used for specific purposes in the public worship of Israel: mourning, thanksgiving, praise of God, and so on.

It is generally recognized that many of the psalms were used for ritual purposes, especially in the Temple worship at Jerusalem. Many of the psalms express a deep awareness of the individual person ("The Lord is my Shepherd") or a single cry for mercy and aid ("My God, my God, why have you forsaken me?"), but there is strong evidence that many were written to be sung congregationally or antiphonally by a congregation. Some psalms are structurally antiphonal in that they repeat a single phrase after each verse, a phrase the congregation repeated in response to a leader who sang the verses. Psalm 136 is a good example of this:

51 *The Blind Harper of Leiden,* detail from the tomb of Patenemheb. Saqqara, c. 1340–1330 B.C. Limestone bas-relief, height 11½" (29 cm). Rijksmuseum van Oudheden, Leiden, Netherlands. The instrument may be similar to the harp mentioned in the Book of Psalms.

PSALM 136

O give thanks to the Lord, for he is good,
    for his steadfast love endures for ever.
O give thanks to the God of gods,
    for his steadfast love endures for ever.
O give thanks to the Lord of lords,
    for his steadfast love endures for ever;

to him who alone does great wonders,
    for his steadfast love endures for ever;
to him who by understanding made the
        heavens,
    for his steadfast love endures for ever;
to him who spread out the earth upon the
        waters,
    for his steadfast love endures for ever;
to him who made the great lights,
    for his steadfast love endures for ever;
the sun to rule over the day,
    for his steadfast love endures for ever;

the moon and stars to rule over the night,
    for his steadfast love endures for ever;

to him who smote the first-born of Egypt,
    for his steadfast love endures for ever;
and brought Israel out from among them,
    for his steadfast love endures for ever;
with a strong hand and an outstretched arm,
    for his steadfast love endures for ever;
to him who divided the Red Sea in sunder,
    for his steadfast love endures for ever;
and made Israel pass through the midst of it,
    for his steadfast love endures for ever;
but overthrew Pharaoh and his host in the
        Red Sea,
    for his steadfast love endures for ever;
to him who led his people through the
        wilderness,
    for his steadfast love endures for ever;
to him who smote great kings,
    for his steadfast love endures for ever;
and slew famous kings,
    for his steadfast love endures for ever;
Sihon, king of the Amorites,
    for his steadfast love endures for ever;
and Og, king of Bashan,
    for his steadfast love endures for ever;
and gave their land as a heritage,
    for his steadfast love endures for ever;
a heritage to Israel his servant,
    for his steadfast love endures for ever;

It is he who remembered us in our low estate,
    for his steadfast love endures for ever;
and rescued us from our foes,
    for his steadfast love endures for ever;
he who gives food to all flesh,
    for his steadfast love endures for ever;

O give thanks to the God of heaven,
    for his steadfast love endures for ever.

Psalm 138 specifically alludes to the singing of hymns in the Temple:

PSALM 138

I give thee thanks, O Lord with my whole
        heart;
    before the gods I sing thy praise;
I bow down toward thy holy temple
    and give thanks to thy name for thy
        steadfast love and thy faithfulness;
for thou hast exalted above everything
    thy name and thy word.
On the day I called, thou didst answer me,
    my strength of soul thou didst increase.

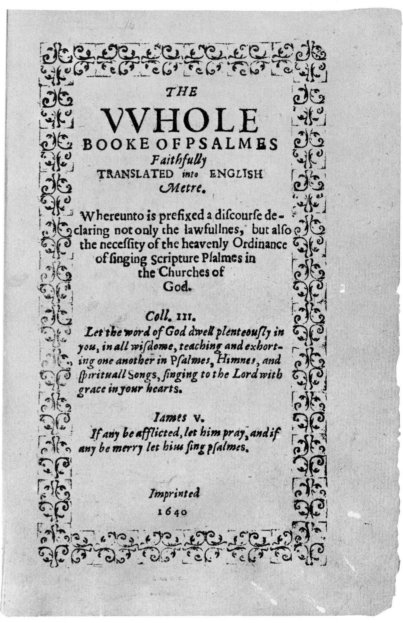

THE

VVHOLE

BOOKE OF PSALMES
Faithfully
TRANSLATED *into* ENGLISH
Metre.

Whereunto is prefixed a difcourse de-
claring not only the lawfulnes, but alfo
the neceffity of the heavenly Ordinance
of finging Scripture Pfalmes in
the Churches of
God.

Coll. III.
*Let the word of God dwell plenteoufly in
you, in all wifdome, teaching and exhort-
ing one another in Pfalmes, Himnes, and
fpirituall Songs, finging to the Lord with
grace in your hearts.*

Iames V.
*If any be afflicted, let him pray, and if
any be merry let him fing pfalmes.*

Imprinted
1640

52 Title page of the *Bay Psalm Book*. Cambridge, Massachusetts, 1640. Rare Books and Manuscripts Division, New York Public Library. Note that the title page describes an introductory essay that insists on the "lawfullnes" and "necessity" of singing the psalms in church worship.

All the kings of the earth shall praise thee, O
    Lord,
    for they have heard the words of thy mouth;
and they shall sing of the ways of the Lord,
    for great is the glory of the Lord.
For though the Lord is high, he regards the
    lowly;
    but the haughty he knows from afar.

Though I walk in the midst of trouble,
    thou dost preserve my life;
thou dost stretch out thy hand against the wrath
    of my enemies,
    and thy right hand delivers me.
The Lord will fulfil his purpose for me;
    thy steadfast love, O Lord, endures for ever.
    Do not forsake the work of thy hands.

The Book of Psalms has continued to be the hymnbook and prayer book of both Judaism and Christianity. Psalms make up a large part of the daily worship of devout Jews. The weekly singing of the entire Book of Psalms is at the heart of Christian monastic worship. The many beautiful illustrated psalters that have been preserved from the Middle Ages testify to the central importance of the psalms in Christianity. During the Reformation the psalms were considered the chief source of formal prayer for the church. The first book printed in the English colonies in North America was the *Bay Psalm Book* [52]. To this day, even outside the church, the psalms continue to inspire; for example, there are Igor Stravinsky's *Symphony of Psalms* of 1930 (based on the Latin Vulgate version of the psalms) and Leonard Bernstein's *Chichester Psalms* of 1965 (based on the Hebrew text of the psalms).

The Book of Job

However close God is to his people, he is ultimately beyond human comprehension. The mysteriousness of God's relationship to humanity is described with poetic intensity in the Book of Job. The Book of Job (written probably after the 5th century B.C.) is the only example of dialogue genre in Hebrew literature. The prologue of the book, which sets the stage for the dialogue itself, describes Job, a pious and holy man, reduced from great wealth to abject poverty and from health to leprosy so that God can test Job's faith to quiet the jibes of a skeptic Satan. Job refuses either to curse God or deny his faith in him.

The great bulk of the book records the speeches of the friends of Job as they come to "comfort" him in his affliction [53]. To each of their explanations of his state of dejection and misery Job answers with contrary evidence to refute them. The crux of this argument is in the form of a dilemma: suffering is visited on the impious as a punishment from God, but, since Job is just, why does he suffer? His friends maintain

that he must be guilty before God and they advise Job to confess this fact. Job vehemently insists on his innocence before God. Since the Hebrew religion had no clear idea of a heaven, it was not possible for Job to argue that he would be rewarded in the next life. Indeed, the whole power of the book comes precisely from the fact that there is only this life and "fairness" would seem to demand that the just should flourish. In chapters 32–37, a rather bumptious young man,

53 Fritz Eichenberg. *Job,* from *Ten Wood Engravings from the Old Testament.* 1954. Wood engraving, 13⅜ × 6⅛" (31 × 16 cm). Print Collection, New York Public Library. In this modern woodcut the artist shows Job, protected by an angel, under the omniscient eye of God as he listens to the "comfort" of his three friends. Their unconvincing advice is symbolized by the scrolls at their feet.

Elihu, approaches Job to expound the educative and moral values of suffering. Job, however, will have none of it.

At the end of the book, God enters the dialogue "out of the whirlwind" [54]. In the hand of a lesser artist God would then have solved Job's theological problem, but, as the British writer G. K. Chesterton once said, the enigmas of God are even darker than the enigmas of Job. Rather than answer Job's questions about his sufferings, God puts a further question to him: How can you plumb the mystery of human suffering when you cannot even begin to grasp the very fact of existence? Strangely enough, the skepticism of God comforts Job more than the rationalizations of his friends. God's challenge does not answer Job's questions; it merely gives Job a way of living with them. Job is to see life not as a problem to be solved but a mystery to be lived.

The Book of Job, as difficult and, in some ways, as atypical a book as one can find in the Bible, has been a favorite for modern interpretations. Archibald MacLeish even rewrote it as a stage play in 1958 under the title of *J.B.* Job is a very "existentialist" work. It poses God as a "problem." (How can a just God afflict a good person?) It depicts human beings as urgent searchers after the meaning of existence. (The proverbial "patience of Job" is wide of the mark; Job was outraged at his situation and wanted it changed as quickly as possible.) Finally, the Book of Job takes on the most persistent problem of philosophy and theology: Why is there evil in the world? Beyond that, the Book of Job contains some of the most powerful poetry in the Hebrew Bible. The concluding chapters, in which God speaks to Job of the wonders of creation and receives Job's repentance for questioning his intent, are unparalleled in their strength and majesty:

Job 38–42
THE WONDERS OF CREATION

Then the Lord answered Job out of the whirlwind:
"Who is this that darkens counsel by words without
　　knowledge?
Gird up your loins like a man,
　　I will question you, and you shall declare to me.

"Where were you when I laid the foundation of the
　　earth?
　　Tell me, if you have understanding.
Who determined its measurements—surely you
　　know!
　　Or who stretched the line upon it?
On what were its bases sunk,
　　or who laid its cornerstone,
when the morning stars sang together,
　　and all the sons of God shouted for joy?

"Or who shut in the sea with doors,
　　when it burst forth from the womb;
when I made clouds its garment,
　　and thick darkness its swaddling band,
and prescribed bounds for it,
　　and set bars and doors,
and said, 'Thus far shall you come, and no farther,
　　and here shall your proud waves be stayed'?

"Have you commanded the morning since your days
　　began,
　　and caused the dawn to know its place,
that it might take hold of the skirts of the earth,
　　and the wicked be shaken out of it?
It is changed like clay under the seal,
　　and it is dyed like a garment.
From the wicked their light is withheld,
　　and their uplifted arm is broken.

"Have you entered into the springs of the sea,
  or walked in the recesses of the deep?
Have the gates of death been revealed to you,
  or have you seen the gates of deep darkness?
Have you comprehended the expanse of the earth?
  Declare, if you know all this.

"Where is the way to the dwelling of light,
  and where is the place of darkness,
that you may take it to its territory
  and that you may discern the paths to its home?
You know, for you were born then,
  and the number of your days is great!

"Have you entered the storehouses of the snow,
  or have you seen the storehouses of the hail,
which I have reserved for the time of trouble,
  for the day of battle and war?
What is the way to the place where the light is dis-
    tributed,
  or where the east wind is scattered upon the earth?

"Who has cleft a channel for the torrents of rain,
  and a way for the thunderbolt,
to bring rain on a land where no man is,
  on the desert in which there is no man;
to satisfy the waste and desolate land,
  and to make the ground put forth grass?

"Has the rain a father,
  or who has begotten the drops of dew?
From whose womb did the ice come forth,
  and who has given birth to the hoarfrost of
    heaven?
The waters become hard like stone,
  and the face of the deep is frozen.

"Can you bind the chains of the Pleiades,
  or loose the cords of Orion?
Can you lead forth the Mazzaroth in their season,
  or can you guide the Bear with its children?
Do you know the ordinances of the heavens?
  Can you establish their rule on the earth?

"Can you lift up your voice to the clouds,
  that a flood of waters may cover you?
Can you send forth lightnings, that they may go
  and say to you, 'Here we are'?
Who has put wisdom in the clouds,
  or given understanding to the mists?
Who can number the clouds by wisdom?
  Or who can tilt the waterskins of the heavens,
when the dust runs into a mass
  and the clods cleave fast together?.

"Can you hunt the prey for the lion,
  or satisfy the appetite of the young lions,
when they crouch in their dens,

or lie in wait in their covert?
Who provides for the raven its prey,
  when its young ones cry to God,
  and wander about for lack of food?

"Do you know when the mountain goats bring
    forth?
  Do you observe the calving of the hinds?
Can you number the months that they fulfil,
  and do you know the time when they bring forth,
when they crouch, bring forth their offspring,
  and are delivered of their young?
Their young ones become strong, they grow up in
    the open;
  they go forth, and do not return to them.

"Who has let the wild ass go free?
  Who has loosed the bonds of the swift ass,
to whom I have given the steppe for his home,
  and the salt land for his dwelling place?
He scorns the tumult of the city;
  he hears not the shouts of the driver.
He ranges the mountains as his pasture,
  and he searches after every green thing.

"Is the wild ox willing to serve you?
  Will he spend the night at your crib?
Can you bind him in the furrow with ropes,
  or will he harrow the valleys after you?
Will you depend on him because his strength is great,
  and will you leave to him your labor?
Do you have faith in him that he will return,
  and bring your grain to your threshing floor?

"The wings of the ostrich wave proudly;
  but are they the pinions and plumage of love?
For she leaves her eggs to the earth,
  and lets them be warmed on the ground,
forgetting that a foot may crush them,
  and that the wild beast may trample them.
She deals cruelly with her young, as if they were not
    hers;
  though her labor be in vain, yet she has no fear;
because God has made her forget wisdom,
  and given her no share in understanding.
When she rouses herself to flee,
  she laughs at the horse and his rider.

"Do you give the horse his might?
  Do you clothe his neck with strength?
Do you make him leap like the locust?
  His majestic snorting is terrible.
He paws in the valley, and exults in his strength;
  he goes out to meet the weapons.
He laughs at fear, and is not dismayed;
  he does not turn back from the sword.
Upon him rattle the quiver,
  the flashing spear and the javelin.

With fierceness and rage he swallows the ground;
  he cannot stand still at the sound of the trumpet.
When the trumpet sounds, he says 'Aha!'
  He smells the battle from afar,
  the thunder of the captains, and the shouting.

"Is it by your wisdom that the hawk soars,
  and spreads his wings toward the south?
Is it at your command that the eagle mounts up
  and makes his nest on high?
On the rock he dwells and makes his home
  in the fastness of the rocky crag.
Thence he spies out the prey;
  his eyes behold it afar off.
His young ones suck up blood;
  and where the slain are, there is he."

And the Lord said to Job:
"Shall a faultfinder contend with the Almighty?
  He who argues with God, let him answer it."

Then Job answered the Lord:
"Behold, I am of small account; what shall I answer
    thee?
  I lay my hand on my mouth.
I have spoken once, and I will not answer;
  twice, but I will proceed no further."

Then the Lord answered Job out of the whirlwind:
"Gird up your loins like a man;
  I will question you, and you declare to me.
Will you even put me in the wrong?
  Will you condemn me that you may be justified?
Have you an arm like God,
  and can you thunder with a voice like his?

"Deck yourself with majesty and dignity;
  clothe yourself with glory and splendor.
Pour forth the overflowings of your anger,
  and look on every one that is proud, and abase
    him.
Look on every one that is proud, and bring him low;
  and tread down the wicked where they stand.
Hide them all in the dust together;
  bind their faces in the world below.
Then will I also acknowledge to you,
  that your own right hand can give you
    victory.

"Behold, Behemoth,
  which I made as I made you;
  he eats grass like an ox.
Behold, his strength in his loins,
  and his power in the muscles of his belly.
He makes his tail stiff like a cedar;
  the sinews of his thighs are knit together.
His bones are tubes of bronze,
  his limbs like bars of iron.

"He is the first of the works of God;
  let him who made him bring near his sword!
For the mountains yield food for him
  where all the wild beasts play.
Under the lotus plants he lies,
  in the covert of the reeds and in the marsh.
For his shade the lotus trees cover him;
  the willows of the brook surround him.
Behold, if the river is turbulent he is not frightened;
  he is confident though Jordan rushes against his
    mouth.
Can one take him with hooks,
  or pierce his nose with a snare?

"Can you draw out Leviathan with a fishhook,
  or press down his tongue with a cord?
Can you put a rope in his nose,
  or pierce his jaw with a hook?
Will he make many supplications to you?
  Will he speak to you soft words?
Will he make a covenant with you
  to take him for your servant for ever?
Will you play with him as with a bird,
  or will you put him on leash for your maidens?
Will traders bargain over him?
  Will they divide him up among the merchants?
Can you fill his skin with harpoons,
  or his head with fishing spears?
Lay hands on him;
  think of the battle; you will not do it again!
Behold, the hope of a man is disappointed;
  he is laid low even at the sight of him.
No one is so fierce that he dares to stir him up.
  Who then is he that can stand before me?
Who has given to me, that I should repay him?
  Whatever is under the whole heaven is mine.

"I will not keep silence concerning his limbs,
  or his mighty strength, or his goodly frame.
Who can strip off his outer garment?
  Who can penetrate his double coat of mail?
Who can open the doors of his face?
  Round about his teeth is terror.
His back is made of rows of shields,
  shut up closely as with a seal.
One is so near to another
  that no air can come between them.
They are joined one to another;
  they clasp each other and cannot be separated.
His sneezings flash forth light,
  and his eyes are like the eyelids of the dawn.
Out of his mouth go flaming torches;
  sparks of fire leap forth.
Out of his nostrils comes forth smoke,
  as from a boiling pot and burning rushes.
His breath kindles coals,
  and a flame comes forth from his mouth.

In his neck abides strength,
    and terror dances before him.
The folds of his flesh cleave together,
    firmly cast upon him and immovable.
His heart is hard as a stone,
    hard as the nether millstone.
When he raises himself up the mighty are afraid;
    at the crashing they are beside themselves.
Though the sword reaches him, it does not avail;
    nor the spear, the dart, or the javelin.
He counts iron as straw,
    and bronze as rotten wood.
The arrow cannot make him flee;
    for him slingstones are turned to stubble.
Clubs are counted as stubble;
    he laughs at the rattle of javelins.
His underparts are like sharp potsherds;
    he spreads himself like a threshing sledge on the
        mire.
He makes the deep boil like a pot;
    he makes the sea like a pot of ointment.
Behind him he leaves a shining wake;
    one would think the deep to be hoary.
Upon earth there is not his like,
    a creature without fear.
He beholds everything that is high;
    he is king over all the sons of pride.''

Then Job answered the Lord:
''I know that thou canst do all things,
    and that no purpose of thine can be
        thwarted.
'Who is this that hides counsel without knowledge?'
Therefore I have uttered what I did not understand,
    things too wonderful for me, which I did not
        know.
'Hear, and I will speak;
    I will question you, and you declare to me.'
I had heard of thee by the hearing of the ear,
    but now my eye sees thee;
therefore I despise myself,
    and repent in dust and ashes.''

After the Lord had spoken these words to Job, the Lord said to Eliphaz the Temanite: "My wrath is kindled against you and against your two friends; for you have not spoken of me what is right, as my servant Job has. Now therefore take seven bulls and seven rams, and go to my servant Job, and offer up for yourselves a burnt offering; and my servant Job shall pray for you, for I will accept his prayer not to deal with you according to your folly; for you have not spoken of me what is right, as my servant Job has." So Eliphaz the Temanite and Bildad the Shuhite and Zophar the Naamathite went and did what the Lord had told them; and the Lord accepted Job's prayer.

And the Lord restored the fortunes of Job, when he had prayed for his friends; and the Lord gave Job twice as much as he had before. Then came to him all his brothers and sisters and all who had known him before, and ate bread with him in his house; and they showed him sympathy and comforted him for all the evil that the Lord had brought upon him; and each of them gave him a piece of money and a ring of gold. And the Lord blessed the latter days of Job more than his beginning; and he had fourteen thousand sheep, six thousand camels, a thousand yoke of oxen, and a thousand she-asses. He had also seven sons and three daughters. And he called the name of the first Jemimah; and the name of the second Keziah; and the name of the third Kerenhappuch. And in all the land there were no women so fair as Job's daughters; and their father gave them inheritance among their brothers. And after this Job lived a hundred and forty years, and saw his sons, and his sons' sons, four generations. And Job died, an old man, and full of days. 📖

The Prophets: God and History

The word "prophet" derives from the Greek *prophetes,* one who speaks for another. That etymological meaning is as good a definition of the biblical prophet as one could hope for: the prophet is one who speaks for God. We normally think of the prophet as one who foretells the future or reveals secret knowledge. Though the biblical prophets did speak of an ideal future age, this was not their primary task or their function in Israelite religion. The Hebrew concept of the prophet was a unique contribution to the history of religion. The prophet was not a seer or an oracle or a diviner but a spokesman for God. This prophetic understanding of religion was to have a profound and lasting influence on the subsequent development of Western religion and culture.

Prophets were not a hereditary religious caste of functionaries as were the priests who received their office by virtue of their birth into the tribe of Levi. Nor were the prophets ordained or commissioned for their task by some religious hierarchy. Prophets felt themselves called by God in unique and mysterious ways. Furthermore, they had no special training for their tasks and, in some cases, were reluctant to undertake the duty of prophetism. The Bible records highly sacred and awe-inspiring language to describe the prophetic call. In the case of Isaiah [55], the Temple itself was the arena:

Isaiah 6:1–8
THE CALL OF ISAIAH

In the year that King Uzziah died I saw the Lord sitting upon a throne, high and lifted up; and his train filled the temple. Above him stood the seraphim; each had six wings: with two he covered his face, and with two he covered his feet, and with two he flew. And one called to another and said:

"Holy, holy, holy is the Lord of hosts;
the whole earth is full of his glory."

55 *Isaiah,* west portal of the Benedictine Abbey of Souillac, France. c. 1110. Isaiah was active as a prophet in and near Jerusalem from about 742 to 701 B.C.

And the foundations of the thresholds shook at the voice of him who called, and the house was filled with smoke. And I said: "Woe is me! For I am lost; for I am a man of unclean lips, and I dwell in the midst of a people of unclean lips; for my eyes have seen the King, the Lord of hosts!"

Then flew one of the seraphim to me, having in his hand a burning coal which he had taken with tongs from the altar. And he touched my mouth, and said: "Behold, this has touched your lips; your guilt is taken away, and your sin forgiven." And I heard the voice of the Lord saying, "Whom shall I send, and who will go for us?" Then I said, "Here am I! Send me."

The call of Jeremiah described in the opening verses of his book shows his reluctance in the face of prophetic responsibility:

Jeremiah 1:1–10
THE CALL OF JEREMIAH

The words of Jeremiah, the son of Hilkiah, of the priests who were in Anathoth in the land of Benjamin, to whom the word of the Lord came in the days of Josiah the son of Amon, king of Judah, in the thirteenth year of his reign. It came also in the days of Jehoiakim the son of Josiah, king of Judah, and until the end of the eleventh year of Zedekiah, the son of Josiah, king of Judah, until the captivity of Jerusalem in the fifth month.

Now the word of the Lord came to me saying,
"Before I formed you in the womb I knew you,
and before you were born I consecrated you;
I appointed you a prophet to the nations."
Then I said, "Ah, Lord God! Behold, I do not know how to speak, for I am only a youth." But the Lord said to me,
"Do not say, 'I am only a youth';
for to all to whom I send you you shall go,
and whatever I command you you shall speak.
Be not afraid of them,
for I am with you to deliver you, says the Lord."
Then the Lord put forth his hand and touched my mouth; and the Lord said to me,
"Behold, I have put my words in your mouth.
See, I have set you this day over nations and over kingdoms,
to pluck up and to break down,
to destroy and to overthrow,
to build and to plant."

The most imagistic and solemn of the prophetic calls is that of the opening chapters of the Book of Ezekiel [56]:

56 Raphael. *The Vision of Ezekiel*. c. 1500. Oil on panel, 40 × 30″ (102 × 76 cm). Pitti Palace, Florence. Raphael depicts the vision that Ezekiel describes in the beginning of his book. The artist simplifies the four-faced figures into an eagle, lion, ox, and man surrounded and supported by angels whose presence shows that this is a heavenly vision. Ezekiel's four figures were, from the beginning of Christianity, taken to represent the four gospels of the New Testament.

Ezekiel 1, 2
THE CALL OF EZEKIEL

In the thirtieth year, in the fourth month, on the fifth day of the month, as I was among the exiles by the river Chebar, the heavens were opened, and I saw visions of God. On the fifth day of the month (it was the fifth year of the exile of King Jehoiakim), the word of the Lord came to Ezekiel the priest, the son of Buzi, in the land of the Chaldeans by the river Chebar; and the hand of the Lord was upon him there.

As I looked, behold, a stormy wind came out of the north, and a great cloud, with brightness round about it, and fire flashing forth continually, and in the midst of the fire, as it were gleaming bronze. And from the midst of it came the likeness of four living creatures. And this was their appearance: they had the form of men, but each had four faces, and each of them had four wings. Their legs were straight, and the soles of their feet were like the sole of a calf's foot; and they sparkled like burnished bronze. Under their wings on their four sides they had human hands. And the four had their faces and their wings thus: their wings touched one another; they went every one straight forward, without turning as they went. As for the likeness of their faces, each had the face of a man in front; the four had the face of a lion on the right side, the four had the face of an ox on the left side, and the four had the face of an eagle at the back. Such were their faces. And their wings were spread out above; each creature had two wings, each of which touched the wing of another, while two covered their bodies. And each went straight forward; wherever the spirit would go, they went, without turning as they went. In the midst of the living creatures there was something that looked like burning coals of fire, like torches moving to and fro among the living creatures; and the fire was bright, and out of the fire went forth lightning. And the living creatures darted to and fro, like a flash of lightning.

Now as I looked at the living creatures, I saw a wheel upon the earth beside the living creatures, one for each of the four of them. As for the appearance of the wheels and their construction: their appearance was like the gleaming of a chrysolite; and the four had the same likeness, their construction being as it were a wheel within a wheel. When they went, they went in any of their four directions without turning as they went. The four wheels had rims and they had spokes; and their rims were full of eyes round about. And when the living creatures went, the wheels went beside them; and when the living creatures rose from the earth, the wheels rose. Wherever the spirit would go, they went, and the wheels rose along with them;

for the spirit of the living creatures was in the wheels. When those went, these went; and when those stood, these stood; and when those rose from the earth, the wheels rose along with them; for the spirit of the living creatures was in the wheels.

Over the heads of the living creatures there was the likeness of a firmament, shining like crystal, spread out above their heads. And under the firmament their wings were stretched out straight, one toward another; and each creature had two wings covering its body. And when they went, I heard the sound of their wings like the sound of many waters, like the thunder of the Almighty, a sound of tumult like the sound of a host; when they stood still, they let down their wings. And there came a voice from above the firmament over their heads; when they stood still, they let down their wings.

And above the firmament over their heads there was the likeness of a throne, in appearance like sapphire; and seated above the likeness of a throne was a likeness as it were of a human form. And upward from what had the appearance of his loins I saw as it were gleaming bronze, like the appearance of fire enclosed round about; and downward from what had the appearance of his loins I saw as it were the appearance of fire, and there was brightness round about him. Like the appearance of the bow that is in the cloud on the day of rain, so was the appearance of the brightness round about.

Such was the appearance of the likeness of the glory of the Lord. And when I saw it, I fell upon my face, and I heard the voice of one speaking.

And he said to me, "Son of man, stand upon your feet, and I will speak with you." And when he spoke to me, the Spirit entered into me and set me upon my feet; and I heard him speaking to me. And he said to me, "Son of man, I send you to the people of Israel, to a nation of rebels, who have rebelled against me; they and their fathers have transgressed against me to this very day. The people also are impudent and stubborn: I send you to them; and you shall say to them, 'Thus says the Lord God.' And whether they hear or refuse to hear (for they are a rebellious house) they will know that there has been a prophet among them. And you, son of man, be not afraid of them, nor be afraid of their words, though briars and thorns are with you and you sit upon scorpions; be not afraid of their words, nor be dismayed at their looks, for they are a rebellious house. And you shall speak my words to them, whether they hear or refuse to hear; for they are a rebellious house.

"But you, son of man, hear what I say to you; be not rebellious like that rebellious house; open your mouth, and eat what I give you." And when I looked, behold, a hand was stretched out to me, and, lo, a written scroll was in it; and he spread it before me; and it had writing on the front and on the back, and there were written on it words of lamentation and mourning and woe.

All these prophets lived after the division of the monarchy following the death of Solomon. In the period before and during the united monarchy, prophetism seems to have had more of an ecstatic character—prophets spoke in trances or to the accompaniment of music. The prophets tended to belong to schools or guilds and were more likely to be attached, though unofficially, to shrines or royal households. In the period of classical prophetism—from the 8th century B.C. on—the office of the prophet developed some unique and distinctive characteristics.

For one thing, the prophets persistently emphasized ethical monotheism together with some tension with (and, indeed, opposition to) the official religion of the priestly worship of the temple and the shrines. A powerful example of this righteous anger against the formalism and corruption of temple worship can be read in Jeremiah's outburst against cultic religion:

Jeremiah 8
THE ANGER OF JEREMIAH

"At that time, says the Lord, the bones of the kings of Judah, the bones of its princes, the bones of the priests, the bones of the prophets, and the bones of the inhabitants of Jerusalem shall be brought out of their tombs; and they shall be spread before the sun and the moon and all the host of heaven, which they have loved and served, which they have gone after, and which they have sought and worshiped; and they shall not be gathered or buried; they shall be as dung on the surface of the ground. Death shall be preferred to life by all the remnant that remains of this evil family in all the places where I have driven them, says the Lord of hosts.

"You shall say to them, Thus says the Lord:
When men fall, do they not rise again?
 If one turns away, does he not return?
Why then has this people turned away
 in perpetual backsliding?
They hold fast to deceit,
 they refuse to return.
I have given heed and listened,
 but they have not spoken aright;
no man repents of his wickedness,
 saying, 'What have I done?'

Every one turns to his own course,
 like a horse plunging headlong into battle.
Even the stork in the heavens
 knows her times;
and the turtledove, swallow, and crane
 keep the time of their coming;
but my people know not
 the ordinance of the Lord.
"How can you say, 'We are wise,
 and the law of the Lord is with us'?
But, behold, the false pen of the scribes
 has made it into a lie.
The wise men shall be put to shame,
 they shall be dismayed and taken;
lo, they have rejected the word of the Lord,
 and what wisdom is in them?
Therefore I will give their wives to others
 and their fields to conquerors,
because from the least to the greatest
 every one is greedy for unjust gain;
from prophet to priest
 every one deals falsely.
They have healed the wound of my people lightly,
 saying, 'Peace, peace,'
 when there is no peace.
Were they ashamed when they committed
  abomination?
 No, they were not at all ashamed;
 they did not know how to blush.
Therefore they shall fall among the fallen;
 when I punish them, they shall be overthrown,
  says the Lord.
When I would gather them, says the Lord,
 there are no grapes on the vine,
 nor figs on the fig tree;
even the leaves are withered,
 and what I gave them has passed away from
  them."

Why do we sit still?
Gather together, let us go into the fortified cities
 and perish there;
for the Lord our God has doomed us to perish,
 and has given us poisoned water to drink,
 because we have sinned against the Lord.
We looked for peace, but no good came,
 for a time of healing, but behold, terror.
"The snorting of their horses is heard from Dan;
 at the sound of the neighing of their stallions
 the whole land quakes.
They come and devour the land and all that fills it,
 the city and those who dwell in it.
For behold, I am sending among you serpents,
 adders which cannot be charmed,
 and they shall bite you," says the Lord.

My grief is beyond healing,
     my heart is sick within me.
Hark, the cry of the daughter of my people
     from the length and breadth of the land:
"Is the Lord not in Zion?
     Is her King not in her?"
"Why have they provoked me to anger with their
          graven images,
     and with their foreign idols?"
"The harvest is past, the summer is ended,
     and we are not saved."
For the wound of the daughter of my people is my
          heart wounded,
   I mourn, and dismay has taken hold
          on me.

Is there no balm in Gilead?
     Is there no physician there?
Why then has the health of the daughter of my
          people
     not been restored?

The classical prophets also tended to think more in universal terms and less in exclusive, nationalistic terms. The classical prophets all affirmed the ancient covenant that God had made with the people of Israel ("I will be your God, you shall be my people"), but they had a clearer sense that the God of Israel was destined to be the God of all people: "And you will say in that day: 'Give thanks to the Lord, call upon his name; make known his deeds among the nations, proclaim that his name is exalted. Sing praises to the Lord, for he has done gloriously; let this be known in all the earth. Shout, and sing for joy, O inhabitant of Zion, for great in your midst is the Holy One of Israel' " (Isaiah 12:4–6).

Finally, the prophets were passionate preachers of social justice. They felt called directly by God; they were commanded to preach. As we saw in the descriptions of their calling, some of them were reluctant to take up the task given them. Most of the prophetic utterances began with the stylized phrase "Thus says the Lord" or "This is the word of the Lord." Precisely because they mediated God's word they felt no social or political restraint on the content of their message. They were called to reprove, correct, and bring back an errant people who were not faithful to the Israelite covenant with God. For that reason they saw in the foreign oppression of their own people a moral evil that affronted the majesty of God's prior intervention on behalf of the people of Israel. Their language could at times be stinging and unyielding:

Amos 5–6
THE MESSAGE TO ISRAEL

Hear this word which I take
     up over you in lamentation, O house of Israel:
"Fallen, no more to rise,
     is the virgin Israel;
forsaken on her land,
     with none to raise her up."

For thus says the Lord God:
"The city that went forth a thousand
     shall have a hundred left,
and that which went forth a hundred
     shall have ten left
     to the house of Israel."

For thus says the Lord to the house of Israel:
"Seek me and live;
     but do not seek Bethel,
and do not enter into Gilgal
     or cross over to Beersheba;
for Gilgal shall surely go into exile,
     and Bethel shall come to nought."

Seek the Lord and live,
     lest he break out like fire in the house of Joseph,
     and it devour, with none to quench it for Bethel,
O you who turn justice to wormwood,
     and cast down righteousness to the earth!

He who made the Pleiades and Orion,
     and turns deep darkness into the morning,
     and darkens the day into night,
who calls for the waters of the sea,
     and pours them out upon·the surface of the earth,
the Lord is his name,
who makes destruction flash forth against the strong,
     so that destruction comes upon the fortress.

They hate him who reproves in the gate,
     and they abhor him who speaks the truth.
Therefore because you trample upon the poor
     and take from him exactions of wheat,
you have built houses of hewn stone,
     but you shall not dwell in them;
you have planted pleasant vineyards,
     but you shall not drink their wine.
For I know how many are your transgressions,
     and how great are your sins—
you who afflict the righteous, who take a bribe,
     and turn aside the needy in the gate.
Therefore he who is prudent will keep silent in such a
          time;
     for it is an evil time.

Seek good, and not evil,
     that you may live;

and so the Lord, the God of hosts, will be with you,
   as you have said.
Hate evil, and love good,
   and establish justice in the gate;
it may be that the Lord, the God of hosts,
   will be gracious to the remnant of Joseph.

Therefore thus says the Lord, the God of hosts, the
   Lord:
In all the squares there shall be wailing;
   and in all the streets they shall say, 'Alas! alas!'
They shall call the farmers to mourning
   and to wailing those who are skilled in
     lamentation,
and in all vineyards there shall be wailing,
   for I will pass through the midst of you,'' says the
   Lord.

Woe to you who desire the day of the Lord!
   Why would you have the day of the Lord?
It is darkness, and not light;
   as if a man fled from a lion,
   and a bear met him;
or went into the house and leaned with his hand
   against the wall,
   and a serpent bit him.
Is not the day of the Lord darkness, and not light,
   and gloom with no brightness in it?

"I hate, I despise your feasts,
   and I take no delight in your solemn assemblies.
Even though you offer me your burnt offerings and
   cereal offerings,
   I will not accept them,
and the peace offerings of your fatted beasts
   I will not look upon.
Take away from me the noise of your songs;
   to the melody of your harps I will not listen.
But let justice roll down like waters,
   and righteousness like an everflowing stream.

"Did you bring to me sacrifices and offerings the forty years in the wilderness, O house of Israel? You shall take up Sakkuth your king, and Kaiwan your star-god, your images, which you made for yourselves; therefore I will take you into exile beyond Damascus," says the Lord, whose name is the God of hosts.

"Woe to those who are at ease in Zion,
   and to those who feel secure on the mountain of
     Samaria,
the notable men of the first of the nations,
   to whom the house of Israel come!
Pass over to Calneh, and see;
   and thence go to Hamath the great;
   then go down to Gath of the Philistines.
Are they better than these kingdoms?

Or is their territory greater than your territory,
O you who put far away the evil day,
   and bring near the seat of violence?
"Woe to those who lie upon beds of ivory,
   and stretch themselves upon their couches,
and eat lambs from the flock,
   and calves from the midst of the stall;
who sing idle songs to the sound of the harp,
   and like David invent for themselves instruments
     of music;
who drink wine in bowls,
   and anoint themselves with the finest oils,
   but are not grieved over the ruin of Joseph!
Therefore they shall now be the first of those to go
   into exile,
   and the revelry of those who stretch themselves
     shall pass away."

The Lord God has sworn by himself
(says the Lord, the God of hosts):
"I abhor the pride of Jacob,
   and hate his strongholds;
   and I will deliver up the city and all that is in it."

And if ten men remain in one house, they shall die. And when a man's kinsman, he who burns him, shall take him up to bring the bones out of the house, and shall say to him who is in the innermost parts of the house, "Is there still any one with you?" he shall say, "No"; and he shall say, "Hush! We must not mention the name of the Lord."

For behold, the Lord commands,
   and the great house shall be smitten into
     fragments,
   and the little house into bits.
Do horses run upon rocks?
   Does one plow the sea with oxen?
But you have turned justice into poison
   and the fruit of righteousness into wormwood—
you who rejoice in Lodebar,
   who say, "Have we not by our own strength
   taken Karnaim for ourselves?"
"For behold, I will raise up against you a nation,
   O house of Israel," says the Lord, the God of
   hosts;
"and they shall oppress you from the entrance of
   Hamath
   to the Brook of the Arabah."

Needless to say, the prophets were not popular with the ruling elite of Israel. Centuries after the age of the classical prophets Jesus would say: "O Jerusalem, Jerusalem, killing the prophets and stoning those who are sent to you!" (Matthew 23:37), echoing the long-held tradition of Israel that the ancient prophets had all died violent deaths because of the severity of their reforming message.

The prophetic message was characterized by its tone of moral censure, its constant threat of divine displeasure, and its call for conversion to the obligations of its religious heritage. The prophetic role of direct mediator of God's word and will to an errant people is a hallmark of Jewish religiousness. One cannot understand the picture of Jesus in the New Testament without reference to it. The tension between Jesus' scrupulous observance of Jewish law and temple ritual and his fierce denunciations of the Jewish rulers is understandable only in light of the prophetic tradition of Israel. When Jesus drove the money-changers from the temple he quoted from both the prophets Isaiah and Jeremiah about the sanctity of God's house and the turning of it into a den of thieves. Perhaps nowhere in the New Testament is the prophetic sense of social justice, ethical religion, and a passion for religious purity so clear as in the famous Sermon on the Mount [57] in the fifth chapter of the Gospel of Matthew.

Matthew 5
SERMON ON THE MOUNT

Seeing the crowds, he went up on the mountain, and when he sat down his disciples came to him. And he opened his mouth and taught them, saying:

"Blessed are the poor in spirit, for theirs is the kingdom of heaven.

"Blessed are those who mourn, for they shall be comforted.

"Blessed are the meek, for they shall inherit the earth.

"Blessed are those who hunger and thirst for righteousness, for they shall be satisfied.

57 Claude Lorrain. *The Sermon on the Mount*. 1656. Oil on canvas, 5'7½" × 8'6¼" (1.71 × 2.6 m). Frick Collection, New York. Jesus is the haloed figure at center on top of the mountain. Paintings done in the 17th century often show listening crowds outdoors—scenes that reflected the outdoor preaching that was common at the time.

"Blessed are the merciful, for they shall obtain mercy.

"Blessed are the pure in heart, for they shall see God.

"Blessed are the peacemakers, for they shall be called sons of God.

"Blessed are those who are persecuted for righteousness' sake, for theirs is the kingdom of heaven.

"Blessed are you when men revile you and persecute you and utter all kinds of evil against you falsely on my account. Rejoice and be glad, for your reward is great in heaven, for so men persecuted the prophets who were before you.

"You are the salt of the earth; but if salt has lost its taste, how shall its saltness be restored? It is no longer good for anything except to be thrown out and trodden under foot by men.

"You are the light of the world. A city set on a hill cannot be hid. Nor do men light a lamp and put it under a bushel, but on a stand, and it gives light to all in the house. Let your light so shine before men, that they may see your good works and give glory to your Father who is in heaven.

"Think not that I have come to abolish the law and the prophets; I have come not to abolish them but to fulfil them. For truly, I say to you, till heaven and earth pass away, not an iota, not a dot, will pass from the law until all is accomplished. Whoever then relaxes one of the least of these commandments and teaches men so, shall be called least in the kingdom of heaven; but he who does them and teaches them shall be called great in the kingdom of heaven. For I tell you, unless your righteousness exceeds that of the scribes and Pharisees, you will never enter the kingdom of heaven.

"You have heard that it was said to the men of old, 'You shall not kill; and whoever kills shall be liable to judgment.' But I say to you that every one who is angry with his brother shall be liable to judgment; whoever insults his brother shall be liable to the council, and whoever says, 'You fool!' shall be liable to the hell of fire. So if you are offering your gift at the altar, and there remember that your brother has something against you, leave your gift there before the altar and go; first be reconciled to your brother, and then come and offer your gift. Make friends quickly with your accuser, while you are going with him to court, lest your accuser hand you over to the judge, and the judge to the guard, and you be put in prison; truly, I say to you, you will never get out till you have paid the last penny.

"You have heard that it was said, 'You shall not commit adultery.' But I say to you that every one who looks at a woman lustfully has already committed adultery with her in his heart. If your right eye causes you to sin, pluck it out and throw it away; it is better that you lose one of your members than that your whole body be thrown into hell. And if your right hand causes you to sin, cut it off and throw it away; it is better that you lose one of your members than that your whole body go into hell.

"It was also said, 'Whoever divorces his wife, let him give her a certificate of divorce.' But I say to you that every one who divorces his wife, except on the ground of unchastity, makes her an adulteress; and whoever marries a divorced woman commits adultery.

"Again you have heard that it was said to the men of old, 'You shall not swear falsely, but shall perform to the Lord what you have sworn.' But I say to you, Do not swear at all, either by heaven, for it is the throne of God, or by the earth, for it is his footstool, or by Jerusalem, for it is the city of the great King. And do not swear by your head, for you cannot make one hair white or black. Let what you say be simply 'Yes' or 'No'; anything more than this comes from evil.

"You have heard that it was said, 'An eye for an eye and a tooth for a tooth.' But I say to you, Do not resist one who is evil. But if any one strikes you on the right cheek, turn to him the other also; and if any one would sue you and take your coat, let him have your cloak as well; and if any one forces you to go one mile, go with him two miles. Give to him who begs from you, and do not refuse him who would borrow from you.

"You have heard that it was said, 'You shall love your neighbor and hate your enemy.' But I say to you, Love your enemies and pray for those who persecute you, so that you may be sons of your Father who is in heaven; for he makes his sun rise on the evil and on the good, and sends rain on the just and on the unjust. For if you love those who love you, what reward have you? Do not even the tax collectors do the same? And if you salute only your brethren, what more are you doing than others? Do not even the Gentiles do the same? You, therefore, must be perfect, as your heavenly Father is perfect." ◗

The later history of Western culture gives ample evidence that the style of prophetic religion has persisted through the ages. It usually appears as a protest "in the name of God" against the vested religious or social powers of the day. When an institution becomes encrusted with privilege or complacency, a prophetic figure may come along to denounce and reform that institution in the name of God and the imperatives of God's justice. Martin Luther's protest against the immobility and decadence of the medieval church may be seen as a prophetic movement, as may the earlier attempts of Saint Francis of Assisi to preach poverty to a materialistic religious culture.

One person of our own era who understood and adopted the prophetic style of religious protest was Martin Luther King, Jr. [58]. When King was in jail in Birmingham, Alabama, as a result of his struggle for the civil rights of black Americans, he wrote a letter to white religious leaders of the city who had accused him of stirring up divisive violence in the city. King's famous letter consciously referred to the prophetic right of the biblical preacher to refuse injustice and to denounce evils:

Martin Luther King, Jr.
from LETTER FROM BIRMINGHAM JAIL

April 16, 1963

My Dear Fellow Clergymen:

While confined here in the Birmingham city jail, I came across your recent statement calling my present activities "unwise and untimely." Seldom do I pause to answer criticism of my work and ideas. If I sought to answer all the criticisms that cross my desk, my secretaries would have little time for anything other than such correspondence in the course of the day, and I would have no time for constructive work. But since I feel that you are men of genuine good will and that your criticisms are sincerely set forth, I want to try to answer your statement in what I hope will be patient and reasonable terms.

58   The Reverend Dr. Martin Luther King, Jr., addresses 70,000 people at a civil rights rally. Soldier Field, Chicago, 1964.

I think I should indicate why I am here in Birmingham, since you have been influenced by the view which argues against "outsiders coming in." I have the honor of serving as president of the Southern Christian Leadership Conference, an organization operating in every southern state, with headquarters in Atlanta, Georgia. We have some eighty-five affiliated organizations across the South, and one of them is the Alabama Christian Movement for Human Rights. Frequently we share staff, educational and financial resources with our affiliates. Several months ago the affiliate here in Birmingham asked us to be on call to engage in a nonviolent direct-action program if such were deemed necessary. We readily consented, and when the hour came we lived up to our promise. So I, along with several members of my staff, am here because I was invited here. I am here because I have organizational ties here.

But more basically, I am in Birmingham because injustice is here. Just as the prophets of the eighth century B.C. left their villages and carried their "thus saith the Lord" far beyond the boundaries of their home towns, and just as the Apostle Paul left his village of Tarsus and carried the gospel of Jesus Christ to the far corners of the Greco-Roman world, so am I compelled to carry the gospel of freedom beyond my own home town. Like Paul, I must constantly respond to the Macedonian call for aid.

Moreover, I am cognizant of the interrelatedness of all communities and states. I cannot sit idly by in Atlanta and not be concerned about what happens in Birmingham. Injustice anywhere is a threat to justice everywhere. We are caught in an inescapable network of mutuality, tied in a single garment of destiny. Whatever affects one directly, affects all indirectly. Never again can we afford to live with the narrow, provincial "outside agitator" idea. Anyone who lives inside the United States can never be considered an outsider anywhere within its bounds. 📖

King's beliefs and his public life had many of the characteristics of the prophetic style. He preached that civil rights come from God; he, like many of the prophets, symbolized his message by dramatic action. As the prophets of old walked naked through a town or shattered pots to show the future of the land of Israel, so King led boycotts, sit-ins, and parades.

King also shared another characteristic with some classical prophets: he died a violent death because of his beliefs.

The Cultural Significance of the Biblical Period

In some ways Solomon is a lesser figure in the biblical tradition than some of the other Hebrew heroes. He was not the father of his people that the patriarch Abraham was. He pales against the mighty figure of the lawgiver Moses. His *persona* is neither as complex nor as attractive as that of his father, King David. He certainly lacked the moral rigor and religious intensity of Jeremiah or Isaiah. Nonetheless, Solomon is a pivotal figure in the history of Israel. In a sense, he stands as a complex symbol for Israel's contribution to later Western culture.

Solomon's reign was the high-water mark of ancient Israel's cultural power. Before his time there was an ascending line of development from tribal origins to a powerful and opulent monarchy. After his time there was a descending line of civil disorder, division, conquest, and subservience. He reshaped the city of Jerusalem, giving it a symbolic character that persists to this day. By building the first great Temple in Jerusalem, he institutionalized the considerable strengths of biblical religion. It was because of the increased power and pressure of the Temple cult that the ancient stories and tales about the patriarchs, the Exodus, and the penetration of the land of Palestine began to be shaped into a literary whole.

Most scholars believe that it was during the period of David and Solomon that the scattered, and largely oral, tradition of Israel began to be remolded into a literary tradition. In short, the Bible, as we know it today, first began to take its present form during the times of Solomon. If the Temple was a great historical achievement, the creative energies unleashed by it resulted in one of Israel's most permanent gifts to our culture: the Bible.

It was the formalism, the richness, and the expensive complexity of the temple cult that the prophets devoted much of their energies to attacking. They did not reject the worship of the Temple (Isaiah, after all, was called while praying in the Temple), but they demanded that it be purified and brought into line with the ethical obligations of the ancient Hebrew covenant. In other words, classical prophetism can only be understood against the background of the priestly religion of the Temple and its later development. A millennium after Solomon, in the stories of Jesus preserved in the New Testament, we can still detect the strong dialectical tension between Temple and prophetism. The public life of Jesus is intelligible only against the long historical tradition of both Temple and prophetic traditions.

As we have already noted, Solomon's reign also bore within it the seeds of social decline and the destruction of the united kingdom. The invasions of the Northern and Southern Kingdoms, the periods of exile and return, the building and rebuilding of the Temple—all contributed to the mighty sense of nostalgia that the people of Israel felt (and still feel) for Jerusalem and its ancient Temple. With the destruction of the Second Temple in A.D. 70, Jerusalem became, not a home for the Jews, but the object of their dreams. "Next year in Jerusalem" they prayed each year during centuries of exile. Nobody can understand the volatile situation in the Middle East without understanding the long Jewish memory of the glory of Jerusalem and its Temple and the hope for their restoration.

Finally, Solomon's achievements made Jerusalem the center of Israel's religion. Jerusalem and its Temple marked the stable point of ancient Israel's life and culture. It is from that center that the great tradition of monotheistic religion in the West springs. Judaism, Christianity, and Islam are all religions of the Book. They all look back to Abraham as to a common father. Islam was born in the deserts of Arabia, but the prophet ended his days in Jerusalem. Christianity was born in the streets and around the sacred precincts of Jerusalem itself. The modern visitor to Jerusalem sees that quickly and clearly. In the old city of Jerusalem, surrounded by the Crusader walls of the Middle Ages, in ten minutes one can walk to major shrines of the three great faiths of the West: the Church of the

59 Jerusalem. The Moslem Dome of the Rock is in the background, with the old city to the left of and behind it. Below the wall is a Jewish cemetery in the Kidron Valley. In the foreground is the Russian Orthodox Church of Saint Mary Magdalene. This view graphically shows the presence of the three major Western faiths in Jerusalem.

Holy Sepulchre, the Western Wall of Herod's Temple, and, on what was once the Temple mount, the Dome of the Rock, a magnificent mosque that marks the spot where tradition has it the Prophet Mohammed ascended to heaven [59]. The swirling crowd of Hasidic Jews, Franciscan friars, veiled Moslem women, pilgrims, Orthodox monks, pious rabbis, and caftaned mullahs tells more about the lasting significance of Jerusalem than words can convey.

By the standards of the great cultures against which we must study the history of Israel—the cultures of Egypt, Assyria, Babylonia, and Persia—the achievement of Solomon for "all his glory" was not impressive. His building program would have been unthinkable without the aid and technology of his neighbors to the North, the Phoenicians. Nor did his reign sustain itself for very long. At the level of human culture, Israel in general and Solomon in particular made no lasting contribution to the great monuments of civilization if one excepts the Bible, which began to take shape during Solomon's time. "If one excepts the Bible . . ." That is a monumentally important "if." The contribution of Israel was precisely in that collection of writings that we call the Bible and the ideas that those writings contain.

This chapter on Jerusalem precedes the two chapters that deal with the far more advanced civilization of Greece. In Greece we find the origins of our politics, philosophy, science, and literary culture. Yet when these two cultures began to merge, much later in history, indeed when Solomon was already a proverbial figure, the tradition of Israel was a determinative factor in the shaping of the ideals and values of the West. The God of this rather insignificant people, cradled in the none-too-loving embrace of hostile civilizations, energized the art and architecture of the Western world and was the fount for the two great religions of the West. The theological culture of Israel provided the ethical ideal of a tradition that is now nearly three thousand years old.

Further Reading

Anchor Bible. Garden City, NY: Doubleday. A continuing series of volumes on each of the books of the Bible by eminent scholars. Excellent.

Anderson, Bernhard W. *Understanding the Old Testament*. 3rd ed. Englewood Cliffs, NJ: Prentice Hall, 1975. The standard college text for biblical study. First-rate scholarship; readable.

Bright, John. *A History of Israel*. Philadelphia: Westminster, 1972. The standard work by an American scholar.

Buttrick, George, et al. *The Interpreter's Dictionary of the Bible*. 4 vols. New York: Abingdon, 1962. Excellent and comprehensive dictionary of the Bible.

DeVaux, Roland. *Ancient Israel: Its Life and Institutions*. New York: McGraw-Hill, 1965. A basic work by an eminent French scholar and archaeologist.

Heschel, Abraham. *The Prophets*. New York: Harper, 1963. A classic study by an outstanding Jewish scholar.

Henn, T. R. *The Bible as Literature*. New York: Oxford, 1970. Good work on literary value of the Bible.

The Interpreter's Bible. New York: Abingdon, 1957. Informative multi-volume commentary on the entire Bible.

May, Herbert. *Oxford Bible Atlas*. New York: Oxford, 1974. Basic for maps of the biblical period.

Pritchard, J. B. *Ancient Near Eastern Texts Relating to the Old Testament*. Princeton, NJ: Princeton University Press, 1969. Anthology of important texts from Egypt, Babylonia, and other areas that shed light on the Bible; indispensable.

Schneidau, Herbert. *Sacred Discontent: The Bible and Western Tradition*. Baton Rouge: Louisiana State University, 1976. A brilliant study of the cultural impact of the Bible on subsequent Western culture.

Suggestions for Listening

Nothing has survived of the actual music performed in biblical times, but we can gain some idea of its character from Jewish liturgical music of later periods. A disc in Philips' *International Series* (PH 6856001) entitled "Jewish Music" offers a good selection of religious chants and hymns from the Hebrew tradition. The same disc also includes music played on the *shofar* (ram's horn), which is the only musical instrument used by Orthodox Jews in divine services after the destruction of the Second Temple in A.D. 70 and the only biblical instrument to survive to the present.

The words of the psalms have provided a source of inspiration for composers of all ages. The music of the later composers does not reflect the music of the biblical period, but it does reflect the power of the poetry of these great writings. Two 20th-century works, in particular, mentioned in the text of this chapter, are worthy of note: Leonard Bernstein's *Chichester Psalms* (1965) and Igor Stravinsky's *Symphony of Psalms* (1930). Both compositions are available conducted by their composers: Bernstein on Columbia MS 6792 and, more recently, on Deutsche Grammofon (DG 2709077); Stravinsky on Columbia MS 6548. Also of particular musical interest is the Hungarian composer Zoltán Kodály's *Psalmus Hungaricus* (1923), available on Hungariton SLPX 11392.

Questions for Further Discussion

1. Solomon's Temple was designed as a space for the God of Israel to inhabit. Churches and synagogues are built as spaces for worshipers. In what basic way do you think architects modify their buildings to reflect these two different attitudes? Since Greek temples were also dwelling places for gods and goddesses, are they functionally close to a temple like that of Solomon?

2. Throughout the Psalms (and other books of the Bible) God is given many titles like "king," "shepherd," "Father," etc. What do these titles say about the nature of Hebrew culture? Do feminist critics of Hebrew religion have a case when they argue that divine imagery in the Bible is too unremittingly masculine?

3. The Book of Job raises the question of the meaning of suffering. Do you accept the notion that suffering is ultimately a mystery about which we can say little, or would you prefer to make a statement about your own understanding of evil in the world? If you were to recast the Job story into modern terms, where would you set the story? Who would make up your cast of characters?

4. The prophets, through fierce language and symbolic action, called down God's judgment on an erring world. Can you imagine a contemporary prophet? How would he or she act out a prophetic message for our age? What do you suspect would be the subject of divine denunciation today?

5. Read through one of the Gospels in the New Testament. Note the significant references to the psalms, the Temple, the general teachings of the Hebrew scriptures. To what degree does Jesus conform to the idea of the Hebrew prophet?

6. Find out more about modern Jerusalem as the city of the three great monotheistic faiths—Judaism, Christianity, and Islam. How do religious concerns affect the politics of the city?

INTERLUDE
Judith and Holofernes

Judith is one of the most interesting heroines of ancient Israel. Her story is simple, but dramatic. Holofernes, general of the Assyrian army, is on a punitive expedition against those who did not help the Assyrians in the war against the Medes. The Jews of Bethulia resist the army of Holofernes as it tries to pass through their city to lay waste the holy city of Jerusalem. Holofernes surrounds Bethulia, sets up a siege, and cuts off the water supply. After 34 days the city is prepared to surrender despite having been told that God will not abandon their cause if they remain true to him in sinlessness. At this crucial point Judith, a pious and wealthy widow, tells her fellow Bethulians that she has a secret plan to free the city.

Judith prays, then removes the widow's weeds she usually wears, dresses her hair, puts on colorful clothes, adorns herself with jewelry, and anoints herself with perfume. Accompanied only by a handmaiden, she leaves the city and approaches the enemy camp. When Assyrian guards stop her, she says that she has run away from Bethulia and that she will tell Holofernes how to conquer the entire hill country without losing even one man. The guards, dazzled by her beauty, at once take her to their general. Also struck by her beauty and breeding, Holofernes readily believes Judith's story. He invites her to a banquet that he intends to end with her seduction. "He shook with passion and was filled with an ardent longing to possess her" (Book of Judith, 12:16). In anticipation of these revels, however, at the banquet he proceeds to drink himself into a stupor. Alone with him, Judith quickly takes his sword and beheads the drunken general. She and her maid slip back into Bethulia, the maid carrying the head in a food bag. The next morning the head of Holofernes is displayed on the city walls. Demoralized and leaderless, the Assyrian army retreats.

Judith's story is told in the Book of Judith, which was originally written in Hebrew but exists now only in Greek manuscripts. The work is difficult to date, but it probably was composed at the end of the 2nd century B.C. As a historical document it is of only limited value. Most scholars believe that behind the moving and elegant story there may be a historical substratum but that the book is meant to be read basically as a moral tale, not an account of an actual event.

The relentlessly masculine character of biblical religion has increasingly been attacked by Jewish, Christian, and secular feminists. It is true that religions based on the Bible—Judaism, Christianity, and Islam—stand alone among the faiths of the world in admitting no feminine deity as a counterpart or consort of a masculine god. Indeed, the God of Israel, reflecting the patriarchal culture of the Hebrews, is usually described in masculine imagery: Father, Lord, Shepherd, King. The Bible also bears witness to the unceasing struggle of the Hebrew prophets against the fertility cults of Canaan with their gods and goddesses and their emphasis on sexuality and fertility. Furthermore, no woman in ancient Israel belonged to the priestly class, and no woman is named among the classical prophets in the Bible.

Though the character of Hebrew religion was undeniably masculine, women did play a role in Hebrew history and in later cultural reflections of that history. They were usually cultural or religious heroines. Thus the Book of Ruth holds up as a model for Israel a non-Hebrew woman who was a paragon of fidelity. The Book of Esther concerns a Jewish woman who ascends the Persian throne and, in the process, becomes a savior to her own people—an event still celebrated in Judaism at the annual feast of *Purim*. Figures like Ruth and Esther expand the characteristics of earlier model heroines of Israel who, like Sarah and Deborah, testified to the vitality and depth of Hebrew religion.

The Book of Judith artfully mixes piety, drama, and violence as it tells of the heroism of another Hebrew woman (the very name *Judith* means "Jewess"). The description of the heroine herself is brief and to the point. "She was a very beautiful and attractive woman. Her husband Manasses had left her gold and silver, male and female slaves, livestock and land, and she lived on her estate. No one spoke ill of her, for she was a very devout woman" (8:7–8).

After her successful foray into the camp of Holofernes Judith sings a hymn of thanksgiving that reflects both her traditional sense of being a woman and her exultation at the audacity of her deed:

The Book of Judith 16:7, 9–11
JUDITH'S HYMN

> It was no young man that brought their champion low;
> no titan struck him down;
> no tall giant set upon him; . . .
> Her sandal entranced his eye,
> her beauty took his heart captive;
> and the sword cut through his neck.
> The Persians shuddered at her daring,
> the Medes were daunted by her boldness.
> Then my oppressed people shouted in triumph, and the enemy were afraid;
>   my weak ones shouted, and the enemy cowered in fear.

The Book of Judith is in neither the Hebrew Bible nor most Protestant versions. Before the time of Christ there were two textual traditions of the Old Testament, the Hebrew and the Greek. The Greek Old Testament, called the Septuagint (which means "seventy," since according to tradition it was translated by seventy wise men), was used by Greek-speaking Jews outside of Jerusalem. It contained a number of books and fragments of books which the Rabbis did not accept when they set the Hebrew *canon* (authentic books) some fifty years after the time of Christ. The early Christian church used the Septuagint, and Saint Jerome included the disputed books in his Latin translation of the Bible, the so-called Vulgate. The Vulgate became the official translation for the Catholic church. At the time of the Protestant Reformation Martin Luther rejected the disputed books of the Septuagint, including the Book of Judith, although he admired its moral power. Many modern Protestant versions of the Bible print the Book of Judith and the other apocryphal works in a section called the Apocrypha, while the Catholic bibles list them as *deuterocanonical* ("belonging to the second canon"). The Book of Judith was read both in Latin and Greek Christianity as an inspired book until the Reformation. It has always been a source for artists and writers who have been attracted by the power of both the story and Judith herself.

It is not surprising that later generations have seen the story of Judith as an allegory of virtue over vice, goodness over evil. The contrast between the temperate, clever Judith and the drunken, deluded Holofernes is too dramatic to resist. Furthermore, in those many periods of Western culture when prowess in war was admired, Judith greatly appealed to those who believed that martial skills must be purified by virtue and faith.

The narrative potential of this combination of purity and violence is clearly what motivated an Anglo-Saxon poet of the 10th century to retell the story of Judith in the language and style of the heroic epic, with its warrior values. The Anglo-Saxon *Judith* is clearly based on the Book of Judith in the Latin Vulgate Bible, but the poet slightly modifies the biblical story to suit contemporary needs and tastes. First, Judith is christianized to the extent that she anachronistically calls on the Christian Trinity rather than the God of the Hebrews. Second, Holofernes' banquet is developed at length—feast descriptions were favorites in Anglo-Saxon epics. The revels of Holofernes become rather more reminiscent of the mead halls of England than the tent of an Assyrian general. During this long scene Judith stands outside the hall, apart from the action. This physical distance emphasizes her spiritual distance from the sensual Holofernes and his cohorts:

from the Anglo-Saxon JUDITH

So the wicked one	
Through the day drenched his followers with wine,	30
The haughty gift-lord, till they lay in swoon;	
His nobles all o'er drenched as they were struck	
To death and every good deed poured out of them.	
So bade the lord of men serve those in hall	
Till the dark night drew near the sons of men.	
Then bade the malice-blind to fetch with speed	
The blessed maid, ring-wreathed, to his bed-rest.	
The attendants quickly did as bade their lord,	
Head of mailed warriors, in a twinkling went	
To the guest chamber, where they Judith found	40
Prudent in soul, and then shield warriors	
Began to lead the pious, the bright maid	
To the tent, the high one, where within at night	
The chief of all times rested, Holofernes,	
Hateful to God the Saviour.	

When Judith beheads Holofernes, the poet describes her as not only a valiant warrior but an instrument of divine retribution. Holofernes, on the other hand, is portrayed as demonic:

from the Anglo-Saxon JUDITH

She, braided locked, then struck the scather-foe
With glittering sword. . . .
        Then the foul carcass lay
Empty behind while the soul went elsewhere
Under the abyss, and there it was condemned,

60 Donatello. *Judith and Holofernes*. c. 1462. Bronze, height with base 7'8" (2.36 m). Piazza della Signoria, Florence.

Tied down to torment ever after, wound
About by serpents, fixed to punishment,
Chained in hell's burning after it went hence. . . .
But there shall dwell ever and ever more
Forth without end in the dark cavern-home,
Deprived for ever of the joys of light.   120

In the final part of the poem (we possess only fragments of a much longer work) Judith, like any triumphant warrior, is given her share of the spoils after the Hebrews rout the fleeing Assyrians, as in the biblical original. But the edifying moralism of the original is turned into pure delight in Judith's military glory as she receives Holofernes' "breast armour broad and ornamented with red gold; all the treasures that the haughty chief possessed, his heritage of circlets and bright gems. . . ."

The artists of the Middle Ages and the Renaissance explored many aspects of the Judith story for widely different purposes and reasons. There was the standard interpretation of Judith as a symbol of fidelity and purity and, as such, prophetic of the Virgin Mary. Such an understanding of the Judith story motivated more than one medieval sculptor to show Judith as a spiritual ancestor of Mary on the facade of a cathedral. By contrast, during the Renaissance, Donatello emphasized both religious and civil values in his famous bronze statue, *Judith and Holofernes,* which today stands outside the Palazzo Vecchio in Florence [60]. In its position in front of the center of Florentine civil power the statue is a conscious symbol of the power of righteousness triumphing over the chaotic destructiveness of lawlessness and vice.

Other artists of the Renaissance were attracted by the violent drama of the story. Andrea Mantegna shows Judith giving her maidservant the head of the slain general as she prepares to leave his tent [61]. Sandro Botticelli did two small tempera panels on the Judith theme. One shows the Assyrians discovering the headless body of Holofernes [62], while another shows Judith and her maid returning to Bethulia in triumph with the head.

61 Andrea Mantegna. *Judith and Holofernes.*
c. 1495. Oil on panel, 11⅞ × 7⅛″ (30 × 18 cm).
National Gallery of Art, Washington (Widener Collection). Judith is about to drop the severed head of Holofernes into the food bag held by her maid.

62 Sandro Botticelli. *Holofernes Dead in His Tent* c. 1475.
Tempera on wood, 12¼ × 10″ (31 × 25 cm). Uffizi, Florence.
The headless body is emphasized by dramatic foreshortening—a continuous decrease in size that gives a three-dimensional effect—and by contrast with the heavy draperies and the elaborate costumes of the horrified viewers.

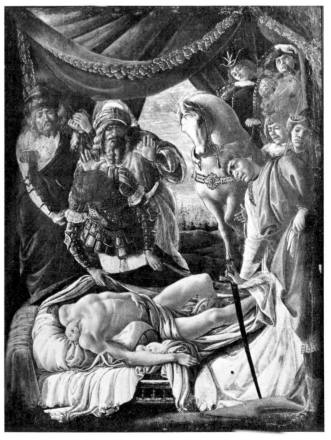

In the late Renaissance Judith attracted the interest of more major artists than we can reasonably discuss. It would be an interesting exercise in comparative cultural study to reflect on the ways these artists handled her story, given their diverse traditions and styles. Judith inspired works by Venetian painters like Giorgione, Titian, and Paolo Veronese. The 16th-century German painter Lucas Cranach did several studies on the Judith theme, as did the slightly later artists Caravaggio and Peter Paul Rubens.

One painter of the late Renaissance who turned to the Judith theme deserves special mention. Artemisia Gentileschi, a 17th-century Roman painter who has been called the "female equivalent of an Old Master" by the feminist critic Germaine Greer, painted the Judith theme at least twice. That she chose that subject should come as no surprise. Her father and his good friend Caravaggio had both painted the subject. Furthermore, Judith undoubtedly appealed in a personal way to a woman who was finding it difficult to make a name for herself in a field dominated by men. Many of Gentileschi's paintings have been lost or misattributed, but we know she portrayed such feminine themes as Susannah and the Elders, Esther, the penitent Magdalene, and Saint Catherine; she also did numerous studies of the Virgin Mary.

Gentileschi's most famous painting is *Judith and Holofernes* [63]. Done in *chiaroscuro* (the technique which strongly contrasts light and dark for dramatic purposes), the painting conveys a tremendous sense of violence as Judith and her maid loom over the drastically foreshortened body of Holofernes. There is a stark contrast between the realistic violence of the beheading and the sensual richness of the silken bed, the jewelry, and the cunning drapery. It is not inconceivable that the painter, herself a rape victim in her youth, poured her own passionate protest into this painting of a woman taking retribution against a would-be defiler.

Although the Protestant Reformers did not regard the Book of Judith as divinely inspired, they recognized a powerful motif of virtue in the story. Martin Luther, who professed an enthusiasm for the dramatization of biblical stories, recommended Judith as a tragic theme worthy of artistic consideration. There are 15th-century plays on the subject, but they begin to increase in number in the next century. Most of these earlier works interest only the drama historian. In our own century, however, authors have turned to the story of Judith to explore themes of contemporary relevance. Lascelles Abercrombie's *Emblems of Love* (1912) uses the story of Judith to preach the cause of suffrage for women. The French dramatist Jean Giraudoux produced a heavily psychological *Judith* (1931) in which Judith becomes a woman of dubious virtue and Holofernes is sympathetically portrayed. Turning Judith into a sexual person had already been anticipated at the beginning of the century by such painters as the Viennese Gustav Klimt, who quite frankly eroticized Judith in his painting [64].

In the realm of music a large number of oratorios (musical compositions for singers, chorus, and orchestra) have been inspired by Judith. Emperor Charles VI of Austria commissioned the Italian librettist Metastasio to compose a libretto on the Judith theme in 1734. Metastasio's *La Betulia liberata* was performed in the royal chapel at Vienna that same year. With the accession of Maria Theresa to the Austrian throne it was fashionable to see her as a latter-day Judith playing to a Holofernes in the person of Frederick the Great of Prussia. Metastasio's libretto touched off a rash of Judith oratorios in the late 18th century, including one based on the Metastasio libretto written by Wolfgang Amadeus Mozart in 1771. In 1823 Beethoven composed three *canons* (compositions in which each voice part imitates the melody exactly and successively, though not always at the same pitch) inspired by texts of the same librettists.

63 Artemisia Gentileschi. *Judith and Holofernes*. c. 1620. Oil on canvas. Uffizi, Florence.

64 Gustav Klimt. *Judith*. 1901. Oil on canvas, 33 × 16½″ (84 × 42 cm). Oesterreichische Galerie, Vienna.

Given the long history of fascination with the Judith story in music it is surprising that it never caught the interest of Verdi or Wagner. The popular 19th-century composer Giacomo Meyerbeer did leave an operatic fragment on the theme which he worked on in 1864. In 1926 Arthur Honegger wrote and saw performed a one-act *Judith*. Two years later Eugene Goossens, scion of a great British musical family, staged his *Judith* using a libretto written earlier by the distinguished British novelist Arnold Bennett.

Looking back over the many attempts to reinterpret the story of Judith in one or other of the arts, we can learn certain valuable lessons. The most basic of these is that the human desire to construct meanings is complex. The story of Judith is, at its simplest, the very old story of good versus evil cast in the form of the "weaker sex" triumphing over brute force. In Western culture this basic symbolic framework takes on quite specific nuances. For traditional religious spirituality Judith becomes prophetic of the Virgin. Her triumph over Holofernes foreshadows the triumph of Christ over the forces of demonic evil. That meaning is not rejected by Renaissance artists, but they superimpose overtones of civic virtue and civic justice. In the post-Renaissance period the specifically religious interpretation gives way to meanings that are more generally moralistic or, as in 18th-century music, political. In our own day a feminist artist, Judy Chicago—echoing a tradition that goes back to Artemisia Gentileschi—has included Judith in her *Dinner Party,* a large-scale artistic ensemble dedicated to heroines of world culture. In this ambitious work, which incorporates such media as ceramics, needlepoint, and china painting, Judith represents all the biblical heroines who emerged from the overwhelmingly patriarchal culture of Hebrew religion.

Also in our own time, the story of Judith has inspired a quite different kind of interpretation. One of the greatest dancers and choreographers of this century, Martha Graham, has explored the character of Judith three times in dance. She first performed an interpretation in 1950 as a solo work. In 1962 she expanded the theme into *The Legend of Judith,* using a full company of dancers; the premiere was in Tel Aviv. Her most recent version of the story was choreographed in 1980 and performed at the Metropolitan Opera House, New York. Graham believes that inner emotion can be revealed through movement; in her dances she acts out the passions we all have but usually do not acknowledge. *The Legend of Judith* [65], is set within

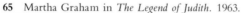

65   Martha Graham in *The Legend of Judith.* 1963.

Judith's mind—the events of the story and the feelings in her heart are portrayed together, as in a dream. The dance gradually moves toward understanding: Judith's soul confronts the past and accepts the consequences of love and of brutality and violence.

This brief discussion of the story of Judith should bring out one point that is important in our cultural tradition. A figure, a symbol, or an idea that triggers cultural reflections in later periods is open to profoundly different cultural "readings" and interpretations. In other words, each great cultural accomplishment of the past nourishes the mind and imagination in various ways at various times. That, in itself, may not be a definition of a "masterpiece," but it does help us understand what a masterpiece must be at its most basic: a work that is good in its own right and also a paradigm for later generations.

Culture is revolutionary when it breaks with the past; it is conservative when it remembers and cherishes the past; it is creative when it sees the past in new and pertinent ways. Culture is all these things. In many ways it brings the past to bear on the present. The pious, moral, militant, violent, wise, prophetic, competent, seductive figure of the Hebrew heroine Judith is a case in point.

Further Reading

Chicago, Judy. *The Dinner Party: A Symbol of Our Heritage.* Garden City, NY: Doubleday Anchor, 1979. A statement about feminist art in general and figures such as Judith in particular.

Cook, Albert. *Judith: An Old English Epic Fragment.* Boston: Heath, 1904.

The Jerusalem Bible. Garden City, NY: Doubleday, 1966. A contemporary Catholic translation.

The New English Bible with the Apocrypha. Oxford and Cambridge, England: Oxford University Press and Cambridge University Press, 1970. A contemporary English Protestant version, newly translated.

Suggestions for Listening

Much of the music discussed in this Interlude is not easily obtainable in recorded form, but two pieces on record represent the best of the Judith tradition. Antonio Vivaldi's *Juditha Triumphans,* a 1716 oratorio by the Baroque Venetian master, has been recorded by the Berlin Chamber Orchestra on Philips 6747173. Wolfgang Amadeus Mozart's *La Betulia liberata,* an oratorio based on the libretto by Metastasio, has been done by the same orchestra and is obtainable on Philips 6703087.

	GENERAL EVENTS	LITERATURE & PHILOSOPHY	ART

3000 B.C. ——————————————————————————————

<table>
<tr><td rowspan="20">BRONZE AGE</td></tr>
</table>

BRONZE AGE

Mycenaean Period

c. 1184 Fall of Troy

1100 ——————————————————————————————

Dark Age

1100 Collapse of Mycenaean Empire

1000 ——————————————————————————————

Heroic Age

1000 Development of Iron Age culture at Athens

c. 900–700 Evolution of Homeric epics *Iliad* and *Odyssey*

1000–900 Protogeometric pottery decoration: bold circular shapes similar to Mycenaean motifs

900–700 Greeks begin colonizing in East and Italy

776 First Olympic Games

c. 775 First Greek colony in Italy founded at Pithekoussai

8th cent. Hesiod, *Works and Days* and *Theogony*

900–700 Geometric pottery decoration: linear designs of zigzags, triangles, diamonds, meanders

750 ——————————————————————————————

IRON AGE (1000 B.C.–)

Age of Colonization

750–600 Greeks found colonies throughout Mediterranean, from Egypt to Black Sea

c. 700 Greeks adapt Phoenician alphabet for their own language

8th cent. Geometric pottery incorporates stylized human figure in painted design; Dipylon amphora

c. 650 Large freestanding sculpture evolves

late 7th cent. Orientalizing styles in vase painting; Corinthian aryballos

c. 650 Archilochus, earliest Greek lyric poet, active

c. 600 *New York Kouros*; Athenians develop narrative style in black-figure vase painting; increased naturalism in Greek art

600 ——————————————————————————————

Archaic Period

c. 590 Solon reforms Athenian constitution

early 6th cent. Sappho, *Poems*

6th cent. Development of Presocratic schools of philosophy: Materialists, Pythagoreans, Dualists, Atomists

c. 550 *Calf-Bearer*
c. 540 *Peplos Kore*
c. 530 *Anavysos Kouros*
c. 525 Exekias, *Suicide of Ajax,* amphora

546 Rule of Pisistratus begins growth of Athenian power; Persian Empire expands to take over Greek colonies in Asia Minor

510 Restoration of democracy at Athens

late 6th cent. Playwriting competition begins

after 525 First official version of Homeric epics written

late 6th cent. Red-figure style of vase painting introduced; *Euphronios Vase*, krater

490 Start of the Persian Wars; forces of King Darius defeated at Marathon

c. 490 *Critian Boy*; turning point between Archaic and Classical periods

480 ——————————————————————————————

Classical Period

480 Xerxes leads a second expedition against Greece; wins battle of Thermopylae and sacks Athens; Greeks defeat Persians decisively at Salamis

479 Greek victories at Plataea and Mycale end Persian Wars

c. 440 Herodotus begins *History of the Persian Wars*

323 ——————————————————————————————

Many dates are approximate

3

Early
Greece

Early music primarily vocal with instrumental accompaniment; use of flute and simple lyre popular

7th cent. Development of aulos (double flute), used to accompany songs

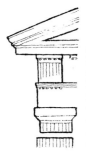

c. 600 Form of Doric temple fully established, derived from early wooden structures; Temple of Hera at Olympia

c. 675 Terpander of Lesbos introduces cithara

c. 550 Basilica at Paestum

c. 540 Temple of Apollo at Corinth

c. 500 Temple of Aphaia, Aegina

586 Sacadas of Argos composes first known purely instrumental work for performance on aulos at Pythian Games in Delphi

c. 550 Pythagoras discovers numerical relationship of music harmonies and our modern musical scale

5th cent. First widespread use of Ionic order

late 5th cent. Earliest surviving fragment of Greek music

One of the major turning points of history is the period around 1000 B.C., the change from the Bronze Age to the Iron Age throughout the Mediterranean area. In the following centuries a culture developed in a small corner of southeastern Europe, Greece, which was to form the foundation of Western civilization. By the 5th century B.C., this culture had produced one of the greatest eras of human achievement.

In certain basic ways, of course, there was some continuity between the Bronze Age and the Iron Age. For example, Athens, which in the 5th century B.C. became the intellectual center of Classical Greece, had been a Mycenaean city long before the Iron Age began. In most significant respects, however, the Iron Age Greeks had to discover for themselves almost all the cultural skills associated with civilization—the visual arts, architecture, literature, philosophy, even the art of writing. The Mycenaeans had known how to write and build and create art. However, their abrupt and violent end around 1100 B.C. was followed by a century of disturbance and confusion that cut off the Bronze Age from the new world of the Iron Age. To follow the first attempts of these Iron Age people to develop an artistic style, organize their societies, and question the nature of the universe is to witness the birth of Western culture.

The history of early Greece falls naturally into three periods, each marked by its own distinctive artistic achievement. During the first three hundred years or so of the Iron Age, development was slow and the Greeks had only limited contact with other Mediterranean peoples. During this period the first great works of literature were created—the epic poems known as the *Iliad* and the *Odyssey*. Because these works treat heroic themes, the early Iron Age in Greece is sometimes known as the Heroic Age.

By the beginning of the 8th century B.C. Greek travelers and merchants had already begun to explore the lands to the east and west. In the next 150 years (c. 750–600 B.C.), called the Age of Colonization, many new ideas and artistic styles were brought to Greece. These foreign influences were finally absorbed in the third era of early Greece, known as the Archaic period (c. 600–480 B.C.). This period, the culmination of the first five hundred years of Greek history, paved the way for the Classical period, discussed in Chapter 4. The Greeks' relationship to the world around them took a decisive turn at the very end of the Archaic period with their victory over the Persians in the wars that lasted from 490 to 479 B.C. The events of the Persian Wars thus end this chapter.

The Heroic Age

During the Mycenaean period most of Greece had been united under a single influence. When the Mycenaeans fell, however, Greece split up into a series of independent regions that corresponded to the geographically separated areas created by the mountain ranges and high hills that crisscross the terrain. Within each of these geographically discrete areas, there developed an urban center that controlled the surrounding countryside. Thus Athens became the dominating force in the geographical region known as Attica; Thebes controlled Boeotia; Sparta controlled Laconia, and so on (see map, page 94). A central urban community of this kind was called by the Greeks of a later period a *polis,* a term generally translated as "city-state."

The *polis* served as focal point for all political, religious, social, and artistic activities within its region. Its citizens felt toward their own individual city a loyalty that was far stronger than any generalized sense of community with their fellow Greeks over the mountains. Each of the leading cities developed its own artistic style, which led to fierce competition and in time bitter and destructive rivalries. The *polis* was, therefore, both the glory and the ruin of Greek civilization, producing on the one hand an unequaled concentration of intellectual and cultural development, on the other a tendency to internal squabbling at the least provocation.

The fragmentation of social and cultural life had a marked effect on the development of Greek mythology and religion. Religion played an important part in Greek life, as Greek art and literature demonstrate, but it was very different in nature from the other religions that influenced our culture, Judaism and Christianity. For one thing, Greek mythology offers no central body of information or teaching corresponding to the Old or New Testaments. Often there are varying versions of the same basic story; even when these versions do not actually contradict one another, they often are difficult to reconcile. For another thing, the very characters of the Greek gods and goddesses often seem confused and self-contradictory. For example, Zeus, President of the Immortals and Father of gods and humans, generally represented the concept of an objective moral code to which both gods and mortals were expected to conform; Zeus imposed justice and supervised the punishment of wrongdoers [66]. Yet this same majestic

66 *Zeus (Poseidon?)*. c. 465
B.C. Bronze, height 6'10"
(2.08 m). National Archaeological Museum, Athens.
Whether this striding god is
Zeus or Poseidon, god of
the sea, the combination of
majestic dignity and physical strength reflects the
Greeks' view of their gods
as superior beings with defi-
nitely human attributes.
This statue, which was
found in the sea off Cape
Artemisium, comes from
the end of the period of this
chapter; it may have been
intended to commemorate
the Greek victory over the
Persians.

ruler was also involved in many love affairs and se-
ductions, in the course of which his behavior was
often undignified and even comical. How could the
Greeks have believed in a champion of morality
whose own moral standards were so lax?

The answer lies in the fact that Greek myth and
religion of later times consist of a mass of folk tales,
primitive customs, and traditional rituals that grew

up during the Heroic Age and were never developed
into a single unified system. Individual cities had their
own mythological traditions, some of them going
back to the Bronze Age, others gradually developing
under the influence of neighboring peoples. Poets
and artists felt free to choose the versions that appealed to their own tastes or helped them to express
their ideas. Later Greeks, it is true, tried to organize

Ancient Greece

all these conflicting beliefs into something resembling order. Father Zeus ruled from Mount Olympus, where he was surrounded by the other principal Olympian deities. His wife Hera was the goddess of marriage and the protectress of the family. His daughter Athena symbolized intelligence and understanding. Aphrodite was the goddess of love, Ares, her lover, the god of war, and so on. But the range and variety of the Greek imagination defied this kind of categorization. The Greeks loved a good story, and so tales that did not fit the ordered scheme continued to circulate.

These contradictions were, of course, perfectly apparent to the Greeks themselves, but they used their religion to illuminate their own lives, rather than to give them divine guidance. One of the clearest examples is the contrast that Greek poets drew between the powers of Apollo and Dionysus, two of the most influential of their gods. Apollo represented logic and order, the power of the mind; Dionysus was the god of the emotions, whose influence, if excessive, could lead to violence and disorder. By worshiping both these forces, the Greeks were acknowledging their obvious dual existence in human nature and trying to strike a prudent balance between them.

The Greek deities served many purposes, therefore, but these purposes were very different from those of the other Western religions. No Greek god, not even Zeus, represents supreme good. At the other end of the moral scale, there is no Greek figure of supreme evil corresponding to the Christian concept of Satan. The Greeks turned to their deities for explanations of both natural phenomena and psychological characteristics they recognized in themselves. At the same time they used their deities as yet another way of enhancing the glory of their individual city-states, as in the case of the cult of Athena at Athens. Problems of human morality required human, rather than divine, solutions. The Greeks turned to art and literature, rather than prayer, as a means of trying to discover them.

The Earliest Greek Literature: Homer

At the beginning of Greek history stand two epic poems which even the quarrelsome Greeks themselves saw as national, indeed universal, in their significance. The *Iliad* and the *Odyssey* have, from the time of the Greeks, been held in the highest esteem.

Homer, their accepted author, is generally regarded as not only the first figure in the Western literary tradition but also one of the greatest. Yet even though Homer's genius is beyond doubt, little else about him is clear. In fact, the many problems and theories connected with the Homeric epics and their creator are generally summed up under the label, "the Homeric Question."

The ancient Greeks themselves were not sure who had composed the *Iliad* and the *Odyssey,* when and where the author had lived, or even if one person was responsible for both of them. In general, tradition ascribed the epics to a blind poet called Homer [67]; almost every city worthy of the name claimed to be his birthplace. Theories about when he had lived

67 *Homer.* Late Hellenistic or Graeco-Roman, c. 150 B.C. Marble, height 16″ (41 cm). Museum of Fine Arts, Boston (H. L. Pierce Fund). Although no one knew what Homer really looked like, the sculptor tried to convey the insight of the blind poet by emphasizing the sense of concentration and venerable old age.

ranged from the time of the Trojan War, around 1250 B.C., to 500 years later.

The problem of who Homer was, and even whether he existed at all, continues to vex scholars to this day. In any case most experts would probably now agree that the creation of the *Iliad* and the *Odyssey* was a highly complex affair. Each of the epics basically consists of a number of shorter folk ballads or "lays" that were combined, gradually evolving over a century or more into the works as we now know them. The first crystallization of these popular tales had probably occurred by around 800 B.C., but the poems were still not in their final form. The first written official version of each epic was probably not made before the late 6th century B.C. The edition of the poems that we now have was made by a scholar working at Alexandria in the 2nd century B.C.

Where, then, in this long development must we place Homer? He may perhaps have been the man who first began to combine the separate lays into a single whole; or perhaps he was the man who sometime after 800 B.C. imposed an artistic unity on the mass of remembered folk tales he had inherited. The differences between the *Iliad* and the *Odyssey* have suggested to a number of commentators that a different "Homer" may have been responsible for the creation or development of each work, but here we are in the realm of speculation. Perhaps after all it would be best to follow the ancient Greeks themselves, contenting ourselves with the belief that at some stage in the evolution of the poems, they were filtered through the imagination of the first great genius of the Western literary tradition, without being too specific about which stage it was.

The power and beauty of these great poems seem almost miraculous in view of the apparently haphazard nature of their creation. Even more astonishing, however, is the fact that throughout most of this long period they were never written down but were composed and passed on by word of mouth. The Greeks of the Iron Age had to rediscover for themselves the art of writing; by the time they had borrowed an alphabet from the Phoenicians and adapted it to their own language—a process barely complete before 700 B.C.—the *Iliad* and *Odyssey* had been created.

That poems of this length and complexity (the *Iliad* alone is more than 15,000 lines long) could be memorized and handed down intact is not of itself unique. Other cultures have had an "oral tradition" of this kind. In fact the process of "oral composition" explains many of the most obvious characteristics of Homeric style. Clearly a *bard,* or poet, who was reciting the poems to an audience would be glad to have a supply of stock lines to fall back on and rest the memory. Listeners would be equally glad to hear familiar words recurring in familiar situations, since it must be remembered that to listen rather than read requires a very special kind of concentration.

Sometimes these repetitions consist of single lines. Warriors killed in battle are often described in the line: "He fell to the ground with a thud and his weapons crashed upon him." Or, to take a particularly characteristic and flavorful example, when one Homeric hero wishes to respond with amazement (and often disapproval) to the words of another, he does so in the line: "What is this word that has escaped the barrier of your teeth?" On occasion, longer passages are repeated verbatim. At a crucial point in the last book of the *Iliad,* Zeus gives his attendant Iris thirteen lines of instructions to take to Achilles, and a few moments later Iris repeats the entire thirteen lines to Achilles himself.

The most frequent repetitions are of phrases and adjectives used as descriptive labels, or *epithets,* applied both to characters and to things. Zeus is described in passage after passage as "the cloud-gatherer" or "father of gods and men," depending on how many words the poet needs to fill out the line. Odysseus is "resourceful" and Achilles is "swift-footed." The sea is "wine-dark" and the dawn "rosy-fingered"—a particularly poetic and effective way of characterizing a phenomenon of nature in human terms.

Of course the use of standard labels of this kind is very different from the general practice of poets, from Aeschylus to the present, who try to find new and original ways of expressing ideas or describing things each time they occur. It is, however, characteristic of works orally composed, and Homer's use of it is often surprisingly subtle.

Another aid to the listening audience, one that is greatly appreciated in addition by the reader, is Homer's masterful use of similes. In general he uses them to describe the unfamiliar in terms of the familiar, comparing the legendary world of his characters to aspects of every day life. Thus in Book II of the *Iliad* the massed Greek forces are compared in quick succession to flocks of birds, leaves and flowers, and insects swarming around pails of milk. Thus the humble listener could be made to feel at home in the heroic world of armies and battles.

All of these literary features are found in both the *Iliad* and the *Odyssey,* which are clearly the result of a single tradition. In spite of their obvious similarities, the two poems are very different in spirit, enough so that some readers believe in two "Homers." The *Iliad* is somber, taut, direct. The concentration of its theme makes it easier to understand, and certainly easier to explain, than the more digressive and light-hearted *Odyssey.* But the *Odyssey* is certainly not a lesser work; if anything its range and breadth of humanity are even greater, and its design is more elaborate.

The principal theme of the *Odyssey* is the return home of the Greek hero Odysseus from the war against Troy. Odysseus' journey, which takes ten years, is filled with adventures involving one-eyed giants, monsters of various kinds, a seductive enchantress, a romantic young girl, a floating island, a trip to the underworld, and many other fairy-tale elements [68]. Into this main narrative is woven a description of the wanderings of Odysseus' son, Telemachus, who, searching for his missing father, visits many of the other Greek leaders who have returned safely from Troy.

In the last half of the poem Odysseus finally returns home in disguise. Without revealing his identity to his ever-faithful wife Penelope, he kills the suitors who have been pestering her for ten years to declare her husband dead and remarry [69]. Homer keeps us waiting almost to the very end for the grand

68 Siren Painter. *Odysseus and the Sirens,* detail of red-figure vase. c. 475 B.C. Terra cotta, height of vase 13⅞" (35 cm). British Museum, London (reproduced by courtesy of the Trustees). Odysseus is tied to the mast of his ship, at his own order, so he can resist the call of the Sirens' song. He has ordered his men to put wax in their ears.

69 Pintoricchio. *Scenes from the Odyssey.* c. 1500. Fresco transferred to canvas, 4′1½″ × 4′11¾″ (1.26 × 1.52 m). National Gallery, London. Telemachus, ignoring Penelope's suitors, is returning to his mother after a journey in search of his father. Penelope is seated at her loom. She has told the eager suitors that she will choose one of them when she finishes weaving a shroud, but each night she unravels the day's work. The ship seen through the window is of the artist's time, not at all like the Greek ship on the vase in figure **68**.

recognition scene between husband and wife. All ends happily, with Penelope, Odysseus, and his aged father Laertes peacefully reunited.

The various episodes of the story are treated with a degree of vividness and realism that is difficult to describe. The short extract below from Book XVII can hardly do justice to so varied a whole, but it may serve to illustrate Homer's unerring choice of detail and his ability to hit exactly the right mood at a crucial moment. At this point in the poem, Odysseus has finally returned to his home after twenty years away. He is disguised as a beggar and accompanied only by a swineherd, Eumaios, who has given him shelter the night before but has not recognized him. Odysseus plans to keep his identity a secret from all except his son until he has disposed of Penelope's suitors. Un-

known and hungry, he has entered the palace and stands talking to Eumaios. But if Odysseus can deceive his friends, his enemies, and even his wife, he cannot deceive his old dog, who has waited almost twenty years to see his master again. In the encounter between man and animal Homer combines an acute realism with universal symbolism. We can easily visualize the scene—the smell of the dung and the tick-ridden dog. At the same time the dog's patience and loyalty take on an emotional power that far transcends the immediate circumstances, while the irony of Odysseus' own position also acquires a broader significance. The themes of hidden identity and the need to deceive even those one loves achieve, by some poetic magic, their most poignant expression in the death of an old dog.

Homer
from ODYSSEY, Book XVII

Now as these two were conversing
  thus with each other, 290
A dog who was lying there raised his
  head and ears. This was
Argos, patient-hearted Odysseus' dog,
  whom he himself
raised, but got no joy of him,
  since before that he went to sacred
Ilion. In the days before,
  the young men had taken him
out to follow goats of the wild,
  and deer, and rabbits;
but now he had been put aside,
  with his master absent,
and lay on the deep pile of dung,
  from the mules and oxen,
which lay abundant before the gates,
  so that the servants
of Odysseus could take it to his great estate,
  for manuring.
There the dog Argos lay in the dung,
  all covered with dog ticks. 300
Now, as he perceived that Odysseus
  had come close to him,
he wagged his tail, and laid both
  his ears back; only
he now no longer had the strength
  to move any closer
to his master, who, watching him
  from a distance, without Eumaios
noticing, secretly wiped a tear away,
  and said to him:
"Eumaios, this is amazing,
  this dog that lies on the dunghill.
The shape of him is splendid,
  and yet I cannot be certain
whether he had the running speed
  to go with this beauty,
or is just one of the kind of table dog
  that gentlemen
keep, and it is only for show that their masters
  care for them." 310
Then, O swineherd Eumaios,
  you said to him in answer:
"This, it is too true, is the dog of a man
  who perished
far away. If he were such,
  in build and performance,
as when Odysseus left him behind,
  when he went to Ilion,
soon you could see his speed and his
  strength for yourself. Never

could any wild animal, in the profound
  depths of the forest,
escape, once he pursued.
  He was very clever at tracking.
But now he is in bad times.
  His master, far from his country,
has perished, and the women are careless,
  and do not look after him;
and serving men, when their masters are no
  longer about, to make them 320
work, are no longer willing to do their
  rightful duties.
For Zeus of the wide brows takes away
  one half of the virtue
from a man, once the day of slavery
  closes upon him."

So he spoke, and went into the
  strongly-settled palace,
and strode straight on, to the great hall
  and the haughty suitors.
But the doom of dark death now closed
  over the dog, Argos,
when, after nineteen years had gone by,
  he had seen Odysseus.

The action of the *Iliad* takes place before that of the *Odyssey,* during the final year of the Greeks' siege of Troy, or Ilium. Its subject is only indirectly concerned with the Trojan War, however, and the poem ends before the episode of the wooden horse and the fall of the city. Its principal theme is stated in the opening lines of Book I, which establish the tragic mood of the work. Here the poet invokes the goddess of poetic inspiration: "Sing, goddess, of the anger of Peleus' son Achilles, which disastrously inflicted countless sufferings on the Greeks, sending the strong souls of many heroes to Hades and leaving their bodies to be devoured by dogs and all birds. . . ."

The subject of the *Iliad,* then, is the anger of Achilles and its consequences. Its message is a direct one: We must be prepared to answer for the results of our own actions and realize that when we act wrongly we will cause suffering both for ourselves and, perhaps more importantly, for those we love. Although the setting of the *Iliad* is heroic, even mythic, the theme of human responsibility is universal.

The story of Achilles' disastrous mistake is told in a basically simple and direct narrative. It begins with a quarrel between Agamemnon, commander-in-chief of the Greek forces, and Achilles, his powerful ally, who resents Agamemnon's overbearing assertion of authority. After a public argument, Achilles decides to punish Agamemnon by withdrawing his military support and retiring to his tent, in the hope that without his aid the Greeks will be unable to defeat the Trojans. In the battles that follow he is proved correct; the Trojans inflict a series of defeats on the Greeks, killing many of their leading warriors.

Agamemnon eventually (Book IX) admits that he behaved too high-handedly and offers Achilles, through intermediaries, not only a handsome apology but a generous financial inducement to return to the fighting and save the Greek cause [70]. Achilles, however, rejects this attempt to make amends and stubbornly nurses his anger as the fighting resumes and Greek casualties mount. Then his dearest friend Patroclus is killed by the Trojan leader Hector, son of their king (Book XVI). Only then does Achilles return to battle, his former anger against Agamemnon now turned against the Trojans in general and Hector in particular.

After killing Hector in single combat (Book XXII), Achilles maltreats Hector's corpse in order to relieve his own sense of guilt at having permitted Patroclus' death. Finally Priam, the old king of Troy, steals into the Greek camp by night to beg for the return of his son's body (Book XXIV). In this encounter with Priam, Achilles at last recognizes and accepts the tragic nature of life and the inevitability of death. His anger melts and he hands over the body of his dead enemy. The *Iliad* ends with the funeral rites of Hector, "tamer of horses."

As is clear even from this brief summary, there is a direct relationship between human actions and their consequences. The gods appear in the *Iliad* and frequently play a part in the action, but at no time can divine intervention save Achilles from paying the price for his unreasonable anger. Furthermore, Achilles' crime is committed not against a divine code of ethics but against human standards of behavior. All

70 Jean Auguste Dominique Ingres. *The Envoys of Agamemnon*. 1801. Oil on canvas, 3'7¼" × 5'1" (1.1 × 1.55 m). Ecole des Beaux-Arts, Paris. The French artist Ingres shows the arrival of Agamemnon's ambassadors in Achilles' tent, an event described in Book IX of the *Iliad*. Achilles, interrupted in the middle of his song, rises in surprise. Patroclus stands behind him. Through the ages artists have responded to the Homeric epics by depicting scenes from them in the styles of their own periods. This picture, with its careful rendering of details like the helmets and Achilles' lyre and chair, is typical of the Neoclassical style of the early 19th century.

his companions, including Patroclus, realize that he is behaving unreasonably.

From its earliest beginnings, therefore, the Greek tradition of morality is in strong contrast to the Judeo-Christian tradition. At the center of the Homeric universe is not God but human beings, who are at least partly in control of their own destiny. If they cannot choose the time when they die, they can at least choose how they live. The standards by which human life will be judged are those established by one's fellow humans. In the *Iliad* the gods serve as divine "umpires." They watch the action and comment on it and at times enforce the rules, but they do not affect the course of history. Humans do not always, however, fully realize the consequences of their behavior. In fact, they often prefer to believe that things happen "according to the will of the gods" rather than because of their own actions. Yet the gods themselves claim no such power. In a remarkable passage at the beginning of Book I of the *Odyssey* we see the world for a moment through the eyes of Zeus as he sits at dinner on Mount Olympus: "How foolish men are! How unjustly they blame the gods! It is their lot to suffer, but because of their own folly they bring upon themselves sufferings over and above what is fated for them. And then they blame the gods." These are hardly words we can imagine coming from the God of the Old Testament.

Human freedom to act is limited in only one way—the way that distinguishes gods from human beings. The gods are immortal; we must die. Destiny, not the gods, decides when and how we die. The power of destiny, of "what must be," is as universal as it is inexplicable. Even Zeus himself is bound by it. At a crucial stage in the battle described in Book XVI of the *Iliad,* Sarpedon, a son of Zeus by a mortal woman, is about to meet death at the hands of Patroclus. As the following passage describes, Zeus' natural inclination to intervene is overruled by his wife Hera, who points out that one doomed by his destiny to death should not be saved. Zeus sheds tears of blood, but he accepts his wife's argument. Homer emphasizes the paradox of his position by describing the despondent god as "father of gods and men" at the very moment when he cannot save his own son [Plate 6, page 121].

Homer
from ILIAD, Book XVI

[Sarpedon] sprang to the ground
   in all his arms from the chariot,

and on the other side Patroklos
   when he saw him leapt down
from his chariot. They as two
   hook-clawed beak-bent vultures
above a tall rock face, high-screaming,
   go for each other,
so now these two, crying aloud,
   encountered together.   430
And watching them the son
   of devious-devising Kronos
was pitiful, and spoke to Hera,
   his wife and his sister:
"Ah me, that it is destined that the
   dearest of men, Sarpedon,
must go down under the hands of
   Menoitios' son Patroklos.
The heart in my breast is balanced
   between two ways as I ponder,
whether I should snatch him out of the
   sorrowful battle
and set him down still alive in the
   rich country of Lykia,
or beat him under at the hands of the
   son of Menoitios."
In turn the lady Hera of the ox eyes
   answered him:
"Majesty, son of Kronos, what sort of thing
   have you spoken?   440
Do you wish to bring back a man
   who is mortal, one long since
doomed by his destiny, from ill-sounding
   death and release him?
Do it, then; but not all the rest of us gods
   shall approve you.
And put away in your thoughts this
   other thing I tell you;
if you bring Sarpedon back to his home,
   still living,
think how then some other one of the
   gods might also
wish to carry his own son out of the
   strong encounter;
since around the great city of Priam
   are fighting many
sons of the immortals. You will waken
   grim resentment among them.
No, but if he is dear to you, and your
   heart mourns for him,   450
then let him be, and let him go down
   in the strong encounter
underneath the hands of Patroklos,
   the son of Menoitios;
but after the soul and the years of his life
   have left him, then send
Death to carry him away, and Sleep,

who is painless,
until they come with him to the
 countryside of broad Lykia
where his brothers and countrymen
 shall give him due burial
with tomb and gravestone. Such is the
 privilege of those who have perished."

She spoke, nor did the father of gods and
 men disobey her;
yet he wept tears of blood that fell to the
 ground, for the sake
of his beloved son, whom now Patroklos
 was presently   460
to kill, by generous Troy and far from the
 land of his fathers.

It is worth examining the Homeric world view at some length, because the *Iliad* and *Odyssey* formed the basis of education and culture throughout the Greek and Roman world; children learned the two poems by heart at school. Ideas changed and developed, but reverence for Homer remained constant. Nor was this reverence limited to the ancient world. In the *Divine Comedy* (*Inferno,* IV), Dante describes Homer as the greatest of all poets. In Raphael's *Parnassus* fresco in the Vatican, he occupies a prominent position to the left of Apollo. The Homeric epics have never ceased to inspire artists, musicians, and writers. One of the most important novels of the 20th century, for example, is James Joyce's *Ulysses* (Odysseus' Latin name).

Homer is not an easy author to read in extracts. Much of the impact of the *Iliad* comes from its majestic length and from the digressions that both enrich the main action and give poignancy to the eventual climax. We feel more deeply for Hector when he is killed in Book XXII and when his corpse is maltreated in Book XXIV because we have seen him with his wife and child in a touching farewell scene in Book VI. Nor is the *Iliad* easy to translate. The sense is clear, of course, but the combination of nobility and directness is difficult to reproduce in English. Nonetheless, the epic scale and the breadth of the original are clearly recognizable in the following translation of the last great episode in the work, the confrontation between Priam and Achilles over the corpse of Hector.

Throughout the long scene Homer maintains the heroic dignity of his characters while allowing us to identify with them as human beings. The pathos of Priam's appeal reaches its height in lines 505–506. Achilles' immediate reaction is as perfectly appropri-

ate as it is unexpected. His own changing moods, which veer from philosophical resignation (lines 549–551) to sudden anger (lines 559–570) to tenderness (lines 592–595) seem to run the gamut of emotional response. How typical it is, too, of a Homeric hero to be practical enough after such an intense encounter to think of dinner and supervise its serving.

Homer
from ILIAD, Book XXIV

[Priam] made straight for the dwelling
where Achilleus the beloved of Zeus was sitting.
 He found him
inside, and his companions were sitting apart, as
 two only,
Automedon the hero and Alkimos, scion of Ares,
were busy beside him. He had just now got
 through with his dinner,
with eating and drinking, and the table still stood
 by. Tall Priam
came in unseen by the other men and stood close
 beside him
and caught the knees of Achilleus in his arms, and
 kissed the hands
that were dangerous and manslaughtering and had
 killed so many
of his sons. As when dense disaster closes on one
 who has murdered   480
a man in his own land, and he comes to the
 country of others,
to a man of substance, and wonder seizes on those
 who behold him,
so Achilleus wondered as he looked on Priam, a
 godlike
man, and the rest of them wondered also, and
 looked at each other.
But now Priam spoke to him in the words of a
 suppliant:
"Achilleus like the gods, remember your father,
 one who
is of years like mine, and on the door-sill of
 sorrowful old age.
And they who dwell nearby encompass him and
 afflict him,
nor is there any to defend him against the wrath,
 the destruction.
Yet surely he, when he hears of you and that you
 are still living,   490
is gladdened within his heart and all his days he is
 hopeful
that he will see his beloved son come home from
 the Troad.
But for me, my destiny was evil. I have had the
 noblest

of sons in Troy, but I say not one of them is left
    to me.
Fifty were my sons, when the sons of the Achaians
    came here.
Nineteen were born to me from the womb of a
    single mother,
and other women bore the rest in my palace; and
    of these
violent Ares broke the strength in the knees of
    most of them,
but one was left me who guarded my city and
    people, that one
you killed a few days since as he fought in defence
    of his country,   500
Hektor; for whose sake I come now to the ships
    of the Achaians
to win him back from you, and I bring you gifts
    beyond number.
Honour then the gods, Achilleus, and take pity
    upon me
remembering your father, yet I am still more
    pitiful;
I have gone through what no other mortal on
    earth has gone through;
I put my lips to the hands of the man who has
    killed my children."

So he spoke, and stirred in the other a passion of
    grieving
for his own father. He took the old man's hand
    and pushed him
gently away, and the two remembered, as Priam
    sat huddled
at the feet of Achilleus and wept close for
    manslaughtering Hektor   510
and Achilleus wept now for his own father, now
    again
for Patroklos. The sound of their mourning moved
    in the house. Then
when great Achilleus had taken full satisfaction in
    sorrow
and the passion for it had gone from his mind and
    body, thereafter
he rose from his chair, and took the old man by
    the hand, and set him
on his feet again, in pity for the grey head and the
    grey beard,
and spoke to him and addressed him in winged
    words: "Ah, unlucky,
surely you have had much evil to endure in your
    spirit.
How could you dare to come alone to the ships of
    the Achaians
and before my eyes, when I am one who have
    killed in such numbers   520

such brave sons of yours? The heart in you is iron.
    Come, then,
and sit down upon this chair, and you and I will
    even let
our sorrows lie still in the heart for all our grieving.
    There is not
any advantage to be won from grim lamentation.
Such is the way the gods spun life for unfortunate
    mortals,
that we live in unhappiness, but the gods
    themselves have no sorrows.
There are two urns that stand on the door-sill of
    Zeus. They are unlike
for the gifts they bestow: an urn of evils, an urn
    of blessings.
If Zeus who delights in thunder mingles these and
    bestows them
on man, he shifts, and moves now in evil, again in
    good fortune.   530
But when Zeus bestows from the urn of sorrows,
    he makes a failure
of man, and the evil hunger drives him over the
    shining
earth, and he wanders respected neither of gods
    nor mortals.
Such were the shining gifts given by the gods to
    Peleus
from his birth, who outshone all men beside for
    his riches
and pride of possession, and was lord over the
    Myrmidons. Thereto
the gods bestowed an immortal wife on him, who
    was mortal.
But even on him the god piled evil also. There
    was not
any generation of strong sons born to him in his
    great house
but a single all-untimely child he had, and I
    give him   540
no care as he grows old, since far from the land of
    my fathers
I sit here in Troy, and bring nothing but sorrow
    to you and your children.
And you, old sir, we are told you prospered once;
    for as much
as Lesbos, Makar's hold, confines to the north
    above it
and Phrygia from the north confines, and
    enormous Hellespont,
of these, old sir, you were lord once in your
    wealth and your children.
But now the Uranian gods brought us, an
    affliction upon you,
forever there is fighting about your city, and men
    killed.

But bear up, nor mourn endlessly in your heart, for there is not

anything to be gained from grief for your son; you will never 550

bring him back; sooner you must go through yet another sorrow."

In answer to him again spoke aged Priam the godlike:

"Do not, beloved of Zeus, make me sit on a chair while Hektor

lies yet forlorn among the shelters; rather with all speed

give him back, so my eyes may behold him, and accept the ransom

we bring you, which is great. You may have joy of it, and go back

to the land of your own fathers, since once you have permitted me

to go on living myself and continue to look on the sunlight."

Then looking darkly at him spoke swift-footed Achilleus:

"No longer stir me up, old sir. I myself am minded 560

to give Hektor back to you. A messenger came to me from Zeus,

my mother, she who bore me, the daughter of the sea's ancient.

I know you, Priam, in my heart, and it does not escape me

that some god led you to the running ships of the Achaians.

For no mortal would dare come to our encampment, not even

one strong in youth. He could not get by the pickets, he could not

lightly unbar the bolt that secures our gateway. Therefore

you must not further make my spirit move in my sorrows,

for fear, old sir, I might not let you alone in my shelter,

suppliant as you are; and be guilty before the god's orders." 570

He spoke, and the old man was frightened and did as he told him.

The son of Peleus bounded to the door of the house like a lion,

nor went alone, but the two henchmen followed attending,

the hero Automedon and Alkimos, those whom Achilleus

honoured beyond all companions after Patroklos dead. These two

now set free from under the yoke the mules and the horses,

and led inside the herald, the old king's crier, and gave him

a chair to sit in, then from the smooth-polished mule wagon

lifted out the innumerable spoils for the head of Hektor,

but left inside it two great cloaks and a finespun tunic 580

to shroud the corpse in when they carried him home. Then Achilleus

called out to his serving-maids to wash the body and anoint it

all over; but take it first aside, since otherwise Priam

might see his son and in the heart's sorrow not hold in his anger

at the sight, and the deep heart in Achilleus be shaken to anger;

that he might not kill Priam and be guilty before the god's orders.

Then when the serving-maids had washed the corpse and anointed it

with olive oil, they threw a fair great cloak and a tunic

about him, and Achilleus himself lifted him and laid him

on a litter, and his friends helped him lift it to the smooth-polished 590

mule wagon. He groaned then, and called by name on his beloved companion:

"Be not angry with me, Patroklos, if you discover,

though you be in the house of Hades, that I gave back great Hektor

to his loved father, for the ransom he gave me was not unworthy.

I will give you your share of the spoils, as much as is fitting."

So spoke great Achilleus and went back into the shelter

and sat down on the elaborate couch from which he had risen,

against the inward wall, and now spoke his word to Priam:

"Your son is given back to you, aged sir, as you asked it.

He lies on a bier. When dawn shows you yourself shall see him 600

as you take him away. Now you and I must remember our supper.

For even Niobe, she of the lovely tresses, remembered

to eat, whose twelve children were destroyed in her palace,

six daughters, and six sons in the pride of their youth, whom Apollo

killed with arrows from his silver bow, being angered

with Niobe, and shaft-showering Artemis killed the daughters;

because Niobe likened herself to Leto of the fair colouring

and said Leto had borne only two, she herself had borne many;

but the two, though they were only two, destroyed all those others.

Nine days long they lay in their blood, nor was there anyone   610

to bury them, for the son of Kronos made stones out of

the people; but on the tenth day the Uranian gods buried them.

But she remembered to eat when she was worn out with weeping.

And now somewhere among the rocks, in the lonely mountains,

in Sipylos, where they say is the resting place of the goddesses

who are nymphs, and dance beside the waters of Acheloios,

there, stone still, she broods on the sorrows that the gods gave her.

Come then, we also, aged magnificent sir, must remember

to eat, and afterwards you may take your beloved son back

to Ilion, and mourn for him; and he will be much lamented."   620

So spoke fleet Achilleus and sprang to his feet and slaughtered

a gleaming sheep, and his friends skinned it and butchered it fairly,

and cut up the meat expertly into small pieces, and spitted them,

and roasted all carefully and took off the pieces.

Automedon took the bread and set it out on the table

in fair baskets, while Achilleus served the meats. And thereon

they put their hands to the good things that lay ready before them.

But when they had put aside their desire for eating and drinking,

Priam, son of Dardanos, gazed upon Achilleus, wondering

at his size and beauty, for he seemed like an outright vision   630

of gods. Achilleus in turn gazed on Dardanian Priam

and wondered, as he saw his brave looks and listened to him talking.

But when they had taken their fill of gazing one on the other,

first of the two to speak was the aged man, Priam the godlike:

"Give me, beloved of Zeus, a place to sleep presently, so that

we may even go to bed and take the pleasure of sweet sleep.

For my eyes have not closed underneath my lids since that time

when my son lost his life beneath your hands, but always

I have been grieving and brooding over my numberless sorrows

and wallowed in the muck about my courtyard's enclosure.   640

Now I have tasted food again and have let the gleaming

wine go down my throat. Before, I had tasted nothing."

He spoke, and Achilleus ordered his serving-maids and companions

to make a bed in the porch's shelter and to lay upon it

fine underbedding of purple, and spread blankets above it

and fleecy robes to be an over-all covering. The maid-servants

went forth from the main house, and in their hands held torches,

and set to work, and presently had two beds made. Achilleus

of the swift feet now looked at Priam and said, sarcastic:

"Sleep outside, aged sir and good friend, for fear some Achaian   650

might come in here on a matter of counsel, since they keep coming

and sitting by me and making plans; as they are supposed to.

But if one of these come through the fleeting black night should notice you,

he would go straight and tell Agamemnon, shepherd of the people,

and there would be delay in the ransoming of the body.

But come, tell me this and count off for me exactly

how many days you intend for the burial of great Hektor.

Tell me, so I myself shall stay still and hold back
    the people."
In answer to him again spoke aged Priam the
    godlike:
"If you are willing that we accomplish a complete
    funeral 660
for great Hektor, this, Achilleus, is what you could
    do and give
me pleasure. For you know surely how we are
    penned in our city,
and wood is far to bring in from the hills, and the
    Trojans are frightened
badly. Nine days we would keep him in our palace
    and mourn him,
and bury him on the tenth day, and the people
    feast by him,
and on the eleventh day we would make the
    grave-barrow for him,
and on the twelfth day fight again; if so we must
    do."

Then in turn swift-footed brilliant Achilleus
    answered him:
"Then all this, aged Priam, shall be done as you
    ask it.
I will hold off our attack for as much time as you
    bid me." 670

So he spoke, and took the aged king by the
    right hand
at the wrist, so that his heart might have no fear.
    Then these two,
Priam and the herald who were both men of close
    counsel,
slept in the place outside the house, in the porch's
    shelter;
but Achilleus slept in the inward corner of the
    strong-built shelter,
and at his side lay Briseis of the fair colouring.

The Visual Arts

Our impressions of the first three hundred years of
Greek art (1000–700 B.C.) are based largely on
painted pottery, hardly a major art form even in later
times, for little else has survived. Of architecture
there is almost no trace. Although small bronze and
ivory statuettes and relief plaques were being made
from the 9th century B.C. on, the earliest surviving
large stone sculptures date to the mid-7th century B.C.

Painted vases, therefore, are our major source of
information about artistic developments. It comes as
something of a surprise to find that Homer's contemporaries decorated their pots with abstract geometric
designs, with no attempt at the qualities most typical
of their literature, vividness and realism. This style
has given its name to the two subdivisions of the period, the Protogeometric (1000–900 B.C.) and the
Geometric (900–700 B.C.).

For the first hundred years, artists decorated their
vases with simple, bold designs consisting mainly of
concentric circles and semicircles [71]. In some ways
this period represents a transition from the end of the
Mycenaean age, but the memory of Mycenaean motifs soon gave way to a new style. If Protogeometric
pottery seems a long way from Greek art of later
centuries, it does show qualities of clarity and order
that reappear later, although in a very different context.

In the Geometric pottery of the following two
centuries (900–700 B.C.) the use of abstract design
continued, but the emphasis changed. Circles and
semicircles were replaced by linear designs, zigzags,
triangles, diamonds, and above all the *meander* (a
maze pattern). The size of the pots increased and their

71 Protogeometric amphora. c. 950 B.C. Height 21¾" (56 cm).
Kerameikos Museum, Athens. The circles and semicircles
typical of this style were drawn with a compass.

shape became increasingly distorted to accommodate more and more bands of geometric design [72].

There is something strangely obsessive about many of these vessels—a sense of artists searching for a subject, meanwhile working out over and over the implications of mathematical formulas. Once again we seem a long way from the achievements of later Greek artists, with their emphasis on realism. Yet precise mathematical relationships lie behind the design of much of the greatest Greek art. The Geometric period is best thought of not as a temporary aberration, a wrong track that was abandoned, but as an expression of the obsession with order and balance so characteristic of Greek culture in general.

By the 8th century B.C. artists had begun to find their way toward the principal subject of later Greek art, the human form. Thus human and animal figures begin to appear among the meanders and zigzags. This is a moment so important in the history of Western art that we should not take it for granted. We have been so conditioned by the art of the ancient Greeks that from the late Geometric period until our own time Western art has been primarily concerned with the depiction of human beings. Landscapes are a popular subject, it is true, and in our own century art has become abstract again. Yet most paintings and sculptures deal with the human form, treated in a more or less realistic way.

This realism may seem so obvious as to be hardly worth stating, but it must be remembered that the art of peoples who were not influenced by the Greeks is very different. Islamic art, for example, deals almost exclusively in abstract design. Indian sculptors depicted their gods and heroes in human form, but they certainly did not treat them realistically. The Hindu god Shiva, for example, is often shown with many arms. It is a tribute to the Greeks' overwhelming influence on our culture that, from the Roman period to the 20th century, artists have accepted the Greeks' decision to make the realistic treatment of the human form the central focus of art, whether the forms were those of mortal people or divine gods and goddesses.

The Greeks themselves did not achieve this naturalism overnight. The first depictions of human beings, which appear on Geometric vases shortly after 800 B.C., are highly stylized. They are painted in silhouette, and a single figure often combines front and side views, the head and legs being shown in profile while the upper half of the body is seen from the front. Clearly these are abstractions of men and women, rather than literal depictions, although the

72 Geometric pitcher. c. 800 B.C. Height 31¼″ (80 cm). National Archaeological Museum, Athens. The bands of decoration cover the entire surface. The lid has a handle in the form of a miniature pitcher, and it too is covered with geometric designs.

artists do sometimes try to distinguish between the sexes by adding small projections below the armpits to represent female breasts.

A number of the vases decorated with stick figures of this kind are of immense size. One of them, the *Dipylon Amphora,* is almost 5 feet (1.53 meters) tall [73]. These vases were set up over tombs to serve as grave markers; they had holes in their bases so that offerings poured into them could seep down to the dead below. The scenes on them frequently show the funeral ceremony. Others show processions of warriors, both on foot and in chariots.

73 *Dipylon Amphora.* c. 750 B.C. Height 5′ (1.53 m). National Archaeological Museum, Athens. This immense vase originally was a grave marker. The main band, between the handles, shows the lying-in-state of the dead man on whose grave the vase stood; on both sides of the bier are mourners tearing their hair in grief. Note the two bands of animals, deer and running goats, in the upper part of the vase.

The Age of Colonization

Throughout the period of Homer and Geometric art, individual city-states were ruled by small groups of aristocrats who concentrated wealth and power in their own hands. Presumably, it is their graves that were marked with great amphoras like the *Dipylon* vase. By the 8th century B.C., however, two developments had occurred. First, two centuries of peace had allowed the individual city-states to become quite prosperous. Second, the continuing rule of a small

hereditary aristocracy left a growing urban population increasingly frustrated. Both increasing wealth and the problem of overpopulation produced a single result, colonization.

Throughout the 8th and 7th centuries, enterprising Greeks went abroad either to make their fortunes or to increase them. To the west, Italy and Sicily were colonized and Greek cities established there. Some of these, like Syracuse in Sicily or Sybaris in southern Italy, became richer and more powerful even than the mother cities from which the colonizers had come. Unfortunately, if inevitably, the settlers took with them not only the culture of their *polis* but their inter-city rivalries, often with disastrous results. To the south and east, cities were also established in Egypt and on the Black Sea.

The most significant wave of colonization was that which moved eastward to the coast of Asia Minor, in some cases back to territory which had been inhabited by the Mycenaeans centuries earlier. From here the colonizers established trade contacts with peoples in the ancient Near East. Within Greece itself the effect on art and life of this expansion to the east was immense. After almost three hundred years of cultural isolation, in a land cut off from its neighbors by mountains and sea, the Greeks were brought face to face with the immensely rich and sophisticated cultures of the ancient Near East. Oriental ideas and artistic styles were seen by the colonizers and carried home by the traders. A growing quantity of eastern artifacts, ivories, jewelry, and metalwork was sent back to the mother cities and even to the Greek cities of Italy. So great was the impact of Near Eastern art on the Greeks from the late 8th century to around 600 B.C., that this period and its style are generally known by the name *Orientalizing*.

Vase Painting at Corinth and Athens

Different Greek cities reacted to Oriental influences in different ways, although all reacted strongly. In particular the growing hostility between the two richest city-states, Athens and Corinth, which two centuries later led to the Peloponnesian War and the fall of Athens, seems already symbolized in the strong differences between their Orientalizing pottery. The Corinthian artists developed a miniature style that made use of a wide variety of eastern motifs—sphinxes, winged human figures, floral designs—all of them arranged in bands covering almost the entire surface of the vase. Individual figures were depicted in the so-called *black-figure technique*. They were first painted in silhouette, in black, and details were then etched in by scratching lines with a fine point. White, yellow, and purple were often used to highlight details, producing a bold and striking effect. After the monotony of Geometric pottery the variety of subject and range of color come as a welcome change.

The small size of the pots made them ideal for export. Corinthian vases have in fact been discovered not only thoughout Greece but in Italy, Egypt, and the Near East. Clearly, any self-respecting woman of the 7th century B.C. wanted an elegant little Corinthian flask [74] for her perfume, oil, or make-up. The vases are well made, the figures lively and the style instantly recognizable as Corinthian—an important factor for commercial success. Corinth's notable political and economic strength throughout the 7th and

early 6th centuries B.C. was, in fact, built on the sale of these little pots and their contents.

In Athens potters were slower to throw off the effects of the Geometric period and less able to develop an all-purpose style like the Corinthian. The vases remain large and the attempts to depict humans and animals, using a combination of the black-figure technique and freehand drawing, are often clumsy. The achievements of later Athenian art are nonetheless clearly foreshadowed in the vitality of the figures and the constant desire of the artists to illustrate events from mythology [75] or daily life, rather than simply to decorate a surface in the Corinthian manner.

By 600 B.C. the narrative style had become established at Athens, and the full-scale use of the black-figure technique permitted the designer greater artistic control. As Athens began to take over an increasing share of the market for painted vases and their

74 Aryballos. Middle Corinthian, c. 625 B.C. State Museums, West Berlin. This little flask held perfumed oil. The black-figure technique and the very Eastern looking panther are characteristic of the Orientalizing style. Also characteristic are the flower-like decorations, which are blobs of paint scored with lines. The musculature and features of the panther are also the result of scoring.

75 *The Blinding of Polyphemus,* detail of proto-Attic amphora. c. 650 B.C. Height of frieze 17″ (43 cm). Museum, Eleusis. The technique is crude, but the artist shows imagination and even humor in depicting an episode from the *Odyssey.* At the center is Odysseus himself, guiding a sharpened, heated pole into the single eye of Polyphemus, the Cyclops, seated drunkenly at the right—note the wine cup in his hand.

contents, Corinth's position inevitably declined, and the trade rivalry that later had devastating results began to develop.

The Beginnings of Greek Sculpture

The influence of Near Eastern and Egyptian models on Greek sculpture is more consistent and easier to trace than on pottery. The first Greek settlers in Egypt were given land around the mid-7th century B.C. by the Egyptian pharaoh Psammetichos I. It is surely no coincidence that the earliest Greek stone sculptures, which date from about the same period, markedly resemble Egyptian cult statues, and were placed in similarly grandiose temples. (The earliest surviving temple, that of Hera at Olympia, dates at least in part to this period.) These stone figures consist of a small number of types repeated over and over. The most popular were the standing female, or *kore,* clad in drapery [76], and the standing male, or *kouros,* always shown nude [77]. This nudity already marks a break with the Egyptian tradition in which

76 *Kore* from Delos, dedicated by Nikandre. c. 650 B.C. Marble. National Archaeological Museum, Athens. Unlike the *kouros,* the figure is completely clothed, though both have the same rigid stance, arms by sides, and wig-like hair.

77 *Kouros.* c. 615 B.C. Marble, height 6'1½" (1.87 m). Metropolitan Museum of Art, New York (Fletcher Fund, 1932).

figures wore loincloths and foreshadows the heroic male nudity of Classical Greek art. The stance of the *kouros* figures, however, was firmly based on Egyptian models. One foot (usually the left) is forward, the arms are by the sides, and the hands are clenched. The elaborate wiglike hair is also Egyptian in inspiration.

By 600 B.C., only a few years after the first appearance of these statues, Greek art had reached a critical stage. After the slow and cautious progress of the Geometric period, the entire character of painting and sculpture had changed. Within the century following 700 B.C. Greek artists had abandoned abstract design for increasing realism. At this point in their development the Greek spirit of independence and inquiry asserted itself. Instead of following their eastern counterparts and repeating the same models and conventions for centuries, Greek painters and sculptors allowed their curiosity to lead them in a new direction, one that changed the history of art. The early stone figures and painted silhouettes had represented human beings, but only in a schematic, stylized form. Beginning in the Archaic period artists used their work to try to answer such questions as: What do human beings really look like? How do perspective and foreshortening work? What in fact is the true nature of appearance? For the first time in history they began to reproduce the human form in a way true to nature rather than merely echoing the achievements of their predecessors.

The Archaic Period

It is tempting to see the works of art and literature of the Archaic period (600–480 B.C.) as steps on the road that leads to the artistic and intellectual achievement in the Classical Age of the 5th and 4th centuries B.C. rather than to appreciate them for their own qualities. This would be to underestimate seriously the vitality of one of the most creative periods in the development of our culture. In some ways, in fact, the spirit of adventure, of striving toward new forms and new ideas, makes the Archaic achievement more exciting, if less perfected, than that of the Classical period. It is better to travel hopefully than to arrive, as Robert Louis Stevenson put it.

The change in Archaic art is, of course, a reflection of similar social changes. The hereditary aristocrats were being replaced as rulers by a new class of rich merchant traders who had made their fortunes in the economic expansion and who won power by playing on the discontent of the oppressed lower classes. These new rulers were called "tyrants"—although the word had none of the unfavorable sense that it now has. Many of them, in fact, were patrons of the arts. The most famous of them all was Pisistratus, who ruled Athens from 546–528 B.C.. Clearly, revolutions like those that brought him and his fellow tyrants to power were likely to produce revolutionary changes in the arts.

Sculpture and Painting

In sculpture there was an astounding progress from the formalized *kouroi* of the early Archaic period, with their flat planes and rigid stances, to the fully rounded figures of the late 6th century, toward the end of the period. Statues like the *Anavysos Kouros* [78] show a careful study of the human anatomy. The conventions remain the same, but the statues have a new life and vigor.

Although most of the male figures are shown in the traditional stance, there are a few important exceptions. The finest is perhaps the famous *Calf-Bearer* [79] from the Athenian Acropolis (the central hill). The essential unity between man and beast is conveyed simply but with great feeling by the diagonals formed by the man's hands and the calf's legs and by the alignment of the two heads.

The finest female figures of the period also come from the Acropolis. The Persians broke them when they sacked Athens in 480 B.C. and then the Athenians buried them when they returned to their city the next year after defeating the Persians. Rediscovered by modern excavators, the figures are among the most impressive of Archaic masterpieces. They show a gradual but sure development from the earliest *korai* to the richness and variety of the work of the late 6th century, with its emphasis on elaborate drapery and delicate details [Plate 7, page 121].

In addition to these freestanding figures, two other kinds of sculpture now appeared: large-scale statues made to decorate temples and carved stone slabs. In both cases sculptors used the technique of *relief* carving: figures do not stand freely, visible from all angles, but are carved into a block of stone, part of which is left as background. In *high relief* the figures project from the background so much as to seem almost three-dimensional. In *low relief* the carving preserves the flat surface of the stone. Although the

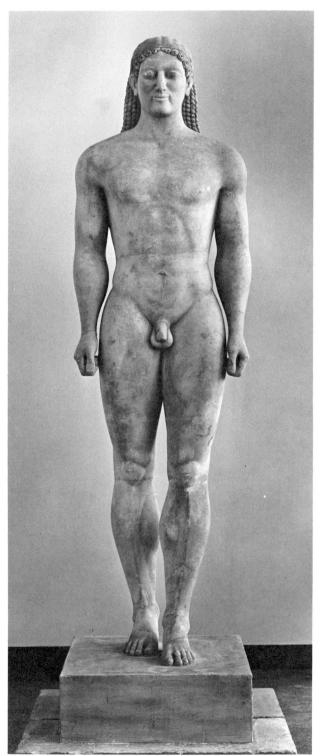

78 *Kouros* from Anavysos. c. 530 B.C. Marble, height 6'4" (1.93 m). National Archaeological Museum, Athens. Note the realism of the muscles and the new sense of power. According to an inscription on the base, this was the tunerary monument to a young man, Kroisos, who had died heroically in battle.

79 *Calf-Bearer*. c. 550 B.C. Marble, height 5'5" (1.65 m). Acropolis Museum, Athens. The archaic smile is softened in this figure. Realism appears in the displacement of the man's hair by the animal's legs and in the amazingly lifelike expression of the calf.

80 Metope showing the decapitation of Medusa. Selinus, c. 540 B.C. Archaeological Museum, Palermo. Medusa was a gorgon whose look turned anyone to stone. Perseus is cutting off her head with the encouragement of Athena, who stands at left. The gorgon's son Pegasus, the winged horse, leaps up at her side. Medusa is shown in the conventional pose indicating rapid motion.

81 Aristokles. *Stele of Aristion.* c. 510 B.C. Height without base 8′ (2.44 m). National Archaeological Museum, Athens. The leather jacket contrasts with the soft folds of the undershirt.

technique is generally used for stone, it can also be applied to metalwork. Temple sculpture, or as it is often called, architectural sculpture, was frequently in high relief, as in the depiction of the decapitation of Medusa from Selinus [80]. Individual carved stone slabs are generally in low relief. Most that have survived were used as grave markers. The workmanship is often of a remarkable subtlety, as on the *stele,* or gravestone, of Aristion [81].

The range of Archaic sculpture is great, and the best pieces communicate something of the excitement of their makers in solving new problems. Almost all of them, however, have in common one feature that often disturbs the modern viewer—the famous "archaic smile." This facial expression, which to our eyes may seem more like a grimace, has been explained in a number of ways. Some believe that it is merely the result of technical inexperience on the part of the sculptors. Others see it as a reflection of the Archaic Greeks' sense of certainty and optimism in facing a world which they seemed increasingly able to control. Whatever its cause, by the

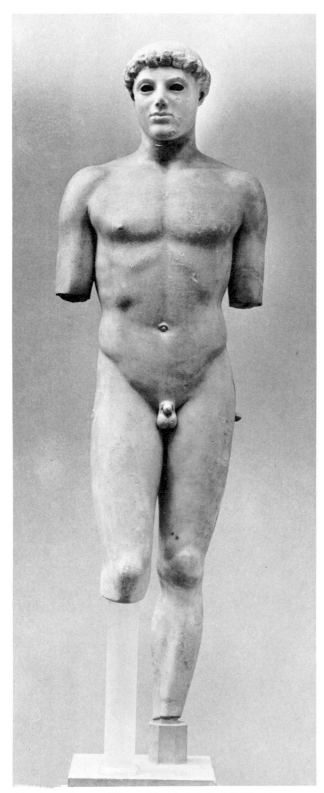

82 *Critian Boy*. c. 490 B.C. Marble, height 34″ (86 cm). Acropolis Museum, Athens. The archaic smile has been superseded by a more natural expression.

83 Exekias. *The Suicide of Ajax*. c. 525 B.C. Black-figure vase, height 21¼″ (54 cm). Musée des Beaux-Arts, Boulogne. Ajax buries his sword in the ground so that he can throw himself onto it. The pathos of the warrior's last moments is emphasized by the empty space around him, the weeping tree, and his now useless shield and helmet.

end of the 6th century B.C., and with the increasing threat posed by the Persians, the archaic smile had begun to fade. It was replaced by the more somber expression of works like the *Critian Boy* [82]. This statue marks a literal "turning point" between the late Archaic world and the early Classical period. For the first time in ancient art the figure is no longer looking or walking straight ahead. The head and the upper part of the body turn slightly; as they do so the weight shifts from one leg to the other and the hips move. Having solved the problem of representing a standing figure in a realistic way, the sculptor has tackled a new and even more complex problem—showing a figure in motion. The consequences of this accomplishment were explored to the full in the Classical period.

By the mid-6th century B.C. the art of vase painting had also made great progress. Works like those of Exekias, perhaps the greatest of black-figure painters, combine superb draftsmanship and immense power of expression [83]. For so restricted a medium, vase painting shows a surprising range. If Exekias's style is serious, somber, sometimes even grim, the style of his contemporary the Amasis painter is relaxed, humorous, and charming.

The end of the 6th century B.C. marks a major development in vase painting with the introduction of the new *red-figure style*. Instead of painting the figures in black silhouette against the red clay of the vase and then etching out the details, the artist paints the background black and leaves the figures in the red color of the clay. Details are now filled in with a brush, allowing much greater variation in fineness or thickness of line. The increased subtlety made possible by this style was used to develop new techniques of foreshortening, perspective, and three-dimensionality [84].

Although some artists continued to produce black-figure works, by the end of the Archaic period around 525 B.C. almost all had turned to the new style. The last Archaic vase painters are among the greatest red-figure artists. Works like the *Euphronios Vase* [see Plate 6, page 121], have a solidity and monumentality that altogether transcend the usual limitations of the medium.

Architecture:
The Doric and Ionic Orders

In architecture, the Archaic period was marked by the construction of a number of major temples in the Doric style or order. This order seems to have been firmly established by 600 B.C., though none of the earlier examples of the evolving style have survived. Important Doric temples include the Temple of Hera at Olympia, the Temple of Apollo at Corinth, and the earliest of the three Doric temples at Paestum, often called the Basilica (meeting hall), though it is

now known to have been dedicated to the goddess Hera [Plate 8, page 122]. The Ionic style of temple architecture, which was widely used in Classical Greece, did not become fully established until later. In the Archaic period Ionic buildings were constructed at such sites as Samos and Ephesus, but most Ionic temples date to the 5th century B.C. and later. For the sake of convenience both the Doric and Ionic orders [85] are described here.

The Doric order is the simpler and the grander of the two. Some of its characteristics seem directly derived from construction methods used in earlier wooden buildings, and its dignity is perhaps in part related to the length of its history. Doric columns have no base but rise directly from the floor of a building. They taper toward the top and have twenty flutes, or vertical grooves. The *capital*, which forms the head of each column, consists of two sections, a spreading convex disc (the *echinus*) and, above, a square block (the *abacus*). The upper part of the temple, or *entablature*, is divided into three sections. The lowest, the *architrave*, is a plain band of rectangular blocks, above which is the *frieze*, consisting of alternating *triglyphs* and *metopes*. The triglyphs are divided by grooves into three vertical bands. The metope panels are sometimes plain, sometimes decorated with sculpture or painting. The building is crowned by a cornice consisting of a horizontal section and two slanting sections meeting at a peak. The long extended triangle thus formed is the *pediment*, often filled with sculptural decoration.

In contrast, the Ionic order is more graceful and more elaborate in architectural details. Ionic columns

84 Kleophrades Painter. Detail of a red-figure vase showing the destruction of Troy. c. 490 B.C. Museo Nazionale, Naples. The elaborate composition and superb details are made possible by the new red-figure technique.

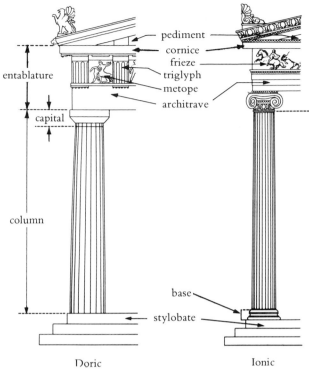

85   The Doric and Ionic orders.

rise from a tiered base and have 24 flutes. These flutes do not meet at a sharp angle as Doric flutes do but are separated by narrow vertical bands. The capitals consist of a pair of spirals, or *volutes.* The architrave is not flat as in the Doric order but is composed of three projecting bands. In place of the Doric triglyphs and metopes is a continuous band often decorated with a running frieze of sculpture.

The differences between the two orders produced different effects. The Doric order suggested simple dignity; the absence of decorative detail drew attention to the weight and massiveness of the Doric temple itself. Ionic temples, on the other hand, conveyed a sense of lightness and delicacy by means of ornate decorations and fanciful carving. The surface of an Ionic temple is as important as its structural design.

Literature: Lyric Poetry

Our knowledge of literary developments between the time of Homer and the Archaic period is very limited. An exception is Hesiod, who probably lived shortly before 700 B.C. He is the author of a poetic account of the origins of the world called the *Theogony* and a rather more down-to-earth work, the

Works and Days, which mainly concerned the disadvantages in being a poor, oppressed (and depressed) farmer in Boeotia, where the climate is "severe in winter, stuffy in summer, good at no time of year." In the Archaic period, however, the same burst of creative energy that revolutionized the visual arts produced a wave of new poets. The medium they chose was lyric verse.

The emergence of lyric poetry was, like developments in the other arts, a sign of the times. The heroic verse of Homer was intended for the ruling class of an aristocratic society, who had the leisure and the inclination to hear of the great and not so great deeds of great men and who were interested in the problems of mighty leaders like Agamemnon and Achilles. Lyric poetry is concerned above all else with the poet's own feelings, emotions, and opinions. The poets of the 6th century B.C. do not hesitate to tell us what they themselves feel about life, death, love, drinking too much wine, or anything else that crosses their minds. Heroes and the glories of battle are no longer the ideal. In the mid-7th century B.C. these thoughts were first expressed by the earliest of the lyric poets, Archilochus:

Archilochus
FRAGMENT 6

Some Thracian is proudly wearing the shield I
    left behind;
It was a fine one, but I had to throw it into a
    bush.
Anyway I saved my life, so why worry about
    the shield?
I can always get another one just as good.

Above all other Greek lyric poets, Sappho has captured the hearts and minds of the following ages. She is the first woman to leave a literary record that reflects her own personal experiences. Her poems have survived only in fragmentary form, and the details of her life remain confused and much disputed. We must be grateful, then, for what we have and not try to overinterpret it.

Sappho was born around 612 B.C. on the island of Lesbos, where she spent most of her life. She seems to have been able to combine the roles of wife and mother with those of poet and teacher; within her own lifetime she was widely respected for her works and surrounded by a group of younger women who presumably came to Lesbos to finish their education, in much the same way that Americans used to go to Paris for a final cultural polish.

The affection between Sappho and her pupils was deep and sincere and is constantly reflected in her poems. The nature of this affection has been debated for centuries. The plain fact is that apart from her poetry we know almost nothing about Sappho herself. Even her appearance is debatable; she is described by one ancient authority as "beautiful day" and by another as short, dark, and ugly. Her fellow poet Alcaeus calls her "violet-haired, pure, and honey-smiling" [86]. Thus those who read Sappho must decide for themselves what the passion of the poems expresses, for passionate they certainly are.

Sappho's chief subject is love; her complete surviving poem is an invocation to Aphrodite, the goddess of love, for help in time of trouble. Elsewhere she gives voice to the contrasting but equally painful agonies of loneliness and of passionate commitment:

86 Circle of the Brygos Painter. *Alcaeus and Sappho*. c. 470 B.C. Antikensammlungen, Munich. The portraits are, of course, purely imaginary, but the lyres that both poets are holding emphasize the close relationship between poetry and music.

Sappho
ALONE

> The moon and Pleiades
> are set. Midnight,
> and time spins away.
> I lie in bed, alone.

Sappho
SEIZURE

> To me he seems like a god
> as he sits facing you and
> hears you near as you speak
> softly and laugh
>
> in a sweet echo that jolts
> the heart in my ribs. For now
> as I look at you my voice
> is empty and
>
> can say nothing as my tongue
> cracks and slender fire is quick
> under my skin. My eyes are dead
> to light, my ears
>
> pound, and sweat pours over me.
> I convulse, paler than grass,
> and feel my mind slip as I
> go close to death.

The note of self-observation is almost clinical in its directness, yet she leaves us in no doubt that the suffering is worthwhile:

Sappho
TO EROS

> From all the offspring
> of the earth and heaven
> love is the most precious.

Sappho's deep feeling for the innocence and vulnerability of the girls who surrounded her is expressed in the following description:

Sappho
THE VIRGIN

> Like a sweet apple reddening on the high
> tip of the topmost branch and forgotten
> by the pickers—no, beyond their reach.
> Like a hyacinth crushed in the mountains
> by shepherds; lying trampled on the earth
> yet blooming purple.

Perhaps Sappho's greatest quality lies in her ability to probe the depths of her own responses and by describing them to understand them. Just as contemporary sculptors and painters sought to understand the workings of their own bodies by depicting them, so Sappho revealed both to herself and to us the workings of her emotions. In the process she wins control over them. Some of her poems have a kind of reluctant resignation that comes only from profound self-understanding.

Sappho
AGE AND LIGHT

Here are fine gifts, children,
O friend, singer on the clear tortoise lyre,

all my flesh is wrinkled with age,
my black hair has faded to white,

my legs can no longer carry me,
once nimble as a fawn's,

but what can I do?
It cannot be undone,

No more than can pink-armed Dawn
not end in darkness on earth,

or keep her love for Tithonos,
who must waste away;

yet I love refinement, and beauty and light
are for me the same as desire for the sun.

The First Philosophers: The Presocrics

The century that saw the expression of the intimate self-revelations of lyric poetry was marked by the development of rational philosophy, which challenged the traditional religious ideas of Homer and Hesiod and scoffed at gods who took human form. If horses and cows had hands and could draw, they would draw gods looking like horses and cows, wrote Xenophanes of Colophon in the second half of the 6th century B.C. Other thinkers began to debate the nature of the universe and try to account for the diversity of the natural world with as few as possible fundamental principles.

There developed a wide variety of schools of thought originated by philosophers generally described by the somewhat confusing label *Presocrics*. The label is accurate in that they all lived and died before the time of Socrates (469–399 B.C.), who, together with his pupil Plato (c. 427–347 B.C.), is the greatest name in Greek philosophy. On the other hand, these 6th-century philosophers had little in common except the time when they lived. Thus it is important to remember that the term "Presocratic" does not describe any single philosophical system.

The earliest school to develop was that of the *Materialists,* who sought to explain all phenomena in terms of one or more elements. Thales of Miletus (c. 585 B.C.), for example, thought that water underlay the changing world of nature. Later, Empedocles of Acragas (c. 495 B.C.) introduced four elements—fire, earth, air, water. The various combinations (through love) and separations (through strife and war) of these elements in a cyclical pattern explained how creatures as well as nations were born, grew, decayed, and died. Anaxagoras of Clazomenae (c. 500 B.C.) postulated an infinite number of small particles, which, however small they might be, always contained not only a dominant substance (for example, bone or water) but also stray bits of other substances in lesser quantities. Unity in nature, he claimed, came from the force of Reason.

The Presocratic philosopher who had the greatest influence on later times was Pythagoras of Samos (c. 550 B.C.). He left his home city for political reasons and settled in southern Italy, where he founded a school of his own. He required his followers to lead pure and devout lives, uniting together to uphold morals and chastity, as well as order and harmony, for the common good. These apparently noble principles did nothing to win him favor from the people among whom he had settled; according to one account he and three hundred of his followers were killed.

It is difficult to know which of the principles of *Pythagoreanism* can be directly attributed to Pythagoras himself and which were added later by his disciples. His chief religious doctrines seem to have been belief in the transmigration of souls and the kinship of all living things, teachings that led to the development of a religious cult which bore his name. In science, his chief contribution was in mathematics. He discovered the numerical relationship of musical harmonies. Our modern musical scale, consisting of an *octave* (a span of eight tones) divided into its constituent parts, derives ultimately from his researches. Inspired by this discovery, Pythagoras went on to claim that mathematical relationships represented the underlying principle of the universe and of morality, the so-called "harmony of the spheres." He is chiefly remembered today for a much less cosmic discovery, the geometrical theorem that bears his name.

In contrast to Pythagoras' belief in universal harmony, the *Dualists* claimed that there existed two separate universes, the world around us, subject to constant change, and another ideal world, perfect and unchanging, which could only be realized through the intellect. The chief proponent of this school was Heraclitus of Ephesus (c. 500 B.C.), who summed up the unpredictable, and therefore unknowable, quality of Nature in the well-known saying, "It is not possible to step twice into the same river." But if the world were too changeable to be known directly, knowledge of the Reason by which the world works was still open to the philosopher. Similarly, Parmedides of Elea (c. 510 B.C.) went so far as to claim that all change, motion, and what we commonly call nature were but a sham and delusion, whereas true reality was all perfect, unchanging, and spherical in shape. His younger pupil, Zeno (c. 490 B.C.), presented a number of difficult paradoxes in support of their doctrines. These paradoxes were later discussed by Plato and Aristotle.

The last and perhaps the greatest school of Presocratic philosophy was that of the *Atomists,* led by Leucippus and Democritus (c. 460 B.C.), who believed that the ultimate, unchangeable reality consisted of atoms (small "indivisible" particles not obvious to the naked eye) and the void (nothingness). Atomism survived into Roman times in the later philosophy of Epicureanism (see pages 210–211) and into the 19th century in the early Atomic Theory of John Dalton. Even in our own times, the great physicist Werner Heisenberg (1901–1976), who astonished the world of science with his discoveries in quantum mechanics, derived his initial inspiration from the Greek Atomists.

Music and Dance
in Early Greece

In comparison with art and literature, the history of Greek music is highly problematic. The very small quantity of evidence is as confusing as it is helpful. Although the frequent references to musical performance make it clear that music played a vital role in all aspects of Greek life, less than a dozen fragments of actual Greek music have survived; the earliest of these dates from the late 5th century B.C. Unfortunately, the problem of understanding the system of notation makes authentic performance of these fragments impossible.

Our inability to re-create even the music we have is particularly frustrating because from the earliest times music was renowned for its emotional and spiritual power. For the Greeks music was of divine origin; the gods themselves had invented musical instruments: Hermes or Apollo the lyre, Athena the flute, and so on. Many of the earliest myths told of the powerful effect of music. Orpheus could move trees and rocks and tame wild beasts by his song; the lyre-playing of Amphion brought stones to life. Nor was music-making reserved for professional performers or women, as so often in later centuries. When, in Book IX of the *Iliad,* Agamemnon's ambassadors arrive at the tent of Achilles they find the great hero playing a lyre, "clear-sounding, splendid and carefully wrought," and entertaining himself by singing "of men's fame." How one would like to have heard that song [see 70].

The first figure in music about whose existence we can be relatively certain was Terpander, who came from the island of Lesbos. Around 675 B.C. he introduced the *cithara,* an elaborate seven-string lyre, to accompany vocal music on ceremonial occasions. The simple lyre, relatively small and easy to hold, had a sounding box made of a whole tortoise shell and sides formed of goat horns or curved pieces of wood. On the other hand, the cithara had a much larger sounding box made of wood, metal, or even ivory and broad hollow sides, to give greater resonance to the sound. The player had to stand while performing on it; the instrument had straps to support it, leaving the player's hands free [87].

Another musical instrument developed about this time was the *aulos,* or double flute [88], which had first been brought into Greece, according to the traditional account, by Olympus, a figure who seems mainly legendary. Like the cithara and lyre, the aulos was generally used to accompany songs.

The little evidence we have suggests that early Greek music was primarily vocal—the instruments were used mainly to accompany the singers. The breakthrough into purely instrumental music seems to have come at the beginning of the Archaic period. We know that in 586 B.C. Sacadas of Argos composed a work to be played on the aulos for the Pythian Games at Delphi—a piece that remained well known and popular for centuries. Also, its character confirms the Greek love of narrative, for it described in music Apollo's fight with the dragon which the Pythian Games commemorated. The information is tantalizing indeed, since this first piece of "program music," the remote ancestor of Richard Strauss' *Til Eulenspiegel* and *Don Quixote,* must have been highly effective for its appeal to have lasted so long.

87 Berlin Painter. Detail of red-figure amphora. Nola, c. 490 B.C. Terra cotta, height of vase 16⅜″ (42 cm). Metropolitan Museum of Art, New York (Fletcher Fund, 1956). This vase, painted at the end of the Archaic period, gives a good idea of the Greeks' enthusiasm for music in general and the cithara in particular. The young musician is singing to his own accompaniment and swaying to the music at the same time.

88 Karneia Painter. Detail of red-figure krater. Ceglie del Campo, c. 410 B.C. Terra cotta. Museo Nazionale, Taranto. A young woman plays the aulos for the god Dionysus. The flowing lines of the dress accentuate her figure. The necklace and bracelets are in low relief.

We know little more of the music of the Archaic period than these odd facts. The lyrics of some of the songs have survived, including some of the choral odes performed in honor of various gods. Apollo and his sister Artemis were thanked for delivery from misfortune by the singing of a *paean,* or solemn invocation to the gods, while the *dithyramb,* or choral hymn to Dionysus, was sung in his honor at public ceremonies. Certainly it is clear that the roles of poet and musician were closely linked. Although we asso-

ciate poets like Anacreon and Sappho with their verses, they were equally well known to their contemporaries as musicians. The combination of words and music is also intimately bound up with the origins of drama (this is a very complex and controversial topic, still not fully understood).

Also closely tied to music was dance, which also played its part in the development of drama. We know both more and less about the early stages of Greek dance than we do about music. On the one

left: 89 Geometric bowl showing dancing. c. 740 B.C. Diameter 6¼″ (16 cm). National Archaeological Museum, Athens. The dancers include both women and men, three playing lyres.

left below: 90 Darius Painter. Darius in council before his expedition against Greece, detail of a krater. c. 335 B.C. Museo Nazionale, Naples. Above the king Greece, symbolized by the figure of a woman, is being entrusted to the protection of the gods. Below, soldiers are collecting booty for a war chest.

dancers apparently made movements reminiscent of the bird, but the steps of the dance had a more specific meaning. According to tradition, it was first performed by Theseus outside the Labyrinth with the boys and girls he had saved by killing the Minotaur (see pages 32–33). The intricate patterns of the dance were supposed to represent the Labyrinth itself. Having accomplished two dangerous feats—killing the Minotaur and finding his way out of the Labyrinth—Theseus still stayed around long enough to lead a complicated performance. Dancing was obviously of great importance to the Greeks.

The Persian Wars

At the beginning of the 5th century B.C. the Greeks had to face the greatest challenge in their history. Their success in meeting the challenge precipitated a decisive break with the world of Archaic culture. In 499 B.C. the Greek cities of Asia Minor, with Athenian support, rebelled against their Persian rulers. The Persian king, Darius, succeeded in checking this revolt; he then resolved to lead a punitive expedition against the mainland Greek cities that had sent help to the eastern cities [90]. In 490 B.C. he took a massive army to Greece; to everyone's surprise, the army was defeated by the Athenians at the Battle of Marathon. After Darius' death in 486 B.C., his son Xerxes launched an even more grandiose expedition in 480 B.C. Xerxes defeated the Spartans at Thermopylae and then attacked and sacked Athens itself. While the city was falling, the Athenians took to their ships, obeying an oracle which enjoined them to "trust to their wooden walls." Eventually, they inflicted a crushing defeat on the Persian navy at nearby Salamis. In 479 B.C., after being conquered on land and sea, at Plataea and Mycale, the Persians returned home, completely beaten.

The Greeks triumphed at least partly because for once they had managed to unite in the face of a common enemy. Their victories inaugurated the greatest

hand, we have from as early as the late Geometric period actual depictions of dances in progress [89], whereas the sound of music of the same period is entirely lost to us. On the other hand, in the Classical period the function of dance remained religious and social, whereas a vast literature on music theory developed, with philosophical implications which became explicit in the writings of Plato and Aristotle; through this literature some information on early music has been preserved.

What we do know about dancing and individual dances suggests that here, as in music and visual arts, telling a story was important. One famous dance was called the *geranos,* from the word for "crane." The

above: Plate 6 Euphronios, painter; Euxitheos, potter. Red-figure calyx krater. c. 515 B.C. Terra cotta; height of vase 18″ (46 cm), diameter 21¾″ (55 cm). Metropolitan Museum of Art, New York (bequest of Joseph H. Durkee, gift of Darius Ogden Mills, and gift of C. Ruxton Love, by exchange, 1972). This masterpiece of red-figure vase painting, generally known as the *Euphronios Vase,* shows the moment when Sarpedon falls in battle during the Trojan War. As his body stiffens in agony, his wounds streaming blood, the twin gods Death (on the right) and Sleep come to his aid. The god Hermes, who leads the souls of the dead to Hades, stands sympathetically behind.

right: Plate 7 *Peplos Kore.* c. 540 B.C. Marble, height 4′ (1.21 m). Acropolis Museum, Athens. The statue is identified by the woolen peplos or mantle the woman is wearing over her dress. The missing left arm was extended. The Greeks painted important parts of their stone statues; traces of paint show here.

121

Plate 8 Basilica at Paestum. c. 550 B.C. This temple to Hera is one of the earliest surviving Greek temples. The bulging columns and spreading capitals are typical of Doric architecture in the Archaic period. (Visible through the columns and above the entablature are columns and part of the pediment of a second temple of Hera beyond, built a century later.)

period in Greek history, the Classical Age. The Greek historian Herodotus (484–420 B.C.) has left us an account of the Persian Wars. It seems appropriate to close the story of the transition from the Heroic Age to the Classical period with his description of some of Greece's most heroic moments.

Herodotus has two claims on our attention. He is the first writer in the Western tradition to devote himself to historical writing rather than epic or lyric poetry, a fact that has earned him the title "Father of History." At the same time he is one of the greatest storytellers, always sustaining the reader's interest, in both the main line of his narrative and the frequent and entertaining digressions. One of these digressions, the tale of Rhampsinitus and the thief, has been described as the first detective story in Western literature.

Herodotus was not a scientific historian in our terms—he had definite weaknesses. He never really understood the finer points of military strategy. He almost always interpreted events in terms of personalities, showing little interest in underlying political or economic causes. His strengths, however, were many. Although his subject involved conflict between Greeks and foreigners, he remained remarkably impartial and free from national prejudice. His natural curiosity about the world around him and about his fellow human beings was buttressed by acute powers of observation. Above all, he recorded as much information as possible, even when versions conflicted. He also tried to provide a reasonable evaluation of the reliability of his sources, so that later readers could form their own opinions.

Herodotus' analysis of the Greek victory was based on a serious philosophical, indeed theological, belief—that the Persians were defeated because they were morally in the wrong. Their moral fault was *hubris,* excessive ambition; thus the Greeks' victory was at the same time a triumph of right over might and a demonstration that the gods themselves would guarantee the triumph of justice. In Book VII Xerxes' uncle, Artabanus, warns him in 480 B.C. not to invade Greece:

> "You know, my lord, that amongst living creatures it is the great ones that God smites with his thunder, out of envy of their pride. The little ones do not vex him. It is always the great buildings and the tall trees which are struck by lightning. It is God's way to bring the lofty low. Often a great army is destroyed by a little one, when God in his envy puts fear into the men's hearts, or sends a

thunderstorm, and they are cut to pieces in a way they do not deserve. For God tolerates pride in none but Himself. Haste is the mother of failure— and for failure we always pay a heavy price; it is in delay our profit lies—perhaps it may not immediately be apparent, but we shall find it, sure enough, as time goes on."

Nevertheless, Xerxes, the personification of *hubris,* presses on and duly arrives at the narrow pass of Thermopylae in central Greece. There a small band of Greek soldiers blocks his road and threatens to hold up the entire Persian army.

Herodotus' account of the battle at Thermopylae is justly famous both as history and as a superb piece of evocative writing. Like Homer, he has the ability to summon up a world of meaning by carefully chosen details—the Spartan soldiers preparing for battle by combing their hair or Dieneces' cooly courageous retort about the arrows.

It is true that the broad sweep of the narrative is sometimes interrupted by the author's wish to include all the relevant information he has collected, as in the case of the history of Ephialtes' later career, which a modern writer would have relegated to a learned footnote. But as the fighting intensifies, so does the tension of the account. With simplicity and dignity Herodotus leads us to the final desperate struggle over the body of the dead Greek commander, one of the first great prose passages in Western literature.

Herodotus
from HISTORY OF THE
PERSIAN WARS, Book VIII

The Persian army was now close to the pass, and the Greeks, suddenly doubting their power to resist, held a conference to consider the advisability of retreat. It was proposed by the Peloponnesians generally that the army should fall back upon the Peloponnese and hold the Isthmus; but when the Phocians and Locrians expressed their indignation at this suggestion, Leonidas gave his voice for staying where they were and sending, at the same time, an appeal for reinforcements to the various states of the confederacy, as their numbers were inadequate to cope with the Persians.

During the conference Xerxes sent a man on horseback to ascertain the strength of the Greek force and to observe what the troops were doing. He had heard before he left Thessaly that a small force was concentrated here, led by the Lacedaemonians under

Leonidas of the house of Heracles. The Persian rider approached the camp and took a thorough survey of all he could see—which was not, however, the whole Greek army; for the men on the further side of the wall which, after its reconstruction, was now guarded, were out of sight. He did, none the less, carefully observe the troops who were stationed on the outside of the wall. At that moment these happened to be the Spartans, and some of them were stripped for exercise, while others were combing their hair. The Persian spy watched them in astonishment; nevertheless he made sure of their numbers, and of everything else he needed to know, as accurately as he could, and then rode quietly off. No one attempted to catch him, or took the least notice of him.

Back in his own camp he told Xerxes what he had seen. Xerxes was bewildered; the truth, namely that the Spartans were preparing themselves to kill and to be killed according to their strength, was beyond his comprehension, and what they were doing seemed to him merely absurd. Accordingly he sent for Demaratus, the son of Ariston, who had come with the army, and questioned him about the spy's report, in the hope of finding out what the unaccountable behaviour of the Spartans might mean. "Once before," Demaratus said, "when we began our march against Greece, you heard me speak of these men. I told you then how I saw this enterprise would turn out, and you laughed at me. I strive for nothing, my lord, more earnestly than to observe the truth in your presence; so hear me once more. These men have come to fight us for possession of the pass, and for that struggle they are preparing. It is the common practice of the Spartans to pay careful attention to their hair when they are about to risk their lives. But I assure you that if you can defeat these men and the rest of the Spartans who are still at home, there is no other people in the world who will dare to stand firm or lift a hand against you. You have now to deal with the finest kingdom in Greece, and with the bravest men."

Xerxes, unable to believe what Demaratus said, asked further how it was possible that so small a force could fight with his army. "My lord," Demaratus replied, "treat me as a liar, if what I have foretold does not take place." But still Xerxes was unconvinced.

For four days Xerxes waited, in constant expectation that the Greeks would make good their escape; then, on the fifth, when still they had made no move and their continued presence seemed mere impudent and reckless folly, he was seized with rage and sent forward the Medes and Cissians with orders to take them alive and bring them into his presence. The Medes charged, and in the struggle which ensued many fell; but others took their places, and in spite of terrible losses refused to be beaten off. They made it plain enough to anyone, and not least to the king himself, that he had in his army many men, indeed, but few soldiers. All day the battle continued; the Medes, after their rough handling, were at length withdrawn and their place was taken by Hydarnes and his picked Persian troops—the King's Immortals—who advanced to the attack in full confidence of bringing the business to a quick and easy end. But, once engaged, they were no more successful than the Medes had been; all went as before, the two armies fighting in a confined space, the Persians using shorter spears than the Greeks and having no advantage from their numbers.

On the Spartan side it was a memorable fight; they were men who understood war pitted against an inexperienced enemy, and amongst the feints they employed was to turn their backs in a body and pretend to be retreating in confusion, whereupon the enemy would come on with a great clatter and roar, supposing the battle won; but the Spartans, just as the Persians were on them, would wheel and face them and inflict in the new struggle innumerable casualties. The Spartans had their losses too, but not many. At last the Persians, finding that their assaults upon the pass, whether by divisions or by any other way they could think of, were all useless, broke off the engagement and withdrew. Xerxes was watching the battle from where he sat; and it is said that in the course of the attacks three times, in terror for his army, he leapt to his feet.

Next day the fighting began again, but with no better success for the Persians, who renewed their onslaught in the hope that the Greeks, being so few in number, might be badly enough disabled by wounds to prevent further resistance. But the Greeks never slackened; their troops were ordered in divisions corresponding to the states from which they came, and each division took its turn in the line except the Phocian, which had been posted to guard the track over the mountains. So when the Persians found that things were no better for them than on the previous day, they once more withdrew.

How to deal with the situation Xerxes had no idea; but while he was still wondering what his next move should be, a man from Malis got himself admitted to his presence. This was Ephialtes, the son of Eurydemus, and he had come, in hope of a rich reward, to tell the king about the track which led over the hills to Thermopylae—and the information he gave was to prove the death of the Greeks who held the pass.

Later on, Ephialtes, in fear of the Spartans, fled to

Thessaly, and during his exile there a price was put upon his head at an assembly of the Amphictyons at Pylae. Some time afterwards he returned to Anticyra, where he was killed by Athenades of Trachis. In point of fact, Athenades killed him not for his treachery but for another reason, which I will explain further on; but the Spartans honoured him none the less on that account. According to another story, which I do not at all believe, it was Onetes, the son of Phanagoras, a native of Carystus, and Corydallus of Anticyra who spoke to Xerxes and showed the Persians the way round by the mountain track; but one may judge which account is the true one, first by the fact that the Amphictyons, who must surely have known everything about it, set a price not upon Onetes and Corydallus but upon Ephialtes of Trachis, and, secondly, by the fact that there is no doubt that the accusation of treachery was the reason for Ephialtes' flight. Certainly Onetes, even though he was not a native of Malis, might have known about the track, if he had spent much time in the neighbourhood—but it was Ephialtes, and no one else, who showed the Persians the way, and I leave his name on record as the guilty one.

Xerxes found Ephialtes' offer most satisfactory. He was delighted with it, and promptly gave orders to Hydarnes to carry out the movement with the troops under his command. They left camp about the time the lamps are lit.

The track was originally discovered by the Malians of the neighbourhood; they afterwards used it to help the Thessalians, taking them over it to attack Phocis at the time when the Phocians were protected from invasion by the wall which they had built across the pass. That was a long time ago, and no good ever came of it since. The track begins at the Asopus, the stream which flows through the narrow gorge, and, running along the ridge of the mountain—which, like the track itself, is called Anopaea—ends at Alpenus, the first Locrian settlement as one comes from Malis, near the rock known as Black-Buttocks' Stone and the seats of the Cercopes. Just here is the narrowest part of the pass.

This then, was the mountain track which the Persians took, after crossing the Asopus. They marched throughout the night, with the mountains of Oeta on their right hand and those of Trachis on their left. By early dawn they were at the summit of the ridge, near the spot where the Phocians, as I mentioned before, stood on guard with a thousand men, to watch the track and protect their country. The Phocians were ready enough to undertake this service, and had, indeed, volunteered for it to Leonidas, knowing that the pass at Thermopylae was held as I have already described.

The ascent of the Persians had been concealed by the oak-woods which cover this part of the mountain range, and it was only when they reached the top that the Phocians became aware of their approach; for there was not a breath of wind, and the marching feet made a loud swishing and rustling in the fallen leaves. Leaping to their feet, the Phocians were in the act of arming themselves when the enemy was upon them. The Persians were surprised at the sight of troops preparing to resist; they had not expected any opposition—yet here was a body of men barring their way. Hydarnes asked Ephialtes who they were, for his first uncomfortable thought was that they might be Spartans; but on learning the truth he prepared to engage them. The Persian arrows flew thick and fast, and the Phocians, supposing themselves to be the main object of the attack, hurriedly withdrew to the highest point of the mountain, where they made ready to face destruction. The Persians, however, with Ephialtes and Hydarnes paid no further attention to them, but passed on along the descending track with all possible speed.

The Greeks at Thermopylae had their first warning of the death that was coming with the dawn from the seer Megistias, who read their doom in the victims of sacrifice; deserters, too, had begun to come in during the night with news of the Persian movement to take them in the rear, and, just as day was breaking, the look-out men had come running from the hills. At once a conference was held, and opinions were divided, some urging that they must on no account abandon their post, others taking the opposite view. The result was that the army split; some dispersed, the men returning to their various homes, and others made ready to stand by Leonidas.

There is another account which says that Leonidas himself dismissed a part of his force, to spare their lives, but thought it unbecoming for the Spartans under his command to desert the post which they had originally come to guard. I myself am inclined to think that he dismissed them when he realized that they had no heart for the fight and were unwilling to take their share of the danger; at the same time honour forbade that he himself should go. And indeed by remaining at his post he left a great name behind him, and Sparta did not lose her prosperity, as might otherwise have happened; for right at the outset of the war the Spartans had been told by the oracle, when they asked for advice, that either their city must be laid waste by the foreigner or one of their kings be killed. The prophecy was in hexameter verse and ran as follows:

Hear your fate, O dwellers in Sparta of the wide spaces;
Either your famed, great town must be sacked by
    Perseus' sons.

Or, if that be not, the whole land of Lacedaemon
Shall mourn the death of a king of the house of Heracles,
For not the strength of lions or of bulls shall hold him,
Strength against strength; for he has the power of Zeus,
And will not be checked till one of these two he has
consumed.

I believe it was the thought of this oracle, combined with his wish to lay up for the Spartans a treasure of fame in which no other city should share, that made Leonidas dismiss those troops; I do not think that they deserted, or went off without orders, because of a difference of opinion. Moreover, I am strongly supported in this view by the case of Megistias, the seer from Acarnania who foretold the coming doom by his inspection of the sacrificial victims: this man—he was said to be descended from Melampus—was with the army, and quite plainly received orders from Leonidas to quit Thermopylae, to save him from sharing the army's fate. But he refused to go, sending away instead an only son of his, who was serving with the forces.

Thus it was that the confederate troops, by Leonidas' orders, abandoned their posts and left the pass, all except the Thespians and the Thebans who remained with the Spartans. The Thebans were detained by Leonidas as hostages very much against their will—unlike the loyal Thespians, who refused to desert Leonidas and his men, but stayed, and died with them. They were under the command of Demophilus the son of Diadromes.

In the morning Xerxes poured a libation to the rising sun, and then waited till about the time of the filling of the market-place, when he began to move forward. This was according to Ephialtes' instructions, for the way down from the ridge is much shorter and more direct than the long and circuitous ascent. As the Persian army advanced to the assault, the Greeks under Leonidas, knowing that the fight would be their last, pressed forward into the wider part of the pass much further than they had done before; in the previous days' fighting they had been holding the wall and making sorties from behind it into the narrow neck, but now they left the confined space and battle was joined on more open ground. Many of the invaders fell; behind them the company commanders plied their whips, driving the men remorselessly on. Many fell into the sea and were drowned, and still more were trampled to death by their friends. No one could count the number of the dead. The Greeks, who knew that the enemy were on their way round by the mountain track and that death was inevitable, fought with reckless desperation, exerting every ounce of strength that was in them against the invader. By this time most of their spears were broken, and they were killing Persians with their swords.

In the course of that fight Leonidas fell, having fought like a man indeed. Many distinguished Spartans were killed at his side—their names, like the names of all the three hundred, I have made myself acquainted with, because they deserve to be remembered. Amongst the Persian dead, too, were many men of high distinction—for instance, two brothers of Xerxes, Habrocomes and Hyperanthes, both of them sons of Darius by Artanes' daughter Phratagune.

There was a bitter struggle over the body of Leonidas; four times the Greeks drove the enemy off, and at last by their valour succeeded in dragging it away. So it went on, until the fresh troops with Ephialtes were close at hand; and then, when the Greeks knew that they had come, the character of the fighting changed. They withdrew again into the narrow neck of the pass, behind the walls, and took up a position in a single compact body—all except the Thebans—on the little hill at the entrance to the pass, where the stone lion in memory of Leonidas stands to-day. Here they resisted to the last, with their swords, if they had them, and, if not, with their hands and teeth, until the Persians, coming on from the front over the ruins of the wall and closing in from behind, finally overwhelmed them.

Of all the Spartans and Thespians who fought so valiantly on that day, the most signal proof of courage was given by the Spartan Dieneces. It is said that before the battle he was told by a native of Trachis that, when the Persians shot their arrows, there were so many of them that they hid the sun. Dieneces, however, quite unmoved by the thought of the terrible strength of the Persian army, merely remarked: "This is pleasant news that the stranger from Trachis brings us: for if the Persians hide the sun, we shall have our battle in the shade." He is said to have left on record other sayings, too, of a similar kind, by which he will be remembered. After Dieneces the greatest distinction was won by the two Spartan brothers, Alpheus and Maron, the sons of Orsiphantus; and of the Thespians the man to gain the highest glory was a certain Dithyrambus, the son of Harmatides.

The dead were buried where they fell, and with them the men who had been killed before those dismissed by Leonidas left the pass. Over them is this inscription, in honour of the whole force:

Four thousand here from Pelops' land
Against three million once did stand.

The Spartans have a special epitaph; it runs:

Go tell the Spartans, you who read:
We took their orders, and are dead.

For the seer Megistias there is the following:

I was Megistias once, who died
When the Mede passed Spercheius' tide.
I knew death near, yet would not save
Myself, but share the Spartans' grave.

Further Reading

Boardman, J. *The Greek Overseas*. Baltimore: Penguin, 1973. A vivid and informative account of the development and effects of Greek colonization.

Burn, A. R. *The Lyric Age of Greece*. London: Arnold, 1960. Historical, cultural, and literary events in 7th- and 6th-century B.C. Greece discussed in a major study.

Bury, J. B., and R. Meiggs. *A History of Greece to the Death of Alexander the Great*. 4th ed. New York: St. Martin's, 1975. The best single-volume history of ancient Greece.

Charbonneaux, M., and V. Charbonneaux. *Archaic Greek Art*. New York: Braziller, 1971. A lavishly illustrated survey of all forms of Archaic art.

Coldstream, J. N. *Geometric Greece*. London: Methuen, 1977. A technical but readable account of all aspects of life in Geometric Greece.

Johnston, A. *The Emergence of Greece*. Oxford: Elsevier-Phaidon, 1976. Primarily an up-to-date account of the archaeology of early Greece, the book also gives an excellent synthesis of history and art.

Luce, J. V. *Homer and the Heroic Age*. New York: Harper, 1975. A masterly account of the historical background of the Homeric epics, although the author's view that Homer's world chiefly reflects that of the Mycenaeans is by no means universally shared.

Page, D. L. *Sappho and Alcaeus*. Oxford: Oxford University Press, 1955. A study of the poets which includes translations of most of the surviving fragments of their works.

Renault, Mary. *The Praise Singer*. New York: Pantheon, 1978. A novel of the life of a Greek bard and of Athens and other cities in the 6th century B.C., with the poet Simonides as narrator.

Wace, J. B., and F. H. Stubbings. *A Companion to Homer*. New York: St. Martin's, 1962. A collection of essays discussing many aspects of the Homeric epics, historical, literary, and archaeological.

Suggestions for Listening

Because evidence for the actual sound of Greek music is very scanty, the few recorded examples of modern reconstructions are discussed in the Suggestions for Listening following Chapter 4.

The number of composers in more recent times who have chosen Greek poems or subjects for their works is legion. The *Iliad* and *Odyssey* have provided the theme for a great number of operas, from Claudio Monteverdi's *Il Ritorno d'Ulisse in Patria* (*The Return of Odysseus to his Native Land*) of 1641, available on Telefunken 4635024, to Michael Tippett's *King Priam* of 1962 (not yet recorded). Sappho's poems have been set to music by several composers, including the 20th-century Italian Luigi Dallapiccola; the only opera of any note devoted to her is Charles Gounod's *Sapho* (1851).

Questions for Further Discussion

1. Although the Homeric epics primarily reflect a man's world, they also give much information on the role of women in early Greek society—so much that in the 19th century Samuel Butler even suggested that the *Odyssey* might have been written by a woman. What actual evidence is there in the *Iliad* and *Odyssey* about the position of women in Homer's time?

2. Many of the most elaborate works of art of the Geometric period are concerned with funeral ceremonies. To what extent does the culture of our own day make use of art in a funerary context? Does it reflect on the general attitude of own own time to life and death?

3. Examine some of the paradoxes of Zeno. Try to identify their fallacies.

4. The period of colonization was one of the most productive and formative in Greek history. How did Greek colonization differ from the colonization by England, France, and other European nations in the 17th, 18th, and 19th centuries? How did the differences affect its results?

5. Sappho's friends and students formed an exclusively female group bound together by intellectual and emotional ties. Later ages have sometimes had difficulty in understanding and interpreting the nature of this group; thus the name of Sappho's birthplace, Lesbos, has acquired its modern overtones. Where else, either in the past or present, can we find a comparable group that might help to throw light on Sappho's world?

6. Although the Spartans emerge as the heroes of the Battle of Thermopylae, in general their reputation in the Greek world was not so favorable. What were the chief characteristics of life in Sparta, and why have the words "spartan" and "laconic" come to have their present meaning?

		GENERAL EVENTS	LITERATURE & PHILOSOPHY	ART

500 B.C.

c. 490 *Critian Boy;* turning point between Archaic and Classical Periods

480

478 Formation of Delian League; beginning of Athenian empire

480–323 First naturalistic sculpture and painting appear

461 Pericles comes to prominence at Athens

c. 460 Sculptures at Temple of Zeus, Olympia

458 Aeschylus, *Oresteia* trilogy wins first prize in drama festival of Dionysus

454 Treasury of Delian League moved to Athens

450

CLASSICAL PERIOD

Golden Age

443–430 Pericles in full control of Athens

441 Sophocles, *Antigone*

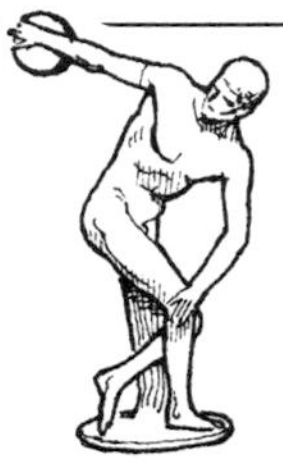

c. 450 Myron, *Discus Thrower*

432 Peloponnesian War begins

429 Pericles dies of plague that devastates Athens

c. 429 Sophocles, *Oedipus the King*

421 Peace of Nicias

c. 421 Euripides, *The Suppliant Women*

c. 440 Polyclitus, *Doryphorus,* treatise *The Canon*

413 Renewed outbreak of Peloponnesian War

c. 420–c. 399 Thucydides, *History of Peloponnesian War*

432 Phidias completes Parthenon sculptures

414 Aristophanes, *The Birds*

411 Aristophanes, *Lysistrata*

late 5th cent. Funerary relief sculpture and white-ground vase painting; lekythos, *Warrior Seated at His Tomb*

404

Late Classical Period

404 Fall of Athens and victory of Sparta

404–403 Rule of Thirty Tyrants

399 Trial and execution of Socrates

387 King's Peace signed

371–362 Ascendancy of Thebes

before 387 Plato, *Republic*

387 Plato founds Academy

c. 350 Scopas, *Pothos*

359–336 Philip II, king of Macedon

c. 385 Xenophon chronicles teachings of Socrates

c. 350 Frescoes, Royal Cemetery at Vergina

338 Macedonians defeat Greeks at Battle of Chaeronea

c. 347–c. 399 Aristotle, *Politics, Metaphysics*

336–323 Alexander the Great, king of Macedon

c. 340 Praxiteles, *Hermes with Infant Dionysus*

331 City of Alexandria founded

335 Aristotle founds Lyceum

c. 325 Lysippus, *Apoxymenos*

323

HELLENISTIC PERIOD

323–281 Wars of Alexander's successors

323–146 Development of realistic portraiture

262 Pergamum becomes independent kingdom

197–156 Eumenes II, king of Pergamum

146 Romans sack Corinth; Greece becomes Roman province

c. 150 *Laocoön;* mosaic, House of Masks, Delos

146

Classical Greece and Its Aftermath

470–456 Libon of Elis, Temple of Zeus at Olympia

c. 500–425 Music serves as accompaniment in dramatic performances

449 Pericles commissions work on Acropolis

447–438 Ictinus and Callicrates, Parthenon

437–432 Mnesicles, Propylaea

c. 427–424 Callicrates, Temple of Athena Nike

421–406 Erechtheum

c. 400 Music dominates dramatic performances

356 Temple of Artemis at Ephesus destroyed by fire and rebuilt

4th cent. Instrumental music becomes popular

c. 350 Theater at Epidaurus

323–146 *Tholos* and other new building forms appear

279 Lighthouse at Alexandria

c. 180–160 Menocrates of Rhodes, Pergamum Altar

late 2nd cent. Earliest surviving Greek music

The victories in the Persian Wars produced a new spirit of optimism and unity in Greece. Divine forces, it appeared, had guaranteed the triumph of right over wrong. There seemed to be no limit to the possibilities of human development. The achievements of the Classical period, which lasted from 479 B.C. to the death of Alexander the Great in 323 B.C., do much to justify the Greeks' proud self-confidence. They certainly represent a level of civilization that has rarely, if ever, been reached since—a level that has been a continuing inspiration to our culture.

Classical civilization reached its high point in Athens during the last half of the 5th century B.C., a time of unparalleled richness in artistic and intellectual achievement that is often called the Golden Age of Greece. To some extent, the importance of the great figures who dominated this period lies in the fact that they were the first in their fields. There are, in fact, few areas of human thought in which the 5th-century Greeks were not pioneers. In subjects as diverse as drama and historiography, town planning and medicine, painting and sculpture, mathematics and government, they laid the foundations of later achievements. Even more astonishing, often they were not merely the first in their fields but also among the greatest of all time. Greek tragedies, for example, are still read and performed today because they give experiences that are as intense emotionally and intellectually as anything in the Western dramatic tradition.

In the Late Classical period, from 404 to 323 B.C., artists and writers continued to explore ideas and styles first outlined in the century before, though in different ways. Greek cultural life was no longer dominated by Athens; a single center no longer governed artistic developments. This 4th-century period was therefore one of greater variety, with individual artists following their own personal visions. The greatest of all Late Classical contributions to our cultural tradition was in the field of philosophy. The works of Plato and Aristotle became the basis of Western thought for the next two thousand years.

Even after the death of Alexander the Great in 323 B.C. and the end of the Classical Age, the Hellenistic period that followed was characterized by an artistic vitality that ultimately drew its inspiration from Classical achievements. Only when Greece was conquered by the Romans in the late 2nd century B.C. did Greek culture cease to have an independent existence.

Although the Roman conquest of Greece ended the glories of the Classical Age, in a way it also perpetuated them by contributing to the melding of Greek culture into the Western humanistic tradition. It was not the Greeks themselves but their conquerors who spread Greek ideas throughout the ancient world—and thus down in time to our own day. These conquerors were first the Macedonians and then, above all, the Romans, possessors of practical skills that they used to construct a world sufficiently at peace for ideas to have a place in it. The Greeks did not live in such a world; we must always remember that the Athenians of the Golden Age existed not in an environment of calm contemplation but in an environment of tension and violence. Their tragic inability to put into practice their own noble ideals and live in peace with other Greeks—the darker side of their genius—proved fatal to their independence; it led to war with the rest of Greece in 431 B.C. and to the fall of Athens in 404 B.C. In this context, the Greek search for order takes on an added significance.

It was the belief that a search for reason and order could succeed that gave a unifying ideal to the immense and varied output of the Classical Age. The central principle of this Classical Ideal was that existence can be ordered and controlled, that human ability can triumph over the apparent chaos of the natural world and create a balanced society. In order to achieve this balance, individual human beings should try to stay within what seem to be reasonable limits, for those who do not are guilty of *hubris,* excessive pride—the same *hubris* of which the Persian leader Xerxes was guilty and for which he paid the price (see page 123). The aim of life should be a perfect equilibrium: everything in due proportion and nothing in excess. "Nothing too much" was one of the most famous Greek proverbs.

The emphasis that the Classical Greeks placed on order affected their spiritual attitudes. Individuals can achieve order, they believed, by understanding why people act as they do and, above all, by understanding the motives for their *own* actions. Thus confidence in the power of both human reason and human self-knowledge was as important as belief in the gods. The greatest of all Greek temples of the Classical Age, the Parthenon, which crowned the Athenian Acropolis [91], was planned not so much to glorify the goddess Athena as to glorify Athens and thus human achievement. Even in their darkest days the Classical Greeks never lost sight of the magnitude of human capability and, perhaps even more important, human potential—a vision that has returned over the centuries to inspire later generations and has certainly not lost its relevance in our own times.

91 The Acropolis, Athens, from the northwest. The Parthenon, temple to Athena, is at the highest point. Below it spreads the monumental gateway, the Propylaea. Far left is the Erechtheum.

Athens in the 5th Century B.C.

The political and cultural center of Greece during the first half of the Classical period was Athens. Here, by the end of the Persian Wars in 479 B.C. the Athenians had emerged as the most powerful people in the Greek world. For one thing, their role in the defeat of the Persians had been a decisive one. For another, their democratic system of government, first established in the late 6th century B.C., was proving to be both effective and stable. It was under Athenian leadership that in the years following the wars a defensive organization of all the Greek city-states was formed to guard against any future attack from outside. The money collected from the participating members was kept in a treasury on the island of Delos, sacred to Apollo and politically neutral. This organization became known as the Delian League.

Within a short time a number of other important city-states, including Thebes, Sparta, and Athens' old trade rival Corinth, began to suspect that the League was serving not so much to protect all of Greece as to strengthen Athenian power. They believed the Athenians were turning an association of free and independent states into an empire of subject peoples. Their suspicions were confirmed when in 454 B.C. the funds of the League were transferred from Delos to Athens and some of the money was used to pay for

Athenian building projects, including the Parthenon. The spirit of Greek unity was starting to dissolve; the Greek world was beginning to divide into two opposing sides: on the one hand Athens and her allies (the cities that remained in the League) and, on the other, the rest of Greece. Conflict was inevitable. The Spartans were finally persuaded to lead an alliance against Athens to check her "imperialistic designs." This war, called the Peloponnesian War after the homeland of the Spartans and their supporters, began in 431 B.C. and was dragged on until 404 B.C.

Our understanding of the Peloponnesian War and its significance owes much to the account by the great historian Thucydides, who himself lived through its calamitous events. Born around 460 B.C., Thucydides played an active part in Athenian politics in the years before the war. In 424 B.C. he was elected general and put in charge of defending the city of Amphipolis in northern Greece. When the city fell to Spartan troops, Thucydides was condemned in his absence and sentenced to exile. He did not return to Athens until 404 B.C.

Thucydides intended his *History of the Peloponnesian War* to describe the entire course of the war to 404 B.C., but he died before completing it; the narrative breaks off at the end of 411 B.C. The work is extremely valuable for its detailed description of events, for although its author was an Athenian he managed to be both accurate and impartial. At the same time, however, Thucydides tried to write more than simply an account of a local war. The *History* was an attempt to analyze human motives and reactions, so that future generations would understand how and why the conflict occurred and, in turn, understand themselves. The work was not meant to entertain by providing digressions and anecdotes but to search out the truth and use it to demonstrate universal principles of human behavior. This emphasis on reason makes Thucydides' work typical of the Classical period. He describes his method and purpose in Book I:

> And with regard to my factual reporting of the events of the war I have made it a principle not to write down the first story that came my way, and not even to be guided by my own general impressions; either I was present myself at the events which I have described or else I heard of them from eye-witnesses whose reports I have checked with as much thoroughness as possible. Not that even so the truth was easy to discover: different eye-witnesses give different accounts of the same events, speaking out of partiality for one side or the other or else from imperfect memories. And it may well be that my history will seem less easy to read because of the absence in it of a romantic element. It will be enough for me, however, if these words of mine are judged useful by those who want to understand clearly the events which happened in the past and which (human nature being what it is) will, at some time or other and in much the same ways, be repeated in the future. My work is not a piece of writing designed to meet the taste of an immediate public, but was done to last for ever.

The hero of Thucydides' account of the years immediately preceding the war is Pericles, the leader whose name symbolizes the achievements of the Athenian Golden Age [92]. An aristocrat by birth, Pericles began his political career in the aftermath of the transfer of the Delian League's funds to Athens. By 443 B.C. he had unofficially assumed the leadership of the Athenian democracy, although he continued democratically to run for reelection every year. Under his guidance the few remaining years of peace were devoted to making visible the glory of Athens by constructing on the Acropolis the majestic buildings that still, though in ruins, evoke the grandeur of Periclean Athens.

Had Pericles continued to lead Athens during the war itself, the final outcome might have been different, but in 430 B.C. the city was ravaged by disease, perhaps bubonic plague, and in 429 B.C. Pericles died. No successor could be found who was capable of winning the respect and support of the majority of his fellow citizens. The war continued indecisively until 421 B.C., when an uneasy peace was signed. Shortly thereafter the Athenians made an ill-advised attempt to replenish their treasury by organizing an unprovoked attack on the wealthy Greek cities of Sicily. The expedition proved a total disaster; thousands of Athenians were killed or taken prisoner. When the war began again in 411 B.C. the Athenian forces were fatally weakened. The end came in 404 B.C. After a siege that left many people dying in the streets, Athens surrendered unconditionally to the Spartans and their allies.

92 Kresilas. *Pericles*. Roman copy after original of c. 440 B.C. Marble. Vatican Museum, Rome. Pericles is wearing a helmet, pushed up over his forehead, because his official rank while leader of Athens was general.

93 Polyclitus the Younger. Theater, Epidaurus. c. 350 B.C. Diameter 373' (113.69 m), orchestra 66' (20.12 m) across.

The Drama Festivals of Dionysus

The tumultuous years of the 5th century B.C., passing from the spirit of euphoria which followed the ending of the Persian Wars to the mood of doubt and self-questioning of 404 B.C., may seem unlikely to have produced the kind of intellectual concentration characteristic of Classical Greek drama. Yet it was, in fact, in the plays written specifically for performance in the theater of Dionysus at Athens in these years that Classical literature reached its most elevated heights. The tragedies of the three great masters, Aeschylus, Sophocles, and Euripides, not only illustrate the development of contemporary thought but also contain some of the most memorable scenes in the history of the theater.

Tragic drama was not itself an invention of the 5th century B.C. It had evolved over the preceding century from *dithyrambs,* or choral hymns sung in honor of the god Dionysus, and the religious character of its origins was still present in its fully developed form. The plays that have survived from the Classical pe-

riod at Athens were all written for performance at one of the two annual festivals sacred to Dionysus before an audience which consisted of the entire population of the city. To go to the theater was to take part in a religious ritual; the theaters themselves were regarded as sacred ground [93].

Each of the authors of the works given each year normally submitted four plays to be performed consecutively on a single day—three tragedies, or a "trilogy," and a more light-hearted play called a *satyr* play (a satyr was a mythological figure with an animal's ears and tail). The "trilogies" often narrated parts of a single story, although often the three plays were based on different stories with a common theme. At the end of each year's festival the plays were judged and a prize awarded to the winning author.

The dramas were religious not only in time and place but also in nature. The plots, generally drawn from mythology, often dealt with the relationship between the human and the divine. To achieve an appropriate seriousness, the style of performance was lofty and dignified. The actors, who in a sense served as priests of Dionysus, wore masks, elaborate costumes, and raised shoes.

The chorus, whose sacred dithyrambic hymn had been the original starting point in the development of tragedy, retained an important function throughout the 5th century B.C. In some plays, generally the earlier ones, the chorus forms a group centrally involved in the action, as in Aeschylus' *Suppliants* and *Eumenides.* More often, as in Sophocles' *Oedipus the King* or *Antigone,* the chorus represents the point of view of the spectator, rather than that of the characters participating directly in the events on stage; in these plays the chorus reduces to more human terms the intense emotions of the principals and comments on them. Even in the time of Euripides, when dramatic confrontation became more important than extended poetic or philosophical expression, the chorus still retained one important function, that of punctuating the action and dividing it into separate episodes by singing lyric odes whose subject was sometimes only indirectly related to the action of the play.

These aspects of Classical tragedy are a reminder that the surviving texts of the plays represent only a small part of the total experience of the original performances. The words—or at least some of them—have survived; but the music to which the words were sung and which accompanied much of the action, the elaborate choreography to which the chorus moved, indeed the whole grandiose spectacle performed out-of-doors in theaters located in sites of extreme natural beauty before an audience of thousands—all of this can only be recaptured in the imagination. It is perhaps relevant to remember that when, almost two thousand years later, around A.D. 1600, a small group of Florentine intellectuals decided to revive the art of Classical drama, they succeeded instead in inventing opera. Similarly, in the 19th century Richard Wagner was inspired by Greek tragedy to devise his concept of a *Gesamtkunstwerk,* a work of art that combined all the arts into one; he illustrated this concept by writing his dramatic operas.

The Tragedies of Aeschylus

Even if some elements of the surviving Greek dramas are lost, we do have the words. And the differing world views of the authors of these words vividly illustrate the changing fate of 5th-century B.C. Athens. The earliest of the playwrights, Aeschylus (525–456 B.C.), died before the lofty aspirations of the early

years of the Classical period could be shaken by contemporary events. His work shows a deep awareness of human weakness and the dangers of power (he had himself fought at the Battle of Marathon in 490 B.C.), but he retains an enduring belief that in the end right will triumph. In Aeschylus' plays the process of learning what is right is painful: one must suffer to learn one's errors; yet the process is inevitable, controlled by a divine force of justice personified under the name of Zeus. Aeschylus expresses the power of Zeus and the necessity to submit to the force he represents in these lines from *Agamemnon*:

Aeschylus
from AGAMEMNON

Zeus: whatever he may be, if this name   160
pleases him in invocation,
thus I call upon him.
I have pondered everything
yet I cannot find a way,
only Zeus, to cast this dead weight of ignorance
finally from out my brain.

He who in time long ago was great,
throbbing with gigantic strength,
shall be as if he never were, unspoken.   170
He who followed him has found
his master, and is gone.
Cry aloud without fear the victory of Zeus,
you will not have failed the truth:

Zeus, who guided men to think,
who has laid it down that wisdom
comes alone through suffering.
Still there drips in sleep against the heart
grief of memory; against   180
our pleasure we are temperate.
From the gods who sit in grandeur
grace comes somehow violent.

The essential optimism of Aeschylus' philosophy must be kept in mind because the actual course of the events he describes is often violent and bloody. Perhaps his most impressive plays are the three that form the *Oresteia* trilogy. This trilogy, the only complete one that has survived, won first prize in the festival of 458 B.C. at Athens. The subject of the trilogy is nothing less than the growth of civilization, represented by the gradual transition from a primitive law of "vendetta" and blood for blood to the rational society of civilized human beings.

The first of the three plays, *Agamemnon,* presents the first of these systems in operation. King Agamemnon returns to his homeland, Argos, after leading the Greeks to victory at Troy. Ten years earlier, on the way to Troy, he had been forced to choose either to abandon the campaign because of unfavorable tides or to obtain an easy passage by sacrificing his daughter Iphigenia. (The situation may seem contrived, but it clearly symbolizes a conflict between public and personal responsibilities.) After considerable hesitation and self-doubt he had chosen to sacrifice his daughter. On his return home at the end of the Trojan War, he pays the price for her death by being murdered by his wife Clytemnestra [94]. Her ostensible motive is vengeance for Iphigenia's death, but an equally powerful, if less noble, one is her desire to replace Agamemnon both as husband and king by her lover Aegisthus. Thus Aeschylus shows us that even the "law of the jungle" is not always as simple as it may seem, while at the same time the punishment of one crime creates in its turn another crime to be punished. If Agamemnon's murder of his daughter merits vengeance, then so does Clytemnestra's murder of her husband. Violence breeds violence.

The second play, *The Libation Bearers,* shows us the effects of the operation of this principle on Agamemnon and Clytemnestra's son, Orestes. After spending years in exile Orestes returns to Argos to avenge his father's death by killing his mother. Although a further murder can accomplish nothing except the transfer of blood guilt to Orestes himself,

94 Dokimasia Painter. *The Murder of Agamemnon,* detail of red-figure krater. Attic, c. 470–465 B.C. Terra cotta. Museum of Fine Arts, Boston (William Francis Warden Fund). Aegisthus strikes the blow in this version of the story, with Clytemnestra standing behind him grasping an axe. Agamemnon, killed as he was about to take a bath, is wearing only a light robe.

the primitive law of "vendetta" requires him to act. With the encouragement of his sister Electra, he kills Clytemnestra. His punishment follows immediately. He is driven mad by the Furies, the implacable goddesses of vengeance, who hound him from his home.

The Furies themselves give their name to the third play, in which they are tactfully called *The Eumenides,* or "the kindly ones." In his resolution of the tragedy of Orestes and his family, Aeschylus makes it clear that violence can only be brought to an end by the power of reason and persuasion. After a period of tormented wandering, Orestes comes finally to Athens where he stands trial for the murder of his mother before a jury of Athenians, presided over by Athena herself. The Furies insist on his condemnation on the principle of blood for blood, but Orestes is defended by Apollo, the god of reason, and finally acquitted by his fellow human beings. Thus the long series of murders is brought to an end, and the apparently inevitable violence and despair of the earlier plays is finally dispelled by the power of persuasion and human reason, which—admittedly with the help of Athena and Apollo—have managed to bring civilization and order out of primeval chaos.

In spite of all of the horror of the earlier plays, therefore, the *Oresteia* ends on a positive note. Aeschylus affirms his belief that progress can be achieved by reason and order. This gradual progression from darkness to light is handled throughout the three plays with unfailing skill. Aeschylus matches the grandeur of his conception with majestic language. His rugged style makes him sometimes difficult to understand, but all the verbal effects are used to dramatic purpose. The piling up of images and complexity of expression produce an emotional tension that has never been surpassed.

That tension can only be fully experienced by reading—or, better still, seeing—if not the whole trilogy, at least a complete play. The following scene from *The Libation Bearers* may, however, give some idea of how masterfully Aeschylus was able to handle a dramatic situation. It is set at the tomb of Agamemnon where Orestes and Electra, together with the Chorus of serving women, lament their father's murder and work themselves into the frenzy required for the murder of their mother. The fusing of poetry and drama into a single long emotional crescendo represents Aeschylus at his most powerfully effective.

The three participants, Orestes, Electra, and the Chorus, begin from three points of view which are slightly different. The Chorus speaks for the age-old tradition of blood for blood (lines 312, 400–404) to reinforce Orestes in the performance of what they see as his duty (lines 375–379). Electra remains obsessed throughout by the memory of her dead father (lines 332–339) and consumed with hatred for her mother (lines 429–433). Orestes begins in a mood of doubt (lines 315–322) and regret for what might have been (lines 345–353), but under the influence of the others his frenzy mounts to the great cry of line 438: "Let me but take her life and die for it." By the last lines all participants are in a condition that can only be described as beyond reason. As so often in drama, incidentally, the whole scene benefits enormously from being read out loud rather than scanned in silence.

Aeschylus
from THE LIBATION BEARERS

CHORUS   Almighty Destinies, by the will
   of Zeus let these things
   be done, in the turning of Justice.
   For the word of hatred spoken, let hate
   be a word fulfilled. The spirit of Right   310
   cries out aloud and extracts atonement
   due: blood stroke for the stroke of blood
   shall be paid. Who acts, shall endure. So speaks
   the voice of the age-old wisdom.
ORESTES   Father, O my dread father, what
     thing
   can I say, can I accomplish
   from this far place where I stand, to mark
   and reach you there in your chamber
   with light that will match your dark?
   Yet it is called an action   320
   of grace to mourn in style for the house,
   once great, of the sons of Atreus.
CHORUS   Child, when the fire burns
   and tears with teeth at the dead man
   it can not wear out the heart of will.
   He shows his wrath in the after-
   days. One dies, and is dirged.
   Light falls on the man who killed him.
   He is hunted down by the deathsong
   for sires slain and for fathers,   330
   disturbed, and stern, and enormous.
ELECTRA   Hear me, my father; hear in turn
   all the tears of my sorrows.
   Two children stand at your tomb to sing
   the burden of your death chant.
   Your grave is shelter to suppliants,
   shelter to the outdriven.
   What here is good; what escape from grief?
   Can we outwrestle disaster?

CHORUS   Yet from such as this the god, if he
   will,   340
   can work out strains that are fairer.
   For dirges chanted over the grave
   the winner's song in the lordly house;
   bring home to new arms the beloved.
ORESTES   If only at Ilium,
   father, and by some Lycian's hands
   you had gone down at the spear's stroke,
   you would have left high fame in your house,
   in the going forth of your children
   eyes' admiration;   350
   founded the deep piled bank of earth
   for grave by the doubled water
   with light lift for your household;
CHORUS   loved then by those he loved
   down there beneath the ground
   who died as heroes, he would have held
   state, and a lord's majesty,
   vassal only to those most great,
   the Kings of the under darkness.
   For he was King on earth when he lived   360
   over those whose hands held power of life
   and death, and the staff of authority.
ELECTRA   No, but not under Troy's
   ramparts, father, should you have died,
   nor, with the rest of the spearstruck hordes
   have found your grave by Scamandrus'
     crossing.
   Sooner, his murderers
   should have been killed, as he was,
   by those they loved, and have found their death,
   and men remote from this outrage   370
   had heard the distant story.
CHORUS   Child, child, you are dreaming, since
     dreaming is a light
   pastime, of fortune more golden than gold
   or the Blessed Ones north of the North Wind.
   But the stroke of the twofold lash is
     pounding
   close, and powers gather under ground
   to give aid. The hands of those who are lords
   are unclean, and these are accursed.
   Power grows on the side of the children.
ORESTES   This cry has come to your ear   380
   like a deep driven arrow.
   Zeus, Zeus, force up from below
   ground the delayed destruction
   on the hard heart and the daring
   hand, for the right of our fathers.
CHORUS   May I claim right to close the deathsong
   chanted in glory across
   the man speared and the woman
   dying. Why darken what deep within me
     forever

flitters? Long since against the heart's 390
stem a bitter wind has blown
thin anger and burdened hatred.

ELECTRA   May Zeus, from all shoulder's strength,
pound down his fist upon them,
ohay, smash their heads.
Let the land once more believe.
There has been wrong done, I ask for right.
Hear me, Earth. Hear me, grandeurs of
Darkness.

CHORUS   It is but law that when the red drops
have been spilled 400
upon the ground they cry aloud for fresh
blood. For the death act calls out on Fury
to bring out of those who were slain before
new ruin on ruin accomplished.

ORESTES   Hear me, you lordships of the world
below.
Behold in assembled power, curses come from
the dead,
behold the last of the sons of Atreus, foundering
lost, without future, cast
from house and right. O god, where shall we
turn?

CHORUS   The heart jumped in me once again 410
to hear this unhappy prayer.
I was disconsolate then
and the deep heart within
darkened to hear you speak it.
But when strength came back hope lifted
me again, and the sorrow
was gone and the light was on me.

ELECTRA   Of what thing can we speak, and strike
more close,
than of the sorrows they who bore us have
given?
So let her fawn if she likes. It softens not. 420
For we are bloody like the wolf
and savage born from the savage mother.

CHORUS   I struck my breast in the stroke-style of
the Arian,
the Cissian mourning woman,
and the hail-beat of the drifting fists was there
to see
as the rising pace went in a pattern of blows
downward and upward until the crashing
strokes
played on my hammered, my all-stricken head.

ELECTRA   O cruel, cruel
all daring mother, in cruel processional 430
with all his citizens gone,
with all sorrow for him forgotten
you dared bury your unbewept lord.

ORESTES   O all unworthy of him, that you tell me.
Shall she not pay for this dishonor

for all the immortals,
for all my own hands can do?
Let me but take her life and die for it.

CHORUS   Know then, they hobbled him beneath
the armpits,
with his own hands. She wrought so, in his
burial 440
to make his death a burden
beyond your strength to carry.
The mutilation of your father. Hear it.

ELECTRA   You tell of how my father was
murdered. Meanwhile I
stood apart, dishonored, nothing worth,
in the dark corner, as you would kennel a
vicious dog,
and burst in an outrush of tears, that came that
day
where smiles would not, and hid the streaming
of my grief.
Hear such, and carve the letters of it on your
heart. 450

CHORUS   Let words such as these
drip deep in your ears, but on a quiet heart.
So far all stands as it stands;
what is to come, yourself burn to know.
You must be hard, give no ground, to win
home.

ORESTES   I speak to you. Be with those you love,
my father.

ELECTRA   And I, all in my tears, ask with him.

CHORUS   We gather into murmurous revolt. Hear
us, hear. Come back into the light.
Be with us against those we hate. 460

ORESTES   Warstrength shall collide with
warstrength; right with right.

ELECTRA   O gods, be just in what you bring to
pass.

CHORUS   My flesh crawls as I listen to them pray.
The day of doom has waited long.
They call for it. It may come.
O pain grown into the race
and blood-dripping stroke
and grinding cry of disaster,
moaning and impossible weight to bear.
Sickness that fights all remedy. 470
Here in the house there lies
the cure for this, not to be brought
from outside, never from others
but in themselves, through the fierce wreck and
bloodshed.
Here is a song sung to the gods beneath us.
Hear then, you blessed ones under the ground,
and answer these prayers with strength on our
side,
free gift for your children's conquest.

Sophocles: *Oedipus the King*

The life of Sophocles (496–406 B.C.) spanned both the glories and the disasters of the 5th century B.C. Of the three great tragic poets, Sophocles was the most prosperous and successful; he was a personal friend of Pericles. He is said to have written 123 plays, but only seven have survived, all of them from the end of his career. They all express a much less positive vision of life than that of Aeschylus. His philosophy is not easy to extract from his work, since he is more concerned with exploring and developing the individual characters in his dramas than with expounding a point of view; in general, he seems to combine an awareness of the tragic consequences of individual mistakes with a belief in the collective ability and dignity of the human race.

The following famous chorus from *Antigone*, which glorifies human achievement, seems to reflect the self-confidence of its age. It was written around 441 B.C., when Pericles had come to power and while the Parthenon, a visible symbol of Athenian splendor, was being built. But in its last two lines there is a note of caution which qualifies the optimism of the picture, and we are reminded of the individual's responsibility to choose between good and evil.

Sophocles
from ANTIGONE

> Wonders are many in the world, and the wonder
>> of all is man.
>> With his bit in the teeth of the storm and his
>> faith in a fragile prow,
> Far he sails, where the waves leap white-fanged,
>> wroth at his plan.
>> And he has his will of the earth by the
>> strength of his hand on the plough.   340
>
> The birds, the clan of the light heart, he snares
>> with his woven cord,
>> And the beasts with wary eyes, and the
>> stealthy fish in the sea;
> That shaggy freedom-lover, the horse, obeys his
>> word,
>> And the sullen bull must serve him, for
>> cunning of wit is he.   350
>
> Against all ills providing, he tempers the dark
>> and the light,
>> The creeping siege of the frost and the
>> arrows of sleet and rain,
> The grievous wounds of the daytime and the
>> fever that steals in the night;
>> Only against Death man arms himself in vain.

> With speech and wind-swift thought he builds
>> the State to his mood,
>> Prospering while he honors the gods and the
>> laws of the land.
> Yet in his rashness often he scorns the ways that
>> are good—
>> May such as walk with evil be far from my
>> hearth and hand!   370

Paradoxically, however, the choice between good and evil is never clear or easy and is sometimes impossible. More than any of his contemporaries, Sophocles emphasizes how much lies outside our own control, in the hands of destiny or the gods. His insistence that we respect and revere the forces that we cannot see or understand makes him the most traditionally religious of the tragedians. These ambiguities appear in his best-known play, *Oedipus the King*, which has stood ever since Classical times as a symbol of Greek tragic drama [95]. A century after it was first performed around 429 B.C., Aristotle used it as his model when, in the *Poetics*, he discussed the nature of tragedy. Its unities of time, place, and action, the inexorable drive of the story with its inevitable yet profoundly tragic conclusion, the beauty of its poetry—all these have made *Oedipus the King* a true classic, in all senses. Its impact has lasted down to our own time [96, 97]; it had a notable effect on the ideas of Sigmund Freud. Yet in spite of the universal admiration which the play has excited, its message is far from clear.

The story concerns Oedipus, doomed even before his birth to kill his father and marry his mother, his attempts to avoid fate, and his final discovery that he has failed. If the play seems, in part, to be saying that

95 Scene from the Oedipus story. c. 1475. Manuscript illumination. Biblioteca Nazionale Marciana, Venice. The tragedy of Oedipus remained a favorite story long after Sophocles' time. In the 1st century A.D. the Roman philosopher Seneca wrote a play called *Oedipus,* and this miniature showing Jocasta's death and Oedipus' self-blinding comes from a 15th-century edition of it.

96 A modern performance of *Oedipus the King* in the ancient theater at Delphi. 1951. The columns in the background are the ruins of the Temple of Apollo.

97 The Old Vic production of *Oedipus Rex*. London, 1945. Laurence Olivier as Oedipus; Sybil Thorndike as Jocasta.

we cannot avoid our destiny, it leaves unanswered the question of whether we deserve that destiny or not. Certainly Oedipus does not choose deliberately to kill his father and marry his mother, even though unknowingly everything he does leads to this end. Then why does he deserve to suffer for his actions?

One of the traditional answers to this question can be found in Aristotle's analysis of tragedy in the *Poetics*. Referring particularly to *Oedipus*, Aristotle makes the point that the downfall of a tragic figure is generally the result of a tragic flaw (the Greek word is *hamartia*) in his character. Thus Oedipus' pride and stubbornness in insisting on discovering who he is (lines 1076–1084) and the anger he shows in the process (lines 345–349, 532–542) bring about the final disastrous revelation. In this way the flaws, or weaknesses, in his character overcome his good points and destroy him.

As a description of Oedipus' behavior, this explanation is convincing enough, but it fails to provide a satisfactory account of the original causes of his condition. Perhaps the message of the play is, in fact, that there are some aspects of existence beyond our understanding, aspects that operate by principles outside our range of experience. If this is so, and many literary critics would deny it, Sophocles seems to be describing the final helplessness of humanity in the face of forces that we cannot control and warning against too great a belief in self-reliance. Certainly we must never make the mistake of overrating our ability to know, like Oedipus' wife and mother Jocasta, who believes that she can disregard the ominous warnings of oracles and prophets. In lines 707–725 she pours scorn on their power and uses reason to prove them wrong. Yet she does not know that her own words contradict themselves and that everything which she claims to be false is in fact true.

Jocasta's lines provide an impressive example of the device of *dramatic irony*, which Sophocles employs frequently. The term is used to describe situations or speeches that have one meaning to the characters in the play but a very different one to the audience. Thus at the very moment when Jocasta convinces herself that the oracles are false we know that they are true. The same dramatic irony characterizes the situation of Oedipus throughout the play. From his dignified appearance in the opening scene, his words are filled with a double significance. When, in line 61, he tells the chorus that "None there is among you as sick as I," his statement has, unknown to him, a terrible truth. The great curse he pro-

nounces on the polluter of the city in lines 216–275 is, of course, unknowingly pronounced on himself. As the tension mounts and the truth becomes apparent to everyone, only Oedipus remains unable to see it, and every word he utters takes on a dire significance hidden from him.

When the final truth is out, and Oedipus sees it for the first time by another stroke of Sophoclean irony, he blinds himself. The end of the play is a gradual unwinding of the tension. As the broken king prepares to go into perpetual exile, the Chorus reminds us of the instability of success and happiness, leaving us to interpret for ourselves the moral of Oedipus' fate. The complete play, translated by Albert Cook, is reproduced below.

Sophocles
OEDIPUS THE KING
Characters

OEDIPUS, *king of Thebes*
A PRIEST
CREON, *brother-in-law of Oedipus*
CHORUS *of Theban elders*
TEIRESIAS, *a prophet*
JOCASTA, *sister of Creon, wife of Oedipus*
MESSENGER
SERVANT *of Laius, father of Oedipus*
SECOND MESSENGER
(*silent*) ANTIGONE *and* ISMENE, *daughters of Oedipus*

SCENE. *Before the palace of Oedipus at Thebes. In front of the large central doors, an altar; and an altar near each of the two side doors. On the altar steps are seated suppliants—old men, youths, and young boys—dressed in white tunics and cloaks, their hair bound with white fillets. They have laid on the altars olive branches wreathed with wool-fillets.*

The old PRIEST OF ZEUS *stands alone facing the central doors of the palace. The doors open, and* OEDIPUS, *followed by two attendants who stand at either door, enters and looks about.*

OEDIPUS   O children, last born stock of ancient Cadmus,
What petitions are these you bring to me
With garlands on your suppliant olive branches?
The whole city teems with incense fumes,
Teems with prayers for healing and with groans.
Thinking it best, children, to hear all this
Not from some messenger, I came myself,
The world renowned and glorious Oedipus.
But tell me, aged priest, since you are fit
To speak before these men, how stand you here,   10

In fear or want? Tell me, as I desire
To do my all; hard hearted I would be
To feel no sympathy for such a prayer.
PRIEST   O Oedipus, ruler of my land, you see
How old we are who stand in supplication
Before your altars here, some not yet strong
For lengthy flight, some heavy with age,
Priests, as I of Zeus, and choice young men.
The rest of the tribe sits with wreathed
        branches,
In market places, at Pallas' two temples,   20
And at prophetic embers by the river.
The city, as you see, now shakes too greatly
And cannot raise her head out of the depths
Above the gory swell. She wastes in blight,
Blight on earth's fruitful blooms and grazing
        flocks,
And on the barren birth pangs of the
        women.
The fever god has fallen on the city,
And drives it, a most hated pestilence
Through whom the home of Cadmus is made
        empty.
Black Hades is enriched with wails and
        groans.   30
Not that we think you equal to the gods
These boys and I sit suppliant at your hearth,
But judging you first of men in the trials of life,
And in the human intercourse with spirits:—
You are the one who came to Cadmus' city
And freed us from the tribute which we paid
To the harsh-singing Sphinx. And that you did
Knowing nothing else, unschooled by us.
But people say and think it was some god
That helped you to set our life upright.
Now Oedipus, most powerful of all,   40
We all are turned here toward you, we beseech
        you,
Find us some strength, whether from one of the
        gods
You hear an omen, or know one from a man.
For the experienced I see will best
Make good plans grow from evil circumstance.
Come, best of mortal men, raise up the state.
Come, prove your fame, since now this land of
        ours
Calls you savior for your previous zeal.
O never let our memory of your reign
Be that we first stood straight and later fell,   50
But to security raise up this state.
With favoring omen once you gave us luck;
Be now as good again; for if henceforth
You rule as now, you will be this country's
        king,
Better it is to rule men than a desert,

Since nothing is either ship or fortress tower
Bare of men who together dwell within.
OEDIPUS   O piteous children, I am not ignorant
Of what you come desiring. Well I know
You are all sick, and in your sickness none   60
There is among you as sick as I,
For your pain comes to one man alone,
To him and to none other, but my soul
Groans for the state, for myself, and for you.
You do not wake a man who is sunk in sleep;
Know that already I have shed many tears,
And travelled many wandering roads of
        thought.
Well have I sought, and found one remedy;
And this I did: the son of Menoeceus,
Creon, my brother-in-law, I sent away   70
Unto Apollo's Pythian halls to find
What I might do or say to save the state.
The days are measured out that he is gone;
It troubles me how he fares. Longer than usual
He has been away, more than the fitting time.
But when he comes, then evil I shall be,
If all the god reveals I fail to do.
PRIEST   You speak at the right time. These men
        just now
Signal to me that Creon is approaching.
OEDIPUS   O Lord Apollo, grant that he may
        come   80
In saving fortune shining as in eye.
PRIEST   Glad news he brings, it seems, or else his
        head
Would not be crowned with leafy, berried bay.
OEDIPUS   We will soon know. He is close enough
        to hear.—
Prince, my kinsman, son of Menoeceus,
What oracle do you bring us from the god?
CREON   A good one. For I say that even burdens
If they chance to turn out right, will all be well.
OEDIPUS   Yet what is the oracle? Your present
        word
Makes me neither bold nor apprehensive.   90
CREON   If you wish to hear in front of this crowd
I am ready to speak, or we can go within.
OEDIPUS   Speak forth to all. The sorrow that I
        bear
Is greater for these men than for my life.
CREON   May I tell you what I heard from the
        god?
Lord Phoebus clearly bids us to drive out,
And not to leave uncured within this country,
A pollution we have nourished in our land.
OEDIPUS   With what purgation? What kind of
        misfortune?
CREON   Banish the man, or quit slaughter with
        slaughter   100

In cleansing, since this blood rains on the state.

OEDIPUS   Who is this man whose fate the god
         reveals?

CREON   Laius, my lord, was formerly the guide
Of this our land before you steered this city.

OEDIPUS   I know him by hearsay, but I never saw
         him.

CREON   Since he was slain, the god now plainly
         bids us
To punish his murderers, whoever they may be.

OEDIPUS   Where are they on the earth? How shall
         we find
This indiscernible track of ancient guilt?

CREON   In this land, said Apollo. What is
         sought   110
Can be apprehended; the unobserved escapes.

OEDIPUS   Did Laius fall at home on this bloody
         end?
Or in the fields, or in some foreign land?

CREON   As a pilgrim, the god said, he left his
         tribe
And once away from home, returned no more.

OEDIPUS   Was there no messenger, no fellow
         wayfarer
Who saw, from whom an inquirer might get
         aid?

CREON   They are all dead, save one, who fled in
         fear
And he knows only one thing sure to tell.

OEDIPUS   What is that? We may learn many facts
         from one   120
If we might take for hope a short beginning.

CREON   Robbers, Apollo said, met there and killed
         him
Not by the strength of one, but many hands.

OEDIPUS   How did the robber unless something
         from here
Was at work with silver, reach this point of
         daring?

CREON   These facts are all conjecture. Laius dead,
There rose in evils no avenger for him.

OEDIPUS   But when the king had fallen slain, what
         trouble
Prevented you from finding all this out?

CREON   The subtle-singing Sphinx made us
         let go   130
What was unclear to search at our own feet.

OEDIPUS   Well then, I will make this clear
         afresh
From the start. Phoebus was right, you were
         right
To take this present interest in the dead.
Justly it is you see me as your ally
Avenging alike this country and the god.
Not for the sake of some distant friends,

But for myself I will disperse this filth.
Whoever it was who killed that man
With the same hand may wish to do vengeance
         on me.   140
And so assisting Laius I aid myself.
But hurry quickly, children, stand up now
From the altar steps, raising these suppliant
         boughs.
Let someone gather Cadmus' people here
To learn that I will do all, whether at last
With Phoebus' help we are shown saved or
         fallen.

PRIEST   Come, children, let us stand. We came here
First for the sake of what this man proclaims.
Phoebus it was who sent these prophecies
And he will come to save us from the
         plague.   150

CHORUS

Strophe A

O sweet-tongued voice of Zeus, in what spirit
         do you come
From Pytho rich in gold
To glorious Thebes? I am torn on the rack,
         dread shakes my fearful mind,
Apollo of Delos, hail!
As I stand in awe of you, what need, either new
Do you bring to the full for me, or old in the
         turning times of the year?
Tell me, O child of golden Hope, undying
         Voice!

Antistrophe A

First on you do I call, daughter of Zeus,
         undying Athene
And your sister who guards our land,   160
Artemis, seated upon the throne renowned of
         our circled Place,
And Phoebus who darts afar;
Shine forth to me, thrice warder-off of death;
If ever in time before when ruin rushed upon
         the state,
The flame of sorrow you drove beyond our
         bounds, come also now.

Strophe B

O woe! Unnumbered that I bear
The sorrows are! My whole host is sick, nor is
         there a sword of thought
To ward off pain. The growing fruits   170
Of glorious earth wax not, nor women
Withstand in childbirth shrieking pangs.
Life on life you may see, which, like the well-
         winged bird,
Faster than stubborn fire, speed
To the strand of the evening god.

Antistrophe B
Unnumbered of the city die.   180
Unpitied babies bearing death lie unmoaned on
    the ground.
Grey-haired mothers and young wives
From all sides at the altar's edge
Lift up a wail beseeching, for their mournful
    woes.
The prayer for healing shines blent with a
    grieving cry;
Wherefore, O golden daughter of Zeus,
Send us your succour with its beaming face.

Strophe C
Grant that fiery Ares, who now with no brazen
    shield   190
Flames round me in shouting attack
May turn his back in running flight from our
    land,
May be borne with fair wind
To Amphitrite's great chamber
Or to the hostile port
Of the Thracian surge.
For even if night leaves any ill undone
It is brought to pass and comes to be in the day.
O Zeus who bear the fire   200
And rule the lightning's might,
Strike him beneath your thunderbolt with death!

Antistrophe C
O lord Apollo, would that you might come and
    scatter forth
Untamed darts from your twirling golden bow;
Bring succour from the plague; may the
    flashing
Beams come of Artemis,
With which she glances through the Lycian
    hills.
Also on him I call whose hair is held in gold,
Who gives a name to this land,   210
Bacchus of winy face, whom maidens hail!
Draw near with your flaming Maenad band
And the aid of your gladsome torch
Against the plague, dishonoured among the
    gods.
OEDIPUS   You pray; if for what you pray you
    would be willing
To hear and take my words, to nurse the
    plague,
You may get succour and relief from evils.
A stranger to this tale I now speak forth,
A stranger to the deed, for not alone   220
Could I have tracked it far without some clue,
But now that I am enrolled a citizen
Latest among the citizens of Thebes

To all you sons of Cadmus I proclaim
Whoever of you knows at what man's hand
Laius, the son of Labdacus, met his death,
I order him to tell me all, and even
If he fears, to clear the charge and he will suffer
No injury, but leave the land unharmed.
If someone knows the murderer to be an
    alien   230
From foreign soil, let him not be silent;
I will give him a reward, my thanks besides.
But if you stay in silence and from fear
For self or friend thrust aside my command,
Hear now from me what I shall do for this;
I charge that none who dwell within this land
Whereof I hold the power and the throne
Give this man shelter whoever he may be,
Or speak to him, or share with him in prayer
Or sacrifice, or serve him lustral rites,   240
But drive him, all, out of your homes, for he
Is this pollution on us, as Apollo
Revealed to me just now in oracle.
I am therefore the ally of the god
And of the murdered man. And now I pray
That the murderer, whether he hides alone
Or with his partners, may, evil coward,
Wear out in luckless ills his wretched life.
I further pray, that, if at my own hearth
He dwells known to me in my own home,   250
I may suffer myself the curse I just now
    uttered.
And you I charge to bring all this to pass
For me, and for the god, and for our land
Which now lies fruitless, godless, and corrupt.
Even if Phoebus had not urged this affair,
Not rightly did you let it go unpurged
When one both noble and a king was murdered!
You should have sought it out. Since now I
    reign
Holding the power which he had held before
    me,
Having the selfsame wife and marriage
    bed—   260
And if his seed had not met barren fortune
We should be linked by offspring from one
    mother;
But as it was, fate leapt upon his head.
Therefore in this, as if for my own father
I fight for him, and shall attempt all
Searching to seize the hand which shed that
    blood,
For Labdacus' son, before him Polydorus,
And ancient Cadmus, and Agenor of old.
And those who fail to do this, I pray the gods
May give them neither harvest from their
    earth   270

Nor children from their wives, but may they be
Destroyed by a fate like this one, or a worse.
You other Thebans, who cherish these
   commands,
May Justice, the ally of a righteous cause,
And all the gods be always on your side.

CHORUS   By the oath you laid on me, my king, I
   speak.
I killed not Laius, nor can show who killed
   him.
Phoebus it was who sent this question to us,
And he should answer who has done the deed.

OEDIPUS   Your words are just, but to compel the
   gods   280
In what they do not wish, no man can do.

CHORUS   I would tell what seems to me our
   second course.

OEDIPUS   If there is a third, fail not to tell it too.

CHORUS   Lord Teiresias I know, who sees this best
Like lord Apollo; in surveying this,
One might, my lord, find out from him most
   clearly.

OEDIPUS   Even this I did not neglect; I have done
   it already.
At Creon's word I twice sent messengers.
It is a wonder he has been gone so long.

CHORUS   And also there are rumors, faint
   and old.   290

OEDIPUS   What are they? I must search out every
   tale.

CHORUS   They say there were some travellers who
   killed him.

OEDIPUS   So I have heard, but no one sees a
   witness.

CHORUS   If his mind knows a particle of fear
He will not long withstand such curse as yours.

OEDIPUS   He fears no speech who fears not such a
   deed.

CHORUS   But here is the man who will convict the
   guilty.
Here are these men leading the divine prophet
In whom alone of men the truth is born.

OEDIPUS   O you who ponder all, Teiresias,   300
Both what is taught and what cannot be
   spoken,
What is of heaven and what trod on the earth,
Even if you are blind, you know what plague
Clings to the state, and, master, you alone
We find as her protector and her saviour.
Apollo, if the messengers have not told you,
Answered our question, that release would
   come
From this disease only if we make sure
Of Laius' slayers and slay them in return
Or drive them out as exiles from the land.

But you now, grudge us neither voice of
   birds   310
Nor any way you have of prophecy.
Save yourself and the state; save me as well.
Save everything polluted by the dead.
We are in your hands; it is the noblest task
To help a man with all your means and powers.

TEIRESIAS   Alas! Alas! How terrible to be wise,
Where it does the seer no good. Too well I
   know
And have forgot this, or would not have come
   here.

OEDIPUS   What is this? How fainthearted you have
   come!

TEIRESIAS   Let me go home; it is best for you to
   bear   320
Your burden, and I mine, if you will heed me.

OEDIPUS   You speak what is lawless, and hateful to
   the state
Which raised you, when you deprive her of
   your answer.

TEIRESIAS   And I see that your speech does not
   proceed
In season; I shall not undergo the same.

OEDIPUS   Don't by the gods turn back when you
   are wise,
When all we suppliants lie prostrate before you.

TEIRESIAS   And all unwise; I never shall reveal
My evils, so that I may not tell yours.

OEDIPUS   What do you say? You know, but will
   not speak?   330
Would you betray us and destroy the state?

TEIRESIAS   I will not hurt you or me. Why in vain
Do you probe this? You will not find out from
   me.

OEDIPUS   Worst of evil men, you would enrage
A stone itself. Will you never speak,
But stay so untouched and so inconclusive?

TEIRESIAS   You blame my anger and do not see
   that
With which you live in common, but upbraid
   me.

OEDIPUS   Who would not be enraged to hear these
   words
By which you now dishonor this our city?   340

TEIRESIAS   Of itself this will come, though I hide it
   in silence.

OEDIPUS   Then you should tell me what it is will
   come.

TEIRESIAS   I shall speak no more. If further you
   desire,
Rage on in wildest anger of your soul.

OEDIPUS   I shall omit nothing I understand
I am so angry. Know that you seem to me
Creator of the deed and worker too

In all short of the slaughter; if you were not blind,
I would say this crime was your work alone.

TEIRESIAS   Really? Abide yourself by the decree   350
You just proclaimed, I tell you! From this day
Henceforth address neither these men nor me.
You are the godless defiler of this land.

OEDIPUS   You push so bold and taunting in your speech;
And how do you think to get away with this?

TEIRESIAS   I have got away. I nurse my strength in truth.

OEDIPUS   Who taught you this? Not from your art you got it.

TEIRESIAS   From you. You had me speak against my will.

OEDIPUS   What word? Say again, so I may better learn.

TEIRESIAS   Didn't you get it before? Or do you bait me?   360

OEDIPUS   I don't remember it. Speak forth again.

TEIRESIAS   You are the slayer whom you seek, I say.

OEDIPUS   Not twice you speak such bitter words unpunished.

TEIRESIAS   Shall I speak more to make you angrier still?

OEDIPUS   Do what you will, your words will be in vain.

TEIRESIAS   I say you have forgot that you are joined
With those most dear to you in deepest shame
And do not see where you are in sin.

OEDIPUS   Do you think you will always say such things in joy?

TEIRESIAS   Surely, if strength abides in what is true.

OEDIPUS   It does, for all but you, this not for you   370
Because your ears and mind and eyes are blind.

TEIRESIAS   Wretched you are to make such taunts, for soon
All men will cast the selfsame taunts on you.

OEDIPUS   You live in entire night, could do no harm
To me or any man who sees the day.

TEIRESIAS   Not at my hands will it be your fate to fall.
Apollo suffices, whose concern it is to do this.

OEDIPUS   Are these devices yours, or are they Creon's?

TEIRESIAS   Creon is not your trouble; you are yourself.

OEDIPUS   O riches, empire, skill surpassing skill   380

In all the numerous rivalries of life,
How great a grudge there is stored up against you
If for this kingship, which the city gave,
Their gift, not my request, into my hands—
For this, the trusted Creon, my friend from the start
Desires to creep by stealth and cast me out
Taking a seer like this, a weaver of wiles,
A crooked swindler who has got his eyes
On gain alone, but in his art is blind.
Come, tell us, in what clearly are you a prophet?   390
How is it, when the weave-songed bitch was here
You uttered no salvation for these people?
Surely the riddle then could not be solved
By some chance comer; it needed prophecy.
You did not clarify that with birds
Or knowledge from a god; but when I came,
The ignorant Oedipus, I silenced her,
Not taught by birds, but winning by my wits,
Whom you are now attempting to depose,
Thinking to minister near Creon's throne.   400
I think that to your woe you and that plotter
Will purge the land, and if you were not old
Punishment would teach you what you plot.

CHORUS   It seems to us, O Oedipus our king,
Both this man's words and yours were said in anger.
Such is not our need, but to find out
How best we shall discharge Apollo's orders.

TEIRESIAS   Even if you are king, the right to answer
Should be free to all; of that I too am king.
I live not as your slave, but as Apollo's.   410
And not with Creon's wards shall I be counted.
I say, since you have taunted even my blindness,
You have eyes, but see not where in evil you are
Nor where you dwell, nor whom you are living with.
Do you know from whom you spring? And you forget
You are an enemy to your own kin
Both those beneath and those above the earth.
Your mother's and father's curse, with double goad
And dreaded foot shall drive you from this land.
You who now see straight shall then be blind,
And there shall be no harbour for your cry   420
With which all Mount Cithaeron soon shall ring,

When you have learned the wedding where you sailed
At home, into no port, by voyage fair.
A throng of other ills you do not know
Shall equal you to yourself and to your children.
Throw mud on this, on Creon, on my voice—
Yet there shall never be a mortal man
Eradicated more wretchedly than you.

OEDIPUS   Shall these unbearable words be heard from him?
Go to perdition! Hurry! Off, away,   430
Turn back again and from this house depart.

TEIRESIAS   If you had not called me, I should not have come.

OEDIPUS   I did not know that you would speak such folly
Or I would not soon have brought you to my house.

TEIRESIAS   And such a fool I am, as it seems to you.
But to the parents who bore you I seem wise.

OEDIPUS   What parents? Wait! What mortals gave me birth?

TEIRESIAS   This day shall be your birth and your destruction.

OEDIPUS   All things you say in riddles and unclear.

TEIRESIAS   Are you not he who best can search this out?   440

OEDIPUS   Mock, if you wish, the skill that made me great.

TEIRESIAS   This is the very fortune that destroyed you.

OEDIPUS   Well, if I saved the city, I do not care.

TEIRESIAS   I am going now. You, boy, be my guide.

OEDIPUS   Yes, let him guide you. Here you are in the way.
When you are gone you will give no more trouble.

TEIRESIAS   I go when I have said what I came to say
Without fear of your frown; you cannot destroy me.
I say, the very man whom you long seek
With threats and announcements about Laius' murder—   450
This man is here. He seems an alien stranger,
But soon he shall be revealed of Theban birth,
Nor at this circumstance shall he be pleased.
He shall be blind who sees, shall be a beggar
Who now is rich, shall make his way abroad
Feeling the ground before him with a staff.
He shall be revealed at once as brother
And father to his own children, husband and son

To his mother, his father's kin and murderer.   460
Go in and ponder that. If I am wrong,
Say then that I know nothing of prophecy.

CHORUS
Strophe A
Who is the man the Delphic rock said with oracular voice
Unspeakable crimes performed with his gory hands?
It is time for him now to speed
His foot in flight, more strong
Than horses swift as the storm.
For girt in arms upon him springs
With fire and lightning, Zeus' son   470
And behind him, terrible,
Come the unerring Fates.

Antistrophe A
From snowy Parnassus just now the word flashed clear
To track the obscure man by every way,
For he wanders under the wild
Forest, and into caves
And cliff rocks, like a bull,
Reft on his way, with care on care
Trying to shun the prophecy
Come from the earth's mid-navel;   480
But about him flutters the ever living doom.

Strophe B
Terrible, terrible things the wise bird-augur stirs.
I neither approve nor deny, at a loss for what to say,
I flutter in hopes and fears, see neither here nor ahead;
For what strife has lain
On Labdacus' sons or Polybus' that I have found ever before   490
Or now, whereby I may run for the sons of Labdacus
In sure proof against Oedipus' public fame
As avenger for dark death?

Antistrophe B
Zeus and Apollo surely understand and know
The affairs of mortal men, but that a mortal seer
Knows more than I, there is no proof. Though a man   500
May surpass a man in knowledge,
Never shall I agree, till I see the word true, when men blame Oedipus,
For there came upon him once clear the winged maiden
And wise he was seen, by sure test sweet for the state.   510

So never shall my mind judge him evil guilt.

CREON   Men of our city, I have heard dread words
That Oedipus our king accuses me.
I am here indignant. If in the present troubles
He thinks that he has suffered at my hands
One word or deed tending to injury
I do not crave the long-spanned age of life
To bear this rumor, for it is no simple wrong
The damage of this accusation brings me;   520
It brings the greatest, if I am called a traitor
To you and my friends, a traitor to the state.

CHORUS   Come now, for this reproach perhaps was forced
By anger, rather than considered thought.

CREON   And was the idea voiced that my advice
Persuaded the prophet to give false accounts?

CHORUS   Such was said. I know not to what intent.

CREON   Was this accusation laid against me
From straightforward eyes and straightforward mind?

CHORUS   I do not know. I see not what my masters do;   530
But here he is now, coming from the house.

OEDIPUS   How dare you come here? Do you own a face
So bold that you can come before my house
When you are clearly the murderer of this man
And manifestly pirate of my throne?
Come, say before the gods, did you see in me
A coward or a fool, that you plotted this?
Or did you think I would not see your wiles
Creeping upon me, or knowing, would not ward off?
Surely your machination is absurd   540
Without a crowd of friends to hunt a throne
Which is captured only by wealth and many men.

CREON   Do you know what you do? Hear answer to your charges
On the other side. Judge only what you know.

OEDIPUS   Your speech is clever, but I learn it ill
Since I have found you harsh and grievous toward me.

CREON   This very matter hear me first explain.

OEDIPUS   Tell me not this one thing: you are not false.

CREON   If you think stubbornness a good possession
Apart from judgment, you do not think right.   550

OEDIPUS   If you think you can do a kinsman evil
Without the penalty, you have no sense.

CREON   I agree with you. What you have said is just.
Tell me what you say you have suffered from me.

OEDIPUS   Did you, or did you not, advise my need
Was summoning that prophet person here?

CREON   And still is. I hold still the same opinion.

OEDIPUS   How long a time now has it been since Laius—

CREON   Performed what deed? I do not understand.

OEDIPUS   —Disappeared to his ruin at deadly hands.   560

CREON   Far in the past the count of years would run.

OEDIPUS   Was this same seer at that time practising?

CREON   As wise as now, and equally respected.

OEDIPUS   At that time did he ever mention me?

CREON   Never when I stood near enough to hear.

OEDIPUS   But did you not make inquiry of the murder?

CREON   We did, of course, and got no information.

OEDIPUS   How is it that this seer did not utter this then?

CREON   When I don't know, as now, I would keep still.

OEDIPUS   This much you know full well, and so should speak:—   570

CREON   What is that? If I know, I will not refuse.

OEDIPUS   This: If he had not first conferred with you
He never would have said that I killed Laius.

CREON   If he says this, you know yourself, I think;
I learn as much from you as you from me.

OEDIPUS   Learn then: I never shall be found a slayer.

CREON   What then, are you the husband of my sister?

OEDIPUS   What you have asked is plain beyond denial.

CREON   Do you rule this land with her in equal sway?

OEDIPUS   All she desires she obtains from me.   580

CREON   Am I with you two not an equal third?

OEDIPUS   In just that do you prove a treacherous friend.

CREON   No, if, like me, you reason with yourself.
Consider this fact first: would any man
Choose, do you think, to have his rule in fear
Rather than doze unharmed with the same power?
For my part I have never been desirous

Of being king instead of acting king.
Nor any other man has, wise and prudent.
For now I obtain all from you without fear.   590
If I were king, I would do much unwilling.
How then could kingship sweeter be for me
Than rule and power devoid of any pain?
I am not yet so much deceived to want
Goods besides those I profitably enjoy.
Now I am hailed and gladdened by all men.
Now those who want from you speak out
   to me,
Since all their chances' outcome dwells therein.
How then would I relinquish what I have
To get those gains? My mind runs not
   so bad.   600
I am prudent yet, no lover of such plots,
Nor would I ever endure others' treason.
And first as proof of this go on to Pytho;
See if I told you truly the oracle.
Next proof: see if I plotted with the seer;
If you find so at all, put me to death
With my vote for my guilt as well as yours.
Do not convict me just on unclear conjecture.
It is not right to think capriciously
The good are bad, nor that the bad are
   good.   610
It is the same to cast out a noble friend,
I say, as one's own life, which best he loves.
The facts, though, you will safely know in time,
Since time alone can show the just man just,
But you can know a criminal in one day.

CHORUS   A cautious man would say he has spoken
   well.
   O king, the quick to think are never sure.

OEDIPUS   When the plotter, swift, approaches me
   in stealth
   I too in counterplot must be as swift.
If I wait in repose, the plotter's ends   620
Are brought to pass and mine will then have
   erred.

CREON   What do you want then? To cast me from
   the land?

OEDIPUS   Least of all that. My wish is you should
   die,
   Not flee to exemplify what envy is.

CREON   Do you say this? Will you neither trust
   nor yield?

OEDIPUS   [No, for I think that you deserve no
   trust.]

CREON   You seem not wise to me

OEDIPUS   I am for me.

CREON   You should be for me too.

OEDIPUS   No, you are evil.

CREON   Yes, if you understand nothing.

OEDIPUS   Yet I must rule.

CREON   Not when you rule badly.

OEDIPUS   O city, city!

CREON   It is my city too, not yours alone.   630

CHORUS   Stop, princes. I see Jocasta coming
   Out of the house at the right time for you.
   With her you must settle the dispute at hand.

JOCASTA   O wretched men, what unconsidered
   feud
   Of tongues have you aroused? Are you not
   ashamed,
   The state so sick, to stir up private ills?
   Are you not going home? And you as well?
   Will you turn a small pain into a great?

CREON   My blood sister, Oedipus your husband
   Claims he will judge against me two
   dread ills: 640
   Thrust me from the fatherland or take and
   kill me.

OEDIPUS   I will, my wife; I caught him in the act
   Doing evil to my person with evil skill.

CREON   Now may I not rejoice but die accursed
   If ever I did any of what you accuse me.

JOCASTA   O, by the gods, believe him, Oedipus.
   First, in reverence for his oath to the gods,
   Next, for my sake and theirs who stand before
   you.

CHORUS   Hear my entreaty, lord. Consider and
   consent.

OEDIPUS   What wish should I then grant?   650

CHORUS   Respect the man, no fool before, who
   now in oath is strong.

OEDIPUS   You know what you desire?

CHORUS   I know.

OEDIPUS   Say what you mean.

CHORUS   Your friend who has sworn do not
   dishonour
   By casting guilt for dark report.

OEDIPUS   Know well that when you ask this grant
   from me,
   You ask my death or exile from the land.

CHORUS   No, by the god foremost among the
   gods,   660
   The Sun, may I perish by the utmost doom
   Godless and friendless, if I have this in mind.
   But ah, the withering earth wears down
   My wretched soul, if to these ills
   Of old are added ills from both of you.

OEDIPUS   Then let him go, though surely I must die
   Or be thrust dishonoured from this land by
   force.   670
   Your grievous voice I pity, not that man's;
   Wherever he may be, he will be hated.

CREON   Sullen you are to yield, as you are heavy
   When you exceed in wrath. Natures like these
   Are justly sorest for themselves to bear.

OEDIPUS   Will you not go and leave me?

CREON   I am on my way.

You know me not, but these men see me just.

CHORUS   O queen, why do you delay to bring this
man indoors?

JOCASTA   I want to learn what happened here.   680

CHORUS: Unknown suspicion rose from talk, and
the unjust devours.

JOCASTA   In both of them?

CHORUS   Just so.

JOCASTA   What was the talk?

CHORUS   Enough, enough! When the land is
pained

It seems to me at this point we should stop.

OEDIPUS   Do you see where you have come?
Though your intent

Is good, you slacken off and blunt my heart.

CHORUS   O lord, I have said not once alone,

Know that I clearly would be mad   690

And wandering in mind, to turn away

You who steered along the right,

When she was torn with trouble, our beloved
state.

O may you now become in health her guide.

JOCASTA   By the gods, lord, tell me on what
account

You have set yourself in so great an anger.

OEDIPUS   I shall tell you, wife; I respect you more
than these men.   700

Because of Creon, since he has plotted against
me.

JOCASTA   Say clearly, if you can; how started the
quarrel?

OEDIPUS   He says that I stand as the murderer of
Laius.

JOCASTA   He knows himself, or learned from
someone else?

OEDIPUS   No, but he sent a rascal prophet here.

He keeps his own mouth clean in what concerns
him.

JOCASTA   Now free yourself of what you said, and
listen.

Learn from me, no mortal man exists

Who knows prophetic art for your affairs,

And I shall briefly show you proof of this: 710

An oracle came once to Laius. I do not say

From Phoebus himself, but from his ministers

That his fate would be at his son's hand to
die—

A child, who would be born from him and me.

And yet, as the rumor says, they were strangers,

Robbers who killed him where three highways
meet.

But three days had not passed from the child's
birth

When Laius pierced and tied together his ankles,

And cast him by others' hands on a pathless
mountain.

Therein Apollo did not bring to pass   720

That the child murder his father, nor for Laius

The dread he feared, to die at his son's hand.

Such did prophetic oracles determine.

Pay no attention to them. For the god

Will easily make clear the need he seeks.

OEDIPUS   What wandering of soul, what stirring of
mind

Holds me, my wife, in what I have just heard!

JOCASTA   What care has turned you back that you
say this?

OEDIPUS   I thought I heard you mention this, that
Laius

Was slaughtered at the place where three
highways meet.   730

JOCASTA   That was the talk. The rumour has not
ceased.

OEDIPUS   Where is this place where such a sorrow
was?

JOCASTA   The country's name is Phocis. A split
road

Leads to one place from Delphi and Daulia.

OEDIPUS   And how much time has passed since
these events?

JOCASTA   The news was heralded in the city
scarcely

A little while before you came to rule.

OEDIPUS   O Zeus, what have you planned to do
to me?

JOCASTA   What passion is this in you, Oedipus?

OEDIPUS   Don't ask me that yet. Tell me about
Laius.   740

What did he look like? How old was he when
murdered?

JOCASTA   A tall man, with his hair just brushed
with white.

His shape and form differed not far from yours.

OEDIPUS   Alas! Alas! I think unwittingly

I have just laid dread curses on my head.

JOCASTA   What are you saying? I shrink to behold
you, lord.

OEDIPUS   I am terribly afraid the seer can see.

That will be clearer if you say one thing more.

JOCASTA   Though I shrink, if I know what you
ask, I will answer.

OEDIPUS   Did he set forth with few attendants
then,   750

Or many soldiers, since he was a king?

JOCASTA   They were five altogether among them.

One was a herald. One chariot bore Laius.

OEDIPUS   Alas! All this is clear now. Tell me, my
wife,

Who was the man who told these stories to
	you?
JOCASTA   One servant, who alone escaped,
	returned.
OEDIPUS   Is he by chance now present in our
	house?
JOCASTA   Not now. Right from the time when he
	returned
	To see you ruling and Laius dead,
	Touching my hand in suppliance, he implored
		me 760
	To send him to fields and to pastures of sheep
	That he might be farthest from the sight of this
		city.
	So I sent him away, since he was worthy
	For a slave, to bear a greater grant than this.
OEDIPUS   How then could he return to us with
	speed?
JOCASTA   It can be done. But why would you
	order this?
OEDIPUS   O lady, I fear I have said too much.
	On this account I now desire to see him.
JOCASTA   Then he shall come. But I myself deserve
	To learn what it is the troubles you, my
		lord. 770
OEDIPUS   And you shall not be prevented, since
	my fears
	Have come to such a point. For who is closer
	That I may speak to in this fate than you?
	Polybus of Corinth was my father,
	My mother, Dorian Merope. I was held there
	Chief citizen of all, till such a fate
	Befell me—as it is, worthy of wonder,
	But surely not deserving my excitement.
	A man at a banquet overdrunk with wine
	Said in drink I was a false son to my father. 780
	The weight I held that day I scarcely bore,
	But on the next day I went home and asked
	My father and mother of it. In bitter anger
	They took the reproach from him who had let
		it fly.
	I was pleased at their actions; nevertheless
	The rumour always rankled; and spread abroad.
	In secret from mother and father I set out
	Toward Delphi. Phoebus sent me away
		ungraced
	In what I came for, but other wretched things
	Terrible and grievous, he revealed in
		answer; 790
	That I must wed my mother and produce
	An unendurable race for men to see,
	That I should kill the father who begot me.
	When I heard this response, Corinth I fled
	Henceforth to measure her land by stars alone.
	I went where I should never see the disgrace

Of my evil oracles be brought to pass,
And on my journey to that place I came
At which you say this king had met his death.
My wife, I shall speak the truth to you. My
	way 800
Led to a place close by the triple road.
There a herald met me, and a man
Seated on colt-drawn chariot, as you said.
There both the guide and the old man himself
Thrust me with driving force out of the path.
And I in anger struck the one who pushed me,
The driver. Then the old man, when he saw
	me,
Watched when I passed, and from his chariot
Struck me full on the head with double goad.
I paid him back and more. From this very
	hand 810
A swift blow of my staff rolled him right out
Of the middle of his seat onto his back.
I killed them all. But if relationship
Existed between this stranger and Laius,
What man now is wretcheder than I?
What man is cursed by a more evil fate?
No stranger or citizen could now receive me
Within his home, or even speak to me,
But thrust me out; and no one but myself
Brought down these curses on my head.   820
The bed of the slain man I now defile
With hands that killed him. Am I evil by birth?
Am I not utterly vile if I must flee
And cannot see my family in my flight
Nor tread my homeland soil, or else be joined
In marriage to my mother, kill my father,
Polybus, who sired me and brought me up?
Would not a man judge right to say of me
That this was sent on me by some cruel spirit?
O never, holy reverence of the gods,   830
May I behold that day, but may I go
Away from mortal men, before I see
Such a stain of circumstance come to me.
CHORUS   My lord, for us these facts are full of
	dread.
	Until you hear the witness, stay in hope.
OEPIDUS   And just so much is all I have of hope,
	Only to wait until the shepherd comes.
JOCASTA   What, then, do you desire to hear him
	speak?
OEPIDUS   I will tell you, if his story is found to be
	The same as yours, I would escape the
		sorrow. 840
JOCASTA   What unusual word did you hear
	from me?
OEPIDUS   You said he said that they were highway
	robbers
	Who murdered him. Now, if he still says

The selfsame number, I could not have killed
  him,
Since one man does not equal many men.
But if he speaks of a single lonely traveller,
The scale of guilt now clearly falls to me.
JOCASTA   However, know the word was set forth
    thus
And it is not in him now to take it back;
This tale the city heard, not I alone.   850
But if he diverges from his previous story,
Even then, my lord, he could not show Laius'
    murder
To have been fulfilled properly. Apollo
Said he would die at the hands of my own son.
Surely that wretched child could not have killed
  him,
But he himself met death some time before.
Therefore, in any prophecy henceforth
I would not look to this side or to that.
OEPIDUS   Your thoughts ring true, but still let
    someone go
To summon the peasant. Do not neglect
    this.   860
JOCASTA   I shall send without delay. But let us
    enter.
I would do nothing that did not please you.

CHORUS
    Strophe A
May fate come on me as I bear
Holy pureness in all word and deed,
For which the lofty striding laws were set
    down,
Born through the heavenly air
Whereof the Olympian sky alone the father was;
No mortal spawn of mankind gave them birth,
Nor may oblivion ever lull them down;   870
Mighty in them the god is, and he does not
    age.

    Antistrophe A
Pride breeds the tyrant.
Pride, once overfilled with many things in vain,
Neither in season nor fit for man,
Scaling the sheerest height
Hurls to a dire fate
Where no foothold is found.
I pray the god may never stop the rivalry   880
That works well for the state.
The god as my protector I shall never cease to
    hold.

    Strophe B
But if a man goes forth haughty in word or deed
With no fear of the Right
Nor pious to the spirits' shrines,

May evil doom seize him
For his ill-fated pride,
If he does not fairly win his gain
Or works unholy deeds,   890
Or, in bold folly lays on the sacred profane
    hands.
For when such acts occur, what man may boast
Ever to ward off from his life darts of the gods?
If practices like these are in respect,
Why then must I dance the sacred dance?

    Antistrophe B
Never again in worship shall I go
To Delphi, holy navel of the earth,
Nor to the temple at Abae,
Nor to Olympia,   900
If these prophecies do not become
Examples for all men.
O Zeus, our king, if so you are rightly called,
Ruler of all things, may they not escape
You and your forever deathless power.
Men now hold light the fading oracles
Told about Laius long ago
And nowhere is Apollo clearly honored;
Things divine are going down to ruin.   910

JOCASTA   Lords of this land, the thought has come
    to me
To visit the spirits' shrines, bearing in hand
These suppliant boughs and offerings of incense.
For Oedipus raises his soul too high
With all distresses; nor, as a sane man should,
Does he confirm the new by things of old,
But stands at the speaker's will if he speaks
    terrors.
And so, because my advice can do no more,
To you, Lycian Apollo—for you are nearest—
A suppliant, I have come here with these
    prayers,   920
That you may find some pure deliverance for
    us:
We all now shrink to see him struck in fear,
That man who is the pilot of our ship.
MESSENGER   Strangers, could I learn from one of
    you
Where is the house of Oedipus the king?
Or best, if you know, say where he is himself.
CHORUS   This is his house, stranger; he dwells
    inside;
This woman is the mother of his children.
MESSENGER   May she be always blessed among the
    blest,
Since she is the fruitful wife of Oedipus.   930
JOCASTA   So may you, stranger, also be. You
    deserve
As much for your graceful greeting. But tell me

What you have come to search for or to show.

MESSENGER   Good news for your house and your husband, lady.

JOCASTA   What is it then? And from whom have you come?

MESSENGER   From Corinth. And the message I will tell
Will surely gladden you—and vex you, perhaps.

JOCASTA   What is it? What is this double force it holds?

MESSENGER   The men who dwell in the Isthmian country
Have spoken to establish him their king.   940

JOCASTA   What is that? Is not old Polybus still ruling?

MESSENGER   Not he. For death now holds him in the tomb.

JOCASTA   What do you say, old man? Is Polybus dead?

MESSENGER   If I speak not the truth, I am ready to die.

JOCASTA   O handmaid, go right away and tell your master
The news. Where are you, prophecies of the gods?
For this man Oedipus has trembled long,
And shunned him lest he kill him. Now the man
Is killed by fate and not by Oedipus.

OEPIDUS   O Jocasta, my most beloved wife,   950
Why have you sent for me within the house?

JOCASTA   Listen to this man, and while you hear him, think
To what have come Apollo's holy prophecies.

OEPIDUS   Who is this man? Why would he speak to me?

JOCASTA   From Corinth he has come, to announce that your father
Polybus no longer lives, but is dead.

OEPIDUS   What do you say, stranger? Tell me this yourself.

MESSENGER   If I must first announce my message clearly,
Know surely that the man is dead and gone.

OEPIDUS   Did he die by treachery or chance disease?   960

MESSENGER   A slight scale tilt can lull the old to rest.

OEDIPUS   The poor man, it seems, died by disease.

MESSENGER   And by the full measure of lengthy time.

OEDIPUS   Alas, alas! Why then do any seek
Pytho's prophetic art, my wife, or hear
The shrieking birds on high, by whose report
I was to slay my father? Now he lies

Dead beneath the earth, and here am I
Who have not touched the blade. Unless in longing
For me he died, and in this sense was killed by me.   970
Polybus has packed away these oracles
In his rest in Hades. They are now worth nothing.

JOCASTA   Did I not tell you that some time ago?

OEDIPUS   You did, but I was led astray by fear.

JOCASTA   Henceforth put nothing of this on your heart.

OEDIPUS   Why must I not still shrink from my mother's bed?

JOCASTA   What should man fear, whose life is ruled by fate,
For whom there is clear foreknowledge of nothing?
It is best to live by chance, however you can.
Be not afraid of marriage with your mother;   980
Already many mortals in their dreams
Have shared their mother's bed. But he who counts
This dream as nothing, easiest bears his life.

OEDIPUS   All that you say would be indeed propitious,
If my mother were not alive. But since she is,
I still must shrink, however well you speak.

JOCASTA   And yet your father's tomb is a great eye.

OEDIPUS   A great eye indeed. But I fear her who lives.

MESSENGER   Who is this woman that you are afraid of?

OEDIPUS   Merope, old man, with whom Polybus lived.   990

MESSENGER   What is it in her that moves you to fear?

OEDIPUS   A dread oracle, stranger, sent by the god.

MESSENGER   Can it be told, or must no other know?

OEDIPUS   It surely can. Apollo told me once
That I must join in intercourse with my mother
And shed with my own hands my father's blood.
Because of this, long since I have kept far
Away from Corinth—and happily—but yet
It would be most sweet to see my parents' faces.

MESSENGER   Was this your fear in shunning your own city?   1000

OEDIPUS   I wished, too, old man, not to slay my father.

MESSENGER   Why then have I not freed you from this fear,

Since I have come with friendly mind, my lord?

OEDIPUS   Yes, and take thanks from me, which you deserve.

MESSENGER   And this is just the thing for which I came,
That when you got back home I might fare well.

OEDIPUS   Never shall I go where my parents are.

MESSENGER   My son, you clearly know not what you do.

OEDIPUS   How is that, old man? By the gods, let me know.

MESSENGER   If for these tales you shrink from going home.   1010

OEDIPUS   I tremble lest what Phoebus said comes true.

MESSENGER   Lest you incur pollution from your parents?

OEDIPUS   That is the thing, old man, that always haunts me.

MESSENGER   Well, do you know that surely you fear nothing?

OEDIPUS   How so? If I am the son of those who bore me.

MESSENGER   Since Polybus was no relation to you.

OEDIPUS   What do you say? Was Polybus not my father?

MESSENGER   No more than this man here but just so much.

OEDIPUS   How does he who begot me equal nothing?

MESSENGER   That man was not your father, any more than I am.

OEDIPUS   Well then, why was it he called me his son?   1020

MESSENGER   Long ago he got you as a gift from me.

OEDIPUS   Though from another's hand, yet so much he loved me!

MESSENGER   His previous childlessness led him to that.

OEDIPUS   Had you bought or found me when you gave me to him?

MESSENGER   I found you in Cithaeron's folds and glens.

OEDIPUS   Why were you travelling in those regions?

MESSENGER   I guarded there a flock of mountain sheep.

OEDIPUS   Were you a shepherd, wandering for pay?

MESSENGER   Yes, and your saviour too, child, at that time   1030

OEDIPUS   What pain gripped me, that you took me in your arms?

MESSENGER   The ankles of your feet will tell you that.

OEDIPUS   Alas, why do you mention that old trouble?

MESSENGER   I freed you when your ankles were pierced together.

OEDIPUS   A terrible shame from my swaddling clothes I got.

MESSENGER   Your very name you got from this misfortune.

OEDIPUS   By the gods, did my mother or father do it? Speak.

MESSENGER   I know not. He who gave you knows better than I.

OEDIPUS   You didn't find me, but took me from another?

MESSENGER   That's right. Another shepherd gave you to me.   1040

OEDIPUS   Who was he? Can you tell me who he was?

MESSENGER   Surely. He belonged to the household of Laius.

OEDIPUS   The man who ruled this land once long ago?

MESSENGER   Just so. He was a herd in that man's service.

OEDIPUS   Is this man still alive, so I could see him?

MESSENGER   You dwellers in this country should know best.

OEDIPUS   Is there any one of you who stand before me
Who knows the shepherd of whom this man speaks?
If you have seen him in the fields or here,
Speak forth; the time has come to find this out.   1050

CHORUS   I think the man you seek is no one else
Than the shepherd you were so eager to see before.
Jocasta here might best inform us that.

OEDIPUS   My wife, do you know the man we just ordered
To come here? Is it of him that this man speaks?

JOCASTA   Why ask of whom he spoke? Think nothing of it.
Brood not in vain on what has just been said.

OEDIPUS   It could not be that when I have got such clues,
I should not shed clear light upon my birth.

JOCASTA   Don't, by the gods, investigate this more   1060
If you care for your own life. I am sick enough.

OEDIPUS   Take courage. Even if I am found a slave
For three generations, your birth will not be base.

JOCASTA   Still, I beseech you, hear me. Don't do this.

OEDIPUS   I will hear of nothing but finding out the truth.

JOCASTA   I know full well and tell you what is best.

OEDIPUS   Well, then, this best, for some time now, has given me pain.

JOCASTA   O ill-fated man, may you never know who you are.

OEDIPUS   Will someone bring the shepherd to me here?

And let this lady rejoice in her opulent birth.   1070

JOCASTA   Alas, alas, hapless man. I have this alone
To tell you, and nothing else forevermore.

CHORUS   O Oedipus, where has the woman gone
In the rush of her wild grief? I am afraid
Evil will break forth out of this silence.

OEDIPUS   Let whatever will break forth. I plan to see
The seed of my descent, however small.
My wife, perhaps, because a noblewoman
Looks down with shame upon my lowly birth.
I would not be dishonoured to call myself
The son of Fortune, giver of the good.   1080
She is my mother. The years, her other children,
Have marked me sometimes small and sometimes great.
Such was I born! I shall prove no other man,
Nor shall I cease to search out my descent.

CHORUS

Strophe

If I am a prophet and can know in mind,
Cithaeron, by tomorrow's full moon   1090
You shall not fail, by mount Olympus,
To find that Oedipus, as a native of your land,
Shall honour you for nurse and mother.
And to you we dance in choral song because you bring
Fair gifts to him our king.
Hail, Phoebus, may all this please you.

Antistrophe

Who, child, who bore you in the lengthy span of years?
One close to Pan who roams the mountain woods,   1100
One of Apollo's bedfellows?
For all wild pastures in mountain glens to him are dear.
Was Hermes your father, who Cyllene sways,
Or did Bacchus, dwelling on the mountain peaks,

Take you a foundling from some nymph
Of those by springs of Helicon, with whom he sports the most?

OEDIPUS   If I may guess, although I never met him,   1110
I think, elders, I see that shepherd coming
Whom we have long sought, as in the measure
Of lengthy age he accords with him we wait for.
Besides, the men who lead him I recognize
As servants of my house. You may perhaps
Know better than I if you have seen him before.

CHORUS   Be assured, I know him as a shepherd
As trusted as any other in Laius' service.

OEDIPUS   Stranger from Corinth, I will ask you first,
Is this the man you said?

MESSENGER   You are looking at him.   1120

OEDIPUS   You there, old man, look here and answer me
What I shall ask you. Were you ever with Laius?

SERVANT   I was a slave, not bought but reared at home.

OEDIPUS   What work concerned you? What was your way of life?

SERVANT   Most of my life I spent among the flocks.

OEDIPUS   In what place most of all was your usual pasture?

SERVANT   Sometimes Cithaeron, or the ground nearby.

OEDIPUS   Do you know this man before you here at all?

SERVANT   Doing what? And of what man do you speak?

OEDIPUS   The one before you. Have you ever had congress with him?   1130

SERVANT   Not to say so at once from memory.

MESSENGER   That is no wonder, master, but I shall remind him,
Clearly, who knows me not; yet will I know
That he knew once the region of Cithaeron.
He with a double flock and I with one
Dwelt there in company for three whole years
During the six months' time from spring to fall.
When winter came, I drove into my fold
My flock, and he drove his to Laius' pens.
Do I speak right, or did it not happen so?   1140

SERVANT   You speak the truth, though it was long ago.

MESSENGER   Come now, do you recall you gave me then
A child for me to rear as my own son?

SERVANT   What is that? Why do you ask me this?

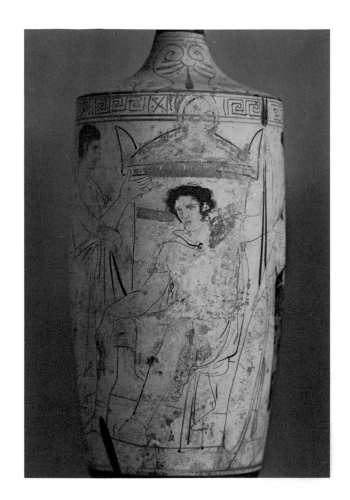

right: Plate 9 Reed Painter. *Warrior Seated at His Tomb*. Late 5th century B.C. White-ground lekythos, height 18⅞″ (48 cm). National Archaeological Museum, Athens. A youth is at one side. On the other side is a young woman who holds the warrior's shield and helmet.

below: Plate 10 Temple of Athena Nike, Athens. 427–424 B.C. This is the view approaching the Acropolis from the southwest, with the temple to the right and the Propylaea to the left.

left: **Plate 11** Praxiteles. *Hermes with the Infant Dionysus.*
c. 340 B.C. Marble, height 7′1″ (2.16 m). Museum, Olympia.
Hermes' missing right arm held a bunch of grapes just out of
the baby's reach.

below: **Plate 12** *Dionysus on a Panther,* from the House of
Masks, Delos. 2nd century B.C. Mosaic, 42⅛″ (108 cm) square.
By careful use of foreshortening and shading the artist creates
an astonishingly three-dimensional effect.

MESSENGER   This is the man, my friend, who then
     was young.
SERVANT   Go to destruction! Will you not be
     quiet?
OEDIPUS   Come, scold him not, old man. These
     words of yours
   Deserve a scolding more than this man's do.
SERVANT   In what, most noble master, do I wrong?
OEDIPUS   Not to tell of the child he asks
     about.   1150
SERVANT   He speaks in ignorance, he toils in vain.
OEDIPUS   If you will not speak freely, you will
     under torture.
SERVANT   Don't, by the gods, outrage an old man
     like me.
OEDIPUS   Will someone quickly twist back this
     fellow's arms?
SERVANT   Alas, what for? What do you want to
     know?
OEDIPUS   Did you give this man the child of
     whom he asks?
SERVANT   I did. Would I had perished on that day!
OEDIPUS   You will come to that unless you tell the
     truth.
SERVANT   I come to far greater ruin if I speak.
OEDIPUS   This man, it seems, is trying
     to delay.   1160
SERVANT   Not I. I said before I gave it to him.
OEDIPUS   Where did you get it? At home or from
     someone else?
SERVANT   It was not mine. I got him from a man.
OEDIPUS   Which of these citizens? Where did he
     live?
SERVANT   O master, by the gods, ask me no more.
OEDIPUS   You are done for if I ask you this again.
SERVANT   Well then, he was born of the house of
     Laius.
OEDIPUS   One of his slaves, or born of his own
     race?
SERVANT   Alas, to speak I am on the brink of
     horror.
OEDIPUS   And I to hear. But still it must
     be heard.   1170
SERVANT   Well, then, they say it was his child.
     Your wife
   Who dwells within could best say how this
     stands.
OEDIPUS   Was it she who gave him to you?
SERVANT   Yes, my lord.
OEDIPUS   For what intent?
SERVANT   So I could put it away.
OEDIPUS   When she bore him, the wretch.
SERVANT   She feared bad oracles.
OEDIPUS   What were they?
SERVANT   They said he should kill his father.

OEDIPUS   Why did you give him up to this old
     man?
SERVANT   I pitied him, master, and thought he
     would take him away
   To another land, the one from which he came.
   But he saved him for greatest woe. If you are
     he   1180
   Whom this man speaks of, you were born
     curst by fate.
OEDIPUS   Alas, alas! All things are now come true.
   O light, for the last time now I look upon you;
   I am shown to be born from those I ought not
     to have been.
   I married the woman I should not have married,
   I killed the man whom I should not have killed.

CHORUS
   Strophe A
   Alas, generations of mortal men!
   How equal to nothing do I number you in life!
   Who, O who, is the man
   Who bears more of bliss   1190
   Than just the seeming so,
   And then, like a waning sun, to fall away?
   When I know your example,
   Your guiding spirit, yours, wretched Oedipus,
   I call no mortal blest.

   Antistrophe A
   He is the one, O Zeus,
   Who peerless shot his bow and won well-fated
     bliss,
   Who destroyed the hook-clawed maiden,
   The oracle-singing Sphinx,   1200
   And stood a tower for our land from death;
   For this you are called our king,
   Oedipus, are highest-honoured here,
   And over great Thebes hold sway.

   Strophe B
   And now who is more wretched for men to
     hear,
   Who so lives in wild plagues, who dwells in
     pains,
   In utter change of life?
   Alas for glorious Oedipus!
   The selfsame port of rest
   Was gained by bridegroom father and his
     son,   1210
   How, O how did your father's furrows ever
     bear you, suffering man?
   How have they endured silence for so long?

   Antistrophe B
   You are found out, unwilling, by all seeing
     Time.

It judges your unmarried marriage where for
    long
Begetter and begot have been the same.
Alas, child of Laius,
Would I had never seen you.
As one who pours from his mouth a dirge I
    wail,
To speak the truth, through you I breathed new
    life,   1220
And now through you I lulled my eye to sleep.
SECOND MESSENGER   O men most honoured always
    of this land
What deeds you shall hear, what shall you
    behold!
What grief shall stir you up, if by your kinship
You are still concerned for the house of
    Labdacus!
I think neither Danube nor any other river
Could wash this palace clean, so many ills
Lie hidden there which now will come to light.
They were done by will, not fate; and sorrows
    hurt   1230
The most when we ourselves appear to choose
    them.
CHORUS   What we heard before causes no little
    sorrow.
What can you say which adds to that a burden?
SECOND MESSENGER   This is the fastest way to tell
    the tale;
Hear it: Jocasta, your divine queen, is dead.
CHORUS   O sorrowful woman! From what cause
    did she die?
SECOND MESSENGER   By her own hand. The most
    painful of the action
Occurred away, not for your eyes to see.
But still, so far as I have memory
You shall learn the sufferings of that wretched
    woman: 1240
How she passed on through the door enraged
And rushed straight forward to her nuptial bed,
Clutching her hair's ends with both her hands.
Once inside the doors she shut herself in
And called on Laius, who has long been dead,
Having remembrance of their seed of old
By which he died himself and left her a mother
To bear an evil brood to his own son.
She moaned the bed on which by double curse
She bore husband to husband, children
    to child.   1250
How thereafter she perished I do not know,
For Oedipus burst in on her with a shriek,
And because of him we could not see her woe.
We looked on him alone as he rushed around.
Pacing about, he asked us to give him a sword,
Asked where he might find the wife no wife,

A mother whose plowfield bore him and his
    children.
Some spirit was guiding him in his frenzy,
For none of the men who are close at hand did
    so.
With a horrible shout, as if led on by
    someone,   1260
He leapt on the double doors, from their
    sockets
Broke hollow bolts aside, and dashed within.
There we beheld his wife hung by her neck
From twisted cords, swinging to and fro.
When he saw her, wretched man, he terribly
    groaned
And slackened the hanging noose. When the
    poor woman
Lay on the ground, what happened was dread
    to see.
He tore the golden brooch pins from her
    clothes,
And raised them up, and struck his own
    eyeballs,   1270
Shouting such words as these "No more shall
    you
Behold the evils I have suffered and done.
Be dark from now on, since you saw before
What you should not, and knew not what you
    should."
Moaning such cries, not once but many times
He raised and struck his eyes. The bloody
    pupils
Bedewed his beard. The gore oozed not in
    drops,
But poured in a black shower, a hail of blood.
From both of them these woes have broken
    out,   1280
Not for just one, but man and wife together.
The bliss of old that formerly prevailed
Was bliss indeed, but now upon this day
Lamentation, madness, death, and shame—
No evil that can be named is not at hand.
CHORUS   Is the wretched man in any rest now
    from pain?
SECOND MESSENGER   He shouts for someone to
    open up the doors
And show to all Cadmeans his father's slayer,
His mother's—I should not speak the unholy
    word.
He says he will hurl himself from the land, no
    more   1290
To dwell cursed in the house by his own curse.
Yet he needs strength and someone who will
    guide him.
His sickness is too great to bear. He will show
    it to you

For the fastenings of the doors are opening up,
And such a spectacle you will soon behold
As would make even one who abhors it take
    pity.
CHORUS   O terrible suffering for men to see,
Most terrible of all that I
Have ever come upon. O wretched man,
What madness overcame you, what springing
    daimon   1300
Greater than the greatest for men
Has caused your evil-daimoned fate?
Alas, alas, grievous one,
But I cannot bear to behold you, though I
    desire
To ask you much, much to find out,
Much to see,
You make me shudder so!
OEDIPUS   Alas, alas, I am grieved!
Where on earth, so wretched, shall I go?
Where does my voice fly through the air,   1310
O Fate, where have you bounded?
CHORUS   To dreadful end, not to be heard or seen.

Strophe A
OEDIPUS   O cloud of dark
That shrouds me off, has come to pass,
    unspeakable,
Invincible, that blows no favoring blast.
Woe,
O woe again, the goad that pierces me,
Of the sting of evil now, and memory of
    before.
CHORUS   No wonder it is that among so many
    pains
You should both mourn and bear a double
    evil.   1320

Antistrophe A
OEDIPUS   Ah, friend,
You are my steadfast servant still,
You still remain to care for me, blind.
Alas! Alas!
You are not hid from me; I know you clearly,
And though in darkness, still I hear your voice.
CHORUS   O dreadful doer, how did you so endure
To quench your eyes? What daimon drove you
    on?

Strophe B
OEDIPUS   Apollo it was, Apollo, friends
Who brought to pass these evil, evil woes of
    mine.   1330
The hand of no one struck my eyes but
    wretched me.
For why should I see,
When nothing sweet there is to see with sight?
CHORUS   This is just as you say.

OEDIPUS   What more is there for me to see,
My friends, what to love,
What joy to hear a greeting?
Lead me at once away from here,   1340
Lead me away, friends, wretched as I am,
Accursed, and hated most
Of mortals to the gods.
CHORUS   Wretched alike in mind and in your
    fortune,
How I wish that I had never known you.

Antistrophe B
OEDIPUS   May he perish, whoever freed me
From fierce bonds on my feet,   1350
Snatched me from death and saved me, doing
    me no joy.
For if then I had died, I should not be
So great a grief to friends and to myself.
CHORUS   This also is my wish.
OEDIPUS   I would not have come to murder my
    father,
Nor have been called among men
The bridegroom of her from whom I was born.
But as it is I am godless, child of
    unholiness,   1360
Wretched sire in common with my father.
And if there is any evil older than evil left,
It is the lot of Oedipus.
CHORUS   I know not how I could give you good
    advice,
For you would be better dead than living blind.
OEDIPUS   That how things are was not done for
    the best—
Teach me not this, or give me more
    advice.   1370
If I had sight, I know not with what eyes
I could ever face my father among the dead,
Or my wretched mother. What I have done to
    them
Is too great for a noose to expiate.
Do you think the sight of my children would
    be a joy
For me to see, born as they were to me?
No, never for these eyes of mine to see.
Nor the city, nor the tower, nor the sacred
Statues of gods; of these I deprive myself,
Noblest among the Thebans, born and
    bred,   1380
Now suffering everything. I tell you all
To exile me as impious, shown by the gods
Untouchable and of the race of Laius.
When I uncovered such a stain on me,
Could I look with steady eyes upon the people?
No, No! And if there were a way to block
The spring of hearing, I would not forbear
To lock up wholly this my wretched body.

I should be blind and deaf.—For it is sweet
When thought can dwell outside our evils.   1390
Alas, Cithaeron, why did you shelter me?
Why did you not take and kill me at once, so I
Might never reveal to men whence I was born?
O Polybus, O Corinth, O my father's halls,
Ancient in fable, what an outer fairness,
A festering of evils, you raised in me.
For now I am evil found, and born of evil.
O the three paths! Alas the hidden glen,
The grove of oak, the narrow triple roads
That drank from my own hands my father's
      blood.   1400
Do you remember any of the deeds
I did before you then on my way here
And what I after did? O wedlock, wedlock!
You gave me birth, and then spawned in return
Issue from the selfsame seed; you revealed
Father, brother, children, in blood relation,
The bride both wife and mother, and whatever
Actions are done most shameful among men.
But it is wrong to speak what is not good to
      do.
By the gods, hide me at once outside our
      land,   1410
Or murder me, or hurl me in the sea
Where you shall never look on me again.
Come, venture to lay your hands on this
      wretched man.
Do it. Be not afraid. No mortal man
There is, except myself, to bear my evils.
CHORUS   Here is Creon, just in time for what you
      ask
   To work and to advise, for he alone
   Is left in place of you to guard the land.
OEDIPUS   Alas, what word, then, shall I tell this
      man?
   What righteous ground of trust is clear
      in me,   1420
   As in the past in all I have done him evil?
CREON   Oedipus, I have not come to laugh at you,
   Nor to reproach you for your former wrongs.
      (To the attendants)
   If you defer no longer to mortal offspring,
   Respect at least the all-nourishing flame
   Of Apollo, lord of the sun. Fear to display
   So great a pestilence, which neither earth
   Nor holy rain nor light will well receive.
   But you, conduct him to the house at once.
   It is most pious for the kin alone   1430
   To hear and to behold the family sins.
OEDIPUS   By the gods, since you have plucked me
      from my fear,
   Most noble, facing this most vile man,
   Hear me one word—I will speak for you, not me.

CREON   What desire do you so persist to get?
OEDIPUS   As soon as you can, hurl me from this
      land
   To where no mortal man will ever greet me.
CREON   I would do all this, be sure. But I want
      first
   To find out from the god what must be done.
OEDIPUS   His oracle, at least, is wholly clear;   1440
   Leave me to ruin, an impious parricide.
CREON   Thus spake the oracle. Still, as we stand
   It is better to find out sure what we should do.
OEDIPUS   Will you inquire about so wretched a
      man?
CREON   Yes. You will surely put trust in the god.
OEDIPUS   I order you and beg you, give the
      woman
   Now in the house such burial as you yourself
   Would want. Do last rites justly for your kin.
   But may this city never be condemned—
   My father's realm—because I live within.   1450
   Let me live in the mountains where Cithaeron
   Yonder has fame of me, which father and
      mother
   When they were alive established as my
      tomb.
   There I may die by those who sought to kill
      me.
   And yet this much I know, neither a sickness
   Nor anything else can kill me. I would not
   Be saved from death, except for some dread
      evil.
   Well, let my fate go wherever it may.
   As for my sons, Creon, assume no trouble;
   They are men and will have no difficulty   1460
   Of living wherever they may be.
   O my poor grievous daughters, who never
      knew
   Their dinner table set apart from me,
   But always shared in everything I touched—
   Take care of them for me, and first of all
   Allow me to touch them and bemoan our ills.
   Grant it, lord,
   Grant it, noble. If with my hand I touch
      them
   I would think I had them just as when I could
      see.   1470

      (Creon's attendants bring in ANTIGONE
      and ISMENE.)

What's that?
By the gods, can it be I hear my dear ones
      weeping?
And have you taken pity on me, Creon?
Have you had my darling children sent to me?
Do I speak right?

CREON   You do. For it was I who brought them here,
Knowing this present joy your joy of old.
OEDIPUS   May you fare well. For their coming may the spirit
That watches over you be better than mine.
My children, where are you? Come to me, come   1480
Into your brother's hands, that brought about
Your father's eyes, once bright, to see like this.
Your father, children, who, seeing and knowing nothing,
Became a father whence he was got himself.
I weep also for you—I cannot see you—
To think of the bitter life in days to come
Which you will have to lead among mankind.
What citizens' gatherings will you approach?
What festivals attend, where you will not cry   1490
When you go home, instead of gay rejoicing?
And when you arrive at marriageable age,
What man, my daughters, will there be to chance you,
Incurring such reproaches on his head,
Disgraceful to my children and to yours?
What evil will be absent, when your father
Killed his own father, sowed seed in her who bore him,
From whom he was born himself, and equally
Has fathered you whence he himself was born.
Such will be the reproaches. Who then will wed you?   1500
My children, there is no one for you. Clearly
You must decay in barrenness, unwed.
Son of Menoeceus—since you are alone
Left as a father to them, for we who produced them
Are both in ruin—see that you never let
These girls wander as beggars without husbands,
Let them not fall into such woes as mine.
But pity them, seeing how young they are
To be bereft of all except your aid.
Grant this, my noble friend, with a touch of your hand.   1510
My children, if your minds were now mature,
I would give you much advice. But, pray this for me,
To live as the time allows, to find a life
Better than that your siring father had.
CREON   You have wept enough here, come, and go inside the house.
OEDIPUS   I must obey, though nothing sweet.

CREON   All things are good in their time.
OEDIPUS   Do you know in what way I go?
CREON   Tell me, I'll know when I hear.
OEDIPUS   Send me outside the land.
CREON   You ask what the god will do.
OEDIPUS   But to the gods I am hated.
CREON   Still, it will soon be done.
OEDIPUS   Then you agree?
CREON   What I think not I would not say in vain.   1520
OEDIPUS   Now lead me away.
CREON   Come then, but let the children go.
OEDIPUS   Do not take them from me.
CREON   Wish not to govern all,
For what you ruled will not follow you through life.
CHORUS   Dwellers in native Thebes, behold this Oedipus
Who solved the famous riddle, was your mightiest man.
What citizen on his lot did not with envy gaze?
See to how great a surge of dread fate he has come!
So I would say a mortal man, while he is watching
To see the final day, can have no happiness
Till he pass the bound of life, nor be relieved of pain.   1530

Euripides

The significance for the Athenians themselves of the Chorus' final message at the end of *Oedipus the King,* warning against the dangers of success, emerges in full force in the work of Euripides (c. 484–406 B.C.). Although only a little younger than Sophocles, Euripides expresses all the weariness and disillusion of the war-torn years at the end of the 5th century B.C. Of all the tragedians he is perhaps the closest to our own time, with his concern for realism and his determination to expose social, political, and religious injustices.

Although Euripides admits the existence of irrational forces in the universe which can be personified in the form of gods and goddesses, he certainly does not regard them as worthy of respect and worship. This skepticism won him the charge of impiety. His plays show characters frequently pushed to the limits of endurance; their reactions show a new concern for psychological truth. In particular, Euripides exhibits a profound sympathy and understanding for the problems of women who live in a society dominated by men. Characters like Medea and Phaedra challenge many of the basic premises of contemporary Athenian society.

Euripides' deepest hatred is reserved for war and its senseless misery. Like the other dramatists he draws the subject matter of his plays from traditional myths, but the lines delivered by the actors must have sounded in their hearers' ears with a terrible relevance. *The Suppliant Women* was probably written in 421 B.C., when ten years of indecisive fighting had produced nothing but an uneasy truce. Its subject is the recovery by Theseus, ruler of Athens, of the bodies of seven chiefs killed fighting at Thebes in order to return them to their families for burial. He yields to their mothers—the women of the title—who beg him to recover the bodies. The audience would have little need to be reminded of the grief of wives and mothers or of the kind of political processes which produced years of futile fighting. Ironically enough, Euripides puts some of the most perceptive comments into the mouth of a Theban herald, the representative of forces hostile to Theseus, the hero of the play. The herald presents the arguments against war briefly but convincingly. Indeed, they retain their force for us today; the gap between the ballot box and the realities of political action is certainly still a feature of all democratic systems of government.

Euripides
from THE SUPPLIANT WOMEN

Think carefully, and do not grow enraged at my
Advice, because you rule a city that is free,
And in exchange of heated words flex muscles
    too.
The hope that springs from arms is unreliable
As many cities have learned in their excess
    of wrath.
For when war comes to be put to vote before
    the folk,   480
No one weighs carefully the thought of his
    own death;
He turns aside to others this calamity.
But if death stood before our eyes on voting
    day,
Spear-crazy Greece would never be at brink
    of ruin.
And yet of these two words—the good, the bad—
    we men,
All of us, know which is the better and how
    much

More good peace gives to mortal souls
    than bloody war.
Peace, the first and best beloved by all the Muses,
But hateful to the Avengers, loves to have
    good children,
Loves to have wealth; we evil fools discard
    them both   490
Whenever we choose war, enslaving men and
    cities.

The Theban's appeal to common sense is rejected, however. After a violent campaign Theseus brings back the dead and returns them to their mothers and children. The subsequent scene of mourning, among the most harrowing in Greek tragedy, reveals Euripides' ability to identify with the point of view of women. Unlike Aeschylus and Sophocles, whose works are dominated by strong female figures like Clytemnestra, Electra, and Jocasta, Euripides brings us closer to the grief of ordinary wives and mothers who, together with their children, are perhaps the true victims of war.

Euripides
from THE SUPPLIANT WOMEN

CHORUS Oh, oh!
    Here are the bones of my dead sons;
    They're carried here; take me, handmaidens,
    Old, strengthless woman—there's no force
        Left in me, for I grieve.
    I've lived a long time, but I'm pining   1110
    Away in death because of sorrow.
    What greater suffering can you find
    Than this for mortals,
        To look on children dead?
BOYS I bring, I bring,
    Poor mother, father's bones from the fire,
    A weight not light because of woes.
        I put my all in a little space.
CHORUS Oh, oh!
    Where do you bring what calls the
        tears   1120
        To a mother dear of the ones who died?
    A little heap of ash instead of bodies
        Once famous in Mycenae?
BOYS Childless, childless!
    And I am wretched, bereft of my poor
        father,
    I shall be orphaned in a barren home,
        Not cherished in my father's hands.
CHORUS Oh, oh!
    Where is my childbirth labor?
    Where is the joy of marriages?   1130
    The care a mother gives, her sleepless vigils,
    Sweet kisses on the mouth?

BOYS They're gone, they are no more; oimoi,
        my father!
    They're gone.
CHORUS The air above us holds them now,
    Melted to ash of fire,
    They've winged their way to Hades.
BOYS Father, don't you hear your children's
        moans?
    Shall I ever, shield on arm, avenge your
        death?
    May justice for my father come, god
        willing.
CHORUS Not yet does evil sleep.   1140
    Ah woes! Enough of sorrow,
    Enough of pain there is for me.
BOYS The waters of Asopus will yet receive
        me,
    A general of the Danaids in brazen armor,
    Avenger of my dead father.
    I seem to see you still, father, before my
        eyes . . .
CHORUS Placing a sweet kiss upon your cheek.
BOYS And the bracing courage of your words
    Is gone, borne in the air.
CHORUS The grief of two he left his
        mother.   1150
    But grief for your father will never leave
        you.
BOYS I have so great a weight that it has killed
        me.
CHORUS Come, I shall sprinkle the beloved
        dust around my breast.
BOYS I weep as I hear this word,
    Most hateful; it has touched my heart.
CHORUS O child, you have gone; no more
    Shall I look on you, the dear delight of a
        mother.

Yet even this sorrow is not allowed to bring the
violence to an end. In the very last scene of the play
the goddess Athena appears and, far from announc-
ing peace, proclaims instead that the descendants of
the dead warriors will in turn mount an expedition
against Thebes to avenge their fathers. The optimism
of Aeschylus has been entirely reversed in this vision
of continuing bloodshed, as inevitable as it is devastating.

If Aeschylus' belief in human progress is more
noble, Euripides is certainly more realistic. Although
unpopular in his own time, he later became the most
widely read of the three tragedians. As a result, more
of his plays have been preserved (nineteen in all),
plays with a wide range of emotional expression.
They extend from romantic comedies like *Helen* and

Iphigenia in Taurus to the profoundly disturbing
Bacchae, his last completed play, in which Euripides
the rationalist explores the inadequacy of reason as
the sole approach to life. In this acknowledgment of
the power of emotion to overwhelm the order and
balance so typical of the Classical ideal, he is most
clearly speaking for his times.

Aristophanes

Euripides was not, of course, the only Athenian to
realize the futility of war. The plays of Aristophanes
(c. 450–385 B.C.), the greatest comic poet of 5th-
century B.C. Athens, deal with the same theme. His
work combines political satire with a strong vein of
fantasy.

In *The Birds,* produced in 414 B.C., two Athenians
decide to leave their city and find a better place to
live. They join forces with the birds and build a new
city in mid-air called Cloudcuckooland. But the city
cuts off contact between gods and humans by blocking the path of the steam rising from sacrifices. The
gods are forced to come to terms with the new city
and Zeus hands over his scepter of authority to the
birds.

This is simple escapism, but *Lysistrata,* written a
few years later, in 411 B.C., deals with the problem of
how to prevent war in a more practical fashion. In the
course of the play the main protagonist, Lysistrata,
persuades her fellow women of Athens to refuse to
make love with their husbands until peace is made.
At the same time her followers seize the Acropolis.
The men, teased and frustrated, finally give in and
envoys are summoned from Sparta. The play ends
with the Athenians and Spartans dancing together for
joy at the new peace which has been concluded.

The Visual Arts

Like the writers and thinkers of their time, artists of
the mid-5th century B.C. were concerned with ideas
of balance and order. Very early Classical works like
the *Critian Boy* [see 82] showed a new interest in realism, and the sculptors who came later began to explore the exciting possibilities of representing the
human body in motion.

Among the most famous 5th-century sculptors
working at Athens was Myron. Although none of his
sculptures has survived, there are a number of later
copies of one of his most famous pieces, the *Discus*

Thrower [98]. The original, which was made around 450 B.C., is typical of its age in combining realistic treatment of an action with an idealized portrayal of the athlete himself.

While striving for naturalism, artists like Myron tried also to create a new standard of human beauty by controlling the human form according to principles of proportion, symmetry, and balance. Around 440 B.C., one of the greatest of Classical sculptors, Polyclitus of Argos, devised a mathematical formula for representing the perfect male body, an ideal canon of proportion, and wrote a book about it. The idea behind *The Canon* was that ideal beauty consisted of a precise relationship between the various parts of the body. Polyclitus' book must have set forth the details of his system of proportion. To illustrate his theory, he also produced a bronze statue of a young man holding a spear, the *Doryphoros*. Both book and original statue are lost; only later copies of the *Doryphoros* survive [99].

We do not know, therefore, exactly what Polyclitus' system was. Nevertheless, we have some indication in the writings of a later philosopher, Chrysippus (c. 280–207 B.C.), who wrote that "beauty consists of the

98   Myron. *Discobolos (Discus Thrower)*. Roman copy after bronze original of c. 450 B.C. Marble, lifesize. National Museum, Rome.

proportion of the parts; of finger to finger; of all the fingers to the palm and the wrist; of those to the forearm; of the forearm to the upper arm; and of all these parts to one another, as set forth in *The Canon* of Polyclitus." Even if the exact relationships are lost, what was important about Polyclitus' ideal—and what made it so characteristic of the Classical vision as a whole—was that it depended on precisely ordered and balanced interrelationships of the various parts of the human body. Furthermore, the ideal beauty which this created was not produced by nature, but by the power of the human intellect.

99 Polyclitus. *Doryphoros (Spear Bearer)*. Roman Copy after original of c. 440 B.C. Marble, height 6'6" (1.98 m). National Museum, Naples.

100 Grave stele of Crito and Timarista. c. 420 B.C. Marble. Museum, Rhodes.

In the late 5th century B.C., sculpture and vase painting were characterized by a growing concern with the individual rather than a generalized ideal. Artists began to depict the emotional responses of ordinary people to life and death, instead of approaching these responses indirectly through the use of myths. Thus, death and mourning became increasingly common subjects.

Among the most touching works to survive from the period are a number of *lekythoi,* or oil flasks, which were used for funerary offerings [Plate 9, page 155]. They are painted with mourning or graveside scenes, on a white rather than red background. The figures are depicted with quiet and calm dignity but with considerable feeling. This personal rather than public response to death is found also on the *steles,* or gravemarkers, of the very end of the 5th century B.C., which show a grief which is perhaps resigned but still intense [100].

Architecture

In architecture, as in sculpture, designers were concerned with proportion and the interrelationship of the various parts that constitute a complete structure. Nowhere is this more apparent than in the Temple of Zeus at Olympia [101], the first great artistic achievement of the years following the Persian Wars, begun in 470 B.C. and finished by 456 B.C. By the time of its completion it was also the largest Doric temple in mainland Greece. The architect of this temple, Libon of Elis, clearly intended it to illustrate the new Classical preoccupation with proportion. The distance from the center of one column to the center of the next, called the *intercolumniation,* was the unit of measurement for the whole temple. Thus the height of each column is equal to two intercolumniations, and the combined length of a triglyph and a metope equals half an intercolumniation.

The theme of order, implicit in the architecture of the temple, became explicit in the sculpture that decorated it. At the center of the west pediment, standing calmly amidst a fight raging between Lapiths and Centaurs, was the figure of Apollo, the god of reason, exerting his authority by a single confident gesture [102].

Like the works of Aeschylus, the sculptures from Olympia express a conviction that justice will triumph and that the gods will enforce it. The art of the second half of the 5th century B.C., however, is more concerned with human achievement than divine will. Pericles' building program for the Acropolis, or citadel of Athens, represents the supreme expression in visual terms of Classical ideals [103].

This greatest of all Classical artistic achievements has a special grandeur and poignancy. The splendor of its conception and execution has survived the vicissitudes of time; the great temple to Athena, the Parthenon, remains to this day an incomparable symbol of the Golden Age of Greece. Yet it was built during years of growing division and hostility in the Greek world—the last sculpture was barely in place before the outbreak of the Peloponnesian War in 431 B.C. Pericles died in 429 B.C., but fighting and build-

opposite below: 101 Reconstruction drawing of east facade, Temple of Zeus, Olympia. c. 470–456 B.C. The pediment shows Zeus between two contestants prior to a chariot race.

right: 102 Apollo intervenes in the battle between the Lapiths and Centaurs, from the west pediment of the Temple of Zeus, Olympia. c. 470–456 B.C. Museum, Olympia.

below: 103 Model reconstruction of the Acropolis. Royal Ontario Museum, Toronto. Most of the smaller buildings no longer exist, leaving an unobstructed view of the Parthenon that was not possible in ancient times (see **91** and **104** and Plate 10).

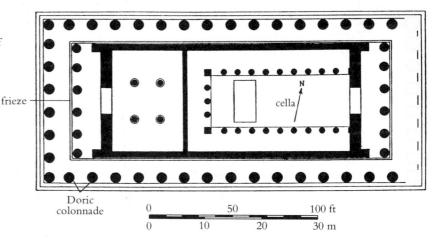

104 Ictinus and Callicrates. The Parthenon, Athens. 447–432 B.C. Height of columns 34′ (10.36 m). At right is a plan of the temple.

frieze

cella

N

Doric colonnade

0   50   100 ft
0   10   20   30 m

ing both dragged on. The Erechtheum, the final temple to be completed, was not finished until 406 B.C., two years before the end of the war and the fall of Athens. Pericles had intended the whole program to perpetuate the memory of Athens' glorious achievements, but instead it is a reminder of the gulf between Classical high ideals and the realities of political existence in 5th-century B.C. Greece.

Even the funding of the Parthenon symbolizes this gap, since it was paid for at least in part from the treasury of the Delian League (see page 131). The transfer of the League's funds to Athens in 454 B.C. clearly indicated Pericles' imperialist intentions, as did the use to which he put them. It is ironic that the supreme monument of Periclean Athens was built with money originally intended for a pan-Hellenic League. It is even more ironic that Athens' further highhanded behavior created a spirit of ill feeling and distrust throughout the Greek world which led inevitably to the outbreak of the Peloponnesian War—a war that effectively destroyed the Athenian glory that the Parthenon had been intended to symbolize.

The great outcrop of rock that forms the Acropolis was an obvious choice by Pericles for the Parthenon and the other buildings planned with it. The site, which towers above the rest of the city, had served as a center for Athenian life from Mycenaean times, when a fortress was built on it. Throughout the Archaic period a series of temples had been constructed there, the last of them destroyed by the Persians in 480 B.C.

Work on the Acropolis was begun in 449 B.C. under the direction of Phidias, the greatest sculptor of his day and a personal friend of Pericles. The Parthenon [104] was the first building to be constructed; its architects were Ictinus and Callicrates (the name of the temple comes from the Greek *parthenos,* or virgin, that is, the goddess Athena). It was built between 447 and 438 B.C.; its sculptural decoration was complete by 432 B.C. Even larger than the Temple of Zeus at Olympia, the building combines the Doric order of its columns (seventeen on the sides and eight on the ends) with some Ionic features, including a continuous running frieze inside the outer colonnade, at the top of the temple wall and inner colonnades. The design incorporates a number of refinements intended to prevent any sense of monotony or heaviness and give to the building an air of richness and grace. Like earlier Doric columns, those of the Parthenon are thickest at the point two-thirds from the top and then taper slightly to the base, a device called *entasis.* In addition, all the columns tilt slightly toward each other (it has been calculated that they would all meet if extended upward for 2 miles, or 3.2 kilometers). The columns at the corners are thicker and closer together than the others and the entablature leans outwards. The flat floor is not really flat at all but convex. All these refinements are, of course, extremely subtle and barely visible to the naked eye. The perfection of their execution, requiring incredible precision of mathematical calculation, is the highest possible tribute to the Classical search for order.

The sculptural decoration of the Parthenon occupied three parts of the building and made use of three different techniques of carving. The figures in the pediments are freestanding; the frieze is carved in low relief; the metopes are in high relief (see page 171). The Ionic frieze, 520 feet (158.6 meters) long, is carved in low relief; it depicts a procession which took place every four years on the occasion of the Great Panathenaic Festival. It shows Athenians walking and riding to the Acropolis in a ceremony during which an ancient wooden statue of Athena was presented with a new robe. The variety of movement, gesture, and rhythm achieved in the relatively limited technique of low relief makes the frieze among the greatest treasures of Greek art [105]. At the beginning of the 19th century, most of the frieze, together with

105 Equestrian group, detail of Parthenon frieze (north face). c. 442–432 B.C. Pentelic marble, height 41⅜" (106 cm). British Museum, London (reproduced by courtesy of the Trustees). The composition is elaborate but clear. The riders, with their calm, typically Classical expressions, are shown in various positions: note especially the last figure on the right.

other Parthenon sculptures, was removed from the building by the British Ambassador to Constantinople, Lord Elgin; these are now in the British Museum. (All the sculptures from the Parthenon that are in the British Museum are generally known as the Elgin Marbles.)

Equally impressive are the surviving figures from the east and west pediments, which are freestanding.

They show, respectively, the birth of Athena and her contest with Poseidon, god of the sea, to decide which of them should be patron deity of the city. They are badly damaged; even so, statues like the reclining figure known as Dionysus [106] or the group of three goddesses [107], all from the east pediment, show a combination of idealism and naturalism which has never been surpassed. The anatomy of

right: 106 *Dionysus,* from Parthenon east pediment. c. 438–432 B.C. Marble, over lifesize. British Museum, London (reproduced by courtesy of the Trustees). This reclining figure is a superb blend of relaxed naturalism and idealism.

below: 107 *Three Goddesses,* from Parthenon east pediment. c. 438–432 B.C. Marble, over lifesize. British Museum, London (reproduced by courtesy of the Trustees). The robes show the sculptor's technical virtuosity in carving drapery.

the figures and the drapery which in some cases covers them are both treated realistically, even in places where the details of the workmanship would have been barely visible to the spectator below. The realism is combined, however, with a characteristically Classical preoccupation with proportion and balance; the result is sculptures that achieve an almost perfect blend of the two elements of the Classical style: ideal beauty is represented in realistic terms.

In contrast to the frieze, the technique employed on the metopes is high relief, so high, in fact, that some of the figures seem almost completely detached from their background. These metopes, which illustrate a number of mythological battles, represent a lower level of achievement, although some are more successful than others at reconciling scenes of violence and Classical idealism. The most impressive ones show episodes from the battle between Lapiths and Centaurs [108], the same story which we saw on the west pediment at Olympia.

The monumental entrance to the Acropolis, the Propylaea [109], was begun in 437 B.C. and finished on the eve of the outbreak of war, although probably only by a modification of the architect Mnesicles' original plan. An unusual feature of its design is that both Doric and Ionic columns are used, the Doric

above: 108 *Lapith and Centaur,* metope from Parthenon (south face). c. 448–442 B.C. Pentelic marble, height 4′4¼″ (1.34 m). British Museum, London (reproduced by courtesy of the Trustees). The assailed Lapith has dropped to one knee.

below: 109 Mnesicles. Propylaea, Athens, west front. 437–431 B.C. This is the view from the Temple of Athena Nike. Note the contrast between the simple Doric columns of the facade and the Ionic columns that line the center passageway.

ones visible from the front and the back and the Ionic ones lining the passageway through the outer porch.

A visitor climbing the Acropolis can see to the right of the Propylaea the little Ionic Temple of Athena Nike, or Athena, goddess of Victory [Plate 10, page 155]. Constructed during the first part of the war, probably between 427 and 424 B.C., it was decorated with reliefs showing the Athenian victories over the Persians of more than fifty years earlier. This unusual use of historical rather than mythological events was presumably intended to remind contemporary viewers of past Athenian successes at a time when such reassurance would have been more than welcome.

The other major building on the Acropolis is the Erechtheum [110], an Ionic temple of complex design which was begun in 421 B.C. but not completed until 406 B.C. The chief technical problem facing the architect, whose identity is unknown, was the uneven ground level of the site. The problem was solved by creating a building with entrances on different levels. The nature of the building itself produced other design problems. The Erechtheum had to commemorate a whole series of elaborate religious events and honor a number of different deities. One of its four chambers housed the ancient wooden statue of Athena that was at the center of the Great Panathenaic Festival shown on the Parthenon frieze. Elsewhere in the temple were altars to Poseidon and Erechtheus, an early Athenian king; to the legendary Athenian hero Butes; and to Hephaistos, the god of the forge. Furthermore, the design had to incorporate the marks in the ground made by Poseidon's trident during the competition with Athena, as shown on the west pediment of the Parthenon, and the site of the grave of another early, and probably legendary, Athenian king, Cecrops. The result of all this was a building whose complex plan is still not fully understood. In fact, the exact identification of the inner chambers remains in doubt.

The decoration of the temple is both elaborate and delicate, almost fragile. Its most well-known feature is the South Porch, where the roof rests not on columns but on the famous *caryatids,* statues of young girls [111]. These graceful figures, who stand gravely upright with one knee slightly bent as if to sustain the weight of the roof, represent the most complete attempt until then to conceal the structural functions of a column behind its form.

In many respects innovations such as these make the Erechtheum as representative of the mood of the late 5th century B.C. as the confident Parthenon is of the mood of a generation earlier. The apparent lack of a coherent overall plan and the blurring of traditional distinctions between architecture and sculpture, structure and decoration, seem to question traditional architectural values in a way that parallels the doubts of Euripides and his contemporaries.

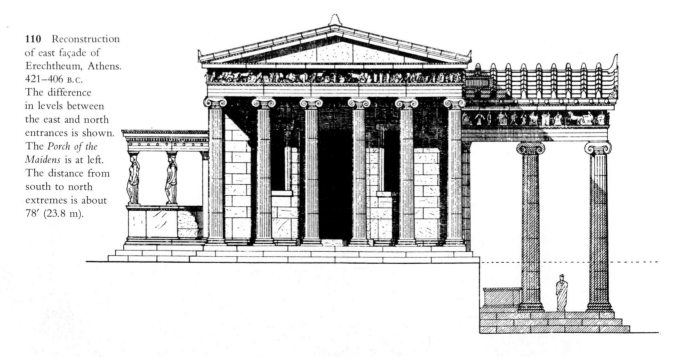

110 Reconstruction of east façade of Erechtheum, Athens. 421–406 B.C. The difference in levels between the east and north entrances is shown. The *Porch of the Maidens* is at left. The distance from south to north extremes is about 78′ (23.8 m).

The Late Classical Period

With the end of the Peloponnesian War in 404 B.C. and the fall of Athenian democracy, both art and political life were to be affected by an atmosphere of considerable confusion. Though Athens had been removed as the dominating force in Greece, there was no successor among her rivals. The vacuum was not filled until the mid-4th century with the appearance on the scene of Philip of Macedon. Earlier, a disastrous series of skirmishes among Sparta, Thebes, Athens, Corinth, and Argos had been temporarily suspended by the intervention of the Great King of the Persians himself, and the so-called King's Peace was signed in 387 B.C. But after a brief respite, the Thebans decisively defeated the Spartan forces at Leuctra in 371 B.C. and remained for a few years the dominating force in Greek political life.

With the accession of Philip in Macedon in 359 B.C., however, the balance of power in Greece began to change. The hitherto backward northern kingdom of Macedon began to exert a new unifying influence, despite opposition in Thebes and in Athens, where the great Athenian orator Demosthenes led the resistance. In 338 B.C., at the Battle of Chaeronea (see map, page 94), Philip defeated Athenian and Theban forces and unified all the cities of Greece, with the exception of Sparta, in an alliance known as the League of Corinth.

Even before his assassination in 336 B.C., Philip had developed schemes for enlarging his empire by attacking Persia. His son and successor, Alexander, carried them out. He spent the ten years from 333 B.C. until his own death in 323 B.C. in an amazing series of campaigns across Asia, destroying the Persian Empire and reaching as far as India. The effects of the breakup of this new Macedonian Empire after the death of Alexander were to be felt throughout the Hellenistic period that followed.

The Philosophies of Socrates and Plato

The intellectual and cultural spirit of the new century was foreshadowed in its very first year in an event at Athens. In 399 B.C. the philosopher Socrates was charged with impiety and corruption of the young, found guilty, and executed. Yet the ideas that Socrates represented—concern with the fate of the individual and the questioning of traditional values—could not be killed so easily. They had already begun to spread at the end of the 5th century B.C. and came to dominate the culture of the 4th century B.C.

Socrates is one of the most important figures in Greek history. He is also one of the most difficult to understand clearly. Much of the philosophy of the Greeks and of later ages and cultures has been inspired by his life and teachings. Yet Socrates himself

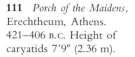

111 *Porch of the Maidens,* Erechtheum, Athens. 421–406 B.C. Height of caryatids 7′9″ (2.36 m).

wrote nothing; most of what we know of him comes from the works of his disciple, Plato. Socrates was born around 469 B.C., the son of a sculptor and a midwife; in later life he claimed to have followed his mother's profession in being a "midwife to ideas." He seems first to have been interested in natural science, but he soon turned to the problems of human behavior and morality. Unlike the sophists, the professional philosophers of the day, he never took money for teaching, nor did he ever found a school. Instead he went around Athens, to both public places like the markets and the gymnasia and private gatherings, talking and arguing, testing traditional ideas by subjecting them to a barrage of questions—as he put it, "following the argument wherever it led." Socrates gradually gained a circle of enthusiastic followers, drawn mainly from the young. At the same time he acquired many enemies, disturbed by both his challenge to established morality and the uncompromising persistence with which he interrogated those who upheld it. Socrates was no respecter of the pride or dignity of others, and his search for the truth inevitably exposed the ignorance of his opponents.

Among Socrates' supporters were a number who had taken part in an unpopular and tyrannical political coup at Athens immediately following the Peloponnesian War. The rule of the so-called Thirty Tyrants lasted only from 404 to 403 B.C.; it ended with the death or expulsion of its leading figures. The return of democracy gave Socrates' enemies a chance to take advantage of the hostility felt toward those who had "collaborated" with the tyrants; thus in 399 B.C. he was put on trial.

It seems probable that to some degree the trial was intended for show and that those who voted for the death sentence never seriously thought it would be carried out. Socrates was urged by his friends to escape from prison, and the authorities themselves offered him every opportunity to do so. However, the strength of his own morality and his reverence for the laws of his city prohibited him from doing so. After a final discussion with his friends he was put to death by the administration of a draught of hemlock.

Many of Socrates' disciples tried to preserve his memory by writing accounts of his life and teachings. The works of only two have survived. One of these is the Greek historian Xenophon, whose *Apology, Symposium,* and *Memorabilia* are interesting, if superficial. The other is Plato, who, together with his pupil Aristotle, stands at the forefront of the whole intellectual tradition of Western civilization.

The dialogues of Plato claim to record the teachings of Socrates. Indeed, in almost all of them Socrates himself appears, arguing with his opponents and presenting his own ideas. How much of Plato's picture of Socrates is historical truth and how much is Plato's invention, however, is debatable. The Socratic problem has been almost as much discussed as the identity of Homer. In general, modern opinion supports the view that in the early dialogues Plato tried to preserve something of his master's views and methods, while in the later ones he used Socrates as the spokesman for his own ideas.

There can certainly be no doubt that Plato was deeply impressed by Socrates' life and death. Born in 428 B.C., he was drawn by other members of his aristocratic family into the Socratic circle. Plato was present at the trial of Socrates, whose speech in his own defense he records in the *Apology,* one of three works that describe Socrates' last days. In the *Crito,* set in prison, Socrates explains why he refuses to escape. The *Phaedo* gives an account of his last day, spent discussing with his friends the immortality of the soul, and his death.

These three works probably bring us closest to the historical figure of Socrates, although Plato makes it clear that he himself was not present at the events described in the *Phaedo.* The long discussion of life and death, then, probably introduces ideas that were Plato's own rather than his master's. Nevertheless, the down-to-earth tone of Socrates' words coupled with his saintly bearing as the moment of death approaches clearly reflect something of his unique character. In the following extract from the *Phaedo* a number of ideas appear which Plato developed further in later works. The belief in the immortality of the soul is reinforced by a conviction that during life the soul is trapped in the body and thereby prevented from attaining its full powers. This emphasis on the superiority of spiritual rather than material values had a great appeal to Christian philosophers.

Plato
from PHAEDO

[Socrates is speaking.] "Now then, I want to give the proof at once, to you as my judges, why I think it likely that one who has spent his life in philosophy should be confident when he is going to die, and have good hopes that he will win the greatest blessings in the next world when he has ended: so Simmias and Cebes my judges, I will try to show how this could be true.

"The fact is, those who tackle philosophy aright are simply and solely practising dying, practising death, all the time, but nobody sees it. If this is true, then it would surely be unreasonable that they should earnestly do this and nothing else all their lives, yet when death comes they should object to what they had been so long earnestly practising."

Simmias laughed at this, and said, "I don't feel like laughing just now, Socrates, but you have made me laugh. I think the many if they heard that would say, 'That's a good one for the philosophers!' And other people in my city would heartily agree that philosophers are really suffering from a wish to die, and now they have found them out, that they richly deserve it!"

"That would be true, Simmias," said Socrates, "except the words 'found out.' For they have not found out in what sense the real philosophers wish to die and deserve to die, and what kind of death it is. Let us say good-bye to them," he went on, "and ask ourselves: Do we think there is such a thing as death?"

"Certainly," Simmias put in.

"Is it anything more than the separation of the soul from the body?" said Socrates. "Death is, that the body separates from the soul, and remains by itself apart from the soul, and the soul, separated from the body, exists by itself apart from the body. Is death anything but that?"

"No," he said, "that is what death is."

"Then consider, my good friend, if you agree with me here, for I think this is the best way to understand the question we are examining. Do you think it the part of a philosopher to be earnestly concerned with what are called pleasures, such as these—eating and drinking, for example?"

"Not at all," said Simmias.

"The pleasures of love, then?"

"Oh no."

"Well, do you suppose a man like that regards the other bodily indulgences as precious? Getting fine clothes and shoes and other bodily adornments—ought he to price them high or low, beyond whatever share of them it is absolutely necessary to have?"

"Low, I think," he said, "if he is a true philosopher."

"Then in general," he said, "do you think that such a man's concern is not for the body, but as far as he can he stands aloof from that and turns towards the soul?"

"I do."

"Then firstly, is it not clear that in such things the philosopher as much as possible sets free the soul from communion with the body, more than other men?"

"So it appears."

"And I suppose, Simmias, it must seem to most men that he who has no pleasure in such things and takes no share in them does not deserve to live, but he is getting pretty close to death if he does not care about pleasures which he has by means of the body."

"Quite true, indeed."

"Well then, what about the actual getting of wisdom? Is the body in the way or not, if a man takes it with him as companion in the search? I mean, for example, is there any truth for men in their sight and hearing? Or as poets are forever dinning into our ears, do we hear nothing and see nothing exactly? Yet if these of our bodily senses are not exact and clear, the others will hardly be, for they are all inferior to these, don't you think so?"

"Certainly," he said.

"Then," said he, "when does the soul get hold of the truth? For whenever the soul tries to examine anything in company with the body, it is plain that it is deceived by it."

"Quite true."

"Then is it not clear that in reasoning, if anywhere, something of the realities becomes visible to it?"

"Yes."

"And I suppose it reasons best when none of these senses disturbs it, hearing or sight, or pain, or pleasure indeed, but when it is completely by itself and says good-bye to the body, and so far as possible has no dealings with it, when it reaches out and grasps that which really is."

"That is true."

"And is it not then that the philosopher's soul chiefly holds the body cheap and escapes from it, while it seeks to be by itself?"

"So it seems."

"Let us pass on, Simmias. Do we say there is such a thing as justice by itself, or not?"

"We do say so, certainly!"

"Such a thing as the good and beautiful?"

"Of course!"

"And did you ever see one of them with your eyes?"

"Never," said he.

"By any other sense of those the body has did you ever grasp them? I mean all such things, greatness, health, strength, in short everything that really is the nature of things whatever they are: Is it through the body that the real truth is perceived? Or is this better—whoever of us prepares himself most completely and most exactly to comprehend each thing which he examines would come nearest to knowing each one?"

"Certainly."

"And would he do that most purely who should approach each with his intelligence alone, not adding sight to intelligence, or dragging in any other sense along with reasoning, but using the intelligence uncontaminated alone by itself, while he tries to hunt out each essence uncontaminated, keeping clear of eyes and ears and, one might say, of the whole body, because he thinks the body disturbs him and hinders the soul from getting possession of truth and wisdom when body and soul are companions—is not this the man, Simmias, if anyone, who will hit reality?"

"Nothing could be more true, Socrates," said Simmias.

"Then from all this," said Socrates, "genuine philosophers must come to some such opinion as follows, so as to make to one another statements such as these: 'A sort of direct path, so to speak, seems to take us to the conclusion that so long as we have the body with us in our enquiry, and our soul is mixed up with so great an evil, we shall never attain sufficiently what we desire, and that, we say, is the truth. For the body provides thousands of busy distractions because of its necessary food; besides, if diseases fall upon us, they hinder us from the pursuit of the real. With loves and desires and fears and all kinds of fancies and much rubbish, it infects us, and really and truly makes us, as they say, unable to think one little bit about anything at any time. Indeed, wars and factions and battles all come from the body and its desires, and from nothing else. For the desire of getting wealth causes all wars, and we are compelled to desire wealth by the body, being slaves to its culture; therefore we have no leisure for philosophy, from all these reasons. Chief of all is that if we do have some leisure, and turn away from the body to speculate on something, in our searches it is everywhere interfering, it causes confusion and disturbance, and dazzles us so that it will not let us see the truth; so in fact we see that if we are ever to know anything purely we must get rid of it, and examine the real things by the soul alone; and then, it seems, after we are dead, as the reasoning shows, not while we live, we shall possess that which we desire, lovers of which we say we are, namely wisdom. For if it is impossible in company with the body to know anything purely, one thing of two follows: either knowledge is possible nowhere, or only after death; for then alone the soul will be quite by itself apart from the body, but not before. And while we are alive, we shall be nearest to knowing, as it seems, if as far as possible we have no commerce or communion with the body which is not absolutely necessary, and if we are not infected with its nature, but keep ourselves pure from it, until God himself shall set us free. And so, pure and rid of the body's foolishness, we shall probably be in the company of those like ourselves, and shall know through our own selves complete incontamination,

and that is perhaps the truth. But for the impure to grasp the pure is not, it seems, allowed.' So we must think, Simmias, and so we must say to one another, all who are rightly lovers of learning; don't you agree?"

"Assuredly, Socrates."

"Then," said Socrates, "if this is true, my comrade, there is great hope that when I arrive where I am travelling, there if anywhere I shall sufficiently possess that for which all our study has been pursued in this past life. So the journey which has been commanded for me is made with good hope, and the same for any other man who believes he has got his mind purified, as I may call it."

"Certainly," replied Simmias.

"And is not purification really that which has been mentioned so often in our discussion, to separate as far as possible the soul from the body, and to accustom it to collect itself together out of the body in every part, and to dwell alone by itself as far as it can, both at this present and in the future, being freed from the body as if from a prison?"

"By all means," said he.

"Then is not this called death—a freeing and separation of soul from body?"

"Not a doubt of that," said he.

"But to set it free, as we say, is the chief endeavour of those who rightly love wisdom, nay of those alone, and the very care and practice of the philosophers is nothing but the freeing and separation of soul from body, don't you think so?"

"It appears to be so."

"Then, as I said at first, it would be absurd for a man preparing himself in his life to be as near as possible to death, so to live, and then when death came, to object?"

"Of course."

"Then in fact, Simmias," he said, "those who rightly love wisdom are practising dying, and death to them is the least terrible thing in the world. Look at it in this way: If they are everywhere at enmity with the body, and desire the soul to be alone by itself, and if, when this very thing happens, they shall fear and object—would not that be wholly unreasonable? Should they not willingly go to a place where there is good hope of finding what they were in love with all through life (and they loved wisdom), and of ridding themselves of the companion which they hated? When human favourites and wives and sons have died, many have been willing to go down to the grave, drawn by the hope of seeing there those they used to desire, and of being with them; but one who is really in love with wisdom and holds firm to this same hope, that he will find it in the grave, and nowhere else worth speaking of—will he then fret at dying and not go thither rejoicing? We must surely think, my comrade, that he will go rejoicing, if he is really a philosopher; he will surely believe that he will find wisdom in its purity there and there alone. If this is true, would it not be most unreasonable, as I said just now, if such a one feared death?"

"Unreasonable, I do declare," said he.

The *Phaedo* ends with one of the most famous of all passages in Greek literature, the description of Socrates' death [112]. His last words have been interpreted in many different ways. Asclepius was the god of healing, and Socrates may perhaps be reminding his friends that death, by releasing the soul, is the final cure of bodily ills.

Plato
from PHAEDO

. . . he got up and retired into another room for the bath, and Criton went after him, telling us to wait. So we waited discussing and talking together about what had been said, or sometimes speaking of the great misfortune which had befallen us, for we felt really as if we had lost a father and had to spend the rest of our lives as orphans. When he had bathed, and his children had been brought to see him—for he had two little sons, and one big—and when the women of his family had come, he talked to them before Criton and gave what instructions he wished. Then he asked the women and children to go, and came back to us. It was now near sunset, for he had spent a long time within. He came and sat down after his bath, and he had not talked long after this when the servant of the Eleven came in, and standing by him said, "O Socrates! I have not to complain of you as I do of others, that they are angry with me, and curse me, because I bring them word to drink their potion, which my officers make me do! But I have always found you in this time most generous and gentle, and the best man who ever came here. And now too, I know well you are not angry with me, for you know who are responsible, and you keep it for them. Now you know what I came to tell you, so farewell, and try to bear as well as you can what can't be helped."

Then he turned and was going out, with tears running down his cheeks. And Socrates looked up at him and said, "Farewell to you also, I will do so." Then, at the same time turning to us, "What a nice fellow!" he said. "All the time he has been coming and talking to me, a real good sort, and now how generously he sheds tears for me! Come along, Criton, let's obey him. Someone bring the potion, if the stuff has been ground; if not, let the fellow grind it."

Then Criton said, "But, Socrates, I think the sun is still over the hills, it has not set yet. Yes, and I know of others who, having been told to drink the poison, have done it very late; they had dinner first and a good one, and some enjoyed the company of any they wanted. Please don't be in a hurry, there is time to spare."

112 Jacques Louis David. *The Death of Socrates*. 1787. Oil on canvas, 4'3" × 6'5¼" (1.3 × 1.96 m). Metropolitan Museum of Art, New York (Wolfe Fund, 1931). This is a Neoclassical interpretation of the scene described by Plato in the *Phaedo*.

But Socrates said, "Those you speak of have very good reason for doing that, for they think they will gain by doing it; and I have good reasons why I won't do it. For I think I shall gain nothing by drinking a little later, only that I shall think myself a fool for clinging to life and sparing when the cask's empty. Come along," he said, "do what I tell you, if you please."

And Criton, hearing this, nodded to the boy who stood near. The boy went out, and after spending a long time, came in with the man who was to give the poison carrying it ground ready in a cup. Socrates caught sight of the man and said, "Here, my good man, you know about these things; what must I do?"

"Just drink it," he said, "and walk about till your legs get heavy, then lie down. In that way the drug will act of itself."

At the same time, he held out the cup to Socrates, and he took it quite cheerfully, Echecrates, not a tremble, not a change in colour or looks; but looking full at the man under his brows, as he used to do, he asked him, "What do you say about this drink? What of a libation to someone? Is that allowed, or not?"

He said, "We only grind so much as we think enough for a moderate potion."

"I understand," he said, "but at least, I suppose, it is allowed to offer a prayer to the gods and that must be done, for good luck in the migration from here to there. Then that is my prayer, and so may it be!"

With these words he put the cup to his lips and, quite easy and contented, drank it up. So far most of us had been able to hold back our tears pretty well; but when we saw him begin drinking and end drinking, we could no longer. I burst into a flood of tears for all I could do, so I wrapped up my face and cried myself out; not for him indeed, but for my own misfortune in losing such a man and such a comrade. Criton had got up and gone out even before I did, for he could not hold the tears in. Apollodoros had never ceased weeping all this time, and now he burst out into loud sobs, and by his weeping and lamentations completely broke down every man there except Socrates himself. He only said, "What a scene! You amaze me. That's just why I sent the women away, to keep them from making a scene like this. I've heard that one ought to make an end in decent silence. Quiet yourselves and endure."

When we heard him we felt ashamed and restrained our tears. He walked about, and when he said that his legs were feeling heavy, he lay down on his back, as the man told him to do; at the same time the one who gave him the potion felt him, and after a while examined his feet and legs; then pinching a foot hard, he asked if he felt anything; he said no. After this, again, he pressed the shins; and, moving up like this, he showed us that he was growing cold and stiff. Again he felt him, and told us that when it came to his heart, he would be gone. Already the cold had come nearly as far as the abdomen, when Socrates threw off the covering from his face—for he had covered it over—and said, the last words he uttered, "Criton," he said, "we owe a cock to Asclepios; pay it without fail."

"That indeed shall be done," said Criton. "Have you anything more to say?"

When Criton had asked this, Socrates gave no further answer, but after a little time, he stirred, and the man uncovered him, and his eyes were still. Criton, seeing this, closed the mouth and eyelids.

This was the end of our comrade, Echecrates, a man, as we would say, of all then living we had ever met, the noblest and the wisest and most just. ◆

After Socrates' death, Plato left Athens, horrified at the society that had sanctioned the execution, and spent a number of years in traveling. He returned in 387 B.C. and founded the Academy, the first permanent institution in Western civilization devoted to education and research, and thus the forerunner of all our universities. Its curriculum concentrated on mathematics, law, and political theory. Its purpose was to produce experts for the service of the state. Some twenty years later, in 368 B.C., Plato was invited to Sicily to put his political theories into practice by turning Syracuse into a model kingdom and its young ruler, Dionysius II, into a philosopher king. Predictably, the attempt was a dismal failure, and by 366 B.C. he was back in Athens. Apart from a second visit to Syracuse in 362 B.C., equally unsuccessful, he seems to have spent the rest of his life in Athens, teaching and writing. He died there in 347 B.C.

Much of Plato's writing deals with political theory and the construction of an ideal society. The belief in an ideal is, in fact, characteristic of most of his work. It is most clearly expressed in his Theory of Forms, according to which in a higher dimension of existence there are perfect Forms of which all the phenomena we perceive in the world around us represent pale reflections. There can be no doubt that Plato's vision of an ideal society is far too authoritarian for most tastes, involving among other restrictions the careful breeding of children, the censorship of music and poetry, and the abolition of private property. In fairness to Plato, however, it must be remembered that his works are intended not as a set of instructions to be followed literally but as a challenge to think seriously about how our lives should be organized.

Furthermore, the disadvantages of democratic government had become all too clear during the last years of the 5th century B.C. If Plato's attempt to redress the balance seems to veer excessively in the other direction, it may in part have been inspired by the continuing chaos of 4th-century Greek politics.

The most complete statement of the Platonic solution to political problems is *The Republic,* a massive work in ten books. It begins with a discussion between Socrates and his friends on the nature of justice and proceeds to explore the operation of justice within society. From here, under the guidance of Socrates, the argument shifts to the subject of the ideal society, which is defined in the terms just described. The role of education and the function of the philosopher within this society are discussed in detail and then described by Socrates in an elaborate metaphor or, as he calls it, a parable, which is probably the most famous part of the work. In this "Allegory of the Cave" Socrates imagines a group of people who live, as it were, chained to the ground in an underground cave in such a way that they can only see shadows of reality projected onto the inner wall of the cave by the fire light behind them [113]. Since they have been accustomed to seeing nothing but shadows all their lives they have no way of comprehending the real world outside the cave. It is therefore the task of the philosopher, who is already free from the chains of misconception, to liberate the others and educate them in such a way as to set them free from the imprisonment of the senses.

The "Allegory of the Cave" illustrates not only Plato's philosophical position but also his literary style. Of all the great philosophers, Plato is perhaps the easiest to read because his style is deceptively simple. The ease with which the most complex ideas are communicated is, in fact, a measure of his literary genius. The use of the dialogue form brings the discussions to life, the individuals taking part are characterized with the lightest of touches, and the argument is generally clear and easy to follow. Furthermore, his choice of an extended metaphor to express a complex intellectual concept represents a remarkable combination of philosophy and artistry.

Plato
from THE REPUBLIC, Book VII
The Allegory of the Cave

"Next, then," I said, "take the following parable of education and ignorance as a picture of the condition of our nature. Imagine mankind as dwelling in an underground cave with a long entrance open to the light across the whole width of the cave; in this they have been from childhood, with necks and legs fettered, so they have to stay where they are. They cannot move their heads round because of the fetters, and they can only look forward, but light comes to them from fire burning behind them higher up at a distance. Between the fire and the prisoners is a road

113 Diagram illustrating Plato's "Allegory of the Cave" in *The Republic, Book VII.*

THE CAVE

THE FIRE

THE ROADWAY

DIFFUSED DAYLIGHT

THE ROUGH ASCENT TO SUNLIGHT

above their level, and along it imagine a low wall has been built, as puppet showmen have screens in front of their people over which they work their puppets."

"I see," he said.

"See, then, bearers carrying along this wall all sorts of articles which they hold projecting above the wall, statues of men and other living things, made of stone or wood and all kinds of stuff, some of the bearers speaking and some silent, as you might expect."

"What a remarkable image," he said, "and what remarkable prisoners!"

"Just like ourselves," I said. "For, first of all, tell me this: What do you think such people would have seen of themselves and each other except their shadows, which the fire cast on the opposite wall of the cave?"

"I don't see how they could see anything else," said he, "if they were compelled to keep their heads unmoving all their lives!"

"Very well, what of the things being carried along? Would not this be the same?"

"Of course it would."

"Suppose the prisoners were able to talk together, don't you think that when they named the shadows which they saw passing they would believe they were naming things?"

"Necessarily."

"Then if their prison had an echo from the opposite wall, whenever one of the passing bearers uttered a sound, would they not suppose that the passing shadow must be making the sound? Don't you think so?"

"Indeed I do," he said.

"If so," said I, "such persons would certainly believe that there were no realities except those shadows of handmade things."

"So it must be," said he.

"Now consider," said I, "what their release would be like, and their cure from these fetters and their folly; let us imagine whether it might naturally be something like this. One might be released, and compelled suddenly to stand up and turn his neck round, and to walk and look towards the firelight; all this would hurt him, and he would be too much dazzled to see distinctly those things whose shadows he had seen before. What do you think he would say, if someone told him that what he saw before was foolery, but now he saw more rightly, being a bit nearer reality and turned towards what was a little more real? What if he were shown each of the passing things, and compelled by questions to answer what each one was? Don't you think he would be puzzled, and believe what he saw before was more true than what was shown to him now?"

"Far more," he said.

"Then suppose he were compelled to look towards the real light, it would hurt his eyes, and he would escape by turning them away to the things which he was able to look at, and these he would believe to be clearer than what was being shown to him."

"Just so," said he.

"Suppose, now," said I, "that someone should drag him thence by force, up the rough ascent, the steep way up, and never stop until he could drag him out into the light of the sun, would he not be distressed and furious at being dragged; and when he came into the light, the brilliance would fill his eyes and he would not be able to see even one of the things now called real?"

"That he would not," said he, "all of a sudden."

"He would have to get used to it, surely, I think, if he is to see the things above. First he would most easily look at shadows, after that images of mankind and the rest in water, lastly the things themselves. After this he would find it easier to survey by night the heavens themselves and all that is in them, gazing at the light of the stars and moon, rather than by day the sun and the sun's light."

"Of course."

"Last of all, I suppose, the sun; he could look on the sun itself by itself in its own place, and see what it is like, not reflections of it in water or as it appears in some alien setting."

"Necessarily," said he.

"And only after all this he might reason about it, how this is he who provides seasons and years, and is set over all there is in the visible region, and he is in a manner the cause of all things which they saw."

"Yes, it is clear," said he, "that after all that, he would come to this last."

"Very good. Let him be reminded of his first habitation, and what was wisdom in that place, and of his fellow-prisoners there; don't you think he would bless himself for the change, and pity them?"

"Yes, indeed."

"And if there were honours and praises among them and prizes for the one who saw the passing things most sharply and remembered best which of them used to come before and which after and which together, and from these was best able to prophesy accordingly what was going to come—do you believe he would set his desire on that, and envy those who were honoured men or potentates among them? Would he not feel as Homer says, and heartily desire rather to be serf of some landless man on earth and to endure anything in the world, rather than to opine as they did and to live in that way?"

"Yes indeed," said he, "he would rather accept anything than live like that."

"Then again," I said, "just consider; if such a one should go down again and sit on his old seat, would he not get his eyes full of darkness coming in suddenly out of the sun?"

"Very much so," said he.

"And if he should have to compete with those who had been always prisoners, by laying down the law about those shadows while he was blinking before his eyes were settled down—and it would take a good long time to get used to things—wouldn't they all laugh at him and say he had spoiled his eyesight by going up there, and it was not worth-while so much as to try to go up? And would they not kill anyone who tried to release them and take them up, if they could somehow lay hands on him and kill him?"

"That they would!" said he.

"Then we must apply this image, my dear Glaucon," said I, "to all we have been saying. The world of our sight is like the habitation in prison, the firelight there to the sunlight here, the ascent and the view of the upper world is the rising of the soul into the world of mind; put it so and you will not be far from my own surmise, since that is what you want to hear; but God knows if it is really true. At least, what appears to me is, that in the world of the known, last of all, is the idea of the good, and with what toil to be seen! And seen, this must be inferred to be the cause of all right and beautiful things for all, which gives birth to light and the king of light in the world of sight, and, in the world of mind, herself the queen produces truth and reason; and she must be seen by one who is to act with reason publicly or privately."

"I believe as you do," he said, "in so far as I am able."

"Then believe also, as I do," said I, "and do not be surprised, that those who come thither are not willing to have part in the affairs of men, but their souls ever strive to remain above; for that surely may be expected if our parable fits the case."

"Quite so," he said.

"Well then," said I, "do you think it surprising if one leaving divine contemplations and passing to the evils of men is awkward and appears to be a great fool, while he is still blinking—not yet accustomed to the darkness around him, but compelled to struggle in law courts or elsewhere about shadows of justice, or the images which make the shadows, and to quarrel about notions of justice in those who have never seen justice itself?"

"Not surprising at all," said he.

"But any man of sense," I said, "would remember that the eyes are doubly confused from two different causes, both in passing from light to darkness and from darkness to light; and believing that the same things happen with regard to the soul also, whenever

he sees a soul confused and unable to discern anything he would not just laugh carelessly; he would examine whether it had come out of a more brilliant life, and if it were darkened by the strangeness; or whether it had come out of greater ignorance into a more brilliant light, and if it were dazzled with the brighter illumination. Then only would he congratulate the one soul upon its happy experience and way of life, and pity the other; but if he must laugh, his laugh would be a less downright laugh than his laughter at the soul which came out of the light above."

Aristotle's Lyceum

Plato's most gifted pupil, Aristotle (384–322 B.C.), continued to develop his master's doctrines, at first wholeheartedly and later critically, for at least twenty years. In 335 B.C. Aristotle founded a school in competition with Plato's Academy, the Lyceum, severing fundamental ties with Plato from then on. Aristotle in effect introduced a rival philosophy—one that has attracted thinking minds ever since. Indeed, in the 19th century the English poet Samuel Taylor Coleridge was to comment, with much truth, that one was born either a "Platonist" or an "Aristotelian."

The Lyceum seems to have been organized with typically Aristotelian efficiency. In the morning Aristotle himself lectured to the full-time students, many of whom came from other parts of Greece to attend his courses and work on the projects he was directing. In the afternoon the students pursued their research in the library, museum, and map collection attached to the Lyceum, while Aristotle gave more general lectures to the public. His custom of strolling along the Lyceum's circular walkways, immersed in profound contemplation or discourse, gained his school the name *Peripatetic,* or the "walking" school.

As a philosopher Aristotle was the great systematizer. He wrote on every topic of serious study of the time. Many of his classifications have remained valid to this day, although some of the disciplines, such as psychology and physics, have severed their ties with philosophy and have become important sciences in their own right.

The most complex of Aristotle's works is probably the *Metaphysics,* in which he deals with his chief dispute with Plato, which concerned the Theory of Forms. Plato had postulated a higher dimension of existence for the Ideal Forms and thereby created a split between the apparent reality which we perceive and the genuine reality which we can only know by philosophical contemplation. Moreover, knowledge of these forms depended on a theory of "remembering" them from previous existences. Aristotle, on the other hand, claimed that the forms were actually present in the objects we see around us, thereby eliminating the split between the two realities.

Elsewhere in the *Metaphysics* Aristotle discusses the nature of God, whom he describes as "thought thinking of itself" and "the Unmoved Mover." The nature of the physical universe ruled over by this supreme being is further explored in the *Physics,* which is concerned with the elements which compose the universe and the laws by which they operate.

As for Aristotle's contribution to practical philosophy, the *Ethics* is a useful handbook for those not fortunate enough to have been born perfect. According to Aristotle, in our lifelong attempt to attain happiness we can best manage to live well by the constant application of a few elementary rules of conduct. Of course the earlier we begin the discipline, the more we can make such rules second nature, or habit (*ethos*), and the more smoothly will the course of life proceed. One of these rules, the so-called doctrine of the Golden Mean, which recommends moderation rather than extremes, is in fact an amplification of the Classical principle of "nothing too much."

Like Plato in *The Republic,* Aristotle extended his analysis of individual human beings to the workings of society as a whole. He rejected the temptation to follow Plato's example and construct his own ideal state; rather, in his practical fashion he devoted his attention to existing systems of government. The chief purpose of government, he believed, should be the common good of all. When the state becomes subjected to the selfish interests of certain classes or elements, a perverted form of government arises: oligarchy, when the state is dominated by the rich and few; tyranny, when it is dominated by the base and the rich; democracy, when it is dominated by the many, the poor, and the mob. Aristotle rigorously appraised even these perverted forms for whatever value they might have, at least temporarily, as viable forms of government.

Other important works by Aristotle include the *Rhetoric,* which prescribes the ideal model of oratory, and the *Poetics,* which does the same for poetry and includes the famous definition of tragedy mentioned earlier (see page 140). Briefly, Aristotle's formula for tragedy is as follows: the tragic hero, who must be noble, through some undetected "tragic flaw" in character meets with a bad end involving the reversal of fortune and sometimes death. The audience, through various emotional and intellectual relations with this tragic figure, undergoes a "cleansing" or "purgation" of the soul, called *catharsis.* Critics of this analysis sometimes complain that Aristotle was trying to read his own very subjective formulas into the Greek tragedies of the time. This is not entirely just, since Aristotle was probably writing for future tragedians, prescribing what ought to be rather than what was.

Aristotle's influence on later ages was vast, although not continuous. Philip of Macedon employed him to tutor young Alexander, but the effect on the young conqueror was probably minimal. Thereafter his works were lost and not recovered until the 1st century B.C., when they were used by the Roman statesman and thinker Cicero (106–43 B.C.). During the Middle Ages, they were translated into Latin and Arabic and became a philosophical basis for Christian theology. Saint Thomas Aquinas' synthesis of Aristotelian philosophy and Christian doctrine still remains the official philosophical position of the Catholic Church.

In philosophy, theology, and scientific and intellectual thought as a whole, many of the distinctions first applied by Aristotle were rediscovered in the early Renaissance and are still valid today. Indeed, no survey such as this can begin to do justice to one described by Dante as "the master of those who know." In the more than two thousand years since his death only Leonardo da Vinci has come near to equaling his creative range [114].

Music and the Visual Arts

Both Plato and Aristotle found a place for music in their ideal states; their comments on it provide some information on the status of Greek music in the late Classical period. Throughout the 5th century B.C., music had played an important part in dramatic performances but had been generally subordinated to the poetry. By the end of the Peloponnesian War, however, the musical aspect of tragedy had begun to predominate. It is interesting to note that Euripides was criticized by his contemporaries for the lack of form and symmetry and the overemotionalism of his music, not of his verse. With its release from the function of mere accompaniment, instrumental music became especially popular in the 4th century B.C.

114 Rembrandt. *Aristotle with a Bust of Homer.* 1653. Oil on canvas, 4′8½″ × 4′5¼″ (1.44 × 1.37 m). Metropolitan Museum of Art, New York (purchased with special funds and gifts of friends of the Museum). In this painting the great Dutch painter brings together the first and the last great names in the Greek intellectual tradition.

The actual sound of Greek music and the principles according to which it was composed are not easy to reconstruct or understand. The numerical relationship of notes to one another established by Pythagoras (see page 117) was used to divide the basic unit of an octave (series of eight notes) into smaller intervals named after their positions in relation to the lowest note in the octave. The interval known as a *fourth,* for example, represents the space between the lowest note and the fourth note up the octave. The intervals were then combined to form a series of scales, or *modes.* Each was given a name and was associated with a particular emotional range. Thus the Dorian mode was serious and warlike, the Phrygian exciting and emotional, and the Mixolydian plaintive and pathetic. It was on the basis of the kind of music likely to be written in a particular mode that Plato permitted some modes in his ideal state and prohibited others.

The unit with which Greek music was constructed was the *tetrachord,* a group of four notes of which the two outer ones are a perfect fourth apart and the inner ones variably spaced. The combination of two tetrachords formed a mode. The Dorian mode, for example, consisted of the following two tetrachords:

The Lydian mode was composed of two different tetrachords:

The origin of the modes and their relationship to one another is uncertain; it was disputed even in ancient times. The situation has not been made easier by the fact that medieval church music adopted the same system of mathematical construction and even some of the same names, but applied them to different modes. Nor do we know much more about Greek concepts of rhythm and harmony. It is probably safest to conclude that although we can form some idea of the importance the Classical Greeks themselves ascribed to music and even understand some of its philosophical implications, we are a long way from being able to recreate its actual sound.

Our knowledge of the visual arts in the 4th century B.C. is similarly incomplete. Greek fresco painting of the period has been entirely lost, though recent discoveries in northern Greece at the Royal Cemetery of Vergina suggest that some of it may yet be found again [115]. In sculpture, fortunately, Roman copies of lost original statues enable us to form a fairly good estimate of the main developments. It is clear that Plato's interest in the fate of the individual soul finds its parallel in the sculptural treatment of the human form. Facial expressions become more human, often characterized by a mood of dreamy tenderness. Technical skill in depicting drapery and the anatomy beneath are put to the service of a new virtuosity. The three sculptors who dominated the art of the 4th century B.C. are Praxiteles, Scopas, and Lysippus.

The influence of Praxiteles on his contemporaries was immense. His particular brand of gentle melan-

below: 115 *Pluto Seizing Persephone,* detail of wall painting from Royal Tomb I, Vergina. Mid-4th century B.C. This unique example of late Classical monumental painting was discovered by the Greek archaeologist Manolis Andronikos in 1977. It shows a remarkable fluency and freedom of technique.

right: 116 Praxiteles. *Aphrodite of Cyrene.* Roman copy of c. 100 B.C. Marble, height 5′ (1.52 m). National Museum, Rome. This copy was found by chance in the Roman baths at Cyrene, North Africa. The statue is also called *Venus Anadyomene,* the Roman name for Aphrodite and a Greek word meaning "rising up from the sea," often used in referring to Aphrodite because she was supposed to have arisen from the sea at her birth. The porpoise is a reminder of the goddess' oceanic associations.

choly is well illustrated by the *Hermes* at Olympia that is generally attributed to him [Plate 11, page 156]. Equally important is his famous statue of Aphrodite nude [116], of which some fifty copies have survived. This represents the discovery of the female body as an object of beauty in itself; it was also one of the first attempts in Western art to introduce the element of sensuality into the portrayal of the female form.

The art of Scopas was more dramatic, with an emphasis on emotion and intensity. Roman copies of his statue of *Pothos,* or Desire [117], allow comparison of this yearning figure with Praxiteles' more relaxed *Hermes.*

The impact of Lysippus was as much on succeeding periods as on his own time. One of his chief claims to fame was as the official portraitist of Alexander the Great. Lysippus' very individual characteristics—a new, more attenuated system of proportion, greater concern for realism, and the large scale of many of his works—had a profound effect later on Hellenistic art [118].

below: 117   Scopas. *Pothos.* Roman copy after original of c. 350 B.C. Marble. Palazzo dei Conservatori, Rome.

right: 118   Lysippus. *Apoxyomenos (The Scraper).* Roman copy after bronze original of c. 330 B.C. Marble, height 6′9″ (2.06 m). Vatican Museums, Rome. The young athlete is cleaning off sweat and dirt with a tool called a *strigil.*

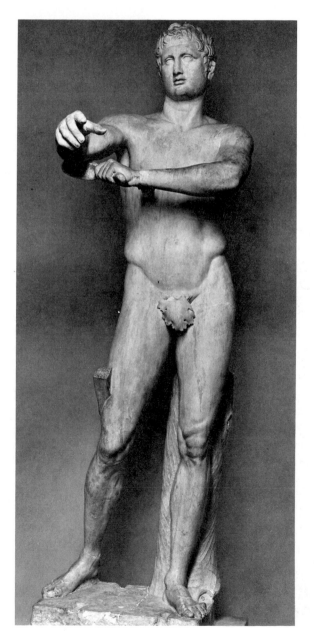

119 Theodoros of Phokaia. Tholos of the Sanctuary of Athena Pronaia, Delphi. c. 390 B.C. Marble and limestone; diameter of cella 28′2⅝″ (8.6 m), present height 27′2½″ (8.29 m). This is one of the first circular designs in Greek architecture. Originally, twenty Doric columns encircled the temple and ten Corinthian columns were set against the wall of the cella within.

In architecture, as in the arts generally, the Late Classical period was one of innovation. The great sanctuaries at Olympia and Delphi were expanded and new building forms were invented, including the *tholos,* or circular building [119]. The most grandiose work of the century was probably the Temple of Artemis at Ephesus, destroyed by fire in 356 B.C. and rebuilt on the same massive scale as before.

Although the Greeks of the 4th century B.C. lacked the certainty and self-confidence of their predecessors, their culture shows no lack of ideas or inspiration. Furthermore, even before Alexander's death the Macedonian Empire had spread Greek culture throughout the Mediterranean world. If Athens itself had lost any real political or commercial importance, the ideas of its great innovators began to affect an ever-growing number of people.

When Alexander died in the summer of 323 B.C., the division of his empire into separate independent kingdoms spread Greek culture even more widely. The kingdoms of the Seleucids in Syria and the Ptole-

mies in Egypt are the true successors to Periclean Athens. Even as far away as India sculptors and town planners were influenced by ideas developed by Athenians of the 5th and 4th centuries B.C.

In due course, the cultural achievement of Classical Greece was absorbed and reborn in Rome, as Chapter 5 will show. Meanwhile, in the period known as the Hellenistic Age, which lasted from the death of Alexander to the Roman conquest of Greece in 146 B.C., that achievement took a new turn.

The Hellenistic Period

The inability of Alexander's generals to agree on a single successor after his death made the division of the Macedonian Empire inevitable. The four most important kingdoms that split off, Syria (the kingdom of the Seleucids), Egypt, Pergamum, and Macedonia itself (see map, opposite), were soon at loggerheads and remained so until they were finally conquered by Rome. Each of them, however, in its own way continued the spread of Greek culture, as the name of the period implies (it is derived from the verb "to Hellenize," or to spread Greek influence).

The greatest of all centers of Greek learning was in the Egyptian city of Alexandria, where Ptolemy, Alexander's former personal staff officer and bodyguard, planned a large institute for scholarship known as the Temple of the Muses, or the Museum. The Library at the Museum contained everything of importance ever written in Greek, up to seven hundred thousand separate works, according to contemporary authorities. Its destruction by fire when Julius Caesar besieged the city in 47 B.C. must surely be one of the greatest intellectual disasters in the history of Western culture.

In Asia Minor and farther east in Syria the Hellenistic rulers of the new kingdoms fostered Greek art and literature as one means of holding foreign influences at bay. Libraries were built at Pergamum and the Syrian capital of Antioch, and philosophers from Greece were encouraged to visit the new centers of learning and lecture there. In this way Greek ideas not only retained their hold but began to make an impression on more remote peoples even farther east. The first Buddhist monumental sculpture, which is called Gandharan after the Indian province of Gandhara where it developed, made use of Greek styles and techniques. There is even a classic Buddhist religious work called *The Questions of King Milinda* in which a local Greek ruler, probably called Menandros, is described exchanging ideas with a Buddhist sage, ending with the ruler's conversion to Buddhism— one example of the failure of Greek ideas to convince.

Yet, however much literature and philosophy could do to maintain the importance of Greek culture, it was primarily to the visual arts that Hellenistic rulers turned. In doing so they inaugurated the last great period of Greek art.

The most powerful influence on the period immediately following Alexander's death was the memory of his life. The daring and immensity of his conquests, his own heroic personality, the new world that he had sought to create—all these produced a spirit of adventure and experiment. Artists of the Hellenistic period sought not so much to equal or surpass their Classical predecessors in the familiar forms as to discover new subjects and invent new

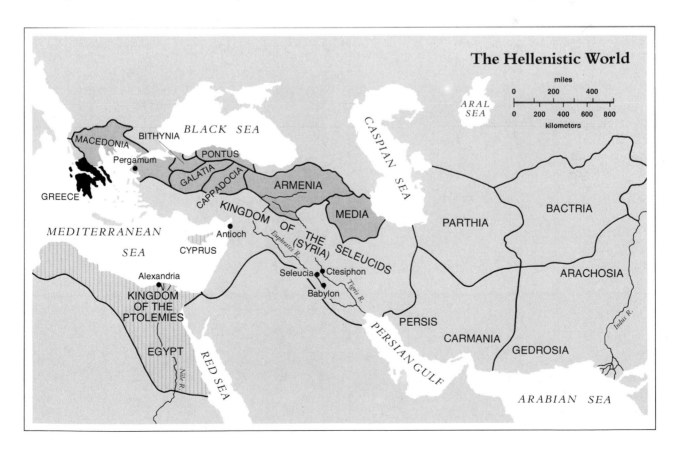

techniques. The development of realistic portraiture dates to this period [120, 121], as does the construction of buildings like the Lighthouse at Alexandria [122], in its day the tallest tower ever built and one of the Seven Wonders of the World.

The all-pervading spirit of the Classical Age had been order. Now artists began to discover the delights of freedom. Classical art was calm and restrained, but Hellenistic art was emotional and expressive. Classical artists sought clarity and balance even in showing scenes of violence, but Hellenistic artists allowed themselves to depict riotous confusion involving strong contrasts of light and shade and the appearance of perpetual motion. It is not surprising that the term *baroque,* originally used to describe the

extravagant European art of the 17th century A.D., is often applied to the art of the Hellenistic period.

The artists responsible for these innovations created their works for a new kind of patron. Most of the great works of the Classical period had been produced for the state, with the result that the principal themes and inspirations were religious and political. With the disintegration of the Macedonian Empire and the establishment of prosperous kindgoms at Pergamum, Antioch, and elsewhere, there developed a group of powerful rulers and wealthy businessmen who commissioned works either to provide lavish decoration for their cities or to adorn their private palaces and villas. The artist was no longer responsible to humanity and to the gods, but to whoever paid

below: 120 *Alexander the Great.* Pergamum, c. 160 B.C. Marble. Archaeological Museum, Istanbul. Note the emotional quality of the eyes and mouth, emphasized by the set of the head.

right: 121 *Old Market Woman.* 2nd century B.C. Marble, height 4′1½″ (1.26 m). Metropolitan Museum of Art, New York (Rogers Fund, 1909). The stark realism of the statue, with bent back and strained expression, is typical of Hellenistic art— a long way from the ideal beauty of the Classical period.

for the work. As a result, the artist was encouraged to develop new techniques and surpass the achievements of rivals.

At the same time, the change in the artist's social role produced a change in the function of the work. Whereas in the Classical period architects had devoted themselves to the construction of temples and religious sanctuaries, the Hellenistic age is notable for its market places and theaters, as well as for scientific and technical buildings like the Tower of the Winds at Athens and the Lighthouse at Alexandria [see 122].

Among the rich cities of Hellenistic Asia, none was richer than Pergamum, ruled by a dynasty of kings known as the Attalids. Pergamum was founded in the early 3rd century B.C. and reached the high point of its greatness in the reign of Eumenes II (197–159 B.C.). The layout of the chief buildings in the city represents a rejection of the Classical concepts of order and balance. Unlike the Periclean buildings on the Athenian Acropolis, the buildings in Pergamum were placed independently of one another with a new and theatrical use of space. The theater itself, set on a steep slope, seemed to be falling dramatically down the hillside [123].

left: 122 Reconstruction of the Lighthouse on Pharos, north of Alexandria harbor. 279 B.C. Original height 440′ (134.2 m). The beam of light from the lantern at top was intensified by a system of reflectors. The name of the island, Pharos, became, and still is, another word for lighthouse or beacon to guide seafarers.

below: 123 Reconstruction model of Upper City, Pergamum. State Museums, East Berlin. The steeply sloping theater is at left; the altar to Zeus is in the center foreground.

The chief religious shrine of Pergamum was the immense altar to Zeus [124], erected by Eumenes II around 180 B.C. to commemorate the victories of his father, Attalus I, over the Gauls. Its base is decorated with a colossal frieze depicting the battle of the gods and giants. The triumphant figure of Zeus presumably stands as a symbol for the victorious king of Pergamum. The drama and violence of the battle find perfect expression in the tangled, writhing bodies, which leap out of the frieze in high relief, and in the intensity of the gestures and facial expressions [125]. The immense emotional impact of the scenes may prevent us from appreciating the remarkable skill of the artists, some of whom were brought from Athens to work on the project. However, the movement of the figures is very far from random and the surface of the stone has been carefully worked to reproduce the texture of hair, skin, fabric, metal, and so on.

124 Reconstruction model of the Great Altar to Zeus, Pergamum. c. 180 B.C. State Museums, East Berlin.

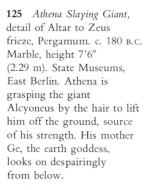

125 *Athena Slaying Giant,* detail of Altar to Zeus frieze, Pergamum. c. 180 B.C. Marble, height 7′6″ (2.29 m). State Museums, East Berlin. Athena is grasping the giant Alcyoneus by the hair to lift him off the ground, source of his strength. His mother Ge, the earth goddess, looks on despairingly from below.

right: 126 Agesander, Athenodorus, and Polydorus of Rhodes. *Laocoön Group.* c. 150 B.C. Marble, height 8′ (2.44 m). Vatican Museums, Rome. This statue was uncovered in 1506 in the ruins of Nero's Golden House. Note the similarity between Laocoön's head and the head of the giant Alcyoneus on the Pergamum frieze. The sons were made relatively small probably to indicate that, though they were grown men, they were sons.

below: 127 Earring. 4th–3rd century B.C. Gold, height 2⅜″ (6 cm). British Museum. The exquisite workmanship shows in this actual-size view. On either side are figures of Eros, a winged god of love. Above them are tiny female figures cut off at the knee.

The Altar of Zeus represents the most complete illustration of the principles and practice of Hellenistic art. It is, of course, a work on a grand, even grandiose, scale, intended to impress a wide public. But many of its characteristics occur in freestanding pieces of sculpture like the *Laocoön* [126]. This famous work shows the Trojan priest Laocoon, punished by the gods for his attempt to warn his people against bringing into their city the wooden horse left by the Greeks. To silence the priest, Apollo sends two sea serpents to strangle him and his sons. The large piece is superbly composed, with the three figures bound together by the sinuous curves of the serpents; each of them turns in a different direction under the agony of the creatures' coils.

The same richness of technique and elaborate design can be found in more intimate art works of the period. Hellenistic jewelry, for example, shows a lavish use of figures in high relief or independently moving in space [127]. The texture of the gold is often enriched by precious stones, which in many cases came from territories opened up by the conquests of Alexander. Hellenistic painting, like that of the Classical period, is lost, but the mosaic decorations made for private houses are rich in color and use illusionistic devices to suggest depth and space [Plate 12, page 156].

By the end of the Hellenistic period both artists and public seemed a little weary of so much richness and elaboration and returned to some of the principles of Classical art. At the same time the gradual conquest of the Hellenistic kingdoms by Rome and their absorption into the Roman Empire produced a new synthesis in which the achievements of Classical and Hellenistic Greece fused with the native Italian culture and passed on to later ages.

Further Reading

Burn, A. R. *Alexander the Great and the Hellenistic Empire.* London: Macmillan, 1947. A clearly written introduction to the period that is both brief and entertaining.

Cornford, F. M. *Before and After Socrates.* Cambridge: Cambridge University Press, 1960. Reprint of an earlier work written in 1932 by the great Plato scholar; not always easy, but rewarding.

Flacelière, R. *Daily Life in Greece at the Time of Pericles.* New York: Macmillan, 1965. A fascinating account filled with information and intelligently illustrated.

Kitto, H. D. F. *The Greeks.* Rev. ed. Baltimore: Penguin, 1957. This book, often unconventional and even controversial in its views, remains the best and most stimulating single-volume introduction to Greek culture in all its aspects.

Lattimore, R. *The Poetry of Greek Tragedy.* Baltimore: John Hopkins, 1958. A sensitive study of Greek tragedy from a literary point of view.

Ling, R. *The Greek World.* Oxford: Elsevier-Phaidon, 1976. Handsomely illustrated, a good introduction to the art and archaeology of Classical Greece.

Pickard-Cambridge, A. W. *The Dramatic Festivals of Athens.* 2nd ed. Oxford: Oxford University Press, 1968. One of the standard works on Greek drama. Perhaps more for the specialist than the general reader but contains much valuable information.

Renault, Mary. *The Nature of Alexander.* New York: Pantheon Books, 1975. A beautifully illustrated biography by the noted author of a number of novels about the ancient world, including two about Alexander, *Fire from Heaven* and *The Persian Boy.*

Schefold, K. *The Art of Classical Greece.* New York: Crown, 1967. Closely argued and not always easy to read; its detailed study and analysis of the art of the period provides far more than a simple survey.

Taplin, O. *The Stagecraft of Aeschylus.* Oxford: Oxford University Press, 1977. Discusses the work of all three of the Greek tragedians as plays rather than as poetry and is an up-to-date examination of problems in the staging of Greek drama. Often highly technical but very illuminating.

Tarn, W. W. *Alexander the Great.* Boston: Beacon, 1956. In two volumes, the first containing the narrative and the second sources and special studies. Even the reader who does not want the details of the second part should read the narrative, a classic account.

Taylor, A. E. *Plato: The Man and His Work.* London: Methuen, 1948. A masterly examination of Plato and his philosophy, still enlightening even if it does not reflect the most recent scholarship.

Suggestions for Listening

Apart from two fragments from the 5th century B.C., one of doubtful authenticity, the earliest Greek music to have survived dates to the late 2nd century B.C. Two hymns to Apollo were found on the walls of the Treasury at Delphi and a *skolion* (drinking song) was found carved on the tombstone of Seikilos, who died in Asia Minor around 100 B.C. All three pieces have been reconstructed and performed, and a number of recordings are available. Probably the most reliable one is that in Volume 1 of the *History of Music in Sound,* produced jointly by the Oxford University Press and RCA.

But beyond these tantalizing fragments is silence. One of the great creative achievements in our humanistic tradition is lost, probably forever. At various times in the history of music, composers have tried to imagine the effects produced by a Greek drama performed with music, in order to imitate it. The earliest surviving opera, Jacopo Peri's *Euridice* of 1600 (available on Telefunken 2635014), is the result of Renaissance curiosity about the Greeks, while Carl Orff's versions of *Antigone* and *Oedipus the King* represent 20th-century interpretations. Other composers have handled Greek dramatic subjects with greater freedom, retaining the stories but interpreting them in their own style. Perhaps the most powerful of all works based on a Greek play is Richard Strauss' *Elektra,* first performed in 1908 and available in a superb recording on London 1269. Although Strauss and his librettist Hugo von Hoffmansthal approached their subject from a modern point of view, incorporating ideas from the works of Freud and others, the shattering emotional impact of *Elektra* perhaps goes some way toward reproducing the original effect of the tragedies when first performed.

Another 20th-century composer, Igor Stravinsky, set a Latin version of *Oedipus the King* to music in his *Oedipus*

Rex (1927), available on London 1168. Although very different in spirit from Strauss' opera, Stravinsky's score is in its own way equally impressive, if more austere. Elsewhere he tried to recapture a different aspect of the Greek world, the sense of the balance and clarity that are so closely identified with the Classical period. Two of his ballet scores, *Orpheus* (1948) and the beautiful *Apollon Musagète,* or *Apollo Leader of the Muses* (1928), are available on Columbia MS 6646 in versions conducted by the composer.

Martha Graham's ballet *Clytemnestra,* inspired by the *Oresteia,* is one of the great classics of modern dance as well as a reminder of the expressive power dance can bring to the reenactment of ancient myths.

Questions for Further Discussion

1. Ever since the 4th century B.C., thinking human beings have categorized themselves—and others—as either "Platonists" or "Aristotelians." What are the chief distinctions between the two? Do they still have any validity in our own time?
2. On a very few occasions in the history of our culture a single city has, for a short time, produced a large number of great artists, writers, and thinkers—Athens in the 5th century B.C., for example, or Florence in the Renaissance. What kind of conditions made this possible? Could they be reproduced artificially, and, if so, should they be?
3. Greek mythology, and the dramas based on it, covers a wide range of human experience, but not all of it. What are some of the aspects of life which apparently did *not* interest the Greeks?
4. Thucydides wrote his *History of the Peloponnesian War* in the belief that people could learn from the mistakes of the past and thereby live better lives. If he was wrong—and events seem to show him so—what other justification is there for writing and reading history?
5. From the very beginning, Greek sculptors were accustomed to carve their male figures nude, and by the 4th century B.C. were also producing nude female figures. What does the Greek obsession with the naked body suggest about their world view? How does it compare with our own?
6. The Greek word for Greece is *Hellas* and for its peoples *Hellenes.* Why do we use the word "Greece," and what does it tell us about the transmission of Greek culture?

GENERAL EVENTS

LITERATURE & PHILOSOPHY

753 B.C.

753 B.C. Founding of Rome (traditional date)

c. 700 Development of Etruscan culture

509

ROMAN REPUBLIC

Conquest of Italy and Mediterranean

509 Expulsion of Etruscan kings and foundation of Roman Republic

c. 390 Sack of Rome by Gauls

264–241 First Punic War: Roman conquest of Sicily, Sardinia, Corsica

218–201 Second Punic War: Roman conquest of Spain

146 Destruction of Carthage: Africa becomes Roman province. Sack of Corinth: Greece becomes Roman province

c. 200–160 B.C. Ennius, *Annales,* epic poem; Plautus, *Mostellaria,* Roman comedy; Terence, Roman comedies

2d cent. Epicureanism and Stoicism imported to Rome

133

Political Crisis at Rome

90–88 Social War

82–81 Sulla dictator at Rome

60 First Triumvirate: Pompey, Caesar, Crassus

58–56 Caesar conquers Gaul

48 Battle of Pharsalus: war of Caesar and Pompey ends in death of Pompey. Caesar meets Cleopatra in Egypt

46–44 Caesar rules Rome as dictator until assassinated

43 Second Triumvirate: Antony, Lepidus, Octavian

c. 65–43 Lucretius, *On the Nature of Things,* Epicurean poem; Cicero, orations and philosophical essays; Catullus, lyric poems; Caesar, *Commentaries,* on Gallic wars

31

31 Battle of Actium won by Octavian

30 Death of Antony and Cleopatra

27–14 Octavian under name of Augustus rules as first Roman emperor

c. 27 B.C.–A.D. 14 Horace, *Odes* and *Ars Poetica;* Vergil, *Aeneid, Georgics, Eclogues;* Ovid, *Metamorphoses,* mythological tales; Livy, *Annals of the Roman People*

B.C.
- - - - - - - - - - -
A.D.

Stability

c. 6 Birth of Jesus; crucified c. A.D. 30

A.D. 14–68 Julio-Claudian emperors: Tiberius, Caligula, Claudius, Nero

69–96 Flavian emperors: Vespasian, Titus, Domitian

70 Capture of Jerusalem by Titus; destruction of Solomon's Temple

79 Destruction of Pompeii and Herculaneum

96–138 Adoptive emperors: Nerva, Trajan, Hadrian, et al.

138–192 Antonine emperors: Antoninus Pius, Marcus Aurelius, et al.

c. A.D. 100–150 Tacitus, *History;* Juvenal, *Satires;* Pliny the Younger, *Letters;* Suetonius, *Lives of the Caesars;* Epictetus, *Enchiridion,* on Stoicism

c. 166–179 Marcus Aurelius, *Meditations,* on Stoicism

ROMAN EMPIRE

180

Disintegration

193–235 Severan emperors: Septimius Severus, Caracalla, et al.

212 Edict of Caracalla

284

Reconstruction and Decline

284–305 Reign of Diocletian; return of civil order

301 Edict of Diocletian, fixing wages and prices

305 Constantius and Galerius rule as joint emperors

307–337 Reign of Constantine; sole emperor after 324

330 Founding of Constantinople

409–455 Vandals and Visigoths invade Italy, Spain, Gaul, Africa

476 Romulus Augustulus forced to abdicate as last Western Roman emperor

476 A.D.

The Roman Legacy

ART	ARCHITECTURE	MUSIC

c. 650–500 B.C.
Influence of Greek and
Orientalizing styles
on Etruscan art

late 6th cent.
Etruscan
Apollo,
from Veii

c. 616–509 B.C.
Etruscans drain
marshes, build temples,
construct roads

Extension of Greek
trumpet into Roman
tuba, used in games,
processions, battles

c. 2d cent. B.C. Greek
music becomes popular
at Rome

1st cent. Discovery
of concrete

1st cent. Realistic
portraiture; *Portrait
of Cicero*

c. 82 Sulla commissions
Sanctuary of Fortuna
Primagenia,
Praeneste

c. 30 B.C.–A.D. 30
Villa of Mysteries
frescoes, Pompeii

c. 20 *View of a Garden,*
fresco from Augustus'
villa, Prima Porta

13–9 *Ara Pacis*

Use of arch,
vault, dome,
principles of stress/
counterstress

c. A.D. 14
*Augustus
of Prima
Porta*

1st cent. A.D. Pont du
Gard, Nîmes; atrium-
style houses at Pompeii

c. 126 Pantheon,
Rome

Decline of realism

300–305 Diocletian's
palace, Split

306–315 Basilica of
Constantine, Rome

324–330 Colossal head
from Basilica of
Constantine, Rome

The Importance of Rome

The contribution of Rome to the development of Western civilization is tremendous. In fields like language, laws, politics, religion, and art Roman culture continues to affect our lives. The road network of modern Europe is based upon one planned and built by the Romans some two thousand years ago; the alphabet we use is the Roman alphabet; and the division of the year into twelve months of unequal length is a modified form of the calendar introduced by Julius Caesar in 46 B.C. Even after the fall of the Roman Empire the city of Rome stood for centuries as the symbol of civilization itself; later empires deliberately shaped themselves upon the Roman model.

The enormous impact of Rome upon our culture is partly due to the industrious and determined character of the Romans themselves, who very early in their history saw themselves as the divinely appointed rulers of the world. In the course of fulfilling their mission they spread Roman culture from the north of England to Africa, from Spain to India (see map below). This Romanization of the entire known world permitted the spread of ideas the Romans had drawn from other peoples. It was through the Romans that Greek art and literature were handed down into the Western tradition, and not from the Greeks themselves. The rapid spread of Christianity in the 4th century A.D. was a result of the decision of the Roman emperors to adopt it as the official religion of the Roman Empire. In these and in other respects, the legacy Rome was to pass on to Western civilization had been inherited from its predecessors.

The Romans themselves were surprisingly modest about their own cultural achievements, in fact, be-

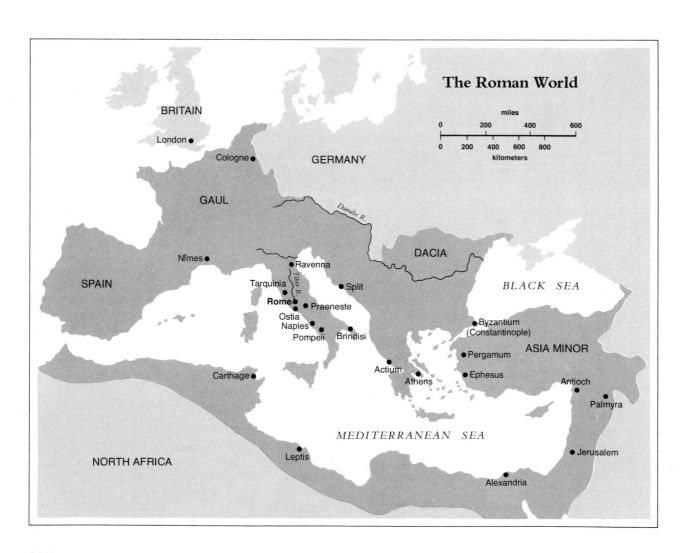

The Roman World

128 Gladiatorial contest with orchestra of hydraulic organ, trumpet, and horn players. Mosaic from villa near Zliten, North Africa, c. A.D. 70. Museum of Antiquities, Tripoli.

lieving that their strengths lay in good government and military prowess rather than in artistic and intellectual attainments. This rather uncharacteristic humility is clearly expressed in a famous passage from the *Aeneid,* the epic poem by Vergil to be discussed in detail later in this chapter. This passage, which summarizes Rome's destiny, transmits a clear message: Rome should get on with the job of ruling the world and leave luxuries like sculpture and astronomy to others.

> Let others fashion from bronze more lifelike, breathing images—
> For so they shall—and evoke living faces from marble;
> Others excel as orators, others track with their instruments
> The planets circling in heaven and predict when stars will appear.
> But, Romans, never forget that government is your medium!
> Be this your art:—to practise men in the habit of peace,
> Generosity to the conquered, and firmness against aggressors.

It is easy but unfair to accept the Romans' estimate of themselves as uncreative without questioning it. True, in some fields the Roman contribution was not very impressive. What little we know about Roman music, for example, suggests that its loss is hardly a serious one. It was intended mainly for performance at religious events like weddings and funerals, and as a background for social occasions. Musicians were often brought into aristocratic homes to provide after-dinner entertainment at a party, and individual performers, frequently women, would play before small groups in a domestic setting. Small bands of traveling musicians, playing on pipes and such percussion instruments as cymbals and tambourines, provided background music for the acrobats and jugglers who performed in public squares and during gladiatorial contests [128].

Nonetheless, for the Romans music certainly had none of the intellectual and philosophical significance it bore for the Greeks, and when Roman writers mention musical performances it is often to complain about the noise. The only serious development in Roman music was the extension of the Greek trumpet into a longer and louder bronze instrument known as the *tuba,* which was used on public occasions like games and processions and in battle, when an especially powerful type some 4 feet (1.2 meters) long gave the signals for attack and retreat. The sound was not pleasant.

In general, Roman music-lovers contented themselves with Greek music played on Greek instruments. Although serious music began to grow in popularity with the spread of Greek culture, it always remained an aristocratic rather than popular taste. The emperor Nero's love of music, coupled with his insistence on giving public concerts on the lyre, may even have hastened his downfall.

In areas other than music, the Roman achievement is considerable. There is no doubt that Roman art and literature rarely show the originality of their Greek predecessors, but originality is not the only artistic virtue, nor is its absence always a defect. The Roman genius, in fact, lay precisely in absorbing and assimilating influences from outside and going on to create from them something typically Roman. The lyric poetry of 1st-century-B.C. writers like Catullus was inspired by the works of Sappho, Alcaeus, and other Greek poets of the 6th century B.C., but nothing could be more Roman in spirit than Catullus' poems. In architecture, the Romans achieved a style that is one of the most impressive of all our legacies from the ancient world.

It is useful to emphasize the very real value of Roman art and literature because there has been a tendency since the 19th century to exalt the Greek cultural achievement at the expense of the Roman. All agree on the superior quality of Roman roads, sewers, and acqueducts; Roman sculpture or drama has in general been less highly rated, mainly because of comparisons with that of the Greeks. Any study of Roman culture inevitably involves examining the influences which went to make it up, and it is necessary always to remember the Roman ability to absorb and combine outside ideas and create something fresh from them.

Rome's history was a long one, beginning with the foundation of the city in the 8th century B.C. As the empire grew, Roman civilization developed along with it, assimilating the cultures of the peoples who fell under Roman domination. But long before the Romans conquered Greece or anywhere else, they were themselves conquered by the Etruscans, and the story of Rome's rise to power truly begins with the impact on Roman life made by Etruscan rule there.

The Etruscans and Their Art

The late 8th century B.C. was a time of great activity in Italy. The Greeks had reached the south coast and the island of Sicily. In the valley of the river Tiber, farmers and herdsmen of a group of tribes known as the Latins (origin of the name of the language spoken by the Romans throughout their history) were establishing small village settlements, one of which was to become the future imperial city of Rome. The most flourishing area at the time, however, was to the north of Rome, where in central Italy a new culture—the Etruscan—was appearing.

The Etruscans are among the most intriguing of ancient peoples, and ever since early Roman times

129 *Capitoline She-Wolf.* Etruscan, late 6th or early 5th century B.C. Bronze, length 4′4″ (1.32 m). Capitoline Museum, Rome. Although this statue or one very like it became the mascot of Rome, it was probably made by an Etruscan craftsman. The twins Romulus and Remus, legendary founders of the city, were added during the Renaissance.

scholars have argued about who they were, where they came from, and what language they spoke. Even today, in spite of the discoveries of modern archaeologists, we still know little about the origins of the Etruscans and their language has still not been deciphered. By 700 B.C. they had established themselves in the part of Italy named for them, Tuscany; but it is not clear whether they arrived from abroad or whether their culture was merely a more developed form of an earlier Italian one. The ancient Greeks and Romans believed that the Etruscans had come to Italy from the East, perhaps from Lydia, an ancient kingdom in Asia Minor. Indeed, many aspects of their life and much of their art have pronounced Eastern characteristics. In other ways, however, the Etruscans have much in common with their predecessors in central Italy. Even so, no other culture related to the Etruscans' has ever been found. Whatever their origins, they were to have a major effect upon Italian life, and on the growth of Rome and its culture in particular [129].

From the very beginning of their history the Etruscans showed an outstanding sophistication and technological ability. The sumptuous gold treasures buried in their tombs are evidence both of their material prosperity and of their superb craftsmanship. The commercial contacts of the Etruscans extended over most of the western Mediterranean and in Italy itself Etruscan cities like Cerveteri and Tarquinia developed rich artistic traditions [Plate 13, page 221]. Much Etruscan art shows the presence of Greek ideas. The Etruscans, like the Greeks, were strongly affected by orientalizing influences. Nonetheless, Etruscan art has its own special character, a kind of elemental force almost primitive in spirit, although the craftsmanship and techniques are highly sophisticated. Unlike the Greeks, the Etruscans were less interested in intellectual problems of proportion or understanding how the human body works, than in producing an immediate impact upon the viewer. The famous statue of Apollo found in 1916 at Veii [130] is unquestionably related to Greek models, but the tension of the god's pose and the sinister quality of his smile produce an effect of great power in a typically Etruscan way. Other Etruscan art is more relaxed, showing a love of nature rarely found in Greek art. The wonderful paintings in the Tomb of Hunting and Fishing at Tarquinia [Plate 14, page 221] convey a marvelous sense of light and air, the hazy blue background evoking all the sensations of sea and spray.

This immensely gifted people was bound to exert

130 *Apollo of Veii*. Etruscan, late 6th or early 5th century B.C. Terra cotta, height 5′10″ (1.78 m). Museo Nazionale di Villa Giulia, Rome.

a strong influence on the development of civilization in Italy; Etruscan occupation of Rome from 616 to 510 B.C. marks a turning point in Roman history. According to later tradition, the city of Rome had been founded in 753 B.C. and was ruled in its earliest days by kings (in actual fact Rome was probably not much more than a small country town for most of this period). The later Romans' own grandiose picture of the early regal days of their city was intended to glamorize its origins, but only with the arrival of the Etruscans did anything like an urban center begin to develop. Etruscan engineers drained a large marshy area, previously uninhabitable, which became the community's center, the future Roman Forum. They built temples and shrines and constructed roads. Under Etruscan instruction new crafts developed and guilds were established, including those of the bronze workers, goldsmiths, and carpenters. Among other innovations the Etruscans introduced a number of things we are accustomed to think of as typically Roman, including public games like chariot racing and even the toga, the most characteristic form of Roman dress.

Most important, however, was the fact that under Etruscan domination the Romans found themselves for the first time in contact with the larger world. Instead of being simple villagers living in a small community governed by tribal chiefs they became part of a large cultural unit with links throughout Italy and abroad. Within a hundred years Rome had truly learned the lessons of Etruscan technology and culture, had driven out the Etruscans, and had begun her unrelenting climb to power.

The rise of Rome signaled the decline of the Etruscans throughout Italy. In the centuries following their expulsion from Rome in 510 B.C., their cities were conquered and their territory taken over by the Romans. In the 1st century B.C. they automatically received the right of Roman citizenship and became absorbed into the Roman Empire. The gradual col-lapse of their world is mirrored in later Etruscan art. The wall paintings in the tombs become increasingly gloomy, suggesting that for an Etruscan of the 4th or 3rd century B.C. the misfortunes of this life were followed by the tortures of the next in an underworld ruled by demons and monsters. The old couple from Volterra whose anxious faces are so vividly depicted on the lid of their sarcophagus [131] give us some idea of the troubled spirit of the final days of Etruscan culture.

Republican Rome

The end of Etruscan rule brought a change in the system of Roman government. Instead of choosing a new king, Rome constituted itself a republic, governed by the people somewhat along the lines of the Greek city-states, although less democratically. Two chief magistrates or consuls were elected for a one-year term by all the male citizens, but the principal assembly, the Senate, drew most of its members from Roman aristocratic families. From the very beginning, therefore, power was concentrated in the hands of the upper class, the patricians, although the lower class (the plebeians) was permitted to form its own assembly. The leaders elected by the plebeian assembly, the tribunes, represented the plebeians' interests and protected them against state officials who treated them unjustly. The meeting place for both the Senate and the assemblies of the people was the

131 Lid of a funerary urn showing the dead couple whose ashes it contains. Etruscan, 1st century B.C. Terra cotta, length 18½″ (47 cm). Museo Guarnacci, Volterra.

132 Aerial view of the Roman forum—center of the political, economic, and religious life of the Roman world—as it appears today.

forum, the large open space at the foot of the Palatine and Capitoline hills that had been drained and made habitable by the Etruscans [132].

From the founding of the Roman Republic to its bloody end in the civil wars following the murder of Julius Caesar in 44 B.C., its history was dominated by agitation for political equality. Yet, the first major confrontation, the conflict between patricians and plebeians, never seriously endangered political stability in Rome or military campaigns abroad. Both sides showed a flexibility and spirit of compromise that produced a gradual growth in plebeian power while avoiding any split disastrous enough to interrupt Rome's growing domination of the Italian peninsula. The final plebeian victory came in 287 B.C. with the passage of the Hortensian Law, which made the decisions of the plebeian assembly binding on the entire Senate and Roman people. By then most of Italy had already fallen under Roman control.

Increasing power brought increasing problems. In the 3rd and 2nd centuries B.C. Rome began to build its empire abroad. By the 1st century B.C. the whole Hellenistic world had been conquered. From Spain to the Middle East stretched a vast territory consisting of subject provinces, protectorates, and nominally free kingdoms, all of which depended on Roman good will and Roman administrative efficiency.

Unfortunately, the Romans had been too busy in acquiring their empire to think very hard about how to rule it; the results were frequently chaotic. Provincial administration was incompetent and often corrupt. The long series of wars had hardened the Roman character, leading to insensitivity and, frequently, brutality in the treatment of conquered peoples. This situation was not helped by increasing political instability at home. The old balance of power struck between the patricians and plebeians was being increasingly disturbed by the rise of a middle class, many of whom were plebeians who had made their fortunes in the wars. Against this background were fought bitter struggles that eventually caused the collapse of the Republic.

By the 1st century B.C. it was apparent that the political system which had been devised for a thriving but small city five hundred years earlier was hopelessly inadequate for a vast empire. Discontent among Rome's Italian allies (*socii*) led to open revolt. Although the Romans were victorious in the Social War of 90–88 B.C. the cost in lives and economic stability was tremendous. The ineffectiveness of the Senate and the frustration of the Roman people led to a series of struggles among the leading statesmen for supreme power. The Roman general Sulla ruled as dictator for a brief and violent period beginning in 82 B.C., but suddenly resigned three years later, in 79 B.C. There followed a long-drawn-out series of political skirmishes between Pompey, the self-appointed defender of the Senate, and Julius Caesar, culminating in Caesar's withdrawal to Gaul and subsequent return to Rome in 49 B.C. After a short but bitter conflict Caesar defeated Pompey in 48 B.C. at the Battle of Pharsalus and returned to Rome as dictator, only to be assassinated himself in 44 B.C. The civil wars that followed brought the Republic to its unlamented end.

The years of almost uninterrupted violence had a profound effect upon the Roman character, and the relief felt when a new era dawned under the first emperor, Augustus, can only be fully appreciated in this light. Yet the figures who dominated the events of the late Republic—or were dominated by them—are among the most fascinating in Roman history. Julius Caesar (100–44 B.C.) is perhaps the most famous Roman of them all. Brilliant politician, skilled general, expert administrator and organizer, he was also able to write the history of his own military campaigns, in his *Commentaries,* in a simple but gripping style. In the four years during which he ruled Rome he did much to repair the damage of the previous decades. His assassination on March 15, 44 B.C., at the hands of a band of devoted republicans served only to prolong Rome's agony for another thirteen years—as well as providing Shakespeare with the plot for one of his best-known plays.

Among the most lasting achievements of Julius Caesar's dictatorship and of Roman culture in general was the creation of a single unified code of civil law, the *Ius Civile*. The science of law is one of the few original creations of Roman literature. The earliest legal code of the Republic was the so-called Law of the Twelve Tables of 451–450 B.C. By the time of Caesar, however, most of this law had become either irrelevant or out of date and had been replaced by a mass of later legislation, much of it contradictory and confusing. Caesar's *Ius Civile,* produced with the help of the most eminent legal experts of the day, served as the model for later times. The most complete collection of Roman law was, in fact, made during Byzantine times by the Byzantine emperor Justinian I (A.D. 527–565).

Perhaps the most endearing figure of the late Republic was Marcus Tullius Cicero (106–43 B.C.), who first made his reputation as a lawyer. He is certainly the figure of this period about whom we know the most, for he took part in a number of important legal cases and embarked on a political career. In 63 B.C., he served as consul. A few years later, the severity with which he had put down a plot against the government during his consulship earned him a short period in exile as the result of the scheming of a rival political faction. He returned in triumph, however, and in the struggle between Pompey and Caesar supported Pompey, although Caesar seems to have forgiven him. Cicero never really trusted Caesar, in spite of his admiration for the dictator's abilities. His mixed feelings are well expressed in a letter to his friend Atticus after having dined Caesar, by then the ruler of the Roman world:

> Quite a guest, although I have no regrets and everything went very well indeed. . . . He was taking medicine for his digestion, so he ate and drank without worrying and seemed perfectly at ease. It was a lavish dinner, excellently served and in addition well prepared and seasoned with good conversation, very agreeable, you know. What can I say? We were human beings together. But he's not the kind of guest to whom you'd say "it's been fun, come again on the way back." Once is enough! We talked about nothing serious, a lot about literature: he seemed to enjoy it and have a good time. So now you know about how I entertained him—or rather had him billeted on me. It was a nuisance, as I said, but not unpleasant.

From letters like these we can derive an incomparably vivid picture of Cicero and his world. Almost 900 were published, most of them after his death. If they often reveal Cicero's weaknesses—his vanity, his inability to make a decision, his stubbornness—they confirm his humanity and sensitivity. For his contemporaries and for later ages his chief fame was nevertheless as an orator. Although the cases and causes that prompted his speeches have ceased to have any but historical interest, the power of a Ciceronian oration can still thrill the responsive reader, especially when it is read aloud.

Roman Comedy

The Romans put most of their energy into political and military affairs, leaving little time for art or literature. By the 3rd century B.C., when most of the Mediterranean was under their control and they could afford to relax, they were overwhelmed intellectually and artistically by the Greeks. Conquest of the Hellenistic kingdoms of the East and of Greece itself brought the Romans into contact with Hellenistic Greek culture (see pages 186–192). Thus, from the 3rd century B.C. most Roman works of art followed Greek models in form and content. Roman plays were based on Greek originals, Roman temples imitated Greek buildings, and Roman sculpture and painting depicted episodes from Greek mythology.

Greek influence extends to the works of Ennius (239–169 B.C.), known to later Romans as the father of Roman poetry. Almost all of his works are lost, but from later accounts Ennius' tragedies appear to have been adapted from Greek models. His major work was the *Annals,* an epic chronicle of the history of Rome, in which for the first time a Greek metrical scheme was used to write Latin verse.

The two comic playwrights Plautus (c. 254–184 B.C.) and Terence (c. 195–159 B.C.) are the first Roman writers whose works have survived in quantity. Their plays are adaptations of Greek comedies [133]. Plautus, the more boisterous of the two, is fond of comic songs and farcical intrigues. Terence's style is more refined and his characters show greater realism. It says something about the taste of the Roman public that Plautus was by far the more successful. In later times, however, Terence's sophisticated style was much admired. His plays were studied and imitated both during the Middle Ages and in more recent times. Both authors were fond of extremely

elaborate plots involving mistaken identities, identical twins, and general confusion, with everything sorted out in the last scene.

General confusion is certainly an element in Plautus' *Mostellaria (The Haunted House),* in which the action revolves around the sudden return home from abroad of Theopropides, an elderly Athenian gentleman. Theopropides' son Philolaches has taken advantage of his father's absence to install in the family house his girlfriend as well as a male friend, Callidamates, who has brought along his own girl, Delphium. When Theopropides arrives back unexpectedly the morning after a wild party, it is up to the cunning slave Tranio to save the situation by inventing a ghost that he claims is haunting the house.

Although its plot is based on a lost Greek play, *The Haunted House* is thoroughly Roman in spirit. Plautus succeeds in breathing new life into a rather predictable story line. Our attention is held not by the suspense of the situation—it is clear that sooner or later the old father is bound to find out what has been going on, and more than probable that he will eventually extend grudging forgiveness to both son

133 Group of actors back-stage preparing to perform a comedy. Pompeii. Mosaic, 23¼ × 32½" (59 × 83 cm). Museo Nazionale, Naples. The figure at right is putting on his costume; note his mask on the table and others on the floor.

and slave—but by Plautus' ability to create amusing and lively characters. Although there is little in the way of psychological insight, Plautus gives his figures a crude vigor and their dialogue has an earthy humor that is a far cry from the rather tired elegance of the Greek comedies from which he borrowed. Like many other writers in the history of Western literature, Plautus produced original plays by building on the examples of his predecessors—a tradition that continued through the 16th and 17th centuries, when French and English writers (including Shakespeare) turned to Plautus for material. (The old man who avoids his "haunted" house was an element in the highly successful 1960s musical comedy *A Funny Thing Happened on the Way to the Forum,* which has interpolations from half a dozen plays by Plautus.)

In Act II of *The Haunted House* we meet many of the characters in the play. Philolaches and Callidamates are spoiled young men-about-town, expert in eating, drinking, and making love, but useless when it comes to taking decisive action. Delphium, who plays only a small part in this scene, is the prototype of the dumb girlfriend. Theopropides, the crusty old father, is another stock comic character. The central figure is, of course, Tranio, the wily slave who is all things to all people and who finds time for a comforting word to Delphium in the middle of organizing the cowardly Philolaches' retreat. In the long scene that closes the act he rises to heights of bloodcurdling comic invention before he manages to scare Theopropides away. More eloquent and resourceful than his masters, Tranio's irrepressible energy and doleful sense of humor make an immediate appeal to our sympathies.

Plautus
from THE HAUNTED HOUSE
Act II

Enter TRANIO *from left, excited.*

TRANIO   Great Jupiter is trying with all his power and might to bring me and our young master Philolaches to ruin. Our hope's all shot. There is no place anywhere for confidence. Even the Goddess of Safety herself couldn't save us if she tried. I've just seen a mighty mountain of misery and misfortune over at the harbor. The master's returned from abroad and Tranio is all washed up. [*To the audience*] Is there anyone of you guys who would like to make a little loose change? All he has 10 to do is let himself be nailed on the cross in my place today. Where are all your tough-skinned, hard-as-nails roughnecks, or those mugs who'll

go right under the enemy's siege-works to earn two bits, or those human pin-cushions who'll let their bodies be pierced by ten spears at a time? I'll give a prize of a thousand dollars to the first fellow who dashes up to the cross, but on this one condition, that his feet and hands should be nailed double. After that's been done, he can come and ask 20 me to pay him the cash right off. But I—oh, but I'm out of luck if I don't rush straight home.

PHILOLACHES   Hooray! Here comes the grub. There's Tranio coming back from the harbor.

TRANIO   [*panting*]   Philolaches!

PHILOLACHES   What's the matter?

TRANIO   You and me both—

PHILOLACHES   You and me, what?

TRANIO   We're dead ducks!

PHILOLACHES   What do you mean?   30

TRANIO   Your father's here!

PHILOLACHES   What's that you've said?

TRANIO   Our goose is cooked. I say your father has come.

PHILOLACHES   Where is he? Tell me.

TRANIO   Where is he? He's here.

PHILOLACHES   Who says so? Who saw him?

TRANIO   I saw him myself, I'm telling you.

PHILOLACHES   Good night! What do I do now?

TRANIO   Why the devil are you asking me what 40 you do? You're lying on the couch.

PHILOLACHES   Did you really see him?

TRANIO   I tell you I did.

PHILOLACHES   You're absolutely sure?

TRANIO   Surest thing alive.

PHILOLACHES   I'm sunk if what you say is true!

TRANIO   What good would it do me to tell a lie?

PHILOLACHES   What am I to do now?

TRANIO   Order all this stuff to be cleared out of here. Who's that sleeping over there?   50

PHILOLACHES   It's Callidamates. Wake him up, Delphium.

DELPHIUM   [*shakes him*]   Callidamates, Callidamates, wake up!

CALLIDAMATES   I'm awake. Gimme a drink.

DELPHIUM   Wake up! Philolaches' father is back from abroad!

CALLIDAMATES   [*holding up a wine glass*]   Here's to the old boy's health.

PHILOLACHES   He's healthy, all right, but I'm 60 more dead than alive.

CALLIDAMATES   Dead and alive? That's impossible.

[*Drops back to sleep.*]

PHILOLACHES   For heaven's sake! Please get up! My father has come back!

CALLIDAMATES   Your father's come back? Tell him to go 'way again. What business he got coming back here?

[*Drops back to sleep.*] 70

PHILOLACHES What am I to do? My father will be here in a minute to find me miserably drunk, the house full of party guests and women. It's a wretched business not to start digging a well until thirst has got you by the throat. That's the way I am, miserably trying to think up what to do, now that my father is upon me.

TRANIO Just look at that! He's put his head down and is dead to the world. Wake him up!

PHILOLACHES [*shakes him*] Won't you wake up? 80 I'm telling you my father will be here any minute.

CALLIDAMATES [*starts up, shouting*] What's that you say? Your father? Gimme my sandals! I'll get my sword and by God, I'll kill your father!

PHILOLACHES Oh, you're ruining everything!

DELPHIUM Hush up, please!

PHILOLACHES [*to some slaves*] Lift him up right away and drag him inside.

CALLIDAMATES [*as he is carried into the house, struggling*] By God, I'll use you for a chamber pot if you 90 don't bring me a chamber pot!

PHILOLACHES Good night!

TRANIO Don't be downhearted. I'll doctor up this trouble all right.

PHILOLACHES I'm sunk!

TRANIO Oh, be quiet! I'll think up some way to straighten everything out. Are you satisfied if I fix things so that when your father comes, he not only won't go inside, but will even run for dear life far away from the house? You folks just go on 100 inside and clear all these things out of here as quick as you can.

PHILOLACHES Where shall I be?

TRANIO Where you want most to be. You'll be with this girl and with that one.

DELPHIUM Hadn't we better leave?

TRANIO You're not going *this* far, Delphium. [*With a gesture of thumb and forefinger*] You can go on drinking inside the house, and not one drop less than you would otherwise. 110

PHILOLACHES Oh dear! I'm worried stiff about how these sweet words of yours will turn out.

TRANIO Can't you calm down and do what I tell you?

PHILOLACHES I guess I can.

TRANIO First of all, you go inside, Philematium, and you too, Delphium.

DELPHIUM We'll both do just as you wish.

[*They go in.*]

TRANIO May Jupiter grant that you really do 120 so! (*To* PHILOLACHES) Now you pay careful attention to what I want done. First of all, see that the house is locked up tight right away. And don't you let anyone make a sound inside.

PHILOLACHES I'll see to that.

TRANIO Just as though there isn't a soul living in the house.

PHILOLACHES All right.

TRANIO And don't let anybody answer when the old man knocks at the door. 130

PHILOLACHES Is that all?

TRANIO Have someone bring that Spartan house key out to me. I'll lock up the house from the outside.

PHILOLACHES I'm entrusting myself and my hopes to your protection, Tranio.

[*Enters house.*]

TRANIO It doesn't matter a darn whether it's the patron or the client that tries to help a fellow, if he has no daring in his heart. Just anybody, 140 whether he is good or bad, finds it easy to do some wicked act on the shortest notice; but the thing to look out for, and what really takes a clever fellow, is that what he has planned and done for a wicked purpose should all turn out peacefully and without trouble, so that he won't get into some mess that will make him sorry he's alive. Now I'll fix things so that all the storm we've raised here will turn out quietly and peacefully and not cause us any trouble at all. 150

SPHAERIO, *Theopropides' slave, comes out of the house.*

But what are you coming out for, Sphaerio?

SPHAERIO *holds out the Spartan key.*

All right, all right. You've obeyed orders perfectly.

SPHAERIO He told me to beg you just as hard as I could to scare his father off any way at all, so that he won't come inside to him.

TRANIO Well, you can tell him this. I'll fix it so that the old man won't even dare to look at the 160 house, but will cover his head and run away in absolute terror. Give me the key and go back inside and lock the door. I'll lock it from the outside also.

SPHAERIO *goes in.*

Now you can tell him to come on. I'll play such games with the old man while he's still here and alive that they'll beat any funeral games which he'll get after he's dead. I'll move away from the door this way and watch from here at a distance, 170 so that I can spring my bundle of tricks on the old boy when he comes.

Enter THEOPROPIDES *from left, accompanied by two slaves carrying his baggage.*

THEOPROPIDES I'm surely grateful to you, Neptune, for having let me get away from you by the skin of my teeth, and just make it home. But if there ever is a time after this when you catch me placing so much as my foot upon your waters, I give you full permission to do to me then and there what you tried to do to me just now. I'm off you for good from this day on. I've already trusted you all that I was ever going to.

TRANIO [aside] Well, well, Neptune, you certainly made a dreadful mistake when you missed so fine an opportunity.

THEOPROPIDES After three years in Egypt I've got back home. I guess my family will be glad to see me back.

TRANIO [aside] By heavens, they would be lots gladder to see a messenger reporting that you were dead!

THEOPROPIDES [reaches the door] What's the meaning of this? The door is locked in the daytime. I'll knock. [Knocks.] Say, isn't there anyone to open the door? [He pounds and kicks on the door.]

TRANIO [approaching] Who is this man who has come up so close to our house?

THEOPROPIDES [aside] Why, this is my own slave Tranio.

TRANIO O Theopropides! How are you, master? I'm so glad to see you back safe. Have you been quite all right?

THEOPROPIDES Quite all right, as you see.

TRANIO That's just fine.

THEOPROPIDES But how about you folks? Have you gone crazy?

TRANIO What do you mean?

THEOPROPIDES Why, here you are, walking in the street with not a soul keeping watch in the house and no one to unlock the door or even answer. Why, I almost broke this whole door down by banging on it.

TRANIO Hey, did you touch this house?

THEOPROPIDES Why shouldn't I touch it? I'm telling you I almost broke the door down banging on it.

TRANIO [horrified] You touched it?

THEOPROPIDES I did touch it, I'm telling you, and I banged on it.

TRANIO [groaning] Oh!

THEOPROPIDES What's wrong?

TRANIO That's simply dreadful!

THEOPROPIDES What is the matter?

TRANIO I just can't tell you what a dreadful, what an awful thing you've done.

THEOPROPIDES What do you mean?

TRANIO [pulling him away from the house] Start running, for heaven's sake, and get away from the house! Run this way! Run here! In this direction, toward me!

He starts running; THEOPROPIDES *follows.*

Did you really touch that door?

THEOPROPIDES How in the world could I bang on it without touching it?

TRANIO Good heavens! You've absolutely ruined———

THEOPROPIDES Ruined whom?

TRANIO Your entire household!

THEOPROPIDES Damn you for those ill-omened words!

TRANIO I'm afraid you won't be able to clear yourself and your family.

THEOPROPIDES What for? What is this news you're bringing me all of a sudden?

TRANIO Say, tell those two fellows to get away from there.

THEOPROPIDES [to the slaves] You may go.

TRANIO And don't you fellows dare touch the house. Touch the ground the way I do.

He bends down and presses his hands on the ground. The slaves leave.

THEOPROPIDES By heavens, won't you please tell me what all this business means?

TRANIO For seven months now nobody has set foot inside this house, ever since we moved out.

THEOPROPIDES Speak up! What did you do that for?

TRANIO Look around you and make sure there isn't anybody listening in on what we say.

THEOPROPIDES [looking around] It's perfectly safe.

TRANIO Better look around again.

THEOPROPIDES There's nobody around. You can speak now.

TRANIO A murder has been committed.

THEOPROPIDES What's that? I don't understand.

TRANIO A murder has been committed, I'm telling you—long ago, a really ancient crime.

THEOPROPIDES An ancient crime?

TRANIO Oh, we've only just lately discovered that it happened.

THEOPROPIDES What is this crime you're talking about, you rascal? Who did it? Speak up!

TRANIO A host overpowered his guest and murdered him. I guess it must have been that fellow who sold you this house.

THEOPROPIDES Murdered him?

TRANIO Then he stole this guest's gold and he buried this guest right on the spot, here in this house.

THEOPROPIDES What makes you think this really happened?

TRANIO I'll tell you. Listen. Your son had had dinner out and after he came back home from dinner, we all of us go off to bed. We fall asleep. It just happened that I had forgotten to put out the lamp. And then he screams all of a sudden, awfully loud.

THEOPROPIDES Who screams? My son?

TRANIO Sh! Shut up, listen now. He said that 290 the dead man came to him in his sleep.

THEOPROPIDES Oh, in his sleep, you say.

TRANIO Yes. But listen now. He said that the dead man spoke to him like this.

THEOPROPIDES In his sleep?

TRANIO It would sure be a funny thing if he spoke to him while he was awake, seeing that he was killed sixty years ago. Sometimes you're just too dumb for words. Can't you keep still?

THEOPROPIDES All right. I'll keep still.   300

TRANIO Now listen to what that dead man said to him. "I am a stranger from across the seas, a Transmarinian. Here do I dwell. This dwelling is assigned to me, for Orcus has refused to admit me to Acheron, because I am prematurely deprived of life. Through violated faith was I ensnared. My host slew me here and buried me secretly in this house without due funeral rites—that accursed man—for the sake of my gold. Now you must get you hence. This house is damned, this dwelling is 310 accursed!" And all the excitements, all the terrible things that have been happening here, I could hardly tell you in a year.

A noise is heard within.

THEOPROPIDES Sh! Sh! [*Moves toward door.*]

TRANIO Why, what in the world is the matter?

THEOPROPIDES There was a noise at the door.

TRANIO [*as if talking to the ghost within*] He's the one that knocked.

THEOPROPIDES [*terrified*] I haven't a drop of 320 blood left. The dead are summoning me to Acheron while I'm still alive!

TRANIO [*aside*] I'm finished! Those folks in there will ruin my whole plan. I'm just dreadfully afraid that the old man will catch me at it.

THEOPROPIDES What are you talking to yourself for?

TRANIO Get away from the door! Run away, I beg you, for heaven's sake!

THEOPROPIDES [*bewildered*] Where shall I run 330 away? Why don't you run, too?

TRANIO I have nothing to fear. I have made my peace with the dead.

VOICE WITHIN Hey, Tranio.

TRANIO [*going to the door*] You'll not call me, if you're wise. I didn't do anything wrong and I didn't bang on this door.

THEOPROPIDES Why are you so excited, Tranio? Whom are you talking to?

TRANIO Oh, were you the one that called me? 340

God help me, but I thought that dead man was complaining because you had knocked on the door. But what are you still standing here for and not doing what I'm telling you to do?

THEOPROPIDES What shall I do?

TRANIO Don't look behind you. Run away! Cover your head!

THEOPROPIDES Why don't you run?

TRANIO I have made my peace with the dead.

THEOPROPIDES I know. But how about a mo- 350 ment ago? Why were you so scared?

TRANIO Don't bother about me, I'm telling you. I'll take care of myself. You just keep on going and run away as hard as you can, and pray to Hercules.

THEOPROPIDES [*running off to the right*] Hercules, I pray to you!

TRANIO And so do I pray—that he'll make you drop dead today, my old fellow. Great gods, I appeal to you! What a mess of trouble I have 360 cooked up today!

Lyric Poetry: Catullus

When educated Romans of the late Republic stopped to think about something other than politics it was likely to be love. Roman lyric poetry, often on a romantic theme, is one of the most rewarding genres of Latin literature. The first great Roman lyric poet, Catullus (c. 80–54 B.C.), is one of the best-loved of all Roman authors. Instead of philosophical or historical themes, he returned to a traditional subject from Sappho's time—personal experience—and charted the course of his own love affair with a girl whom he calls Lesbia. Among his works are 25 short poems describing the course of his relationship that range from the ecstasy of its early stages to the disillusionment and despair of the final breakup. The clarity of his style is the perfect counterpart to the directness with which he expresses his emotions. In a poem like this ode to Lesbia his use of language achieves a musical beauty.

Catullus
V

My darling, let us live
  And love for ever.
They with no love to give,
  Who feel no fever,
Who have no tale to tell
  But one of warning—
The pack of them might sell
  For half a farthing.

The sunset's dying ray
  Has its returning,
But fires of our brief day
  Shall end their burning
In night where joy and pain
  Are past recalling—
So kiss me, kiss again—
  The night is falling.

Kiss me and kiss again,
  Nor spare thy kisses.
Let thousand kisses rain
  A thousand blisses.
Then, when ten thousand more
  Their strength have wasted,
Let's wipe out all the score
  Of what we've tasted:
Lest we should count our bliss
  To our undoing,
Or others grudge the kiss
  On kiss accruing.

But the contentment was not to last. Lesbia has lost interest, although Catullus continues to protest his love:

Catullus
LXXXVII

None could ever say that she,
Lesbia! was so loved by me.
Never all the world around
Faith so true as mine was found:
If no longer it endures
(Would it did!) the fault is yours.
I can never think again
Well of you: I try in vain:
But—be false—do what you will—
Lesbia! I must love you still.

The poet's desperation increases as he realizes the hopelessness of his cause, but it is one thing to see the sensible course of action and another to follow it.

Catullus
LXXV

The office of my heart is still to love
  When I would hate.
Time and again your faithlessness I prove
  Proven too late.
Your ways might mend, yet my contempt could
    never
  Be now undone.
Yet crimes repeated cannot stop this fever
  From burning on.

At last he can take no more, and the last of the Lesbia poems express bitterness and hatred:

Catullus
LVIII

She that I loved, that face,
  Those hands, that hair,
Dearer than all my race,
  As dear as fair—
See her where throngs parade
  Th' imperial route,
Plying her skill unpaid—
  Rome's prostitute.

These poems, personal though they are, are not simply an outpouring of feelings. Catullus makes his own experiences universal. However trivial one man's unhappy love affair may seem in the context of the grim world of the late Republic, Lesbia's inconstancy has achieved a timelessness unequaled by many more serious events.

Art and Architecture

In the visual arts as in literature, the late Republic shows the translation of Greek styles into new Roman forms. The political scene was dominated by individuals like Cicero and Caesar; their individualism was captured in portrait busts that were both realistic and psychologically revealing. To some extent these realistic portraits are based on such Etruscan models as the heads of the old couple on the Volterra sarcophagus [see 131] rather than on Hellenistic portraits, which idealized their subjects. However, the subtlety and understanding shown in portraits like those of Cicero, Caesar, and Hadrian represent a typically Roman combination and amplification of others' styles. In many respects, indeed, Roman portraiture represents Roman art at its most creative and sensitive. It certainly opened up new expressive possibilities, as artists discovered how to use physical appearance to convey something about character. Many of the best Roman portraits serve as revealing psychological documents, expressing, for example, Cicero's self-satisfaction as well as his humanity [134], or Hadrian's brooding aloofness, which does not completely hide his vulnerability [135]. Realistic details like the lines at the corners of the eyes and mouth, the hollows in the cheeks, or the set of the lips are used to express both outer appearance and

above: 134 *Bust of Cicero*. Roman, 1st century B.C. Uffizi, Florence. This portrait of one of the leading figures of the late Republic suggests the ability of Roman sculptors of the period to capture both likeness and character. Cicero is portrayed as thoughtful and preoccupied.

above right: 135 *Bust of the Emperor Hadrian*. Roman, c. A.D. 120. Marble. Museo Nazionale, Rome. Hadrian's complex character was recognized in his own time and makes a special appeal to ours. With this portrait bust the sculptor attempted to capture something of the reticent, brooding spirit of this architect-philosopher-ruler.

right: 136 Plan of the Sanctuary of Fortuna Primigenia, Praeneste (Palestrina). This vast complex, constructed by Sulla after his destruction of the city in 82 B.C., is a series of six immense terraces crowned by a semicircular structure in front of which stood an altar.

inner character. The new skill, as it developed, could of course be put to propaganda use, and statesmen and politicians soon learned that they could project their chosen self-image through their portraits.

The powerful political figures of the period also used the medium of architecture to express their authority. The huge sanctuary constructed by Sulla at Praeneste (modern Palestrina) around 82 B.C. has all the qualities of symmetry and grandeur we associate with later Roman imperial architecture although it took its inspiration from massive Hellenistic building programs such as that at Pergamum [136] Caesar himself had a large area in the center of Rome cleared for the construction of a forum, or public meeting place, to be named after him. In time it was dwarfed by later monumental fora, but it had initiated the construction of public buildings for personal display and glory.

Roman Philosophy

The Romans produced little in the way of original philosophical writing. Their practical nature made them suspicious of professional philosophers and unable to appreciate the rather subtle delights involved in arguing both sides of a complex moral or ethical question. In consequence most of the great Roman philosophical writers devoted their energies to expounding Greek philosophy to a Roman audience. The two principal schools of philosophy to make an impact at Rome, Epicureanism and Stoicism, were both imported from Greece.

Epicureanism never really gained many followers, in spite of the efforts of the poet Lucretius (99–55 B.C.), who expounded its doctrines to a Roman audience in his brilliant poem *On the Nature of Things (De rerum natura)*. A remarkable synthesis of poetry and philosophy, this work alone is probably responsible for whatever admiration the Romans could muster for a system of thought so different from their own traditional virtues of simplicity and seriousness. According to Epicurus (341–271 B.C.), the founder of the school, the correct goal and principle of human actions is pleasure. Although Epicureanism stresses moderation and prudence in the pursuit of pleasure, the Romans insisted on thinking of the philosophy as a typically Greek enthusiasm for self-indulgence and debauchery.

Lucretius tried to correct this impression by emphasizing the profoundly intellectual and rational aspects of Epicureanism. Its principal teaching was that the gods, if they exist, play no part in human affairs or in the phenomena of nature; as a result we can live our lives free from superstitious fear of the unknown and the threat of divine retribution. The Epicurean theory of matter explains the universe in purely physical terms. It describes the universe as made up of two elements: small particles of matter, or atoms, and empty space. The atoms are completely solid, possessing the qualities of size, shape, and mass, and can be neither split nor destroyed. Their joining together to form complex structures is entirely caused by their random swerving in space, without interference from the gods. As a result human life can be lived in complete freedom; we can face the challenges of existence and even natural disasters like earthquakes or plagues with complete serenity, since their occurrence is random and outside our control. According to Epicurus, at death the atoms that make up our body separate, and neither body, mind, nor soul survives. Since no part of us is in any way immortal, we should have no fear of death, which offers no threat of punishment in a future world but brings only the complete ending of any sensation.

Epicureanism's rejection of a divine force in the world and its campaign against superstition probably appealed to the Romans as little as its claim that the best life was one of pleasure and calm composure. The hard-headed practical moralizing of the Roman mentality found far more appeal in the other school of philosophy imported into Rome from Greece, Stoicism. The Stoics taught that the world was governed by Reason and that Divine Providence watched over the virtuous, never allowing them to suffer evil. The key to becoming virtuous lay in willing or desiring only that which was under one's own control. Thus riches, power, or even physical health—all subject to the whims of Fortune—were excluded as objects of desire. For the Stoic all that counted was that which was subject to the individual's will.

Although Stoicism had already won a following at Rome by the 1st century B.C. and was discussed by Cicero in his philosophical writings, its chief literary exponents came slightly later. Seneca (8 B.C.–A.D. 65) wrote a number of essays on Stoic morality. He had an opportunity, and the necessity, to practice the moral fortitude about which he wrote when his former pupil, the emperor Nero, ordered him to commit suicide, since the taking of one's own life was fully sanctioned by Stoic philosophers. Perhaps the most impressive of all Stoic writers is Epictetus (c. A.D. 50–134), a former slave who established a school of philosophy in Rome and then in Greece. In his *Encheiridion (Handbook)* he recommends an absolute trust in Divine Providence, to be maintained through every misfortune. For Epictetus the philosopher represented the spokesman of Providence itself "taking the human race for his children."

Epictetus' teachings exerted a profound influence on the last great Stoic, the emperor Marcus Aurelius (A.D. 121–180), who was constantly plagued with the difficulty of being a Stoic and an emperor at the same time. Delicate in health, sentimental, inclined to be disillusioned by the weaknesses of others, Marcus Aurelius struggled hard to maintain the balance between his public duty and his personal convictions. While on military duty he composed his *Meditations,* which are less a philosophical treatise than an account of his own attempt to live the life of a Stoic. As many of his observations make clear, this was no easy task: "Tell yourself every morning 'Today I shall meet the officious, the ungrateful, the bullying, the treacherous, the envious, the selfish. All of them behave like this because they do not know the difference between good and bad.'"

Yet, even though Stoicism continued to attract a number of Roman intellectuals, the great majority of Romans remained immune to the appeal of a philosophical life. Both in the 1st century B.C. and later, the very superstition both Stoicism and Epicureanism sought to combat remained deeply ingrained in the Roman character. Festivals in honor of traditional deities were celebrated until long after the advent of Christianity. Rituals that tried to read the future by the traditional examination of animals' entrails and other time-honored methods continued to be popular. If the Romans had paused more often to meditate on the nature of existence, they would probably have had less time to civilize the world.

The Age of Augustus

With the assassination of Julius Caesar a brief respite from civil war was followed by further turmoil [137]. Caesar's lieutenant, Mark Antony, led the campaign to avenge his death and punish the conspirators. He was joined in this by Caesar's young great-nephew, Octavius, who had been named by Caesar as his heir and had recently arrived in Rome from the provinces. It soon became apparent that Antony and Octavius (or Octavian, to use the name he now took) were unlikely to coexist very happily. After the final defeat of the conspirators in 42 B.C. a temporary peace was obtained by putting Octavian in charge of the western provinces and sending Antony to the East. A final confrontation could not be long delayed, and Antony's fatal involvement with Cleopatra alienated much of his support at Rome. The end came in 31 B.C., at the Battle of Actium. The forces of Antony, reinforced by those of Cleopatra, were routed, and the couple commited suicide. Octavian was left as sole ruler of the Roman world, a world that was now in ruins. His victory marked the end of the Roman Republic.

When Octavian took supreme control after the Battle of Actium, Rome had been continuously in-

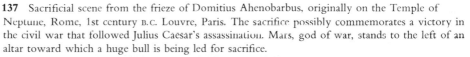

137 Sacrificial scene from the frieze of Domitius Ahenobarbus, originally on the Temple of Neptune, Rome, 1st century B.C. Louvre, Paris. The sacrifice possibly commemorates a victory in the civil war that followed Julius Caesar's assassination. Mars, god of war, stands to the left of an altar toward which a huge bull is being led for sacrifice.

volved both in civil and external wars for much of a century. The political and cultural institutions of Roman life were beyond repair, the economy was wrecked, and large areas of Italy were in complete turmoil. By the time of his death in A.D. 14, Rome had achieved a peace and prosperity unequaled in its history before or after. The art and literature created during his rule represents the peak of the Roman cultural achievement. To the Romans of his own time it seemed that a new Golden Age had dawned, and for centuries afterward his memory was revered. As the first Roman emperor, Octavian inaugurated the second great period in Roman history—the Empire, which lasted technically from 27 B.C., when he assumed the title Augustus, until A.D. 476, when the last Roman emperor was overthrown. In many ways, however, the period began with the Battle of Actium and continued in the subsequent Western and Byzantine empires.

Augustus' cultural achievement was stupendous, but it could only have been accomplished in a world at peace. Perhaps Augustus' greatest achievement, then, was to restore calm and dignity to Roman life. Once again the Romans were inspired with a sense of destiny and purpose, and the results are visible in their art.

Augustan Literature: Vergil

Augustus himself played an active part in supporting and encouraging the writers and artists of his day; many of their works echo the chief themes of Augustan politics—the return of peace, the importance of the land and agriculture, the putting aside of ostentation and luxury in favor of a simple life, and above all the belief in Rome's destiny as world ruler. Many of the greatest works of Roman sculpture commemorate Augustus and his deeds; Horace and Vergil sing his praises in their poems. It is sometimes said that much of this art was propaganda, organized by the emperor to present the most favorable picture possible of his reign. Even the greatest works of the time do relate in some way or other to the Augustan world view, and it is difficult to imagine a poet whose philosophy differed radically from that of the emperor being able to give voice to it. But we have no reason to doubt the sincerity of the gratitude felt toward Augustus or the strength of what seems to have been an almost universal feeling that at last a new era had dawned. In any case, from the time of Augustus art at Rome became in large measure offi-

cial. Most of Roman architecture and sculpture of the period was public, commissioned by the state, and served state purposes.

The greater the artist, the more complex was the response to the Augustan vision. The greatest of all Roman poets, Publius Vergilius Maro (70–19 B.C.), devoted the last ten years of his life to the composition of an epic poem intended to honor Rome, and, by implication, Augustus. The result was the *Aeneid,* one of the great poems of the world, not completely finished at the poet's death. For much of the Middle Ages, Vergil himself was held in the highest reverence. A succession of great poets has regarded him as their master—Dante, Tasso, Milton, among others. Probably no work of literature in the entire tradition of Western culture has been more loved and revered than the *Aeneid*—described by T. S. Eliot as *the classic* of Western society—yet its significance is complex and by no means universally agreed upon.

The *Aeneid* was not Vergil's first poem. The earliest authentic works that have survived are ten short pastoral poems known as the *Eclogues* or sometimes the *Bucolics,* which deal with the joys and sorrows of the country and the shepherds and herdsmen who live there. Vergil himself was the son of a farmer; his deep love of the land emerges also in his next work, the four books of the *Georgics* (29 B.C.). Their most obvious purpose is to serve as a practical guide to farming, and they offer helpful advice on such subjects as cattle breeding and beekeeping as well as a deep conviction that the strength of Italy lies in its agricultural richness. In a great passage in the second book of the *Georgics* Vergil hails the "ancient earth, great mother of crops and men." He does not disguise the hardships of the farmer's life, the poverty, hard work, and frequent disappointments, but still feels that only life in the country brings true peace and contentment [138].

The spirit of the *Georgics* clearly matched Augustus' plans for an agricultural revival. Indeed, it was probably the emperor himself who commissioned Vergil to write an epic poem that would be to Roman literature what the *Iliad* and *Odyssey* were for Greek: a national epic. The task was immense. Vergil had to find a subject that would do appropriate honor to Rome and its past as well as commemorate the achievements of Augustus. The *Aeneid* is not a perfect poem (on his deathbed Vergil ordered his friends to destroy it), but in some ways it surpasses even the high expectations Augustus must have had for it. Vergil succeeded in providing Rome with its national

138 View of a garden, from the villa of Augustus at Prima Porta. c. 20 B.C. Fresco, detail. Museo Nazionale Romano, Rome. The peaceful scene, with its abundance of fruit and flowers, reflects the interest in country life expressed in Vergil's *Eclogues* and *Georgics*.

epic and stands as a worthy successor to Homer. At the same time, he created a profoundly moving study of the nature of human destiny and personal responsibility.

The *Aeneid* is divided into twelve books. Its hero is a Trojan prince, Aeneas, who flees from the ruins of burning Troy and sails west to Italy to found a new city, the predecessor of Rome. Vergil's choice was significant: Aeneas' Trojan birth establishes connections with the world of Homer; his arrival in Italy involves the origins of Rome; and the theme of a fresh beginning born, as it were, out of the ashes of the past corresponds perfectly to the Augustan mood of revival. We first meet Aeneas and his followers in the middle of his journey from Troy to Italy, caught in a storm that casts them up on the coast of North Africa. They make their way to the city of Carthage, where they are given shelter by the Carthaginian ruler, Queen Dido. At a dinner in his honor Aeneas describes the fall of Troy (Book II) and his wanderings from Troy to Carthage (Book III), in the course of which his father Anchises had died.

In Book IV, perhaps the best known, the action resumes where it had broken off at the end of Book I. The tragic love that develops between Dido and Aeneas tempts Aeneas to stay in Carthage and thereby abandon his mission to found a new home in Italy. But a divine messenger is sent to remind Aeneas of his responsibilities. He leaves after an agonizing encounter with Dido, and the distraught queen kills herself.

Book V brings the Trojans to Italy. In Book VI, Aeneas journeys to the underworld to hear from the spirit of his father the destiny of Rome. This tremendous episode provides the turning point of the poem. Before it we see Aeneas, and he sees himself, as a man prone to human weaknesses and subject to human feelings. After Anchises' revelations, Aeneas' humanity is replaced by a sense of mission and the weary, suffering Trojan exile becomes transformed into a "man of destiny."

In Books VII and VIII the Trojans arrive at the river Tiber and Aeneas visits the future site of Rome while the Italian peoples prepare to resist the Trojan invaders. The last four books describe in detail the war between the Trojans and the Latins, in the course of which there are losses on both sides. The *Aeneid* ends with the death of the great Italian warrior Turnus and the final victory of Aeneas.

It is tempting to see Aeneas as the archetype of Augustus; certainly Vergil must have intended us to draw some parallels. Other historical analogies can

139 *Death of Dido* from the *Vatican Vergil*. 5th century. Manuscript illustration. Vatican Library, Rome.

also be found: Dido and Cleopatra, for example, have much in common. The *Aeneid* is, however, far more than an allegorical retelling of the events leading up to the foundation of the empire. Put briefly, Aeneas undertakes a responsibility for which initially he has no real enthusiasm and which costs him and others considerable suffering. It would have been much easier for him to have stayed in Carthage, or settled somewhere else along his way, rather than push forward under difficult circumstances into a foreign land where he and his followers were not welcome.

Once he has accepted his mission, however, he fulfils it conscientiously and in the process learns to sublimate his own personal desires to a common good. If this is indeed a portrait of Augustus, it represents a much more complex view of his character than we might expect. And Vergil goes further. If greatness can only be acquired by sacrificing human individuals, is it worth the price? Is the future glory of Rome a sufficient excuse for the cruel and unmanly treatment of Dido? Readers will provide their own answers. Vergil's might have been that the sacrifices were probably worth it, but only just. Much, of course, depends on individual views on the nature and purpose of existence, and for Vergil there is no doubt that life is essentially tragic. The prevailing mood of the poem is one of melancholy regret for the sadness of human lives and the inevitability of human suffering.

The language in which all this is expressed is of majestic dignity and sustained beauty. The tone is less varied than Homer's: there are, for example, no moments of comic relief and none of Homer's exulting in the sheer physical prowess of his heroes. As poetry, though, the *Aeneid* touches chords and explores depths of human experience few other writers have managed to reach.

Scenes like the confrontation between Dido and Aeneas in Book IV have inspired artists and musicians through the ages. Memorable musical versions have been provided by composers as different as Henry Purcell and Hector Berlioz; Dido's death has been represented many times in art [139, 140]. The scene begins as Aeneas has received the divine message to continue on his journey. He says nothing to Dido for the moment and makes his preparations for departure. The queen cannot be fooled so easily; in a frenzy of grief and rage, she accuses him of deserting her. Vergil conveys all the pathos of Dido's wounded love in lines 327–330, where she confesses that if Aeneas had given her a child the blow of his departure would have been less. Aeneas' response seems cold and indicates for the first time in the *Aeneid* the sacrifice of personal feelings his mission requires. His appeal to common sense and the will of the gods only enrages Dido further; she dismisses him with words of furious contempt. The most poignant moment in the scene, however, is reserved for the last four lines,

140 Joshua Reynolds. *The Death of Dido.* 1781. Oil on canvas, 4'8" × 7'10" (1.42 × 2.39 m). Buckingham Palace. By gracious permission of Her Majesty the Queen.

in which we are shown Aeneas' terrible dilemma. Faced with the choice between love and duty he has chosen duty, but only at the price of personal anguish. This translation is by C. Day Lewis.

Vergil
from the AENEID, Book IV

But who can ever hoodwink a woman in
    love? The queen,
Apprehensive even when things went well, now
    sensed his deception,
Got wind of what was going to happen. That
    mischievous Rumour,
Whispering the fleet was preparing to sail, put
    her in a frenzy.
Distraught, she witlessly wandered about the
    city, raving   300
Like some Bacchante driven wild, when the
    emblems of sanctity
Stir, by the shouts of "Hail, Bacchus!" and
    drawn to Cithaeron
At night by the din of revellers, at the triennial
    orgies.
Finding Aeneas at last, she cried, before he
    could speak:—
  Unfaithful man, did you think you could do
    such a dreadful thing
And keep it dark? yes, skulk from my land
    without one word?
Our love, the vows you made me—do these
    not give you pause,

Nor even the thought of Dido meeting a painful
    death?
Now, in the dead of winter, to be getting your
    ships ready
And hurrying to set sail when northerly gales
    are blowing,   310
You heartless one! Suppose the fields were not
    foreign, the home was
Not strange that you are bound for, suppose
    Troy stood as of old,
Would you be sailing for Troy, now, in this
    stormy weather?
Am I your reason for going? By these tears, by
    the hand you gave me—
They are all I have left, to-day, in my
    misery—I implore you,
And by our union of hearts, by our marriage
    hardly begun,
If I have ever helped you at all, if anything
About me pleased you, be sad for our broken
    home, forgo
Your purpose, I beg you, unless it's too late for
    prayers of mine!
Because of you, the Libyan tribes and the
    Nomad chieftains   320
Hate me, the Tyrians are hostile: because of you
    I have lost
My old reputation for faithfulness—the one
    thing that could have made me
Immortal. Oh, I am dying! To what, my guest,
    are you leaving me?

"Guest"—that is all I may call you now, who
    have called you husband.
Why do I linger here? Shall I wait till my
    brother, Pygmalion,
Destroys this place, or Iarbas leads me away
    captive?
If even I might have conceived a child by you
    before
You went away, a little Aeneas to play in the
    palace
And, in spite of all this, to remind me of you
    by his looks, oh then
I should not feel so utterly finished and desolate. 330
    She had spoken. Aeneas, mindful of Jove's
    words, kept his eyes
Unyielding, and with a great effort repressed his
    feeling for her.
In the end he managed to answer:—
    Dido, I'll never pretend
You have not been good to me, deserving of
    everything
You can claim. I shall not regret my memories
    of Elissa
As long as I breathe, as long as I remember my
    own self.
For my conduct—this, briefly: I did not look to
    make off from here
In secret—do not suppose it; nor did I offer you
    marriage
At any time or consent to be bound by a
    marriage contract.
If fate allowed me to be my own master, and
    gave me   340
Free will to choose my way of life, to solve my
    problems,
Old Troy would be my first choice: I would
    restore it, and honour
My people's relics—the high halls of Priam
    perpetuated,
Troy given back to its conquered sons, a
    renaissant city,
Had been my task. But now Apollo and the
    Lycian
Oracle have told me that Italy is our bourne.
There lies my heart, my homeland. You, a
    Phoenician, are held by
These Carthaginian towers, by the charm of
    your Libyan city:
So can you grudge us Trojans our vision of
    settling down
In Italy? We too may seek a kingdom abroad.   350
Often as night envelops the earth in dewy
    darkness,
Often as star-rise, the troubled ghost of my
    father, Anchises,

Comes to me in my dreams, warns me and
    frightens me.
I am disturbed no less by the wrong I am doing
    Ascanius,
Defrauding him of his destined realm in
    Hesperia.
What's more, just now the courier of heaven,
    sent by Jupiter—
I swear it on your life and mine—conveyed to
    me, swiftly flying,
His orders: I saw the god, as clear as day, with
    my own eyes,
Entering the city, and these ears drank in the
    words he uttered.
No more reproaches, then—they only torture
    us both.   360
God's will, not mine, says "Italy".
    All the while he was speaking she gazed at
    him askance,
Her glances flickering over him, eyes exploring
    the whole man
In deadly silence. Now, furiously, she burst
    out:—
    Faithless and false! No goddess mothered
    you, no Dardanus
Your ancestor! I believe harsh Caucasus begat
    you
On a flint-hearted rock and Hyrcanian tigers
    suckled you.
Why should I hide my feelings? What worse can
    there be to keep them for?
Not one sigh from him when I wept! Not a
    softer glance!
Did he yield an inch, or a tear, in pity for her
    who loves him?   370
I don't know what to say first. It has come to
    this,—not Juno,
Not Jove himself can view my plight with the
    eye of justice.
Nowhere is it safe to be trustful. I took him, a
    castaway,
A pauper, and shared my kingdom with him—I
    must have been mad—
Rescued his lost fleet, rescued his friends from
    death.
Oh, I'm on fire and drifting! And now Apollo's
    prophecies,
Lycian oracles, couriers of heaven sent by
    Jupiter
With stern commands—all these order you to
    betray me.
Oh, of course this is just the sort of transaction
    that troubles the calm of
The gods. I'll not keep you, nor probe the
    dishonesty of your words,   380

Chase your Italy, then! Go, sail to your realm
    overseas!
I only hope that, if the just spirits have any power,
Marooned on some mid-sea rock you may
    drink the full cup of agony
And often cry out for Dido. I'll dog you, from
    far, with the death-fires;
And when cold death has parted my soul from
    my body, my spectre
Will be wherever you are. You shall pay for the
    evil you've done me.
The tale of your punishment will come to me
    down in the shades.
    With these words Dido suddenly ended, and
    sick at heart
Turned from him, tore herself away from his
    eyes, ran indoors,
While he hung back in dread of a still worse
    scene, although   390
He had much to say. Her maids bore up the
    fainting queen
Into her marble chamber and laid her down on
    the bed.
    But the god-fearing Aeneas, much as he
    longed to soothe
Her anguish with consolation, with words that
    would end her troubles,
Heavily sighing, his heart melting from love of
    her,
Nevertheless obeyed the gods and went off to
    his fleet.

No account of the *Aeneid* would be complete
without an extract from Book VI, which was to have
a powerful influence on Dante. It describes Aeneas'
journey to the underworld led by his guide, the Sibyl
of Cumae, to learn of the future destiny both of himself and of Rome. As in *The Epic of Gilgamesh* and the
Odyssey, the poet uses a journey to represent a voyage of the spirit. The opening lines of this extract
evoke magnificently the melancholy gloom of the
underworld; as Aeneas comes to the river of the dead
the poet emphasizes the sadness of those trying to
cross it by the pathos of his images (lines 309–312).
Aeneas' journey is necessary because he has to con-
front his past and come to terms with it before he can
move on to his heroic future destiny. As the Sibyl
leads him through the ranks of the dead he meets
Palinurus, an old comrade who had fallen overboard
on the way from Troy and drowned. The most emotional encounter, however, is with Dido. Now it is
Aeneas who weeps and pleads, while Dido neither
looks at him nor speaks.

Vergil
from the AENEID, Book VI

You gods who rule the kingdom of souls!
    You soundless shades!
Chaos, and Phlegethon! O mute wide leagues of
    Nightland!—
Grant me to tell what I have heard! With your
    assent
May I reveal what lies deep in the gloom of the
    Underworld!
    Dimly through the shadows and dark
    solitudes they wended,
Through the void domiciles of Dis, the bodiless
    regions:
Just as, through fitful moonbeams, under the
    moon's thin light,   270
A path lies in a forest, when Jove has palled the
    sky
With gloom, and the night's blackness has bled
    the world of colour.
See! At the very porch and entrance way to
    Orcus
Grief and ever-haunting Anxiety make their
    bed:
Here dwell pallid Diseases, here morose Old
    Age,
With Fear, ill-prompting Hunger, and squalid
    Indigence,
Shapes horrible to look at, Death and Agony;
Sleep, too, which is the cousin of Death; and
    Guilty Joys,
And there, against the threshold, War, the
    bringer of Death:
Here are the iron cells of the Furies, and lunatic
    Strife
Whose viperine hair is caught up with a
    headband soaked in blood.   280
    In the open a huge dark elm tree spreads
    wide its immemorial
Branches like arms, whereon, according to old
    wives' tales,
Roost the unsolid Dreams, clinging everywhere
    under its foliage.
Besides, many varieties of monsters can be found
Stabled here at the doors—Centaurs and
    freakish Scyllas,
Briareus with his hundred hands, the Lernaean
    Hydra
That hisses terribly and the flame-throwing
    Chimaera,
Gorgons and Harpies, and the ghost of three-
    bodied Geryon.
Now did Aeneas shake with a spasm of fear,
    and drawing   290

His sword, offered its edge against the creatures'
    onset:
Had not his learned guide assured him they
    were but incorporeal
Existences floating there, forms with no
    substance behind them,
He'd have attacked them, and wildly winnowed
    with steel mere shadows.
    From here is the road that leads to the dismal
      waters of Acheron.
Here a whirlpool boils with mud and immense
    swirlings
Of water, spouting up all the slimy sand of
    Cocytus.
A dreadful ferryman looks after the river
    crossing,
Charon: Appallingly filthy he is, with a bush of
    unkempt
White beard upon his chin, with eyes like jets
    of fire;   300
And a dirty cloak draggles down, knotted about
    his shoulders.
He poles the boat, he looks after the sails, he is
    all the crew
Of the rust-coloured wherry which takes the
    dead across—
An ancient now, but a god's old age is green
    and sappy.
This way came fast and streaming up to the
    bank the whole throng:
Matrons and men were there, and there were
    great-heart heroes
Finished with earthly life, boys and unmarried
    maidens,
Young men laid on the pyre before their
    parents' eyes;
Multitudinous as the leaves that fall in a forest
At the first frost of autumn, or the birds that
    out of the deep sea   310
Fly to land in migrant flocks, when the cold of
    the year
Has sent them overseas in search of a warmer
    climate.
So they all stood, each begging to be ferried
    across first,
Their hands stretched out in longing for the
    shore beyond the river.
But the surly ferryman embarks now this, now
    that group,
While others he keeps away at a distance from
    the shingle.
Aeneas, being astonished and moved by the
    great stir, said:—
    Tell me, O Sibyl, what means this
      rendezvous at the river?

What purpose have these souls? By what
    distinction are some
Turned back, while other souls sweep over the
    wan water?   320
    To which the long-lived Sibyl uttered this
    brief reply:—
    O son of Anchises' loins and true-born
      offspring of heaven,
What you see is the mere of Cocytus, the
    Stygian marsh
By whose mystery even the gods, having
    sworn, are afraid to be forsworn.
All this crowd you see are the helpless ones, the
    unburied:
That ferryman is Charon: the ones he conveys
    have had burial.
None may be taken across from bank to
    awesome bank of
That harsh-voiced river until his bones are laid to rest.
Otherwise, he must haunt this place for a
    hundred years
Before he's allowed to revisit the longed-for
    stream at last.   330
    The son of Anchises paused and stood stock
    still, in deep
Meditation, pierced to the heart by pity for their
    hard fortune.
He saw there, sorrowing because deprived of
    death's fulfilment,
Leucaspis and Orontes, the commodore of the
    Lycian
Squadron, who had gone down, their ship being
    lost with all hands
In a squall, sailing with him the stormy seas
    from Troy.
    And look! yonder was roaming the
      helmsman, Palinurus,
Who, on their recent voyage, while watching
    the stars, had fallen
From the afterdeck, thrown off the ship there in
    mid-passage.
A sombre form in the deep shadows, Aeneas
    barely   340
Recognised him; then accosted:—
    Which of the gods, Palinurus,
Snatched you away from us and made you
    drown in the midsea?
Oh, tell me! For Apollo, whom never before
    had I found
Untruthful, did delude my mind with this one
    answer,
Foretelling that you would make your passage
    to Italy
Unharmed by sea. Is it thus he fulfils a sacred
    promise?

Palinurus replied:—
The oracle of Phoebus has not tricked you,
My captain, son of Anchises; nor was I
    drowned by a god.
It was an accident: I slipped, and the violent shock
Of my fall broke off the tiller to which I was
    holding firmly   350
As helmsman, and steering the ship. By the
    wild seas I swear
That not on my own account was I frightened
    nearly so much as
Lest your ship, thus crippled, its helmsman
    overboard,
Lose steerage-way and founder amid the
    mountainous waves.
Three stormy nights did the South wind
    furiously drive me along
Over the limitless waters: on the fourth day I just
Caught sight of Italy, being lifted high on a
    wave crest.
Little by little I swam to the shore. I was all but safe,
When, as I clung to the rough-edged cliff top,
    my fingers crooked
And my soaking garments weighing me down,
    some barbarous natives   360
Attacked me with swords, in their ignorance
    thinking that I was a rich prize.
Now the waves have me, the winds keep
    tossing me up on the shore again.
So now, by the sweet light and breath of
    heaven above
I implore you, and by your father, by your
    hopes for growing Ascanius
Redeem me from this doom, unconquered one!
    Please sprinkle
Dust on my corpse—you can do it and quickly
    get back to port Velia:
Or else, if way there is, some way that your
    heavenly mother
Is showing you (not, for sure, without the
    assent of deity
Would you be going to cross the swampy
    Stygian stream),
Give poor Palinurus your hand, take me with
    you across the water   370
So that at least I may rest in the quiet place, in
    death.
    Thus did the phantom speak, and the Sibyl
        began to speak thus:—
    This longing of yours, Palinurus, has carried
        you quite away.
Shall you, unburied, view the Styx, the austere
    river
Of the Infernal gods, or come to its bank
    unbidden?

Give up this hope that the course of fate can be
    swerved by prayer.
But hear and remember my words, to console
    you in your hard fortune.
I say that the neighbouring peoples, compelled
    by portents from heaven
Occurring in every township, shall expiate your
    death,
Shall give you burial and offer the solemn dues
    to your grave,   380
And the place shall keep the name of Palinurus
    for ever.
    Her sayings eased for a while the anguish of
        his sad heart;
He forgot his cares in the joy of giving his
    name to a region.
    So they resumed their interrupted journey,
        and drew near
The river. Now when the ferryman, from out
    on the Styx, espied them
Threading the soundless wood and making fast
    for the bank,
He hailed them, aggressively shouting at them
    before they could speak:—
    Whoever you are that approaches my river,
        carrying a weapon,
Halt there! Keep your distance, and tell me why
    you are come!
This is the land of ghosts, of sleep and
    somnolent night: 390
The living are not permitted to use the Stygian
    ferry.
Not with impunity did I take Hercules,
When he came, upon this water, nor Theseus,
    nor Pirithous,
Though their stock was divine and their powers
    were irresistible.
Hercules wished to drag off on a leash the
    watch-dog of Hades,
Even from our monarch's throne, and dragged
    it away trembling:
The others essayed to kidnap our queen from
    her lord's bedchamber.
    The priestess of Apollo answered him
        shortly, thus:—
    There is no such duplicity here, so set your
        mind at rest;
These weapons offer no violence: the huge
    watch-dog in his kennel   400
May go on barking for ever and scaring the
    bloodless dead,
Prosperpine keep her uncle's house,
    unthreatened in chastity.
Trojan Aeneas, renowned for war and a duteous
    heart,

Comes down to meet his father in the shades of
    the Underworld.
If you are quite unmoved by the spectacle of
    such great faith,
This you must recognise—
    And here she disclosed the golden
Bough which was hid in her robe. His angry
    mood calms down.
No more is said. Charon is struck with awe to see
After so long that magic gift, the bough fate-
    given;
He turns his sombre boat and poles it towards
    the bank.   410
Then, displacing the souls who were seated
    along its benches
And clearing the gangways, to make room for
    the big frame of Aeneas,
He takes him on board. The ramshackle craft
    creaked under his weight
And let in through its seams great swashes of
    muddy water.
At last, getting the Sibyl and the hero safe
    across,
He landed them amidst wan reeds on a dreary
    mud flat.
    Huge Cerberus, monstrously couched in a
    cave confronting them,
Made the whole region echo with his three-
    throated barking.
The Sibyl, seeing the snakes bristling upon his
    neck now,
Threw him for bait a cake of honey and wheat
    infused with   420
Sedative drugs. The creature, crazy with hunger,
    opened
Its three mouths, gobbled the bait; then its huge
    body relaxed
And lay, sprawled out on the ground, the whole
    length of its cave kennel.
Aeneas, passing its entrance, the watch-dog
    neutralised,
Strode rapidly from the bank of that river of no
    return.
    At once were voices heard, a sound of
    mewling and wailing,
Ghosts of infants sobbing there at the threshold,
    infants
From whom a dark day stole their share of
    delicious life,
Snatched them away from the breast, gave them
    sour death to drink.
Next to them were those condemned to death
    on a false charge.   430
Yet every place is duly allotted and judgment is
    given.

Minos, as president, summons a jury of the
    dead: he hears
Every charge, examines the record of each; he
    shakes the urn.
Next again are located the sorrowful ones who
    killed
Themselves, throwing their lives away, not
    driven by guilt
But because they loathed living: how they
    would like to be
In the world above now, enduring poverty and
    hard trials!
God's law forbids: that unlovely fen with its
    glooming water
Corrals them there, the nine rings of Styx corral
    them in.
Not far from here can be seen, extending in all
    directions,   440
The vale of mourning—such is the name it
    bears: a region
Where those consumed by the wasting torments
    of merciless love
Haunt the sequestered alleys and myrtle groves
    that give them
Cover; death itself cannot cure them of love's
    disease.
Here Aeneas descried Phaedra and Procris, sad
Eriphyle displaying the wounds her heartless
    son once dealt her,
Evadne and Pasiphae; with them goes
    Laodamia;
Here too is Caeneus, once a young man, but
    next a woman
And now changed back by fate to his original
    sex.
Amongst them, with her death-wound still
    bleeding, through the deep wood   450
Was straying Phoenician Dido. Now when the
    Trojan leader
Found himself near her and knew that the form
    he glimpsed through the shadows
Was hers—as early in the month one sees, or
    imagines he sees,
Through a wrack of cloud the new moon rising
    and glimmering—
He shed some tears, and addressed her in
    tender, loving tones:—
    Poor, unhappy Dido, so the message was
    true that came to me
Saying you'd put an end to your life with the
    sword and were dead?
Oh god! was it death I brought you, then? I
    swear by the stars,
By the powers above, by whatever is sacred in
    the Underworld,

left: **Plate 13** Fibula from the Regolini-Galassi tomb at Cerveteri. Etruscan, c. 650 B.C. Gold, length 12½″ (32 cm). Vatican Museums, Rome. The elaborate relief on this large pin for fastening clothing uses Eastern motifs.

below: **Plate 14** Wall painting from the Tomb of Hunting and Fishing, Tarquinia. c. 520 B.C. Fresco. Men, fish, and birds are all rendered naturalistically, with acute observation. Note the bird perched on the waves to the left of the diving fish and the hunter at right.

Plate 15 Wall paintings from the Villa of the Mysteries, Pompeii. c. 60 B.C. Frescoes. Probably no ancient work of art has been more argued about than these paintings. They seem to relate to the cult of the Greek god Dionysus and the importance of the cult for girls approaching marriage, but many of the details are difficult to interpret. There is no argument, however, about the high quality of the paintings.

It was not of my own will, Dido, I left your
    land.   460
Heaven's commands, which now force me to
    traverse the shades,
This sour and derelict region, this pit of
    darkness, drove me
Imperiously from your side. I did not, could not
    imagine
My going would ever bring such terrible agony
    on you.
Don't move away! Oh, let me see you a little
    longer!
To fly from me, when this is the last word fate
    allows us!
    Thus did Aeneas speak, trying to soften the
    wild-eyed,
Passionate-hearted ghost, and brought the tears
    to his own eyes.
She would not turn to him; she kept her gaze
    on the ground,
And her countenance remained as stubborn to
    his appeal   470
As if it were carved from recalcitrant flint or a
    crag of marble.

At last she flung away, hating him still, and
    vanished
Into the shadowy wood where her first
    husband, Sychaeus,
Understands her unhappiness and gives her an
    equal love.
None the less did Aeneas, hard hit by her
    piteous fate,
Weep after her from afar, as she went, with
    tears of compassion.

Augustan Sculpture

Many of the characteristics of Vergil's poetry can also be found in contemporary sculpture. In a relief from one of the most important works of the period, the *Ara Pacis* (Altar of Peace), Aeneas himself performs a sacrifice on his arrival in Italy in front of a small shrine that contains two sacred images bought from Troy [141]. More significantly, the *Ara Pacis* depicts the abundance of nature that could flourish again in the peace of the Augustan age. The altar, begun on

141 Aeneas sacrificing, from the Ara Pacis, Rome. 13–9 B.C. Marble. Aeneas is depicted in the manner of a Classical Greek god; the landscape and elaborate relief detail are typical of late Hellenistic art.

Augustus' return to Rome in 13 B.C. after a visit to the provinces, was dedicated on January 30, 9 B.C., at a ceremony which is shown in the surrounding reliefs [142]. The procession making its way to the sacrifice is divided into two parts. On the south side Augustus leads the way, accompanied by priests and followed by the members of his family; the north side shows senators and other dignitaries. The lower part of the walls is decorated with a rich band of fruit and floral motifs, luxuriantly intertwined, amid which swans are placed. The actual entrance to the altar is flanked by two reliefs—on the right, the one showing Aeneas, and on the left, Romulus and Remus.

The *Ara Pacis* is perhaps the single most comprehensive statement of how Augustus wanted his contemporaries—and future generations—to see his reign. The altar is dedicated neither to Jupiter or Mars nor to Augustus himself but to the spirit of Peace. Augustus is shown as the first among equals rather than supreme ruler; although he leads the procession, he is marked by no special richness of dress. The presence of Augustus' family indicates that he intends his successor to be drawn from among them, and that they have a special role to play in public affairs. The reliefs of Aeneas and of Romulus and Remus relate the entire ceremony to Rome's glorious past. Further reliefs at the back showing the Earth Mother and the goddess of war emphasize the abundance of the land and the need for vigilance. The rich vegetation of the lower band is a constant reminder of the rewards of agriculture, rewards that can be enjoyed once more in the peace to which the whole altar is dedicated.

Amazingly enough, this detailed political and social message is expressed without pretentiousness and with superb workmanship. The style is deliberately and self-consciously "classical," based on works like the Parthenon frieze. To depict the new Golden Age of Augustus, his artists have chosen the artistic language of the Golden Age of Athens, although with a Roman accent. The figures in the procession, for instance, are portrayed far more realistically than those in the sculpture of 5th-century-B.C. Athens.

142 *Ara Pacis* of Augustus, Rome. 13–9 B.C. Marble, 36 × 33′ (11 × 10 m). The central doorway, through which the altar itself is just visible, is flanked by the reliefs showing Romulus and Remus and Aeneas. On the right-hand side is the procession led by Augustus. The altar originally stood on the ancient Via Flaminia. Fragments were discovered in the 16th century; the remaining pieces were located in 1937 and 1938 and the structure was reconstructed near the mausoleum of Augustus.

The elaborate message illustrated by the *Ara Pacis* can also be seen in the best-preserved statue of the emperor himself, the *Augustus of Prima Porta,* so called after the spot where an imperial villa containing the statue was excavated [143]. The statue probably dates from about the time of the emperor's death; the face is in the full vigor of life, calm and determined. The stance is one of quiet authority. The ornately carved breastplate recalls one of the chief events of Augustus' reign. In 20 B.C. he defeated the Parthians, an eastern tribe, and recaptured from them the Roman standards that had been lost in battle in 53 B.C. On that occasion Rome had suffered one of the greatest military defeats in its history, and Augustus'

victory played an important part in restoring national pride. The breastplate shows a bearded Parthian handing back the eagle-crowned standard to a Roman soldier. The cupid on a dolphin at Augustus' feet serves two purposes. The symbol of the goddess Venus, it connects Augustus and his family with Aeneas (whose mother was Venus) and thereby with the origins of Rome. At the same time it looks to the future by representing Augustus' grandson Gaius, who was born the year of the victory over the Parthians and was at one time considered a possible successor to his grandfather.

The choice of his successor was the one problem that Augustus never managed to solve to his own satisfaction. The death of other candidates forced him to fall back reluctantly on his unpopular stepson Tiberius—a problem that was to recur thoughout the long history of the empire, since no really effective mechanism was ever devised for guaranteeing a peaceful transfer of power. (As early as the reign of Claudius [A.D. 41–54], the right to choose a new emperor was seized by the army.) In every other respect the Augustan age was one of high attainment. In the visual arts, Augustan artists set the styles that dominated succeeding generations, while writers like the poets Vergil, Horace, Ovid, and Propertius, and the historian Livy established a Golden Age of Latin literature.

Curiously enough, perhaps the only person to feel any real doubts about the Augustan achievement may have been Augustus himself. The Roman writer and gossip Suetonius (A.D. c. 69–c. 160) tells us that as the emperor lay dying he ordered a slave to bring a mirror so that he could comb his hair. He looked at himself, then turned to some friends standing by and asked, "Tell me, have I played my part in the comedy of life well enough?"

Life in the Roman Empire

The Evidence of Pompeii

The 1st and 2nd centuries A.D. are probably the best-documented times in the whole of classical antiquity. From the many literary sources and the wealth of art and architecture that has survived, it is possible to reconstruct a detailed picture of life in imperial Rome. Even more complete is our knowledge of a prosperous but unimportant little town some 150 miles (240 kilometers) south of Rome that owes its world-wide

143 *Augustus of Prima Porta.* c. A.D. 14. Marble, height 6'8" (2.03 m). Vatican Museums, Rome.

144 Aerial view of the excavated portion of Pompeii as it appears today. The long open rectangular space in the lower center is the forum. The total area is 166 acres (67.23 hectares). Although excavations at Pompeii have been in progress for more than two hundred years, some two fifths of the city is still buried.

145 Cast of a woman trapped in volcanic pumice during the eruption of Mount Vesuvius at Pompeii, A.D. 79. Museo Nazionale, Naples.

fame to the circumstances of its destruction [144]. On August 24 in the year A.D. 79, the volcano Vesuvius above the Gulf of Naples erupted and a number of small towns were buried, the nearer ones under flowing lava and those some distance away under pumice and ash. By far the most famous is Pompeii, situated some 10 miles (16 kilometers) southeast of the erupting peak. Excavation first began there more than two hundred years ago. The finds preserved by the volcanic debris give us a rich and vivid impression of the way of life in a provincial town of the early empire—from the temples in which the Pompeians worshiped and the baths in which they cleaned themselves to their food on the fatal day [145, 146].

An eyewitness report about the eruption comes from two letters written by the Roman politician and literary figure Pliny the Younger (A.D. 62–before 114)—so called to distinguish him from his uncle, Pliny the Elder (A.D. 23–79). The two were in fact together at Misenum on the Bay of Naples on the day of the eruption. Pliny's uncle was much interested in natural phenomena (his chief work was a *Natural History* in 37 volumes); to investigate for himself the nature of the explosion he made his way toward Vesuvius, where he was suffocated to death by the fumes. The younger Pliny stayed behind with his mother and in a letter to the historian Tacitus a little while later described the events of the next few hours:

Pliny the Younger
LETTER TO TACITUS ON THE ERUPTION OF VESUVIUS

You say that the letter I wrote at your request about the death of my uncle makes you want to hear about the terrors, and dangers as well, which I endured, having been left behind at Misenum—I had started on that topic but broken off. "Though my mind shudders to remember, I shall begin." After my uncle departed I spent the rest of the day on my studies; it was for that purpose I had stayed. Then I took a bath, ate dinner, and went to bed; but my sleep was restless and brief. For a number of days before this there had been a quivering of the ground, not so fearful because it was common in Campania. On that night, however, it became so violent that everything seemed not so much to move as to be overturned. My mother came rushing into my bedroom; I was just getting up, intending in my turn to arouse her if she were asleep. We sat down in the rather narrow courtyard of the house lying between the sea and the buildings. I don't know whether I should call it iron nerves or folly—I was only seventeen: I called for a book of Titus Livy and as if at ease I read it and even copied some passages, as I had been doing. Then one of my uncle's friends, who had recently come from Spain to visit him, when he saw my mother and me sitting there, and me actually reading a book, rebuked her apathy and my unconcern. But I was as intent on my book as ever.

It was now the first hour of day, but the light was still faint and doubtful. The adjacent buildings now began to collapse, and there was great, indeed inevitable, danger of being involved in the ruins; for though the place was open, it was narrow. Then at last we decided to leave the town. The dismayed crowd came after us; it preferred following someone else's decision rather than its own; in panic that is practically the same as wisdom. So as we went off we were crowded and shoved along by a huge mob of followers. When we got out beyond the buildings we halted. We saw many strange and fearful sights there. For the carriages we had ordered brought for us, though on perfectly level ground, kept rolling back and forth; even when the wheels were chocked with stones they would not stand still. Moreover the sea appeared to be sucked back and to be repelled by the vibration of the earth; the shoreline was much farther out than usual, and many specimens of marine life were caught on the dry sands. On the other side a black and frightful cloud, rent by twisting and quivering paths of fire, gaped open in huge patterns of flames; it was like sheet lightning, but far worse. Then indeed that friend from Spain whom I have mentioned spoke to us more sharply and insistently: "If your brother and uncle still lives, he wants you to be saved; if he has died, his wish was that you should survive him; so why do you delay to make your escape?" We replied that we would not allow ourselves to think of our own safety while still uncertain of his. Without waiting any longer he rushed off and left the danger behind at top speed.

Soon thereafter the cloud I have described began to descend to the earth and to cover the sea; it had encircled Capri and hidden it from view, and had blotted out the promontory of Misenum. Then my mother began to plead, urge, and order me to make my escape as best I could, for I could, being young; she, weighed down with years and weakness, would die happy if she had not been the cause of death to me. I replied that I would not find safety except in her company; then I took her hand and made her walk faster. She obeyed with difficulty and scolded herself for slowing me. Now ashes, though thin as yet, began to fall. I looked back; a dense fog was looming up behind us; it poured over the ground like a river as it followed. "Let us turn aside," said I, "lest, if we should fall on the road, we should be trampled in the darkness by the throng of those going our way." We barely had time to consider the thought, when night was upon us, not such a night as when there is no moon or there are clouds, but such as in a closed place with the lights put out. One could hear the wailing of women, the crying of children, the shouting of men; they called each other, some their parents, others their children, still others their mates, and sought to recognize each other by their voices. Some lamented their own fate, others the fate of their loved ones. There were even those who in fear of death prayed for death. Many raised their hands to the gods; more held that there were nowhere gods any more and that this was that eternal and final night of the universe.

146 Carbonized dates, walnuts, sunflower seeds, and bread from Pompeii, August 24, A.D. 79. Museo Nazionale, Naples.

Nor were those lacking who exaggerated real dangers with feigned and lying terrors. Men appeared who reported that part of Misenum was buried in ruins, and part of it in flames; it was false, but found credulous listeners.

It lightened a little; this seemed to us not daylight but a sign of approaching fire. But the fire stopped some distance away; darkness came on again, again ashes, thick and heavy. We got up repeatedly to shake these off; otherwise we would have been buried and crushed by the weight. I might boast that not a groan, not a cowardly word, escaped from my lips in the midst of such dangers, were it not that I believed I was perishing along with everything else, and everything else along with me; a wretched and yet a real consolation for having to die. At last the fog dissipated into smoke or mist, and then vanished; soon there was real daylight; the sun even shone, though wanly, as when there is an eclipse. Our still trembling eyes found everything changed, buried in deep ashes as if in snow. We returned to Misenum and attended to our physical needs as best we could; then we spent a night in suspense between hope and fear. Fear was the stronger, for the trembling of the earth continued, and many, crazed by their sufferings, were mocking their own woes and others' by awful predictions. But as for us, though we had suffered dangers and anticipated others, we had not even then any thought of going away until we should have word of my uncle.

You will read this account, far from worthy of history, without any intention of incorporating it; and you must blame yourself, since you insisted on having it, if it shall seem not even worthy of a letter. 📖

With a few exceptions, like the frescoes in the Villa of the Mysteries [Plate 15, page 222], the works of art unearthed at Pompeii are not masterpieces. Their importance lies precisely in the fact that they show us how the ordinary Pompeian lived, worked, and played [147]. The general picture is very impressive. Cool, comfortable houses were decorated with charming frescoes [148] and mosaics and included quiet gardens, remote from the noise of busy streets and watered by fountains. The household silver and other domestic ornaments found in the ruins of houses were often of very high quality. Although the population of Pompeii was only 20,000 there were no fewer than three sets of public baths, a theater, a concert hall, an amphitheater large enough to seat the entire population, and a more-than-adequate number of brothels. The forum was closed to traffic, and the major public buildings ranged around it include a splendid basilica or large hall that served as both stock exchange and law courts. Life must have been extremely comfortable at Pompeii, even though it was far from the most prosperous of the towns buried by Vesuvius. Although only a small part of Herculaneum has been excavated, some mansions [149] found there far surpass the houses of Pompeii. In the last few years work has begun at Oplontis, where a

147 Peristyle of the House of the Silver Wedding, Pompeii. 1st century A.D. The open plan of substantial houses such as this helped keep the interior cool in summer; the adjoining rooms were closed off by folding doors in winter.

superbly decorated villa has already come to light.

Apart from its historic importance, the excavation of Pompeii in the 18th and 19th centuries had a profound effect upon contemporary writers and artists. Johann Wolfgang von Goethe visited the site in 1787 and wrote of the buried city that "of all the disasters there have been in this world, few have provided so much delight to posterity." Johann Winckelmann (1717–1768), sometimes called the father of archaeology, used material from the excavations in his *History of Ancient Art*. Artists like Ingres, David, and Canova were influenced by Pompeian paintings and sculptures; on a more popular level a style of Wedgwood china was based on Pompeian motifs. Countless poets and novelists of the 19th century either set episodes in the excavations at Pompeii or tried to imagine what life there was like in Roman times. An irreverent, if characteristic, reaction was that of Mark Twain in *Innocents Abroad* (1869):

> The sun shines as brightly down on old Pompeii today as it did when Christ was born in Bethlehem, and its streets are cleaner a hundred times than ever Pompeian saw them in her prime. I know whereof I speak—for in the great, chief thoroughfares (Merchant Street and the Street of Fortune) have I not seen with my own eyes how for two hundred years at least the pavements were not repaired!—how ruts five and even ten inches

above: 148 Architectural painting from the cubiculum wall of a villa at Boscoreale, Italy. 1st century B.C. Fresco. Metropolitan Museum of Art, New York (Rogers Fund, 1903).

right: 149 Langdon & Wilson. J. Paul Getty Museum, Malibu, California. 1974. The museum is a recreation of the Villa dei Papiri, a Roman villa just south of Herculaneum. The villa was explored through tunnels in the 18th century but still remains underground.

LIFE IN THE ROMAN EMPIRE **229**

deep were worn into the thick flagstones by the chariot-wheels of generations of swindled tax-payers? And do I not know by these signs that street commissioners of Pompeii never attended to their business, and that if they never mended the pavements they never cleaned them? And, besides, is it not the inborn nature of street commissioners to avoid their duty whenever they get a chance? I wish I knew the name of the last one that held office in Pompeii so that I could give him a blast. I speak with feeling on this subject, because I caught my foot in one of those ruts, and the sadness that came over me when I saw the first poor skeleton, with ashes and lava sticking to it, was tempered by the reflection that maybe that party was the street commissioner.

More in keeping with the general response are the lines that begin Percy Bysshe Shelley's "Ode to Naples":

I stood within the city disinterred;
  And heard the autumnal leaves like light footfalls
Of spirits passing through the streets; and heard
  The mountain's slumberous voice at intervals
    Thrill through those roofless halls;
The oracular thunder penetrating shook
  The listening soul in my suspended blood;
I felt that Earth out of her deep heart spoke—
  I felt, but heard not:—through white columns glowed
    The isle-sustaining ocean-flood,
A plane of light between two heavens of azure!

The Architectural Grandeur of Imperial Rome

All the charm and comfort of Pompeii pale before the grandeur of imperial Rome itself, where both public buildings and private houses were constructed in numbers and on a scale that still remains impressive [150]. The Roman achievement in both architecture and engineering had a lasting effect on the development of later architectural styles. In particular their

150 Model of ancient Rome as it was in about A.D. 320. Museo della Civiltà, Rome. In the right center is the emperor's palace on the Palatine Hill, with the Colosseum above and the mammoth Basilica of Constantine at the upper left.

use of the arch, probably borrowed from the Etruscans, was widely imitated, and pseudo-Roman triumphal arches have sprung up in such unlikely places as the Champs Élysées in Paris and Washington Square in New York. The original triumphal arches commemorated military victories [151]; each was a permanent version of the temporary wooden arch erected to celebrate the return to the capital of a victorious general.

Equally important was the use of internal arches and vaults [152] to provide roofs for structures of increasing size and complexity. Greek and Republican Roman temples had been relatively small, partly because of the difficulties involved in roofing a large space without supports. With the invention of concrete in the 1st century B.C. and growing understanding of the principles of stress and counterstress, Roman architects were able to experiment with elaborate new forms, many of which—like the barrel vault and the dome—were to pass into the Western architectural tradition.

The Greeks had rarely built arches, but the Etruscans used them as early as the 5th century B.C., and the Romans may well have borrowed the arch form from them. From the 2nd century B.C. on, stone arches were regularly used for bridges and aqueducts. Vaults of small size were often used for domestic buildings, and by the time of Augustus architects had begun to construct larger-scale barrel vaults, semicylindrical in shape, two or more of which could intersect to roof a large area. The dome, which is really a hemispherical vault, became increasingly popular with the building of the vast public baths of imperial Rome. Using both bricks and concrete, architects could combine vaults, barrel vaults, and domes to construct very elaborate buildings capable of holding thousands of people at a time. The inside and outside surfaces of the buildings were then covered with a marble facing to conceal the elaborate internal support structures.

Much of the work of these architects was destroyed during the barbarian invasions of the 5th and

151 Arch of Titus, Rome. A.D. 81. Height 47′4″ (14.43 m). This structure commemorates the Roman capture of Jerusalem in A.D. 70. (Two reliefs from this arch are shown in figures **45** and **46,** page 52.)

152 *Top:* Simple arch composed of wedge-shaped blocks or *voussoirs* and *keystone*; the curve of the arch rises from the *springers* on either side. *Center:* Tunnel or barrel vault composed of a series of arches. *Bottom:* Dome composed of a series of arches intersecting each other around a central axis.

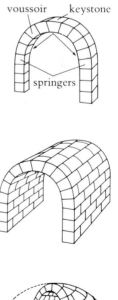

6th centuries A.D. and more was wrecked in the Renaissance by builders looking for bricks or marble. But by great good fortune one of the most superb of all imperial structures has been preserved almost intact. The Pantheon [153] was built around 126, during the reign of Hadrian (117–138) to a design by the emperor himself. An austere and majestic exterior portico is supported on granite columns with Corinthian capitals [154]. It leads into the central rotunda, an astonishing construction approximately 142 feet (43.3 meters) high and wide in which a huge concrete dome rests on a wall interrupted by a series of niches. The building's only light source is a huge *oculus* (eye) at the top of the dome, an opening 30 feet (9.2 meters) across. The proportions of the building are very carefully calculated and contribute to its air of balance. The height of the dome from the ground, for example, is exactly equal to its width [155].

The Pantheon was dwarfed by the huge complex of buildings which made up the imperial fora. Completed by the beginning of the 2nd century A.D., they formed a vast architectural design unsurpassed in an-

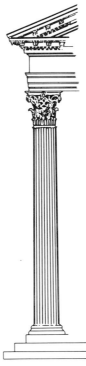

above: 153 Pantheon, Rome. c. A.D. 126. Height of portico 59′ (17.98 m).

left: 154 Corinthian capital. This elaborate bell-shape design, decorated with acanthus leaves, first became commonly used in Hellenistic times. It was especially popular with Roman architects, who in general preferred it to either the Doric or Ionic style (see figure **85,** page 115).

232 THE ROMAN LEGACY

155 Gian Paolo Panini. *Interior of the Pantheon, Rome*. c. 1750. Oil on canvas, 4'2½" × 3'3" (1.28 × .99 m). National Gallery of Art, Washington (Samuel H. Kress Collection).

tiquity and barely equaled since [156]. Elsewhere in the city baths, theaters, temples, race tracks, and libraries catered to the needs and fancies of a huge urban population. In many of these buildings architects continued to experiment with new techniques of construction, and architectural principles developed in Rome were applied throughout the Roman Empire. From Spain to the Middle East theaters, amphitheaters, and other public structures were erected according to the same basic designs, leaving a permanent record of construction methods for later generations.

Urban life on such a scale required a constant supply of one of the basic human necessities, water. Their system of aqueducts is one of the most impressive of the Romans' engineering achievements. A vast network of pipes brought millions of gallons of water a day into Rome, distributing it to public fountains and baths and to the private villas of the wealthy. At the same time a system of covered street drains was built, eliminating the open drains that had been usual before Roman times. These open drains

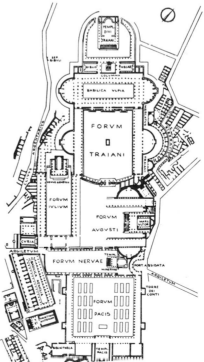

156 Plan of the imperial fora, Rome. Unlike the Republican forum, which served as a public meeting place, these huge complexes were constructed as monuments to the emperors who commissioned them.

were to return during the medieval period, when many of the Roman engineering skills were gone.

With the passage of time, most of the aqueducts that supplied ancient Rome have been demolished or have collapsed. Elsewhere in the Roman Empire, however, examples have survived that give some idea of Roman engineering skill. The famous Pont du Gard [157], which can still be seen in southern France, was probably first constructed during the reign of Augustus. It carried the aqueduct that supplied the Roman city of Nîmes with water—a hundred gallons (387.5 liters) a day for each inhabitant—and was made of uncemented stone. The largest blocks weigh 2 tons (1.8 metric tons).

Even with the provision of such facilities, imperial Rome suffered from overcrowding. The average Roman lived in an apartment block, of which there were some 45,000. Most of these have long since disappeared, although their appearance can be reconstructed from examples excavated at Ostia, Rome's port [158]. The height of the apartment blocks was controlled by law to prevent the construction of unsafe buildings, but it was not unheard of for a building to collapse and fire was a constant danger. No doubt the grandeur of the public buildings in Rome was intended at least in part to distract the poorer Romans from thoughts of their humble private residences.

157   Pont du Gard, near Nîmes in southern France. Late 1st century B.C. Length 902′ (274.93 m), height 161′ (49.07 m). Note the careful positioning of the three rows of arches along the top of which ran the water channel. The whole aqueduct was 25 miles (40 kilometers) long. This section carried the water over the river Gard.

158 Reconstruction drawing of the garden façade of the Insula dei Dipinti, an apartment block in Ostia, the seaport of ancient Rome.

Rome as the Object of Satire

Life in this huge metropolis had many of the problems of big-city living today: noise, traffic jams, dirty streets, and overcrowding were all constant sources of complaint. A particularly bitter protest comes from the Roman satirist Juvenal (c. 60–c. 130 A.D.). Born in the provinces, he came to Rome, where he served as a magistrate and irritated the current emperor, Domitian—not a difficult task. After a period of exile, probably in Egypt, he returned to Rome and lived in considerable poverty. Toward the end of his life, however, his circumstances improved. His sixteen *Satires* make it perfectly clear that Juvenal liked neither Rome nor Romans. He tells us that he writes out of fierce outrage at the corruption and decadence of his day, the depraved aristocracy, the general greed and meanness. "At such a time who could *not* write satire?" His fiercest loathing is reserved for foreigners, although in the sixth *Satire* he launches a particularly virulent attack against women in one of the archetypal documents of misogyny.

Juvenal himself does not emerge as a very pleasant character and his obsessive hatred frequently verges on the psychopathic. As a satirical poet, though, he is among the greatest in Western literature, and strongly influenced many of his successors, including Jonathan Swift. Few other writers can make better or more powerful use of biting sarcasm, irony, and outright invective. In the third *Satire* he turns his weapons against Rome itself. An imaginary friend has decided that he can stand life there no longer, and as he leaves for the country (symbolized in the first lines of this extract by towns like Praeneste and Gabii) he catalogues some of the reasons for his departure.

Juvenal
from the third SATIRE

"Who, in Praeneste's cool, or the wooded
    Volsinian uplands,
Who, on Tivoli's heights, or a small town
    like Gabii, say,
Fears the collapse of his house? But Rome is
    supported on pipestems,
Matchsticks; it's cheaper, so, for the landlord
    to shore up his ruins,
Patch up the old cracked walls, and notify all
    the tenants   195
They can sleep secure, though the beams are
    in ruins above them.
No, the place to live is out there, where no
    cry of *Fire!*
Sounds the alarm of the night, with a
    neighbor yelling for water,
Moving his chattels and goods, and the
    whole third story is smoking.
This you'll never know: for if the ground
    floor is scared first,
You are the last to burn, up there where the
    eaves of the attic
Keep off the rain, and the doves are brooding
    over their nest eggs. . . .

"Here in town the sick die from insomnia
    mostly.
Undigested food, on a stomach burning with
    ulcers,
Brings on listlessness, but who can sleep in a
    flophouse?
Who but the rich can afford sleep and a
    garden apartment?   235
That's the source of infection. The wheels
    creak by on the narrow

Streets of the wards, the drivers squabble and
    brawl when they're stopped,
More than enough to frustrate the drowsiest
    son of a sea cow.
When his business calls, the crowd makes
    way, as the rich man,
Carried high in his car, rides over them,
    reading or writing,
Even taking a snooze, perhaps, for the
    motion's composing.
Still, he gets where he wants before we do;
    for all of our hurry
Traffic gets in our way, in front, around and
    behind us.
Somebody gives me a shove with an elbow,
    or two-by-four scantling.
One clunks my head with a beam, another
    cracks down with a beer keg.   245
Mud is thick on my shins, I am trampled by
    somebody's big feet.
Now what?—a soldier grinds his hobnails
    into my toes.
    "Don't you see the mob rushing along to
    the handout?
There are a hundred guests, each one with
    his kitchen servant.
Even Samson himself could hardly carry
    those burdens,
Pots and pans some poor little slave tries to
    keep on his head, while he hurries
Hoping to keep the fire alive by the wind of
    his running.
Tunics, new-darned, are ripped to shreds;
    there's the flash of a fir beam
Huge on some great dray, and another carries
    a pine tree,
Nodding above our heads and threatening
    death to the people.   255
What will be left of the mob, if that cart of
    Ligurian marble
Breaks its axle down and dumps its load on
    these swarms?
Who will identify limbs or bones? The poor
    man's cadaver,
Crushed, disappears like his breath. And
    meanwhile, at home, his household
Washes the dishes, and puffs up the fire, with
    all kinds of a clatter
Over the smeared flesh-scrapers, the flasks of
    oil, and the towels.
So the boys rush around, while their late
    master is sitting,
Newly come to the bank of the Styx, afraid
    of the filthy
Ferryman there, since he has no fare, not
    even a copper

In his dead mouth to pay for the ride
    through that muddy whirlpool.   265
    "Look at other things, the various dangers
    of nighttime.
How high it is to the cornice that breaks, and
    a chunk beats my brains out,
Or some slob heaves a jar, broken or
    cracked, from a window.
Bang! It comes down with a crash and
    proves its weight on the sidewalk.
You are a thoughtless fool, unmindful of
    sudden disaster,
If you don't make your will before you go
    out to have dinner.
There are as many deaths in the night as
    there are open windows
Where you pass by; if you're wise, you will
    pray, in your wretched devotions,
People may be content with no more than
    emptying slop jars."

The End of
the Roman Empire

Few historical subjects have been as much discussed
as the fall of the Roman Empire. It is not even possible to agree on when it fell, let alone why. The traditional date, A.D. 476, marks the deposition of the last Roman emperor, Romulus Augustulus. By that time, however, the political unity of the empire had already disintegrated. Perhaps the beginning of the end was A.D. 330, when the emperor Constantine moved the capital from Rome to a new city on the Bosphorus, Constantinople, although in another sense the move represented a new development as much as a conclusion. It might even be possible to argue that Constantine's successors in the East, the Byzantine emperors, were the successors of Augustus and that there is a continuous tradition from the beginning of the empire in 31 B.C. to the fall of Constantinople in A.D. 1453.

Fascinating though the question is, in a sense it is theoretical rather than practical. The Roman Empire did not fall overnight. Many of the causes for its long decline are obvious though not always easy to order in importance. One important factor was the growing power and changing character of the army. The larger it became, the more necessary it was to recruit troops from the more distant provinces—Germans, Illyrians, and others, the very people the army was supposed to be holding in check. Most of these soldiers had never been anywhere near Rome. They felt no loyalty to the empire, no reason to defend Roman interests. A succession of emperors had to buy their support by raising their pay and promising gifts of lands. At the same time, the army came to play an increasingly prominent part in the choice of a new emperor, and, since the army itself was largely non-Roman, so were many of the emperors chosen. Emperors of the 3rd and 4th centuries included Africans, Thracians, a Syrian, and an Arab, men unlikely to feel any strong reason to place the interests of Rome over those of themselves and their men.

Throughout this late period the empire was increasingly threatened from outside. To the west, barbarian tribes like the Huns, the Goths, and the Alemanni began to penetrate farther and farther into its defenses and even to sack Rome itself. Meanwhile, in the East, Roman armies were continually involved in resisting the growing power of the Persians. In many parts of the empire it became clear that Rome could provide no help against invaders, and some of the provinces set themselves up as independent states with their own armies.

Problems like these inevitably had a devastating effect upon the economy. Taxes increased and the value of money declined. The constant threat of invasion or civil war made trade impossible. What funds there were went for the support of the army, and the general standard of living suffered a steady decline. The eastern provinces, the old Hellenistic kingdoms, suffered rather less than the rest of the empire, since they were protected in part by the wealth accumu-lated over the centuries and by their long tradition of civilization. As a result Italy sank to the level of a province rather than remaining the center of the imperial administration.

Total collapse was prevented by the efforts of two emperors: Diocletian, who ruled from A.D. 284 to 305, and Constantine, who ruled from 306 to 337. Both men were masterly organizers who realized that the only way to save the empire was to impose the most stringent controls on every aspect of life—social, administrative, and economic. In 301 the Edict of Diocletian was passed, establishing fixed maximums for the sale of goods and for wages. A vast bureaucracy was set up to collect taxes and administer the provinces. The emperor himself became once again the focal point of the empire, but to protect himself from the dangers of coups and assassinations, he never appeared in public. As a result an elaborate court with complex rituals developed, and the emperor's claim to semidivine status invested him with a new religious authority.

Late Roman Art and Architecture

Even if the emperor did not show himself to his subjects, he could impress them in other ways, and the reigns of Diocletian and Constantine marked the last great age of Roman architecture. The immense Basilica of Constantine [159], with its central nave rising to a height of 100 feet (30.5 meters), is now in ruins, but in its day this assembly hall must have been a power-

159 Basilica of Constantine, the last great imperial building in Rome. Begun in A.D. 306 by Maxentius, it was finished by Constantine after 315. Only the northern side is still standing; the central nave and south aisle collapsed during antiquity.

160 Head of the colossal statue of Constantine that stood in the Basilica of Constantine, Rome. A.D. 324–330. Marble, height 8′6″ (2.59 m). Palazzo dei Conservatori, Rome. The massive and majestic simplicity of this portrait is very different from the detailed observation of earlier, much smaller Roman portraits like those of Cicero and Hadrian (figures **134, 135**), illustrating the new belief in the emperor as God's regent on earth.

ful reminder of the emperor's authority. It also contained a 30-foot (9.2-meter) statue of the emperor himself [160]. The palace Diocletian had built for him at Split, on the Adriatic coast, is constructed on the plan of a military camp, with enormous central avenues dividing it into four quarters [161]. The decoration makes use of Eastern motifs, and the whole design is far from the classical style of earlier times.

In sculpture, too, classical forms and styles were increasingly abandoned. Realistic portraiture and naturalistic drapery were neglected, and sculptors no longer tried to express depth or reality in their relief carving. The lack of perspective and precision in their work foreshadows the art of the early Middle Ages [162]. The general abandonment of classical ideas these artistic changes indicate went along with a waning of interest in Stoicism and Epicureanism and a new enthusiasm for Eastern religious cults. Traditional Roman religion had always been organized by the state, and from the time of the late Republic some Romans had sought a more personal religious satisfaction in the worship of Eastern deities. During the last stages of the empire strong cults developed around the Phrygian goddess Cybele, the Egyptian Isis, and the sun god Mithras.

The appearance and eventual triumph of Christianity is outside the scope of this account, but its emergence as the official religion of the empire played a final and decisive part in bringing to an end the classical era. Pagan art, pagan literature, and pagan culture as a whole represented forces and ideals Christianity strongly rejected, and the art of the early Christians is fundamentally different in its inspiration. Yet even the fathers of the early Church, implacable opponents of paganism, could not fail to be moved by the end of so great a cultural tradition. Jerome writes at the beginning of the 5th century A.D., in a letter to Augustine:

> I once wanted to turn to the Book of Ezekiel and provide a commentary which I had promised to some enthusiastic readers, but, as I began dictating, my mind was distracted by thoughts of the devastation of the western provinces and in particular that of Rome itself. As the proverb says, "I could not even think of a word," and for a long time I kept silent, knowing that this was the time for tears.

The memory of Rome's greatness lived on through the succeeding ages of turmoil and achievement and the classical spirit survived, to be reborn triumphantly in the Renaissance.

161 Reconstruction model of the Palace of Diocletian at Split, Yugoslavia. A.D. 300–305. Museo della Civiltà Romana, Rome. Note the octagonal dome of the emperor's mausoleum.

162 *Constantine Receiving Homage from the Senate,* frieze on the Arch of Constantine, Rome. A.D. 315. Marble, 3'4" × 17'6" (1.02 × 5.33 m). On both sides of the emperor (seated in the center) his officials distribute money to the crowds below. The simplified style, in which most of the puppetlike figures are shown frontally, foreshadows Byzantine and medieval art and is certainly very different from the style of earlier reliefs (figures **141, 142**).

Further Reading

Brendel, O. J. *Etruscan Art.* Baltimore: Penguin, 1978. The most up-to-date survey of Etruscan painting and sculpture, with numerous illustrations.

Brion, M. *Pompeii and Herculaneum: The Glory and the Grief.* London: Elek, 1960. A popular but scholarly account of the excavations of the buried cities and of life there in Roman times. Entertaining and informative.

Commager, S., ed. *Virgil, a Collection of Critical Essays.* Englewood Cliffs, NJ: Prentice-Hall, 1966. The literature on Vergil is immense and wide-ranging, but this volume of essays provides a useful survey of modern critical approaches and suggests some further directions for the interested reader to explore.

Dudley, D. R. *The Civilization of Rome.* New York: Mentor, 1962. A handy one-volume survey of Roman culture, more useful for history than for art or literature.

Graves, Robert. *I, Claudius* and *Claudius the God.* Baltimore: Penguin, 1977. These two historical novels, originally published in 1934, are recreations of the Roman world that are both scholarly and thoroughly absorbing. Highly recommended.

Hanfmann, G. M. A. *Roman Art.* New York: Norton, 1975. The best introduction to the subject, with a very full selection of illustrations, sensitive comments, and up-to-date bibliographical notes.

Kahler, H. *Rome and Her Empire.* London: Methuen, 1963. A more technical survey of Roman art of the imperial period with a fine selection of color plates.

Luck, G. *The Latin Love-Elegy.* London: Methuen, 1959. A detailed study of Catullus and his successors that is easier to follow if the reader has some knowledge of Latin.

Otis, B. *Virgil: A Study in Civilized Poetry.* Oxford: Oxford University Press, 1964. Perhaps the single most important book on Vergil to appear in recent years. Sensitive and perceptive, it merits careful reading.

Pallottino, M. *The Etruscans*. Baltimore: Penguin, 1975. A revised version of the standard work by the most eminent Etruscologist of our time, covering all aspects of Etruscan culture. Especially good on the language.

Reich, J. *Italy Before Rome*. Oxford: Elsevier/Phaidon, 1979. A survey of Italy in the early Iron Age that includes an account of recent archaeological discoveries. Many illustrations in color.

Rose, H. J. *A Handbook of Latin Literature*. New York: Dutton, third edition, 1961. A good single-volume account.

Scullard, H. H. *From the Gracchi to Nero*. Third edition. London: Methuen, 1970. A useful survey of the history of the late Republic and the early empire, reflecting the state of modern scholarly opinion.

Vickers, M. *The Roman World*. Oxford: Elsevier/Phaidon, 1977. A fully illustrated account of Roman art and archaeology, also valuable for its discussion of the rediscovery of classical antiquity in the Renaissance.

Wilder, Thornton. *Ides of March*. New York: Grosset & Dunlap, 1956. A brilliant and engrossing fictional narration of the last days of Julius Caesar.

Yourcenar, Marguerite. *Memoirs of Hadrian*. New York: Farrar, Straus, 1963. A superb evocation of the personality of one of the truly extraordinary Romans.

Suggestions for Listening

Apart from occasional literary references and the discovery at Pompeii and elsewhere of some musical instruments, we know very little about Roman music or how it was made. Cultured Romans would in any event have turned to Greek music for intellectual pleasure, and so distinguished a nonprofessional lyre-player and singer as Nero would doubtless have performed only Greek works. The local composers' output would have been encountered in more popular form on such public occasions as theatrical performances, games, and processions.

Roman history and literature, however, provided as rich and frequent inspiration for later composers as for writers and artists. Nero himself figured prominently in at least one early opera, Claudio Monteverdi's *L'incoronazione di Poppea (The Coronation of Poppea),* which was first produced in 1642 in Venice and concerns the emperor's mistress Poppea who replaces the empress and assumes her place on the throne. Cleopatra has appeared frequently on the operatic stage both alone and with her eminent lovers—in Handel's *Julius Caesar* (1724), Domenico Cimarosa's *Cleopatra* of 1791, in the 1914 *Cléopâtre* of Jules Massenet (who also wrote an opera titled *Roma* two years earlier),

and Samuel Barber's *Antony and Cleopatra* (1966), among others.

Robert Schumann wrote a *Julius Caesar Overture,* and both Marc Blitzstein and Darius Milhaud wrote incidental music for Shakespeare's *Julius Caesar.* The distinguished American composer Virgil Thomson, among others, has written incidental music for Shakespeare's *Antony and Cleopatra.*

One further work illustrates the impact of Roman literature—in this case Vergil's *Aeneid*—on the Western artistic tradition. Between 1856 and 1858 the French composer Hector Berlioz created a mammoth operatic work, *The Trojans,* that has come to be appreciated as one of the magnificent peaks of 19th-century musical drama. It is available in a superb recorded performance on Philips 6709002.

Questions for Further Discussion

1. Art and literature were never at the center of Roman life, but always took second place to more practical affairs. What effects did this have upon the development of Roman culture, and to what extent were the Romans justified in seeing the arts as a distraction from the real world?

2. In what ways have the Roman political and legal systems influenced Western systems of government, in particular that of the United States? How and why were the Romans chosen as models?

3. What kind of evidence do we have for the origins of the Etruscans, and what conclusions does it suggest? Is there any chance that the mysteries of Etruscan origins and the Etruscan language will ever be fully understood?

4. How sympathetic a hero is Aeneas, and how does our opinion of his character influence our interpretation of the *Aeneid?*

5. What are the chief problems presented by the frescoes in the Villa of the Mysteries at Pompeii, and what are some of the solutions scholars have proposed? What light do the frescoes throw on the role of women and marriage in Roman times?

6. It is sometimes said that late imperial Rome and America in the late 20th century share many of the same weaknesses, including an indifference to the arts, an inability to adapt traditional values to changing times, and the lack of a satisfactory relationship between the individual and society as a whole. How far are these charges justified, and what (if anything) can be learned from the Roman example?

INTERLUDE

Antony and Cleopatra

Cleopatra (69–30 B.C.), who combined her personal romantic activities with her position as queen of Egypt, shocked beyond measure the Romans who knew about her—particularly since her lovers included such distinguished Roman leaders as Julius Caesar and Mark Antony. Women played an important role in the life of the Roman family and certain patrician women wielded formidable political and economic power behind the scenes, but they took an active part in public only rarely. The wives of public figures were expected to set an example of domestic rectitude and respectability that would both inspire others and aid their husbands' careers. Julius Caesar expressed the contemporary view succinctly when he divorced his wife after a widely discussed scandal in which she may have been involved: "Caesar's wife must be above suspicion."

At the same time, there was in operation a double standard that by no means disappeared with the fall of the Roman Empire. Men about town frequently turned to women other than their wives—often quite publicly—for sophisticated attentions a Roman matron was hardly expected to cultivate. Among the most notorious of these courtesans was none other than Catullus' beloved Lesbia—almost certainly the infamous Clodia, a woman as beautiful and intelligent as she was ruthless.

Even so, in the Rome of the 1st century B.C. there was widespread respect for virtue and morality, and Cleopatra for the Romans was both a threat and a shocking figure. When her exotic career ended with a dramatic death, it was inevitable that she would become—for the Romans and for later ages—the symbol of the glamorous Eastern beauty, seductive but dangerous. She continues to intrigue graphic artists, writers, and theater audiences. Shakespeare's version of the story of the doomed lovers in *Antony and Cleopatra* remains the most spectacularly poetic—and perhaps most dramatic—one. We have seen (page 240) that Cleopatra has remained a frequent subject for writers of opera. She and her first Roman conquest inspired one of Bernard Shaw's wittiest and most sparkling comedies, *Caesar and Cleopatra,* also made into a classic motion picture [163].

But there is a considerable difference between most of these later accounts and the facts of history. The real Cleopatra was chiefly interested in power, not in love. The last ruler of an independent Egypt, she was the culmination of two great traditions. By blood she was a Macedonian and thus the heir of Alexander the Great; her native tongue was Greek. At the same time she saw herself as the successor of the pharaohs and like them descended from the sun god Ra. Her self-appointed mission was to

163 *Above:* Claude Rains as Julius Caesar and Vivien Leigh, portraying a Cleopatra who is still a child, meet for the first time between the paws of the Sphinx in the 1946 film version of Bernard Shaw's *Caesar and Cleopatra. Right:* Leigh is a more mature and more regal queen of Egypt to Laurence Olivier's Antony in the production of Shakespeare's *Antony and Cleopatra* at the Ziegfeld Theatre, New York, 1951.

fulfill Alexander's dream of uniting East and West in a single great empire. The first stage in accomplishing this was to be the conquest of Rome, with subsequent victories intended to establish a worldwide kingdom with Cleopatra as supreme ruler. But Egypt, although rich, had little military power and could never have provided an army strong enough to challenge Roman might. Only by setting the Romans against themselves could she hope to overthrow the Roman Empire. To accomplish her vision of world domination she had to find herself a Roman with whom to join forces, and she threw all her considerable abilities into the attempt.

Her remarkable beauty was the most immediately visible of her advantages, and she was willing to exploit it, but she was in addition a woman of notable intellectual gifts, widely read in literature and philosophy, a brilliant administrator, and determined, even ruthless, in character. At the time of her alliance with Antony, contemporary Romans followed the lead of Octavian in describing her as an Oriental tyrant, sunk in depravity and prone to every vice. The intensity of their hatred for her reveals their genuine fear that, of all Rome's enemies, she could come the closest to overthrowing Roman rule [164].

164 The fact that no authentic portrait of either Antony or Cleopatra has survived can probably be credited to the wishes of the emperor Augustus. The coins the couple had minted nevertheless give some idea of their appearance. *Right:* Coin with the profile of Mark Antony. 41 B.C. Silver, diameter ¾″ (1.9 cm). British Museum, London (reproduced by courtesy of the Trustees). *Far right:* Coin with the profile of Cleopatra. Diameter 1″ (2.5 cm). Cabinet des Medailles, Paris.

165 André Bauchant. *Cleopatra's Barge.* 1939. Oil on canvas, 32 × 39⅜" (81 × 100 cm). Museum of Modern Art, New York (Abby Aldrich Rockefeller Fund).

Her first victim had been Julius Caesar. After his defeat of Pompey in 47 B.C. Caesar made his way to Egypt to arbitrate a dispute between the pharoah, Ptolemy XII, and his sister Cleopatra; in accordance with Egyptian custom, they were married to each other. Caesar also hoped to collect some money owed him by the couple's deceased father, Ptolemy XI. Both his financial demands and his support of Cleopatra naturally won him the enmity of the young Ptolemy. After a series of skirmishes, in the course of which Caesar himself narrowly escaped death several times, Ptolemy's troops were defeated and the king himself killed. By this time Rome was anxiously awaiting Caesar's return, but he delayed his departure and spent several weeks traveling in Egypt with Cleopatra. By the time he left, the queen was pregnant. When her son was born she named him Caesarion and took him to Rome to join his father. Although Caesar showered her with presents and honors, he was careful to go no further, and any hopes she might have had of an eventual marriage were ended by his assassination.

As Cleopatra surveyed the new situation created by Caesar's death, it must soon have been apparent to her that an even more likely candidate for her attentions was Mark Antony. Antony had been Caesar's faithful lieutenant and after the defeat of Caesar's assassins in 42 B.C. had been placed in command of the East. A man of great personality and abilities, he was characterized by moderation and good sense in his political and military achievements. His Roman virtues of leadership and courage were counterbalanced by a streak of sensuality and self-indulgence, and it was on these that Cleopatra counted. In 40 B.C., she traveled to Cydnus in Asia Minor, and there the two met for the first time [165]. Shakespeare immortalized the encounter in a superb description spoken by Antony's friend Enobarbus in *Antony and Cleopatra:*

William Shakespeare
from **ANTONY AND CLEOPATRA, Act II, Scene 2**

ENOBARBUS   The barge she sat in, like a burnished throne,
  Burned on the water: the poop was beaten gold,

Purple the sails, and so perfumed that
The winds were love-sick with them; the oars were silver,
Which to the tune of flutes kept stroke, and made   200
The water which they beat to follow faster,
As amorous of their strokes. For her own person,
It beggared all description: she did lie
In her pavilion, cloth-of-gold, of tissue,
O'er-picturing that Venus where we see   205
The fancy outwork nature. On each side her,
Stood pretty dimpled boys, like smiling Cupids,
With divers coloured fans, whose wind did seem
To glow the delicate cheeks which they did cool,
And what they undid did.
AGRIPPA   O rare for Antony!   210
ENOBARBUS   Her gentlewomen, like the Nereides,
So many mermaids, tended her i' th' eyes,
And made their bends adornings. At the helm,
A seeming mermaid steers. The silken tackle
Swell with the touches of those flower-soft hands,   215
That yarely frame the office. From the barge
A strange invisible perfume hits the sense
Of the adjacent wharfs. The city cast
Her people out upon her; and Antony,
Enthroned i' th' market place, did sit alone,   220
Whistling to th' air; which but for vacancy
Had gone to gaze on Cleopatra too,
And made a gap in nature.
AGRIPPA   Rare Egyptian!
ENOBARBUS   Upon her landing, Antony sent to her,
Invited her to supper. She replied,   225
It should be better he became her guest;
Which she entreated. Our courteous Antony,
Whom ne'er the word of no woman heard speak,
Being barbered ten times o'er, goes to the feast;
And for his ordinary pays his heart,   230
For what his eyes eat only.
AGRIPPA   Royal wench;
She made great Caesar lay his sword to bed.
He ploughed her, and she cropped.

At the banquet that followed their first meeting Cleopatra made every effort to impress Antony with both her beauty and her wealth. According to one story, probably apocryphal, during the meal she removed a priceless pearl earring and dropped it into her glass of wine, in which it dissolved. She then casually drank the wine, showing her indifference to the value of the pearl. True or not, the episode was depicted from the Renaissance on by a number of artists, including Alessandro Allori (1535–1607) and Giovanni Battista Tiepolo (1696–1770) [166].

Within a year Cleopatra had borne Antony twins, but her initial success was frustrated by the plans of Octavian, who in 39 B.C. persuaded Antony to try to patch up their growing differences by marrying his sister Octavia. By all accounts this remarkably diplomatic woman performed miracles in restraining Antony's wilder impulses and in keeping the peace between her new husband and her brother; from 39 to 37 B.C. Octavia and Antony lived peacefully at Athens, administering the Eastern provinces and strengthening the frontiers. The news of their marriage must

166 Giovanni Battista Tiepolo. *The Banquet of Antony and Cleopatra.* 1745–1750. Oil on canvas, 26⅛ × 16″ (67 × 41 cm). National-museum, Stockholm. This master painter of the Venetian school was fascinated by the elaborate splendor surrounding the first encounter of Antony and Cleopatra. He produced a number of smaller paintings and sketches—of which this is one—on the subject as well as a great series of frescoes in the Palazzo Labia, Venice.

have been a considerable shock to Cleopatra. In the following brief scene from Shakespeare's play, Cleopatra is reassured by the description from a messenger of Antony's new wife and comforts herself with the thought of her own superior beauty. The real Cleopatra must have been much less certain of her eventual triumph. Unlike Shakespeare's character, she was fully aware that Antony was being forced to choose not merely between two women but between a military and political alliance either with herself or with Octavia.

William Shakespeare
from ANTONY AND CLEOPATRA, Act III, Scene 3

Alexandria. CLEOPATRA's *palace. Enter* CLEOPATRA, CHARMIAN, IRAS, *and* ALEXAS.
CLEOPATRA   Where is the fellow?
ALEXAS   Half afeard to come.
CLEOPATRA   Go to, go to.
Enter MESSENGER.
                                         Come hither sir.
ALEXAS   Good Majesty,
 Herod of Jewry dare not look upon you
 But when you are well pleased.
CLEOPATRA   That Herod's head
 I'll have: but how, when Antony is gone,   5
 Through whom I might command it? Come thou near.
MESSENGER   Most gracious Majesty.
CLEOPATRA   Didst thou behold
 Octavia?

MESSENGER	Ay dread Queen.	
CLEOPATRA	Where?	10
MESSENGER	Madam in Rome,	

I looked her in the face; and saw her led
Between her brother and Mark Antony.

CLEOPATRA   Is she as tall as me?

MESSENGER   She is not madam.

CLEOPATRA   Didst hear her speak? Is she shrill-tongued or low?   15

MESSENGER   Madam, I heard her speak, she is low-voiced.

CLEOPATRA   That's not so good: he cannot like her long.

CHARMIAN   Like her? O Isis! 'Tis impossible.

CLEOPATRA   I think so, Charmian. Dull of tongue, and dwarfish.
What majesty is in her gait? Remember   20
If e'er thou look'dst on majesty.

MESSENGER   She creeps.
Her motion and her station are as one.
She shows a body, rather than a life,
A statue, than a breather.

CLEOPATRA   Is this certain?

MESSENGER   Or I have no observance.

CHARMIAN   Three in Egypt   25
Cannot make better note.

CLEOPATRA   He's very knowing;
I do perceive't; there's nothing in her yet.
The fellow has good judgement.

CHARMIAN   Excellent.

CLEOPATRA   Guess at her years, I prithee.

MESSENGER   Madam,
She was a widow—

CLEOPATRA   Widow? Charmian, hark.   30

MESSENGER   And I do think she's thirty.

CLEOPATRA   Bear'st thou her face in mind? Is't long or round?

MESSENGER   Round even to faultiness.

CLEOPATRA   For the most part too, they are foolish that are so.
Her hair what colour?   35

MESSENGER   Brown madam; and her forehead
As low as she would wish it.

CLEOPATRA   There's gold for thee.
Thou must not take my former sharpness ill,
I will employ thee back again. I find thee
Most fit for business. Go, make thee ready,   40
Our letters are prepared.   [*Exit* MESSENGER.]

Cleopatra's optimism was nonetheless justified. After three years with Octavia, Antony became restless. He had long had in mind an expedition that would accomplish Julius Caesar's dream of conquering the Parthians and at the same time increase his own prestige. In 36 B.C. he mustered an army of almost a hundred thousand men and set off, leaving Octavia behind and summoning Cleopatra to join him in Syria. The expedition was a complete failure, and the loss of a third of his forces seriously undermined Antony's reputation as a military leader. Back at Rome, the prestige of Octavian, by now embittered by Antony's treatment of his sister, was growing and Antony decided to strengthen his weakening position by cementing his alliance with Cleopatra. At an elaborate ceremony in Alexandria in 34 B.C. he formalized their political union by the so-called Donations of Alexandria. Cleopatra's eldest child, Caesarion, was publicly acknowledged Julius Caesar's son and was made joint ruler with his mother of Egypt and Cyprus. Antony's own children by Cleopatra were given other kingdoms.

The effect of this news at Rome was predictably disastrous for Antony's cause. Roman indignation at Antony's submission to the hated queen's plans for a universal kingdom under her rule was adroitly fanned by Octavian, who showed the same skillful control of propaganda he was later to demonstrate during his reign as Augustus. Octavian managed to obtain and publish his rival's will (in which Antony instructed that he be buried in Alexandria with Cleopatra at his side), which served to inflame still further Roman resentment against the noble Roman who had allowed himself to be so completely seduced. Although neither Octavian or Antony had any legal political status by now, Octavian's agents organized the taking of an oath of allegiance to their master throughout Italy. Armed with this vote of confidence, Octavian formally declared war on Egypt and launched an expedition against the joint forces of Antony and Cleopatra. The decisive engagement took place in September 31 B.C. at Actium in western Greece [167]. Shortly after the beginning of the battle, which took place at sea, Antony's forces deserted. Antony and Cleopatra fled back to Egypt in total defeat.

The account of the Battle of Actium provided by Vergil in Book VIII of the *Aeneid,* in the form of a description of the decorations on Aeneas' shield, is hardly impartial: it was written in accordance with the official version provided by Octavian, by then styled Augustus, and it is difficult not to sense the emperor leaning over the poet's shoulder as he wrote. As a literal description of the events it is thus not very successful, but it does provide a fascinating illustration of the Augustan propaganda machine at work. Augustus is described as having the support of both his country and the gods, while Antony is surrounded with the Oriental paraphernalia of his "Egyptian wife." Vergil permits himself a sarcastic reference to Antony's "triumphs in the East," and the description of the animal gods of the Egyptians would automatically send a shudder through any respectable Roman reader. Propaganda has never drawn its strength from its accuracy, of course, and although Vergil describes the flight of the Egyptian, Indian, Arabian, and Sabaean ships, it was in fact Antony's Roman galleys that turned and fled.

167 Roman warship with legionary soldiers, scene from a bas-relief of the Battle of Actium. Late 1st century B.C. Marble. Vatican Museums, Rome. One of the heavy craft that took part in the decisive engagement at Actium (symbolized by the crocodile), this vessel has two banks of oars, each probably worked by several rowers.

Vergil
from the AENEID, Book VIII

The center showed the battle of Actium—   675
the bronze-clad ships attacking in a line,
Leucata seething, and billows bright with gold.
Augustus led the Italians into battle
with Senate and people, with gods both small and great.
He stood in the sternsheets. Flame poured from his brows   680
exultant; above him dawned his father's star.
Elsewhere, Agrippa, blessed by gods and winds,
swooped down with his fleet; that proud ensign of war,
the naval crown, shone bright upon his brow.
There Antony, like some savage, gaudy sheik,   685
hero of Araby and the Sea of Pearls,
led Egypt, the lords of the East, and Bactria;
behind him (God forfend!) his Gypsy Queen.
The fleets advanced full speed; then oars aback
in a welter of foam, while spiked rams ripped the wave.   690
Then—out to sea! As were the Isles of Greece
torn loose and floating, or Alp attacking Alp,
so huge, so tall, were the battling men-o'-war.
Men lobbed the fireball; iron spear-points fell
like rain; fresh bloodshed reddened Neptune's realm.   695
Her majesty rang her gong for battle stations,
not yet aware of twin asps at her back.
Weird gods, fantastic shapes, the dog Anubis,
stood in phalanx against Minerva, Neptune,
and Venus. Mars raged up and down the lines,   700
chiseled in steel; the Dirae hung in heaven,
and Discord in torn gown strode grinning by,
trailed by Bellona with her blood-stained lash.
Apollo of Actium watched and bent his bow
above the scene: Egyptians, Indians all,   705
Sabaeans, and every Arab fled in terror.
Her majesty herself prayed for a wind,
made sail, cast off the sheets, and let them run.
Amid the carnage Vulcan had carved her pale
with impending death, riding the wind and wave.   710
And there, to the south, the Nile, grief-stricken, great,
offering haven, waving the conquered home
to hiding spots in his blue creeks and bays.
But Caesar, riding through Rome in triple triumph,
promised immortal gifts to Italy's gods: 715
three hundred major shrines in all the city.
The streets were loud with cheers and joyful noise.
Women filled every temple with hymn and prayer,
and slaughtered oxen strewed the altar grounds.
Caesar, sitting by Phoebus' marble threshold,   720
canvassed the gifts a world by that proud door
had laid. Long files of captive peoples passed,
in speech outlandish, as in dress and arms.
Here were Numidians, Berbers in burnoose,
Levantines, bowmen from the steppes, all carved   725
by Vulcan; there Euphrates (gentled now),

men of land's end: Walloons, the horned Rhine,
proud Cossacks, Araxes grumbling at his bridge.

Within a few months Octavian had followed Antony to Egypt and defeated the
new forces remaining to him, leaving Antony little choice but suicide [168]. Memorable
though Shakespeare's version of Antony's death is, a modern poet has provided
an especially poignant insight into his last moments. Constantine Cavafy
(1863–1933), a Greek by descent, was born, lived, and died in Alexandria, the scene
of Antony's former triumphs and of his suicide. In his brief "Antony's Ending"
Cavafy captures something of the ambivalence and alienation of the doomed Roman
who comes fully to understand himself only in total defeat.

Constantine Cavafy
ANTONY'S ENDING

But when he heard the women wailing,
lamenting his sorry state—
Madam with her oriental gestures
and her slaves with their barbarous Greek—
the pride in his soul rose up,
his Italian blood sickened with disgust
and all he'd worshipped blindly till then
his wild Alexandrian life—
now seemed dull and alien.
And he said: "Stop wailing for me.
It's all wrong, that kind of thing.
You ought to be singing my praises
for having been a great ruler,
a man of wealth and glory.
And if I'm down now, I haven't fallen humbly,
but as a Roman conquered by a Roman."

168 *Deaths of Antony and Cleopatra,*
from a French translation of
Boccaccio's *De Claris Mulieribus,* 1401.
Manuscript illumination. Bibliothèque
Nationale, Paris.

169 Michelangelo. *Cleopatra.* Drawing. Galleria Buonarroti, Florence. In the absence of any real evidence, Michelangelo's imaginary portrait cannot be criticized for lack of accuracy, although to some it may seem a bit lacking in strength of will. The serpent alludes, of course, to the manner of her death.

A meeting was arranged between Octavian and Cleopatra, but if the queen made a last desperate attempt to win over her conqueror, it was unsuccessful. When it became clear that Octavian was only keeping her alive so he could exhibit her in his triumphal procession at Rome, she committed suicide. Her eldest son, Caesarion, was killed—Octavian was taking no chances—but her two children by Antony were taken to Rome, where they walked before Octavian's chariot in his triumphal procession.

Cleopatra's death, caused by the deadly bite of a snake smuggled to her in a basket of figs by her attendants Iras and Charmian, has been popular with artists [169] but found its most famous depiction in language, in the final scene of Shakespeare's play:

William Shakespeare
from **ANTONY AND CLEOPATRA, Act V, Scene 2**

CLEOPATRA   Give me my robe, put on my crown, I have
  Immortal longings in me. Now no more
  The juice of Egypt's grape shall moist this lip.   285
  Yare, yare, good Iras; quick. Methinks I hear
  Antony call; I see him rouse himself
  To praise my noble act. I hear him mock
  The luck of Caesar, which the gods give men
  To excuse their after wrath. Husband, I come.   290
  Now to that name my courage prove my title.
  I am fire and air; my other elements
  I give to baser life. So, have you done?
  Come then, and take the last warmth of my lips.
  Farewell kind Charmian—Iras, long farewell.   295
                      [*Kisses them.* IRAS *falls and dies*]

Have I the aspic in my lips? Dost fall?
If thou and nature can so gently part,
The stroke of death is as a lover's pinch,
Which hurts, and is desired. Dost thou lie still?
If thus thou vanishest, thou tell'st the world   300
It is not worth leave-taking.
CHARMIAN   Dissolve thick cloud, and rain, that I may say
The gods themselves do weep.
CLEOPATRA   This proves me base.
If she first meet the curled Antony,
He'll make demand of her, and spend that kiss   305
Which is my heaven to have. Come thou mortal wretch.

                              [*Applies an asp to her breast*]

With thy sharp teeth this know intrinsicate
Of life at once untie. Poor venomous fool,
Be angry, and dispatch. O couldst thou speak,
That I might hear thee call great Caesar ass,   310
Unpolicied.
CHARMIAN   O eastern star!
CLEOPATRA   Peace, peace.
Dost thou not see my baby at my breast,
That sucks the nurse asleep?
CHARMIAN   O break! O break!
CLEOPATRA   As sweet as balm, as soft as air, as gentle—
O Antony! Nay I will take thee too.   315

                         [*Applies another asp to her arm*]

What should I stay—   [*Dies*]

Further Reading

Bradford, E. *Cleopatra.* New York: Harcourt Brace Jovanovich, 1972. Lavishly illustrated, readable if sometimes superficial description of Cleopatra's life and times.

Grant, M. *Cleopatra.* London: Weidenfeld and Nicolson, 1972. A more scholarly account of Cleopatra's career, well documented and with useful notes. The genealogical tables at the end are helpful.

Ludwig, Emil. *Cleopatra: The Story of a Queen.* New York: Bantam Books, 1959. The English translation of a book first published in German in 1937. More historical novel than accurate account, it provides a highly imaginative, and frequently imagined, picture of its subject.

Marsh, F. B. *A History of the Roman World 146–30 B.C.* 3rd ed. London: Methuen, 1963. This standard account of the fall of the Roman Republic discusses Cleopatra's life and character at some length.

Syme, R. *The Roman Revolution.* Oxford: Oxford University Press, 1939. A magnificent work of scholarship that traces the decline of freedom at Rome and the rise of Augustus and in the process throws much valuable light on Antony and Cleopatra.

	GENERAL EVENTS	LITERATURE & PHILOSOPHY	ART

64 A.D.

<table>
<tr><td rowspan="5" style="writing-mode: vertical-lr">EARLY CHRISTIAN ERA</td><td rowspan="2">Period of Persecution</td><td>

250 Persecution of Christians under Decius

286 Diocletion divides Roman Empire into East and West parts ruled by himself and Maximian

305 Abdication of Diocletian and Maximian; Constantius and Galerius rule as joint emperors

307–327 Reign of Constantine
</td><td>

c. 67 Apostle Paul, bearer of Christian message throughout Mediterranean, martyred at Rome
</td><td></td></tr>
</table>

313

Period of Recognition

313 Edict of Milan, giving Christians freedom of religion

324 Constantine convenes Council of Nicaea

330 Constantine dedicates new capital of Roman Empire on site of Byzantium, naming it Constantinople

337 Constantine is baptized a Christian on his deathbed

383 Ostrogoths accept Christianity

c. 350 *Codex Sinaiticus*, earliest extant Greek codex of New Testament

c. 374–404 Saint John Chrysostom active as writer and preacher

c. 386 Saint Jerome translates Bible into Latin

c. 390 Obelisk of Theodosius erected in Hippodrome at Constantinople

395

Growth of Empire

395 Division of Roman Empire begun by Diocletian becomes total separation

4th–5th cent. Decline of Western Roman Empire

410 Visigoths sack Rome

455 Vandals sack Rome

476 Romulus Augustulus forced to abdicate as last Western Roman emperor; Ostrogoths rule Italy

493–526 Theodoric the Ostrogoth reigns in Italy

527–565 Reign of Justinian as Eastern Roman emperor in Constantinople

532 Nika revolt; civil disorders in Constantinople

c. 533 Justinian codifies Roman Law

540 Belisarius conquers Ostrogoths in Italy for Justinian; Ravenna comes under Byzantine rule

397 Augustine of Hippo, *The Confessions*

413–426 Augustine of Hippo, *The City of God*

c. 522–524 Boethius, *The Consolation of Philosophy*, allegorical treatise; translation of Aristotle's writings

524 Execution of Boethius by Theodoric the Ostrogoth

c. 562 Procopius, *History of the Wars, The Buildings, Secret History*

c. 415 Theodosius II moves gilded horses and chariot from Rome to Hippodrome

c. 425 Mosaics at Mausoleum of Galla Placidia, Ravenna

c. 450 Dome mosaic in Orthodox Baptistery, Ravenna

6th cent. Art tied to theological doctrine and liturgical practice of Orthodox Church

c. 547 Ivory throne of Archbishop Maximian, given by Justinian for San Vitale

c. 550 Mosaics at Sant' Apollinare Nuovo and San Vitale, Ravenna; *Metamorphosis of Christ*, apse mosaic from Katholikon, Monastery of Saint Catherine, Mount Sinai

BYZANTINE ERA

565

Territorial Decline

730–843 Iconoclastic Controversy: ban on religious imagery

800 Pope Leo III crowns first Western Roman emperor (Charlemagne) at Rome since 5th cent.

730–843 Ban on religious imagery; most earlier pictographic art destroyed

900

Second Growth

988–989 Russians accept Christianity

1054 Eastern and Western Church formally split

Renewal of icon tradition

1100

Final Decline

1204 Crusaders sack Constantinople on way to Holy Land

1453 Constantinople falls to Ottoman Turks, ending Byzantine Empire; Church of Hagia Sophia becomes a mosque

12th cent. Mosaics at Palermo, Sicily

c. 1410 Rublev active as painter of icons in Moscow

1453

The World of Byzantium

c. 324 Constantine has stadium
in Constantinople enlarged
to form Hippodrome

c. 326 Holy Sepulchre,
Jerusalem

c. 333 Old Saint Peter's Basilica,
Vatican

Use of basilica plan and central
plan with dome

after 350 Beginnings of Byzantine
music, based probably
on Syriac and Hebrew music

386 Saint Ambrose of Milan
begins use of vernacular hymns
in church

c. 450 Mausoleum of Galla
Placidia, Neonian and
Arian Baptisteries, Ravenna

c. 493–526 Sant' Apollinare
Nuovo, Ravenna

c. 526–547 San Vitale,
Ravenna

526 Theodoric's Tomb, Ravenna

527 Hagia Eirene,
Constantinople, begun

532–537 Anthemius of Tralles
and Isidore of Miletus rebuild
Hagia Sophia, Constantinople,
combining basilica plan and
central plan with dome

549 Sant' Apollinare in Classe

c. 550 Stephanos, Monastery
of Saint Catherine, Mount Sinai

590–602 Gregorian Chant
established at Rome during papacy
of Gregory the Great

7th cent. Golden Age of
Byzantine hymnody

1063 Saint Mark's, Venice, begun

11th cent. Codification of Greek
liturgy; musical modifications
decline

c. 1166 Church of the
Intercession of the Virgin,
near Vladimir, Russia;
"onion dome" adapted
from central dome

The Rise of Christianity and Decline of Rome

The Message of Paul

The greatest missionary of the religion of Jesus was the Apostle Paul. After his conversion to Christianity, Paul traveled to the major cities of the Mediterranean—called by the Romans *mare nostrum* (our sea)—from about A.D. 49 until A.D. 60. Paul's message was that Jesus was the anointed (the Greek word *christ* and the Hebrew word *messiah* both mean "anointed one") savior of the world. This religious teaching took hold in both Jewish and Gentile circles in various cities of the empire, including Rome itself. The fascination and the resistance of those in the Roman world who heard the strange new ideas from the little-regarded backwater of Jerusalem are suggested by a passage from the New Testament:

Acts 17: 16–34
PAUL SPEAKS TO THE ATHENIANS

Now while Paul was waiting for them at Athens, his spirit was provoked within him as he saw that the city was full of idols. So he argued in the synagogue with the Jews and the devout persons, and in the market place every day with those who chanced to be there. Some also of the Epicurean and Stoic philosophers met him. And some said, "What would this babbler say?" Others said, "He seems to be a preacher of foreign divinities"— because he preached Jesus and the resurrection. And they took hold of him and brought him to the Areopagus [Ares' or Mars' hill], saying, "May we know what this new teaching is which you present? For you bring some strange things to our ears; we wish to know therefore what these things mean." Now all the Athenians and the foreigners who lived there spent their time in nothing except telling or hearing something new.

So Paul, standing in the middle of the Areopagus, said: "Men of Athens, I perceive that in every way you are very religious. For as I passed along, and observed the objects of your worship, I found also an altar with this inscription, 'To an unknown god.' What therefore you worship as unknown, this I proclaim to you. The God who made the world and everything in it, being Lord of heaven and earth, does not live in shrines made by man, nor is he served by human hands, as though he needed anything, since he himself gives to all men life and breath and everything. And he made from one every nation of men to live on all the face of the earth, having determined allotted periods and the boundaries of their habitation, that they should seek God, in the hope that they might feel after him and find him. Yet he is not far from each one of us, for

'In him we live and move and have our being';
as even some of your poets have said.
'For we are indeed his offspring.'

Being then God's offspring, we ought not to think that the Deity is like gold, or silver, or stone, a representation by the art and imagination of man. The times of ignorance God overlooked, but now he commands all men everywhere to repent, because he has fixed a day on which he will judge the world in righteousness by a man whom he has appointed, and of this he has given assurance to all men by raising him from the dead."

Now when they heard of the resurrection of the dead, some mocked; but others said, "We will hear you again about this." So Paul went out from among them. But some men joined him and believed, among them Dionysius the Areopagite and a woman named Damaris and others with them.

There are many reasons for the widespread success of Christianity in the 1st-century A.D. Roman world. The Roman Empire was at peace; there was a common language in it; the roads were relatively safe and the Mediterranean was free of marauding pirates. The widespread interest in various Oriental philosophies and religions testifies to a hunger for religious experience and a passive dissatisfaction with the emotional content of official Roman religion. Christianity also appealed to all segments of society from the massive slave population of Rome to the intellectuals. And, unlike Mithraism (an Oriental religion popular with the military), it permitted female members.

Roman authorities were relatively tolerant of most religious ideas, but Christianity's insistence that only the God of the Christians could be worshiped seemed to them a subversive and dangerous idea. Such preaching struck at the heart of the Roman notion of *pietas*—the virtue by which children were bound to their parents by love and obedience, by which the parents in turn were bound to the state, and by which the state was bound to the gods of Rome. To deny those gods was to subvert the social "glue" that held the empire together. As a consequence of this distrust, Roman emperors from Nero in the 1st century to Diocletian in the late 3rd century intermittently persecuted Christians and outlawed the Christian religion. At times the persecutions were empire-wide

170 *Christ Teaching Among the Apostles.* c. A.D. 300. Wall painting, 1'3" × 4'3" (.38 × 1.3 m). Cemetery of Domitilla, Rome. Note the young beardless Christ in this early representation (compare figure **193**).

and bloodily oppressive (as, for example, the persecution of Decius in A.D. 250), while at other periods the persecutions were localized and sporadic.

The spread of Christianity nevertheless continued. At the beginning of the 4th century (and after a fierce but ineffectual persecution in 303 under the Emperor Diocletian) the Emperor Constantine issued an edict of toleration (the Edict of Milan, A.D. 313) for the Christians. By the middle of the 4th century Christianity was the state religion of the empire [170].

Constantine became formally a Christian only on his deathbed, but his interest in the religion had been manifest and generous. He drew Christianity closer to the state and provided it the freedom to expend some of the energies that had been suppressed during the times of the persecutions.

Two of the most famous churches in Christendom are associated with the reign of the Emperor Constantine. The present Saint Peter's Basilica in the Vatican rests on the remains of a basilica dedicated in 326. We do not have a fully articulated plan of that church, but its main outlines are clear. The faithful would enter into a courtyard called an *atrium* around which was a colonnaded arcade and from there through a vestibule into the church proper. The basilica, modeled after secular counterparts in Rome [see 159], featured a long central *nave* with two parallel side aisles. The nave was intersected at one end by a *transept,* the roof of which was pitched with wooden trusses and supported by the outer walls and the columned interiors. High up on the walls above the arches and below the roof was the so-called *clerestory,* windows

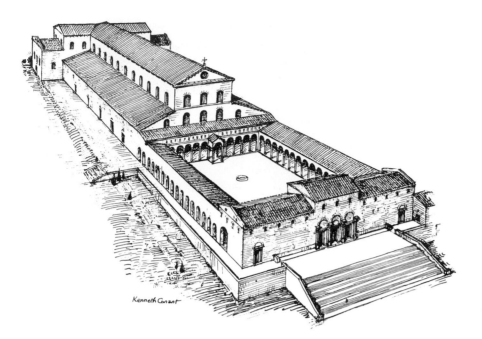

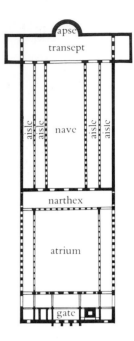

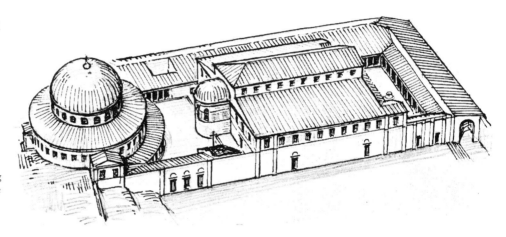

above left: 171 Old Saint Peter's Basilica, Rome. c. A.D. 333. Length of grand axis 835′ (254.5 m), width of transept 295′ (86.87 m). Reconstruction study by Kenneth J. Conant.

above right: 172 Plan of Old Saint Peter's Basilica.

right: 173 Church of the Holy Sepulchre, Jerusalem, as it appeared in about A.D. 345. Reconstruction drawing by Kenneth J. Conant. Note that the basilica church has given way to a domed building.

that provided most of the interior illumination. This basilica-type church [171, 172] became a model from which many of the features of later church architecture evolved.

The other famous church built in the Constantinian period is the church of the Holy Sepulchre in Jerusalem [173]. This church was also built in the basilica style, its atrium in front of the basilica hall, but with a significant addition. Behind the basilica was a domed structure that covered—it was believed—the rocky place where the body of Christ had been buried for three days. The domelike structure was utilized in Christian architecture as an adaptation of existing

domed structures in pagan Rome, most notably the Pantheon [see 153] and some of the vast baths.

The period between Saint Paul and Constantine saw the Roman Empire slip from undisputed mastery of the known world to a tottering and endangered realm. Economic problems and threats from the barbarians at the borders of the empire threatened the stability of the far-flung outreaches of Roman control, and the 4th and 5th centuries saw the gradual but inexorable decline of the empire in the West. The last Roman emperor in the West died at Ravenna in 476, by which time imperial power had already shifted to Constantinople in the East (see map).

Augustine of Hippo

The greatest writer of the Christian Latin West, Augustine of Hippo, was a witness to this decline. Born in 354 in North Africa (then part of the Roman provinces), Augustine received a thorough classical education in Africa and in Rome. He was converted to Christianity in Milan and soon afterward returned to his native country, where he was named bishop of Hippo in 390. When the Vandals sacked Rome in 410, the pagan world was aghast and many blamed the rise of Christianity for this event. Partially as a response to this charge, Augustine wrote *The City of God* as an attempt to show that history had a direction willed by God and that "in the end" all would be made right as the city of man gave way to the city of God. This work, packed with reflections on scripture, philosophy, and pagan wisdom, is often cited as one of the most influential philosophies of history written in the Western world.

Indeed, it is difficult to overestimate the intellectual impact of Augustine of Hippo on the subsequent cultural history of the West. His influence within Christianity is without parallel. Until Thomas Aquinas in the 13th century, all Christian theologians started from explicitly Augustinian premises. Even Thomas did not shake off his debt to Augustine, although he replaced Augustine's strong Platonic orientation with a more empirical Aristotelian one. Augustine emphasized the absolute majesty of God, the immutability of the Divine will, and the flawed state of the human condition (notions synthesized

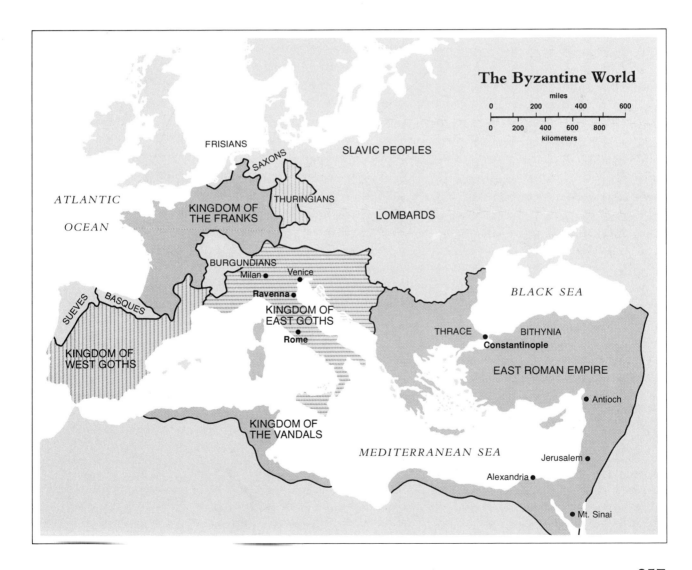

from Paul). These tenets received a powerful reformulation in the Protestant Reformation by Martin Luther (who as a Catholic friar had lived under the rule of Saint Augustine) and by John Calvin, a profound student of Augustine's theological writings.

Augustine also made a notable impact beyond theology. *The City of God,* begun about 412, was an attempt to formulate a coherent and all-embracing philosophy of history, the first such attempt in the West. For Augustine history moves on a straight line in a direction from its origin in God until it ends, again in God, at the consummation of history in the Last Judgment. Augustine rejected the older notion that history repeats itself endlessly in cycles. His reading of the Bible convinced him that humanity had an origin, played out its story, and would terminate. The city of man would be judged and the city of God would be saved. Subsequent philosophers of history have secularized this view but, with very few exceptions (Vico, a 17th-century Italian philosopher, was one), have maintained the outlines of Augustine's framework to some extent. "A bright future," "An atomic wasteland of the future," and "Classless society" are all statements about the end of history, all statements that echo, however dimly, the world view of Augustine.

Augustine also invented the genre of self-reflective writing in the West. *Noverim me ut noverim Te* (I would know myself that I might know Thee) Augustine writes of God in *The Confessions*. Before Augustine's time, memoirs related a life in terms of social, political, or military affairs (as Caesar's *Gallic Wars* did), but Augustine's intimate self-scrutiny of the significance of life was new in Western culture. There would not be another work like *The Confessions* until Petrarch, an indefatigable student of Augustine, wrote his *Letter to Posterity* (pages 434–438) in the mid-14th century. The Renaissance writers, an extremely self-conscious generation, were devoted students of Augustine's stately Latin prose; even the great later autobiographies of our inherited culture—those of Gibbon, Mill, Newman—are literary and spiritual descendants of Augustine's.

Augustine's *The Confessions* is a compelling analysis of his spiritual and intellectual development from his youth until the time of his conversion to Christianity and readiness to return to his native Africa. The title must be understood in a triple sense—a confession of sin, an act of faith in God, and a confession of praise—so it is appropriate that Augustine wrote his book as a prayer to God.

Although strongly autobiographical, *The Confessions* is actually a long meditation by Augustine on the hidden grace of God as his life is shaped toward its appointed end. Augustine "confesses" to God (and the reader) how his early drive for fame as a teacher of rhetoric, his flirtation with the Manichean sect with its belief in two gods of evil and good, his liaison with a woman that resulted in the birth of a son, and his restless movement from North Africa to Rome and Milan were all part of a seamless web of circumstance that made up an individual life. Interspersed in the narrative line of his early life are Augustine's reflections on the most basic philosophical and theological questions of the day, always linked to his own experience. In the selection in this book, Augustine meditates on the "strange phenomenon" of the mind's inability completely to rule the will. And this is no mere exercise in speculation: Augustine is concerned about his own unruly will and its tendency toward evil, and about his inability to lead a sexually chaste life. Augustine always moves from general principle to a specific application in his own life and experience.

If *The Confessions* can be said to be the beginning of autobiography, beyond that historic importance it is classic and singular in its balance of immense learning, searching speculation, and intense self-scrutiny. It is a work concerned first of all with meaning at the deepest philosophical level, and its full power is evident only to the reader who will take the time to enter Augustine's line of argument.

The passages reprinted here mark two high points in the work. The first (VIII: 9-12) relates Augustine's final intellectual struggles before his conversion to Christianity. The passage resounds with many of Augustine's leading preoccupations—the problem of evil, his concern for sexual continence, the desire to believe—and culminates with his conversion at the home of his Christian friend Alypius in Milan.

The second passage (IX: 10-11) tells poignantly of the last days of his mother Monica as she and her son wait for a ship at Rome's seaport, Ostia, to go back to North Africa. Generations of writers and readers alike have been moved by the powerful description of the "mystical vision and conversation" between Augustine and his mother as they look over the port city. Modern visitors to Ostia and its extensive archaeological remains can still envision the town as it was in Augustine's day. On one of the buildings is affixed a large marble plaque with the opening lines of the passage carved in it.

Saint Augustine
THE CONFESSIONS
from Book VIII

9

Why does this strange phenomenon occur? What causes it? O Lord in your mercy give me light to see, for it may be that the answer to my question lies in the secret punishment of man and in the penitence which casts a deep shadow on the sons of Adam. Why does this strange phenomenon occur? What causes it? The mind gives an order to the body and is at once obeyed, but when it gives an order to itself, it is resisted. The mind commands the hand to move and is so readily obeyed that the order can scarcely be distinguished from its execution. Yet the mind is mind and the hand is part of the body. But when the mind commands the mind to make an act of will, these two are one and the same and yet the order is not obeyed. Why does this happen? What is the cause of it? The mind orders itself to make an act of will, and it would not give this order unless it willed to do so; yet it does not carry out its own command. But it does not fully will to do this thing and therefore its orders are not fully given. It gives the order only in so far as it wills, and in so far as it does not will the order is not carried out. For the will commands that an act of will should be made, and it gives this command to itself, not to some other will. The reason, then, why the command is not obeyed is that it is not given with the full will. For if the will were full, it would not command itself to be full, since it would be so already. It is therefore no strange phenomenon partly to will to do something and partly to will not to do it. It is a disease of the mind, which does not wholly rise to the heights where it is lifted by the truth, because it is weighed down by habit. So there are two wills in us, because neither by itself is the whole will, and each possesses what the other lacks.

10

*There are many abroad who talk of their own fantasies and lead men's minds astray.** They assert that because they have observed that there are two wills at odds with each other when we try to reach a decision, we must therefore have two minds of different natures, one good, the other evil. *Let them vanish at God's presence as the smoke vanishes.* As long as they hold these evil beliefs they are evil themselves, but even they will be good if they see the truth and accept it, so that your apostle may say to them *Once you were all darkness; now, in the Lord you are all daylight.* These people want to be light, not in the Lord, but in themselves, because they think that the nature of the soul is the same

*Italics indicate biblical quotations.

as God. In this way their darkness becomes denser still, because in their abominable arrogance they have separated themselves still further from you, who are *the true Light which enlightens every soul born into the world.* I say to them, "Take care what you say, and blush for shame. Enter God's presence, and find there enlightenment; *here is no room for downcast looks.*"

When I was trying to reach a decision about serving the Lord my God, as I had long intended to do, it was I who willed to take this course and again it was I who willed not to take it. It was I and I alone. But I neither willed to do it nor refused to do it with my full will. So I was at odds with myself. I was throwing myself into confusion. All this happened to me although I did not want it, but it did not prove that there was some second mind in me besides my own. It only meant that my mind was being punished. *My action did not come from me, but from the sinful principle that dwells in me.* It was part of the punishment of a sin freely committed by Adam, my first father.

If there were as many different natures in us as there are conflicting wills, we should have a great many more natures than merely two. Suppose that someone is trying to decide whether to go to the theatre or to the Manichees' meeting-house. The Manichees will say, "Clearly he has two natures, the good one bringing him here to us and the bad one leading him away. Otherwise, how can you explain this dilemma of two opposing wills?" I say that the will to attend their meetings is just as bad as the will to go off to the theatre, but in their opinion it can only be a good will that leads a man to come to them. Suppose then that one of us is wavering between two conflicting wills and cannot make up his mind whether to go to the theatre or to our church. Will not the Manichees be embarrassed to know what to say? Either they must admit—which they will not do—that it is a good will which brings a man to our church, just as in their opinion it is a good will which brings their own communicants and adherents to their church; or they must presume that there are two evil natures and two evil minds in conflict in one man. If they think this, they will disprove their own theory that there is one good and one evil will in man. The only alternative is for them to be converted to the truth and to cease to deny that when a man tries to make a decision, he has one soul which is torn between conflicting wills.

So let us hear no more of their assertion, when they observe two wills in conflict in one man, that there are two opposing minds in him, one good and the other bad, and that they are in conflict because they spring from two opposing substances and two opposing principles. For you, O God of truth, prove that they are utterly wrong. You demolish their arguments and confound them completely. It may be that both the wills are bad. For instance, a man may be trying to decide whether to commit murder by poison or by stabbing; whether he should swindle another man out of one part of his property or another, that is, if he cannot obtain both; whether he should spend his money extravagantly on pleasure or hoard it like a miser; or whether he should go to the games in the circus or to the theatre, when there is a performance at both places on the same day. In this last case there may be a third possibility, that he should go and rob another person's house, if he has the chance. There may even be a fourth choice open to him, because he may wonder whether to go and commit adultery, if the occasion arises at the same time. These possibilities may all occur at the same moment and all may seem equally desirable. The man cannot do all these things at once, and his mind is torn between four wills which cannot be reconciled—perhaps more than four, because there are a great many things that he might wish to do. But the Manichees do not claim that there are as many different substances in us as this.

It is just the same when the wills are good. If I question the Manichees whether it is good to find pleasure in reading Paul's Epistles or in the tranquil enjoyment of a Psalm or in a discussion of the Gospel, they will reply in each case that it is good. Supposing, then, that a man finds all these things equally attractive and the chance to do all of them occurs at the same time, is it not true that as long as he cannot make up his mind which of them he most wants to do his heart is torn between several different desires? All these different desires are good, yet they are in conflict with each other until he chooses a single course to which the will may apply itself as a single whole, so that it is no longer split into several different wills.

The same is true when the higher part of our nature aspires after eternal bliss while our lower self is held back by the love of temporal pleasure. It is the same soul that wills both, but it wills neither of them with the full force of the will. So it is wrenched in two and suffers great trials, because while truth teaches it to prefer one course, habit prevents it from relinquishing the other.

11

This was the nature of my sickness. I was in torment, reproaching myself more bitterly than ever as I twisted and turned in my chain. I hoped that my chain might be broken once and for all, because it was only a small thing that held me now. All the same it held me. And you, O Lord, never ceased to watch over my secret heart. In your stern mercy you lashed me with the twin scourge of fear and shame in case I should give way once more and the worn and slender remnant of my chain should not be broken but gain new strength and bind me all the faster. In my heart I kept saying "Let it be now, let it be now!," and merely by saying this I was on the point of making the resolution. I was on the point of making it, but I did not succeed. Yet I did not fall back into my old state. I stood on the brink of resolution, waiting to take fresh breath. I tried again and came a little nearer to my goal, and then a little nearer still, so that I could almost reach out and grasp it. But I did not reach it. I could not reach out to it or grasp it, because I held back from the step by which I should die to death and become alive to life. My lower instincts, which had taken firm hold of me, were stronger than the higher, which were untried. And the closer I came to the moment which was to mark the great change in me, the more I shrank from it in horror. But it did not drive me back or turn me from my purpose: it merely left me hanging in suspense.

I was held back by mere trifles, the most paltry inanities, all my old attachments. They plucked at my garment of flesh and whispered, "Are you going to dismiss us? From this moment we shall never be with you again, for ever and ever. From this moment you will never again be allowed to do this thing or that, for evermore." What was it, my God, that they meant when they whispered "this thing or that?" Things so sordid and so shameful that I beg you in your mercy to keep the soul of your servant free from them! These voices, as I heard them, seemed less than half as loud as they had been before. They no longer barred my way, blatantly contradictory, but their mutterings seemed to reach me from behind, as though they were stealthily plucking at my back, trying to make me turn my head when I wanted to go forward. Yet, in my state of indecision, they kept me from tearing myself away, from shaking myself free of them and leaping across the barrier to the other side, where you were calling me. Habit was too strong for me when it asked, "Do you think you can live without these things?"

But by now the voice of habit was very faint. I had turned my eyes elsewhere, and while I stood trembling at the barrier, on the other side I could see the chaste beauty of Continence in all her serene, unsullied joy, as she modestly beckoned me to cross over and to hesitate no more. She stretched out loving hands to welcome and embrace me, holding up a host of good examples to my sight. With her were countless boys and girls, great numbers of the young and people of all ages, staid widows and women still virgins in old age. And in their midst was Continence herself, not barren but a fruitful mother of children, of joys born of you, O Lord, her Spouse. She smiled at me to give me courage, as though she were saying, "Can you not do what these men and these women do? Do you think they find the strength to do it in themselves and not in the Lord their God? It was the Lord their God who gave me to them. Why do you try to stand in your own strength and fail? Cast yourself upon God and have no fear. He will not shrink away and let you fall. Cast yourself upon him without fear, for he will welcome you and cure you of your ills." I was overcome with shame, because I was still listening to the futile mutterings of my lower self and I was still hanging in suspense. And again Continence seemed to say, "Close your ears to the unclean whispers of your body, so that it may be mortified. It tells you of things that delight you, but not such things as the law of the Lord your God has to tell."

In this way I wrangled with myself, in my own heart, about my own self. And all the while Alypius stayed at my side, silently awaiting the outcome of this agitation that was new in me.

12

I probed the hidden depths of my soul and wrung its pitiful secrets from it, and when I mustered them all before the eyes of my heart, a great storm broke within me, bringing with it a great deluge of tears. I stood up and left Alypius so that I might weep and cry to my heart's content, for it occurred to me that tears were best shed in solitude. I moved away far enough to avoid being embarrassed even by his presence. He must have realized what my feelings were, for I suppose I had said something and he had known from the sound of my voice that I was ready to burst into tears. So I stood up and left him where we had been sitting, utterly bewildered. Somehow I flung myself down beneath a fig tree and gave way to the tears which now streamed from my eyes, the sacrifice that is acceptable to you. I had much to say to you, my God, not in these very words but in this strain: *Lord, will you never be content? Must we always taste your vengeance? Forget the long record of our sins.* For I felt that I was still the captive of my sins, and in my misery I kept crying "How long shall I go on saying 'tomorrow, tomorrow'? Why not now? Why not make an end of my ugly sins at this moment?"

I was asking myself these questions, weeping all the while with the most bitter sorrow in my heart, when all at once I heard the sing-song voice of a child in a nearby house. Whether it was the voice of a boy or a girl I cannot say, but again and again it repeated the refrain "Take it and read, take it and read." At this I looked up, thinking hard whether there was any kind of game in which children used to chant words

like these, but I could not remember ever hearing them before. I stemmed my flood of tears and stood up, telling myself that this could only be a divine command to open my book of Scripture and read the first passage on which my eyes should fall. For I had heard the story of Antony, and I remembered how he had happened to go into a church while the Gospel was being read and had taken it as a counsel addressed to himself when he heard the words *Go home and sell all that belongs to you. Give it to the poor, and so the treasure you have shall be in heaven; then come back and follow me.* By this divine pronouncement he had at once been converted to you.

So I hurried back to the place where Alypius was sitting, for when I stood up to move away I had put down the book containing Paul's Epistles. I seized it and opened it, and in silence I read the first passage on which my eyes fell: *Not in revelling and drunkenness, not in lust and wantonness, not in quarrels and rivalries. Rather, arm yourselves with the Lord Jesus Christ; spend no more thought on nature and nature's appetites.* I had no wish to read more and no need to do so. For in an instant, as I came to the end of the sentence, it was as though the light of confidence flooded into my heart and all the darkness of doubt was dispelled.

I marked the place with my finger or by some other sign and closed the book. My looks now were quite calm as I told Alypius what had happened to me. He too told me what he had been feeling, which of course I did not know. He asked to see what I had read. I showed it to him and he read on beyond the text which I had read. I did not know what followed, but it was this: *Find room among you for a man of over-delicate conscience.* Alypius applied this to himself and told me so. This admonition was enough to give him strength, and without suffering the distress of hesitation he made his resolution and took this good purpose to himself. And it very well suited his moral character, which had long been far, far better than my own.

Then we went in and told my mother, who was overjoyed. And when we went on to describe how it had all happened, she was jubilant with triumph and glorified you, *who are powerful enough, and more than powerful enough, to carry out your purpose beyond all our hopes and dreams.* For she saw that you had granted her far more than she used to ask in her tearful prayers and plaintive lamentations. You converted me to yourself, so that I no longer desired a wife or placed any hope in this world but stood firmly upon the rule of faith, where you had shown me to her in a dream so many years before. And you *turned her sadness into rejoicing,* into joy far fuller than her dearest wish, far sweeter and more chaste than any she had hoped to find in children begotten of my flesh.

10

Not long before the day on which she was to leave this life—you knew which day it was to be, O Lord, though we did not—my mother and I were alone, leaning from a window which overlooked the garden in the courtyard of the house where we were staying at Ostia. We were waiting there after our long and tiring journey, away from the crowd, to refresh ourselves before our sea-voyage. I believe that what I am going to tell happened through the secret working of your providence. For we were talking alone together and our conversation was serene and joyful. *We had forgotten what we had left behind and were intent on what lay before us.* In the presence of Truth, which is yourself, we were wondering what the eternal life of the saints would be like, that life which *no eye has seen, no ear has heard, no human heart conceived.* But we laid the lips of our hearts to the heavenly stream that flows from your fountain, *the source of all life* which is *in you,* so that as far as it was in our power to do so we might be sprinkled with its waters and in some sense reach an understanding of this great mystery.

Our conversation led us to the conclusion that no bodily pleasure, however great it might be and whatever earthly light might shed lustre upon it, was worthy of comparison, or even of mention, beside the happiness of the life of the saints. As the flame of love burned stronger in us and raised us higher towards the eternal God, our thoughts ranged over the whole compass of material things in their various degrees, up to the heavens themselves, from which the sun and the moon and the stars shine down upon the earth. Higher still we climbed, thinking and speaking all the while in wonder at all that you have made. At length we came to our own souls and passed beyond them to that place of everlasting plenty, where you feed Israel for ever with the food of truth. There life is that Wisdom by which all these things that we know are made, all things that ever have been and all that are yet to be. But that Wisdom is not made: it is as it has always been and as it will be for ever—or, rather, I should not say that it *has been* or *will be,* for it simply *is,* because eternity is not in the past or in the future. And while we spoke of the eternal Wisdom, longing for it and straining for it with all the strength of our hearts, for one fleeting instant we reached out and touched it. Then with a sigh, leaving *our spiritual harvest* bound to it, we returned to the sound of our own speech, in which each word has a beginning and an ending—far, far different from your Word, our Lord, who abides in himself for ever, yet never grows old and gives new life to all things.

And so our discussion went on. Suppose, we said, that the tumult of a man's flesh were to cease and all that his thoughts can conceive, of earth, of water, and of air, should no longer speak to him; suppose that the heavens and even his own soul were silent, no longer thinking of itself but passing beyond; suppose that his dreams and the visions of his imagination spoke no more and that every tongue and every sign and all that is transient grew silent—for all these things have the same message to tell, if only we can hear it, and their message is this: We did not make ourselves, but he who abides for ever made us. Suppose, we said, that after giving us this message and bidding us listen to him who made them, they fell silent and he alone should speak to us, not through them but in his own voice, so that we should hear him speaking, not by any tongue of the flesh or by an angel's voice, not in the sound of thunder or in some veiled parable, but in his own voice, the voice of the one whom we love in all these created things; suppose that we heard him himself, with none of these things between ourselves and him, just as in that brief moment my mother and I had reached out in thought and touched the eternal Wisdom which abides over all things; suppose that this state were to continue and all other visions of things inferior were to be removed, so that this single vision entranced and absorbed the one who beheld it and enveloped him in inward joys in such a way that for him life was eternally the same as that instant of understanding for which we had longed so much—would not this be what we are to understand by the words *Come and share the joy of your Lord?* But when is it to be? Is it to be when *we all rise again, but not all of us will undergo the change?*

This was the purport of our talk, though we did not speak in these precise words or exactly as I have reported them. Yet you know, O Lord, that as we talked that day, the world, for all its pleasures, seemed a paltry place compared with the life that we spoke of. And then my mother said, "My son, for my part I find no further pleasure in this life. What I am still to do or why I am here in the world, I do not know, for I have no more to hope for on this earth. There was one reason, and one alone, why I wished to remain a little longer in this life, and that was to see you a Catholic Christian before I died. God has granted my wish and more besides, for I now see you as his servant, spurning such happiness as the world can give. What is left for me to do in this world?"

11

I scarcely remember what answer I gave her. It was about five days after this, or not much more, that she took to her bed with a fever. One day during her illness she had a fainting fit and lost consciousness for a short time. We hurried to her bedside, but she soon regained consciousness and looked up at my brother and me as we stood beside her. With a puzzled look she asked, "Where was I?" Then watching us closely as we stood there speechless with grief, she said, "You will bury your mother here." I said nothing, trying hard to hold back my tears, but my brother said something to the effect that he wished for her sake that she would die in her own country, not abroad. When she heard this, she looked at him anxiously and her eyes reproached him for his worldly thoughts. She turned to me and said, "See how he talks!" and then, speaking to both of us, she went on, "It does not matter where you bury my body. Do not let that worry you! All I ask of you is that, wherever you may be, you should remember me at the altar of the Lord."

Although she hardly had the strength to speak, she managed to make us understand her wishes and then fell silent, for her illness was becoming worse and she was in great pain. But I was thinking of your gifts, O God. Unseen by us you plant them like seeds in the hearts of your faithful and they grow to bear wonderful fruits. This thought filled me with joy and I thanked you for your gifts, for I had always known, and well remembered now, my mother's great anxiety to be buried beside her husband's body in the grave which she had provided and prepared for herself. Because they had lived in the greatest harmony, she had always wanted this extra happiness. She had wanted it to be said of them that, after her journeyings across the sea, it had been granted to her that the earthly remains of husband and wife should be joined as one and covered by the same earth. How little the human mind can understand God's purpose! I did not know when it was that your good gifts had borne their full fruit and her heart had begun to renounce this vain desire, but I was both surprised and pleased to find that it was so. And yet, when we talked at the window and she asked, "What is left for me to do in this world?," it was clear that she had no desire to die in her own country. Afterwards I also heard that one day during our stay at Ostia, when I was absent, she had talked in a motherly way to some of my friends and had spoken to them of the contempt of this life and the blessings of death. They were astonished to find such courage in a woman—it was your gift to her, O Lord—and asked whether she was not frightened at the thought of leaving her body so far from her own country. "Nothing is far from God," she replied, "and I need have no fear that he will not know where to find me when he comes to raise me to life at the end of the world."

And so on the ninth day of her illness, when she was fifty-six and I was thirty-three, her pious and devoted soul was set free from the body. 📖

The Ascendancy of Byzantium

The Emperor Constantine dedicated a Greek trading town on the Bosporus as his eastern capital in May 330, changing its name from Byzantium to Constantinople (the city of Constantine). It contained a mix of pagan, Christian, and Greek elements. Constantine built churches and monasteries as well as the obligatory palaces, fora, markets, and civic monuments, although only a few foundations and other archaeological remains have survived.

Constantine's choice of Byzantium for what he intended as the "New Rome" proved felicitous. Rome itself was reduced to a shadow of its former glory by the 5th century. Among the other major possibilities, Alexandria in Egypt had long been suffering an economic decline in this period and Antioch was eventually devastated by an earthquake in 525.

Constantinople had some obvious geographic advantages for a major city: it straddled the most prominent land route between Asia and Europe. It also had a deep-water port with natural shelter. It guarded the passage between the Mediterranean and the Black Sea (see map, page 257). The surrounding countryside was rich in woodlands and natural springs of drinkable water. The neighboring areas of Europe (Thrace) and Asia (Bithynia) were rich in agricultural lands, providing the city a ready food supply.

Justinian and Theodora

Justinian became emperor in Constantinople in 527. He fully intended to restore the empire to a state of grandeur. In this he was aided by his beautiful and ruthless wife Theodora. A former dancer and prostitute whose ascent to the royal purple "cannot be applauded as the triumph of feminine virtue," as the 18th-century English historian Edward Gibbon observed rather starchily, Theodora was a tough-minded and capable woman who added strength and resolve to the grandiose ideas of the emperor. She was Justinian's equal, and perhaps more.

The reign of Justinian and Theodora was impressive, if profligate, by any standard. The emperor encouraged Persian monks residing in China to bring back silkworms for the introduction of the silk industry into the West. Because the silk industry of China was a fiercely guarded monopoly, the monks accomplished this rather dangerous mission by smuggling silkworm eggs out of the country in hollow tubes, and within a decade the silk industry in the Western world rivaled that of China.

Justinian also revised and codified Roman law, a gigantic undertaking of scholarship and research. Roman law had evolved over a thousand-year period, and by Justinian's time was a vast jumble of unorganized and often contradictory decisions, decrees, statutes, opinions, and legal codes. Under the aegis of the emperor, a legal scholar named Tribonian produced order out of this chaos. First a *Code* that summarized all imperial decrees from the time of Hadrian (in the 2nd century) to the time of Justinian was published. The *Code* was followed by the *Pandects* (digest), which synthesized a vast quantity of legal opinion and scholarship from the past. Finally came the *Institutes,* a legal collection broken down into four categories by which the laws concerning persons, things, actions, and personal wrongs (in other words, criminal law) were set forth. The body of this legal revision became the basis for the law courts of the empire and, in later centuries, the basis for the use of Roman law in the West.

Justinian and Theodora were fiercely partisan Christians who took a keen interest in theology and ecclesiastical governance. Justinian's fanatical devotion prompted him to shut down the last surviving Platonic academy in the world on the grounds that its paganism was inimical to the true religion. His own personal life—despite evidences of cruelty and capriciousness—was austere and abstemious, influenced by the presence of so many monks in the city of Constantinople. His generosity to the church was great, with his largess shown most clearly in openhanded patronage of church-building. Hagia Sophia, his most famous project, has become legendary for the beauty and opulence of its decoration.

Hagia Sophia: Monument and Symbol

Hagia Sophia (Greek for "Holy Wisdom") was the principal church of Constantinople. It had been destroyed twice, once by fire and—during Justinian's reign—during the terrible civil disorders of the Nika revolt in 532 that devastated most of the European side of the city. Soon afterward Justinian decided to rebuild the church using the plans of two architects, Anthemius of Tralles and Isidore of Miletus. Work began in 532 and the new edifice was solemnly dedicated five years later in the presence of Justinian and Theodora.

The church of Hagia Sophia was a stunning architectural achievement that combined the longitudinal shape of the Roman basilica with a domed central plan. Two centuries earlier Constantine had used both the dome and basilica shapes in the church of the Holy Sepulchre in Jerusalem, as we have seen, but he had not joined them into a unity. In still earlier domed buildings in the Roman world such as the Pantheon and Santa Costanza, the dome rested on a circular drum. This gave the dome solidity but limited its height and expansiveness. Anthemius and Isidore solved this problem by the use of *pendentives* [174], triangular masonry devices that carried the weight of the dome on massive piers rather than straight down to the drum. In the church of Hagia Sophia the central dome was abutted by two half domes so that a person looking down at the building from above might see a nave in the form of an oval instead of a quadrangle [175, 176].

The church—184 feet (55.2 meters) high, 41 feet (12.3 meters) higher than the Pantheon—retained a hint of the old basilica style as a result of the columned side aisles and the *matroneum* gallery for female worshipers in the triforium space above the

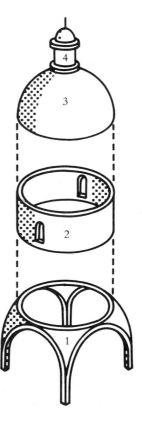

174 Dome construction: 1. pendentive; 2. drum; 3. cupola; 4. lantern.

arches of the aisles, but the overwhelming visual impression came from the massive dome. Since the pendentives reduced the weight of the dome, the area between drum and dome could be pierced by forty windows that made the dome seem to hang in space. Light streamed into the church from the windows and refracted off the rich mosaics and colored marbles that covered the interior [Plate 16, page 287].

Light, in fact, was a key theoretical element behind the entire conception of Hagia Sophia. Light is the symbol of divine wisdom in the philosophy of both Plato and the New Testament. A common metaphor in pagan and biblical wisdom had the sun and its rays represent the eternity of God and his illumination of mortals. The suffusion of light was an element in the Hagia Sophia that went far beyond the functional

left: 175 Justinian presenting a model of Hagia Sophia to the enthroned Madonna, detail from the lunette over the south vestibule door of Hagia Sophia. 10th century. Mosaic.
below: 176 Anthemius of Tralles and Isidore of Miletus. Hagia Sophia, Constantinople (Istanbul). 532–537, 553–563. Exterior view from the southeast. The towers, of Turkish inspiration, are of later date.

need to illuminate the interior of the church. Light refracting in the church created a spiritual ambiance analogous to that of heaven, where the faithful would be bathed in the actual light of God.

The sequence of the various parts of the worship service at Constantinople—the *liturgy*—was developed from the efforts of Saint John Chrysostom (345–407), patriarch of the city in the century before Justinian. The official liturgy of Byzantine Christianity is still the Divine Liturgy of Saint John Chrysostom, modified and added to over the centuries. In that liturgy, the worshiping community visualized itself as standing in the forecourt of heaven when it worshiped in the church. Amid the swirling incense, the glittering light, and the stately *a cappella* chants of the clergy and people comes a sense of participation with the household of heaven standing before God. A fragment from the liturgy—added during the reign of Justinian's successor Justin II (565–578)—underscores the point dramatically. Note the characteristic cry of *Wisdom!* and the description of the congregation as mystically present in heaven:

PRIEST Wisdom! That ever being guarded by Thy power, we may give glory to thee, Father, Son, and Holy Spirit, now and forevermore.
CONGREGATION Amen. Let us here who represent the mystic Cherubim in singing the thrice holy hymn to the life-giving Trinity now lay aside every earthly care.

So that we may welcome the King of the universe who comes escorted by invisible armies of angels. Alleluia. Alleluia. Alleluia.

Hagia Sophia was enriched by subsequent emperors, and after repairs were made to the dome in 989 new mosaics were added to the church. After the fall of Constantinople in 1453 the Turks turned the church into a mosque; the mosaics were whitewashed or plastered over since the Koran prohibits the use of images. When the mosque was converted to a museum by the modern Turkish state, some of the mosaics were uncovered, and we can get some sense of the splendor of the original interior.

Other monuments bear the mark of Justinian's creative efforts. His church of the Holy Apostles [177], built on the site of an earlier church of the same name destroyed by an earthquake, did not survive the fall of the city in 1453 but did serve as a model for the church of Saint Mark in Venice, as a comparison of surviving illustrations with Saint Mark's shows clearly [178]. Near the church of the Hagia Sophia is the church of Hagia Eirene (Holy Peace), now a mosque, whose architecture also shows the combination of basilica and dome. The church dedicated to the martyr saints Sergius and Bacchus, begun in 527, was a preliminary study for the later Hagia Sophia. In all, Justinian built more than twenty-five churches and convents in Constantinople. His program of secular architecture included an impressive waterconduit system that still exists.

The Games at Byzantium

Part of the Romans' legacy to Byzantium was a taste for spectator sports. The ancient Greeks had preferred individual participation in athletics, and the status of victorious athletes was high. The Romans held chariot races and gladiatorial combat on a massive scale before a vast public. The charioteers and fighters were generally slaves or criminals, however, since no respectable Roman citizen would compete in public. Prizes were very large; a successful gladiator or charioteer could easily amass a fortune and become the idol of a rabid clique. The enthusiasm of the public was further stimulated by the division of the charioteers into four teams—the Reds, Whites, Blues, and Greens—each supported and cheered by its partisans.

In Byzantium, the gladiatorial and animal combats so popular in Rome were suppressed. It was hardly in accordance with Christian principles to watch men or men and animals tear each other to pieces for the entertainment of others. To this extent at least, the Byzantine games in the time of Justinian were a notable improvement over their predecessors. Chariot races, staged in the racetrack of Byzantium, the Hippodrome, before tremendous crowds, nevertheless soon came to dominate Byzantine life in ways that may seem strange to us today. Enthusiasm for one's own team and contempt for the supporters of a rival one is not unknown today among spectators at sports events and can sometimes lead to violent demonstrations and fighting. But the Byzantine crowds combined sport and religion in a way that illustrates vividly and disturbingly the obsession of the Byzantine populace with theological argument. By A.D. 500 the number of teams had been reduced from four to two, the Blues and the Greens, each upholding and racing in support of a different doctrine. The Greens fought for Monophysitism (the belief that Christ had only one, divine nature) while the Blues were staunch upholders of the dual nature of Christ—both human and divine.

It is scarcely credible now that a debate of such subtlety and complexity, worthy of the attention of the most sophisticated theologian, should have become associated with chariot racers and their supporters. Nevertheless, the partisanship reached a level of popular frenzy which thankfully remains unequaled since. Every inhabitant of Byzantium became an adherent of one team or the other and followed its fortunes both in the Hippodrome and elsewhere. Supporters adopted styles of dress by which they could easily be recognized: some of the Blues, for example, shaved their heads in the front and let their hair grow long at the back in imitation of the barbarian Huns.

By the time of Justinian the Blues had acquired the support of the emperor himself, although Theodora was rumored to follow her father's allegiance to the Greens. The Hippodrome, decorated with art treasures from Greece, Rome, and Egypt, now became the center of political life in Byzantium. Enlargement of an earlier stadium had been one of Constantine's first projects after the move of the capital to Byzantium in 324, and the Hippodrome in Justinian's time not only accommodated most of the population of

above: 177 *The Ascension,* detail of miniature showing the five-domed Church of the Holy Apostles in Constantinople, from the collection of Homilies on the Virgin by James of Kokkinobaphos. 12th century. Manuscript illumination. Bibliothèque Nationale, Paris. The destroyed church was the model for Saint Mark's in Venice.

right: 178 Main façade of the Basilica of Saint Mark, Venice. Begun 1063.

the city but also included stables and living quarters for the charioteers. Emperor and empress had their own private boxes [179] that could be entered directly from the palace and resembled small houses, with private and public rooms, more than mere viewing stands. The center of the stadium was called the *spina;* around it lay the racing track, which consisted of a bed of stone covered with sand. The spina was adorned with statues of famous charioteers [180] and masterpieces by such famous artists of the past as Phidias. Above the emperor's box was a chariot drawn by four gilt horses made of an alloy of copper, silver, and gold, thought to have been the work of the great 4th-century-B.C. sculptor Lysippus [181]. It had been taken to Rome by Nero and was moved to Byzantium in the early 5th century A.D. by Theodosius II. During the Fourth Crusade, in 1204, the horses made another journey when they were taken by the Venetians to decorate the entrance porch of the church of Saint Mark, although even this did not end their wanderings. At the end of the 18th century they were removed by Napoleon and taken to Paris, only to return after Napoleon's defeat in 1815 yet again to Venice, where they are still to be seen.

The Hippodrome and the factions associated with it were the cause of a particularly violent riot in January 532 known as the Nika Revolt after the password *Nika* (Conquer) used by some of the rioters. A vivid

above: 179 Detail of relief from the Obelisk of Theodosius, which once stood in the spina of the Hippodrome of Constantinople. c. A.D. 390. The relief shows the emperor in the royal box, surrounded by his family, holding a wreathed crown for a winning charioteer.

right: 180 The ruins of the Hippodrome of Constantinople in the 16th century, from an engraving by Onofrio Panvinio in the *Imperium Orientale* by Anselmo Banduri. Book page 11 × 16½″ (28 × 42 cm). Rare Book Room, University of Illinois at Urbana-Champaign.

181 Four horses of Greek origin. 1st century A.D. Gilt bronze, life-size. Basilica of Saint Mark, Venice. These gilt horses once stood over the emperor's box in the Hippodrome at Constantinople.

account has been preserved in the writings of the great Byzantine historian Procopius, who himself served on the staff of Belisarius, the foremost of Justinian's generals. Procopius was born at Caesarea in Palestine around 500 and accompanied Belisarius on his travels in Persia, Africa, and Italy. Procopius' task was to write an official history of the campaigns. This *History of the Wars* reflects his official status and with *The Buildings,* which describes the chief architectural achievements of Justinian's reign, paints a generally favorable portrait of both Justinian and Theodora. His other surviving work, the *Secret History,* was not intended for publication in his lifetime. It retraces the events covered in the *History of the Wars,* this time in the form of a virulent and sustained attack on the emperor and his wife. The antecedents and character of Theodora are described in scurrilous detail, while Justinian is blamed for every kind of disaster from bankruptcy to earthquakes.

Hints of Procopius' true point of view appear even in the following extract from his official history.

Justinian emerges as weak and vacillating, incapable of taking firm action and only prevented from fleeing the city by the intervention of Theodora. The true hero of the episode is Belisarius, for whom Procopius seems to have felt a genuine respect and admiration. In general, however, and with the exception of the *Secret History,* Procopius' works are notable for a clarity and well-balanced judgment that make him a worthy successor to the great historians of Classical Greece.

Procopius
from **HISTORY OF THE WARS**

About the same time a popular uprising suddenly broke out in Byzantium, which turned out, contrary to expectation, to be very serious, and which ended by greatly harming both the people and the Senate. This is how it came about. The population in every city has long since been divided into Blues and Greens, but it is only recently that for the sake of these names and the benches on which they sit when at the games, they spend their money and subject themselves to physical violence of the most bitter kind, and will even die a death of the utmost dishonor. They fight against those sitting opposite them, not knowing why they put themselves into this danger, yet knowing full well that even if they overcome their enemies in the fight it remains for them to be dragged off to prison at once, and then to perish after horrible torture. They have a senseless hatred of their neighbors, which is perpetual and never ending, and it yields neither to marriage connection nor to ties of family nor to bonds of friendship, even if the opposing sides in this matter of colors are brothers or something similar. They care for nothing, human or divine, in comparison with victory in their engagements. If a sacrilege to God is committed by anyone, or if the laws and the state are assailed by friends or enemies, they do not think it their affair, even though they may actually be short of food and in desperate straits because of their attacks on the state, so long as it goes well for their "party"—for this is the name they give to their fellow insurgents. And women share with them in this pollution also, not only following their husbands, but even opposing them if necessary, even though they never go near the theater at all or have any other reason to spur them on. For my part, I can only call this a disease of the soul. This then is the state of affairs in the cities and in every citizen body.

At that time the officers controlling the people in Byzantium carried off some of the insurgents to death. But the two sides joined together and made an agreement between themselves. They seized the prisoners and then went straight to the prison and released all those who were imprisoned there for rebellion or on any other foolishness. The servants attending the city officers were killed for no reason, and any loyal citizens that were there fled to the mainland opposite. The city was fired, as if it had fallen into enemy hands. The church of Sophia, the baths of Zeuxippus, and the part of the royal palace from the entrance porch to the so-called house of Ares were burned down and destroyed, and besides these both the great porticoes which go to the market place called after Constantine, many houses, and a great deal of treasure belonging to rich men. The Emperor and his consort and some of the senators shut themselves up and waited in the palace. The people passed around among themselves as their watchword "Conquer," and from this the rebellion has taken its name until the present day.

At that time the prætorian prefect was John, the Cappadocian, and Tribonian, the Pamphylian, was the Emperor's assessor (the Romans call this man "quæstor"). One of these two, John, had no experience in liberal conversation and education. He learned nothing from his attendance at the grammarian's except grammar, and that badly. But he was the most capable man of our time, as far as native wit goes. He could always recognize what ought to be done and find a way out of difficulties. But he was the wickedest man on earth and used his native ability to this end; no respect for God or man ever entered his head—instead he sought to destroy many men's lives and raze whole cities for the sake of gain. In a short time he amassed a great deal of money and flung himself into an endless drinking bout. He would plunder the property of subjects of the Empire until it was time for lunch, and then he would idle away the rest of the time in drunkenness and in wanton acts of the flesh. He could not restrain himself; he would go on eating until he was sick. He was always ready to steal money, and even readier to waste and squander it. This was what John was like. Tribonian, on the other hand, was both possessed of native wit and as well educated as any of his contemporaries, but he was extraordinarily greedy for money and was always capable of selling justice for gain; and every day, as a general rule, he spent his time repealing some laws and proposing others, selling either service to applicants, according to their need.

While the people carried on its internal war over the names of the colors, no one paid any attention to the harm that these two men were doing to the state. But when the factions joined, as I have mentioned above, and took up the rebellion together, they openly reviled them all over the city and went around looking for them to kill them. So the Emperor, wishing to conciliate the people, immediately deprived both of their office. He made Phocas, a patrician, prætorian prefect, a man of great intelligence and well able to preserve justice. He ordered Basilides to hold the office of quæstor, a man known among the patricians for fairness and notable in other ways. But the rebellion did not abate under them either. On the fifth day of the rebellion, about evening, the Emperor Justinian told Hypatius and Pompeius, the nephews of the late Emperor Anastasius, to go home at once, either suspecting that they were plotting some mischief against his person or because fate was actually leading them to this. But they were afraid that—as did actually happen—the people might force them to assume the throne, and they said that they would not be doing right if they abandoned their Emperor when he was in such danger. When the Emperor Justinian heard this he was confirmed in his suspicions and commanded them to go at once. So these two men went home and stayed there for the night.

On the following day at sunrise the people discovered that both of them had left the palace where they had been staying. The whole mob therefore set off after them at a run, and made to proclaim Hypatius Emperor, and would have brought him to the Forum to take over the power. But Hypatius' wife, Maria, who was an intelligent woman well known for her wisdom, clung to her husband and would not let him go. She cried and wailed and told all her friends that the people were leading him to his death. But the people were very violent and against her will she had to let her husband go; and the mob brought him against his will to the Forum of Constantine and called on him to adopt the purple. Putting a golden wreath on his head (for they had no diadem nor any other of the Emperor's customary appendages), they proclaimed him Emperor of Rome. But now the senators were assembling, those of them who had not been left in the royal palace, and many expressed the opinion that they should go to the palace and fight. But a senator called Origen came forward and said this: "Our present crisis, Romans, can only be resolved by war. But war and imperial power are generally agreed to be the greatest things in the world. And important actions are not such as to be settled by a momentary crisis, but only by wise counsels and physical effort, displayed by men over a long period. So if we are to attack the enemy, our fate will be standing on a razor's edge, and we shall be staking our all in a moment of time, and in what follows we shall either abase ourselves before Fortune or else revile her utterly—for when men act in haste their actions generally fall under the power of Fortune. But if we take our time in settling the present crisis, we shall not be able to take Justinian in the palace, even if we wish—he will soon enough be glad if someone lets him escape. For when authority is ignored it ebbs away, its strength diminishing day by day. We have other palaces, the Placillianai and that called after Helen, from which this Emperor ought to carry on the war and settle everything else for the best." These were Origen's words. But the rest were more impetuous, as a crowd usually is, and thought that the present moment was the best time; Hypatius (for he was fated to come to a bad end) was in the lead in urging them to lead the way to the Hippodrome. But some say that he came there on purpose, because he was well disposed to the Emperor.

The Emperor's companions were debating whether it would be better for them to stay or to flee by ship. Many arguments were put forward on both sides. The Empress Theodora said: "As to whether it is unseemly for a woman to be bold among men, or to be daring when others are full of fear, I do not think that the present crisis allows us to consider the matter. For in extreme danger the only vital thing is to deal with the situation in the best way. For my part, I consider that now of all times flight would be bad, even if it brings safety. Once a man is born he cannot escape dying, but for one who has held the imperial power it would be unbearable to become a fugitive. May I never be parted from this purple, and may I never live to see the day when men who meet me will not address me as their sovereign. If you wish to be saved, Emperor, that is not difficult. We have great resources of wealth; there is the sea, here are the boats. But take care lest when you have saved yourself you wish that you could have death instead of your safety. I agree with the old saying, 'Royalty is a good winding sheet.'" At these words from the Empress they were all inspired with courage and began to debate how they could defend themselves if anyone attacked them. Now the soldiers, including those who were stationed at the Emperor's residence, were not well disposed to the Emperor and did not want to take part in the fighting openly; they were waiting for the outcome of events. The Emperor put all his hope in Belisarius and Mundus. One of the two, Belisarius, had just returned from the Persian war, and among his powerful and remarkable suite he had a large number of spearsmen and guards who had been trained in battle and in enemy engagements. Mundus, appointed general of the Illyrians, had been summoned back to Byzantium for some purpose, and by some chance happened to have brought with him Erul barbarians.

So when Hypatius came to the Hippodrome, he went straight up to where it is customary for the Emperor to sit, and he sat down on the imperial throne, from which the Emperor always watched the equestrian and athletic contests. Mundus came from the palace through the gate which is called the "Snail" from its spiral descent. Belisarius first made straight for Hypatius and the imperial throne, and when he came to the nearby enclosure where there have always been soldiers on guard, he shouted to the soldiers to open the gate for him as quickly as possible, so that he could reach the usurper. But the soldiers had decided to help neither side until one of them was clearly on top; they pretended not to hear and put him off. So Belisarius turned back to the Emperor and assured him that all was lost, for the soldiers garrisoning the palace were in rebellion against him. So the Emperor told him to go to the Chalce and the propylæa there. So Belisarius, with great difficulty and not without considerable effort and danger, made his way up to the stadium. When he came to the Blue portico, which is on the right of the Emperor's throne, he wanted to get to Hypatius first, but there was a small door there which was closed and guarded inside by Hypatius' soldiers, and he was afraid that while he was struggling in the confined space, the crowd might join forces, kill him and his men, and have an easy and effortless path to the Emperor. He decided that he must attack the crowd standing in the Hippodrome, which was of enormous size and pushing and shoving in great disorder, and he drew his sword from its scabbard and telling the rest to do the same he advanced against them at a run, shouting. The crowd was massed together anyhow, in no sort of battle order, and when they saw armed soldiers with a great reputation for valor and war experience mercilessly brandishing their swords, they turned to flight. In the shouting which naturally ensued, Mundus, who was standing nearby wishing to join in the affray (he was a man of great daring and energy), but not knowing what to do in the circumstances, deduced that Belisarius was engaged in it, and immediately entered the Hippodrome by the gate called the Gate of Death. Then Hypatius' supporters were hit on all sides and cut to pieces. When the defeat became obvious, and many of the people had already been killed, Boraedes and Justus, cousins of the Emperor Justinian, pulled Hypatius down from the throne, no one daring to raise a hand against them, and took him and handed him over to the Emperor with Pompeius. More than thirty thousand of the people died on that day. The Emperor ordered the two to be kept under close arrest. At this Pompeius wept and moaned in a most pitiful way, for he was not at all the sort of man accustomed to such misfortunes. But Hypatius rebuked him and said that men about to die without justice ought not to lament. He said that in the beginning they had been forced against their will by the people, and that later when they came to the Hippodrome they had meant no harm to the Emperor. But the soldiers killed both of them on the following day and threw their bodies into the sea. The Emperor proscribed their money for the treasury, together with that of all the senators who had supported them. Later, however, he restored to all of them, including the sons of Hypatius and Pompeius, the rank which they formerly held and such of their money as he had not given to certain of his friends. This was the end of the revolt in Byzantium. ▬

Ravenna

For all the beautiful remains that we may see in modern Istanbul—especially the impressive Hagia Sophia—it is still Ravenna that provides us the more complete archaeological and monumental picture of the period of Justinian and of the Byzantine world. Ravenna is a rather small, not particularly attractive city on the northeast Adriatic coast of Italy (see map, page 257). In 402 the Roman emperor Honorius made Ravenna the capital of the western empire because of the hazardous conditions in Rome. In 476 the Ostrogoth king Odoacer conquered Ravenna, bringing to an end the line of Roman emperors in the West. From then until 540 the Ostrogoths ruled Ravenna until they were defeated by Belisarius, commander-in-chief of Justinian's army.

Boethius

In this twilight period between the death of the last Roman emperor and the arrival of Justinian's troops an important figure who bridged the gap between classical paganism and Christianity lived and died. Anicius Manlius Severinus Boethius was a highly educated Roman who entered the service of the Goth king Theodoric in 522. Imprisoned for reasons that are not clear, Boethius wrote a treatise called *The Consolation of Philosophy* while awaiting execution. Cast as a dialogue between Lady Philosophy and the author on the philosophical and religious basis for human freedom, the work blends the spirit of the Book of Job with Roman Stoicism. Attempting to console him for his sad state of disgrace and imprisonment, Lady Philosophy demands that the author avoid self-pity, that he face his troubles with serenity and hope. Insisting that a provident God overcomes all evil, Philosophy insists that blind fate has no control over humanity. She explains that human freedom exists along with an all-knowing God and that good will triumph. Although Christian themes permeate the work, there is no explicit mention of Christian doctrine. What one does sense is the recasting of Roman thought into Christian patterns. In a way, *The Consolation of Philosophy* is one of the last works of the late Roman period. It reflects the elegance of Roman expression, the burgeoning hope of Christianity, and the sense of terrible sadness that must have afflicted any sensitive Roman in this period.

The Consolation of Philosophy was one of the most widely read and influential works of the Middle Ages (Chaucer made an English translation of it from an already-existing French version). Its message of hope and faith was liberally quoted by every major medieval thinker from Thomas Aquinas to Dante Alighieri.

Boethius sets out a basic problem and provides an answer that would become normative Christian thought for subsequent centuries. In *The Consolation* Boethius asks how one can reconcile human freedom with the notion of an all-knowing God. To put it another way: If God knows what we do before we do it, how can we be said to be free agents who must accept responsibility for personal acts? The answer, Boethius insists through Lady Philosophy, is to look at the problem from the point of view of God, not from the human vantage point. God lives in eternity. Eternity does not mean a "long time" with a past and a future. Eternity means "no time": God lives in an eternal moment that for Him is a "now." In that sense God doesn't "foresee" the future. There is no future for God. God sees everything in one simple moment that is only past, present, and future from the human point of view. Boethius says that God does not exercise *praevidentia* (seeing things before they happen) but *providence* (seeing all things in the simultaneity of their happening). Thus God, in a single eternal, ineffable moment, grasps all activity, which for us is a long sequence of events. More specifically, in that moment, God sees our choices, the events that follow from them, and the ultimate consequences of those choices.

The consolation of Boethius, as Lady Philosophy explains it, rests in the fact that people do act with freedom, that they are not in the hands of an indifferent fate, and that the ultimate meaning of life rests with the all-seeing presence of a Person, not a blind force.

The excerpt from *The Consolation* that follows is from the final chapter of the last book of the work (Book V, 6), where Lady Philosophy sums up her discussion with Boethius by offering him this "consolation." It is her assurance that his life, even while awaiting execution in a prison cell, was not the product of a blind fate or an uncaring force in the universe.

The language of the selection, with its discussion of time, eternity, free will, and the nature of God, echoes the great philosophical tradition of Plato and Aristotle (Boethius had translated the latter's works) as well as the Stoicism of Cicero and the theological reflections of Augustine. It is a fitting end to the intellectual tradition of the late Roman Empire in the West.

Boethius
from THE CONSOLATION
OF PHILOSOPHY, Book V, 6

"Since, then, as was shown a little while ago, everything which is known is known not according to its own nature but according to the nature of those comprehending it, let us now examine, so far as is allowable, what is the nature of the divine substance, so that we may be able to recognize what kind of knowledge his is. Now that God is eternal is the common judgement of all who live by reason. Therefore let us consider, what is eternity; for this makes plain to us both the divine nature and the divine knowledge. Eternity, then, is the whole, simultaneous and perfect possession of boundless life, which becomes clearer by comparison with temporal things. For whatever lives in time proceeds in the present from the past into the future, and there is nothing established in time which can embrace the whole space of its life equally, but tomorrow surely it does not yet grasp, while yesterday it has already lost. And in this day to day life you live no more than in that moving and transitory moment. Therefore whatever endures the condition of time, although, as Aristotle thought concerning the world, it neither began ever to be nor ceases to be, and although its life is drawn out with the infinity of time, yet it is not yet such that it may rightly be believed to be eternal. For it does not simultaneously comprehend and embrace the whole space of its life, though it be infinite, but it possesses the future not yet, the past no longer. Whatever therefore comprehends and possesses at once the whole fullness of boundless life, and is such that neither is anything future lacking from it, nor has anything past flowed away, that is rightly held to be eternal, and that must necessarily both always be present to itself, possessing itself in the present, and hold as present the infinity of moving time.

"And therefore those are not right who, when they hear that Plato thought this world neither had a beginning in time nor would have an end, think that in this way the created world is made co-eternal with the Creator. For it is one thing to be drawn out through a life without bounds, which is what Plato attributes to the world, but it is a different thing to have embraced at once the whole presence of boundless life, which it is clear is the property of the divine mind. Nor should God seem to be more ancient than created things by some amount of time, but rather by his own simplicity of nature. For this present nature of unmoving life that infinite movement of temporal things imitates, and since it cannot fully represent and equal it, it fails from immobility into motion, it shrinks from the simplicity of that present into the infinite quantity of the future and the past and, since it cannot possess at once the whole fullness of its life, in this very respect, that it in some way never ceases to be, it seems to emulate to some degree which it cannot fully express, by binding itself to the sort of present of this brief and fleeting moment, a present which since it wears a kind of likeness of that permanent present, grants to whatsoever things it touches that they should seem to be. But since it could not be permanent, it seized on the infinite journeying of time, and in that way became such that it should continue by going on a life the fullness of which it could not embrace by being permanent. And so if we should wish to give things names befitting them, then following Plato we should say that God indeed is eternal, but that the world is perpetual.

"Since then every judgement comprehends those things subject to it according to its own nature, and God has an always eternal and present nature, then his knowledge too, surpassing all movement of time, is permanent in the simplicity of his present, and embracing all the infinite spaces of the future and the past, considers them in his simple act of knowledge as though they were now going on. So if you should wish to consider his foreknowledge, by which he discerns all things, you will more rightly judge it to be not foreknowledge as it were of the future but knowledge of a never-passing instant. And therefore it is called not prevision (*praevidentia*) but providence (*providentia*), because set far from the lowest of things it looks forward on all things as though from the highest peak of the world. Why then do you require those things to be made necessary which are scanned by the light of God's sight, when not even men make necessary those things they see? After all, your looking at them does not confer any necessity on those things you presently see, does it?"

"Not at all."

"But if the comparison of the divine and the human present is a proper one, just as you see certain things in this your temporal present, so he perceives all things in his eternal one. And therefore this divine foreknowledge does not alter the proper nature of things, but sees them present to him just such as in time they will at some future point come to be. Nor does he confuse the ways things are to be judged, but with one glance of his mind distinguishes both those things necessarily coming to be and those not necessarily coming to be, just as you, when you see at one and the same time that a man is walking on the ground and that the sun is rising in the sky, although the two things are seen simultaneously, yet you distinguish them, and judge the first to be voluntary, the second necessary. So then the divine perception looking down on all things does not disturb at all the quality of things that are present indeed to him but future with reference to imposed conditions of time. So it is that it is not opinion but a knowledge grounded rather upon truth, when he knows that something is going to happen, something which he is also aware lacks all necessity of happening.

"If at this point you were to say that what God sees is going to occur cannot not occur, and that what cannot not occur happens from necessity, and so bind me to this word "necessity," I will admit that this is a matter indeed of the firmest truth, but one which scarcely anyone except a theologian could tackle. For I shall say in answer that the same future event, when it is related to divine knowledge, is necessary, but when it is considered in its own nature it seems to be utterly and absolutely free. For there are really two necessities, the one simple, as that it is necessary that all men are mortal; the other conditional, as for example, if you know that someone is walking, it is necessary that he is walking. Whatever anyone knows cannot be otherwise than as it is known, but this conditional necessity by no means carries with it that other simple kind. For this sort of necessity is not caused by a thing's proper nature but by the addition of the condition; for no necessity forces him to go who walks of his own will, even though it is necessary that he is going at the time when he is walking. Now in the same way, if providence sees anything as present, that must necessarily be, even if it possesses no necessity of its nature. But God beholds those future events which happen because of the freedom of the will, as present; they therefore, related to the divine perception, become necessary through the condition of the divine knowledge, but considered in themselves do not lose the absolute freedom of their nature. Therefore all those things which God foreknows will come to be, will without doubt come to be, but certain of them proceed from free will, and although they do come to be, yet in happening they do not lose their proper nature, according to which, before they happened, they might also not have happened. What then does it matter that they are not necessary, since on account of the condition of the divine knowledge it will turn out in all respects like necessity? Surely as much as those things I put before you a moment ago, the rising sun and the walking man: while these things are happening, they cannot not happen, but of the two one, even before it happened, was bound to happen, while the other was not. So also, those things God possesses as present, beyond doubt will happen, but of them the one kind is consequent upon the necessity of things, the other upon the power of those doing them. So therefore we were not wrong in saying that these, if related to the divine knowledge, are necessary, if considered in themselves, are free from the bonds of necessity, just as everything which lies open to the senses, if you relate it to the reason, is universal, if you look at it by itself, is singular.

"But if, you will say, it lies in my power to change my intention, I shall make nonsense of providence, since what providence foreknows, I shall perhaps have changed. I shall reply that you can indeed alter your intention, but since the truth of providence sees in its present both that you can do so, and whether you will do so and in what direction you will change, you cannot avoid the divine prescience, just as you could not escape the sight of an eye that was present, even though of your own free will you changed to different courses of action. What then will you say? Will the divine knowledge be changed by my disposition, so that, since I want to do this at one time and that at another, it too alternates from this kind of knowledge to that? Not at all. For the divine perception runs ahead over every future event and turns it back and recalls it to the present of its own knowledge, and does not alternate, as you suggest, foreknowing now this, now that, but itself remaining still anticipates and embraces your changes at one stroke. And God possesses this present instant of comprehension and sight of all things not from the issuing of future events but from his own simplicity. In this way that too is resolved which you suggested a little while ago, that it is not right that our future actions should be said to provide the cause of the knowledge of God. For the nature of his knowledge as we have described it, embracing all things in a present act of knowing, establishes a measure for everything, but owes nothing to later events. These things being so, the freedom of the will remains to mortals, inviolate, nor are laws proposing rewards and punishments for wills free from all necessity unjust. There remains also as an observer from on high foreknowing all things, God, and the always present eternity of his sight runs along with the future quality of our actions dispensing rewards for the good and punishments for the wicked. Nor vainly are our hopes placed in God, nor our prayers, which when they are right cannot be ineffectual. Turn away then from vices, cultivate virtues, lift up your mind to righteous hopes, offer up humble prayers to heaven. A great necessity is solemnly ordained for you if you do not want to deceive yourselves, to do good, when you act before the eyes of a judge who sees all things."

Art and Architecture

Ravenna is a repository of monuments that reflect its late-Roman, barbarian Gothic, and Byzantine history. The mausoleum (burial chapel) of Galla Placidia (who reigned as regent from 430 to 450) was built at the end of the Roman period of Ravenna's history [182]. Once thought to be the tomb of the empress (hence its name), it is more likely a votive chapel to Saint Lawrence originally attached to the nearby church of the Holy Cross. The huge sarcophagi in the building are probably medieval. This small chapel in the shape of a cross, very plain on the outside, shows the architectural tendency to combine the basilica-style nave with the structure of a dome (it even uses a modified pendentive form) used later in monumental structures like Hagia Sophia.

The importance of Galla Placidia rests in the complete and breathtakingly beautiful mosaics that decorate the walls and ceiling. The north niche, just above

182 The so-called Mausoleum of Galla Placidia, Ravenna. Early 5th century. The building has sunk more than a meter—about 4 feet—into the marshy soil, thus making the building seem rather smaller than it must originally have appeared.

183 *The Good Shepherd,* from the Mausoleum of Galla Placidia, Ravenna. 5th century. Mosaic. The "Persian-rug" motif can be seen in the vaulting above the lunette mosaic.

the entrance, has a *lunette* mosaic depicting Christ as the Good Shepherd [183]. Clothed in royal purple and with a gold staff in his hand, the figure of Christ has a courtly, almost languid elegance that refines the more rustic depictions of the Good Shepherd theme in earlier Roman Christian art. The vaulting of both the apse and the dome is covered with a deep blue mosaic interspersed with stylized sunbursts and stars in gold. This "Persian-rug" motif symbolized the heavens, the dwelling place of God. Since the *tesserae,* the small cubes that make up the mosaic, are not set fully flush in the wall, the surfaces of the mosaic are irregular. These surfaces thus refract and break up the light in the chapel, especially from flickering lamps and candles. (The translucent alabaster windows now in the chapel were installed in the 20th century.)

Opposite the lunette of the Good Shepherd is another lunette that depicts the deacon martyr of the Roman Church, Saint Lawrence, who stands next to the gridiron that was the instrument of his death. Beyond the gridiron is an open cabinet containing codices of the four gospels [184]. The spaces above these mosaics are filled with figures of the apostles. Between these are symbols of the search for religious understanding—deer, doves, fountains. In the arches, more spectacular and often overlooked are the abstract interlocking designs (called *guilloche*) with their brightness and *trompe l'oeil* (trick-the-eye) quality.

184 *The Martyrdom of Saint Lawrence,* from the Mausoleum of Galla Placidia, Ravenna. 5th century. Mosaic. The window above is one of the modern alabaster ones. According to tradition, Saint Lawrence was roasted to death on a gridiron. He was one of the most revered saints in early Christianity.

276 THE WORLD OF BYZANTIUM

185 The Neonian (Orthodox) Baptistery of the Ravenna Cathedral, including baptismal font. Early 5th century. Originally each of the eight sides had a door, the arch of which is still visible.

The two baptisteries of Ravenna represent a major religious division of the time between the Orthodox Christians, who accepted the divinity of Christ, and the Arian Christians, who did not. The Neonian Baptistery [185], built by Orthodox Christians in the early 5th century next to the ancient cathedral of the city, is octagonal—as were most baptisteries, because of their derivation from Roman bath houses. The ceiling mosaic, directly over the baptismal pool, is particularly striking. The lower register of the mosaic, above the windows, shows floral designs based on common Roman decorative motifs. Just above are a circle of empty thrones interspersed with altars with biblical codices open on them [186]. In the band above are the apostles, who seem to be walking in a stately procession around the circle of the dome. In the central disc is a mosaic of the baptism of Christ by John the Baptist in the Jordan River. The spirit of the river is depicted as Neptune.

The mosaic ensemble in the ceiling was designed to reflect the beliefs of the participants in the ceremonies below. The circling apostles reminded the candidates for baptism that the church was founded on the apostles; the convert's baptism was a promise that one day they would dwell with the apostles in heaven. Finally, the codices on the altars taught of the sources of their belief, while the empty thrones promised the new Christians a place in the heavenly

186 Ceiling mosaic of the Orthodox Baptistery, Ravenna. Mid-5th century. The original mosaic work begins with the arched floral motifs above the present windows, the stucco motifs and columns between the windows are of much later date.

187 Dome of the Arian Baptistery, Ravenna, showing the baptism of Christ with the outer band of twelve apostles in procession toward the "cross of glory." c. 520. Mosaic. The detail below shows the head of the River Jordan figure with its claws.

Jerusalem. The art, then, was not merely decorative but, in the words of a modern Orthodox thinker, "theology in color."

The Arian Baptistery, built by the Goths toward the end of the 5th century, is much more severely decorated. Again the traditional scene of Christ's baptism is in the central disc of the ceiling mosaic. Here the figure of the River Jordan has lobsterlike claws sprouting from his head—a curiously pagan marine touch [187]. The twelve apostles in the lower register are divided into two groups, one led by Peter and the other by Paul. These two groups converge at a throne bearing a jeweled cross (the crucifix with the body of Christ on the cross is very uncommon in this period) that represents in a single symbol the passion and the resurrection of Christ.

Theodoric, the emperor of the Goths who had executed Boethius and reigned from 493 to 526, was buried in a massive mausoleum that may still be seen on the outskirts of Ravenna [188]. The most famous extant monument of Theodoric's reign aside from his mausoleum is the church of Sant' Apollinare Nuovo, originally called the Church of the Redeemer, the palace church of Theodoric. This church is constructed in the severe basilica style: a wide nave with

188 Tomb of Theodoric, Ravenna. Early 6th century. The cap of the mausoleum is a great stone about 36' (11 m) in diameter and 10' (3 m) high. Inside is a huge porphyry coffin, now pillaged, that contained the king's body. Theodoric maintained peace in Italy during his reign.

189 South-wall mosaic, Sant' Apollinare Nuovo, Ravenna. Early 6th century. The procession of male saints is in the lower register, with prophets and apostles between the windows and scenes from the Gospels in the upper register. Details are shown in figures **191** and **192**.

190 North-wall mosaic, Sant' Apollinare Nuovo, Ravenna. The procession of female saints is in the lower register, with scenes from the life of Christ in the upper register. Details are shown in figures **193** and **194**.

two side aisles partitioned off from the nave by double columns of marble. The apse decorations have been destroyed, but the walls of the basilica, richly ornamented with mosaics, can be seen. The mosaics, however, are of two different dates and reflect in one building both the Roman and Byzantine styles of art. On each side of the aisles, in the spaces just above the aisle arches, are processions of male and female saints, each procession facing toward the apse and main altar [189, 190]. They move to an enthroned Christ on one side and toward a Madonna and Child on the other. These mosaics were added to the church when the

top: 191 Mosaic of Theodoric's palace *(palatium),* detail of south-wall mosaic, Sant'Apollinare Nuovo, Ravenna. The curtains replaced the earlier figures in the mosaic.

above: 192 Detail of figure 191. The first and third columns from the left still show hands, and outlines of heads can be see faintly above the curtain rods.

lower level. The gospel sequence is more Roman in inspiration, more severe and simple. Certain themes of earlier Roman Christian iconography are evident. The procession of saints, most likely erected by artists from a Constantinople studio, is much more lush, reverent, and static in tone. The orientalizing element is especially noteworthy in the depiction of the Three Magi (with their Phrygian caps) who offer gifts to the Christ Child [194].

The church of San Vitale most clearly testifies to the presence of Justinian in Ravenna [195]. Dedicated by Bishop Maximian in 547, it had been begun by Bishop Ecclesius in 526, the year Justinian came to

193 Jesus calling the first apostles, Peter and Andrew, detail of north-wall upper-register mosaic, Sant' Apollinare Nuovo, Ravenna. Note the youthful beardless Jesus and the Roman togas (compare figure 170).

building passed from the Goths into Byzantine hands in the reign of Justinian. The depiction of Theodoric's palace [191], in fact, still shows evidence of Orthodox censorship. In the arched spaces one can still see traces of halos of now-excised Arian saints (or perhaps members of Theodoric's court). On several columns of the mosaic can be seen the hands of figures that have now been replaced by decorative twisted draperies [192]. The next register above has a line of prophetic figures. At the level of the clerestory windows there are scenes from the New Testament—the miracles of Christ on one side [193] and scenes from his passion on the other. These mosaics are very different in style from the procession of sainted martyrs on the

194 The Magi bearing gifts, detail of north-wall mosaic, Sant' Apollinare Nuovo, Ravenna. Christian legend had already given these figures the names that can be seen at the top of the mosaic: Balthasar, Melchior, and Caspar. Saint Apollinaris was a 2nd-century Phrygian bishop who defended the Christian faith in an address to the Roman emperor Marcus Aurelius.

the throne, while the Goths still ruled Ravenna. The church is octagonal, with only the barest hint of basilica length. How different it is may be seen by comparing it with Sant'Apollinare in Classe (the ancient seaport of Ravenna), built at roughly the same time [196]. The octagon has another octagon within it. This interior octagon, supported by columned arches and containing a second-story *matroneum* (women's gallery), is the structural basis for the dome. The dome is supported on the octagonal walls by small vaults called *squinches* that cut across the angles of each part of the octagon.

The most arresting characteristic of San Vitale, apart from its intricate and not fully understood architectural design, is its stunning program of mosaics. In the apse is a great mosaic of Christ the Panto-

above right: 195 San Vitale, Ravenna. c. 530–548. Aerial view. This complex building was to be the inspiration for Charlemagne's church at Aachen (see pages 297–299).

right: 196 Sant' Apollinare in Classe, Ravenna. c. 549. Aerial view. The tower is an early-medieval addition.

crator, the one who sustains all things in his hands [197]. Christ is portrayed as a beardless young man, clothed in royal purple. He holds in his left hand a book with seven seals (a reference to the book of Revelation) and offers the crown of martyrdom to Saint Vitalis with his right. Flanked by the two archangels, Christ is offered a model of the church by the bishop, Ecclesius, who laid its foundations. Above the figures are symbolic representations of the four rivers of paradise.

The mosaics to the left and right of the apse mosaic represent the royal couple as regents of Christ on earth. On the left wall of the sanctuary is a mosaic depicting Justinian and his attendants [198]. It is not merely accidental nor an exercise of simple piety that the soldiers carry a shield with *chi* and *rho* (the first Greek letters in the name of Christ) or that there are twelve attendants or that the figure of the emperor divides clergy and laity. The emperor considered himself the regent of Christ, an attitude summed up

in the *iconographic,* or symbolic, program: Justinian represents Christ on earth and his power balances both church and state. The only figure identified in the mosaic is Bishop (later Archbishop) Maximian flanked by his clergy who include a deacon with a jeweled gospel and a subdeacon with a chained incense pot.

Opposite the emperor's retinue, the Empress Theodora and her attendants look across at the imperial group [199; plate 17, page 287]. Theodora holds a chalice to complement the bread basket (paten) held by the emperor. At the hem of Theodora's gown is a small scene of the Magi bringing gifts to the Christ Child. Scholars disagree whether the two mosaics represent the royal couple bringing the eucharistic gifts for the celebration of the liturgy or the donation of the sacred vessels for the church. It was a custom for the rulers to give such gifts to the more important churches of their realm. The fact that the empress seems to be leaving her palace (two male functionaries of the court are ushering her out) makes the latter interpretation the more probable one. The women at Theodora's left are striking; those to the extreme left are stereotyped, but the two closest to the empress appear more individualized, leading some art historians to suggest that they are idealized portraits of two of Theodora's closest friends: the wife and daughter of the conqueror of Ravenna, Belisarius.

The royal generosity extended not only to the building and decoration of the church of San Vitale. An ivory throne, now preserved in the episcopal museum of Ravenna, was a gift of the emperor to Bishop Maximian, the ecclesiastical ruler of Ravenna when San Vitale was dedicated [200]. A close stylistic analysis of the carving on the throne has led scholars to see the work of at least four different artists on the

above: 197 Christ enthroned, with Saints Vitalis and Ecclesius, ceiling mosaic, San Vitale, Ravenna. c. 530.

right: 198 Emperor Justinian and courtiers, wall mosaic, San Vitale, Ravenna. c. 547.

282

left: 199 Empress Theodora and retinue, wall mosaic, San Vitale, Ravenna. c. 547.

below: 200 Bishop's throne (cathedra) of Maximian. c. 546–556. Ivory panels on wood frame; height 4′11″ (1.5 m), width 1′11⅝″ (.6 m). Archepiscopal Museum, Ravenna.

panels, probably in Constantinople. The front of the throne bears portraits of John the Baptist and the four Evangelists while the back has scenes from the New Testament with sides showing episodes from the Old Testament of the life of Joseph. The purely decorative elements of trailing vines and animals show the style of a different hand, probably Syrian. The bishop's throne (*cathedra* in Latin; a cathedral is a church where a bishop presides) bears a small monogram: *Maximian, Bishop.*

The entire ensemble of San Vitale, with its pierced capitals typical of the Byzantine style, its elaborate mosaic portraits of saints and prophets, its lunette mosaics of Old Testament prefigurements of the Eucharist, and monumental mosaic scenes, is a living testimony to the rich fusion of imperial, Christian, and middle Eastern cultural impulses. San Vitale is a microcosm of the sociopolitical vision of Byzantium fused with the religious world view of early Christianity.

Saint Catherine's Monastery at Mount Sinai

Justinian is remembered not only in Constantinople and Ravenna but also in the Near East, where he founded a monastery that is still in use some fifteen hundred years later—a living link back to the Byzantine world.

In her *Peregrinatio,* that wonderfully tireless traveler of the 4th century, Etheria, describes a visit to the forbidding desert of the Sinai to pray at the site where God appeared to Moses in a burning bush (that, Etheria assures us, "is still alive to this day and throws out shoots") and to climb the mountain

where the Law was given to Moses. She says that there was a church at the spot of the burning bush with some hermits living nearby to tend it and see to the needs of pilgrim visitors. More than a century later the Emperor Justinian built a monastery fortress

century. The codex—from the middle of the 4th century—was given by the monks to the Tsar of Russia. In 1933 the Soviet Government sold it for £100,000 to the British Museum, where it remains today, a precious document.

The monastery is surrounded by heavy fortified walls, the main part of which date from before Justinian's time. Within those walls are some modern buildings, including a fireproof structure that houses the monastery's library and icon collections. The monastic church, the Katholikon, dates from the time of Justinian, as recently discovered inscriptions carved into the wooden trusses in the ceiling of the church prove. Even the name of the architect—Stephanos—was uncovered. This church thus is unique: signed 6th-century ecclesiastical architecture.

The great central mosaic of the church's apse also dates from the period of Justinian. The subject is the transfiguration of Christ (*metamorphosis* in Greek), a rare choice for the period [Plate 18, page 288]. The foremost authority on Sinaitic art, Kurt Weitzmann, believes the theme of the transfiguration was chosen to emphasize both the human and the divine nature of Christ, since that era engaged in so many controversies about the precise relationship of the divine and human in Christ. A medallion portrait of King David directly below the figure of Christ depicts that ancient king in the royal purple and golden diadem of a Byzantine emperor, an anachronistic touch that both exalted the emperor and reminded the viewer that the emperor was regent of Christ on this earth.

One of the more spectacular holdings of the monastery is its vast collections of religious icons. Because of the iconoclastic controversies of the 8th and 9th centuries in the Byzantine Empire almost no pictorial art remains from the period before the 8th century. Sinai survived the purges of the "image-breakers" (iconoclasts) that engulfed the rest of the Byzantine world because of its extreme isolation. At Sinai, a range of icons that date from Justinian's time to the modern period can be seen. In a real sense, the icons of the monastery of Saint Catherine show the entire evolution of icon painting.

The Greek word *icon* means image. In the Byzantine Christian tradition *icon* means a painting of a religious figure or a religious scene which is used in the

at the foot of Mount Sinai and some pilgrimage chapels on the slopes of the mountain [201]. An Arabic inscription over one of the gates tells the story:

> The pious king Justinian, of the Greek Church, in the expectation of divine assistance and in the hope of divine promises, built the monastery of Mount Sinai and the Church of the Colloquoy [a church over the spot where Moses spoke to God in the burning bush] to his eternal memory and that of his wife, Theodora, so that all the earth and all its inhabitants should become the heritage of God; for the Lord is the best of masters. The building was finished in the thirtieth year of his reign and he gave the monastery a superior named Dukhas. This took place in 6021st year after Adam, the 527th year [by the calendar] of the era of Christ the Savior.

Because of a number of factors—most important its extreme isolation and the very dry weather—the monastery is an immense repository of ancient Byzantine art and culture. It preserves, as well as the oldest icons in Christianity, some of Justinian's architecture. The monastery is also famous as the site of the rediscovery of the earliest Greek codex of the New Testament hitherto found. Called the *Codex Sinaiticus,* it was discovered in the monastery by the German scholar Konstantin von Tischendorf in the 19th

public worship (the liturgy) of the church. Icons are not primarily decorative and they are didactic only in a secondary sense: for the Orthodox Christian faithful the icon is a window into the world of the sacred. Just as Jesus Christ was in the flesh but imaged God in eternity, so the icon is a "thing" but permits a glimpse into the timeless world of religious mystery. One stands before the icon and speaks through its image to the reality beyond it. This explains why the figures in an icon are usually portrayed full-front with no shadow or sense of three-dimensionality. The figures "speak" directly and frontally to the viewer against a hieratic background of gold.

This iconic style becomes clear by an examination of an icon of Christ that may well have been sent to his new monastery by Justinian himself [202]. The icon is done by the *encaustic* method of painting (a technique common in the Roman world for funerary portraits): painting with molten wax that has been colored by pigments. Christ, looking directly at the viewer, is robed in royal purple; in his left hand he holds a jeweled codex and with his right hand he blesses the viewer. Another icon, the *Virgin Enthroned with Two Saints,* from this same period is also worth notice [203]. The flanking saints in military garb are most probably Theodore and George. The angels that traditionally flank the enthroned Virgin in earlier representations are here relegated to the background while the saints, almost like an honor guard, appear on either side of the seated Virgin, who presents her son to the viewer. The convention of the Madonna on a throne presenting the Christ Child, a venerable one, is repeated, with variations, through the entire history of Christian art.

These two icons are a sample from a large number found at Sinai that can be dated from before the 10th century. The later icons of the same monastery have not yet been published, but the entire corpus repre-

202 *Christ Pantocrator.* c. 500–550. Encaustic on wood panel, 32¾ × 17¾″ (84 × 46 cm). Monastery of Saint Catherine, Mount Sinai.

203 *Virgin Enthroned with Two Saints.* 6th century. Encaustic on wood panel, 26¾ × 19⅜″ (69 × 50 cm). Monastery of Saint Catherine, Mount Sinai.

sents a continuous tradition of Byzantine art and piety. Mount Sinai is unique in its great tradition of historical continuity. Despite the rise of Islam, the harshness of the atmosphere, the vicissitudes of history, and the changing culture of the modern world, the monastery fortress at Sinai is living testimony to a style of life and a religiosity with an unbroken history to the time of Justinian's building program.

The Persistence of Byzantine Culture

It is simplistic to describe Byzantine art as unchanging—it underwent regional, intellectual, social, and iconographic changes—but a person who visits a modern Greek or Russian Orthodox church is struck more by the similarities than by the dissimilarities with the art of early medieval Constantinople. Furthermore, the immediately recognizable Byzantine style can be found in the history of art in areas as geographically diverse as Sicily in southern Italy and the far-eastern reaches of Russia. What explains this basic persistence of style and outlook?

First of all, until it fell to the Turks in 1453, Constantinople exerted an extraordinary cultural influence over the rest of the Eastern Christian world. Russian emissaries sent to Constantinople in the late 10th century to inquire about religion brought back to Russia both favorable reports about Byzantine Christianity and a taste for the Byzantine style of religious art. It was the impact of services in Hagia Sophia that most impressed the delegates of Prince Vladimir, the first Christian ruler in Russia. Although art in Christian Russia was to develop its own regional variations, it was still closely tied to the art of Constantinople; Russian "onion-dome" churches, for example, are native adaptations of the central-dome churches of Byzantium [204].

Russia, in fact, accepted Christianity about 150 years after the ban on icons was lifted in Constantinople in 843. By this time the second "golden age" of Byzantine art was well under way. By the 11th century Byzantine artists were not only working in Russia but had also established schools of icon painting in such centers as Kiev [205]. By the end of the century these schools had passed into the hands of Russian monks, but their stylistic roots remained the artistic

204 Church of the Intercession of the Virgin, near Vladimir, U.S.S.R. c. 1166. In this structure Byzantine ideas are changed into a typically Russian idiom.

205 Andrei Rublev. Icon of the Old Testament Trinity. 1422–1427. State Tretyakov Gallery, Moscow. The three angelic visitors of Genesis 18 are shown prefiguring the Christian Trinity.

right: Plate 16 Anthemius of Tralles and Isidore of Miletus. Hagia Sophia, Constantinople (Istanbul). 532–537, 553–563. This view of the interior, looking toward the apse, shows how the windows between drum and dome give an impression of floating lightness that continues down, reinforced by the other windows, to the floor.

below: Plate 17 Empress Theodora, detail of wall mosaic, San Vitale, Ravenna. c. 547. This is a detail of figure **199, page 283.**

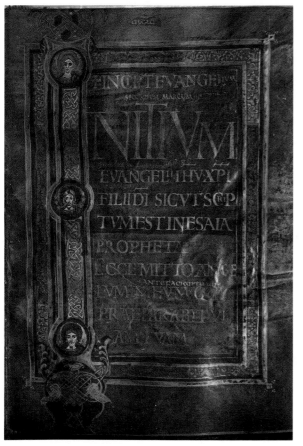

above: Plate 18 *The Transfiguration of Christ,* mosaic in apse of church at Monastery of Saint Catherine, Mount Sinai. 6th century.

left: Plate 19 Title page of the Gospel of Saint Mark, from the *Centula Evangeliary.* Aachen, late 8th century. Manuscript illumination, 13⅝ × 9½" (35 × 25 cm). Bibliothèque Municipale, Abbeville. The parchment used for this book made for the Centula Monastery was dyed purple. Note that the lettering shows a familiarity with the lettering on Roman monuments.

ideas of Byzantium. Even after the Mongol invasions of Russia in 1240, Russian religious art continued to have close ties to the Greek world, although less with Constantinople than with the monastic centers of Mount Athos and Salonica in Greece.

Byzantine influence was also very strong in Italy. We have already seen the influence of Justinian's court on Ravenna. Although northern Italy fell to Lombard rule in the 8th century, Byzantine influence continued in the south of Italy for the next five hundred years. During the iconoclastic controversy in the East many Greek artisans went into exile in Italy, where their work is still to be seen. Even while the Kingdom of Sicily was under Norman rule in the 12th century, Byzantine artisans were still active—as the great mosaics of Monreale, Cefalù [206], and Palermo testify. In northern Italy, especially in Venice, the trade routes to the East and the effects of the Crusades permitted a strong presence of Byzantine art, as the mosaics of the church of Saint Mark's (as well as Byzantine art looted when the Crusaders entered Constantinople in 1204) and the cathedral on the nearby island of Torcello attest. We shall see in later chapters the impact of this artistic presence on panel

206 Christ Pantocrator, detail of apse mosaic, cathedral, Cefalù. c. 1148. Christ Pantocrator, the one who sustains all things in his hands, is common in Byzantine art. This kind of cosmic Christ, rather than a suffering one, was a mark of Byzantine Christianity. The open book begins, in Greek and Latin, with the gospel phrase "I am the Light of the world."

painting in Italy. Until the revolutionary changes by Cimabue and Giotto at the end of the 13th century, the pervasive influence of this style was so great that Italian painting up to that time is often characterized as Italo-Byzantine.

There is another reason that Byzantine aesthetics seem so changeless over the centuries. From the time of Justinian (and even more so after controversies of the 8th and 9th centuries) Byzantine art was intimately tied to the theology and liturgical practices of the Orthodox church. The use of icons, for example, is not merely a pious practice but a deep-rooted part of the faith. Each year the Orthodox church celebrated a feast commemorating the triumph of the Icon party called the Feast of the Triumph of Orthodoxy.

Art, then, is tied to theological doctrine and liturgical practice. Because of the innate conservatism of the theological tradition, innovation either in theology or in art was discouraged. The ideal of the artist was not to try something new but to infuse his work with a spirit of deep spirituality and unwavering reverence. This art, while extremely conservative, was never stagnant. The artists strove for fidelity to the past as their aesthetic criterion. As art historian André Grabar has noted: "Their role can be compared to that of musical performers in our day, who do not feel that their importance is diminished by the fact that they limit their talent to the interpretation of other people's work, since each interpretation contains original nuances."

This attitude of theological conservatism and aesthetic stability helps explain why, for example, the art of icon-painting is considered a holy occupation in the Eastern Orthodox church. Today, when a new Orthodox church is built the congregation may commission from a monk or icon-painter the necessary icons for the interior of the church. The expeditions of scholars who went to Saint Catherine's monastery to study the treasures there recall the sadness they felt at the funeral of a monk, Father Demetrios, in 1958. The last icon-painter in the monastery, he marked the end of a tradition that stretched back nearly fifteen hundred years.

Travelers to Mount Athos in Greece can visit (with some difficulty) the small monastic communities (*sketes*) on the south of the peninsula, where monastic icon painters still work at their art. In our century there has been a renaissance in the appreciation of this style of painting. In Greece there has been a modern attempt to purge icon painting of Western influences (especially those of the Renaissance and the

Baroque periods) in order to recover a more authentic link with the great Byzantine tradition of the past. Even in the Soviet Union, which for decades was indifferent to its religious heritage, there has been a surge of interest in the treasures of past religious art. This has resulted in careful conservation of the icons in Russia, exhibits of the art in the museums of Russia and abroad, and an intense scholarly study of this heritage.

Byzantine culture was not confined to artistic concerns. We have already seen that Justinian made an important contribution to legal studies. Constantinople also had a literary, philosophical, and theological culture. Although Justinian closed the pagan academies, later Byzantine emperors encouraged humanistic and theological studies. While the links between Constantinople and the West were strained over the centuries, those links did remain. At first a good deal of Greek learning came into the West (after having been lost in the early Middle Ages) through the agency of Arabic sources. The philosophical writings of Aristotle became available to Westerners in the late 12th and early 13th centuries in the form of Latin translations of Arabic translations of the Greek: Aristotle came to the University of Paris from the Moslem centers of learning in Spain and northern Africa. Not until the 15th century did Greek become a widely known language in the West; Petrarch and Boccaccio in the 14th century had a difficult time finding anyone to teach them the language. By the 15th century this had changed. One factor contributing to the Renaissance love for the classics was the presence of Greek-speaking scholars from Constantinople in Italy.

The importance of this reinfusion of Greek culture can be seen easily enough by looking at the great libraries of 15th-century Italy. Of the nearly four thousand books in the Vatican library listed in a catalogue of 1484, a thousand were in Greek, most of them from Constantinople. The core of the great library of Saint Mark's in Venice was Cardinal Bessarion's collection of Greek books, brought from the East when he went to the Council of Ferrara–Florence to discuss the union of the Greek and Latin churches in 1438. Bessarion brought with him, in addition to his books, a noted Platonic scholar, Genistos Plethon, who lectured on Platonic philosophy for the delighted Florentines. This event prompted Cosimo de' Medici to subsidize the collection, translation, and study of Plato's philosophy under the direction of Marsilio Ficino. Ficino's Platonic Academy, supported by Medici money, became a rallying point for the study of philosophical ideas.

The fall of Constantinople to the Turks in 1453 brought a flood of émigré Greek scholars to the West, in particular to Italy. The presence of these scholars enhanced the already considerable interest in Greek studies. Greek refugee scholars soon held chairs at the various *studia* (schools) of the leading Italian cities. These scholars taught language, edited texts, wrote commentaries, and fostered an interest not only in Greek pagan learning but also in the literature of the Greek Fathers of the Church. By the end of the 15th century the famous Aldine press in Venice was publishing a whole series of Greek classics to meet the great demand for such works. This new source of learning and scholarship spread rapidly throughout Western Europe so that by the early 16th century the

207 A Russian Orthodox Christmas service in Moscow. Note the elaborate icon screen, called an iconostasis, which separates the congregation from the altar. At the most solemn part of a service, the gates, now open behind the priest, are closed.

290

study of Greek was an ordinary but central part of both humanistic and theological education.

The cultural world view of Justinian's Constantinople is preserved directly in the conservative traditionalism of Orthodox religious art [207] and indirectly by Constantinople's gift of Greek learning to Europe during the Renaissance. The great social and political power of the Byzantine Empire ended in the 15th century although it had been in decline since the end of the 12th century. Only the great monuments remain to remind us of a splendid and opulent culture now gone but once active and vigorous for nearly a thousand years.

Further Reading

Beckwith, John. *The Art of Constantinople*. New York: Phaidon, 1961. A brief survey of Byzantine art from A.D. 330 to 1453 with good illustrations.

Gibbon, Edward. *The Decline and Fall of the Roman Empire*. Many editions; the standard version is in 9 vols., edited by J. Bury in 1914. This monumental work, first published in 1776, is still the single best work on the period of Rome's decline. For a panoramic view of the period in this chapter and an example of how English should be written, it is unparalleled.

Grabar, André. *Byzantium: Byzantine Art in the Middle Ages*. London: Methuen, 1966. A sensitive and original study of Byzantine art and culture by an acknowledged expert in the field.

————. *The Golden Age of Justinian*. New York: Odyssey, 1967. A splendid work by one of the best scholars in the field.

MacDonald, William. *Early Christian and Byzantine Architecture*. New York: Braziller, 1967. A handy survey with good photographs and schematics of important buildings.

Sherrard, P. *Constantinople*. Oxford: Oxford University Press, 1965. An important study for its historical learning.

Simson, Otto von. *The Sacred Fortress*. Chicago: University of Chicago Press, 1948. The best book on the artistic heritage of Ravenna.

Talbot Rice, David, and Tamara Talbot Rice. *Icons and Their History*. London: Thames and Hudson, 1974. Fine scholarship with good bibliographies and beautiful plates.

Vidal, Gore. *Julian*. New York: Vintage, 1977. This novel, originally published in 1964, is a brilliant evocation of Christianity and Classicism in conflict toward the end of the Roman Empire.

Ware, Timothy. *The Orthodox Church*. Baltimore: Penguin Paperback, 1969. A reliable, nontechnical survey.

Suggestions for Listening

Byzantine music is much less well known in the West than the great tradition of medieval religious music, Gregorian Chant. Byzantine music is nevertheless a living tradition of the Orthodox Church. Modern versions of Byzantine chant show the influences of the centuries but allow us to catch the peculiarities of the music, which is in spirit somewhat closer to Jewish and Oriental music than to the religious chants of the West. One of the most interesting and atmospheric recordings of Byzantine music was actually made on Mount Athos in Greece, a recording of the Easter Liturgy sung by the monastic community of Athos (DG ARC 2533413). Another record, Philips 6830194, is a setting of the Liturgy of Saint John Chrysostom.

The words of the Liturgy of Saint John Chrysostom have also been set to music by modern composers, particularly those with a personal attachment to the Orthodox Church. Tchaikovsky, normally associated with intensely dramatic and romantic music, wrote a setting of the Byzantine Liturgy (Angel SZ 3876). Sergei Rachmaninoff's version of the Liturgy is available on Angel S 3864.

Questions for Futher Discussion

1. Augustine's *Confessions* is an intensely introspective work. Augustine tends to scrutinize himself in the light of his religious belief. A modern writer might be more psychological in self-scrutiny. How would a psychologically oriented person look at the life and problems of Augustine, especially with respect to his preoccupation with evil?

2. Certain buildings have become landmarks in the history of Western culture. Hagia Sophia is one of these. Compare the use of space in the Parthenon, Pantheon, Solomon's Temple, and Hagia Sophia.

3. Although mosaics and paintings are very similar (colored pictures on flat surfaces bound by defined planes), they are also very different as visual experiences. Compare a painting depicting a scene similar to that of one of the mosaics in this chapter with the mosaic and list the differences you see.

4. Reread the account of the riots in Constantinople by the historian Procopius. Does the account have anything in common with incidents in our own urban experience? Can large-scale organized sports be a catalyst for social upheaval, and why?

5. The icon had a sacred use. Do we normally "use" art for a sacred (or even a secular) purpose, or do we now only "enjoy" art? Explain.

	GENERAL EVENTS	LITERATURE & PHILOSOPHY	ART

650

Rise of the Franks

714–741 Charles Martel, grandfather of Charlemagne, reigns as first ruler of Frankish kingdom

732 Charles Martel defeats Moslems at Battle of Poitiers

741–768 Reign of Pepin the Short, father of Charlemagne

735 Death of Venerable Bede, author of *Ecclesiastical History of the English People* and other religious writings

8th–9th cent. Irish *Book of Kells*

768

Carolingian Period

768 Charlemagne ascends Frankish throne

772–778 Charlemagne's military campaigns against Moslem Emirates

778 Battle of Roncesvalles

c. 790 Charlemagne settles his court at Aachen (Aix-la-Chapelle)

800 Charlemagne crowned Holy Roman emperor at Rome by Pope Leo III

814 Death of Charlemagne

910 Founding of monastery at Cluny

987–996 Reign of Hugh Capet in France ends Carolingian line of succession

after 780 Carolingian minuscule form of lettering developed

781 Charlemagne opens palace school, importing such scholars as Theodulf of Orléans and Alcuin of York

785 Alcuin, *Sacramentary*

after 814 Carolingian monasteries adopt *Rule* of Saint Benedict of Nursia (480–547?)

821 Einhard, *Vita Caroli (Life of Charlemagne)*

Illuminated manuscripts and carved ivories prevalent

c. 775 *Centula Evangeliary* and *Dagulf Psalter*

800–810 *Gospel Book of Charlemagne*

early 9th cent. *Crucifixion Ivory*, done at palace school of Charlemagne

c. 820–830 *Utrecht Psalter*

1000

Romanesque Period

11th cent. Pilgrimages become very popular

1066 Norman invasion of England by William the Conqueror

1096–1099 First Crusade; capture of Jerusalem by Christians

c. 1098 *Song of Roland, chanson de geste* inspired by Battle of Roncesvalles, written down after 300 yrs. of oral tradition

12th cent. Development of liturgical drama

c. 1125 Saint Bernard of Clairvaux denounces extravagances of Romanesque decoration

1100–1125 Sculptures at Abbey Church of Saint-Pierre, Moissac

1120–1132 Sculptures at Abbey Church of La Madeleine, Vézelay

c. 1140 Portal sculptures at Priory Church, Saint-Gilles-du-Gard

1140

1165 Charlemagne canonized at Cathedral of Aachen

1187 Sultan Saladin conquers Jerusalem

1202–1204 Fourth Crusade; sack of Constantinople by crusaders

1270 Eighth Crusade

1291 Fall of Acre, last Christian stronghold in Holy Land

14th–15th cent. Play cycles performed outside the church; *Everyman* (15th cent.), morality play

c. 1165 Reliquary of Charlemagne and candelabra commissioned for Aachen cathedral by Frederick Barbarossa for canonization of Charlemagne

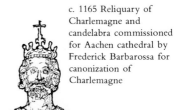

1400

ARCHITECTURE   **MUSIC**

Monastic complexes become important
centers in rural life

The Age of Charlemagne

c. 795 Palace and chapel of
Charlemagne at Aachen

c. 800 Monasteries become
centers for encouragement of
sacred music; theoretical
study of music at
Charlemagne's palace school

9th cent. Use of semi-dramatic
trope in liturgical music;
Quem Quaeritis trope
introduced into Easter Mass

c. 810 Gregorian plain
chant *(cantus planus)*
obligatory in
Charlemagne's churches

c. 820 Plan for Abbey of Saint Gall,
the "ideal" monastery

822 Earliest
documented church organ

Use of massive
walls and piers, rounded
arches, and minimal windows

c. 1071–1112 Pilgrimage church at
Santiago de Compostela, Spain

c. 1080–1130 Church of Saint Sernin,
Toulouse, pilgrimage center

1088–1130 Great Third
Church at Cluny

1096–1120 Abbey Church of
La Madeleine, Vézelay

11th–12th cent. Gregorian
chant codified

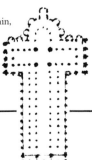

Charlemagne as Ruler and Diplomat

Charles the Great (742?–814)—known to subsequent history as Charlemagne—was crowned emperor of the Roman Empire in Saint Peter's Basilica at Rome on Christmas Day A.D. 800 by Pope Leo III, in the first imperial coronation in the West since the late 6th century [208]. The papal coronation was rebellion in the eyes of the Byzantine court, and the emperor in Constantinople considered Charlemagne a usurper, but this act marked the revival of the Roman Empire in the West.

Leo III had compelling reasons to be grateful to Charlemagne. Driven from Rome by a conspiracy and riot in 799, he had taken refuge at Charlemagne's court and was restored to the holy see by the king's Frankish troops. Charlemagne had also created a buffer zone between the Christian West and the Moslems of Spain by his many conquests in southern France. He had destroyed the Longobard kingdom of northern Italy, which had been a consistent threat to the independence of papal rule in the center of Italy. His bloodily persistent wars against the Saxons of northern Germany had reduced the threat of these barbarian warriors and made possible their eventual Christianization [209]. His coastal defenses on the northern shores offered some protection against the incursions of the dreaded Vikings, who made regular coastal raids from their fjord strongholds in Scandinavia (see map opposite).

Charlemagne was not only a conquerer; he was also an able administrator of lands brought under his

209 Charlemagne having a church built, detail from Charlemagne window, Chartres Cathedral. Early 13th century. According to legend, Charlemagne ordered a church built in honor of Saint James, who had helped him conquer Pamplona. (Another detail from this window is in Plate 20, page 353.)

subjugation [210]. He modified and adapted the classic Roman administrative machinery to fit the needs of his own kingdom. Charlemagne's rule was essentially feudal—structured in a hierarchical fashion, with lesser rulers bound by acts of fealty to higher ones. Lesser rulers were generally large landowners who derived their right to own and rule their land from their tie to the emperor. Charlemagne also maintained a number of vassal dependents at his court who acted as counselors at home and as legates to execute and oversee the imperial will abroad. From his palace the emperor regularly issued *capitularies* (from the Latin *capitulum,* clause), legal decrees modeled on the old imperial Roman decrees [211]. These capitularies were detailed sets of instructions that touched on a wide variety of secular and religious issues. Those that have survived give us some sense of what life was like in the very early medieval period. The legates of the emperor carried the capitularies to the various regions of the empire and reported back on their acceptance and implementation. This burgeoning *bureaucratic* system required a class of civil servants with a reasonable level of literacy, an important factor in the cultivation of letters that was so much a part of the so-called Carolingian Renaissance.

208 The coronation of Charlemagne, detail of scenes from the life of Charlemagne, from Vincent de Beauvais' *Le Miroir Historial.* 15th century. Manuscript illumination. Musée Condé, Chantilly.

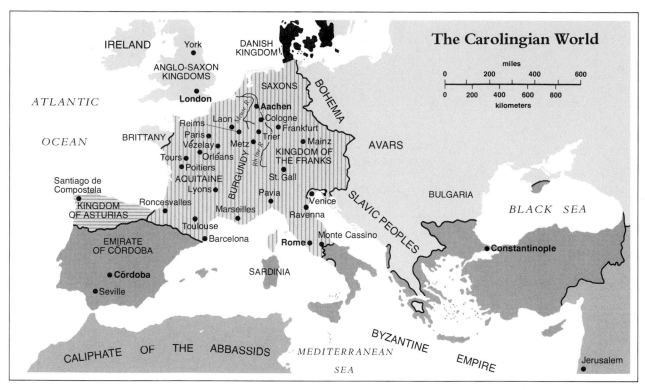

The Carolingian World

left: 210 Equestrian statuette of Charlemagne (?). 9th century. Bronze with traces of gilt, height 9½″ (24 cm). Louvre, Paris. This small figure, for centuries in the treasury of the cathedral of Metz, dates to the Carolingian period although the horse is a 16th-century replacement and the sword is modern. The emperor carries the imperial orb, signifying rule, in his left hand; the sword represents his power.

below: 211 Charlemagne's seal. 9th century. Archives Nationales, Paris. This seal—a Roman gem with the head of an emperor or a philosopher—would have been impressed on molten wax to certify documents. The inscription reads *Christ, protect Charles, the King of the Franks.*

The popular view of the early Middle Ages—often referred to as the Dark Ages—is of a period of isolated and ignorant peoples with little contact outside the confines of their own immediate surroundings, and at times that was indeed the general condition of life. Nonetheless, it is important to note that in the late 8th and early 9th centuries Charlemagne not only ruled over an immense kingdom (all of modern-day France, Germany, the Low Countries, and Italy as far south as Calabria) but also had extensive diplomatic contact outside that kingdom. Charlemagne maintained regular, if somewhat testy, diplomatic relations with the emperor in Constantinople (at one point he tried to negotiate a marriage between himself and the Byzantine empress Irene in order to consolidate the two empires). Envoys from Constantinople were regularly received in his palace at Aachen, and Charlemagne learned Greek well enough to understand the envoys speaking their own tongue.

Charlemagne's relationship with the rulers of Islamic kingdoms is interesting. Islam had spread all along the southern Mediterranean coast in the preceding century. Arabs were in complete command of all the Middle East, North Africa, and most of the Iberian peninsula. Charlemagne's grandfather Charles Martel (Charles the Hammer) had defeated the Moslems decisively at the battle of Poitiers in 732, thus halting an Islamic challenge from Spain to the rest of Europe. Charlemagne himself had fought the Moslems of the Córdoba caliphate on the Franco–Spanish borders; the battle of Roncesvalles (778) was the historical basis for the later epic poem the *Song of Roland*.

Despite his warlike relationship with Moslems in the West, Charlemagne had close diplomatic ties with the great Harun al-Rashid, the caliph of Baghdad. In 787 Charlemagne sent an embassy to the caliph to beg protection for the holy places of the Christians in Moslem-held Palestine. The caliph (of *Thousand and One Nights* fame) received the Frankish legates and their gifts (mainly bolts of the much-prized Frisian cloth) with welcome and sent an elephant back to the emperor as a gesture of friendship. This gift actually arrived at Aachen and lived there for a few years before succumbing to the harsh winter climate. Charlemagne's negotiations were successful. From a pair of Palestinian monks he received the keys to the church of the Holy Sepulchre and other major Christian shrines, an important symbolic act that made the emperor the official guardian of the holiest shrines in Christendom.

212 Silver *denier* minted during Charlemagne's reign. c. 804. Coin Collection, State Museums, East Berlin. One side of the coin carried a relief of the emperor's head and the inscription "Charles the Emperor." Deniers were struck at the royal mint at Frankfurt.

Charlemagne's reign was also conspicuous for its economic developments. He stabilized the currency system of his kingdom. The silver *denier* struck at the royal mint in Frankfurt after 804 became the standard coin of the time [212]; its presence in archaeological finds from Russia to England testifies to its widespread use and the faith traders had in it.

Trade and commerce were vigorous. Charlemagne welcomed Jewish immigration into his kingdom to provide a merchant class for commerce. There were annual trade fairs at Saint Denis near Paris, at which English merchants could buy foodstuffs, honey, and wine from the Carolingian estates. A similar fair was held each year at Pavia, an important town of the old Lombard kingdom of northern Italy. Port cities such as Marseilles provided mercantile contacts with the Moslems of Spain and North Africa. Jewish merchants operated as middlemen in France for markets throughout the Near East. The chief of Charlemagne's mission to Harun al-Rashid's court was a Jew named Isaac who had the linguistic ability and geographic background to make the trip to Baghdad and back—with an elephant—at a time when travel was a risky enterprise. Rivers such as the Rhine and the Moselle were utilized as important trade routes. One of the most sought-after articles from the Frankish kingdom was the iron broadsword produced from forges in and around the city of Cologne and sold to Arabs in the Middle East through Jewish merchants at the port cities. Vivid testimony to their value can be read in the repeated embargoes (imposed under penalty of death) decreed by Charlemagne against their export to the land of the Vikings, who put them too often to effective use against their Frankish manufacturers in coastal raids on North Sea towns and trading posts.

213 Model reconstruction of Charlemagne's palace at Aachen. Römisch-Germanisches Zentralmuseum, Mainz. The *aula regis* with its long connecting gallery is in the foreground. The royal chapel is the octagonal building in the left background.

Charlemagne's Palace at Aachen

Beyond his immediate commercial, military, and political goals, Charlemagne had an overwhelming desire to model his kingdom on that of ancient Rome. His coronation in Rome symbolized the fusion of the ancient imperial ideal with the notion of Christian destiny. It was not accidental that Charlemagne's favorite book—he had it read to him frequently at meals—was Augustine's *The City of God*. One highly visible way of making concrete this ideal was to build a capital. For years Charlemagne and his court, like that of his Frankish ancestors, moved from place to place during the year. Wherever he stopped, there was his *palatium* (palace). After 789 Charlemagne settled permanently at a site between the Meuse and Rhine rivers where there were abundant hot springs for bathing. The name of the town was Aachen, a corruption of the Latin *aquae* (waters); in French it is called Aix-la-Chapelle.

At Aachen Charlemagne built his palace and royal chapel [213]. Except for the chapel (incorporated into the present cathedral), all the buildings of Charlemagne's palace have been destroyed and the Aachen city hall (itself built in the 14th century) covers the palace site. From excavations and contemporary documents we can reconstruct the general outlines. The palace itself was a long one-story building; its main room was the large *aula regalis* (royal hall), which measured roughly 140 by 60 feet (42.7 by 18.3 meters). So richly decorated that even the fastidious and sophisticated Byzantine legates were favorably impressed, the room had as its focal point at the western end the emperor's throne. In front of the palace was an open courtyard around which were outbuildings and apartments for the imperial retinue. Around the year 800 the courtyard held a great bronze statue of Theodoric, once king of the Ravenna Ostrogoths, that Charlemagne had brought back from Ravenna to adorn his palace.

The *aula regalis* was joined to Charlemagne's chapel by a long wooden gallery. This royal chapel was probably built around 795. With sixteen exterior walls, the chapel was a central-plan church based on an octagon [214], its model undoubtedly the church of San Vitale in Ravenna [see figure 195, page 281], which Charlemagne had visited and admired. The octagon formed the main nave of the church, which was surrounded by *cloisters;* the building itself was two-storied. At the eastern end of the chapel was an altar dedicated to the Savior, with a chapel dedicated to the Virgin directly below it. The central space was crowned with an octagonal cupola the lower part of which was pierced by windows, the main source of light in the church. The outside of the church was plain and severe; the inside was richly ornamented with marbles brought to Aachen from Ravenna and Rome. The interior of the cupola was decorated with a rich mosaic depicting Christ and the twenty-four elders of the Apocalypse (now destroyed; the present mosaics in the chapel are modern copies) while the other planes of the interior were covered with frescoes (now also destroyed). The railing of the upper gallery was made from bronze screens that are still in place, wrought in geometrical forms.

The chapel included two objects that emphasized its royal status: the most important relic of the kingdom, Saint Martin of Tours' cape, and a throne. Charlemagne's throne was on the second floor, opposite the chapel of the Savior. From this vantage point the emperor could observe the liturgical services being conducted in the Savior chapel and at the same time view the Virgin chapel with its rich collection of relics.

Charlemagne's throne, with its curved back and armrests, was mounted by six stone steps [215]. This arrangement was obviously taken from King Solomon's throne as described in the Bible (I Kings 10:18–19). Charlemagne was to be thought of as the "new Solomon" who, like his ancient prototype, was an ambitious builder, a sagacious lawgiver, and the symbol of national unity. That this analogy was not an idle fancy is proved by a letter from Alcuin, Charlemagne's friend and tutor, to the emperor in anticipation of his return to Aachen: "May I soon be allowed to come with palms, accompanied with children singing psalms, to meet your triumphant glory, and to see once more your beloved face in the Jerusalem of our most dear fatherland, wherein is the temple set up to God by this most wise Solomon."

214 Interior of chapel of Charlemagne, Aachen. This view is eastward toward the emperor's tribune (second story center) from the side of the double altars. The mosaics above and the band of inscriptions at the lower level are modern.

215 Charlemagne's throne in the royal chapel, Aachen. To emphasize the sacredness of the place, relics of saints were placed under the throne and in the capitals of two Corinthian columns to the front of the throne. The steps echo Solomon's throne as described in I Kings 10:18–19.

Learning in the Time of Charlemagne

At Aachen Charlemagne opened his famous "palace school," an institution that was a prime factor in initiating what has been called the Carolingian Renaissance. Literacy in Western Europe before the time of Charlemagne was rather spotty; it existed, but hardly thrived, in certain monastic centers that kept alive the old tradition of humanistic learning taken from ancient Rome. Original scholarship was rare, although monastic copyists did keep alive the tradition of literary conservation. Charlemagne himself could not write. His contemporary and biographer Einhard, who wrote the *Vita Caroli* (The Life of Charles)— the first secular biography of post-Roman Europe— provides us a touching portrait of the emperor's attempts to learn:

> Under [Alcuin] the emperor spent much time and effort in studying rhetoric, dialectic, and especially astrology. He applied himself to mathematics and traced the course of the stars with great

attention and care. He also tried to learn to write. With this object in view he kept writing tablets and notebooks under the pillows on his bed, so that he could try his hand at forming letters during his leisure moments; but, although he tried very hard, he had begun too late in life and he made little progress.

The scholars and teachers Charlemagne brought to Aachen provide some clues as to the various locales in which early medieval learning had survived. Peter of Pisa and Paul the Deacon (from Lombardy) came to teach grammar and rhetoric at his school since they had had contact with the surviving liberal arts curriculum in Italy. Theodulf of Orleans was a theologian and poet. He had studied in the surviving Christian kingdom of Spain and was an heir to the encyclopedic tradition of Isadore of Seville and his followers. Finally and most importantly, Charlemagne brought an Anglo-Saxon, Alcuin of York, to Aachen after meeting him in Italy in 781. Alcuin had been trained in the English intellectual tradition of the Venerable Bede (died 735), the most prominent intellectual of his day, a monk who had welded together the study of humane letters and biblical scholarship. These scholar-teachers were hired by Charlemagne for several purposes.

First, Charlemagne wished to establish a system of education for the young of his kingdom. The primary purpose of these schools was to develop literacy, Alcuin of York developed a curriculum for them. He insisted that humane learning should consist of those studies which developed logic and science. It was from this distinction that later medieval pedagogues developed the two courses of studies for all schooling prior to the university: the *trivium* (grammar, rhetoric, and dialectic) and the *quadrivium* (arithmetic, geometry, music, and astronomy). These subjects remained at the heart of the school curriculum from the medieval period until modern times. (The now much-neglected "classical education" has its roots in this basic plan of learning.)

Few books were available and writing was done on slates or waxed tablets since parchment was expensive. In grammar, some of the texts of the Latin grammarian Priscian might be studied and then applied to passages from Latin prose writers. In rhetoric, the work of Cicero was studied, or Quintilian's *Institutio Oratoria* if available. For dialectics, some of the work of Aristotle might be read in the Latin translation of Boethius. In arithmetic, multiplication and division was learned and perhaps there was some

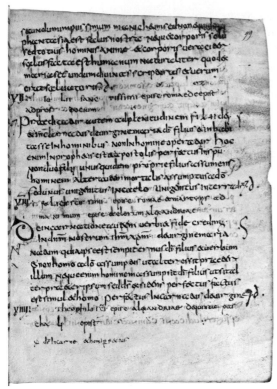

216 Manuscript with notations added in Alcuin's handwriting (right margin and bottom line). Bibliothèque Nationale, Paris.

It was mainly Alcuin of York who worked at the task of revising the liturgical books [216]. Alcuin published a book of extracts of Old and New Testament passages in Latin for public reading during Mass. He sent for books from Rome in order to publish a sacramentary, the book of prayers and rites for the administration of the sacraments of the church. Alcuin's *Sacramentary* was made obligatory for the churches of the Frankish kingdom in 785. Charlemagne made the Roman chant (called *Gregorian* after Pope Gregory the Great, who was said to have initiated such chants in the end of the 6th century) obligatory in all the churches of his realm. Alcuin also attempted to correct scribal errors in the Vulgate Bible (the Latin version of Saint Jerome) by a comparative reading of manuscripts, a gigantic task he never completed.

The revisions and reforms of Alcuin and Charlemagne may seem minor achievements today, but it is difficult to overestimate their importance in the development of the intellectual life of Europe. At a time when there was no uniformity of liturgical practice, Alcuin's reforms gave strong support to Roman usage, which would contribute mightily to the power and prestige of Rome and the papacy in subsequent centuries. Further, Alcuin's labors set a standard for textual studies and emendations that would influence the literary tradition of Europe for centuries to come.

Beyond the practical need for literacy there was a further aim of education in this period. It was generally believed that all learning would lead to a better grasp of revealed truth—the Bible. The study of profane letters (by and large the literature of Rome) was a necessary first step toward the full study of the Bible. The study of grammar would set out the rules of writing, while dialectics would help distinguish true from false propositions. Models for such study were sought in the works of Cicero, Statius, Ovid, Lucan, and Vergil. These principles of correct writing and argumentation could then be applied to the study of the Bible in order to get closer to its truth. The pursuit of analysis, definition, and verbal clarity are the roots from which the scholastic form of philosophy would spring in the High Middle Ages. Scholasticism, which dominated European intellectual life until the eve of the Renaissance, had its first beginnings in the educational methodology established by Alcuin and his companions.

These educational enterprises were not centered exclusively at the palace school at Aachen. Under Charlemagne's direction Alcuin developed a system

practice on the *abacus* since the Latin numerals were clumsy to compute with pen and paper. Arithmetic also included some practice in chronology as students were taught to compute the variable dates of Easter and might conclude with a study of the allegorical meaning of numbers. Geometry was based on the study of Euclid. Astronomy was derived from the Roman writer Pliny, with some attention to Bede's work. Music was the theoretical study of scale, proportion, the harmony of the universe, and the "music of the spheres." Music at this period was distinguished from *cantus,* which was the practical knowledge of chants and hymns for church use. In general, all study was based largely on the rote mastery of texts.

Beyond the foundation of schools, Charlemagne needed scholars to reform existing texts and to halt their terrible corruption, especially those used in church worship. Literary revival was closely connected with liturgical revival. Part of Charlemagne's educational reform envisioned people who would read aloud and sing in church from decent, reliable texts. Literacy was conceived of as a necessary prelude for intelligible worship.

of schools throughout the Frankish Empire, schools centered in both monasteries and towns. Attempts were also made to attach them to parish churches in the rural areas. The monastic school at Metz became a center for singing and liturgical study; schools at Lyons, Orleans, Mainz, Tours, and Laon had centers for teaching children rudimentary literary skills and offered some opportunity for further study in the liberal arts and the study of scripture. The establishment of these schools was accomplished by a steady stream of decrees and capitularies emanating from the Aachen palace. A circular letter, written most likely by Alcuin, called *De Litteris Colendis (On the Cultivation of Learning)* encouraged monks to study the Bible and to teach the young to do the same. A capitulary of 798 insisted that prelates and country clergy alike start schools for children.

This program of renewal in educational matters was an ideal set forth at a time when education was at a low ebb in Europe. Charlemagne tried to reverse the trend and in so doing encouraged real hope for an educated class in his time. His efforts were not entirely successful; many of his reforms came to naught in the generations after him when Europe slipped back into violence and ignorance. But in Charlemagne's own lifetime there was a heady optimism about education. We can catch some of the enthusiasm in a letter Alcuin sent to Charlemagne in 799:

> If many people became imbued with your ideas a new Athens would be established in Francia— nay, an Athens fairer than the Athens of old, for it would be ennobled by the teachings of Christ, and ours would surpass all the wisdom of the ancient academy. For this had only for its instruction the disciples of Plato; yet, moulded by the seven liberal arts, it shone with constant splendour. But ours would be endowed as well with the sevenfold fullness of the Holy Spirit, and would surpass all secular wisdom in dignity. . . .

The Visual Arts

Given Charlemagne's preoccupation with literary culture, it should not be surprising that a great deal of artistic effort should have been expended on the production and illumination of manuscripts. Carolingian manuscripts were made of parchment (treated animal skins, mainly from cows and sheep) since papyrus was unavailable and the technical process of making paper was not known at this period. For very fine

books the parchment was dyed purple and the letters were painted on with silver and gold pigments. This type of opulent manuscript was common enough in Charlemagne's time and the *Centula Evangeliary* (an evangeliary is a gospel book), produced at a workshop of the palace school at Aachen, was done in this style [Plate 19, page 288]. The intricate border decorations on this manuscript indicate that the fantastic decorative techniques of Celtic artists (like those who did the famous *Book of Kells*) were known to the artisans of the late 8th century.

While a good deal of decoration of Carolingian manuscripts shows the influence of Irish models, the illustrations often show other influences. This is strikingly apparent in the illustrations of the *Gospel Book of Charlemagne* (800–810), where it is clear that the artists were conscious of the Roman style [217]. The page showing the four evangelists with their symbolic emblems is strikingly classical: the four evangelists are toga-clad like ancient Roman consuls. There is some evidence that the artist attempted some experiment in three-dimensionality. The wooded

217 The four Evangelists and their symbols, from the *Gospel Book of Charlemagne*. Palace school of Charlemagne. Aachen, early 9th century. Manuscript illumination. Cathedral Treasury, Aachen.

background in the receding part of the upper two illustrations tends to bring the evangelists forward and thus diminish the flatness we associate both with Byzantine and Celtic illustrations.

The *Utrecht Psalter* (so called because its present home is the University of Utrecht in Holland) has been called the masterpiece of the Carolingian Renaissance. Executed at Reims sometime around 820 to 840, it contains the whole psalter with wonderfully free and playful pen drawings around the text of the psalms. The figures are free from any hieratic stiffness; they are mobile and show a nervous energy. The illustration for Psalm 148, for example, has a scene at the bottom of the page showing various figures "praising God with horn and cymbals" [218]. There are two other interesting aspects of the same illustration. One is that the figures are in the act of praising Christ, who stands at the apex of the illustration with the symbols of his resurrection (the stafflike

cross in his hand). Although the psalms speak of the praise of God, for the medieval Christian the "hidden" or true meaning of the scriptures was that they speak in a prefigurative way of Christ. Thus the psalmist who praises God is a "shadow" of the church which praises Christ.

A second thing to note in this illustration is the bottom-center scene of an organ with two men working the bellows to supply the air. An anecdote in a not-very-reliable biography of the emperor, Notker the Stammerer's *De Carolo Magno,* sheds some light on this: "These same [Greek envoys] brought with them every kind of organ, as well as other instruments. These were all examined by the craftsmen of the most sagacious Charlemagne to see just what was new about them. Then the craftsmen reproduced them with the greatest possible accuracy. The chief of these was that most remarkable of organs ever possessed by musicians which, when its bronze windchests were filled and its oxhide bellows blew through its pipes of bronze, equaled with its deep note the roar of thunder, and yet which, for very sweetness, could resemble the soft tinkle of a lyre or a cymbal. This is, however, neither the time nor the place to tell of where it was set up, how long it lasted, and the way in which it was destroyed in the general cataclysm which befell the state." (Notker was not terribly careful with facts: The organ had actually been a gift to Pepin the Short from the emperor Constantine V in 757.)

The style of the *Utrecht Psalter* has much in common with early Christian illustration. The lavish purple-and-silver manuscripts show a conscious imitation of Byzantine taste. We have also noted the influence of Celtic illustration. Carolingian manuscript art thus had a certain international flavor, and the various styles and borrowings give ample testimony to the cosmopolitan character of Charlemagne's culture. This universality diminished in the next century; not until the period of the so-called International Style in the 14th century would such a broad eclecticism again be seen in Europe.

One other art form that developed from the Carolingian love for the book is ivory carving. This technique was not unique to Charlemagne's time; it was known in the ancient world and highly valued in Byzantium, as noted in the discussion of Maximian's throne at Ravenna in Chapter 6 (see pages 282–283). The ivories that have survived from Charlemagne's time were used for book covers. One beautiful example of the ivory carver's art is a crucifixion panel

218 Page from the *Utrecht Psalter*. Hautvillers (near Reims), c. 820–840. Pen and ink on vellum, 12⅞ × 10″ (33 × 26 cm). University Library, Utrecht. This page is typical of the fast, nervous style of the unknown illustrator who did similar symbolic drawings for the whole of the psalter.

219 *Crucifixion.* Palace school of Charlemagne. Early 9th century. Ivory, 9⅞ × 6⅛″ (25 × 16 cm). Treasury, cathedral of Saint Just, Narbonne. Such ivories were used as book covers for evangeliaries and other illustrated works.

made at the palace workshop at Aachen sometime in the early 9th century [219]. Note the crowded scenes that surround the crucifixion event. Reading clockwise from the bottom left, one sees the Last Supper, the betrayal in the garden, and, at the top, a soldier piercing Jesus' side. As a balance at the top right another soldier offers Jesus a wine-soaked sponge on a lance. Below that scene is one of the women at the tomb and, at the bottom, of the incredulity of Thomas. Framing these scenes above are the ascension of Christ on the left and Pentecost on the right, the two scenes separated by a stylized sun and moon. The entire ivory is framed with geometric and abstract floral designs. The composition indicates that the carver had seen some examples of early Christian

carving, while the beardless Christ and the flow of the drapery indicate familiarity with Byzantine art.

One surviving Carolingian manuscript that allows us to see both illumination and ivory work is the *Dagulf Psalter,* made as a gift for Pope Hadrian I, who reigned from 772 to 795. The psalms are not illustrated like the ones in the *Utrecht Psalter;* instead the illustrator begins a tradition which will be fairly normal for psalters in the future: he enlarges and illuminates the initial letter of the first, 51st, and 101st psalms. The *B* of the first word of Psalm 1, *Beatus vir qui* (Blessed is the man who), is enlarged and decorated in the swelling style of Celtic illumination; the same patterns are echoed on the page margin [220].

220 Beginning of Psalm 1, from the *Dagulf Psalter.* Late 8th century. Manuscript illumination, 7½ × 4⅝″ (19 × 12 cm). National Library, Vienna. The total conception of this page is close to that of the *Centula Evangeliary* (see Plate 19, page 288); with its clear debt to Celtic illustration technique in the borders and within the letter *B.*

221 Cover panels for the *Dagulf Psalter*. Late 8th century. Ivory, 6⅝ × 3⅛″ (17 × 8 cm). Louvre, Paris.

The ivory covers of the psalter have been preserved and are now in the Louvre [221]. Rather than the usual crowded scenes of most of these covers, the ivories from the *Dagulf Psalter* are composed of two scenes on each of the panels; the scenes make references to both the psalter and the papal connection. The panel on the left shows David and his court; below, David is shown singing one of his psalms to the accompaniment of his lyre. The right panel depicts Saint Jerome receiving a letter from Pope Damasus instructing him to correct the psalter; the scene below depicts Jerome in the act of working on the psalter while a grateful clergy looks on.

One other advance in manuscript production during the Carolingian period was in the area of fine handwriting or, as it is more technically known, calligraphy. Handwriting before the Carolingian period was cluttered, unformed, and cramped. It was very hard to read because of its erratic flourishes and its lack of symmetry. After 780 scribes in Carolingian

scriptoria began to develop a precise and rounded form of lettering that became known as the Carolingian *minuscule* [222], as opposed to the *majuscule* or capital letter. This form of lettering was so crisp and legible that it soon became a standard form of manuscript writing. Even in the 15th century, the Florentine humanists preferred the minuscule calligraphy for their manuscripts. When printing became popular in the early 16th century, printers soon designed type fonts to conform to Carolingian minuscule. It overcame Gothic type in popularity and is the ancestor of modern standard lettering systems.

The loving care lavished on books at this period should not surprise us. In an age of mass-produced (and throw-away) book culture it is difficult to appreciate how precious a book was in the Carolingian period and how much human effort went into the production of a single work. Try to imagine the effort involved in using a hand-dipped pen and copying out, letter by letter, on pieces of treated animal

222 Two examples of minuscule calligraphy. *Left:* Section of a list, possibly of a library at Würzburg, Germany. c. 800. Bodleian Library, Oxford. *Right:* Section of a manuscript, *Lindau Gospels,* Saint Gall, Switzerland. Late 9th century. Pierpont Morgan Library, New York.

223 Two scribes at work, from the *Book of Pericopes of Henry III.* 1030–1040. Manuscript illumination. Staatsbibliothek, Bremen. Pericopes are liturgical lessons to be read on certain days during religious services. The scribes are working in a scriptorium (see page 310).

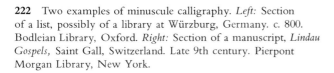

skin the whole 150 psalms or the entire four gospels of the Bible [223].

Beyond the sheer energy required to produce a book was a further difference between their culture and ours. We are a people who accept ideas only after testing and reflection. We do not accept the past as authority. The early medieval person was far more respectful of the wisdom of the past. Books represented authority, especially the Bible. Holy Scripture not only represented a plan of salvation; it was the authoritative word about the nature of reality and the structure of human existence. It was a commonplace in the medieval world that God had written "two books": the book of nature and the book of the Scriptures. Each had inexhaustible reserves of wisdom. In reproducing the book of Scripture there was a natural impulse to try to imitate the beauty of the book of nature, since in the creation of beauty one was imitating the creative genius of God.

Benedictine Monasticism

Monasticism—from the Greek *monos* (alone)—was an integral part of Christianity from the 3rd century on. Monasticism came into the West from the great Eastern tradition of asceticism (self-denial) and eremitism (the solitary life). Its development in the West was very complex, and we cannot speak of any one form of monasticism as predominant before the time of Charlemagne.

Celtic monasticism in Ireland was characterized both by austere living and by a rather lively intellectual tradition. Monasticism in Italy was far more simple and rude. Some of the monasteries on the continent were lax, and Europe was full of wandering monks. No rule of life predominated in the 6th and 7th centuries. Monastic life styles varied not only from country to country but also from monastery to monastery.

224 Saint Benedict of Nursia, detail from a fresco in the Catacomb of Hermes, Rome. 8th century. This is the earliest known—of course idealized—portrait of the saint.

The Rule of Saint Benedict

One strain of European monasticism derived from a rule of life written in Italy by Benedict of Nursia (480–547?) in the early 6th century [224]. Although it borrows from early monastic rules and was applied only to a small proportion of monasteries for a century after its publication, the Rule of Saint Benedict eventually became the Magna Carta of monasticism in the West. Charlemagne had Alcuin of York bring the Rule to his kingdom and impose it on the monasteries of the Frankish kingdom to reform them and impose on them some sense of regular observance. In fact, the earliest copy of the Rule of Saint Benedict we possess today (a 9th-century manuscript preserved in the monastery of Saint Gall) is a copy of a copy Charlemagne had made in 814 from Saint Benedict's autograph copy preserved at the abbey of Monte Cassino in Italy (now lost).

The Rule of Saint Benedict consists of a prologue and 73 chapters (some only a few sentences long) which set out the ideal of monastic life. Monks (the brethren) are to live a family life in community under the direction of a freely elected father (the abbot) for the purpose of being schooled in religious perfection. They are to possess nothing of their own (poverty); they are to live in one monastery and not wander (stability); their life is to be one of obedience to the abbot; and they are to remain unmarried (chastity). Their daily life is to be a balance of common prayer, work, and study. Their prayer life centered around duly appointed hours of liturgical praise of God that were to mark the intervals of the day. This prayer, called the "Divine Office," consisted of the public recitation of psalms, hymns, and prayers with readings from the Holy Scriptures. The offices were interspersed throughout the day and were central to the monks' life. The periods of public liturgical prayer themselves set off the times for reading, study, and the manual labor that was done for the good of the community and its sustenance [225, 226]. The life style of Benedictine monasticism can be summed up in its motto: *ora et labora* (pray and work).

The daily life of the monk was determined by sunrise and sunset (as it was for most people in those days). Here is a typical day—called the *horarium*—in an early medieval monastery. The italicized words designate the names for the liturgical hours of the day:

Horarium Monasticum

2:00 A.M.	Rise
2:10–3:30	*Nocturns* (later called *Matins;* the longest office of the day)
3:30–5:00	Private reading and study
5:00–5:45	*Lauds* (the second office; also called "morning prayer")
5:45–8:15	Private reading and *Prime* (the first of the short offices of the day); at times, there was communal Mass at this time and, in some places, a light breakfast, depending on the season
8:15–2:30	Work punctuated by short offices of *Tierce, Sext,* and *None* (literally the third, sixth, and ninth hours)
2:30–3:15	Dinner
3:15–4:15	Reading and private religious exercises
4:15–4:45	*Vespers*—break—*Compline* (night prayers)
5:15–6:00	To bed for the night.

225 Simon, Abbot of Saint Albans, reading at his book-chest. 14th century. Manuscript illumination. British Library, London. Simon founded the library of his abbey in England.

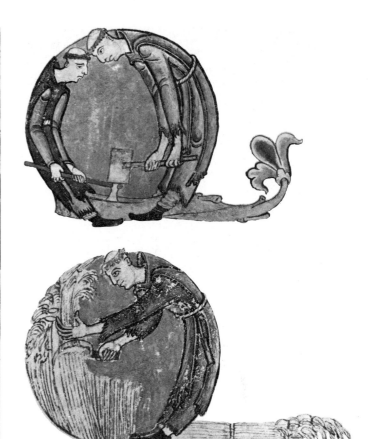

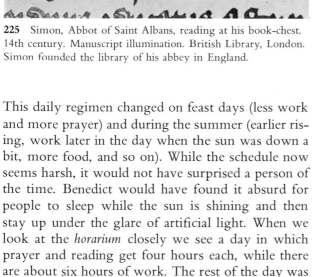

226 Monks splitting wood and a monk reaping wheat. 12th century. Manuscript illuminations, each about 2½ × 4″ (6.5 × 10 cm). Bibliothèque Municipale, Dijon. Initial letter Q's.

This daily regimen changed on feast days (less work and more prayer) and during the summer (earlier rising, work later in the day when the sun was down a bit, more food, and so on). While the schedule now seems harsh, it would not have surprised a person of the time. Benedict would have found it absurd for people to sleep while the sun is shining and then stay up under the glare of artificial light. When we look at the *horarium* closely we see a day in which prayer and reading get four hours each, while there are about six hours of work. The rest of the day was devoted to personal chores, eating, and the like.

The triumph of the Benedictine monastic style of life (the early Middle Ages has been called by some historians the Benedictine centuries) is to be found in its sensible balance between the extreme asceticism of Eastern monastic practices and the unstructured life of Western monasticism before the Benedictine reforms. There was an even balance of prayer, manual labor, and intellectual life. Seven brief selections from the Rule of Saint Benedict can give us a sense of this balanced spiritual pragmatism:

Saint Benedict
from **THE RULE OF SAINT BENEDICT**

Chapter 1
The Different Kinds of Monks and Their Customs

There are four kinds of monks. First are the Cenobites, those who live in a monastery waging their war under a rule and an abbot.

Second are the Anchorites (hermits) who are not neophytes. They have spent much time in the monastery testing themselves and learning to fight against the devil. They have prepared themselves in the fraternal line of battle for the single combat of the hermit. They have laid the foundation to fight, with the aid of God, against their own bodily and spiritual vices.

Third are the Sarabaites (the worst kind), unschooled by any rule, untested, as gold is by fire, but soft as lead, living in and of the world, openly lying to God through their tonsure (shaved heads). They live together in twos or threes, more often alone, without a shepherd in their own fold, not the Lord's. Their only law is the pleasure of their desires, and whatever they wish or choose they call holy. They consider whatever they dislike unlawful.

Fourth are the gyratory monks. All their lives they wander in different countries staying in various monasteries for three or four days at a time. They are restless, servants to the seduction of their own will and appetites, and are much worse in all things than the Sarabaites. It is better to be silent as to their wretched life style than to speak.

Casting these aside, let us with God's help establish a rule for Cenobites who are the best kind of monks.

Chapter 22
How the Monks Are to Sleep

All the monks shall sleep in separate beds. All shall receive bedding, allotted by the abbot, appropriate to their environment. If possible they should all sleep in one room. However, if there are too many for this, they will be grouped in tens or twenties, a senior in charge of each group. Let a candle burn throughout the night. They will sleep in their robes, belted but with no knives, thus preventing injury in slumber. The monks then will always be prepared to rise at the signal and hurry to the Divine Office. But they must make haste with gravity and modesty.

The younger brothers should not be next to each other. Rather their beds should be interspersed with those of their elders. When they arise for the Divine Office, they ought to encourage each other, for the sleepy make many excuses.

Chapter 31
The Cellarer

One of the monks should be chosen cellarer—a man who is wise, mature, sober, not gluttonous, not arrogant, not argumentative, not disrespectful, not procrastinating and not wasteful. He must fear God and be like a father to the whole community.

He will take care of everything, but will do all under the abbot's orders, making sure he does not offend any of the brothers. If a brother makes an unreasonable request, he must not reject it out of hand but humbly and reasonably turn it down.

He must look after his own soul, as the apostle says, "For he who discharges his service well shall win for himself a good place" (I Timothy 3:13). He

will care for the sick, children, the poor and guests knowing for certain that he will be held accountable on Judgment Day.

He will think of all the monastery's property as if they were consecrated chalices. He must never neglect any of his charges, nor be greedy, nor lavishly wasteful of the monastery's goods. He must do everything with restraint and as the abbot directs.

Above all, he must have humility. If he has nothing to give, his response (to the request) should be a good word, for, "A good word is better than the best gift" (Ecclesiastes 18:17). Let him have under his care all that is delegated to him by the abbot, but not what is another's province. He will provide the brothers with their food allowance, but without delay or arbitrariness, so they may not be scandalized. He must remember what he might deserve: "Who shall scandalize one of these little ones, it were better for him that a millstone be hanged about his neck, and that he should be drowned in the depth of the sea" (Matthew 18:6).

He should be given assistants if the monastery is large, so he may perform his duties without worry. Things should be both requested and distributed at convenient times so no one will be bothered or upset in God's house.

Chapter 39
Food Apportionment

We believe that two cooked dishes will satisfy the daily needs at each meal—at the sixth and ninth hours. If some brothers cannot eat one, then they may eat the other. Two dishes must be enough for all. A third dish may appear if fresh fruit or vegetables are available. Whether it be eaten at one meal or two (dinner and supper), a pound of bread will be allotted to each monk daily. If supper is to be served, the cellarer will reserve a third of the ration for that meal.

If the monks have worked harder than usual, the abbot shall decree, if he thinks it wise, an increase in the ration. But care must be taken against excessive eating so that no one is laid low by gastric upset. Nothing is more contrary to being a Christian than gluttony. "Take heed to yourselves, lest your hearts be overcharged with surfeiting" (Luke 21:34).

Young boys shall receive smaller portions than their elders—maintaining frugality in all. Except for the sick, no one is to eat the flesh of quadrupeds.

Chapter 55
Clothing and Shoes

Suitable clothing shall be given the monks, dependent on the climate. In cold regions more will be required than in warm. All this will be decided by the abbot. However, in temperate regions, we believe that each monk will make do with a cowl and tunic—heavy for winter, light (or worn) for summer. He should also have a shift for labor and shoes for the feet.

Monks should not complain of the color or texture of their clothing. It shall be whatever is available in the surrounding countryside or whatever is cheapest.

The abbot shall see to it so that the clothes are not too short but properly sized to the wearer. When new clothes are handed out, the monks shall turn in their old ones. These will be stored in the wardrobe for the poor. Each monk needs only two each of tunics and cowls, so he will be prepared for night wear and washing. Anything else is superfluous and should be banished. Shoes and other garments will also be returned when replaced. Those who must travel are to be given leggings. Afterwards these are to be washed and returned. On these trips they should have better quality cowls and tunics than usual; these are to be returned after use.

Bedding shall consist of a mattress, coverlet, blanket and pillow. The abbot will make frequent inspections of the bedding to prevent hoarding. Any infractions are subject to the severest discipline and, so that this vice of private ownership may be cut away at the roots, the abbot is to furnish all necessities: cowl, tunic, shoes, stockings, belt, knife, pen, needle, towel and writing tablet. With these, any excuse for need will be vanquished.

The abbot must always remember, "And distribution was made to everyone according to his need" (Acts 4:35). He should take into account the frailties of those in need and not the hostility of the envious. In everything he should think of the retribution of God.

Chapter 66
The Porter of the Monastery

A wise old monk should guard the gates of the monastery. He shall know how to receive and answer a question, and be old enough so he will not be able to wander far. His cell should be nearby; thus, all who arrive will find someone to give information.

When someone knocks, or a poor man calls, the porter shall answer, "Thanks be to God," or ask for a blessing. With all the courtesy of the fear of God, he should reply to a question humbly and with charity. If he needs help (in his duties) he should be given a younger assistant.

The monastery should be planned, if possible, with all the necessities—water, mill, garden, shops—within the walls. Thus the monks will not need to wander about outside, for this is not good for their

souls. We wish this Rule to be read frequently to the community so none may plead ignorance and make excuses.

Chapter 73
All Perfection Is Not Herein Attained

We have composed this Rule so that, through its observance in monasteries, we may know we have made some progress in pursuit of virtue and the commencement of a monastic life. For those who are hurrying to attain a truly holy life, there are the works of the Holy Fathers. The following of these will lead a man to heights of perfection. For what page or word of the Bible is not a perfect rule for temporal life? What book of the Fathers does not proclaim that by a straight path we shall find God? What else but examples of the virtue of good living, obedient monks are the *Collations, Institutions, Lives* of the Saints, of the Holy Fathers, and the Rule of Saint Basil? We who are slothful, bad living and careless should be ashamed. Whoever you are, if you wish to follow the path to God, make use of this little Rule for beginners. Thus at length you will come to the heights of doctrine and virtue under God's guidance. Amen! ◖

The Carolingian Monastery

In the period between Saint Benedict and Charlemagne the Benedictine monastery underwent a complex evolution. Originally the monasteries were made up of small communities with fewer than fifteen members who led a life of prayer and work in a rather simple setting. With the decline of city life and the disorders brought on by the repeated invasions of the barbarians after the 5th century, the monastery became increasingly a center of life for rural populations. Monasteries not only kept learning alive and worship intact but were also called on to become a shelter for the traveler, a rudimentary hospital for the sick, a place of refuge in time of invasion, a granary for the farmer, a center of law for both religious and civil courts, and a place that could provide agricultural services such as milling and brewing.

This expansion of services, making the monastery into what has been called a "miniature civic center," inevitably changed the physical character of the monastery compound itself. By Charlemagne's time the monastery was an intricate complex of buildings suitable for the many tasks it was called upon to perform. One vivid example of the complexity of the Carolingian monastery can be gained by a study of a plan for an ideal monastery developed about 820 at the Benedictine abbey of Saint Gall in present-day Switzerland [227].

In the Saint Gall plan the monastic church dominated the area. Set off with its two round towers, it was a basilica-style church with numerous entrances for the use of the monks. To the south of the church was a rectangular garden space surrounded by a covered walkway (the *cloister*) from which radiated the monk's dormitory, dining hall *(refectory),* and kitchens. To the north of the church were a copying room *(scriptorium),* a separate house for the abbot, a school for youths and young novices, and a guest house. To the extreme south of the church were ranged workshops, barns, and other utilitarian outbuildings. To the east beyond the church were an infirmary and separate house for aspirant monks (the *novitiate*), gardens, poultry houses, and the community cemetery.

Romanesque Style

The plan of Saint Gall was never realized in stone, but the Benedictines did participate in ambitious architectural works after the Carolingian period. In the 11th century, after a long period of desolation and warfare, Europe began to stir with new life. Pilgrimages became very popular as travel became safe. Pilgrimage routes—in particular to sites in Spain, England, and Italy—crisscrossed Europe. Crusades were mounted to free the holy places of the Middle East

227 Plan for an ideal monastery. c. 820. Reconstruction interpretation developed by Walter Horn and Ernest Born from the manuscript in the library of the former monastery of Saint Gall. The original plan, 3′8″ (112 cm) across, was drawn to scale on vellum. It shows a monastery on a site 480 × 640′ (146 × 195 m), which was to house some 120 monks and 170 serfs. The plan was intended to be a guide for future monasteries, and so it was for centuries, greatly influencing monastery design.

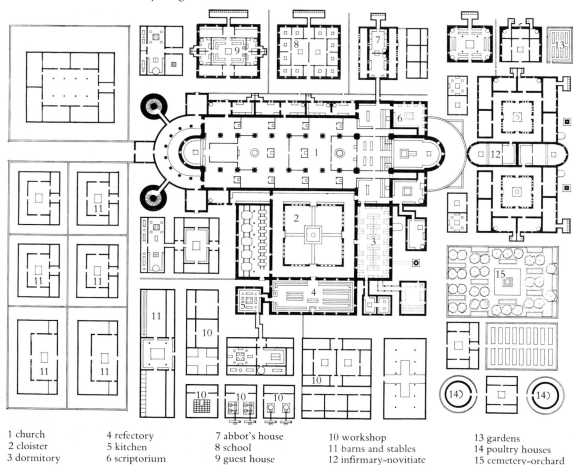

1 church	4 refectory	7 abbot's house	10 workshop	13 gardens
2 cloister	5 kitchen	8 school	11 barns and stables	14 poultry houses
3 dormitory	6 scriptorium	9 guest house	12 infirmary-novitiate	15 cemetery-orchard

from the Moslems so that pilgrims could journey in peace to the most desired goal of the pilgrim: Jerusalem. In this period monks built and maintained pilgrimage churches and hostels on the major routes of the pilgrims.

The building style of this period (roughly from 1000 to 1200) is called Romanesque because the architecture was larger and more "Roman"-looking than the work done in the earlier medieval centuries. The two most striking characteristics of this architecture were the use of heavy stone arches and generous exterior decoration, mainly sculpture. The Romanesque style had two obvious advantages. One was that the use of heavy stone and masonry walls permitted larger and more spacious interiors. Secondly, the heavy walls could support stone arches (mainly the Roman barrel arch, at least in France and Spain [See figure 152, page 231]), which in turn permitted fireproof stone and masonry roofs. Long experience had shown that basilica-style churches, with their wooden trusses and wooden roofs, were notoriously susceptible to destruction by fire.

Romanesque architecture sprouted all over Europe, and while it showed great regional variation its main lines are clear enough. The Benedictine pilgrimage church of Saint Sernin in Toulouse was designed to accommodate the large number of pilgrims as they made their way to the famous shrine of Santiago de Compostela in Spain. A glimpse at the floor plan [228] and the interior [229] shows clearly

228 Floor plan of the church of Saint Sernin, Toulouse. Notice the ample aisles for easy passage of groups of pilgrims around the entire church. The radiating chapels around the ambulatory permitted many services to be held simultaneously.

229 Interior of the church of Saint Sernin, Toulouse. c. 1080–1120. The massive vaulting of the roof of the nave is called barrel vaulting or tunnel vaulting for obvious reasons. Its heavy stonework required thick supporting walls. The galleries with their own vaults helped support these cut-stone vaults over the nave.

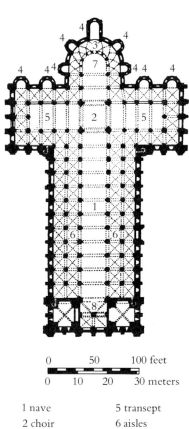

0   50   100 feet

0   10   20   30 meters

1 nave   5 transept
2 choir   6 aisles
3 ambulatory   7 apse
4 chapels   8 narthex

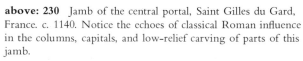

above: 230 Jamb of the central portal, Saint Gilles du Gard, France. c. 1140. Notice the echoes of classical Roman influence in the columns, capitals, and low-relief carving of parts of this jamb.

above right: 231 *Demon of Luxury,* nave capital sculpture, abbey church of La Madeleine, Vézelay. c. 1130. This figure is not untypical of the extravagant imagination reflected in Romanesque sculpture.

right: 232 The prophet Jeremiah, trumeau of south portal, Saint Pierre, Moissac. Early 12th century. Notice the sinuous curve of his figure as the prophet inclines toward the church while he holds his prophetic scroll. The lions reflect the influence of the Islamic art of southern Spain.

that the generous interior space was articulated in such a manner that large numbers of persons besides the monastic community could move freely through the building. For example, the floor plan allows for an aisle parallel to the nave to go completely around the church. In that fashion the monastic choir, which extended out into the nave, was circumvented by the faithful—who could make a complete circle of the church without disturbing the monks.

Exterior church decoration was almost unknown in the Carolingian period, but during the Romanesque period there was a veritable explosion of exterior sculpture. The lack of interior light (precluded by the thick solid walls needed for the roof vaulting) drove the artist outside, in a sense. A favorite area of

233 Pentecost scene, tympanum, abbey church of La Madeleine, Vézelay. c. 1120–1132.

decoration was the *portal* or doorway, since the crowds would pass through the doors to enter the church and receive edifying instruction in the process. The artist might decorate a door jamb [230], a capital [231], or the central supporting post of a portal, the *trumeau* [232].

The fullest iconographic program of the Romanesque sculptor can usually be found in the *tympanum* of the portal; Romanesque churches in France offer many splendid examples of this elaborated art. The sculptural program over the inner west door of the Benedictine abbey church of Sainte Madeleine at Vézelay is representative of the elaborated art in stone [233].

The Vézelay tympanum depicts Christ, ascending into heaven, giving his church the mission to preach the gospel to the entire world. Christ, in the center almond-shape *mandorla,* sends the power of the Holy Spirit into the apostles who cluster on either side and just below with copies of the gospel in their hands. Below the apostles the lintel stone depicts the peoples of the world, including fanciful races known to the sculptor only through the legendary travel books and encyclopedias that circulated in Europe. The theme of the exotic peoples to be healed by the gospel is repeated in the eight arching compartments above the central scene, which depict strange peoples, lepers, cripples, and others who need to hear the gos-

pel. The outer *archivolts* depict the signs of the Zodiac and the symbolic seasons of the year, a reminder that the gospel depicted in the central scene is to be preached "in season and out"; these symbolic medallions are interspersed with mythical and fantastic beasts. The outer archivolts are purely decorative, derived perhaps from Islamic sources known to the artists through the Moslem architecture of Spain.

Romanesque was a European phenomenon—its variant forms in Italy, Germany, and England give ample testimony—and a summing-up of much of European culture between the end of the Carolingian period and the rise of city life and the Gothic style in the late 12th century. The roots of the Romanesque were in the Benedictine tradition of service, scholarship, and solidity. Churches like Vézelay also manifest the period's concern with travel, expansion, and the attendant knowledge that comes from such mobility. When reaction came against the more extravagant forms of Romanesque decoration it came from Bernard of Clairvaux (1090–1153), who was primarily a monastic reformer. Bernard was horrified by the fantastic nature of Romanesque sculpture since he felt so many "and so marvelous are the varieties of diverse shapes that we are more tempted to read in the marbles than in the Book and to spend our whole day wondering at these things rather than meditating on the Law of God." Even Bernard's strictures testify to the close relationship between the Benedictines and the Romanesque (especially the French Romanesque), which is another reason the period after Charlemagne and before the primacy of the city can be called simply the Benedictine age.

Monasticism and Gregorian Chant

The main occupation of the monk was the *Opus Dei* (work of God)—the liturgical common prayer of the monasteric *horarium*; life centered around the monastic church where the monks gathered seven times a day for prayer. The centrality of the liturgy also explains why copying, correcting, and illuminating manuscripts was such an important part of monastic life. Texts were needed for religious services as well as for spiritual reading. The monks were encouraged to study the scriptures as a lifelong occupation. For the monk this work was *lectio divina* (divine reading) and was central to the development of himself as a monk. This monastic imperative encouraged the study of the Bible and such ancillary disciplines (grammar, criticism, and the like) as necessary for the study of Scripture. From the 7th century on, monastic scriptoria were busily engaged in copying a wealth of material, both sacred and profane.

The monasteries were also centers for the development of sacred music. We have already seen that Charlemagne was interested in church music. His biographer Einhard tells us that the emperor "made careful reforms in the way in which the psalms were chanted and the lessons read. He was himself an expert at both of these exercises but he never read the lesson in public and he would sing only with the rest of the congregation and then in a low voice." Charlemagne's keen interest in music explains why certain monasteries of his reign—notably those at Metz and Trier—became centers for church music.

Charlemagne brought monks from Rome to stabilize and reform church music in his kingdom as part of his overall plan of liturgical renovation. In the earlier period of Christianity's growth quite diverse traditions of ecclesiastical music developed in various parts of the West. Roman music represented one tradition—later called *Gregorian* chant after Pope Gregory the Great (540–604) who was erroneously believed to have codified the music in the late 6th century. Milan had its own musical tradition, known as *Ambrosian* music—in honor of Saint Ambrose, who had been a noted hymn writer, as Saint Augus-

tine attests in the *Confessions*. There was a peculiar regional style of music in Spain known as *Mozarabic* chant, while the Franks also had their own peculiar style of chant. All of these styles derive from earlier models of music which have their roots in Hebrew, Greco-Roman, and Byzantine styles. Lack of adequate documentation now permits only an educated reconstruction of this early music and its original development.

Gregorian chant as we know it today was not codified until the 11th and 12th centuries, so it is rather difficult to reconstruct precisely the music of Charlemagne's court. It was probably a mixture of Roman and Frankish styles of singing. It was *monophonic*—that is, one or many voices sang a single melodic line—and more often than not lacked musical accompaniment in the monastic churches. Most scholars believe that the majority of the music consisted of simple chants for the recitation of the psalms at the Divine Office; more elaborate forms were used for the hymns of the Office and the Mass chants. The music was simply called *cantus planus,* plainsong or plain chant.

In its more elementary form the chant consisted of a single note for each syllable of a word. The basic symbols used to notate Gregorian chant were called *neums.* Using the Gregorian notational system with its four-line staff and the opening line of Psalm 109, *Dixit Dominus Domino Meo, sede a dextris meis* (The Lord said to my Lord: sit on my right hand), a line of syllabic chant would look like this:

1. Di-xit Dóminus Dómino mé- o : * Séde a déxtris mé- is.

Even in the earliest form of chants, the final word of a phrase was emphasized by the addition of one or two extra notes, as above. Later, more notes were added to the final words or syllables for elaboration and variation. For example, see the nine treatments of the word *meis* in the elaborated version below of the chant shown above.

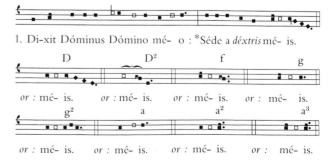

1. Di-xit Dóminus Dómino mé- o : *Séde a *déxtris* mé- is.

The simplicity of syllabic chant should not be regarded as useful only for the monotonous chanting of psalm verses. Very simple yet hauntingly melodic Gregorian compositions still exist that do not use elaborate cadences while relying on simple syllabic notes. A fine example is the Gregorian melody for the Lord's Prayer, reproduced here in modern notation. No rests are indicated in the musical text; the singer should simply breathe on a skipped note (it is presumed that not all would skip the same note) so that the music flows without pause. Ordinarily, these chants would be sung *a capella* (without musical accompaniment).

Gregorian Chant

Our Fa-ther, who art in heav-en, hal-lowed be thy name; thy king-dom come; thy will be done on earth as it is in heav-en. Give us this day our dai-ly bread; and for-give us our tres-pass-es as we for-give those who tres-pass a-gainst us; and lead us not in-to temp-ta-tion, but de-liv-er us from e-vil.

Certain phrases, especially words of acclamation (like *Alleluia*) or the word at the end of a line, were elaborated beyond the few notes provided in syllabic chant. This extensive elaboration of a final syllable (or any syllable) by a chain of intricate notes was called a *melisma*. An example of melismatic chant may be noted in the elaboration of the final *ia* of the Easter *Alleluia* sung at the Easter Mass:

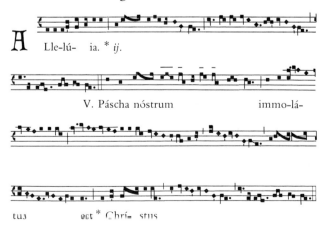

A Lle-lú- ia. * ij.

V. Páscha nóstrum immo-lá-

tus oct * Chrí- stus

Liturgical Music and the Rise of Drama

The Liturgical Trope

One development connected with melismatic chant which evolved in the Carolingian period was the *trope*. Since books were scarce, monks memorized a great deal of liturgical chant. As an aid to memorization and, also, to provide some variety in the chant, words would be added to the long melismas. These words, tropes, would be verbal elaborations of the content of the text. Thus, for example, if there was a melismatic *Kyrie Eleison* (the Greek "Lord, have mercy on us" retained in the Latin Mass) with an elaboration of notes for the syllable *rie* of *Kyrie,* it became customary to add words such as *sanctus* (holy), *dominus* (lord), and the like, which were sung to the tune of the melisma. The use of tropes grew rapidly and became standard in liturgical music until they were removed from the liturgy at the time of the Counter-Reformation in the 16th century.

Scholars have pointed to the interpolation of tropes into liturgical music as the origin of drama in the Western world. There had been drama in the classical and Byzantine worlds, of course, but drama in Europe developed from the liturgy of the medieval church after it largely had been lost (or suppressed) in the very early Middle Ages.

A 9th-century manuscript (preserved at the monastery of Saint Gall) preserves an early trope that was added to the music of the Easter entrance hymn (the *Introit*) for Mass. It is in the form of a short dialogue and seems to have been sung by either two different singers or two choirs. It is called the *Quem Quæritis* trope from its opening lines:

THE *QUEM-QUÆRITIS* TROPE

De Resurrectione Domini	Of the Lord's Resurrection
Int[errogatio]: *Quem quæritis in sepulchro, [o] Christicolæ?*	Question [of the angels]: *Whom seek ye in the sepulchre, O followers of Christ?*
R[esponsio]: *Jesum Nazarenum crucifixum, o cælicolæ.*	Answer [of the Marys]: *Jesus of Nazareth, which was crucified, O celestial ones.*
[Angeli:] *Non est hic; surrexit, sicut prædixerat.*	[The angels:] *He is not here; he is risen, just as he foretold.*

Ite, nuntiate quia	*Go, announce that he*
surrexit de	*is risen from the*
sepulchro.	*sepulchre.*

Very shortly after the introduction of this trope into the Easter Mass the short interrogation began to be acted out, not at Mass but at the end of *Matins*, the night office of Easter. The dialogue was not greatly enlarged but the directions for its singing were elaborated into a short play. The following is from a manuscript for services held at a monastery at Tours:

SEMI-DRAMATIC TROPE
[Easter]

After this [the third responsory] let two boys, in albs [vestments], one at the right of the altar, the other at the left, sing:

Whom seek ye in the sepulchre, O followers of Christ?

Let three chaplains, garbed in white dalmatics [outer vestments], with covered heads, standing before the altar, reply:

Jesus of Nazareth, which was crucified, O celestial ones.

Then the boys:

He is not here; he is risen, just as he foretold.
Go, announce that he is risen from the dead.

Then those three, approaching the altar and looking within, turning towards the choir, say in a loud voice:

Alleluia, the Lord is risen!

After this the cantor begins:

We praise thee, O God.

By the 11th and 12th centuries the dialogue was elaborated beyond the words of scripture and more personages were added. By the 12th century the stories became more elaborate; this text is set around two fictional characters, the *peregrini* or pilgrims, who witness the Gospel events:

PEREGRINI
[Monday of Passion Week]

Observe, son: The office of the Wayfarers [to Emmaus] should at this point be performed in the following manner.

Let two of the lower row, whose names may be written on the bulletin-board at the pleasure of the scribe, clothed in tunics and copes, go across, carrying staffs and wallets in the likeness of travelers; and let them have caps upon their heads and be bearded. Let them advance from the vestry singing the hymn:

Jesus, our Redeemer,
Love and Ardent Desire,
God, Creator of all things,
Man in these final times,

What mercy has o'erwhelmed thee
That thou shouldst bear our sins,
Enduring a cruel death
In order to free us from death,

Entering the gates of Hell,
Releasing thy captives,
Conqueror in a glorious triumph,
Sitting at the right hand of the Father!

Let sheer compassion impel thee
To overcome our wrong-doing
With forbearance, and to satisfy us,
Our desire thereby fulfilled, with thy countenance.

Be thou our joy,
Who wilt be our reward!
In thee be our glory
Through all ages, forever!

coming at a slow pace, through the right aisle of the church, as far as the western doors, and taking their stand at the head of the procession. And when they shall have sung the [above-quoted] hymn to the line "Our desire thereby fulfilled, with thy countenance," then let a priest from the upper row, whose name has been written on the bulletin-board, clothed in an alb and an amice, barefooted, bearing the cross upon his right shoulder, with a downcast countenance, come up to them through the right aisle of the church, and let him suddenly stand with them and say:

What manner of communications are these that ye have one to another as ye walk and are sad?

Let the wayfarers, as if in wonder, and gazing at him, say:

Art thou only a stranger in Jerusalem, and hast not known the things which are come to pass there in these days?

Let the priest inquire:

What things?

Let the wayfarers reply:

Concerning Jesus of Nazareth, which was a prophet, mighty in deed before God and all the people, how the chief priests and our rulers delivered him up to be condemned to death, and have crucified him, and beside all this, to-day is the third day since these things were done.

Let the priest, looking fixedly at both, say:

O fools! and slow of heart to believe all that the prophets have spoken! Ought not Christ to have suffered these things, and to enter into his glory?

With these words, immediately let the priest walk away, making as though he would go further, and let the wayfarers, hastening, following after him, detain him as if inviting and urging him to be their guest, pointing to the village with their staffs, and saying:

Abide with us, for it is toward evening, and the day is now far spent. The sun declining towards the west urges that thou accept our hospitality; for we are pleased with what thou sayest to us concerning the resurrection of our Master.

And thus singing, let them lead him to the structure in the middle of the nave of the church, prepared in the likeness of the village of Emmaus. When they have ascended into it, and are seated at the table ready there, and the Lord, sitting between them, has broken bread unto them, and has been recognized by them through his breaking of the bread, then let him suddenly vanish out of their sight. Moreover, let them, rising up as if dumfounded, with faces turned towards each other, mournfully sing:

Alleluia!

with the verse:

Was not our heart burning within us while he was talking by the way, and while he opened to us the scriptures! Alas! wretched we! where were our senses when we did not comprehend!

Having repeated this, let them turn themselves toward the pulpit and sing this verse:

Tell us, Mary,
What hast thou seen on the way?

Then let one from the upper row, clothed in a dalmatic and an amice, his head bound about after the fashion of a woman, answer:

The sepulchre of the living Christ,
And the glory of the Resurrected One, saw!
Angelic witnesses,
The sudarium and the vestments!

Then let him hold up to view and unfold a muslin cloth from one side, to represent the sudarium [burial cloth], and another muslin cloth from the other side, to represent the vestments; and let him cast them before the main entrance to the choir. Then let him say:

Christ is risen, my hope!
He goes before his disciples into Galilee!

Then let the choir sing the remaining two verses, which follow:

It is better to believe a single truthful Mary
Then all the lying host of the Jews!

We know that Christ is risen
From the dead in very truth!
Do thou, O Victor King, have mercy on us!

And, in the meanwhile, let Mary and the Wayfarers withdraw.

It was but a step to remove these plays from the church proper and begin to perform them out-of-doors. By the 14th century there were sizable cycles of these plays performed at various times of the year, some of which told most of the major stories of the Bible from Adam to the Last Judgment. The repertory also began to expand to show lives of the saints and allegorical plays such as *Everyman* to illustrate the struggle of virtue and vice.

The Morality Play: *Everyman*

Everyman is a 15th-century play that may well be a translation from an earlier Dutch play. The subject is no longer a redoing of a biblical theme. Now we have rather personified abstractions representing a theme dear to the medieval heart: the *psychomachia*— the struggle for the soul. The unprepared reader of *Everyman* will note the heavy-handed allegorizing and moralizing (complete with a "Doctor" who makes a final appearance to point up the moral of the play) with some sense of estrangement, but the more astute student will also note the stark dignity of the play, the earnestness with which it is constructed, and the economy of its structure. Written in rather spare rhyming couplets, *Everyman* is a good example of the transitional play which forms a link between the earlier liturgical drama and the more secular drama which was to come at the end of the English medieval period.

The plot of *Everyman* is simplicity itself; it is quickly summarized by the messenger who opens the play. Everyman must face God in final judgment after death. None of the aids and friends of this life will support Everyman, as the speeches of the allegorical figures of Fellowship and others make clear. The strengths for Everyman come from the aiding virtues of Confession, Good Deeds, and Knowledge. The story, however, is not the central core of this play; the themes that run through the entire play are what should engage our attention. First is the common medieval notion of life itself as a pilgrimage, a notion that comes up again and again. It is embedded not only in the medieval penchant for pilgrimage but the use of that term (as one sees, for example, in Chaucer) as a metaphor. Second, the notion of the inevitability of death as the defining action of human life is omnipresent in medieval culture. *Everyman* has an extremely intense *memento mori* ("Keep death before your eyes!") motif. Finally, medieval theology puts great emphasis on the will of the human being in the attainment of salvation. It is not faith (this virtue is presumed) that will save Everyman; his or her willingness to learn (Knowledge), act (Good Deeds), and convert (Confession) will make the difference between salvation and damnation.

The Messenger says that *Everyman* is "By figure a moral play." It is meant not merely to instruct on the content of religion (as does a mystery play) but to instruct for the purposes of moral conversion. The earlier mystery plays usually point out a moral at the end of the performance. The morality uses its resources to moralize throughout the play.

The one lingering element from the liturgy one still sees in a play like *Everyman* is its pageant quality: the dramatic force of the presentation is enhanced by the solemn wearing of gowns, the stately pace of the speeches, and the seriousness of the message. The play depends less on props and place. Morality plays did not evolve directly out of liturgical drama (they may owe something to the study of earlier plays based on the classics studied in schools) but the liturgical overtones are not totally absent.

EVERYMAN

HERE BEGINNETH A TREATISE HOW THE HIGH FATHER OF HEAVEN SENDETH DEATH TO SUMMON EVERY CREATURE TO COME AND GIVE ACCOUNT OF THEIR LIVES IN THIS WORLD, AND IS IN MANNER OF A MORAL PLAY.

MESSENGER   I pray you all give your
    audience,
  And hear this matter with reverence,

234 Everyman, with Death at his shoulder, is tempted by the allegorical figure of Beauty. *Everyman,* Salzburg Festival, Austria, 1980.

By figure° a moral play: *in form*
The *Summoning of Everyman* called it is,
That of our lives and ending shows   5
How transitory we be all day.°   *always*
This matter is wondrous precious,
But the intent of it is more gracious,
And sweet to bear away.
The story saith: Man, in the beginning   10
Look well, and take good heed to the
    ending,
Be you never so gay!
Ye think sin in the beginning full sweet,
Which in the end causeth the soul to
    weep,
When the body lieth in clay.   20
Here shall you see how Fellowship and
    Jollity,
Both Strength, Pleasure, and Beauty,
Will fade from thee as flower in May;
For ye shall hear how our Heaven King
Calleth Everyman to a general
    reckoning: 20
Give audience, and hear what he doth
    say.   [*Exit*]

[GOD *speaketh*]

GOD   I perceive, here in my majesty,
    How that all creatures be to me
        unkind,°   *ungrateful*
    Living without dread in worldly
        prosperity:
    Of ghostly sight the people be so blind,   25
    Drowned in sin, they know me not for
        their God;
    In worldly riches is all their mind,
    They fear not my righteousness, the sharp
        rod.
    My law that I showed, when I for them died,
    They forget clean, and shedding of my
        blood red;   30
    I hanged between two, it cannot be
        denied;
    To get them life I suffered to be dead;
    I healed their feet, with thorns hurt was
        my head.
    I could do no more than I did, truly;
    And now I see the people do clean
        forsake me: 35
    They use the seven deadly sins damnable,
    As pride, covetise, wrath, and
        lechery°   *covetousness*

8 But the purpose of it is more devout.
25 In spiritual vision.
32 I consented to die.

Now in the world be made commendable;
And thus they leave of angels the heavenly
    company.
Every man liveth so after his own pleasure,   40
And yet of their life they be nothing sure:
I see the more that I them forbear
The worse they be from year to year.
All that liveth appaireth° fast;   *degenerates*
Therefore I will, in all the haste,   45
Have a reckoning of every man's person;
For, and° I leave the people thus alone   *if*
In their life and wicked tempests,°   *tumults*
Verily they will become much worse than
    beasts;
For now one would by envy
    another up eat;   50
Charity they do all clean forget.
I hoped well that every man
In my glory should make his mansion,
And thereto I had them all elect;
But now I see, like traitors deject,°   *abject*
They thank me not for the pleasure
    that I to° them meant   *for*
Nor yet for their being that I them have
    lent.
I proffered the people great multitude of
    mercy,
And few there be that asketh
    it heartily.°   *earnestly*
They be so cumbered with worldly riches   60
That needs on them I must do justice,
On every man living without fear.
Where art thou, Death, thou mighty
    messenger?

[*Enter* DEATH]

DEATH   Almighty God, I am here at your
    will,
    Your commandment to fulfil.   65
GOD   Go thou to Everyman,
    And show him, in my name,
    A pilgrimage he must on him take,
    Which he in no wise may escape;
    And that he bring with him
        a sure reckoning   70
    Without delay or any tarrying.   [GOD
        withdraws]
DEATH   Lord, I will in the world
        go run overall,°   *everywhere*
    And cruelly outsearch both great and
        small;
    Every man will I beset that liveth beastly
    Out of God's laws, and dreadeth not folly.   75

41 And yet their lives are by no means secure.

He that loveth riches I will strike with my
    dart,
His sight to blind, and from heaven
    to depart°—   *separate*
Except that alms be his good friend—
In hell for to dwell, world without end.
Lo, yonder I see Everyman walking.   80
Full little he thinketh on my coming;
His mind is on fleshly lusts and his
    treasure,
And great pain it shall cause him to
    endure
Before the Lord, Heaven King.

             [*Enter* EVERYMAN]

Everyman, stand still!
    Whither art thou going   85
Thus gaily? Hast thou thy Maker forget?
EVERYMAN   Why askest thou?
    Wouldest thou wit?°   *know*
DEATH   Yea, sir; I will show you:
    In great haste I am sent to thee   90
    From God out of his majesty.
EVERYMAN   What, sent to me?
DEATH   Yea, certainly.
    Though thou have forget him here,
    He thinketh on thee
        in the heavenly sphere,   95
    As, ere we depart, thou shalt know.
EVERYMAN   What desireth God of me?
DEATH   That shall I show thee:
    A reckoning he will needs have
    Without any longer respite.   100
EVERYMAN   To give a reckoning longer
    leisure I crave;
    This blind° matter troubleth my wit.   *obscure*
DEATH   On thee thou must take a long
    journey;
    Therefore thy book of count°
        with thee thou bring,   *account*
    For turn again° thou cannot by   *return*
    no way.
    And look thou be sure of thy reckoning,
    For before God thou shalt answer, and
    show
    Thy many bad deeds, and good but a few;
    How thou hast spent thy life, and in what
    wise,
    Before the chief Lord of paradise.   110
    Have ado that we were in that way,
    For, wit thou well, thou shalt make none
    attorney.

111 i.e., let's see about making that journey.
112 No one [your] advocate.

EVERYMAN   Full unready I am such reckoning
    to give.
    I know thee not. What messenger art
    thou?
DEATH   I am Death,
    that no man dreadeth,   115
    For every man I rest,°   *arrest*
    and no man spareth;
    For it is God's commandment
    That all to me should be obedient.
EVERYMAN   O Death, thou comest when I
    had thee least in mind!
    In thy power it lieth me to save;   120
    Yet of my good° will I give thee,   *goods*
    if thou will be kind:
    Yea, a thousand pound shalt thou have,
    And defer this matter till another day.
DEATH   Everyman, it may not be, by no
    way.
    I set not by° gold, silver, nor   *care not for*
    riches,
    Ne by pope, emperor, king, duke, ne
    princes;
    For, and° I would receive gifts great,   *if*
    All the world I might get;
    But my custom is clean contrary.
    I give thee no respite.
        Come hence, and not tarry.   130
EVERYMAN   Alas, shall I have no longer
    respite?
    I may say Death giveth no warning!
    To think on thee, it maketh my heart sick,
    For all unready is my book of reckoning.
    But twelve year and I might have abiding,   135
    My counting-book I would make so clear
    That my reckoning I should not need to fear.
    Wherefore, Death, I pray thee, for God's
    mercy,
    Spare me till I be provided of remedy.
DEATH   Thee availeth not to
    cry, weep, and pray;   140
    But haste thee lightly that thou were gone
    that journey,
    And prove thy friends if thou can;
    For, wit thou well,
        the tide° abideth no man,   *time*
    And in the world each living creature
    For Adam's sin must die of nature.   145
EVERYMAN   Death, if I should this pilgrimage
    take,

115 Who fears no man.
122 If you defer.
135 If I could stay for just twelve more years.
141 But set off quickly on your journey.
145 In the course of nature.

And my reckoning surely make,
Show me, for saint charity,
Should I not come again shortly?
DEATH   No, Everyman;
    and thou be once there,   150
Thou mayst never more come here,
Trust me verily.
EVERYMAN   O gracious God in the high seat
    celestial,
Have mercy on me in this most need!
Shall I have no company
    from this vale terrestrial   155
Of mine acquaintance, that way me to
    lead?
DEATH   Yea, if any be so hardy
That would go with thee and bear thee
    company.
Hie thee that thou were gone to God's
    magnificence,
Thy reckoning to give before his
    presence.   160
What, weenest° thou thy life   *suppose*
    is given thee,
And thy worldly goods also?
EVERYMAN   I had wend° so, verily.   *supposed*
DEATH   Nay, nay; it was but lent thee;
For as soon as thou art go,°   *gone*
Another a while shall have it,
    and then go therefro,°   *from it*
Even as thou hast done.
Everyman, thou art mad! Thou hast thy
    wits five,
And here on earth will not amend thy life;
For suddenly I do come.   170
EVERYMAN   O wretched caitiff, whither shall
    I flee,
That I might scape this endless sorrow?
Now, gentle Death, spare me till to-
    morrow,
That I may amend me
With good advisement.°   *reflection*
DEATH   Nay, thereto I will not consent,
Nor no man will I respite;
But to the heart suddenly I shall smite
Without any advisement.
And now out of thy sight I will me hie;   180
See thou make thee ready shortly,
For thou mayst say this is the day
That no man living may scape
    away.   [*Exit* DEATH]
EVERYMAN   Alas, I may well weep with sighs
    deep!

Now have I no manner of company   185
To help me in my journey,
    and me to keep;°   *guard*
And also my writing is full unready.
How shall I do now for to excuse me?
I would to God I had never
    be get!°   *been born*
To my soul a full great profit it had be;   190
For now I fear pains huge and great.
The time passeth. Lord, help, that all
    wrought!
For though I mourn it availeth nought.
The day passeth, and is almost ago;°   *gone*
I wot not well what for to do.   195
To whom were I best my complaint to
    make?
What and° I to Fellowship thereof spake,   *if*
And showed him of this sudden chance?
For in him is all mine affiance;°   *trust*
We have in the world so many a day   200
Be good friends in sport and play.
I see him yonder, certainly.
I trust that he will bear me company;
Therefore to him will I speak to ease my
    sorrow.
Well met, good Fellowship,
    and good morrow!   205

[FELLOWSHIP *speaketh*]

FELLOWSHIP   Everyman, good morrow, by
    this day!
Sir, why lookest thou so piteously?
If any thing be amiss, I pray thee me say,
That I may help to remedy.
EVERYMAN   Yea, good Fellowship, yea;   210
I am in great jeopardy.
FELLOWSHIP   My true friend, show to me
    your mind;
I will not forsake thee to my life's end,
In the way of good company.
EVERYMAN   That was well spoken,
    and lovingly.   215
FELLOWSHIP   Sir, I must needs know
    your heaviness;°   *sorrow*
I have pity to see you in any distress.
If any have you wronged, ye shall
    revenged be,
Though I on the ground be slain for
    thee—
Though that I know
    before that I should die.   220
EVERYMAN   Verily, Fellowship, gramercy.

---

148 In the name of holy charity.
150 Hurry up and go

187 *writing,* i.e., the writing of Everyman's accounts.
206 *by this day,* an asseveration.

FELLOWSHIP   Tush! by thy thanks I set not a
        straw.
    Show me your grief, and say no more.
EVERYMAN   If I my heart should to
        you break,°   *open*
    And then you to turn
        your mind from me,   225
    And would not me comfort when ye hear
        me speak,
    Then should I ten times sorrier be.
FELLOWSHIP   Sir, I say as I will do indeed.
EVERYMAN   Then be you a good friend at
        need:
    I have found you true herebefore.   230
FELLOWSHIP   And so ye shall evermore;
    For, in faith, and thou go to hell,
    I will not forsake thee by the way.
EVERYMAN   Ye speak like a good friend; I
        believe you well.
    I shall deserve° it, and I may.   *repay*
FELLOWSHIP   I speak of no deserving, by this
        day!
    For he that will say, and nothing do,
    Is not worthy with good company to go;
    Therefore show me the grief of your
        mind,
    As to your friend most loving and kind.   240
EVERYMAN   I shall show you how it is:
    Commanded I am to go a journey,
    A long way, hard and dangerous,
    And give a strait count,°   *strict account*
        without delay,
    Before the high Judge, Adonai.   245
    Wherefore, I pray you, bear me company,
    As ye have promised, in this journey.
FELLOWSHIP   That is matter indeed. Promise is
        duty;
    But, and I should take such a voyage on
        me,
    I know it well, it should be to my pain;   250
    Also it maketh me afeard, certain.
    But let us take counsel here as well as we
        can,
    For your words would fear°   *frighten*
        a strong man.
EVERYMAN   Why, ye said if I had need
    Ye would me never forsake, quick ne dead,   255
    Though it were to hell, truly.
FELLOWSHIP   So I said, certainly,
    But such pleasures be set aside, the sooth
        to say;
    And also, if we took such a journey,
    When should we come again?   260

245 *Adonai,* a Hebrew name for God.
248 That is a good reason indeed [for asking me].

EVERYMAN   Nay, never again, till the day of
        doom.
FELLOWSHIP   In faith, then will not I come
        there!
    Who hath you these tidings brought?
EVERYMAN   Indeed, Death was with me here.
FELLOWSHIP   Now, by God   265
        that all hath bought,°   *redeemed*
    If Death were the messenger,
    For no man that is living to-day
    I will not go that loath° journey—   *loathsome*
    Not for the father that begat me!
EVERYMAN   Ye promised otherwise,
        pardie.°   *by God*
FELLOWSHIP   I wot well I said so, truly;
    And yet if thou wilt eat, and drink, and
        make good cheer,
    Or haunt to women the lusty company,
    I would not forsake you while the day is
        clear,
    Trust me verily.   275
EVERYMAN   Yea, thereto ye would be ready!
    To go to mirth, solace, and play,
    Your mind will sooner apply,°   *attend*
    Than to bear me company in my long
        journey.
FELLOWSHIP   Now, in good faith, I will not
        that way.   280
    But and thou will murder, or any man
        kill,
    In that I will help thee with a good will.
EVERYMAN   O, that is a simple advice indeed.
    Gentle fellow, help me in my necessity!
    We have loved long, and now I need;   285
    And now, gentle Fellowship, remember
        me.
FELLOWSHIP   Whether ye have loved me or
        no,
    By Saint John, I will not with thee go.
EVERYMAN   Yet, I pray thee, take the labour,
        and do so much for me
    To bring me forward,° for   *escort me*
        saint charity,
    And comfort me till I come without the
        town.
FELLOWSHIP   Nay, and thou would give me a
        new gown,
    I will not a foot with thee go;
    But, and thou had tarried, I would not
        have left thee so.
    And as now God speed thee in thy journey,   295
    For from thee I will depart as fast as I
        may.

273 Or frequent the pleasant company of women.
274 Until daybreak.

EVERYMAN   Whither away, Fellowship? Will thou forsake me?

FELLOWSHIP   Yea, by my fay°! To God I betake° thee.   *faith* / *commend*

EVERYMAN   Farewell, good Fellowship; for thee my heart is sore.
Adieu for ever! I shall see thee no more.   300

FELLOWSHIP   In faith, Everyman, farewell now at the ending;
For you I will remember that parting is mourning.

[*Exit* FELLOWSHIP]

EVERYMAN   Alack! shall we thus depart° indeed—   *part*
Ah, Lady, help!—without any more comfort?
Lo, Fellowship forsaketh me in my most need.   305
For help in this world whither shall I resort?
Fellowship herebefore with me would merry make,
And now little sorrow for me doth he take.
It is said, "In prosperity men friends may find,
Which in adversity be full unkind."   310
Now whither for succour shall I flee,
Sith° that Fellowship hath forsaken me?   *since*
To my kinsmen I will, truly,
Praying them to help me in my necessity;
I believe that they will do so,   315
For kind will creep where it may not go.
I will go say,°   *essay, try*
for yonder I see them.
Where be ye now, my friends and kinsmen?

[*Enter* KINDRED *and* COUSIN]

KINDRED   Here be we now at your commandment.
Cousin, I pray you show us your intent   320
In any wise, and do not spare.

COUSIN   Yea, Everyman, and to us declare
If ye be disposed to go anywhither;°   *anywhere*
For, wit you well, we will live and die together.

KINDRED   In wealth and woe   325
we will with you hold,°   *side*
For over his kin a man may be bold.

316 For kinship will creep where it cannot walk, i.e., blood is thicker than water.
321 Without fail, and do not hold back.
326 For a man may be sure of his kinsfolk.

EVERYMAN   Gramercy, my friends and kinsmen kind.
Now shall I show you the grief of my mind:
I was commanded by a messenger,
That is a high king's chief officer;   330
He bade me go a pilgrimage, to my pain,
And I know well I shall never come again;
Also I must give a reckoning strait,
For I have a great enemy that hath me in wait,
Which intendeth me for to hinder.   335

KINDRED   What account is that which ye must render?
That would I know.

EVERYMAN   Of all my works I must show
How I have lived and my days spent;
Also of ill deeds that I have used°   *practiced*
In my time, sith life was me lent;
And of all virtues that I have refused.
Therefore, I pray you, go thither with me
To help to make mine account, for saint charity.

COUSIN   What, to go thither?
Is that the matter?   345
Nay, Everyman, I had liefer fast bread and water
All this five year and more.

EVERYMAN   Alas, that ever I was bore!°   *born*
For now shall I never be merry,
If that you forsake me.   350

KINDRED   Ah, sir, what ye be a merry man!
Take good heart to you, and make no moan.
But one thing I warn you, by Saint Anne—
As for me, ye shall go alone.

EVERYMAN   My Cousin,
will you not with me go?   355

COUSIN   No, by our Lady! I have the cramp in my toe.
Trust not to me, for, so God me speed,
I will deceive you in your most need.

KINDRED   It availeth not us to tice.
Ye shall have my maid with all my heart;   360
She loveth to go to feasts, there to be nice,°   *wanton*
And to dance, and abroad to start:
I will give her leave to help you in that journey,

334 A great enemy (i.e. the devil) who has me under observation.
346 I had rather fast on bread and water.
351 What a merry man you are!
359 It is no use trying to entice us.
362 Go out and about.

If that you and she may agree.

EVERYMAN   Now show me the very   365
    effect° of your mind: *tenor*
Will you go with me, or abide behind?

KINDRED   Abide behind? Yea, that will I, and
    I may!
Therefore farewell till another
    day. [*Exit* KINDRED]

EVERYMAN   How should I be merry or glad?
For fair promises men to me make,   370
But when I have most need they me
    forsake.
I am deceived; that maketh me sad.

COUSIN   Cousin Everyman, farewell now,
For verily I will not go with you.
Also of mine own an unready reckoning   375
I have to account; therefore I make
    tarrying.
Now God keep thee, for now I
    go. [*Exit* COUSIN]

EVERYMAN   Ah, Jesus, is all come hereto?
Lo, fair words maketh fools fain;
They promise, and nothing will do,
    certain.   380
My kinsmen promised me faithfully
For to abide with me steadfastly,
And now fast away do they flee:
Even so Fellowship promised me.
What friend were best me of to provide? 385
I lose my time here longer to abide.
Yet in my mind a thing there is:
All my life I have loved riches;
If that my Good° now help me might,   *Goods*
He would make my heart full light.   390
I will speak to him in this distress—
Where art thou, my Goods and riches?

[GOODS *speaks from a corner*]

GOODS   Who calleth me? Everyman? What!
    hast thou haste?
I lie here in corners, trussed and piled so
    high,
And in chests I am locked so fast,   395
Also sacked in bags.   Thou mayst see
    with thine eye
I cannot stir; in packs low I lie.
What would you have? Lightly° mĕ   *quickly*
    say.

EVERYMAN   Come hither, Good, in all the
    haste thou may,
For of counsel I must desire thee.   400

GOODS   Sir, and ye in the world have sorrow
    or adversity,

385 To provide myself with.
400 For I must entreat your advice.

That can I help you to remedy shortly.

EVERYMAN   It is another disease°   *trouble*
    that grieveth me;
In this world it is not, I tell thee so.
I am sent for, another way to go,   405
To give a strait count general
Before the highest Jupiter of all;
And all my life I have had joy and
    pleasure in thee,
Therefore, I pray thee, go with me;
For, peradventure, thou mayst
    before God Almighty   410
My reckoning help to clean and purify;
For it is said ever among
That money maketh all right that is wrong.

GOODS   Nay, Everyman, I sing another song.
I follow no man in such voyages;   415
For, and I went with thee,
Thou shouldst fare much the worse for
    me;
For because on me thou did set thy mind,
Thy reckoning I have made blotted°   *obscure*
    and blind,
That thine account thou cannot make
    truly;   420
And that hast thou for the love of me.

EVERYMAN   That would grieve me full sore,
When I should come to that fearful
    answer.
Up, let us go thither together.

GOODS   Nay, not so! I am too brittle,
    I may not endure;   425
I will follow no man one foot, be ye sure.

EVERYMAN   Alas, I have thee loved, and had
    great pleasure
All my life-days on good and treasure.

GOODS   That is to thy damnation, without
    leasing,
For my love is contrary to the love
    everlasting;   430
But if thou had me loved moderately
    during,
As to the poor to give part of me,
Then shouldst thou not in this
    dolour° be,   *distress*
Nor in this great sorrow and care.

EVERYMAN   Lo, now was I deceived   435
    ere I was ware,°   *aware*
And all I may wite misspending of time.

412 For it is sometimes said.
429 Without a lie, i.e. truly.
431–432 But if you had loved me moderately during your lifetime, so as to give part of me to the poor.
436 And I may blame it all on the bad use I have made of my
time.

GOODS What, weenest thou that I am thine?

EVERYMAN I had wend° so.   *supposed*

GOODS Nay, Everyman, I say no.
As for a while I was lent thee;   440
A season thou hast had me in prosperity.
My condition° is man's soul to kill;   *nature*
If I save one, a thousand I do spill.°   *ruin*
Weenest thou that I will follow thee?
Nay, not from this world, verily.   445

EVERYMAN I had wend otherwise.

GOODS Therefore to thy soul Good is a
thief;
For when thou art dead, this is
my guise°—   *practice*
Another to deceive in this same wise
As I have done thee,   450
and all to his soul's reprief.°—   *shame*

EVERYMAN O false Good, cursed may
thou be,
Thou traitor to God, that hast deceived me
And caught me in thy snare!

GOODS Marry, thou brought thyself in care,
Whereof I am glad;   455
I must needs laugh, I cannot be sad.

EVERYMAN Ah, Good, thou hast had
long my heartly° love;   *heartfelt*
I gave thee that which should be the
Lord's above.
But wilt thou not go with me indeed?
I pray thee truth to say.   460

GOODS No, so God me speed!
Therefore farewell, and have good day.

[*Exit* GOODS]

EVERYMAN O, to whom shall I make my
moan
For to go with me in that heavy journey?
First Fellowship said he would   465
with me gone;°   *go*
His words were very pleasant and gay,
But afterward he left me alone.
Then spake I to my kinsmen, all in
despair,
And also they gave me words fair;
They lacked no fair speaking,   470
But all forsook me in the ending.
Then went I to my Goods, that I loved
best,
In hope to have comfort, but there had I
least;
For my Goods sharply did me tell
That he bringeth many into hell.   475
Then of myself I was ashamed,
And so I am worthy to be blamed;
Thus may I well myself hate.

Of whom shall I now counsel take?
I think that I shall never speed   480
Till that I go to my Good Deed.
But, alas, she is so weak
That she can neither go° nor speak;   *walk*
Yet will I venture° on her now.   *gamble*
My Good Deeds, where be you?   485

[GOOD DEEDS *speaks from the ground*]

GOOD DEEDS Here I lie, cold in the ground;
Thy sins hath me sore bound,
That I cannot stir.

EVERYMAN O Good Deeds, I stand in fear!
I must you pray of counsel,   490
For help now should come right well.

GOOD DEEDS Everyman, I have
understanding
That ye be summoned account to make
Before Messias, of Jerusalem King;
And you do by me, that journey   495
with you will I take.

EVERYMAN Therefore I come to you, my
moan to make;
I pray you that ye will go with me.

GOOD DEEDS I would full fain, but I cannot
stand, verily.

EVERYMAN Why, is there anything on
you fall°?   *befallen*

GOOD DEEDS Yea, sir, I may thank you
of° all;   *for*
If ye had perfectly cheered me,
Your book of count full ready had be.
Look, the books of your works and deeds
eke°!   *also*
Behold how they lie under the feet,
To your soul's heaviness.   505

EVERYMAN Our Lord Jesus help me!
For one letter here I cannot see.

GOOD DEEDS There is a blind reckoning in
time of distress.

EVERYMAN Good Deeds, I pray you help me
in this need,
Or else I am for ever damned indeed;   510
Therefore help me to make reckoning
Before the Redeemer of all thing,
That King is, and was, and ever shall.

GOOD DEEDS Everyman, I am sorry of your
fall,
And fain would I help you, and I were
able.   515

491 For help would now be very welcome.
495 If you do as I advise.
501 If you had encouraged me fully.
508 i.e., a sinful person in his hour of need finds that the account of his good deeds is dimly written and difficult to read.

EVERYMAN   Good Deeds, your counsel I pray
   you give me.
GOOD DEEDS   That shall I do verily;
   Though that on my feet I may not go,
   I have a sister that shall with you also,
   Called Knowledge, which shall with you
      abide,   520
   To help you to make that dreadful
      reckoning.

[*Enter* KNOWLEDGE]

KNOWLEDGE   Everyman, I will go with thee,
   and be thy guide,
   In thy most need to go by thy side.
EVERYMAN   In good condition I am now in
   every thing,
   And am wholly content with this good
      thing,
   Thanked be God my creator.
GOOD DEEDS   And when she hath brought
   you there
   Where thou shalt heal thee of thy
      smart,°   *pain*
   Then go you with your reckoning and
      your Good Deeds together,
   For to make you joyful at heart   530
   Before the blessed Trinity.
EVERYMAN   My Good Deeds, gramercy!
   I am well content, certainly,
   With your words sweet.
KNOWLEDGE   Now go we together lovingly   535
   To Confession, that cleansing river.
EVERYMAN   For joy I weep; I would we were
   there!
   But, I pray you, give me cognition°   *knowledge*
   Where dwelleth that holy man,
   Confession.
KNOWLEDGE   In the house of salvation: 540
   We shall find him in that place,
   That shall us comfort, by God's grace.

[KNOWLEDGE *takes* EVERYMAN *to* CONFESSION]

Lo, this is Confession.   Kneel down and
   ask mercy,
For he is in good conceit° with   *esteem*
   God Almighty.
EVERYMAN   O glorious fountain,
   that all uncleanness doth clarify,   545
   Wash from me the spots of vice unclean,
   That on me no sin may be seen.
   I come with Knowledge for my
   redemption,

Redempt with heart and full contrition;
For I am commanded a pilgrimage to take,   550
And great accounts before God to make.
Now I pray you, Shrift,° mother   *confession*
   of salvation,
Help my Good Deeds for my piteous
   exclamation.
CONFESSION   I know your sorrow well,
   Everyman.
   Because with Knowledge ye come to me,   555
   I will you comfort as well as I can,
   And a precious jewel I will give thee,
   Called penance, voider° of adversity;   *expeller*
   Therewith shall your body chastised be,
   With abstinence and perseverance   560
   in God's service.
   Here shall you receive that scourge of me,
   Which is penance strong that ye must
      endure,
   To remember thy Saviour was scourged
   for thee
   With sharp scourges, and suffered it
      patiently;
   So must thou, ere thou scape that   565
   painful pilgrimage.
   Knowledge, keep him in this voyage,
   And by that time Good Deeds will be
      with thee.
   But in any wise be siker° of mercy,   *sure*
   For your time draweth fast;
      and° ye will saved be,   *if*
   Ask God mercy, and he will grant truly.   570
   When with the scourge of penance
      man doth him° bind,   *himself*
   The oil of forgiveness then shall he find.
EVERYMAN   Thanked be God for his gracious
   work!
   For now I will my penance begin;
   This hath rejoiced and lighted° my   *lightened*
   heart,
   Though the knots be painful and hard
   within.
KNOWLEDGE   Everyman, look your penance
   that ye fulfil,
   What pain that ever it to you be;
   And Knowledge shall give you counsel at
   will
   How your account ye shall make clearly.   580
EVERYMAN   O eternal God, O heavenly
   figure,

549 Redeemed by heartfelt and full contrition.
553 In answer to my piteous cry.
569 Draws quickly to an end.
576 Though the knots [of the scourge] be painful and hard to
my body.

520 The meaning of Knowledge here is "acknowledgment or
recognition of sins."
540 i.e., in the church.

O way of righteousness, O goodly vision,
Which descended down in a virgin pure
Because he would every man redeem,
Which Adam forfeited by his disobedience: 585
O blessed Godhead,
    elect and high divine,   *divinity*
Forgive my grievous offence;
Here I cry thee mercy in this presence.
O ghostly treasure, O ransomer and
    redeemer,
Of all the world hope and conductor,   590
Mirror of joy, and founder of mercy,
Which enlumineth heaven
    and earth thereby,°   *besides*
Hear my clamorous complaint, though it
    late be;
Receive my prayers, of thy benignity;
Though I be a sinner most abominable,   595
Yet let my name be written in Moses'
    table.
O Mary, pray to the Maker of all thing,
Me for to help at my ending;
And save me from the power of my
    enemy,
For Death assaileth me strongly.   600
And, Lady, that I may by mean of thy
    prayer
Of your Son's glory to be partner,
By the means of his passion, I it crave;
I beseech you help my soul to save.
Knowledge, give me the scourge of
    penance;   605
My flesh therewith shall give acquittance:
I will now begin, if God give me grace.
KNOWLEDGE   Everyman, God give you
    time and space!°   *opportunity*
Thus I bequeath you in the hands of our
    Saviour;
Now may you make your reckoning sure.   610
EVERYMAN   In the name of the Holy Trinity,
My body sore punished shall be:
Take this, body, for the sin of the flesh!

[*Scourges himself*]

Also° thou delightest to go gay and fresh,   *as*

588 In the presence of this company.
596 Medieval theologians regarded the two tables given on
Sinai as symbols of baptism and penance respectively. Thus
Everyman is asking to be numbered among those who have escaped damnation by doing penance for their sins.
599 i.e., from the devil.
601–603 And, Lady, I beg that through the mediation of thy
prayer I may share in your Son's glory, in consequence of His
passion.
606 *acquittance,* satisfaction (as a part of the sacrament of penance)

And in the way of damnation thou did me
    bring,   615
Therefore suffer now strokes and
    punishing.
Now of penance I will wade the water
    clear,
To save me from purgatory, that sharp
    fire.

[GOOD DEEDS *rises from the ground*]

GOOD DEEDS   I thank God, now I can walk
    and go,
And am delivered of my sickness and woe.   620
Therefore with Everyman I will go, and
    not spare;
His good works I will help him to declare.
KNOWLEDGE   Now, Everyman, be merry and
    glad!
Your Good Deeds whole and sound,   625
Going upright upon the ground.
EVERYMAN   My heart is light, and shall be
    evermore;
Now will I smite faster than I did before.
GOOD DEEDS   Everyman, pilgrim, my special
    friend,
Blessed be thou without end;   630
For thee is preparate° the eternal glory.   *prepared*
Ye have me made whole and sound,
Therefore I will bide by thee
    in every stound.°   *trial*
EVERYMAN   Welcome, my Good Deeds; now I
    hear thy voice,
I weep for very sweetness of love.   635
KNOWLEDGE   Be no more sad, but ever
    rejoice;
God seeth thy living in his throne above.
Put on this garment to thy behoof,°   *advantage*
Which is wet with your tears,
Or else before God you may it miss,   640
When ye to your journey's end come shall.
EVERYMAN   Gentle Knowledge, what do ye it
    call?
KNOWLEDGE   It is a garment of sorrow:
From pain it will you borrow;°   *release*
Contrition it is,   645
That geteth forgiveness;
It pleaseth God passing° well.   *exceedingly*
GOOD DEEDS   Everyman, will you wear it
    for your heal?°   *salvation*
EVERYMAN   Now blessed be Jesu, Mary's
    Son,
For now have I on true contrition.   650
And let us go now without tarrying;
Good Deeds, have we clear our reckoning?

GOOD DEEDS   Yea, indeed, I have it here.

EVERYMAN   Then I trust we need not fear;
  Now, friends, let us not part in twain.   655

KNOWLEDGE   Nay, Everyman, that will we
    not, certain.

GOOD DEEDS   Yet must thou lead with thee
  Three persons of great might.

EVERYMAN   Who should they be?

GOOD DEEDS   Discretion and Strength   660
    they hight,°   *are called*
  And thy Beauty may not abide behind.

KNOWLEDGE   Also ye must call to mind
  Your Five Wits° as for your   *senses*
    counsellors.

GOOD DEEDS   You must have them ready at
    all hours.

EVERYMAN   How shall I get them hither?   665

KNOWLEDGE   You must call them all together,
  And they will hear you
    incontinent.°   *immediately*

EVERYMAN   My friends, come hither and be
    present,
  Discretion, Strength, my Five Wits, and
    Beauty.

[*Enter* BEAUTY, STRENGTH, DISCRETION, *and* FIVE WITS]

BEAUTY   Here at your will we be all ready.   670
  What will ye that we should do?

GOOD DEEDS   That ye would with Everyman
    go,
  And help him in his pilgrimage.
  Advise° you, will ye with him or   *consider*
    not in that voyage?

STRENGTH   We will bring him all thither,   675
  To his help and comfort, ye may believe me.

DISCRETION   So will we go with him all
    together.

EVERYMAN   Almighty God, lofed° may   *praised*
    thou be!
  I give thee laud that I have hither brought
  Strength, Discretion, Beauty, and Five
    Wits.   680
    Lack I nought.
  And my Good Deeds, with Knowledge clear,
  All be in my company at my will here;
  I desire no more to° my business.   *for*

STRENGTH   And I, Strength, will by you
    stand in distress,
  Though thou would in battle fight   685
    on the ground.

FIVE WITS   And though it were through the
    world round,
  We will not depart for sweet ne sour.

687 i.e., in happiness or adversity.

BEAUTY   No more will I unto° death's   *until*
    hour,
  Whatsoever thereof befall.

DISCRETION   Everyman, advise you first of
    all;   690
  Go with a good advisement°   *reflection*
    and deliberation.
  We all give you virtuous monition°   *forewarning*
  That all shall be well.

EVERYMAN   My friends, harken what I will
    tell:
  I pray God reward you in his   695
    heavenly sphere.
  Now harken, all that be here,
  For I will make my testament
  Here before you all present:
  In alms half my good I will give with my
    hands twain
  In the way of charity, with good intent,   700
  And the other half still shall remain
  In queth,° to be returned   *bequest*
    there° it ought to be.   *where*
  This I do in despite of the fiend of hell,
  To go quit out of his peril
  Ever after and this day.   705

KNOWLEDGE   Everyman, harken what I say:
  Go to priesthood, I you advise,
  And receive of him in any wise°   *without fail*
  The holy sacrament and ointment
    together.
  Then shortly see ye turn again hither;   710
  We will all abide you here.

FIVE WITS   Yea, Everyman, hie you that ye
    ready were.
  There is no emperor, king, duke, ne
    baron,
  That of God hath commission°   *authority*
  As hath the least priest in the world   715
    being;°   *living*
  For of the blessed sacraments pure and
    benign
  He beareth the keys,
    and thereof hath the cure°   *charge*
  For man's redemption—it is ever sure—
  Which God for our soul's medicine
  Gave us out of his heart with great   720
    pine.°   *suffering*
  Here in this transitory life, for thee and me,
  The blessed sacraments seven there be:
  Baptism, confirmation, with priesthood
    good,

701–702 The meaning seems to be that Everyman's immov-
able property (i.e., his body) will lie at rest in the earth.
704–705 To go free out of his power today and ever after.
712 Hurry and prepare yourself.

And the sacrament of God's precious flesh
and blood,
Marriage, the holy extreme unction,   725
and penance;
These seven be good to have in
remembrance,
Gracious sacraments of high divinity.

EVERYMAN   Fain would I receive that holy
body,
and meekly to my ghostly° father   *spiritual*
I will go.

FIVE WITS   Everyman, that is the best that ye   730
can do.
God will you to salvation bring,
To us Holy Scripture they do teach,
And converteth man from sin heaven to
reach;
God hath to them more power given   735
Than to any angel that is in heaven.
With five words he may consecrate,
God's body in flesh and blood to make,
And handleth his Maker between his
hands.
The priest bindeth and unbindeth all bands,   740
Both in earth and in heaven.
Thou ministers° all the sacraments   *administer*
seven;
Though we kissed thy feet, thou were
worthy;
Thou art surgeon that cureth sin deadly:
No remedy we find under God   745
But all only priesthood.
Everyman, God gave priests that dignity,
And setteth them in his stead among us to
be;
Thus be they above angels in degree.

[EVERYMAN *goes to the priest to receive*
the last sacraments]

KNOWLEDGE   If priests be good, it is so,
surely.   750
But when Jesus hanged on the cross with
great smart,
There he gave out of his blessed heart
The same sacrament in great torment:
He sold them not to us, that Lord
omnipotent.
Therefore Saint Peter the apostle doth say   755
That Jesu's curse hath all they

Which God their Saviour do buy or sell,
Or they for any money do take or
tell.°   *count out*
Sinful priests giveth the sinners example
bad;
Their children sitteth by other men's fires,   760
I have heard;
And some haunteth women's company
With unclean life, as lusts of lechery:
These be with sin made blind.

FIVE WITS   I trust to God no such may we
find;
Therefore let us priesthood honour,   765
And follow their doctrine for our souls'
succour.
We be their sheep, and they shepherds be
By whom we all be kept in surety.
Peace, for yonder I see Everyman come,
Which hath made true satisfaction.   770

GOOD DEEDS   Methinks it is he indeed.

[*Re-enter* EVERYMAN]

EVERYMAN   Now Jesu be your alder speed!
I have received the sacrament for my
redemption,
And then mine extreme unction:
Blessed be all they that counselled   775
me to take it!
And now, friends, let us go without
longer respite;
I thank God that ye have tarried so long.
Now set each of you on this rood° your   *cross*
hand,
And shortly follow me:
I go before there I would be;   780
God be our guide!

STRENGTH   Everyman, we will not from you
go
Till ye have done this voyage long.

DISCRETION   I, Discretion, will bide by you
also.

KNOWLEDGE   And though this pilgrimage
be never so strong,°   *grievous*
I will never part you fro.°   *from you*

STRENGTH   Everyman, I will be as sure by
thee
As ever I did by Judas Maccabee.

[EVERYMAN *comes to his grave*]

EVERYMAN   Alas, I am so faint I may not
stand;

---

728 i.e., the sacrament.
737 *five words*, i.e., *Hoc est enim corpus meum.*
740 Matt. 16:19.
746 Except only from the priesthood.
750 *it is so*, i.e., that they are above the angels.
755–758 The reference here is to the sin of simony (Acts 8:18ff.).

760 i.e., illegitimate children.
772 Be the helper of you all.
786–787 I will stand by you as steadfastly as ever I did by Judas
Maccabaeus (I Macc, 3).

My limbs under me doth fold.
Friends, let us not turn again to this land, 790
Not for all the world's gold;
For into this cave must I creep
And turn to earth, and there to sleep.
BEAUTY   What, into this grave? Alas!
EVERYMAN   Yea, there shall ye consume, 795
more and less.
BEAUTY   And what, should I smother here?
EVERYMAN   Yea, by my faith, and never
more appear.
In this world live no more we shall,
But in heaven before the highest Lord of
all.
BEAUTY   I cross out all this; adieu, 800
by Saint John!
I take my cap in my lap, and am gone.
EVERYMAN   What, Beauty, whither will ye?
BEAUTY   Peace, I am deaf; I look not behind
me,
Not and thou wouldest give me all the
gold in thy chest.

[*Exit* BEAUTY]

EVERYMAN   Alas, whereto may I trust? 805
Beauty goeth fast away from me;
She promised with me to live and die.
STRENGTH   Everyman, I will thee also forsake
and deny;
Thy game liketh° me not at all.   *pleases*
EVERYMAN   Why, then, ye will forsake me 810
all?
Sweet Strength, tarry a little space.°   *while*
STRENGTH   Nay, sir, by the rood of grace!
I will hie me from thee fast,
Though thou weep till thy heart
to-brast.°   *break*
EVERYMAN   Ye would ever bide by me, ye 815
said.
STRENGTH   Yea, I have you far enough
conveyed.
Ye be old enough, I understand,
Your pilgrimage to take on hand;
I repent me that I hither came.
EVERYMAN   Strength, you to displease 820
I am to blame;
Yet promise is debt, this ye well wot.
STRENGTH   In faith, I care not.
Thou art but a fool to complain;
You spend your speech and waste your
brain.

795 Decay, all of you.
800 I cancel all this, i.e., my promise to stay with you.
801 I doff my cap [so low that it comes] into my lap.
820 I am to blame for displeasing you.

Go thrust thee into the ground!   825

[*Exit* STRENGTH]

EVERYMAN   I had wend surer I should you
have found.
He that trusteth in his Strength
She him deceiveth at the length.
Both Strength and Beauty forsaketh me;
Yet they promised me fair and lovingly.   830
DISCRETION   Everyman, I will after Strength
be gone;
As for me, I will leave you alone.
EVERYMAN   Why, Discretion, will ye forsake me?
DISCRETION   Yea, in faith, I will go from
thee,
For when Strength goeth before   835
I follow after evermore.
EVERYMAN   Yet, I pray thee, for the love of
the Trinity,
Look in my grave once piteously.
DISCRETION   Nay, so nigh will I not come;
Farewell, every one!   840

[*Exit* DISCRETION]

EVERYMAN   O, all thing faileth, save God
alone—
Beauty, Strength, and Discretion;
For when Death bloweth his blast,
They all run from me full fast.
FIVE WITS   Everyman, my leave now   845
of thee I take;
I will follow the other, for here I thee
forsake.
EVERYMAN   Alas, then may I wail and weep,
For I took you for my best friend.
FIVE WITS   I will no longer thee keep;
Now farewell, and there an end.   850

[*Exit* FIVE WITS]

EVERYMAN   O Jesu, help! All hath forsaken me.
GOOD DEEDS   Nay, Everyman; I will bide
with thee.
I will not forsake thee indeed;
Thou shalt find me a good friend at need.
EVERYMAN   Gramercy, Good Deeds!   855
Now may I true friends see.
They have forsaken me, every one;
I loved them better than my Good Deeds
alone.
Knowledge, will ye forsake me also?
KNOWLEDGE   Yea, Everyman, when ye to   860
Death shall go;
But not yet, for no manner of danger.
EVERYMAN   Gramercy, Knowledge, with all
my heart.

KNOWLEDGE   Nay, yet I will not from hence depart
   Till I see where ye shall become.
EVERYMAN   Methink, alas, that I must be gone   865
   To make my reckoning and my debts pay,
   For I see my time is nigh spent away.
   Take example, all ye that this do hear or see,
   How they that I loved best do forsake me,
   Except my Good Deeds that bideth truly.   870
GOOD DEEDS   All earthly things is but vanity:
   Beauty, Strength, and Discretion do man forsake,
   Foolish friends, and kinsmen, that fair spake—
   All fleeth save Good Deeds, and that am I.
EVERYMAN   Have mercy on me, God most mighty;   875
   And stand by me, thou mother and maid, holy Mary.
GOOD DEEDS   Fear not; I will speak for thee.
EVERYMAN   Here I cry God mercy.
GOOD DEEDS   Short our end, and minish our pain;
   Let us go and never come again.   880
EVERYMAN   Into thy hands, Lord, my soul I commend;
   Receive it, Lord, that it be not lost.
   As thou me boughtest, so me defend,
   And save me from the fiend's boast,
   That I may appear with that blessed host   885
   That shall be saved at the day of doom.
   In manus tuas, of mights most
   For ever, *commendo spiritum meum.*

                 [*He sinks into his grave.*]

KNOWLEDGE   Now hath he suffered that we all shall endure;
   The Good Deeds shall make all sure.   890
   Now hath he made ending;
   Methinketh that I hear angels sing,
   And make great joy and melody
   Where Everyman's soul received shall be.
ANGEL   Come, excellent elect spouse, to Jesu!   895
   Hereabove thou shalt go
   Because of thy singular virtue.
   Now the soul is taken the body fro,
   Thy reckoning is crystal-clear.

864 What shall become of you.
879 Shorten our end, and diminish our pain.
887–888 Into thy hands, most mighty One forever, I commend my spirit.
895 Bride of Jesus (a common medieval metaphor to express the idea of the soul's union with God).

Now shalt thou into the heavenly sphere,   900
   Unto the which all ye shall come
   That liveth well before the day of doom.

              [*Enter* DOCTOR]

DOCTOR   This moral men may have in mind
   Ye hearers, take it of worth,° old and young,   *value it*
   And forsake Pride, for he deceiveth you in the end;   905
   And remember Beauty, Five Wits, Strength, and Discretion,
   They all at the last do every man forsake,
   Save his Good Deeds there° doth he take.   *unless*
   But beware, for and they be small
   Before God, he hath no help at all;   910
   None excuse may be there for every man.
   Alas, how shall he do then?
   For after death amends may no man make,
   For then mercy and pity doth him forsake
   If his reckoning be not clear when he doth come,   915
   God will say: *"Ite, maledicti, in ignem eternum."*
   And he that hath his account whole and sound,
   High in heaven he shall be crowned;
   Unto which place God bring us all thither,
   That we may live body and soul together.   920
   Thereto help the Trinity!
   Amen, say ye, for saint charity.

THUS ENDETH THIS MORAL PLAY OF EVERYMAN

The Legend of Charlemagne: *Song of Roland*

Charlemagne's kingdom did not long survive intact after the death of the emperor. By the 10th century, the Frankish kingdom was fractured and Europe reduced to a state worthy of the name "Dark Ages." Anarchy, famine, ignorance, war, and factionalism were constants in 10th-century Europe; Charlemagne's era was looked back to as a long-vanished Golden Age. By the 12th century Charlemagne's reputation was such that he was canonized (in Aachen on December 29, 1165) by the Emperor Frederick Barbarossa. Charlemagne's cult was immensely popular throughout France—especially at the royal abbey of

916 Depart, ye cursed, into everlasting fire (Matt. 25:41).

Saint Denis in Paris, which made many claims of earlier links with the legendary emperor.

A 15th-century oil painting in Aachen depicts an idealized Charlemagne as saint, wearing the crown of the Holy Roman Emperor and carrying a model of the church he had built at Aachen [235]. Frederick Barbarossa commemorated the canonization by commissioning a great wrought-bronze candelabrum to hang in the Aachen cathedral. He also ordered a gold reliquary (now in the Louvre in Paris) to house the bones of one of his saintly predecessor's arms [236]; another reliquary in the form of a portrait bust

that contains fragments of Charlemagne's skull is in the cathedral treasury at Aachen.

The memory of Charlemagne and his epoch was kept more vividly alive, however, in cycles of epic poems and in tales and memoirs developed, embroidered, and disseminated by poets and singers throughout Europe from shortly after Charlemagne's time until the late Middle Ages. These are the famous *chansons de geste* (songs of deeds) or, as some were called, *chansons d'histoire* (songs of history). Of these songs, the oldest extant—as well as the best and most famous—is the *Song of Roland*.

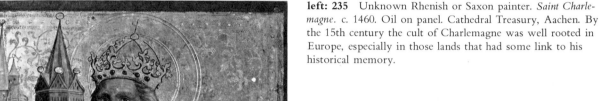

left: 235 Unknown Rhenish or Saxon painter. *Saint Charlemagne*. c. 1460. Oil on panel. Cathedral Treasury, Aachen. By the 15th century the cult of Charlemagne was well rooted in Europe, especially in those lands that had some link to his historical memory.

below: 236 Reliquary of Charlemagne. Bust of Charlemagne after 1349, crown before 1349. Cathedral Treasury. Aachen.

The *Song of Roland* was written sometime late in the 11th century, but behind it lay some three hundred years of oral tradition and earlier poems celebrating a battle between Charlemagne's army and a Moslem force at the Spanish border. Charlemagne did indeed campaign against the emirate of Spain in 777 and 778, without conclusive result. In August 778 Charlemagne's rear guard was ambushed by the Basques while making its way through the Pyrenees after the invasion of Spain. The real extent of that battle (later placed, on not too much evidence, at the town of Roncesvalles) is unclear. Some experts maintain that it was a minor skirmish, remembered in the area in local legends later told and retold (and considerably embroidered in the process) by monks of the monasteries and sanctuaries on the pilgrimage routes to the great shrine of Saint James at Santiago de Compostela in Spain. Other historians insist that the battle was a horrendous bloodbath for the army of Charlemagne and that the tale was carried back to the Frankish cities; the legend was transformed as it was repeated by the descendants of the few survivors.

In any event, by the 11th century the tale was widely known in Europe. Taillefer sang the *Song of Roland* to inspire the Norman army before the Battle of Hastings in 1066, and in 1096 Pope Urban II cited it in an appeal to French patriotism when he attempted to raise armies for a crusade to free the Holy Land. Medieval translations of the poem into German, Norse, and Italo-French attest its widespread popularity outside the French-speaking area.

The *Song of Roland* is an epic poem; its unknown writer or writers had little interest in historical accuracy or geographic niceties. Its subject matter is the glory of the military campaign, the chivalric nature of the true knight, the constant possibility of human deviousness, the clash of good and evil. The poem, although set in the 8th century, reflects the military values and chivalric code of the 11th century.

The story is simple: Moslems attack the retreating rear portion of Charlemagne's army (through an act of betrayal) while it is under the command of Roland, a favorite nephew of the emperor. Roland's army is defeated, but not before he sounds his ivory horn (the *oliphant*) to alert the emperor to the peril [Plate 20, page 353]. . The emperor in turn raises a huge army from throughout Christendom while the Moslems also raise a great force. An epic battle follows; Charlemagne, with divine aid, is victorious.

The *Song of Roland* is some four thousand lines long; it is divided into *laisses* (stanzas), and each line contains ten syllables. It is impossible to reproduce the rhyme in English, since each *laisse* ends with an assonance, so the poem is best read in blank-verse translation—although that loses the recitative quality of the original.

The selection reproduced here begins with Roland's decision to sound his great elephant-tusk horn to alert the troops of the emperor Charlemagne. His closest friend and comrade at-arms Olivier had asked him to do so earlier but had been refused, a stubborn bravery that cost many lives. The tension between Roland's obvious courage and his willfulness should remind the reader of the actions of Achilles in the *Iliad*. When Charlemagne finally vanquishes the Saracens the villainy of Ganelon is discovered through trial by combat. Ganelon's treason (he had betrayed his allies to the Saracens out of a raging hatred for his stepson Roland), Roland's impetuous valor, Olivier's steadfastness, and Charlemagne's friendship with God and overwhelming power over men are all fully explored.

This poem was meant to be heard, not read. It was recited by wandering minstrels—*jongleurs*—to largely illiterate audiences. This fact explains the verse style, the immediacy of the adjectives describing the characters and the situations, and the somewhat repetitive language. The still-unexplained *AOI* at the end of many stanzas may have something to do with the expected reaction of the *jongleur* as he uttered that particular sound to give emphasis to a stanza. (Some sense of the immediacy of the original may be gained by a reader today who declaims some of these stanzas with gesture and appropriate pauses.)

Certain details of this selection merit particular attention. This portion of the poem recounts Charlemagne's arrival on the scene and his victory over the Saracens who are beleaguering the forces commanded by Roland. Most striking is the mixture of military and religious ideals, not an uncommon motif in the medieval period. This mixture is reflected not only in the imagery and in the plot (Charlemagne's prayer keeps the sun from setting in order to allow time for victory, an echo of the biblical siege of Jericho by Joshua) but also in the bellicose Archbishop Turpin. Christian valor is contrasted with Saracen wickedness and treachery; the anti-Moslem bias of the poem is clear. The Moslem Saracens are pagans and idolaters—an odd way to describe the fiercely monotheistic followers of Islam. The *Song of Roland*, like much of the epic tradition from which it springs, is nevertheless devoted to the martial virtues of courage and strength, the comradeship of the battlefield, and the power of great men as well as the venality of evil ones.

from SONG OF ROLAND

128

Count Roland sees the slaughter of his men.
He calls aside Olivier, his comrade:
"Fair lord, dear comrade, in the name of God,
    what now?
You see what good men lie here on the ground.
We well may mourn sweet France the Beautiful,
to be deprived of barons such as these.
Oh king, my friend—if only you were here!
Olivier, my brother, what can we do?
By what means can we get this news to him?"
"I have no notion," says Olivier,   10
"but I'd rather die than have us vilified." AOI

129

Then Roland says: "I'll sound the oliphant,
and Charles, who's moving through the pass,
    will hear it.
I promise you the Franks will then return."
Olivier says: "That would bring great shame
and reprobation down on all your kin,
and this disgrace would last throughout their
    lives!
You wouldn't do a thing when I implored you,
so don't act now to win my gratitude.
No courage is involved in sounding it;   20
already you have bloodied both your arms."
The count replies: "I've struck some lovely
    blows!" AOI

130

Then Roland says: "Our fight is getting rough:
I'll sound my horn—King Charles is sure to
    hear it."
Olivier says: "That would not be knightly.
You didn't deign to, comrade, when I asked
    you,
and were the king here now, we'd be
    unharmed.
The men out yonder shouldn't take the blame."
Olivier says: "By this beard of mine,
if I should see my lovely sister Alde,   30
then *you* shall never lie in her embrace." AOI

131

Then Roland says: "You're angry with
    me—why?"
And he replies: "Companion, you're to blame,

for bravery in no sense is bravado,
and prudence is worth more than recklessness.
Those French are dead because of your caprice;
King Charles will have our services no more.
My lord would be here now, if you'd believed me,
and we'd have put an end to this affray;
Marsilla would be dead or taken captive.   40
But we were doomed to see your prowess,
    Roland;
now Charlemagne will get no help from us
(there'll be no man like him until God judges)
and you shall die, and France shall be disgraced.
Today our loyal comradeship will end:
before the evening falls we'll part in grief." AOI

132

The archbishop overhears them quarreling:
he rakes his horse with spurs of beaten gold,
comes over, and begins to reprimand them:
"Lord Roland, you too, Lord Olivier,   50
I beg of you, for God's sake do not quarrel!
A horn blast cannot save us any more,
but nonetheless it would be well to sound it;
the king will come, and then he can avenge
    us—
the men from Spain will not depart in joy.
Our Frenchmen will dismount here, and on foot
they'll come upon us, dead and hacked to
    pieces,
and lift us up in coffins onto pack-mules,
and weep for us in pity and in grief.
They'll bury us beneath the aisles of churches,   60
where wolves and pigs and dogs won't gnaw
    on us."
"You've spoken very well, sire," answers
    Roland. AOI

133

Count Roland brought the horn up to his
    mouth:
he sets it firmly, blows with all his might.
The peaks are high, the horn's voice carries far;
they hear it echo thirty leagues away.
Charles hears it, too, and all his company:
the king says then: "Our men are in a fight."
And Ganelon replies contentiously:
"Had someone else said that, he'd seem a liar."
AOI   70

134

Count Roland, racked with agony and pain
and great chagrin, now sounds his ivory horn:
bright blood leaps in a torrent from his mouth:
the temple has been ruptured in his brain.

The horn he holds emits a piercing blast:
Charles hears it as he crosses through the pass;
Duke Naimes has heard it, too; the Franks give
    ear.
The king announces: "I hear Roland's horn!
He'd never sound it if he weren't embattled."
Says Ganelon: "There isn't any battle!   80
You're getting old, your hair is streaked and
    white;
such speeches make you sound just like a child.
You're well aware of Roland's great conceit;
it's strange that God has suffered him so long.
Without your orders he once captured Naples:
the Saracens inside came riding out
and then engaged that worthy vassal Roland,
who later flushed the gory field with water—
he did all this to keep it out of sight.
He'll blow that horn all day for just one hare.   90
He's showing off today before his peers—
no army under heaven dares to fight him.
So keep on riding!—Why do you stop here?
For Tere Majur[1] lies far ahead of us." AOI

135

Count Roland's mouth is filling up with blood;
the temple has been ruptured in his brain.
In grief and pain he sounds the oliphant;
Charles hears it, and his Frenchmen listen, too.
The king says then, "That horn is long of
    wind."
Duke Naimes replies, "The baron is attacking!   100
A fight is taking place, of that I'm sure.
This man who tries to stall you has betrayed
    them.
Take up your arms, sing out your battle cry,
and then go save your noble retinue:
you've listened long enough to Roland's plaint!"

136

The emperor has let his horns be sounded:
the French dismount, and then they arm
    themselves
with hauberks and with casques[2] and gilded
    swords.
Their shields are trim, their lances long and
    stout,
their battle pennants crimson, white, and blue.   110
The barons of the army mount their chargers
and spur them briskly, all down through the
    passes.
There is not one who fails to tell his neighbor:
"If we see Roland prior to his death,

[1] The Fatherland; i.e., the Frankish kingdom
[2] Metal helmets for warriors

we'll stand there with him, striking mighty
    blows."
But what's the use?—for they've delayed too
    long.

137

The afternoon and evening are clear:
the armor coruscates against the sun,
those casques and hauberks throw a dazzling
    glare,
as do those shields, ornate with painted flowers,   120
those spears, those battle flags of gold brocade.
Impelled by rage, the emperor rides on,
together with the French, chagrined and
    grieved.
No man there fails to weep with bitterness,
and they are much afraid for Roland's sake.
The king has had Count Ganelon arrested,
and turns him over to his household cooks.
He tells Besgun, the leader of them all:
"Keep watch on him, like any common thug,
for he's betrayed the members of my house."   130
He turned him over to a hundred comrades,
the best and worst together, from the kitchen.
These men plucked out his beard and his
    moustache,
and each one hit him four times with his fist;
they whipped him thoroughly with sticks and
    clubs,
and then they put a chain around his neck
and chained him up exactly like a bear;
in ridicule, they set him on a pack-horse.
They'll guard him this way until Charles
    returns.

138

The hills are high and shadowy and large,   140
the valleys deep, with swiftly running streams.
The trumpets ring out to the front and rear,
all racketing reply to the oliphant.
The emperor rides on, impelled by rage,
as do the Franks, chagrined and furious:
no man among them fails to weep and mourn
and pray to God that He may safeguard Roland
until they all arrive upon the field.
Together with him there, they'll really fight.
But what's the use? They cannot be of help;   150
they stayed too long; they can't get there in
    time. AOI

139

Impelled by rage, King Charles keeps riding on,
his full white beard spread out upon his byrnie.[3]

[3] Coat of chain mail

The Frankish barons all have used their spurs;
not one of them but bitterly regrets
that he is not beside the captain Roland,
now fighting with the Saracens from Spain,
and injured so, I fear his soul won't stay.
But, God—the sixty in his company!
No king or captain has commanded better. AOI 160

140

Count Roland scans the mountains and the hills:
he sees so many dead French lying there,
and like a noble knight he weeps for them.
"My lords and barons, God be merciful,
deliver all your souls to Paradise
and let them lie among the blessed flowers!
I've never seen more worthy knights than
          you—
you all have served me long and faithfully,
and conquered such great lands for Charles's
          sake!
The emperor has raised you, all for naught.   170
My land of France, how very sweet you are—
today laid waste by terrible disaster!
French lords, because of me I see you dying—
I can't reprieve you now, nor save your lives.
May God, who never lied, come to your aid!
Olivier, I won't fail *you,* my brother;
if no one kills me, I shall die of grief.
My lord companion, let's attack once more."

141

Count Roland now goes back into the field,
with Durendal in hand, fights gallantly: 180
he then has cut Faldrun of Pui in two,
as well as twenty-four among their best;
no man will ever want revenge so badly.
Just as the stag will run before the hounds,
the pagans break and run away from Roland.
The archbishop says: "You're doing rather well!
Such gallantry a chevalier should have,
if he's to carry arms and ride a horse.
He must be fierce and powerful in combat—
if not, he isn't worth four deniers[4]—   190
should be instead a monastery monk
and pray the livelong day for all our sins."
"Lay on, don't spare them!" Roland says in
          answer,
and at these words the Franks attack again.
The Christians suffered very heavy losses.

142

The man who knows no captives will be taken,

in such a fight puts up a stout defense:
because of this, the Franks are fierce as lions.
Now see Marsilla make a gallant show.
He sits astride the horse he calls Gaignon;   200
he spurs him briskly, then attacks Bevon
(this man was lord of Beaune and of Dijon).
He breaks his shield and smashes through his
          hauberk
and drops him dead without a *coup de grâce.*[5]
And then he killed Ivon and Ivorie,
together with Gerard of Roussillon.
Count Roland isn't very far away;
he tells the pagan: "May the Lord God damn
          you!
So wrongfully you've slaughtered my
          companions;
before we separate, you'll take a stroke,   210
and from my sword today you'll learn its
          name."
He goes to strike him with a gallant show:
the count swings down and cuts his right hand
          off,
then takes the head of Jurfaleu the Blond
(this pagan was the son of King Marsilla).
The pagans raise the cry: "Help us,
          Mohammed!
And you, our gods, give us revenge on Charles.
He's sent such villains to us in this land—
they'd rather die than leave the battlefield."
One tells another: "Let's get out of here!"   220
And at that word a hundred thousand run.
No matter who may call, they won't come
          back. AOI

145

The pagans, when they see the French are few,
feel proud and reassured among themselves:
"The emperor is wrong," one tells another.
Astride a sorrel horse sits Marganice;
he rakes him briskly with his golden spurs
and strikes Olivier on the back,
lays bare the flesh beneath the shining hauberk
and shoves his lance entirely through his chest,   230
and then he says: "You took a mortal blow!
Great Charles should not have left you at the
          pass,
he's done us wrong, he has no right to boast;
through you alone, our side is well avenged."

146

Olivier feels wounded unto death,
but gripping Halteclere, whose blade was
          polished,

---

[4] Silver coins struck at the royal mint in Frankfurt after 804;
the standard coin of the period; see figure 212, page 296

[5] Close-range dagger thrust to ensure a quick death

strikes Marganice's high-peaked golden casque;
he smashes downward through fleurons and
     gems
and splits the skull wide open to the teeth.
He wrenches free and lets the dead man fall,   240
and afterward he tells him: "Damn you, pagan!
I do not say that Charles has had no loss,
but neither to your wife nor any woman
you've seen back where you came from shall
     you brag
you took a denier of loot from me,
or injured me or anybody else."
Then afterward he calls for help to Roland. AOI

147

Olivier feels injured unto death,
yet he will never have his fill of vengeance:
he battles in the thick crowd like a baron,   250
still shearing through those shafts of spears,
     those bucklers,
and feet and wrists and shoulder-bones and ribs.
Whoever saw him maiming Saracens
and piling dead men one upon the other
would be reminded of a worthy knight.
Not wanting Charles's battle cry forgotten,
he sings out in a loud, clear voice: "Monjoy!"
He calls to him his friend and peer, Count
     Roland:
"My lord companion, come fight here by me;
today in bitter anguish we shall part." AOI   260

148

Count Roland contemplates Olivier:
his face is gray and bloodless, wan and pale,
and from his trunk bright blood is surging out
and dripping down in pools upon the ground.
The count says: "God, I don't know what to
     do.
Your valor was for naught, my lord
     companion—
there'll never be another one like you.
Sweet France, today you're going to be robbed
of loyal men, defeated and destroyed:
all this will do the emperor great harm."   270
And at this word he faints, still on his horse.
     AOI

149

See Roland, who has fainted on his horse,
and, wounded unto death, Olivier,
his vision so impaired by loss of blood
that, whether near or far, he cannot see
enough to recognize a living man;
and so, when he encounters his companion,

he hits him on his jeweled golden casque
and splits it wide apart from crown to nasal,
but doesn't cut into his head at all.   280
On being struck so, Roland studied him,
then asked him in a soft and gentle voice:
"My lord companion, did you mean to do that?
It's Roland, who has been your friend so long:
you gave no sign that you had challenged me."
Olivier says: "Now I hear you speak.
Since I can't see you, God keep you in sight!
I hit you, and I beg you to forgive me."
And Roland says: "I've not been hurt at all,
and here before the Lord I pardon you."   290
And with these words, they bowed to one
     another:
in friendship such as this you see them part.

150

Olivier feels death-pangs coming on;
his eyes have both rolled back into his head,
and his sight and hearing are completely gone.
Dismounting, he lies down upon the ground,
and then confesses all his sins aloud,
with both hands clasped and lifted up toward
     heaven.
He prays that God may grant him Paradise
and give His blessing to sweet France and
     Charles   300
and, most of all, to his companion Roland.
His heart fails; his helmet tumbles down;
his body lies outstretched upon the ground.
The count is dead—he could endure no more.
The baron Roland weeps for him and mourns:
on earth you'll never hear a sadder man.

151

Now Roland, when he sees his friend is dead
and lying there face down upon the ground,
quite softly starts to say farewell to him:
"Your valor was for naught, my lord
     companion!   310
We've been together through the days and years,
and never have you wronged me, nor I you;
since you are dead, it saddens me to live."
And having said these words, the marquis faints
upon his horse, whose name is Veillantif;
but his stirrups of fine gold still hold him on:
whichever way he leans, he cannot fall.

153

Now, Roland, grown embittered in his pain,
goes slashing through the middle of the crowd;
he throws down lifeless twenty men from
     Spain,   320

while Gautier kills six, and Turpin five.
The pagans say: "These men are infamous;
don't let them get away alive, my lords:
whoever fails to rush them is a traitor,
who lets them save themselves, a renegade."
So once more they renew the hue and cry;
from every side they go to the attack. AOI

154

Count Roland is a noble man-at-arms.
Gautier of Hum a splendid chevalier,
the archbishop an experienced campaigner: 330
no one of them will ever leave the others.
Engulfed within the crowd, they cut down
        pagans.
A thousand Saracens get down on foot,
and forty thousand stay upon their horses:
they do not dare come closer, that I know,
but they hurl at them their javelins and spears
and darts and wigars, mizraks, and agers.[6]
The first barrage has killed Count Gautier;
Turpin of Reims—his shield is pierced clear
        through,
his helmet broken, injuring his head,   340
his hauberk torn apart and stripped of mail;
his body has been wounded by four spears;
they kill his destrier[7] from under him.
Great sorrow comes as the archbishop falls.
        AOI

155

Turpin of Reims, when he sees that he's been
        downed
by four spears driven deep into his body,
the brave man leaps back quickly to his feet
and looks toward Roland, then runs up to him
and says this word: "By no means am I beaten;
no loyal man gives up while still alive."   350
He draws Almace, his sword of polished steel;
in the crowd he strikes a thousand blows or
        more.
Charles later on will say he spared no one—
he found about four hundred, all around him,
some only wounded, some who'd been run
        through,
and others who had had their heads cut off.
Thus says the *geste* and he who was afield,
the noble Giles, for whom God brought forth
        wonders.
At the minster[8] of Laon he wrote the charter;
whoever doesn't know that much knows little.   360

[6] Various projectiles used in battle
[7] War horse
[8] Cathedral

156

Count Roland keeps on fighting skillfully,
although his body's hot and drenched with
        sweat:
he feels great pain and torment in his head,
since, when he blew his horn, his temple burst.
Yet he has to know if Charles is coming back:
he draws the ivory horn and sounds it feebly.
The emperor pulled up so he might listen:
"My lords," he says, "it's very bad for us;
today my nephew Roland will be lost.
From his horn blast I can tell he's barely living; 370
whoever wants to get there must ride fast.
So sound your trumpets, all this army has!"
And sixty thousand of them blare so loud,
the mountains ring, the valleys echo back.
The pagans hear it, take it as no joke.
One tells another: "Now we'll have King
        Charles."

157

The pagans say: "The emperor's returning; AOI
just listen to the Frenchmen's trumpets blare!
If Charles comes, it will be the ruin of us—
if Roland lives, our war will start again,   380
and we'll have forfeited our land of Spain."
About four hundred, wearing casques,
        assemble—
and launch one brutal, grim assault on Roland.
This time the count has got his work cut out.
        AOI

158

Count Roland, when he sees them drawing
        near,
becomes so strong and bold and vigilant!
As long as he's alive, he'll never yield.
He sits astride the horse called Veillantif
and rakes him briskly with his fine gold spurs
and wades into the crowd to fight them all,   390
accompanied by Turpin, the archbishop.
One tells another: "Friend, get out of here!
We've heard the trumpets of the men from
        France;
now Charles, the mighty king, is coming back."

159

Count Roland never cared much for a coward
nor a swaggerer nor evil-minded man
nor a knight, if he were not a worthy vassal.
He called out then to Turpin, the archbishop:
"My lord, you are on foot and I am mounted;
for love of you I'll make my stand right here.   400
Together we shall take the good and bad;

no mortal man shall ever make me leave you.
Today, in this assault, the Saracens
shall learn the names Almace and Durendal."
The archbishop says: "Damn him who won't
    fight hard!
When Charles comes back here, he'll avenge us
    well."

160

The pagans cry out: "We were doomed at birth;
a bitter day has dawned for us today!
We've been bereft of all our lords and peers,
the gallant Charles is coming with his host,   410
we hear the clear-voiced trumpets of the French
and the uproar of the battle cry 'Monjoy.'
So great is the ferocity of Roland,
no mortal man will ever vanquish him;
so let us lance at him, then let him be."
They hurl at him a multitude of darts,
befeathered mizraks, wigars, lances, spears—
they burst and penetrated Roland's shield
and ripped his hauberk, shearing off its mail,
but not a one went through into his body.   420
They wounded Veillantif in thirty places
and killed him out from underneath the count.
The pagans take flight then and let him be:
Count Roland is still there upon his feet. AOI

161

The pagans, galled and furious, take flight
and head for Spain, as fast as they can go.
Count Roland is unable to pursue them,
for he has lost his charger Veillantif
and now, despite himself, is left on foot.
He went to give Archbishop Turpin help,   430
unlaced his gilded helmet from his head,
then pulled away his gleaming, lightweight
    hauberk
and cut his under-tunic all to shreds
and stuffed the strips into his gaping wounds.
This done, he took him up against his chest
and on the green grass gently laid him down.
Most softly Roland made him this request:
"Oh noble lord, if you will give me leave—
all our companions, whom we held so dear,
are dead now; we should not abandon them.   440
I want to seek them out, identify them,
and lay them out before you, side by side."
The archbishop tells him: "Go and then return;
this field is yours, I thank God, yours and mine."

162

Now Roland leaves and walks the field alone:
he searches valleys, searches mountain slopes.

He found there Gerier, his friend Gerin,
and then he found Aton and Berenger,
and there he found Sanson and Anseïs;
he found Gerard the Old of Roussillon.   450
The baron picked them up then, pair by pair,
and brought them every one to the archbishop
and placed them in a row before his knees.
The archbishop cannot help himself; he weeps,
then lifts his hand and makes his benediction,
and says thereafter: "Lords, you had no chance;
may God the Glorious bring all your souls
to Paradise among the blessed flowers!
My own death causes me great pain, for I
shall see the mighty emperor no more."   460

163

Now Roland leaves, goes searching through the
    field:
he came upon Olivier, his comrade,
and holding him up tight against his chest
returned as best he could to the archbishop.
He laid him on a shield beside the others;
the archbishop blessed him, gave him
    absolution.
Then all at once despair and pain well up,
and Roland says: "Olivier, fair comrade,
you were the son of wealthy Duke Renier,
who ruled the frontier valley of Runers.   470
To break a lance-shaft or to pierce a shield,
to overcome and terrify the proud,
to counsel and sustain the valorous,
to overcome and terrify the gluttons,
no country ever had a better knight."

164

Count Roland, looking on his lifeless peers
and Olivier, whom he had cared for so,
is seized with tenderness, begins to weep.
The color has all vanished from his face;
he cannot stand, the pain is so intense;   480
despite himself, he falls to earth unconscious.
The archbishop says: "Brave lord, you've come
    to grief."

165

The archbishop, upon seeing Roland faint,
feels sorrow such as he has never felt,
extends his hand and takes the ivory horn.
At Roncesvals there is a running stream;
he wants to fetch some water there for Roland;
with little, stumbling steps he turns away,
but can't go any farther—he's too weak
and has no strength, has lost far too much
    blood.   490

Before a man could walk across an acre,
his heart fails, and he falls upon his face.
With dreadful anguish death comes over him.

166

Count Roland, now regaining consciousness,
gets on his feet, in spite of dreadful pain,
and scans the valleys, scans the mountainsides,
across the green grass, out beyond his
    comrades.
He sees the noble baron lying there—
the archbishop, sent by God in His own name.
Confessing all his sins, with eyes upraised   500
and both hands clasped and lifted up toward
    Heaven,
he prays that God may grant him Paradise.
Now Turpin, Charles's warrior, is dead:
in mighty battles and in moving sermons
he always took the lead against the pagans.
May God bestow on him His holy blessing! AOI

167

Count Roland sees the archbishop on the ground:
he sees the entrails bulging from his body.
His brains are boiling out upon his forehead.
Upon his chest, between the collarbones,   510
he laid crosswise his beautiful white hands,
lamenting him, as was his country's custom:
"Oh noble vassal, well-born chevalier,
I now commend you to celestial Glory.
No man will ever serve Him with such zeal;
no prophet since the days of the Apostles
so kept the laws and drew the hearts of men.
Now may your soul endure no suffering;
may Heaven's gate be opened up for you!"

168

Count Roland realizes death is near: 520
his brains begin to ooze out through his ears.
He prays to God to summon all his peers,
and to the angel Gabriel, himself.
Eschewing blame, he takes the horn in hand
and in the other Durendal, his sword,
and farther than a crossbow fires a bolt,
heads out across a fallow field toward Spain
and climbs a rise. Beneath two lovely trees
stand four enormous marble monoliths.
Upon the green grass he has fallen backward   530
and fainted, for his death is near at hand.

169

The hills are high, and very high the trees;
four massive blocks are there, of gleaming
    marble;

upon green grass Count Roland lies
    unconscious.
And all the while a Saracen is watching:
he lies among the others, feigning death;
he smeared his body and his face with blood.
He rises to his feet and starts to run—
a strong, courageous, handsome man he was;
through pride he enters into mortal folly—   540
and pinning Roland's arms against his chest,
he cries out: "Charles's nephew has been
    vanquished;
I'll take this sword back to Arabia."
And as he pulls, the count revives somewhat.

170

Now Roland feels his sword is being taken
and, opening his eyes, he says to him:
"I know for certain you're not one of us!"
He takes the horn he didn't want to leave
and strikes him on his jeweled golden casque;
he smashes through the steel and skull and
    bones,   550
and bursting both his eyeballs from his head,
he tumbles him down lifeless at his feet
and says to him: "How dared you, heathen
    coward,
lay hands on me, by fair means or by foul?
Whoever hears of this will think you mad.
My ivory horn is split across the bell,
and the crystals and the gold are broken off."

171

Now Roland feels his vision leaving him,
gets to his feet, exerting all his strength;
the color has all vanished from his face.   560
In front of him there is a dull gray stone;
ten times he strikes it, bitter and dismayed:
the steel edge grates, but does not break or
    nick.
"Oh holy Mary, help me!' says the count,
"Oh Durendal, good sword, you've come to
    grief!
When I am dead, you won't be in my care.
I've won with you on many battlefields
and subjugated many spacious lands
now ruled by Charles, whose beard is shot with
    gray.
No man who flees another should possess you!   570
A loyal knight has held you many years;
your equal holy France will never see."

172

Roland strikes the great carnelian stone:
the steel edge grides, but does not break or chip.

And when he sees that he cannot destroy it,
he makes this lamentation to himself:
"Oh Durendal, how dazzling bright you are—
you blaze with light and shimmer in the sun!
King Charles was in the Vales of Moriane
when God in Heaven had His angel tell him   580
that he should give you to a captain-count:
the great and noble king then girded me.
With this I won Anjou and Brittany,
and then I won him both Poitou and Maine.
with this I won him Normandy the Proud,
and then I won Provence and Aquitaine,
and Lombardy, as well as all Romagna.
With this I won Bavaria, all Flanders,
and Burgundy, the Poliani lands,
Constantinople, where they did him homage—   590
in Saxony they do what he commands.
With this I won him Scotland, Ireland too,
and England, which he held as his demesne.
With this I've won so many lands and countries
which now are held by Charles, whose beard is
    white.
I'm full of pain and sorrow for this sword;
I'd rather die than leave it to the pagans.
Oh God, my Father, don't let France be
    shamed!"

173

Roland hammers on a dull gray stone
and breaks off more of it than I can say: 600
the sword grates, but it neither snaps nor splits,
and only bounces back into the air.
The count, on seeing he will never break it,
laments it very softly to himself:
"Oh Durendal, so beautiful and sacred,
within your golden hilt are many relics—
Saint Peter's tooth, some of Saint Basil's blood,
some hair belonging to my lord, Saint Denis,
a remnant, too, of holy Mary's dress.
It isn't right that pagans should possess you;   610
you ought to be attended on by Christians.
You never should be held by one who cowers!
With you I've conquered many spacious lands
now held by Charles, whose beard is streaked
    with white;
through them the emperor is rich and strong."

174

Now Roland feels death coming over him,
descending from his head down to his heart.
He goes beneath a pine tree at a run
and on the green grass stretches out, face down.
He puts his sword and ivory horn beneath him   620
and turns his head to face the pagan host.
He did these things in order to be sure

that Charles, as well as all his men, would say:
"This noble count has died a conqueror."
Repeatedly he goes through his confession,
and for his sins he proffers God his glove. AOI

175

Now Roland is aware his time is up:
he lies upon a steep hill, facing Spain,
and with one hand he beats upon his chest:
"Oh God, against Thy power I have sinned,   630
because of my transgressions, great and small,
committed since the hour I was born
until this day when I have been struck down!"
He lifted up his right-hand glove to God:
from Heaven angels came to him down there.
        AOI

176

Count Roland lay down underneath a pine,
his face turned so that it would point toward
        Spain:
he was caught up in the memory of things—
of many lands he'd valiantly subdued,
of sweet France, of the members of his line,   640
of Charlemagne, his lord, who brought him up;
he cannot help but weep and sigh for these.
But he does not intend to slight himself;
confessing all his sins, he begs God's mercy:
"True Father, Who hath never told a lie,
Who resurrected Lazarus from the dead,
and Who protected Daniel from the lions,
protect the soul in me from every peril
brought on by wrongs I've done throughout
        my life!"
He offered up his right-hand glove to God: 650
Saint Gabriel removed it from his hand.
And with his head inclined upon his arm,
hands clasped together, he has met his end.
Then God sent down his angel Cherubin[9]
and Saint Michael of the Sea and of the Peril;
together with Saint Gabriel they came
and took the count's soul into Paradise.

177

Roland is dead, his soul with God in Heaven.
The emperor arrives at Roncesvals.
There's not a single trace nor footpath there,   660
nor ell, nor even foot of vacant ground,
on which there's not a pagan or a Frank.
"Fair nephew," Charles cries loudly, "where are
        you?
Where's the archbishop, and Count Olivier?

---

[9]Angels who were thought to carry fiery swords

Where is Gerin, and his comrade Gerier?
Where is Anton? and where's Count Berenger?
Ivon and Ivorie, I held so dear?
What's happened to the Gascon, Engelier?
and Duke Sanson? and gallant Anseïs?
and where is Old Gerard of Roussillon?   670
—the twelve peers I permitted to remain?"
But what's the use, when none of them reply?
The king says: "God! I've cause enough to grieve
that I was not here when the battle started!"
He tugs upon his beard like one enraged;
the eyes of all his noble knights shed tears,
and twenty thousand fall down in a faint.
Duke Naimes profoundly pities all of them.

178

There's not a chevalier or baron there
who fails to shed embittered tears of grief;   680
they mourn their sons, their brothers, and their
    nephews,
together with their liege-lords and their friends;
and many fall unconscious to the ground.
Duke Naimes displayed his courage through all
    this,
for he was first to tell the emperor:
"Look up ahead of us, two leagues away—
along the main road you can see the dust,
so many of the pagan host are there.
So ride! Take vengeance for this massacre!"
"Oh God!" says Charles, "already they're so
    far!   690
Permit me what is mine by right and honor;
they've robbed me of the flower of sweet
    France."
The king gives orders to Geboin, Oton,
Thibaud of Reims, and to the count Milon:
"You guard the field—the valleys and the hills.
Leave all the dead exactly as they lie,
make sure no lion or other beast comes near,
and let no groom or serving-man come near.
Prohibit any man from coming near them
till God grants our return upon this field."   700
In fond, soft-spoken tones these men reply:
"Dear lord and rightful emperor, we'll do it!"
They keep with them a thousand chevaliers.
        AOI

179

The emperor has had his trumpets sounded;
then, with his mighty host, the brave lord rides.
The men from Spain have turned their backs to
    them;
they all ride out together in pursuit.
The king, on seeing dusk begin to fall,
dismounts upon the green grass in a field,

prostrates himself, and prays Almighty God   710
that He will make the sun stand still for him,
hold back the night, and let the day go on.
An angel he had spoken with before
came instantly and gave him this command:
"Ride on, Charles, for the light shall not desert
    you.
God knows that you have lost the flower of France;
you may take vengeance on the guilty race."
And at these words, the emperor remounts. AOI

180

For Charlemagne God worked a miracle,
because the sun is standing motionless.   720
The pagans flee, the Franks pursue them hard,
and overtake them at Val-Tenebrus.
They fight them on the run toward Saragossa;
with mighty blows they kill them as they go;
they cut them off from the main roads and the
    lanes.
The river Ebro lies in front of them,
a deep, swift-running, terrifying stream;
there's not a barge or boat or dromond[10] there.
The pagans call on Termagant,[11] their god,
and then leap in, but nothing will protect them.   730
The men in armor are the heaviest,
and numbers of them plummet to the bottom;
the other men go floating off downstream.
The best equipped thus get their fill to drink;
they all are drowned in dreadful agony.
The Frenchmen cry out: "You were luckless,
    Roland!" AOI

181

As soon as Charles sees all the pagans dead
(some killed, a greater number of them drowned)
and rich spoils taken off them by his knights,
the noble king then climbs down to his feet,   740
prostrates himself, and offers thanks to God.
When he gets up again, the sun has set.
"It's time to pitch camp," says the emperor.
"It's too late to go back to Roncesvals.
Our horses are fatigued and ridden down;
unsaddle them and then unbridle them
and turn them out to cool off in this field."
The Franks reply: "Sire, you have spoken well."
        AOI

182

The emperor has picked a place to camp.
The French dismount upon the open land   750

[10]Medieval galley used in the Mediterranean
[11]A mythical pagan god whom the Christians believed the
Moslems worshiped

and pull the saddles off their destriers
and take the gold-trimmed bridles from their
    heads;
then turn them out to graze the thick green grass;
there's nothing else that they can do for them.
The tiredest go to sleep right on the ground:
that night they post no sentinels at all.

183

The emperor has lain down in a meadow.
The brave lord sets his great lance at his head—
tonight he does not wish to be unarmed—
keeps on his shiny, saffron-yellow hauberk,   760
and his jeweled golden helmet, still laced up,
and at his waist Joyeuse, which has no peer:
its brilliance alters thirty times a day.
We've heard a great deal spoken of the lance
with which Our Lord was wounded on the cross;
that lance's head is owned by Charles, thank God;
he had its tip inletted in the pommel.
Because of this distinction and this grace,
the name "Joyeuse" was given to the sword.
The Frankish lords will not forget this fact: 770
they take from it their battle cry, "Monjoy."
Because of this, no race can stand against them.

Further Reading

Almedingen, E. M. *Charlemagne: A Study*. London: Bodley Head, 1968. A readable and thorough biography of the man in relation to his times.

Boussard, Jacques. *The Civilization of Charlemagne*. Translated by Frances Partridge. New York: McGraw-Hill, 1968. A well-illustrated survey with a detailed bibliography of more specialized sources.

Brondsted, Johannes. *The Vikings*. Translated by Kalle Skov. New York: Penguin Books, 1960. A basic survey of the Northmen; with some illustrations in black and white.

Bullough, Donald. *The Age of Charlemagne*. New York: Putnam, 1966. Well-written and lavishly illustrated.

Folz, Robert. *The Coronation of Charlemagne: 25th December 800*. Translated by J. E. Anderson. London: Routledge Kegan Paul, 1974. A detailed but readable study of Charlemagne's imperial ideals.

Henderson, George. *Early Medieval*. New York: Penguin Books, 1972. Part of the "style and civilization" series; an extremely readable and thorough study of artistic styles in the early medieval period with 150 illustrations and a thorough bibliography.

Knowles, David. *Christian Monasticism*. New York: McGraw-Hill, 1969. A readable survey of the history of Christian monasticism by a distinguished monastic historian.

Riche, Pierre. *Daily Life in the World of Charlemagne*. Translated by JoAnn MacNamara. Philadelphia: University of Pennsylvania Press, 1978. A fascinating and indispensable study of all facets of Carolingian life.

Thorpe, Lewis (trans.). *Einhard and Notker the Stammerer: Two Lives of Charlemagne*. New York: Penguin Books, 1969. Basic sources from the period with a good introduction.

Suggestions for Listening

Intense studies over the past hundred years have given scholars and musicians very precise notions about early medieval chant, and many recordings are available for the serious listener. One older collection is the two-record *A Treasury of Gregorian Chants* (SDBR 3159), an anthology of church music sung by a variety of monastic choirs. More useful for study is the Schola Antiqua recording (directed by R. John Blackley) called *A Guide to Gregorian Chant* (VSD 71217). This set has very fine liner notes and a discussion of the origin and development of Gregorian music. The Cappella Musicale of the Milan Cathedral in Italy has recorded representative examples of Ambrosian music in a recording called simply *Ambrosian Chant* (DG ARC 2533158). For a musical setting of a medieval play one might begin with the New York Pro Musica rendering of the *Play of Daniel* (MCA 2504).

Questions for Further Discussion

1. It has often been said that monasticism was a form of counterculture in that it set forth an alternate form of life and community. Do you see similarities (and differences) between monastic communal life and some modern experiments in communal living and/or alternative life styles?

2. We have noted that drama in the early medieval period derived from the liturgy of the church. We also know that Greek tragedy had its roots in the worship of the fertility god Dionysus. Speculate on the reasons that drama should spring forth from corporate religious worship.

3. In the post-Vietnam period it is hard to think of a work of literature that would praise military and chivalrous values with the same enthusiasm as the *Song of Roland*. What kind of values and virtues have you noted as being singled out by contemporary writers or filmmakers when dealing with modern war?

4. What continuities and discontinuities do you see as you compare the aims and methods of Carolingian education with our own?

5. Speculate on the vastly different attitude the Carolingians showed toward books and ours to our own book culture today. List reasons that help explain this difference.

	GENERAL EVENTS	LITERATURE & PHILOSOPHY	ART

768

EARLY MIDDLE AGES

Romanesque Period

987 Paris made center of feudal kingdom of Hugh Capet

1000

11th cent. Capetian kings consolidate power and expand French kingdom

1096–1099 First Crusade; capture of Jerusalem by Christians

12th cent. Golden Age of University of Paris under Saint Thomas Aquinas and other scholastic masters

12th cent. *Notre Dame de Belle Verrière,* stained glass window at Chartres

1113 Abelard begins teaching in Paris; meets Heloise

1121 Abelard, *Sic et Non;* birth of Scholasticism

1140

Early Gothic Period

1141 Saint Bernard of Clairvaux leads condemnation of Abelard at Council of Sens

c. 1145–1170 Tympanum of right door, Royal Portal, Chartres

c. 1150 Universities of Paris and Bologna founded

c. 1163 Oxford University founded

after 1150 Recovery of lost texts by Aristotle and others via Arabic translations

1180 Philip Augustus assumes throne of France; promotes Paris as capital

c. 1190 Maimonides, *Guide for the Perplexed*

1194

HIGH MIDDLE AGES

Mature Gothic Period

1202–1204 Fourth Crusade; crusaders sack Constantinople on way to Holy Land

c. 1209 Cambridge University founded

1215 Magna Carta, limiting powers of king, signed in England

c. 1220 Growth begins of mendicant friars: Franciscans, Dominicans

13th cent. Era of secular poems; Goliardic verse

c. 1200 Charlemagne window at Chartres

c. 1215 *Christ Blessing,* trumeau, south porch, Chartres

c. 1215–c. 1250 Guild windows at Chartres

1258 Robert de Sorbon founds Paris hospice for scholars, forerunner of Sorbonne

1270 Eighth Crusade; death of Saint Louis of France

c. 1271–1293 Marco Polo travels to China and India

1291 Fall of Acre, last Christian stronghold in Holy Land

c. 1267–1273 Aquinas, *Summa Theologica*

1300 Dante exiled from Florence

c. 1303–1321 Dante, *Divine Comedy*

1348–1367 Universities based on Paris model founded in Prague, Vienna, Cracow, Pecs

c. 1385–1400 Chaucer, *The Canterbury Tales*

1400

The High Middle Ages: The Search for Synthesis

10th cent. Organum develops

11th cent. Guido of Arezzo invents musical notation used today

c. 1130 Halt of construction at Great Third Abbey Church of Cluny

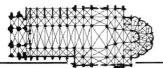

12th cent. Notre Dame School of Paris is center of music study and composition

1140 Abbot Suger begins rebuilding Abbey Church of Saint Denis; Gothic style evolves: use of pointed arch, flying buttress, window tracery

12th–13th cent. French troubadours and trouvères flourish

c. 1163–1250 Cathedral of Notre Dame, Paris

1160 Léonin of Paris, *Magnus Liber Organi*

c. 1180 Philip Augustus commissions Louvre as royal residence and treasury

1181 Pérotin "the Great," director of Notre Dame School of Paris

1194 Chartres cathedral destroyed by fire; rebuilding begins 1195 (ends 1260)

13th cent. German minnesingers flourish

1220–1269 Cathedral of Amiens

c. 1250 Polyphonic motets are principal form of composition

c. 1235 Honnecourt, notebook

1243–1248 Sainte Chapelle, Paris

1247–1568 Cathedral of Beauvais; cathedral of Strasbourg

1399–1439 Spire of Strasbourg cathedral erected

The Significance of Paris

In Roman times Paris was a provincial outpost in the backwaters of the Roman Empire, mainly a cross-roads for the Roman systems of transportation. With the decline of the empire, Paris fell into an obscurity saved from total oblivion in the early Middle Ages by the presence of churches and monasteries (every other social institution had gone into deep decline). Even in the age of Charlemagne, Rome or Aachen, not Paris, was the focal point of cultural and commercial interest. At the end of the brutal 10th century a feudal lord, Hugh Capet, began to consolidate his power into something like a monarchy and the fortunes of Paris began to improve. In 987 Hugh made Paris the center of his kingdom. The Capetian line of kings of the 11th century consolidated their power and added to their kingdom.

This political expansion naturally aided the growth and importance of Paris. By the 12th century, and certainly during the reign of Philip Augustus (who assumed the throne in 1180), the king was truly the king of France and Paris was a royal city, and in the subsequent century the kings of France would be the greatest monarchs of the time. Philip Augustus began building the Louvre [237], now a celebrated museum, as his royal residence and the place for the royal treasury. Additions by Charles V in the 14th century made the Louvre a totally self-sufficient royal city within a city.

From about 1150 to 1300 Paris could well claim to be the center of Western civilization. Beyond its position as a royal seat, it was a strong mercantile center [238]. Its annual trade fair was famous [239]. In addition, Paris gave birth to Gothic architecture, the philosophical and theological tradition known as scholasticism, and the educational community that in time became known as the university. These three creations have their own distinct history but they sprang from a common intellectual impulse: the desire to articulate all knowledge in a systematic manner.

The culture of the Middle Ages, especially as it is manifested in this era, derives from the twin sources of all Western high culture: the humane learning inherited from the culture of Greece and Rome and the accepted faith of the West, which has its origin in the world view of the Judeo-Christian scriptures and re-

237 Limbourg Brothers. The Louvre, detail from the October page of the *Très Riches Heures du Duc de Berry*. c. 1413–1416. Manuscript illumination. Musée Condé, Chantilly. Within this royal residence were rooms for the state treasury and a state prison. The building was constructed by Philip Augustus in the 12th century and continuously embellished by subsequent monarchs.

238 Trade goods entering the city of Paris on the Seine and by the Grand Pont, from the *Life of Saint Denis*. 1317. Manuscript illumination. Bibliothèque Nationale, Paris.

239 The Archbishop of Paris blesses sellers at the annual trade fair, from the *Grandes Chroniques de France*. 14th century. Manuscript illumination. Bibliothèque Nationale, Paris.

ligious world view. This twin stream of intellectual and religious ideas was present in earlier periods of Western history, as already noted in chapters 6 and 7. The flowering of a distinct expression of culture in and around medieval Paris was made possible by a large number of factors. There was a renewed interest in learning, fueled largely by the discovery of

hitherto lost texts from the classical world—especially the writings of Aristotle—which came to the West via the Moslem world. The often ill-fated crusades begun in the 11th century to recover the Holy Land and the increasing vogue for pilgrimages created a certain cosmopolitanism that, in turn, weakened the static feudal society. Religious reforms initiated by new religious orders like that of the Cistercians in the 12th century and the begging friars in the 13th breathed new life into the church.

Beyond these more generalized currents one can also point to individuals of genius who were crucial in the humanistic renaissance of the time. The University of Paris is inextricably linked with the name of Peter Abelard just as scholasticism is associated with the name of Thomas Aquinas. The Gothic style, unlike most art movements, can be pinpointed to a specific time at a particular place and with a single individual. Gothic architecture began near Paris at the Abbey of Saint Denis in the first half of the 12th century under the sponsorship of the head of the abbey, the Abbot Suger (1080–1151).

The Gothic Style

Suger's Building Program for Saint Denis

The Benedictine Abbey of Saint Denis over which Abbot Suger presided from 1122 until his death nearly 29 years later was the focal point for French patriotism. The abbey church—built in the Carolingian times—housed the relics of Saint Denis, a 5th-century martyr who had evangelized the area of Paris before his martyrdom. The crypts of the church served as burial places for Frankish kings and nobles from before the reign of Charlemagne, although it lacked the tomb of Charlemagne himself. One concrete link between the Abbey of Saint Denis and Charlemagne came through a series of literary works. The fictitious *Pèlerinage de Charlemagne* claimed that the relics of the Passion housed at the abbey had been brought there by Charlemagne himself when he returned from a pilgrimage-crusade to the Holy Land. Another work, the *Pseudo-Turpin,* has Charlemagne returning to the Abbey of Saint Denis after his Spanish campaign (the reputed scene of the *Song of Roland*) and proclaiming all France to be under the protection and tutelage of the saint. These two legends were widely believed in the Middle Ages; there is fair evidence that Suger himself accepted their authenticity. The main themes of the legends—pilgrimage, crusades, and the mythical presence of Charlemagne—created a story about the abbey that made it a major Christian shrine as well as one worthy of the royal city of Paris.

The pilgrims and visitors who came to Paris to visit Saint Denis either because of the fame of the abbey's relics or because of the annual *Lendit,* the trade fair held near the precincts of the abbey, soon overwhelmed the capacity of the old Carolingian abbey church. Accordingly in 1124 Suger decided to build a new church to accommodate those who flocked to the popular pilgrimage center. This rebuilding program took the better part of fifteen years and never saw completion. Suger mentions as models two sacred buildings that by his time already had archetypal significance for Christianity. He wanted his church to be as lavish and brilliant as Hagia Sophia in Constantinople [see Plate 16, page 287], which he knew only by reputation, and as loyal to the will of God as the Temple of Solomon [see figures 41, 42, page 48] as it was described in the Bible.

The first phase of Suger's project was basically a demolition and repair job; he had to tear down the more deteriorated parts of the old church and replace them. He reconstructed the western façade of the church and added two towers. In order better to handle the pilgrimage crowds and the increasingly elaborate processions called for in the medieval liturgy, the

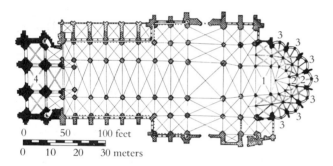

240 Plan of the abbey church of Saint Denis, built about 1140, and photograph of the ambulatory. The Abbot Suger was responsible for those parts of the existing church shaded black in the plan; the piers around the high altar were rebuilt after Suger's time. Note how use of the ribbed vault and the pointed arch in the ambulatory gave scope for the play of light from the lancet windows. Spans of differing widths could be brought easily to the same height.

| 1 choir | 3 chapel |
| 2 ambulatory | 4 narthex |

entrance was given three portals. The *narthex,* the part of the church one enters first, before the nave, was rebuilt and the old nave was to be extended by about 40 feet (12.2 meters). About 1140 Suger abruptly stopped work on the narthex to commence work at the opposite end, the *choir,* the area of the church where the monks sang the Office. By his own reckoning, he spent three years and three months at this new construction. The finished choir made a revolutionary change in architecture in the West.

Suger's choir was surrounded by a double *ambulatory,* an aisle around the apse and behind the high altar. The outer ambulatory had nine radiating chapels to accommodate the increasing number of monks who were priests and thus said Mass on a daily basis. Two tall windows pierced the walls of each chapel so that there was little external masonry wall in relation to the amount of space covered by windows. The chapels were shallow enough to permit the light from the windows to fall on the inner ambulatory [240].

Although Suger's nave was never completed there is some evidence that it would have had characteristics similar to that of the choir: crossed rib vaults with an abundance of stained-glass windows to permit the flooding of light into the church [Plate 21, page 353]. We can get some idea of what that nave might have looked like by looking at churches directly inspired by Saint Denis: the cathedrals of Senlis and Noyons [241] (their bishops were both at the

241 Interior of Noyons Cathedral. The nave was finished between 1285 and 1330. This is a fine example of the older style of Gothic architecture. The walls have four stories instead of the later three: the nave arcade at floor level, the tribune gallery, a triforium, and the clerestory with its windows. The somewhat thick arches of the triforium galleries give way in later Gothic churches to a much more pointed appearance.

242 Interior of the cathedral of Notre Dame, Paris. c. 1163–c. 1250.

consecretion of Saint Denis in 1144), begun respectively in 1153 and 1157, as well as the cathedral of Notre Dame in Paris, the first stone of which was laid in 1163 [242]. This quick emulation of the style of Saint Denis blossomed by the end of the century into a veritable explosion of cathedral-building [243] in the cities and towns radiating out from Paris, the so-called Île de France (see map opposite). The Gothic impulse also so touched other countries that by the end of the 13th century there were fine examples of Gothic architecture in England, Germany, and Italy.

The term *Gothic* merits a word of explanation. It was used first in the 17th century as a pejorative term meaning "barbarous" or "rude" to distinguish buildings that did not follow the classical models of Greece and Rome, a use still current in the mid-18th century.

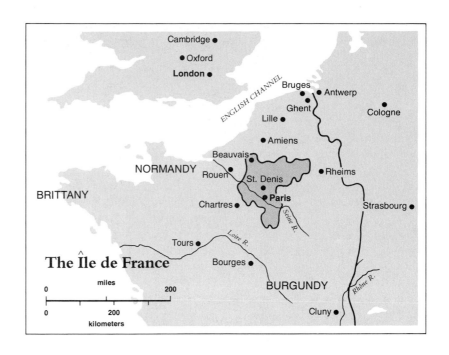

The Île de France

243 The building of many churches, from *The Deeds of Girart de Roussillon*. French, 1448. Manuscript illumination, 15¾ × 11¾″ (40 × 30 cm). Österreichische Nationalbibliothek, Vienna. The big church in the foreground was started at the east end, as almost always was the case, and the chancel is already in use. Work is continuing on the transept and nave. The other churches are at various stages.

It was only as a result of the reappraisal of the medieval period in the last century that the word lost its negative meaning.

It is tempting to say that the common characteristic of these cathedrals was the desire for verticality. We tend to identify the Gothic style with the pointed arch, pinnacles and columns, and increasingly higher walls buttressed from the outside by flying arches to accommodate the weight of a pitched roof and the sheer size of the ascending walls [244]. It is a truism that the medieval builders seem to engage in contests to build higher and higher almost as a matter of civic pride: Chartres (begun in 1194) reached a height of 122 feet (37.2 meters); almost as a response the builders of Amiens (begun 1220) stretched that height to 140 feet (42.7 meters), while Beauvais (begun 1247) pushed verticality almost to the limit with a height of 157 feet (47.9 meters) from the cathedral pavement to the roof arch; indeed, Beauvais had a serious collapse of the roof when the building was barely completed.

That verticality typified Gothic architecture is indisputable, yet Romanesque architects only a generation before Suger had attempted the same verticality, as is evident in such churches as the proposed third abbey church of Cluny [245] or the pilgrimage church at Santiago de Compostela in Spain. What

1 nave arcade 3 clerestory 5 buttress 7 pitched roof 9 pointed arch
2 triforium   4 vault   6 flying buttress 8 pinnacle 10 gargoyle

244 Transverse half sectional drawing of a typical Gothic church (cathedral of Notre Dame, Paris). The height is about 140′ (42.7 m). Note the tiny figure of a person for scale.

245 Hezelo. Nave, third abbey church of Cluny. 1088–1130. Reconstruction drawing by Kenneth J. Conant. This church, never completed, is clear in the intention to seek verticality and spaciousness. Note the rounded arches in the roof and the massive piers. Construction ended some ten years before Suger's revolutionary choir at Saint Denis.

above: **Plate 20** Roland's last deeds, detail from Charlemagne window, Chartres Cathedral. Early 13th century. Roland is shown at right sounding his horn for the last time (lines 366–370) and then trying to break his hallowed sword (lines 561–563). Slain soldiers lie below. The presence of Roland in this window testifies to his eminence in medieval culture. (Another detail from this window is in figure **209,** page 294.)

right: **Plate 21** Interior, abbey church of Saint Denis, Paris. c. 1140. The stained glass now in Saint Denis is not the original, since most of it was destroyed or dispersed in the French Revolution. However, there are historical records that permit us to reconstruct Abbot Suger's original designs.

353

Plate 22 *Notre Dame de Belle Verrière,* Chartres Cathedral. Early 13th century. The heavy vertical and horizontal lines are iron bars for reinforcement. The thinner lines are the leading. Note the painting on the glass in such features as the eyes, nose, and mouth of the Virgin. This window is an excellent example of the famous red-colored glass of the Chartres workshop.

prevented the Romanesque architect from attaining greater verticality was not lack of desire but insufficient technical means. The pointed arch was known in Romanesque architecture but not fully understood. It distributed weight more thoroughly in a downward direction and lessened the need for the massive interior piers of the typical Romanesque church. The size of the piers was further reduced by using buttresses outside the building to prop the interior piers and absorb some of the downward thrust. Furthermore, the downward thrust of the exterior buttresses themselves could be increased by the addition of heavy decorative devices such as spires.

The net result of these technical innovations was to lessen the thickness, weight, and mass of the walls of the Gothic cathedral. This reduction provided an opportunity for greater height with less bulk to absorb the weight of the vaulted roof. Such a reduction made the walls more available as framing devices for the windows that are so characteristic of the period. It has been said, perhaps with some exaggeration, that walls in Gothic cathedrals were replaced by masonry scaffolding for windows [246]. In any case, the basic characteristic of Gothic architecture is not verticality but luminosity. The Gothic may be described as transparent—diaphanous—architecture.

246 Interior of the upper chapel of La Sainte Chapelle, Paris. 1243–1248. Built to house major relics of Christ's Passion, this is a perfect example of Gothic luminosity. It has been restored somewhat, but the overall effect is not unlike that of the original. Sainte Chapelle uniquely illustrates the skeletal nature of Gothic buildings.

The Mysticism of Light

Abbot Suger wrote two short booklets about his stewardship of the abbey and his ideas about the building and decorating program he initiated for the abbey church, extremely important sources for our understanding of the thought that stood behind the actual work of the builder and artist. Underlying Suger's description of the abbey's art treasures and architectural improvements was a theory or (perhaps, better) a theology of beauty. Suger was heavily indebted to his reading of certain mystical treatises written by Dionysius the Areopagite (whom Suger and many of his contemporaries assumed was the Saint Denis for whom the abbey was named), a 5th-century Syrian monk whose works on mystical theology were strongly influenced by neo-Platonic philosophers as well as by Christian doctrine. In the doctrine of the Pseudo-Dionysius (as later generations have called him), every created thing partakes, however imperfectly, of the essence of God. There is an ascending hierarchy of existence that ranges from inert mineral matter to the purity of light, which is God. The Pseudo-Dionysius described all of creation under the category of light: every created thing is a small light that illumines the mind a bit. Ultimately, as light becomes more pure (as one ascends the hierarchy) one gets closer to pure light, which is God.

Suger applied these mystical ideas to all the component parts of his building program. One example will help to show how Suger did this. For the bronze doors of the central portal of Saint Denis, Suger composed a poem that is a handy summary of his notion about light mysticism:

> Whoever thou art, if thou seekest
>   to extol the glory of these doors,
> Marvel not at the gold and the expense
>   but at the craftsmanship of the work.
> Bright is the noble work; but, being
>   nobly bright, the work
> Should brighten the minds so that they
>   may travel, through the true lights,
> To the True Light where Christ is
>   the true door.
>
> In what manner it be inherent in
>   this world the golden door defines;
> The dull mind rises to truth
>   through that which is material
> And, in seeing this light, is resurrected
>   from its former submersion.

The high point of this light mysticism is expressed in the stained-glass window. Suger himself believed that when he finished his nave with its glass windows (never completed in fact) to complement his already finished choir he would have a total structure that would make a single statement: "Bright is that which is brightly coupled with the bright / and bright is the noble edifice which is pervaded by the new light [*lux nova*]." The *lux nova* is of course an allusion to the biblical description of God as the God of light. Suger did not invent stained glass but he fully exploited its possibilities both by encouraging an architecture that could put it to its most advantageous employment and at the same time providing a theory to justify and enhance its use.

No discussion of light and glass in this period can overlook the famous windows of the cathedral of Chartres, a small but important commercial town just south of Paris. When the cathedral was rebuilt after a disastrous fire in 1194 (which destroyed everything except the west façade of the church), the new building gave wide scope to the glazier's art.

When the walls were rebuilt more than 173 windows were installed covering an area of about 2000 square yards (1672 square meters) of surface. It is important to note that, except for some fine details like facial contours, the glass is not painted. The glaziers produced the colors (the blues and reds of Chartres are famous and the tones were never again reproduced exactly) by adding metallic salts to molten glass. Individual pieces were fitted together like a jigsaw puzzle and fixed by leading the pieces together. Individual pieces were rarely larger than 8 feet (2.4 meters) square, but 30-foot (9.2-meter) sections could be bonded together safely in the leading process. The sections were set into stone frames (mullions) and reinforced in place by the use of iron retaining rods. Windows as large as 60 feet (18.3 meters) high could be created in this fashion.

It would be useful at this point to compare the aesthetics of the stained-glass window to the mosaics discussed in Chapter 6. There was a strong element of light mysticism in the art of Byzantine mosaic decoration, derived from some of the same sources later utilized by Abbot Suger: neo-Platonism and the allegorical reading of the Bible. The actual perception of light in the two art forms, however, was radically different. The mosaic refracted light off an opaque surface. The "sacred" aura of the light in a Byzantine church comes from the oddly mysterious breaking up of light as it strikes the irregular surface of the mosaic *tesserae*. The stained-glass window was the medium through which the light was seen directly even if it was subtly muted into diverse colors and combinations of colors.

You can only "read" the meaning of the window by looking at it from the inside with an exterior light source—the sun—illuminating it. It was a more perfectly Platonic analogy of God's relationship to the world and its creatures. The viewer sees an object (the illustrated window) but "through it" is conscious of a distant unseen source (the sun—God) that illumines it and gives it its intelligibility. (*Read* is not a rhetorical verb in this context. It was a commonplace of the period to refer to the stained-glass windows as the "Bible of the Poor" since the unlettered could "read" the biblical stories in their illustrated form in the cathedral.)

A close examination of one window at Chartres will illustrate the complexity of this idea. The *Notre Dame de Belle Verrière* (Our Lady of the Beautiful Window) [Plate 22, page 354], one of the most famous works in the cathedral, is a 12th-century work saved from the rubble of the fire of 1194 and reinstalled in the south choir. The window, with its characteristic pointed arch frame, depicts the Virgin enthroned with the Christ Child surrounded by worshiping angels bearing candles and censers. Directly above her is the dove that represents the Holy Spirit and at the very top a stylized church building representing the cathedral built in her honor.

To the simple viewer the window honored the Virgin, to whom one prayed in time of need and to whom the church was dedicated. The person of some theological sophistication would further recognize the particular scene of the Virgin enthroned as the symbol of Mary as the Seat of Wisdom, a very ancient motif in religious art. The window also has a conceptual link with the exterior sculptural program. In the tympanum of the portal is an enthroned Madonna and Christ Child with two censer-bearing angels. This scene is surrounded by sculptured arches, called *archivolts,* in which there is a symbolic representation of the Seven Liberal Arts [247], which together constitute a shorthand version of the window.

247 Scenes from the life of the Virgin Mary, tympanum of the right door of the royal portal, west façade, Chartres Cathedral. Done between 1145 and 1170, the central panel shows the Virgin and Child as an almost mirror image of the *Belle Verrière* (see Plate 22). The arch over the Virgin has adoring angels while the outer arch *(archivolt)* has symbolic representations of the Seven Liberal Arts with their ancient masters. At the lower left, for example, is Aristotle dipping his pen in ink with the female figure of Dialectic above him. Under the figure of the Virgin are panels showing scenes of the early life of Christ, beginning in the lower left corner with the Annunciation followed by the Visitation, and so on.

The Blessed Virgin depicted as the Seat of Wisdom would be an especially attractive motif for the town of Chartres. The cathedral school was a flourishing center of literary and philosophical studies, studies which emphasized that human learning became wisdom only when it led to the source of wisdom, God. The fact that Mary was depicted here in glass would also call to mind an oft-repeated *exemplum* (moral example) used in medieval preaching and theology. Christ was born of a virgin. He passed through her body as light passes through a window, completely intact without changing the glass. The Christ/light–Mary/glass analogy is an apt and deepened metaphor to be seen in the *Belle Verrière* of Chartres.

That kind of interpretation can be applied profitably to many aspects of Gothic art and architecture. Builders and theologians worked closely while a cathedral was under construction. The church authorities felt it a primary duty not only to build a place suitable for divine worship but also to utilize every opportunity to teach and edify the participating worshiper. The famous Gothic gargoyles [248] are a good example of this blend of functionality and didacticism. These carved beasts served the practical purpose of funneling rainwater off the roofs while, in their extended and jutting positions on the roofs and buttresses, signifying that evil flees the sacred precincts of the church. At a far more ambitious level, the whole decorative scheme of a cathedral was an

248 Grotesques and a gargoyle waterspout on a tower terrace of the cathedral of Notre Dame, Paris.

249 Laon Cathedral from the northeast. Completed 1205. The position of this cathedral on a hilltop over the town would have been enhanced by the seven towers envisioned for it; two (at each end of the transept) were left unfinished.

attempt to tell an integrated story about the history of salvation, a story alluded to in both profane and divine learning. The modern visitor may be overwhelmed by what appears a chaotic jumble of sculptures depicting biblical scenes, allegorical figures, symbols of the labors of the month, signs of the Zodiac, representatives of pagan learning, and panoramic views of Last Judgments; for the medieval viewer the variegated scenes represented a patterned whole. The decoration of the cathedral was, as it were, the common vocabulary of sermons, folk wisdom, and school learning fleshed out in stone.

The Many Meanings
of the Gothic Cathedral

Some theological and philosophical background is crucial for an appreciation of the significance of the Gothic cathedral, but it is a serious oversimplification to view the cathedral only in the light of its intellectual milieu. The cathedral was, after all, the preeminent building in the episcopal towns of the Île de France, as a view of any of the towns shows. The cathedral overwhelms the town either by crowning a hilly site, as at Laon [249], or rising up above the town plain, as at Amiens [250]. The cathedrals were *town* buildings (Saint Denis, a monastic church, is a conspicuous exception) and one might well inquire into their functional place in the life of the town. It is simplistic to think that their presence in the town reflected a credulous faith on the part of the populace or the egomania of the civil and religious builders. In fact, the cathedral served vital social and economic functions in medieval society.

A modern analogy illustrates the social function of architecture and building. Many small towns in America, especially those in rural areas of the South and the Northeast, center their civic and commercial life around a town square. The courthouse symbolically emanates social control (justice), social structures (births, weddings, and deaths are registered there), power (the sheriff, commissioners or aldermen, and the mayor are housed there), and—to a degree—culture, with its adjacent park and military or civic monuments to the founders and war dead.

The better stores, the "uptown" churches, and the other appurtenances of respectability—banks, lawyers' and physicians' offices—cluster about the square. (The urbanization and suburbanization of America has steadily destroyed this basic symmetry, replacing it with a far more diffuse city or suburban pattern where the concept of "center" is less easy to identify.) The cathedral square of the typical European or Latin American town is the ancestor of the courthouse square. The difference is that the medieval cathedral exercised a degree of social control and integration more comprehensive than that of the courthouse.

The cathedral and its power were a serious force that shaped both individual and social life in the town. The individual was baptized in, made a communicant of, married in, and buried from the cathedral. Schooling was obtained from the cathedral school and social services (hospitals, poor relief, orphanages, and so on) directed by the decisions of the

250 Amiens Cathedral. Completed 1269. Called by Marcel Aubert the "rational summit of Gothic art," it rests firmly within the town center, as shown in this aerial view. The plan of the cathedral can also be clearly seen: nave, transept, apse, and radiating chapels.

360

cathedral staff (the *chapter*). The daily and yearly round of life was regulated by the horarium of the cathedral. People rose and ate and went to bed in rhythm with the tolling of the cathedral bell just as they worked or played in line with the feast days of the liturgical calendar of the church year. Citizens could sue and be sued in the church courts, and those same courts dispensed justice on a par with the civil courts; the scenes of the Last Judgment over the central portals of medieval cathedrals referred to more than divine justice.

Far more significant than the social interaction of town and cathedral was the economic impact of the cathedral on the town. The building of a cathedral was an extremely expensive enterprise. When the people of Chartres decided to rebuild their cathedral in 1194 the bishop pledged all of the diocesan revenues for three years (three to five million dollars!) simply to initiate the project [251]. It should be remembered that a town like Chartres was very small in the late 12th century, with no more than ten to fifteen thousand residents in the town itself. Some economic historians have attempted to show that the combination of civic pride and religious enthusiasm that motivated the town to build a cathedral was economically ruinous in the long run. The majority of scholars, however, insist that it was precisely economic gain that was the significant factor in construction. This was surely the case with Chartres.

From the late 9th century Chartres had been a major pilgrimage site. The cathedral possessed a relic of the Virgin (the tunic she wore when Jesus was born) given by Charles the Bald, the great-grandson of Charlemagne, in 876. Relics were very popular throughout the Middle Ages and this particular one was specially important to the pilgrims of the time. The relic had not been destroyed by the fire of 1194, a sure sign in the eyes of the populace that the Virgin wished the church rebuilt. Furthermore, the four great feasts of the Blessed Virgin in the liturgical year

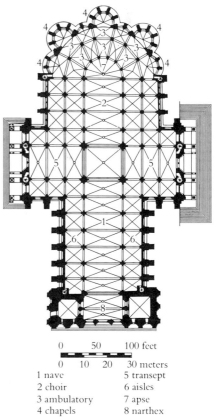

0		50		100 feet
0	10	20		30 meters

1 nave   5 transept
2 choir   6 aisles
3 ambulatory   7 apse
4 chapels   8 narthex

251 West front and floor plan of Chartres Cathedral. 1194–1240. Chartres is almost an archetype in plan of the Gothic cathedral,

(the Purification of Mary on February 2, the Annunciation on March 25, the Assumption on August 15, and the Nativity of the Virgin on September 8) were celebrated in Chartres in conjunction with large trade fairs that drew merchants and customers from all over Europe.

These fairs were held in the shadow of the cathedral and their conduct was protected by legislation issued by the cathedral chapter. Regulations from the chapter, for example, stated that the prized textiles of the area were to be sold near the north portal while the purveyors of fuel, vegetables, fruit, and wine were to be located by the south portal. There were also sellers of images, medals, and other religious objects (forerunners of the modern souvenir) to the pilgrims who came both for the fair and for reasons of devotion. The church, then, was a magnet for outsiders as much as a symbol for the townspeople.

The patrons who donated the windows of Chartres Cathedral also give some indication of the economics of the place. It was only natural that some of the large windows—like a rose window—would be the gift of a royal family or that a tall, pointed *lancet* window like those in the choir would be given by the nobility or the higher clergy. A large number of the windows, however, were donated by the members of the various craft and commercial guilds in the town; their "signature frames" can be found at the bottoms of the windows. The fact that the five large windows in honor of the Virgin in the *chevet,* the east end of the cathedral, were donated by merchants—principally the bakers, butchers, and

253 Bakers, detail of stained-glass window, Chartres Cathedral. c. 1250.

vintners—indicates the significant power of the guilds [252, 253].

The guild, a fraternal society of craftsmen or merchants, was a cross between a modern-day union and a fraternal organization like the Elks or the Knights of Columbus. Members of the guilds put themselves under the patronage of a saint, promised to perform certain charitable works, and acted as a mutual-aid society. Many of the economic guilds appear to have developed out of earlier, more purely religious confraternities. One had to belong to a guild to work at any level beyond day labor. The guild accepted and instructed apprentices; certified master craftsmen; regulated prices, wages, working conditions; and maintained funds for the care of older members and the burial of their dead. The guilds were a crucial part of town life and would remain so well into the modern period. And, as we shall see, the university developed from the guild idea in the 12th century.

The motivation for the building of a medieval cathedral, then, came from theological vision, religious devotion, civic pride, and socioeconomic interest. The actual construction depended on a large number of people. The cathedral chapter decided to construct

252 Vintners, detail of stained-glass window, Chartres Cathedral. c. 1215. This panel, in a larger window donated by the vintners' guild, shows a carter taking casks to market.

a building, raised the money, and hired the master-builder–architect. He in turn was responsible for hiring the various master craftsmen, designing the building, and creating the decorative scheme from ideas generated and approved by the theologians or church officials of the chapter. A great workshop was set up near the proposed site, with each master (mason, stonecutter, glazier) hiring his crew, obtaining his material, and setting up work quarters. Manual and occasional labor was recruited from the local population, but the construction crews were usually migratory groups who traveled from job to job.

The names of a number of master builders, including the builder of Chartres, have been lost, but others have survived in funerary inscriptions, commemora-

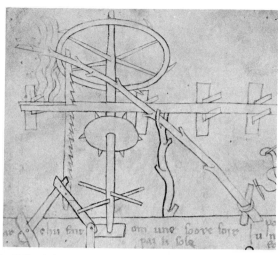

255 Villard de Honnecourt. Sketch for a water-driven saw, from his *Album*. c. 1275. Pen and ink. Bibliothèque Nationale, Paris. Water power had been much used in Europe for hundreds of years before Villard's time. This saw was for cutting the large timbers needed for construction.

254 Villard de Honnecourt. Sketch of a perpetual-motion machine, from his *Album*. c. 1275. Pen and ink. Bibliothèque Nationale, Paris. The mechanism involved the use of mercury in the enclosed arms of the pieces jutting from the wheel to power it perpetually. Villard probably got the idea from Arabic sources, who had learned it from Indian sources. The machine did not work.

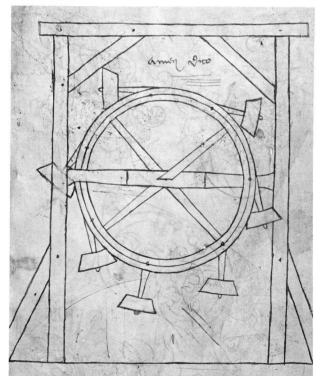

tive plaques, and building records. Notes intended for students of buildings written by Villard de Honnecourt (about 1235), an architect from northern France, preserved in a unique copy at the Bibliothèque Nationale in Paris, provide us a rare glimpse into the skills of a medieval cathedral builder. Villard says in his book that he could teach a willing apprentice a wide range of skills ranging from carpentry and masonry to the more demanding skills of practical geometry and plan drafting. The notebook also has random sketches and ideas jotted down for his own personal use; they include religious figures to serve as models for stonecarvers, and animals and buildings that caught his eye. He visited Rheims and made sketches of the cathedral. He tells of traveling as far as Hungary to get work. While not as complete and wide-ranging as the Renaissance notebooks of Leonardo da Vinci (with which they have often been compared), Villard's notebook reveals a highly skilled, persistently inquisitive, and very inventive man.

The notebook is instructive. Villard was fascinated with the problem of harnessing energy. He sketched a perpetual-motion machine [254] (which didn't work). His notebook contains probably the first example of clockworks in the West. He discovered this mechanism accidentally; what he really wanted was a device to make an angel's statue on a cathedral roof point continually to the sun as it moved across the heavens in a day. He also sketched out a plan for a self-operating mechanical saw [255] to cut the huge timbers needed for buttressing and roofing. One whole page of his notebook is devoted to solving building problems of measurement by the application of what he called "practical geometry" [256].

256 Villard de Honnecourt. Page on "practical geometry," from his *Album*. c. 1275. Pen and ink. Bibliothèque Nationale, Paris. *Top row:* Measuring the diameter of a partly visible column; finding the middle of a circle; cutting the mold of an arch; arching a vault with an outer covering; making an apse with twelve windows; cutting the springing stone of an arch. *Second row:* Bringing together two stones; cutting a voussoir for a round building; cutting an oblique voussoir. *Third row:* Bridging a stream with timbers; laying out a cloister; measuring the width of a river without crossing it; measuring the width of a distant window. *Fourth row:* Placing the cornerstones of a cloister without plumb line or level; dividing a stone into square halves; shaping the screw of a press; making two vessels of different capacities. *Bottom row:* Cutting a regular voussoir.

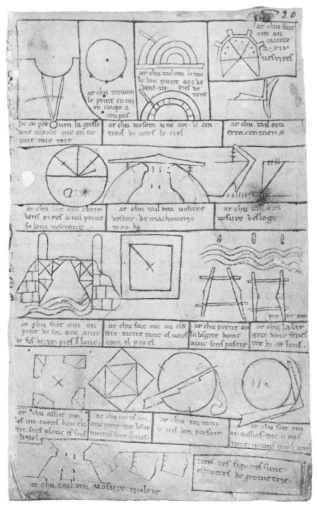

A perusal of Villard's notebook forcefully reminds us of something easily overlooked when studying a culture as distant and alien as that of the medieval era. Our tendency is to emphasize the religious and social significance of a cathedral because that is what first strikes us about such buildings. We also need to emphasize another basic fact: the medieval cathedral is a stunning technological achievement. A single example of this technological virtuosity might make the point with force. The elegant Gothic spire of the Strasbourg Cathedral, finished in 1439, is 466 feet (142.1 meters) high from pavement to tip—as high as a 40-story building [257]. That stone structure remained the highest in Europe until the mid-1960s, when the London Post Office Tower was completed.

Gothic cathedrals were possible only because a very precise knowledge of mathematics, geometry, architectural technology, and other practical sciences was increasingly available and refined for specific ends—a development that brought with it certain inevitable "spinoffs" in the areas of scientific knowledge. Just as, in our age, the space shots "spun off" advances in metallurgy, medicine, and so on, the building of so many cathedrals in a short time brought new solutions and new materials.

The Gothic cathedral is an almost perfect artifact for the study of the humanistic enterprise since it may be approached from so many angles and at so many levels. It was first an architectural and technological achievement. Its ensemble of walls, windows, sculpture, and decoration demonstrated a peculiar way of combining human knowledge and religious faith that provides a basic aesthetic experience to the viewer. It had a fundamental economic and social significance for the community in which it was located. Finally, it was, for those who entered it in faith, a transcendental religious experience of passing from the profane to the sacred world. Henry Adams, in his wonderfully eccentric book *Mont-Saint-Michel and Chartres,* says that only a person coming to Chartres as a pilgrim could understand the building. The pilgrim is a central metaphor for the period whether one speaks of the actual pilgrim on the road to Santiago de Compostela or Canterbury or life itself as a pilgrimage toward God. Pilgrims to Chartres or the other cathedrals were pilgrims in both senses: they traveled to visit a real monument and, at the same time, hoped to find rest and salvation through the act [258]. It is no wonder Abbot Suger should have called Saint Denis *Porta Coeli* (Gate of Heaven): that is exactly what it was meant to be.

left: 257 Strasbourg Cathedral. 1230–1318, spire 1399–1439. It is a mark of the mobility of early builders that the two men who finished the spire were called to Strasbourg from Ulm and Cologne in Germany to do the work. The spire for the other tower has never been built.

right: 258 Christ in the act of blessing, figure from trumeau of main portal, Chartres Cathedral. c. 1215. This statue symbolically blesses every pilgrim who enters the doors of the church (the "gates of heaven").

Music: The School of Notre Dame

It should not be surprising that in an age of artistic and architectural development such as the Gothic the rather austere music of the early church should also undergo development and change. From the time Charlemagne introduced Gregorian chant into the church life of the Frankish kingdom there had been further developments of that musical form. In the 11th century, Guido of Arezzo had worked out a system of musical notation that is the basis for the musical notation used today. Church musicians from the 10th century on also experimented with the single melodic line of plainchant by adding parallel voices at different musical intervals above the line of chant. This first step toward *polyphony*, a musical term for "many voices," is called *organum*. Outside the church, the knightly classes also composed and performed secular music. Some of the melodies of the *troubadours* and *trouvères* have survived, giving us an idea of secular music in the 12th and 13th centuries. The German *minnesingers* (*minne* means "love") of the 13th century utilized traditional church modes and melodies to create both secular and sacred songs.

The school of Notre Dame in Paris was the center of systematic musical study and composition in the 12th century. Léonin's *Magnus Liber Organi* (about 1160) is an important source for our knowledge of music in the period of the Gothic cathedral. Léonin's book was a collection of organum compositions for use during the liturgical services throughout the church year. Léonin's work was carried on by the other great composer of the century, Pérotin, who assumed the directorship of the music school of Notre Dame sometime around 1181.

In general, the Notre Dame organum utilized the basic melodic line of the traditional chant (the *cantus firmus*) while a second melodic line (the *duplum*), a third (*triplum*), and in some cases a fourth (*quadruplum*) voice was added above the melody. These added lines mirrored the rhythmic flow of the cantus firmus. It was soon learned, however, that pleasing and intricate compositions could be created by having the duplum and triplum move in opposition to the cantus firmus. This *counterpoint*—from *contrapunctum* (against the note)—meant, at its most basic level, that a descending series of notes in the cantus firmus would have an ascending series of notes in the melodic lines above it.

One development in the Gothic period deriving from the polyphony of organum was the motet. The motet usually had three voices (in some cases, four). The tenor—from the Latin *tenere* (to hold), another term for cantus firmus—maintained the traditional line, usually derived from an older ecclesiastical chant. Since some of the manuscripts from the period show no words for this tenor position, it has been thought that for many motets the tenor line was the musical accompaniment (perhaps the organ, then an instrument of increasing popularity). Above the tenor were two voices who sang interweaving melodies. In the early 13th century, these melodies were invariably in Latin and were exclusively religious in content. In the late 13th century it was not uncommon to sing the duplum in Latin and the triplum in French. Indeed, the two upper voices could be singing quite distinct songs: a hymn in Latin with a love lyric in French with a tenor voice (or instrument) maintaining an elaborated melody based on the melismas of Gregorian chant.

This increasingly sophisticated music, freed from its monastic binds, is indicative of many of the intellectual currents of the period. It is a technically complex music rooted in the distant past but open to new and somewhat daring innovation, a blend of the traditional and the vernacular—all held together in an intellectually complicated balance of competing elements. Gothic music was an aural expression of the dynamism inherent in the medieval Gothic cathedral.

Scholasticism

The Rise of the Universities

A number of our contemporary institutions have roots in the Middle Ages. Trial by jury is one, constitutional monarchy another. By far the best-known and most widely diffused cultural institution that dates from the Middle Ages, however, is the university. In fact, some of the most prestigious centers of European learning today stand where they were founded eight hundred years ago: Oxford and Cambridge in England; the University of Paris in France; the University of Bologna in Italy. There is also a remarkable continuity between the organization and purposes of the medieval university and our own. The medieval student would be puzzled, to be sure, by the idea of football games, coeducation, degrees in business or agriculture, and well-manicured campuses, were he to visit a modern American university. He would find himself at home with the idea of a liberal arts curriculum, the degrees from the baccalaureate through the master's to the doctorate, and the high cost of textbooks. At a less serious level, he would be well acquainted with drinking parties, fraternities, and friction between town and gown (the phrase itself has a medieval ring). The literature that has come down to us from the period is full of complaints about poor housing, high rents, terrible food, and lack of jobs after graduation. Letters from the Middle Ages between students and parents have an almost uncanny contemporaneity about them. Here is one 14th-century example from parent to son at law school in Orléans, France:

> . . . I have recently discovered that you live dissolutely and slothfully, preferring license to restraint and play to work and strumming a guitar while the others are at their studies, whence it happens that you have but one volume of law while more industrious companions have read several. I

have decided to exhort you herewith to repent utterly of your dissolute and careless ways that you may no longer be called a waster and that your shame may be turned to good repute.

Another son wrote to his parent from the same university at Orléans with a timeless request:

. . . We occupy a good and comely dwelling, next door but one from the schools and marketplace, so that we can go to school every day without wetting our feet. We have good companions in the house with us, well advanced in their studies and of excellent habits—an advantage which we well appreciate, for as the Psalmist says, "with an upright man thou will show thyself upright." Wherefore, lest production cease from lack of material, we beg your paternity to send us by the bearer money for buying parchment, ink, a desk, and the other things which we need, in sufficient amount that we may suffer no want on your account (God forbid!) but finish our studies and return home with honor. The bearer will also take charge of the shoes and stockings which you have to send us, and any news at all.

European universities developed in the late 12th and early 13th centuries along with the emergence of city life. In the earlier medieval period schools were most often associated with the monasteries, which were perforce situated in rural areas. As cities grew in importance, schools also developed at urban monasteries or, increasingly, under the aegis of bishops whose cathedrals were in the towns. The episcopal or cathedral school was a direct offshoot of the increasing importance of towns and the increasing power of bishops, the spiritual leaders of town life. In Italy, where town life had been relatively strong throughout the early Middle Ages and where feudalism never took hold, there was also a tradition of schools controlled by the laity. The center of medical studies in Salerno and the law faculty of Bologna had been in secular hands since the 10th century.

A number of factors help to explain the rapid rise of formal education institutions in the 12th century. First, the increasing complexity of urban life created a demand for an educated class who could join the ranks of administrators and bureaucrats. Urban schools were not simply interested in providing basic literacy. They were designed to produce an educated class who could give support to the socioeconomic structures of society. Those who completed the arts curriculum of a 12th-century cathedral school (like the one at Chartres) could find ready employment in either the civil or the ecclesiastical bureaucracy as lawyers, clerks, or administrators.

There were also intellectual and cultural reasons for the rise of the universities. In the period from 1150 to 1250 came a wholesale discovery and publication of texts from the ancient world. Principal among these were lost books by Aristotle that came to the West through Moslem sources in Spain. Aristotle's writings covered a vast range of subjects ranging from meteorology and physics to logic and philosophy. Furthermore, with a closer relationship between Christian and Arabic scholars, a large amount of scientific and mathematical material was coming into Europe [259]. There was also a renaissance of legal studies centered primarily at Bologna, the one intellectual center that could nearly rival Paris. Finally, there was a new tool being refined by such scholars as Peter Abelard and Peter Lombard: dialectics. Theologians and philosophers began to apply the principles of logic to the study of philosophy and theology. Abelard's book *Sic et Non* (1121) put together conflicting opinions concerning theological matters with contradictory passages from the Bible and the Church Fathers and then attempted to mediate and reconcile the apparent divergences. This method was later refined and stylized into the method which was to become *scholasticism,* so called because it was the

259 A university lecture, detail from compendium of Aristotle's *Nichomachean Ethics.* German, 14th century. Manuscript illumination. State Museums, Berlin. Note the professor in his chair *(cathedra)* expounding a text. Even today, in certain English universities the lower ranks of professors are called readers.

philosophical method of the schools, the communities of scholars at the nascent universities.

The most famous and representative university to emerge in the Middle Ages was the University of Paris. The eminence of Paris rested mainly on the fame of the teachers who came there to teach. At this state of educational development, the teacher really was the school. Students in the 12th century flocked from all over Europe to frequent the lectures of teachers like William of Champeaux (1070–1121) and, later, his former student and vehement critic, Peter Abelard (1079–1142). Besides these famous individual teachers Paris also had some established centers of learning that enjoyed a vast reputation. There were a cathedral school attached to the cathedral of Notre Dame, a theological center associated with the canons of the church of Saint Victor, and a school of arts maintained at the ancient monastery of Sainte Geneviève.

Although it is difficult to assign precise dates, it is safe to say that the university at Paris developed in the final quarter of the 12th and early part of the 13th centuries. Its development began with the masters—*magistri* (teachers)—of the city forming a corporation after the manner of the guilds. At this time the word *universitas* simply meant a guild or corporation. The masters formed the *universitas* in Paris in order to exercise some "quality control" over the teaching profession and the students entrusted to their care. At Bologna the reverse was true. The students formed the *universitas* in order to hire the teachers with the best qualifications and according to the most advantageous financial terms.

The *universitas* soon acquired a certain status in law with a corporate right to borrow money, to sue (and be sued), and to issue official documents. As a legal body the *universitas* could issue stipulations for the conduct of both masters and students. When a student finished the course of studies and passed his examinations the *universitas* would grant him a *licentia docendi* (teaching certificate) that enabled him to enter the ranks of the masters: he was a master of arts (our modern degree has its origin in that designation). After graduation a student could go on to specialized training in law, theology, or medicine. The completion of this specialized training entitled one to be called *doctor* (from the Latin *doctus* [learned]) in his particular field. The modern notion that a professional person (doctor, lawyer, and the like) should be university-trained is an idea derived directly from the usages of the medieval university.

Since the Carolingian period—indeed, earlier—the core of education was the arts curriculum. In the late 12th century in Paris the arts began to be looked on as a prelude to the study of theology. This inevitably caused a degree of tension between the arts faculty and the theology masters. This tension resulted in 1210 in a split, with the masters and students of arts moving their faculty to the Left Bank of the Seine, where they settled in the area intersected by the rue du Fouarre (Straw Street—so named because the students sat on straw during lectures). That part of the Left Bank has traditionally been a student haunt. The Latin Quarter name reminds us of the old language that was once the only tongue used at the university.

By the end of the 12th century Paris was the intellectual center of Europe. Students came from all over Europe to study there. We do not have reliable statistics about their number, but an estimate of five thousand to eight thousand students would not be far from the mark for the early 13th century. The students were organized into *nationes* by their place of national origin. By 1294 there were four recognized *nationes* in Paris: the French, the Picard, the Norman, and the Anglo-German. Student support came from families, pious benefactors, church stipends, or civic grants to underwrite an education. Certain generous patrons provided funds for hospices for scholars, the most famous of which was that underwritten by Robert de Sorbon in 1258 for graduate students in theology; his hospice was the forerunner of the Sorbonne in Paris.

By our standards student life in the 13th century was harsh. Food and lodging were primitive, heating scarce, artificial lighting nonexistent, and income sporadic. The daily schedule was rigorous, made more so by the shortage of books and writing material. An "ideal" student's day, as sketched out in a late medieval pamphlet for student use, now seems rather grim:

A Student's Day
at the University of Paris

4:00 A.M.	Rise
5:00–6:00	Arts lectures
6:00	Mass and breakfast
8:00–10:00	Lectures
11:00–12:00	Disputations before the noon meal
1:00–3:00	"Repetitions"—study of morning lectures with tutors

3:00–5:00	Cursory lectures (generalized lectures on special topics) or disputations
6:00	Supper
7:00–9:00	Study and repetitions; bed at 9:00 P.M.

The masters' lectures consisted of detailed commentaries on certain books the master intended to cover in a given term. Since books were expensive, emphasis was put on note-taking and copying so that the student might build up his own collection of books. Examinations were oral, before a panel of masters. Students were also expected to participate in formal debates (called disputations) as part of their training.

Geoffrey Chaucer provides us an unforgettable, albeit idealized, portrait of the medieval student (the clerk or cleric—many of the students were members of the minor clerical orders of the church) in his Prologue to the *Canterbury Tales:*

A clerk from Oxford was with us also,
Who'd turned to getting knowledge, long ago.
As meagre was his horse as is a rake,
Nor he himself too fat, I'll undertake,
But he looked hollow and went soberly.
Right threadbare was his overcoat; for he
Had got him yet no churchly benefice,
Nor was so worldly as to gain office.
For he would rather have at his bed's head
Some twenty books, all bound in black and red,
Of Aristotle and his philosophy
Than rich robes, fiddle, or gay psaltery.
Yet, and for all he was philosopher,
He had but little gold within his coffer;
But all that he might borrow from a friend
On books and learning he would swiftly spend,
And then he'd pray right busily for the souls
Of those who gave him wherewithal for schools.
Of study took he utmost care and heed.
Not one word spoke he more than was his need;
And that was said in fullest reverence
And short and quick and full of high good sense.
Pregnant of moral virtue was his speech;
And gladly would he learn and gladly teach.

Chaucer's portrait of the lean, pious, poor, zealous student was highly idealized to create a type. We get probably a far more realistic picture of what students were actually doing and thinking about from the considerable amount of popular poetry that comes from the student culture of the medieval period. This poetry depicts a student life we are all familiar with: a poetry of wine, women, song, sharp satires at the expense of pompous professors or poor accommodations, and the occasional episodes of cruelty that most

260 Students taunting a woman, quatrefoil from south transept of the cathedral of Notre Dame, Paris. c. 1260. The woman—perhaps a prostitute—is tied to the "bishop's ladder," a sort of medieval stocks. The figures in front are law officers; the students hurl rocks and mud.

individuals are capable of only when they are banded into groups [260].

The student subculture had also invented a mythical Saint Golias, who was the patron saint of wandering scholars. Verses (called Goliardic verse) were written in honor of the "saint." The poems that have come down to us are a far cry from the sober commentaries on Aristotle's *Metaphysics* that we usually associate with the medieval scholar:

Nature gives to every man
Gifts as she is willing;
I compose my verses when
Good wine I am swilling.
Wine the best for jolly guest
Jolly hosts are filling;
From such wine rare fancies fine
Flow like dews distilling.

There are poets, worthy men,
Shrink from public places,
And in lurking hole or den

Hide their pallid faces;
There they study, sweat, and woo
Pallas and the Graces
But bring forth nothing to view
Worth the girls' embraces!

One of the more interesting collections of these medieval lyrics was discovered in a Bavarian monastery in the early 19th century. The songs in this collection were written in Latin, Old French, and German and seem to date from the late 12th and the 13th centuries. Their subject range was wide but, given the nature of such songs, predictable. There were drinking songs, laments over the loss of love or the trials of fate, hymns in honor of nature, salutes to the end of winter and the coming of the spring, and cheerfully obscene songs of exuberant sexuality. The lyrics reveal a shift of emotions ranging from the happiness of love to the despair of disappointment just as the allusions range from classical learning to medieval piety. One famous song, for example, praises the beautiful powerful virgin in language that echoes the piety of the church. The last line reveals, however, that the poem salutes not Mary but generous Venus.

In 1935 and 1936 the German composer Carl Orff set a number of these poems to music under the title *Carmina Burana*. His brilliantly lively blending of heavy percussion, snatches of ecclesiastical chant, strong choral voices, and vibrant rhythms have made this work a modern concert favorite. The listener receives a good sense of the vibrancy of these medieval lyrics by the use of the modern setting. Since the precise character of student music has not come down to us, Orff's new setting of these lyrics is a fine substitute in learning about the musicality of this popular poetry from the medieval university.

Poems of this sort are products of the highly mobile university population of the period. The community was mobile since there were few permanent structures; when students and masters moved, the *universitas* moved. One of the most powerful weapons the *universitas* possessed was the *cessatio*. If things went bad between the host city and the *universitas* a *cessatio* (closing) could be called and the *universitas* could threaten to move. The *cessatio* was a potent economic tool. When the university closed down in Paris in 1228–1229 (after a quarrel between the civil authorities and the *universitas* as a result of student riots during Lent), the English king, Henry III, was quick to seize his chance to lure the whole *universitas* from Paris to his more benevolent shores:

Greetings to the masters and the whole body of scholars at Paris. Humbly sympathizing with the exceeding tribulations and distresses which you have suffered at Paris under an unjust law, we wish by our pious aid, with reverence to God and His Holy Church, to restore your status to its proper condition of liberty. Wherefore we have concluded to make known to your entire body that if it shall be your pleasure to transfer yourselves to our kingdom of England and to remain there to study we will for this purpose assign to you cities, towns, boroughs, whatsoever you may wish to select, and in every fitting way cause you to rejoice in a state of liberty and tranquility which should please God and fully meet your needs.

Although the entire *universitas* did not accept the king's invitation, many scholars did go to England, where they settled at Cambridge and Oxford. Ironically enough, a migration of students from Oxford to Cambridge in 1209 gave Cambridge greater prestige and a student body large enough to form its own *universitas*.

The reputation of intellectual centers like Oxford, Paris, and Bologna invited imitation in the 13th century. Other universities started up in this period in France, the Low Countries, and the Iberian peninsula, often modeled on the Paris *universitas*. (The Bologna model of having a corporation of students as opposed to a corporation of masters did not gain wide acceptance.) In Italy, universities developed at Siena, Pavia, and Vercelli as offshoots of the University of Bologna. In the 14th century many other European cities founded universities based on the Paris model. Some of these still exist today: Prague (1348), Vienna (1365), Cracow (1364), Pecs in Hungary (1367).

Thomas Aquinas

The Golden Age of the University of Paris was the 13th century, since in that period Paris could lay fair claim to being the intellectual center of the Western world. It is a mark of the international character of medieval university life that some of its most distinguished professors were from outside France: Albert the Great was German; Alexander of Hales was English; Bonaventure and Thomas Aquinas were Italian.

Thomas Aquinas (1225?–1274) was the most famous and influential of the Parisian masters of the 13th century [261]. His intellectual influence went far beyond the lecture halls of Paris and is felt to the present. Born of noble parentage in southern Italy,

261 Andrea da Firenze. *The Triumph of Saint Thomas Aquinas.* c. 1365. Fresco. Spanish Chapel, Santa Maria Novella, Florence. The saint is enthroned between Doctors of the Old and New Testaments, with personifications of the Virtues, Sciences, and Liberal Arts below.

Thomas joined the Preaching Friars of Saint Dominic (the Dominicans) in 1243. From 1245 to 1248 he studied with Albert the Great at both Paris and Cologne. He was made a *magister* of theology in 1258 after completing his doctoral studies. During this same period (from roughly 1256 to 1259) he lectured on theology in Paris. From 1259 to 1268 he was back in Italy, where he lectured and wrote at Orvieto (the papal court for a time), Rome, and Naples. From 1268 to 1272 he held a chair of theology again, when he returned to Naples to teach there. He died two years later on his way to a church council at Lyons in France.

Thomas Aquinas' life ended before he was fifty, but in that span he produced a vast corpus of writings (they fill 40 folio volumes) on theology, philosophy, and biblical studies. It is a mark of his mobility that his masterpiece—the *Summa Theologica*—was composed at Rome, Viterbo, Paris, and Naples, although it was unfinished at his death. While his writings touched on a wide variety of subjects, at root Thomas Aquinas was interested in and made a lifetime study of a very basic problem: How does one harmonize those things that are part of human learning (reason) with those supernatural truths revealed by God in the Bible and through the teaching of the church (revelation)? Aquinas' approach was to steer a middle path through two diametrically opposed opinions, both of which had avid supporters in the Middle Ages: the position of *fideism,* which held that religious faith as an absolute is indifferent to the efforts of human reason (*credo quia absurdum est*—I believe because it is absurd) and *rationalism,* which insists that everything, revelation included, must meet the test of rational human scrutiny. Aquinas wanted to demonstrate what the Gothic cathedral illustrated: that the liberal arts, the things and seasons of the world, and the mysteries revealed by God could be brought into some kind of intellectual harmony based on a single criterion of truth.

For Aquinas, reason finds truth when it sees evidence of truth. The mind judges something true when it has observed a sufficient number of facts to compel it to make that judgment. The mind gives assent to truth on the basis of evidence. Aquinas was convinced that there was a sufficient amount of observable evidence in the world to conclude the existence of God. He proposed five arguments in support of such a position. Still he recognized that such argumentation only yields a very limited understanding of God. Aquinas did not believe that the naked use of reason could ever discover or prove the mysteries about God revealed in the Bible: that God became a man in Jesus Christ or that there was a Trinity of persons in God. God had to tell us that. Our assent to it is not based on evidence, but on the authority of

God who reveals it to us. If we could prove the mysteries of faith, there would have been no need of a revelation and no need of faith.

Thus for Aquinas there is an organic relationship between reason and revelation. Philosophy perfects the human capacity to know and revelation perfects one beyond self by offering salvation and eternal life. Aquinas stated this relationship between reason and revelation at the very beginning of his great work of theology, the *Summa Theologica:*

> I answer that it was necessary for salvation that there be a knowledge revealed by God, beyond the philosophical sciences investigated by human reason. First, because man is directed by God to an end that surpasses the grasp of his reason. . . . But the need must be known first to those who direct their thoughts and actions towards that end. Hence it is necessary for the salvation of man that certain truths which are beyond human reason be made known to him by divine revelation. Even with respect to those truths about God which human reason can investigate, it is necessary that man be taught by a divine revelation. For the truth about God, as human reason can know it, could only be known by a few, and only after a long time, and with many errors; while man's whole salvation, which is in God, depends on the knowledge of that truth. Therefore, in order that the salvation of men might be accomplished fitly and with certitude it is necessary that they be taught divine truths by divine revelation. It is therefore necessary that, beyond the philosophical sciences investigated by reason, there should be a sacred science by way of revelation.

The philosophical tradition Aquinas used in his writing was that of the Greek philosopher Aristotle. He first knew Aristotle's work in Latin translations based on Arabic texts done by Moslem scholars in the south of Spain and North Africa. Later Aquinas was able to use texts translated directly out of Greek by a Flemish friar and sometime companion, William of Moerbeke. Aquinas' use of Aristotle was certainly not a novelty in the Middle Ages. Such Arabic scholars as Avicenna (980–1036) and Averröes of Córdova (1126–98) commented on Aristotle's philosophy and its relationship to the faith of Islam. Jewish thinkers like the famous Moses Maimonides (born in Córdova in 1135, died in Egypt in 1204) made similar attempts to bridge Greek thought and their religious faith. Maimonides wrote his famous *Guide for the Perplexed* to demonstrate the essential compatibility of the Hebrew scriptures with the thought of Aristotle. Maimonides was determined that essentials of the biblical message not be compromised, but he likewise felt that in nonessentials there was room for human reflection. In this task of distinguishing the place of intellect and faith Maimonides anticipated the work of Thomas Aquinas by two generations.

What all of these theologians and philosophers—Islamic, Jewish, and Christian—did was synthesize or reconcile the two streams of human culture we recognize as the two sources of Western civilization: the biblical and the classical.

When we read Aquinas today (the short selection above is not atypical) we get some sense of his stark and rigorous attempt to think things through. For one thing, he offers no stylistic adornment to relieve his philosophical and rational discourse. For another, he makes clear that philosophical reasoning is difficult; it is not a pastime for the incompetent or the intellectually lazy. Yet Aquinas was not a mere machine for logic. He had the temperament of the mystic. Some months before he died he simply put down his pen; when his secretary asked him why he had stopped writing, Aquinas simply said that in prayer and quiet he had had a vision and that what he had written "seemed as straw." Aquinas was a rare combination of intellectual and mystic.

Two other characteristics of the thought of Aquinas should be noted. First, his world view was strongly hierarchical. Everything has its place in the universe, and that place is determined in relationship to God. A rock is good because it *is* (to Aquinas existence was a gift), but an animal is more perfect because it has life and thus shares more of divine attributes. In turn, men and women are better still because they possess mind and will. Angels are closer yet to God because they, like God, are pure spirit.

This hierarchical world view explains other characteristics of Aquinas' thought in particular and medieval thought in general: it is wide-ranging, it is encyclopedic, and in interrelating everything it is synthetic. Everything fits and has its place, meaning, and truth. That a person would speak on psychology, physics, politics, theology, and philosophy with equal authority would strike us as presumptuous, just as any building decorated with symbols from the classics, astrology, the Bible, and scenes from everyday life would now be considered a hodgepodge. Such was not the case in the 13th century, since it was assumed that everything ultimately pointed to God.

Dante's *Divine Comedy*

In any discussion of the culture of the High Middle Ages two descriptive adjectives come immediately to mind: hierarchical and synthetic. It has been a commonplace, for example, to compare the Gothic cathedral and the systematic treatise on philosophy and theology called the *Summa* since Erwin Panofsky first gave the comparison credibility in *Gothic Architecture and Scholasticism* (1951). On close inspection such comparisons may be facile, but they point to truths about this period that are relatively secure. Both the Gothic cathedral and the theology of Aquinas, for example, started from the tangible and sensual ("Nothing comes to the mind except through the senses" is a basic axiom for Aquinas) in order to mount in a hierarchical manner to the light that is God. Again, both writer and architect felt it possible to be universal in their desire to synthesize all human knowledge as prelude and pointer to the full revelation of God. Finally, they both constructed their edifices by the juxtaposition of tensions and syntheses.

If the Gothic cathedral and the *Summa* represent two masterpieces of the hierarchical and synthetic religious humanism of the Middle Ages, the *Divine Comedy* of Dante Alighieri (1265–1321) represents the same masterly achievement in literature. Dante [262] was a Florentine. He was nonetheless deeply influenced by the intellectual currents that emanated from the Paris of his time. As a comfortably fixed young man he devoted himself to a rigorous program of philosophical and theological study in order to enhance his already burgeoning literary talent. He frequented lectures at the Dominican *studium* of Santa Maria Novella in his home city. At an earlier age he had also studied rhetoric at the Franciscan school of Santa Croce in Florence. There is some evidence that he spent time in Bologna, but it is assumed that his studies there were in the arts faculty and not at Bologna's celebrated law school. His studies at Florence's Santa Maria Novella must have been decisive; his thorough knowledge of Aristotle and Thomas Aquinas is evident in every page of his mature writing. Dante's published work gives evidence of a profound culture and a deep love for study. He wrote on the origin and development of language *(De Vulgari Eloquentia),* political theory *(De Monarchia),* and generalized knowledge *(Convivio)* as well as his own poetic aspirations *(Vita Nuova).* His masterpiece, of course, is the *Divine Comedy.*

262 Sandro Botticelli. *Dante.* c. 1480–1485. Oil on canvas, 24¼ × 18½" (54 × 47 cm). Collection Dr. Martin Bodmer, Cologny/Geneva.

Dante was exiled from Florence for political reasons in 1300. In his bitter wanderings in the north of Italy he worked on—and finally brought to conclusion—a long poem to which he gave a bitingly ironical title: *The Comedy of Dante Alighieri, A Florentine by Birth but Not in Behavior.* Dante called his poem a comedy since, as he noted, it had a happy ending and it was written in the popular language of the people. The adjective *divine* was added later; some say by Boccaccio, who in the next generation lectured on the poem in Florence and wrote one of the first biographies of the great poet.

The *Divine Comedy* relates a symbolic journey which the poet begins on Good Friday, 1300, through the world of hell, purgatory, and heaven. In the first two parts of his journey, Dante is guided by the ancient Roman poet Vergil, whose *Aeneid* was

QVI COELVM CECINIT MEDIVMQVE IMVMQVE TRIBVNAL· LVSTRAVITQVE ANIMO CVNCTA POETA SVO· DOCTVS ADEST DANTES SVA QVEM FLORENTIA SAEPE· SENSIT CONSILIIS AC PIETATE PATREM· NIL POTVIT TANTO MORS SAEVA NOCERE POETAE· QVEM VIVVM VIRTVS CARMEN IMAGO FACIT·

263 Domenico di Michelino. *Dante and His Poem.* 1465. Fresco. Florence Cathedral. Dante, holding his *Comedy,* points to Hell, where his journey begins. Behind him is the Mount of Purgatory. At right is Florence (note the recently finished Cathedral with its dome), here a symbol of the heavenly city of Paradise. This fresco is one of several monuments to Dante in Florence. In the detail *(left),* note the angel guarding the entrance to Purgatory, where the seven deadly sins are purged.

such an inspiration to him and from which he borrowed (especially from Book VI, which tells of Aeneas' own journey to the Underworld). From the border at the top of the Mount of Purgatory to the pinnacle of heaven where Dante glimpses the "still point of light" that is God, Dante's guide is Beatrice, a young woman Dante had loved passionately if platonically in his youth [263].

Every significant commentator on the *Comedy* has noted its careful organization. The poem is made up of 100 cantos. The first canto of the *Inferno* serves as an introduction to the whole poem. There are then 33 cantos for each of the three major sections *(Inferno, Purgatorio,* and *Paradiso).* The entire poem is written in a rhyme scheme called *terza rima* (aba, bcb, cdc, and so on) that is almost impossible to duplicate in English because of the shortage of rhyming words in our language. The number three and its multiples, symbols of the Trinity, occur over and over. The *Inferno* is divided into nine regions plus a vestibule, and the same number is found in the *Purgatorio.* Dante's *Paradiso* is constituted by the nine heavens of the Ptolemaic system plus the Empyrean, the highest heaven. This scheme mirrors the whole poem of 99 cantos plus one. The sinners in the *Inferno* are arranged according to whether they sinned by incontinence, violence, or fraud (a division Dante derived from Aristotle's *Ethics*), while the yearning souls of purgatory are divided in three ways according to how they acted or failed to act in relation to love. The saved souls in the *Paradiso* are divided into the lay folk, the active, and the contemplative. Nearest the throne of God, but reflected in the circles of heaven, are the nine categories of angels.

Dante's interest in the symbolic goes beyond his elaborate manipulation of numbers. In the *Inferno* sinners suffer punishments that have symbolic value; their sufferings both punish and instruct. The gluttonous live on heaps of garbage under driving storms of cold rain, while the flatterers are immersed in pools of sewage and the sexually perverse walk burning stretches of sand in an environment as sterile as their attempts at love. Conversely, in the *Paradiso,* the blessed dwell in the circles most symbolic of their virtue. The theologians are in the circle of the sun since they provided such enlightenment to the world, and the holy warriors dwell in the sphere of Mars.

We can better appreciate the density and complexity of Dante's symbolism by looking at a single example. Our common image of Satan is that of a sly tempter (in popular art he is often in formal dress whispering blandishments in a willing ear with just a whiff of sulphur about him) after the manner of Milton's proud, perversely tragic, heroic Satan in *Paradise Lost.* For Dante, Satan is a huge, stupid beast, frozen in a lake of ice in the pit of hell. He beats six batlike wings (a demonic leftover from his angelic existence; see Isaiah 6:1–5) in an ineffectual attempt to escape the frozen pond that is watered by the four rivers of hell. He is grotesquely three-headed (a parody of the Trinity) and his slavering mouths remorselessly chew the bodies of three infamous traitors from sacred and secular history (Judas, Cassius, and Brutus).

Why does Dante portray Satan so grotesquely? It is clear that Dante borrowed some of the picture of Satan from Byzantine mosaics with which he would have been familiar in the Baptistery of Florence [264]. Beyond that, the whole complex of Satan is

264 Hell, detail of mosaic in vault of the Baptistery, Florence Cathedral. 13th century. The giant, who is a Satan figure, his throne, and the serpents are all swallowing up human beings.

heavily weighted with symbolic significance. Satan lies in frozen darkness at a point in the universe farthest from the warmth and light of God. He is the fallen angel of light (Lucifer means "light-bearer"), now encased in a pit in the center of the earth excavated by the force of his own fall from heaven. He is immobile to contrast him with God, who is the mover of all things in the universe. He is totally inarticulate and stupid because he represents, par excellence, all of the souls of hell who have lost what Dante calls "the good of intellect." Satan, and all of the souls in hell, will remain totally unfulfilled as created rational beings because they are cut off from the final source of rational understanding and fulfillment: God. Intellectual estrangement from God is for Dante, as it was for Thomas Aquinas, the essence of damnation. This estrangement is most evident in the case of Satan, who symbolizes in his very being the loss of rationality and all that derives from that fact.

Dante, following a line of thought already developed by Suger and Aquinas, conceived the human journey as a slow ascent to the purity of God by means of the created things of this world. To settle for less than God was, in essence, to fail to return to the natural source of life, God. This explains why light is such a crucial motif in the *Divine Comedy* as it had been in the theories of Abbot Suger. Neither light nor the sources of light (the sun) is ever mentioned in the *Inferno*. The overwhelming visual impression of the *Inferno* is darkness—a darkness that begins when Dante is lost in the "dark wood" of Canto I and continues until he climbs from hell and sees above his head the stars (the word *stars* ends each of the three major parts of the poem) of the Southern Hemisphere. In the ascent of the mountain of purgatory, daylight and sunset are controlling motifs to symbolize the reception and rejection of divine light. In the *Paradiso* the blessed are bathed in the reflected light that comes from God. At the climax of the *Paradiso* the poet has a momentary glimpse of God as a point of light and rather obscurely understands that God, the source of all intelligibility, is the power that also moves the "sun and the other stars."

Within the broad reaches of Dante's philosophical and theological preoccupations the poet still has the concentrated power to sketch unforgettable portraits: the doomed lovers Paolo and Francesca—each of the tercets that tell their story starts with the word *amore* (love)—the haughty political leader Farinata degli Umberti, the pitiable suicide Pier delle Vigne, or the

caricatures of gluttons like Ciacco the Hog. Damned, penitent, or saved, the characters are by turns both symbols and persons. Saint Peter represents the church in the *Paradiso* but also explodes with ferociously human anger at its abuses. Brunetto Latini in the *Inferno* with "his brown-baked features" is a condemned sodomite but still anxious that posterity at least remember his literary accomplishments.

It has been said that a mastery of the *Divine Comedy* would be a mastery of all that was significant about the intellectual culture of the Middle Ages. It is certainly true that the poem, encyclopedic and complex as it is, would provide a primer for any reader interested in the science, political theory, philosophy, literary criticism, and theology of the 13th century as well as a detailed acquaintance with the burning questions of Dante's time. The very comprehensiveness of the poem has often been its major obstacle for the modern reader. Beyond that hurdle is the strangeness of the Dantean world, so at variance with our own: earth-centered, manageably small, sure of its ideas of right and wrong, orthodox in its theology, prescientific in its outlook, Aristotelean in its philosophy. For all that, Dante is not to be read only for his store of medieval lore; he is, as T. S. Eliot once wrote, the most universal of poets. He had a deeply sympathetic appreciation of human aspiration, love and hate, the destiny of humanity, and the meaning of nature and history.

If parts of the *Divine Comedy* make for rough going, certain cantos stand out as unforgettable moments in poetry. These cantos, as an Italian critic once said, have been singled out by critical consensus. Of course this does not mean that the rest is not worth reading. It merely means that the cantos reprinted here give a short but substantial entry into the world of Dante the poet and thinker.

This translation is by the American poet John Ciardi. Each canto is introduced by a translator's summary. Ciardi also wrote the explanatory notes.

Dante Alighieri
from the DIVINE COMEDY

Inferno

Canto I
The Dark Wood of Error
Midway in his allotted threescore years and ten, Dante comes to himself with a start and realizes that he has strayed from the True Way into the Dark Wood of Error (Worldliness). As soon as he has realized his loss,

Dante lifts his eyes and sees the first light of the sunrise (the Sun is the Symbol of Divine Illumination) lighting the shoulders of a little hill (The Mount of Joy). It is the Easter Season, the time of resurrection, and the sun is in its equinoctial rebirth. This juxtaposition of joyous symbols fills Dante with hope and he sets out at once to climb directly up the Mount of Joy, but almost immediately his way is blocked by the Three Beasts of Worldliness: *The Leopard of Malice and Fraud, The Lion of Violence and Ambition,* and *The She-Wolf of Incontinence.* These beasts, and especially the She-Wolf, drive him back despairing into the darkness of error. But just as all seems lost, a figure appears to him. It is the shade of *Virgil,* Dante's symbol of *Human Reason.*

Virgil explains that he has been sent to lead Dante from error. There can, however, be no direct ascent past the beasts: the man who would escape them must go a longer and harder way. First he must descend through Hell (The Recognition of Sin), then he must ascend through Purgatory (The Renunciation of Sin), and only then may he reach the pinnacle of joy and come to the Light of God. Virgil offers to guide Dante, but only as far as Human Reason can go. Another guide (*Beatrice,* symbol of *Divine Love*) must take over for the final ascent, for Human Reason is self-limited. Dante submits himself joyously to Virgil's guidance and they move off.

Midway in our life's journey, I went astray
   from the straight road and woke to find
      myself
   alone in a dark wood. How shall I say   3

what wood that was! I never saw so drear,
   so rank, so arduous a wilderness!
   Its very memory gives a shape to fear.   6

Death could scarce be more bitter than that
      place!
   But since it came to good, I will recount
   all that I found revealed there by God's   9
      grace.

How I came to it I cannot rightly say,
   so drugged and loose with sleep had I
      become
   when I first wandered there from the   12
      True Way.

But at the far end of that valley of evil
   whose maze had sapped my very heart with
      fear
   I found myself before a little hill   15

and lifted up my eyes. Its shoulders glowed
   already with the sweet rays of that planet
   whose virtue leads men straight on every   18
      road,

and the shining strengthened me against the
      fright

whose agony had wracked the lake of my
      heart
   through all the terrors of that piteous night.   21

Just as a swimmer, who with his last breath
   flounders ashore from perilous seas, might
      turn
   to memorize the wide water of his death—   24

so did I turn, my soul still fugitive
   from death's surviving image, to stare down
   that pass that none had ever left alive.   27

And there I lay to rest from my heart's race
   till calm and breath returned to me. Then
      rose
   and pushed up that dead slope at such a pace   30

each footfall rose above the last. And lo!
   almost at the beginning of the rise
   I faced a spotted Leopard, all tremor and   33
      flow

and gaudy pelt. And it would not pass, but
      stood
   so blocking my every turn that time and
      again
   I was on the verge of turning back to the   36
      wood.

This fell at the first widening of the dawn
   as the sun was climbing Aries with those
      stars
   that rode with him to light the new creation.   39

Thus the holy hour and the sweet season
   of commemoration did much to arm my fear
   of that bright murderous beast with their   42
      good omen.

Yet not so much but what I shook with dread
   at sight of a great Lion that broke upon me
   raging with hunger, its enormous head   45

held high as if to strike a mortal terror
   into the very air. And down his track,
   a She-Wolf drove upon me, a starved horror   48

ravening and wasted beyond all belief.
   She seemed a rack for avarice, gaunt and
      craving.
   Oh many the souls she has brought to   51
      endless grief!

She brought such heaviness upon my spirit
   at sight of her savagery and desperation,
   I died from every hope of that high summit.   54

And like a miser—eager in acquisition
   but desperate in self-reproach when Fortune's
      wheel
   turns to the hour of his loss—all tears and   57
      attrition

I wavered back; and still the beast pursued,
  forcing herself against me bit by bit
  till I slid back into the sunless wood. 60

And as I fell to my soul's ruin, a presence
  gathered before me on the discolored air,
  the figure of one who seemed hoarse 63
    from long silence.

At sight of him in that friendless waste I cried:
  "Have pity on me, whatever thing you are,
  whether shade or living man." [265] 66
    And it replied:

"Not man, though man I once was, and my blood
  was Lombard, both my parents Mantuan.
  I was born, though late, *sub Julio,* and bred 69

in Rome under Augustus in the noon
  of the false and lying gods. I was a poet
  and sang of old Anchises' noble son 72

who came to Rome after the burning of Troy.
  But you—why do *you* return to these
    distresses
  instead of climbing that shining Mount 75
    of Joy

which is the seat and first cause of man's bliss?"
  "And are you then that Virgil and that
    fountain
  of purest speech?" My voice grew tremulous: 78

"Glory and light of poets! now may that zeal

and love's apprenticeship that I poured out
  on your heroic verses serve me well! 81

For you are my true master and first author,
  the sole maker from whom I drew the breath
  of that sweet style whose measures have 84
    brought me honor.

See there, immortal sage, the beast I flee.
  For my soul's salvation, I beg you, guard me
    from her,
  for she has struck a mortal tremor 87
    through me."

And he replied, seeing my soul in tears:
  "He must go by another way who would
    escape
  this wilderness, for that mad beast that fleers 90

before you there, suffers no man to pass.
  She tracks down all, kills all, and knows no
    glut,
  but, feeding, she grows hungrier than 93
    she was.

She mates with any beast, and will mate with
    more
  before the Greyhound comes to hunt her
    down.
  He will not feed on lands nor loot, but honor 96

and love and wisdom will make straight
    his way.

265 William Blake. *Dante Running from the Three Beasts.* 1825. Pen and watercolor over pencil, 14½ × 20¾" (37 × 52.4 cm). National Gallery of Victoria, Melbourne (Felton Bequest, 1920). Virgil, seeming almost Christ-like, floats near the terrified Dante, who looks back at the beasts. Blake obviously had the famous Roman statue, the *Capitoline She-Wolf,* in mind when he drew this wolf (see figure **129,** page 198). Blake's last work was illustrating the *Divine Comedy* in 102 watercolor drawings.

He will rise between Feltro and Feltro,
  and in him
shall be the resurrection and new day   99

of that sad Italy for which Nisus died,
  and Turnus, and Euryalus, and the maid
    Camilla.
  He shall hunt her through every nation of   102
    sick pride

till she is driven back forever to Hell
  whence Envy first released her on the world.
  Therefore, for your own good, I think it well 105

you follow me and I will be your guide
  and lead you forth through an eternal place.
  There you shall see the ancient spirits tried 108

in endless pain, and hear their lamentation
  as each bemoans the second death of souls.
  Next you shall see upon a burning mountain   111

souls in fire and yet content in fire,
  knowing that whensoever it may be
  they yet will mount into the blessed choir.   114

To which, if it is still your wish to climb,
  a worthier spirit shall be sent to guide you.
  With her shall I leave you, for the King of   117
    Time,

who reigns on high, forbids me to come there
  since, living, I rebelled against his law.
  He rules the waters and the land and air   120

and there holds court, his city and his throne.
  Oh blessed are they he chooses!" And I
    to him:
  "Poet, by that God to you unknown,   123

lead me this way. Beyond this present ill
  and worse to dread, lead me to Peter's gate
  and be my guide through the sad halls of   126
    Hell."

And he then: "Follow." And he moved ahead
  in silence, and I followed where he led.

NOTES

1. *midway in our life's journey:* The Biblical life span is three-score years and ten. The action opens in Dante's thirty-fifth year, i.e., 1300 A.D.

17. *that planet:* The sun. Ptolemaic astronomers considered it a planet. It is also symbolic of God as He who lights man's way.

31. *each footfall rose above the last:* The literal rendering would be: "So that the fixed foot was ever the lower." "Fixed" has often been translated "right" and an ingenious reasoning can support that reading, but a simpler explanation offers itself and seems more competent: Dante is saying that he climbed with such zeal and haste that every footfall carried him above the last despite the steepness of the climb. At a slow pace, on the other hand, the rear foot might be brought up only as far as the forward foot. This

device of selecting a minute but exactly-centered detail to convey the whole of a larger action is one of the central characteristics of Dante's style.

THE THREE BEASTS: These three beasts undoubtedly are taken from *Jeremiah* v. 6. Many additional and incidental interpretations have been advanced for them, but the central interpretation must remain as noted. They foreshadow the three divisions of Hell (incontinence, violence, and fraud) which Virgil explains at length in Canto XI, 16–111.

38–9. *Aries . . . that rode with him to light the new creation:* The medieval tradition had it that the sun was in Aries at the time of the Creation. The significance of the astronomical and religious conjunction is an important part of Dante's intended allegory. It is just before dawn of Good Friday 1300 A.D. when he awakens in the Dark Wood. Thus his new life begins under Aries, the sign of creation, at dawn (rebirth) and in the Easter season (resurrection). Moreover the moon is full and the sun is in the equinox, conditions that did not fall together on any Friday of 1300. Dante is obviously constructing poetically the perfect Easter as a symbol of his new awakening.

69. *sub Julio:* In the reign of Julius Caesar.

95. *The Greyhound . . . Feltro and Feltro:* Almost certainly refers to Can Grande della Scala (1290–1329), great Italian leader born in Verona, which lies between the towns of Feltre and Montefeltro.

100–101. *Nisus, Turnus, Euryalus, Camilla:* All were killed in the war between the Trojans and the Latins when, according to legend, Aeneas led the survivors of Troy into Italy. Nisus and Euryalus (*Aeneid* IX) were Trojan comrades-in-arms who died together. Camilla (*Aeneid* XI) was the daughter of the Latin king and one of the warrior women. She was killed in a horse charge against the Trojans after displaying great gallantry. Turnus (*Aeneid* XII) was killed by Aeneas in a duel.

110. *the second death:* Damnation. "This is the second death, even the lake of fire." (*Revelation* xx, 14)

118. *forbids me to come there since, living, etc.:* Salvation is only through Christ in Dante's theology. Virgil lived and died before the establishment of Christ's teachings in Rome, and cannot therefore enter Heaven.

125. *Peter's gate:* The gate of Purgatory. (See *Purgatorio* IX, 76 ff.) The gate is guarded by an angel with a gleaming sword. The angel is Peter's vicar (Peter, the first Pope, symbolized all Popes; i.e., Christ's vicar on earth) and is entrusted with the two great keys.

Some commentators argue that this is the gate of Paradise, but Dante mentions no gate beyond this one in his ascent to Heaven. It should be remembered, too, that those who pass the gate of Purgatory have effectively entered Heaven.

The three great gates that figure in the entire journey are: the gate of Hell (Canto III, 1–11), the gate of Dis (Canto VIII, 79–113, and Canto IX, 86–87), and the gate of Purgatory, as above.

Canto III
The Vestibule of Hell
The Opportunists

The Poets pass the Gate of Hell and are immediately assailed by cries of anguish. Dante sees the first of the souls in torment. They are *The Opportunists,* those souls who in life were neither for good nor evil but only for themselves. Mixed with them are those outcasts who took no sides in the Rebellion of the Angels. They are neither in Hell nor out of it. Eternally unclassified, they race round and round pursuing a wavering banner that runs forever before them through the dirty air; and as they run they are pursued by swarms of wasps and hornets, who sting them and produce a constant flow of blood and putrid matter which trickles down the bodies of the sinners and is feasted upon by loathsome worms and maggots who coat the ground.

The law of Dante's Hell is the law of symbolic retribution. As they sinned so are they punished. They took no sides, therefore they are given no place. As they pursued the ever-shifting illusion of their own advantage, changing their courses with every changing wind, so they pursue eternally an elusive, ever-shifting banner. As their sin was a darkness, so they move in darkness. As their own guilty conscience pursued them, so they are pursued by swarms of wasps and hornets. And as their actions were a moral filth, so they run eternally through the filth of worms and maggots which they themselves feed.

Dante recognizes several, among them *Pope Celestine V*, but without delaying to speak to any of these souls, the Poets move on to *Acheron*, the first of the rivers of Hell. Here the newly-arrived souls of the damned gather and wait for monstrous *Charon* to ferry them over to punishment. Charon recognizes Dante as a living man and angrily refuses him passage. Virgil forces Charon to serve them, but Dante swoons with terror, and does not reawaken until he is on the other side.

I AM THE WAY INTO THE CITY OF WOE.
I AM THE WAY TO A FORSAKEN PEOPLE.
I AM THE WAY INTO ETERNAL SORROW.   3

SACRED JUSTICE MOVED MY ARCHITECT.
I WAS RAISED HERE BY DIVINE OMNIPOTENCE,
PRIMORDIAL LOVE AND ULTIMATE INTELLECT.   6

ONLY THOSE ELEMENTS TIME CANNOT WEAR
WERE MADE BEFORE ME, AND BEYOND TIME I
    STAND.
ABANDON ALL HOPE YE WHO ENTER HERE.   9

These mysteries I read cut into stone
    above a gate. And turning I said: "Master,
    what is the meaning of this harsh   12
    inscription?"

And he then as initiate to novice:
    "Here must you put by all division of spirit
    and gather your soul against all cowardice.   15

This is the place I told you to expect.
    Here you shall pass among the fallen people,
    souls who have lost the good of intellect."   18

So saying, he put forth his hand to me,
    and with a gentle and encouraging smile
    he led me through the gate of mystery.   21

Here sighs and cries and wails coiled and
        recoiled
    on the starless air, spilling my soul to tears.
    A confusion of tongues and monstrous   24
    accents toiled

in pain and anger. Voices hoarse and shrill
    and sounds of blows, all intermingled, raised
    tumult and pandemonium that still   27

whirls on the air forever dirty with it
    as if a whirlwind sucked at sand. And I,
    holding my head in horror, cried: "Sweet   30
    Spirit,

what souls are these who run through this black
        haze?"
    And he to me: "These are the nearly soulless
    whose lives concluded neither blame nor   33
    praise.

They are mixed here with that despicable corps
    of angels who were neither for God nor
    Satan,
    but only for themselves. The High Creator   36

scourged them from Heaven for its perfect
        beauty,
    and Hell will not receive them since the
    wicked
    might feel some glory over them." And I: 39

"Master, what gnaws at them so hideously
    their lamentation stuns the very air?"
    "They have no hope of death," he   42
    answered me,

"and in their blind and unattaining state
    their miserable lives have sunk so low
    that they must envy every other fate.   45

No word of them survives their living season.
    Mercy and Justice deny them even a name.
    Let us not speak of them: look,   48
    and pass on."

I saw a banner there upon the mist.
    Circling and circling, it seemed to scorn all
    pause.
    So it ran on, and still behind it pressed   51

a never-ending rout of souls in pain.
    I had not thought death had undone so many
    as passed before me in that mournful train.   54

And some I knew among them; last of all
    I recognized the shadow of that soul
    who, in his cowardice, made the Great   57
    Denial.

At once I understood for certain: these
    were of that retrograde and faithless crew
    hateful to God and to His enemies.   60

These wretches never born and never dead
   ran naked in a swarm of wasps and hornets
   that goaded them the more the more they   63
   fled,

and made their faces stream with bloody gouts
   of pus and tears that dribbled to their feet
   to be swallowed there by loathsome   66
   worms and maggots.

Then looking onward I made out a throng
   assembled on the beach of a wide river,
   whereupon I turned to him: "Master, I long   69

to know what souls these are, and what strange
   usage
   makes them as eager to cross as they seem
   to be
   in this infected light." At which the Sage: 72

"All this shall be made known to you when we
   stand
   on the joyless beach of Acheron." And I
   cast down my eyes, sensing a reprimand   75

in what he said, and so walked at his side
   in silence and ashamed until we came
   through the dead cavern to that sunless tide.   78

There, steering toward us in an ancient ferry
   came an old man with a white bush of hair,
   bellowing: "Woe to you depraved souls!   81
   Bury

here and forever all hope of Paradise:
   I come to lead you to the other shore,
   into eternal dark, into fire and ice.   84

And you who are living yet, I say begone
   from these who are dead." But when he saw
   me stand
   against his violence he began again: 87

"By other windings and by other steerage
   shall you cross to that other shore. Not here!
   Not here!
   A lighter craft than mine must give you   90
   passage."

And my Guide to him: "Charon, bite back your
   spleen:
   this has been willed where what is willed
   must be,
   and is not yours to ask what it may mean."   93

The steersman of that marsh of ruined souls,
   who wore a wheel of flame around each eye,
   stifled the rage that shook his woolly jowls.   96

But those unmanned and naked spirits there
   turned pale with fear and their teeth began to
   chatter
   at sound of his crude bellow. In despair   99

they blasphemed God, their parents, their time
   on earth,
   the race of Adam, and the day and the hour
   and the place and the seed   102
   the womb that gave them birth.

But all together they drew to that grim shore
   where all must come who lose the fear
   of God.
   Weeping and cursing they come for   105
   evermore,

and demon Charon with eyes like burning coals
   herds them in, and with a whistling oar
   flails on the stragglers to his wake of souls.   108

As leaves in autumn loosen and stream down
   until the branch stands bare above its tatters
   spread on the rustling ground, so one by one   111

the evil seed of Adam in its Fall
   cast themselves, at his signal, from the shore
   and streamed away like birds who hear their   114
   call.

So they are gone over that shadowy water,
   and always before they reach the other shore
   a new noise stirs on this, and new throngs   117
   gather.

"My son," the courteous Master said to me,
   "all who die in the shadow of God's wrath
   converge to this from every clime and   120
   country.

And all pass over eagerly, for here
   Divine Justice transforms and spurs them so
   their dread turns wish: they yearn for what   123
   they fear.

No soul in Grace comes ever to this crossing;
   therefore if Charon rages at your presence
   you will understand the reason for his   126
   cursing."

When he had spoken, all the twilight country
   shook so violently, the terror of it
   bathes me with sweat even in memory: 129

the tear-soaked ground gave out a sigh of wind
   that spewed itself in flame on a red sky,
   and all my shattered senses left me. Blind,   132

like one whom sleep comes over in a swoon,
I stumbled into darkness and went down.

NOTES

7–8. *Only those elements time cannot wear:* The Angels, the Empyrean, and the First Matter are the elements time cannot wear, for
they will last to all time. Man, however, in his mortal state, is not
eternal. The Gate of Hell, therefore, was created before man. The
theological point is worth attention. The doctrine of Original Sin

is, of course, one familiar to many creeds. Here, however, it would seem that the preparation for damnation predates Original Sin. True, in one interpretation, Hell was created for the punishment of the Rebellious Angels and not for man. Had man not sinned, he would never have known Hell. But on the other hand, Dante's God was one who knew all, and knew therefore that man would indeed sin. The theological problem is an extremely delicate one.

It is significant, however, that having sinned, man lives out his days on the rind of Hell, and that damnation is forever below his feet. This central concept of man's sinfulness, and, opposed to it, the doctrine of Christ's ever-abounding mercy, are central to all of Dante's theology. Only as man surrenders himself to Divine Love may he hope for salvation, and salvation is open to all who will surrender themselves.

8. *and beyond time I stand:* So odious is sin to God that there can be no end to its just punishment.

9. *Abandon all hope ye who enter here:* The admonition, of course, is to the damned and not to those who come on Heaven-sent errands. The Harrowing of Hell provided the only exemption from this decree, and that only through the direct intercession of Christ.

57. *who, in his cowardice, made the Great Denial:* This is almost certainly intended to be Celestine V, who became Pope in 1294. He was a man of saintly life, but allowed himself to be convinced by a priest named Benedetto that his soul was in danger since no man could live in the world without being damned. In fear for his soul he withdrew from all worldly affairs and renounced the papacy. Benedetto promptly assumed the mantle himself and became Boniface VIII, a Pope who became for Dante a symbol of all the worst corruptions of the church. Dante also blamed Boniface and his intrigues for many of the evils that befell Florence. We shall learn in Canto XIX that the fires of Hell are waiting for Boniface in the pit of the Simoniacs, and we shall be given further evidence of his corruption in Canto XXVII. Celestine's great guilt is that his cowardice (in selfish terror for his own welfare) served as the door through which so much evil entered the church.

80. *an old man:* Charon. He is the ferryman of dead souls across the Acheron in all classical mythology.

88–90. *By other windings:* Charon recognizes Dante not only as a living man but as a soul in grace, and knows, therefore, that the Infernal Ferry was not intended for him. He is probably referring to the fact that souls destined for Purgatory and Heaven assemble not at his ferry point, but on the banks of the Tiber, from which they are transported by an Angel.

100. *they blasphemed God:* The souls of the damned are not permitted to repent, for repentance is a divine grace.

123. *they yearn for what they fear:* Hell (allegorically Sin) is what the souls of the damned really wish for. Hell is their actual and deliberate choice, for divine grace is denied to none who wish for it in their hearts. The damned must, in fact, deliberately harden their hearts to God in order to become damned. Christ's grace is sufficient to save all who wish for it.

133–34. DANTE'S SWOON: This device (repeated at the end of Canto V) serves a double purpose. The first is technical: Dante uses it to cover a transition. We are never told how he crossed Acheron, for that would involve certain narrative matters he can better deal with when he crosses Styx in Canto VII. The second is to provide a point of departure for a theme that is carried through the entire descent: the theme of Dante's emotional reaction to Hell. These two swoons early in the descent show him most susceptible to the grief about him. As he descends, pity leaves him, and he even goes

so far as to add to the torments of one sinner. The allegory is clear: we must harden ourselves against every sympathy for sin.

Canto V
Circle Two
The Carnal

The Poets leave Limbo [the dwelling place of the unbaptized] and enter the *Second Circle.* Here begin the torments of Hell proper, and here, blocking the way, sits *Minos,* the dread and semi-bestial judge of the damned who assigns to each soul its eternal torment. He orders the Poets back; but Virgil silences him as he earlier silenced Charon, and the Poets move on.

They find themselves on a dark ledge swept by a great whirlwind, which spins within it the souls of the *Carnal,* those who betrayed reason to their appetites. Their sin was to abandon themselves to the tempest of their passions: so they are swept forever in the tempest of Hell, forever denied the light of reason and of God. Virgil identifies many among them. *Semiramis* is there, and *Dido, Cleopatra, Helen, Achilles, Paris,* and *Tristan.* Dante sees *Paolo* and *Francesca* swept together, and in the name of love he calls to them to tell their sad story. They pause from their eternal flight to come to him, and Francesca tells their history while Paolo weeps at her side. Dante is so stricken by compassion at their tragic tale that he swoons once again.

So we went down to the second ledge alone;
    a smaller circle of so much greater pain
    the voice of the damned rose in a bestial   3
        moan.

There Minos sits, grinning, grotesque, and hale.
    He examines each lost soul as it arrives
    and delivers his verdict with his coiling tail.   6

That is to say, when the ill-fated soul
    appears before him it confesses all,
    and that grim sorter of the dark and foul   9

decides which place in Hell shall be its end,
    then wraps his twitching tail about himself
    one coil for each degree it must descend.   12

The soul descends and others take its place:
    each crowds in its turn to judgment, each
        confesses,
    each hears its doom and falls away through   15
        space.

"O you who come into this camp of woe,"
    cried Minos when he saw me turn away
    without awaiting his judgment, "watch where you go   18

once you have entered here, and to whom you
        turn!
    Do not be misled by that wide and easy
        passage!"

And my Guide to him: "That is not your concern;

it is his fate to enter every door.
    This has been willed where what is willed must be,
    and is not yours to question. Say no more." 24

Now the choir of anguish, like a wound,
    strikes through the tortured air. Now I have come
    to Hell's full lamentation, sound beyond sound. 27

I came to a place stripped bare of every light
    and roaring on the naked dark like seas
    wracked by a war of winds. Their hellish flight 30

of storm and counterstorm through time foregone,
    sweeps the souls of the damned before its charge.
    Whirling and battering it drives them on, 33

and when they pass the ruined gap of Hell
    through which we had come, their shrieks begin anew.
    There they blaspheme the power of God eternal. 36

And this, I learned, was the never ending flight
    of those who sinned in the flesh, the carnal and lusty
    who betrayed reason to their appetite. 39

As the wings of wintering starlings bear them on
    in their great wheeling flights, just so the blast
    wherries these evil souls through time foregone. 42

Here, there, up, down, they whirl and whirling, strain
    with never a hope of hope to comfort them,
    not of release, but even of less pain. 45

As cranes go over sounding their harsh cry,
    leaving the long streak of their flight in air,
    so come these spirits, wailing as they fly. 48

And watching their shadows lashed by wind, I cried:
    "Master, what souls are these the very air
    lashes with its black whips from side to side?" 51

"The first of these whose history you would know,"
    he answered me, "was Empress of many tongues.

Mad sensuality corrupted her so 54

that to hide the guilt of her debauchery
    she licensed all depravity alike,
    and lust and law were one in her decree. 57

She is Semiramis of whom the tale is told
    how she married Ninus and succeeded him
    to the throne of that wide land the Sultans hold. 60

The other is Dido; faithless to the ashes
    of Sichaeus, she killed herself for love.
    The next whom the eternal tempest lashes 63

is sense-drugged Cleopatra. See Helen there,
    from whom such ill arose. And great Achilles,
    who fought at last with love in the house of prayer. 66

And Paris. And Tristan." As they whirled above
    he pointed out more than a thousand shades
    of those torn from the mortal life by love. 69

I stood there while my Teacher one by one
    named the great knights and ladies of dim time;
    and I was swept by pity and confusion. 72

At last I spoke: "Poet, I should be glad
    to speak a word with those two swept together
    so lightly on the wind and still so sad." 75

And he to me: "Watch them. When next they pass,
    call to them in the name of love that drives
    and damns them here. In that name they will pause." 78

Thus, as soon as the wind in its wild course
    brought them around, I called: "O wearied souls!
    if none forbid it, pause and speak to us." 81

As mating doves that love calls to their nest
    glide through the air with motionless raised wings,
    borne by the sweet desire that fills each breast— 84

Just so those spirits turned on the torn sky
    from the band where Dido whirls across the air;
    such was the power of pity in my cry. 87

"O living creature, gracious, kind, and good,
    going this pilgrimage through the sick night,
    visiting us who stained the earth with blood, 90

were the King of Time our friend, we would
    pray His peace

on you who have pitied us. As long as the wind
will let us pause, ask of us what you please.   93

The town where I was born lies by the shore
where the Po descends into its ocean rest
with its attendant streams in one long murmur.   96

Love, which in gentlest hearts will soonest bloom
seized my lover with passion for that sweet body
from which I was torn unshriven to my doom.   99

Love, which permits no loved one not to love,
took me so strongly with delight in him
that we are one in Hell, as we were above.   102

Love led us to one death. In the depths of Hell
Caïna waits for him who took our lives."
This was the piteous tale they stopped to tell.   105

And when I had heard those world-offended lovers
I bowed my head. At last the Poet spoke:
"What painful thoughts are these
your lowered brow covers?"   108

When at length I answered, I began: "Alas!
What sweetest thoughts, what green and young desire
led these two lovers to this sorry pass."   111

Then turning to those spirits once again,
I said: "Francesca, what you suffer here
melts me to tears of pity and of pain.   114

But tell me: in the time of your sweet sighs
by what appearances found love the way
to lure you to his perilous paradise?"   117

And she: "The double grief of a lost bliss
is to recall its happy hour in pain.
Your Guide and Teacher knows the truth of this.   120

But if there is indeed a soul in Hell
to ask of the beginning of our love
out of his pity, I will weep and tell: 123

On a day for dalliance we read the rhyme
of Lancelot, how love had mastered him.
We were alone with innocence and dim time.   126

Pause after pause that high old story drew
our eyes together while we blushed and paled;
but it was one soft passage overthrew   129

our caution and our hearts. For when we read

how her fond smile was kissed by such a lover,
he who is one with me alive and dead   132

breathed on my lips the tremor of his kiss.
That book, and he who wrote it, was a pander.
That day we read no further." As she said this,   135

the other spirit, who stood by her, wept
so piteously, I felt my senses reel
and faint away with anguish. I was swept   138

by such a swoon as death is, and I fell,
as a corpse might fall, to the dead floor of Hell.

NOTES

2. *a smaller circle:* The pit of Hell tapers like a funnel. The circles of ledges accordingly grow smaller as they descend.

4. *Minos:* Like all the monsters Dante assigns to the various offices of Hell, Minos is drawn from classical mythology. He was the son of Europa and of Zeus, who descended to her in the form of a bull. Minos became a mythological king of Crete, so famous for his wisdom and justice that after death his soul was made judge of the dead. Virgil presents him fulfilling the same office at Aeneas' descent to the underworld. Dante, however, transforms him into an irate and hideous monster with a tail. The transformation may have been suggested by the form Zeus assumed for the rape of Europa—the monster is certainly bullish enough here—but the obvious purpose of the brutalization is to present a figure symbolic of the guilty conscience of the wretches who come before it to make their confessions. Dante freely reshapes his materials to his own purposes.

8. *It confesses all:* Just as the souls appeared eager to cross Acheron, so they are eager to confess even while they dread. Dante is once again making the point that sinners elect their Hell by an act of their own will.

27. *Hell's full lamentation:* It is with the second circle that the real tortures of Hell begin.

34. *the ruined gap of Hell:* See note to Canto II, 53. At the time of the Harrowing of Hell a great earthquake shook the underworld shattering rocks and cliffs. Ruins resulting from the same shock are noted in Canto XII, 34, and Canto XXI, 112 ff. At the beginning of Canto XXIV, the Poets leave the *bolgia* of the Hypocrites by climbing the ruined slabs of a bridge that was shattered by this earthquake.

THE SINNERS OF THE SECOND CIRCLE (THE CARNAL): Here begin the punishments for the various sins of Incontinence (The sins of the She-Wolf). In the second circle are punished those who sinned by excess of sexual passion. Since this is the most natural sin and the sin most nearly associated with love, its punishment is the lightest of all to be found in Hell proper. The Carnal are whirled and buffeted endlessly through the murky air (symbolic of the beclouding of their reason by passion) by a great gale (symbolic of their lust).

53. *Empress of many tongues:* Semiramis, a legendary queen of Assyria who assumed full power at the death of her husband, Ninus.

61. *Dido:* Queen and founder of Carthage. She had vowed to

remain faithful to her husband, Sichaeus, but she fell in love with Aeneas. When Aeneas abandoned her she stabbed herself on a funeral pyre she had had prepared.

According to Dante's own system of punishments, she should be in the Seventh Circle (Canto XIII) with the suicides. The only clue Dante gives to the tempering of her punishment is his statement that "she killed herself for love." Dante always seems readiest to forgive in that name.

65. *Achilles:* He is placed among this company because of his passion for Polyxena, the daughter of Priam. For love of her, he agreed to desert the Greeks and to join the Trojans, but when he went to the temple for the wedding (according to the legend Dante has followed) he was killed by Paris.

74. *those two swept together:* Paolo and Francesca (PAH-oe-loe: Frahn-CHAY-ska).

Dante's treatment of these two lovers is certainly the tenderest and most sympathetic accorded any of the sinners in Hell, and legends immediately began to grow about this pair.

The facts are these. In 1275 Giovanni Malatesta (Djoe-VAH-nee Mahl-ah-TEH-stah) of Rimini, called Giovanni the Lame, a somewhat deformed but brave and powerful warrior, made a political marriage with Francesca, daughter of Guido da Polenta of Ravenna. Francesca came to Rimini and there an amour grew between her and Giovanni's younger brother Paolo. Despite the fact that Paolo had married in 1269 and had become the father of two daughters by 1275, his affair with Francesca continued for many years. It was sometime between 1283 and 1286 that Giovanni surprised them in Francesca's bedroom and killed both of them.

Around these facts the legend has grown that Paolo was sent by Giovanni as his proxy to the marriage, that Francesca thought he was her real bridegroom and accordingly gave him her heart irrevocably at first sight. The legend obviously increases the pathos, but nothing in Dante gives it support.

102. *that we are one in Hell, as we were above:* At many points of *The Inferno* Dante makes clear the principle that the souls of the damned are locked so blindly into their own guilt that none can feel sympathy for another, or find any pleasure in the presence of another. The temptation of many readers is to interpret this line romantically: *i.e.,* that the love of Paolo and Francesca survives Hell itself. The more Dantean interpretation, however, is that they add to one another's anguish (a) as mutual reminders of their sin, and (b) as insubstantial shades of the bodies for which they once felt such great passion.

104. *Caïna waits for him:* Giovanni Malatesta was still alive at the writing. His fate is already decided, however, and upon his death, his soul will fall to Caïna, the first ring of the last circle (Canto XXXII), where lie those who performed acts of treachery against their kin.

124–5. *the rhyme of Lancelot:* The story exists in many forms. The details Dante makes use of are from an Old French version.

126. *dim time:* The original simply reads "We were alone, suspecting nothing." "Dim time" is rhyme-forced, but not wholly outside the legitimate implications of the original, I hope. The old courtly romance may well be thought of as happening in the dim ancient days. The apology, of course, comes after the fact: one does the possible, then argues for justification, and there probably is none.

134. *that book, and he who wrote it, was a pander:* "Galeotto," the Italian word for "pander," is also the Italian rendering of the name of Gallehault, who in the French Romance Dante refers to here, urged Lancelot and Guinevere on to love.

Canto X
Circle Six
The Heretics

As the Poets pass on, one of the damned hears Dante speaking, recognizes him as a Tuscan, and calls to him from one of the fiery tombs. A moment later he appears. He is *Farinata degli Uberti,* a great war-chief of the Tuscan Ghibellines. The majesty and power of his bearing seem to diminish Hell itself. He asks Dante's lineage and recognizes him as an enemy. They begin to talk politics, but are interrupted by another shade, who rises from the same tomb.

This one is *Cavalcante dei Cavalcanti,* father of Guido Cavalcanti, a contemporary poet. If it is genius that leads Dante on his great journey, the shade asks, why is Guido not with him? Can Dante presume to a greater genius than Guido's? Dante replies that he comes this way only with the aid of powers Guido has not sought. His reply is a classic example of many-leveled symbolism as well as an overt criticism of a rival poet. The senior Cavalcanti mistakenly infers from Dante's reply that Guido is dead, and swoons back into the flames.

Farinata, who has not deigned to notice his fellow-sinner, continues from the exact point at which he had been interrupted. It is as if he refuses to recognize the flames in which he is shrouded. He proceeds to prophesy Dante's banishment from Florence, he defends his part in Florentine politics, and then, in answer to Dante's question, he explains how it is that the damned can foresee the future but have no knowledge of the present. He then names others who share his tomb, and Dante takes his leave with considerable respect for his great enemy, pausing only long enough to leave word for Cavalcanti that Guido is still alive.

We go by a secret path along the rim
    of the dark city, between the wall and the
      torments.
    My Master leads me and I follow him.   3

"Supreme Virtue, who through this impious
    land
    wheel me at will down these dark gyres," I
    said,
    "speak to me, for I wish to understand.   6

Tell me, Master, is it permitted to see
    the souls within these tombs? The lids are
      raised,
    and no one stands on guard." And he to
    me: 9

"All shall be sealed forever on the day
    these souls return here from Jehosaphat
    with the bodies they have given once to   12
      clay.

In this dark corner of the morgue of wrath

lie Epicurus and his followers,
who make the soul share in the body's
death.

And here you shall be granted presently
not only your spoken wish, but that other as
well,
which you had thought perhaps to hide from
me."

And I: "Except to speak my thoughts in few
and modest words, as I learned from your
example,
dear Guide, I do not hide my heart from
you."

"O Tuscan, who go living through this place
speaking so decorously, may it please you
pause
a moment on your way, for by the grace

of that high speech in which I hear your birth,
I know you for a son of that noble city
which perhaps I vexed too much
in my time on earth."

These words broke without warning from
inside
one of the burning arks. Caught by surprise,
I turned in fear and drew close to my
Guide.

And he: "Turn around. What are you doing?
Look there:
it is Farinata rising from the flames.
From the waist up his shade will be made
clear."

My eyes were fixed on him already. Erect,
he rose above the flame, great chest, great
brow;
he seemed to hold all Hell in disrespect.

My Guide's prompt hands urged me among the
dim
and smoking sepulchres to that great figure,
and he said to me: "Mind how you speak to
him."

And when I stood alone at the foot of the
tomb,
the great soul stared almost contemptuously,
before he asked: "Of what line do you
come?"

Because I wished to obey, I did not hide
anything from him: whereupon as he
listened,
he raised his brows a little, then replied:

"Bitter enemies were they to me,
to my fathers, and to my party, so that twice
I sent them scattering from high Italy."

"If they were scattered, still from every part
they formed again and returned both times,"
I answered,
"but yours have not yet wholly learned that
art."

At this another shade rose gradually,
visible to the chin. It had raised itself,
I think, upon its knees, and it looked around
me

as if it expected to find through that black air
that blew about me, another traveler.
And weeping when it found no other
there,

turned back. "And if," it cried, "you travel
through
this dungeon of the blind by power of
genius,
where is my son? why is he not with
you?"

And I to him: "Not by myself am I borne
this terrible way. I am led by him who waits
there,
and whom perhaps your Guido held in
scorn."

For by his words and the manner of his
torment
I knew his name already, and could,
therefore,
answer both what he asked and what he
meant.

Instantly he rose to his full height:
"He *held*? What is it you say? Is he dead, then?
Do his eyes no longer fill with that sweet
light?"

And when he saw that I delayed a bit
in answering his question, he fell backwards
into the flame, and rose no more from it.

But that majestic spirit at whose call
I had first paused there, did not change
expression,
nor so much as turn his face to watch him
fall.

"And if," going on from his last words, he said,
"men of my line have yet to learn that art,
that burns me deeper than this flaming bed.

But the face of her who reigns in Hell shall not
be fifty times rekindled in its course
before you learn what griefs attend that art.

And as you hope to find the world again,
tell me: why is that populace so savage
in the edicts they pronounce against my
strain?"

And I to him: "The havoc and the carnage
   that dyed the Arbia red at Montaperti
   have caused these angry cries in our   87
     assemblage."

He sighed and shook his head. "I was not alone
   in that affair," he said, "nor certainly
   would I have joined the rest without good   90
     reason.

But I *was* alone at that time when every other
   consented to the death of Florence; I
   alone with open face defended her."   93

"Ah, so may your soul sometime have rest,"
   I begged him, "solve the riddle that pursues
    me
   through this dark place and leaves   96
     my mind perplexed:

you seem to see in advance all time's intent,
   if I have heard and understood correctly;
   but you seem to lack all knowledge of the   99
     present."

"We see asquint, like those whose twisted sight
   can make out only the far-off," he said,
   "for the King of All still grants us that much   102
    light.

When things draw near, or happen, we perceive
   nothing of them. Except what others
    bring us
   we have no news of those who are alive.   105

So may you understand that all we know
   will be dead forever from that day and hour
   when the portal of the Future is swung to."   108

Then, as if stricken by regret, I said:
   "Now, therefore, will you tell that fallen one
   who asked about his son, that he is not   111
    dead,

and that, if I did not reply more quickly,
   it was because my mind was occupied
   with this confusion you have solved for   114
    me."

And now my Guide was calling me. In haste,
   therefore, I begged that mighty shade to
    name
   the others who lay with him in that chest.   117

And he: "More than a thousand cram this tomb.
   The second Frederick is here, and the
    Cardinal
   of the Ubaldini. Of the rest let us be   120
    dumb."

And he disappeared without more said, and I
   turned back and made my way to the ancient
    Poet,

pondering the words of the dark   123
   prophecy.

He moved along, and then, when we had
    started,
   he turned and said to me, "What troubles
    you?
   Why do you look so vacant and   126
    downhearted?"

And I told him. And he replied: "Well may you
    bear
   those words in mind." Then, pausing, raised
    a finger:
   "Now pay attention to what I tell you   129
    here:

when finally you stand before the ray
   of that Sweet Lady whose bright eye sees all,
   from her you will learn the turnings of   132
    your way."

So saying, he bore left, turning his back
   on the flaming walls, and we passed deeper
    yet
   into the city of pain, along a track   135

that plunged down like a scar into a sink
   which sickened us already with its stink.

NOTES

11. *Jehosaphat:* A valley outside Jerusalem. The popular belief that it would serve as the scene of the Last Judgment was based on *Joel* iii, 2, 12.

14. *Epicurus:* The Greek philosopher. The central aim of his philosophy was to achieve happiness, which he defined as the absence of pain. For Dante this doctrine meant the denial of the Eternal life, since the whole aim of the Epicurean was temporal happiness.

17. *not only your spoken wish, but that other as well:* "All knowing" Virgil is frequently presented as being able to read Dante's mind. The "other wish" is almost certainly Dante's desire to speak to someone from Florence with whom he could discuss politics. Many prominent Florentines were Epicureans.

22. *Tuscan:* Florence lies in the province of Tuscany. Italian, to an extent unknown in America, is a language of dialects, all of them readily identifiable even when they are not well understood by the hearer. Dante's native Tuscan has become the main source of modern official Italian. Two very common sayings still current in Italy are: *"Lingua toscana, lingua di Dio"* (the Tuscan tongue is the language of God) and—to express the perfection of Italian speech—*"Lingua toscana in bocca romana"* (the Tuscan tongue in a Roman mouth).

32–51. *Farinata:* Farinata degli Uberti (DEH-lyee Oob-EHR-tee) was head of the ancient noble house of the Uberti. He became tee) was head of the ancient noble house of the Uberti. He became leader of the Ghibellines of Florence in 1239, and played a large part in expelling the Guelphs in 1248. The Guelphs returned in 1251, but Farinata remained. His arrogant desire to rule singlehanded led to difficulties, however, and he was expelled in 1258. With the aid of the Manfredi of Siena, he gathered a large force and defeated the Guelphs at Montaperti on the River Arbia in 1260.

Re-entering Florence in triumph, he again expelled the Guelphs, but at the Diet of Empoli, held by the victors after the battle of Montaperti, he alone rose in open counsel to resist the general sentiment that Florence should be razed. He died in Florence in 1264. In 1266 the Guelphs once more returned and crushed forever the power of the Uberti, destroying their palaces and issuing special decrees against persons of the Uberti line. In 1283 a decree of heresy was published against Farinata.

26. *that noble city:* Florence.

39. *"Mind how you speak to him"*: The surface interpretation is clearly that Virgil means Dante to show proper respect to so majestic a soul. But the allegorical level is more interesting here. Virgil (as Human Reason) is urging Dante to go forward on his own. These final words then would be an admonition to Dante to guide his speech according to the highest principles.

52. *another shade:* Cavalcante dei Cavalcanti was a famous Epicurean ("like lies with like"). He was the father of Guido Cavalcanti, a poet and friend of Dante. Guido was also Farinata's son-in-law.

61. *Not by myself:* Cavalcanti assumes that the resources of human genius are all that are necessary for such a journey. (It is an assumption that well fits his character as an Epicurean.) Dante replies as a man of religion that other aid is necessary.

63. *whom perhaps your Guido held in scorn:* This reference has not been satisfactorily explained. Virgil is a symbol on many levels—of Classicism, of Religiosity, of Human Reason. Guido might have scorned him on any of these levels, or on all of them. One interpretation might be that Dante wished to present Guido as an example of how skepticism acts as a limitation upon a man of genius. Guido's skepticism does not permit him to see beyond the temporal. He does not see that Virgil (Human Reason expressed as Poetic Wisdom) exists only to lead one to Divine Love, and therefore he cannot undertake the final journey on which Dante has embarked.

70. *and when he saw that I delayed:* Dante's delay is explained in lines 112–114.

79. *her who reigns in Hell:* Hecate or Proserpine. She is also the moon goddess. The sense of this prophecy, therefore, is that Dante will be exiled within fifty full moons. Dante was banished from Florence in 1302, well within the fifty months of the prophecy.

83. *that populace:* The Florentines.

97–108. THE KNOWLEDGE OF THE DAMNED: Dante notes with surprise that Farinata can foresee the future, but that Cavalcante does not know whether his son is presently dead or alive. Farinata explains by outlining a most ingenious detail of the Divine Plan: the damned can see far into the future, but nothing of what is present or *of what has happened.* Thus, after Judgment, when there is no longer any Future, the intellects of the damned will be void.

119. *the second Frederick:* The Emperor Frederick II. In Canto XIII Dante has Pier delle Vigne speak of him as one worthy of honor, but he was commonly reputed to be an Epicurean.

119–120. *the Cardinal of the Ubaldini:* In the original Dante refers to him simply as "il Cardinale." Ottaviano degli Ubaldini (born *circa* 1209, died 1273) became a Cardinal in 1245, but his energies seem to have been directed exclusively to money and political intrigue. When he was refused an important loan by the Ghibellines, he is reported by many historians as having remarked: "I may say that if I have a soul, I have lost it in the cause of the Ghibellines, and no one of them will help me now." The words "If I have a soul" would be enough to make him guilty in Dante's eyes of the charge of heresy.

131. *that Sweet Lady:* Beatrice.

Canto XIII
Circle Seven: Round Two
The Violent Against Themselves

Nessus [a centaur] carries the Poets across the river of boiling blood and leaves them in the Second Round of the Seventh Circle, *The Wood of the Suicides*. Here are punished those who destroyed their own lives and those who destroyed their substance.

The souls of the Suicides are encased in thorny trees whose leaves are eaten by the odious *Harpies,* the overseers of these damned. When the Harpies feed upon them, damaging their leaves and limbs, the wound bleeds. Only as long as the blood flows are the souls of the trees able to speak. Thus, they who destroyed their own bodies are denied a human form; and just as the supreme expression of their lives was self-destruction, so they are permitted to speak only through that which tears and destroys them. Only through their own blood do they find voice. And to add one more dimension to the symbolism, it is the Harpies—defilers of all they touch—who give them their eternally recurring wounds.

The Poets pause before one tree and speak with the soul of *Pier delle Vigne*. In the same wood they see *Jacomo da Sant' Andrea,* and *Lano da Siena,* two famous *Squanderers* and *Destroyers of Goods* pursued by a pack of savage hounds. The hounds overtake *Sant' Andrea,* tear him to pieces and go off carrying his limbs in their teeth, a self-evident symbolic retribution for the violence with which these sinners destroyed their substance in the world. After this scene of horror, Dante speaks to an *Unknown Florentine Suicide* whose soul is inside the bush which was torn by the hound pack when it leaped upon Sant' Andrea.

Nessus had not yet reached the other shore
    when we moved on into a pathless wood
    that twisted upward from Hell's broken
      floor.   3

Its foliage was not verdant, but nearly black.
    The unhealthy branches, gnarled and
      warped and tangled,
    bore poison thorns instead of fruit. The track   6

of those wild beasts that shun the open spaces
    men till between Cecina and Corneto
    runs through no rougher nor more tangled   9
      places.

Here nest the odious Harpies of whom my
      Master
    wrote how they drove Aeneas and his
      companions
    from the Strophades with prophecies of   12
      disaster.

Their wings are wide, their feet clawed, their
      huge bellies

covered with feathers, their necks and faces
    human.
    They croak eternally in the unnatural trees.   15

"Before going on, I would have you
    understand,"
    my Guide began, "we are in the second
    round
    and shall be till we reach the burning sand.   18

Therefore look carefully and you will see
    things in this wood, which, if I told them to
    you
    would shake the confidence you have placed   21
    in me."

I heard cries of lamentation rise and spill
    on every hand, but saw no souls in pain
    in all that waste; and, puzzled, I stood still.   24

I think perhaps he thought that I was thinking
    those cries rose from among the twisted
    roots
    through which the spirits of the damned   27
    were slinking

to hide from us. Therefore my Master said:
    "If you break off a twig, what you will learn
    will drive what you are thinking from your   30
    head."

Puzzled, I raised my hand a bit and slowly
    broke off a branchlet from an enormous
    thorn:
    and the great trunk of it cried: "Why do   33
    you break me?"

And after blood had darkened all the bowl
    of the wound, it cried again: "Why do you
    tear me?
    Is there no pity left in any soul?   36

Men we were, and now we are changed to
    sticks;
    well might your hand have been more
    merciful
    were we no more than souls of lice and   39
    ticks."

As a green branch with one end all aflame
    will hiss and sputter sap out of the other
    as the air escapes—so from that trunk there   42
    came

words and blood together, gout by gout.
    Startled, I dropped the branch that I was
    holding
    and stood transfixed by fear, half turned   45
    about

to my Master, who replied: "O wounded soul,
    could he have believed before what he has seen

in my verses only, you would yet be whole,   48
    for his hand would never have been raised
    against you.
    But knowing this truth could never be
    believed
    till it was seen, I urged him on to do   51

what grieves me now; and I beg to know your
    name,
    that to make you some amends in the sweet
    world
    when he returns, he may refresh your   54
    fame."

And the trunk: "So sweet those words to me
    that I
    cannot be still, and may it not annoy you
    if I seem somewhat lengthy in reply.   57

I am he who held both keys to Frederick's
    heart,
    locking, unlocking with so deft a touch
    that scarce another soul had any part   60

in his most secret thoughts. Through every
    strife
    I was so faithful to my glorious office
    that for it I gave up both sleep and life.   63

That harlot, Envy, who on Caesar's face
    keeps fixed forever her adulterous stare,
    the common plague and vice of court and   66
    palace,

inflamed all minds against me. These inflamed
    so inflamed him that all my happy honors
    were changed to mourning. Then, unjustly   69
    blamed,

my soul, in scorn, and thinking to be free
    of scorn in death, made me at last, though
    just,
    unjust to myself. By the new roots of this   72
    tree

I swear to you that never in word or spirit
    did I break faith to my lord and emperor
    who was so worthy of honor in his merit.   75

If either of you return to the world, speak for
    me,
    to vindicate in the memory of men
    one who lies prostrate from the blows of   78
    Envy."

The Poet stood. Then turned. "Since he is
    silent,"
    he said to me, "do not you waste this hour,
    if you wish to ask about his life or torment." 81

And I replied: "Question him for my part,
    on whatever you think I would do well to hear;

I could not, such compassion chokes my
heart."

The Poet began again: "That this man may
with all his heart do for you what your
words
entreat him to, imprisoned spirit, I pray,   87

tell us how the soul is bound and bent
into these knots, and whether any ever
frees itself from such imprisonment."   90

At that the trunk blew powerfully, and then
the wind became a voice that spoke these
words:
"Briefly is the answer given: when   93

out of the flesh from which it tore itself,
the violent spirit comes to punishment,
Minos assigns it to the seventh shelf.   96

It falls into the wood, and landing there,
wherever fortune flings it, it strikes root,
and there it sprouts, lusty as any tare,   99

shoots up a sapling, and becomes a tree.
The Harpies, feeding on its leaves then, give it
pain and pain's outlet simultaneously.   102

Like the rest, we shall go for our husks on
Judgment Day,
but not that we may wear them, for it is not
just
that a man be given what he throws away.   105

Here shall we drag them and in this mournful
glade
our bodies will dangle to the end of time,
each on the thorns of its tormented shade."   108

We waited by the trunk, but it said no more;
and waiting, we were startled by a noise
that grew through all the wood. Just such a   111
roar

and trembling as one feels when the boar and
chase
approach his stand, the beasts and branches
crashing
and clashing in the heat of the fierce race.   114

And there on the left, running so violently
they broke off every twig in the dark wood,
two torn and naked wraiths went plunging
by me.   117

The leader cried, "Come now, O Death! Come
now!"
And the other, seeing that he was outrun,
cried out: "Your legs were not so ready,   120
Lano,

in the jousts at the Toppo." And suddenly in
his rush,

perhaps because his breath was failing him,
he hid himself inside a thorny bush   123

and cowered among its leaves. Then at his back,
the wood leaped with black bitches, swift as
greyhounds
escaping from their leash, and all the pack   126

sprang on him; with their fangs they opened
him
and tore him savagely, and then withdrew,
carrying his body with them, limb by limb.   129

Then, taking me by the hand across the wood,
my Master led me toward the bush.
Lamenting,
all its fractures blew out words and blood: 132

"O Jacomo da Sant' Andrea!" it said,
"what have you gained in making me your
screen?
What part had I in the foul life you led?"   135

And when my Master had drawn up to it
he said: "Who were you, who through all
your wounds
blow out your blood with your lament, sad   138
spirit?"

And he to us: "You who have come to see
how the outrageous mangling of these
hounds
has torn my boughs and stripped my leaves   141
from me,

O heap them round my ruin! I was born
in the city that tore down Mars and raised
the Baptist.
On that account the God of War has sworn   144

her sorrow shall not end. And were it not
that something of his image still survives
on the bridge across the Arno, some have   147
thought

those citizens who of their love and pain
afterwards rebuilt it from the ashes
left by Attila, would have worked in vain.   150

I am one who has no tale to tell:
I made myself a gibbet of my own lintel."

NOTES

6–10. The reference here is to the Maremma district of Tuscany which lies between the mountains and the sea. The river
Cecina is the northern boundary of this district; Corneto is on
the river Marta, which forms the southern boundary. It is a
wild district of marsh and forest.

10–15. THE HARPIES: These hideous birds with the faces of
malign women were often associated with the Erinyes (Furies).
Their original function in mythology was to snatch away the
souls of men at the command of the Gods. Later, they were

portrayed as defilers of food, and, by extension, of everything they touched. The islands of the Strophades were their legendary abode. Aeneas and his men landed there and fought with the Harpies, who drove them back and pronounced a prophecy of unbearable famine upon them.

18. *The burning sand:* The Third Round of this Circle.

25. *I think perhaps he thought that I was thinking:* The original is "Cred' io ch'ei *credette ch'io credesse."* This sort of word play was considered quite elegant by medieval rhetoricians and by the ornate Sicilian School of poetry. Dante's style is based on a rejection of all such devices in favor of a sparse and direct diction. The best explanation of this unusual instance seems to be that Dante is anticipating his talk with Pier delle Vigne, a rhetorician who, as we shall see, delights in this sort of locution. (An analogous stylistic device is common in opera, where the musical phrase identified with a given character may be sounded by the orchestra when the character is about to appear.)

48. *In my verses only:* The *Aeneid,* Book III, describes a similar bleeding plant. There, Aeneas pulls at a myrtle growing on a Thracian hillside. It bleeds where he breaks it and a voice cries out of the ground. It is the voice of Polydorus, son of Priam and friend of Aeneas. He has been treacherously murdered by the Thracian king.

58. *I am he, etc.:* Pier delle Vigne (Pee-YAIR deh-leh VEE-nyeh) 1190–1249. A famous and once-powerful minister of Emperor Frederick's whole confidence until 1247 when he was accused of treachery and was imprisoned and blinded. He committed suicide to escape further torture. (For Frederick see Canto X.) Pier delle Vigne was famous for his eloquence and for his mastery of the ornate Provencal-inspired Sicilian School of Italian Poetry, and Dante styles his speech accordingly. The double balanced construction of line 59, the repetition of key words in lines 67–69 and 70–72, are characteristic of this rhetorical fashion. It is worth noting, however, that the style changes abruptly in the middle of line 72. There his courtly preamble finished, delle Vigne speaks from the heart, simply and passionately.

58. *who held both keys:* The phrasing unmistakably suggests the Papal keys; delle Vigne may be suggesting that he was to Frederick as the Pope is to God.

64. *Caesar:* Frederick II was of course Caesar of the Roman Empire, but in this generalized context "Caesar" seems to be used as a generic term for any great ruler, *i.e.,* "The harlot, Envy, never turns her attention from those in power."

72. *new roots:* Pier delle Vigne had only been in Hell fifty-one years, a short enough time on the scale of eternity.

98. *wherever fortune flings it:* Just as the soul of the suicide refused to accept divine regulation of its mortal life span, so eternal justice takes no special heed of where the soul falls.

102. *pain and pain's outlet simultaneously:* Suicide also gives pain and its outlet simultaneously.

117 ff. THE VIOLENT AGAINST THEIR SUBSTANCE: They are driven naked through the thorny wood pursued by ravening bitches who tear them to pieces and carry off the limbs. (Obviously the limbs must re-form at some point so that the process can be repeated. For a parallel see Canto XXVIII, the Schismatics. Boccaccio uses an identical device in the Decameron V, vi.) The bitches may be taken as symbolizing conscience, the last besieging creditors of the damned who must satisfy their claims by dividing their wretched bodies, since nothing else is

left them. It is not simply prodigality that places them here but the *violence* of their wasting. This fad of violent wasting, scandalously prevalent in Dante's Florence, is hard to imagine today.

120. *Lano:* Lano da Siena, a famous squanderer. He died at the ford of the river Toppo near Arezzo in 1287 in a battle against the Aretines. Boccaccio writes that he deliberately courted death having squandered all his great wealth and being unwilling to live on in poverty. Thus his companion's jeer probably means: "You were not so ready to run then, Lano: why are you running now?"

133. *Jacomo da Sant' Andrea* (YAH-coe-moe): A Paduan with an infamous lust for laying waste his own goods and those of his neighbors. Arson was his favorite prank. On one occasion, to celebrate the arrival of certain noble guests, he set fire to all the workers' huts and outbuildings of his estate. He was murdered in 1239, probably by assassins hired by Ezzolino (for whom see Canto XII).

131–152. AN ANONYMOUS FLORENTINE SUICIDE: All that is known of him is what he says himself.

143. *the city that tore down Mars and raised the Baptist:* Florence. Mars was the first patron of the city and when the Florentines were converted to Christianity they pulled down his equestrian statue and built a church on the site of his temple. The statue of Mars was placed on a tower beside the Arno. When Totila (see note to line 150) destroyed Florence the tower fell into the Arno and the statue with it. Legend has it that Florence could never have been rebuilt had not the mutilated statue been rescued. It was placed on the Ponte Vecchio but was carried away in the flood of 1333.

150. *Attila:* Dante confuses Attila with Totila, King of the Ostrogoths (died 552). He destroyed Florence in 542. Attila (d. 453), King of the Huns, destroyed many cities of northern Italy, but not Florence.

Canto XXXIII
Circle Nine: Cocytus
Compound Fraud
Round Two: Antenora
The Treacherous to Country
Round Three: Ptolomea
The Treacherous to Guests and Hosts

The sinner who is gnawing his companion's head looks up, wipes his bloody mouth on his victim's hair, and tells his harrowing story. He is *Count Ugolino* and the wretch he gnaws is *Archbishop Ruggieri.* Both are in Antenora for treason. In life they had once plotted together. Then Ruggieri betrayed his fellow-plotter and caused his death, by starvation, along with his four "sons." In the most pathetic and dramatic passage of the *Inferno,* Ugolino details how their prison was sealed and how his "sons" dropped dead before him one by one, weeping for food. His terrible tale serves only to renew his grief and hatred, and he has hardly finished it before he begins to gnaw Ruggieri again with renewed fury. In the immutable Law of Hell, the killer-by-starvation becomes the food of his victim.

The Poets leave Ugolino and enter *Ptolomea,* so named for the Ptolomaeus of *Maccabees,* who murdered his father-in-law at a banquet. Here are punished those who were *Treacherous Against the Ties of Hospitality*. They lie with only half their faces above the ice and their tears freeze in their eye sockets, sealing them with little crystal visors. Thus even the comfort of tears is denied them. Here Dante finds *Friar Alberigo* and *Branca d'Oria,* and discovers the terrible power of Ptolomea: so great is its sin that the souls of the guilty fall to its torments even before they die, leaving their bodies still on earth, inhabited by Demons.

The sinner raised his mouth from his grim repast
 and wiped it on the hair of the bloody head
 whose nape he had all but eaten away. At last 3

he began to speak: "You ask me to renew
 a grief so desperate that the very thought
 of speaking of it tears my heart in two. 6

But if my words may be a seed that bears
 the fruit of infamy for him I gnaw,
 I shall weep, but tell my story through my tears. 9

Who you may be, and by what powers you reach
 into this underworld, I cannot guess,
 but you seem to me a Florentine by your speech. 12

I was Count Ugolino, I must explain;
 this reverend grace is the Archbishop Ruggieri:
 now I will tell you why I gnaw his brain. 15

That I, who trusted him, had to undergo
 imprisonment and death through his treachery,
 you will know already. What you cannot know— 18

that is, the lingering inhumanity
 of the death I suffered—you shall hear in full:
 then judge for yourself if he has injured me. 21

A narrow window in that coop of stone
 now called the Tower of Hunger for my sake
 (within which others yet must pace alone) 24

had shown me several waning moons already
 between its bars, when I slept the evil sleep
 in which the veil of the future parted for me. 27

This beast appeared as master of a hunt
 chasing the wolf and his whelps across the mountain
 that hides Lucca from Pisa. Out in front 30

of the starved and shrewd and avid pack he had placed

Gualandi and Sismondi and Lanfranchi
 to point his prey. The father and sons had raced 33

a brief course only when they failed of breath
 and seemed to weaken; then I thought I saw
 their flanks ripped open by the hounds' fierce teeth. 36

Before the dawn, the dream still in my head,
 I woke and heard my sons, who were there with me,
 cry from their troubled sleep, asking for bread. 39

You are cruelty itself if you can keep
 your tears back at the thought of what foreboding
 stirred in my heart; and if you do not weep, 42

at what are you used to weeping?—The hour when food
 used to be brought, drew near. They were now awake,
 and each was anxious from his dream's dark mood. 45

And from the base of that horrible tower I heard
 the sound of hammers nailing up the gates:
 I stared at my sons' faces without a word. 48

I did not weep: I had turned stone inside.
 They wept. 'What ails you, Father, you look so strange,'
 my little Anselm, youngest of them, cried. 51

But I did not speak a word nor shed a tear:
 not all that day nor all that endless night,
 until I saw another sun appear. 54

When a tiny ray leaked into that dark prison
 and I saw staring back from their four faces
 the terror and the wasting of my own, 57

I bit my hands in helpless grief. And they,
 thinking I chewed myself for hunger, rose
 suddenly together. I heard them say: 60

'Father, it would give us much less pain
 if you ate us: it was you who put upon us
 this sorry flesh; now strip it off again.' 63

I calmed myself to spare them. Ah! hard earth,
 why did you not yawn open? All that day
 and the next we sat in silence. On the fourth, 66

Gaddo, the eldest, fell before me and cried,
 stretched at my feet upon that prison floor:
 'Father, why don't you help me?' There he died. 69

And just as you see me, I saw them fall
 one by one on the fifth day and the sixth.

Then, already blind, I began to crawl 72

from body to body shaking them frantically.
Two days I called their names, and they were dead.
Then fasting overcame my grief and me." 75

His eyes narrowed to slits when he was done,
and he seized the skull again between his teeth
grinding it as a mastiff grinds a bone. 78

Ah, Pisa! foulest blemish on the land
where "si" sound sweet and clear,
since those nearby you are slow to blast
the ground on which you stand, 81

may Caprara and Gorgona drift from place
and dam the flooding Arno at its mouth
until it drowns the last of your foul race! 84

For if to Ugolino falls the censure
for having betrayed your castles, you for your part
should not have put his sons to such a torture: 87

you modern Thebes! those tender lives you spilt—
Brigata, Uguccione, and the others
I mentioned earlier—were too young for guilt! 90

We passed on further, where the frozen mine
entombs another crew in greater pain;
these wraiths are not bent over, but lie supine. 93

Their very weeping closes up their eyes;
and the grief that finds no outlet for its tears
turns inward to increase their agonies: 96

for the first tears that they shed knot instantly
in their eye-sockets, and as they freeze they form
a crystal visor above the cavity. 99

And despite the fact that standing in that place
I had become as numb as any callus,
and all sensation had faded from my face, 102

somehow I felt a wind begin to blow,
whereat I said: "Master, what stirs this wind?
Is not all heat extinguished here below?" 105

And the Master said to me: "Soon you will be
where your own eyes will see the source and cause
and give you their own answer to the mystery." 108

And one of those locked in that icy mall
cried out to us as we passed: "O souls so cruel

that you are sent to the last post of all, 111

relieve me for a little from the pain
of this hard veil; let my heart weep a while
before the weeping freeze my eyes again." 114

And I to him: "If you would have my service,
tell me your name; then if I do not help you
may I descend to the last rim of the ice." 117

"I am Friar Alberigo," he answered therefore,
"the same who called for the fruits from the bad garden.
Here I am given dates for figs full store." 120

"What! Are you dead already?" I said to him.
And he then: "How my body stands in the world
I do not know. So privileged is this rim 123

of Ptolomea, that often souls fall to it
before dark Atropos has cut their thread.
And that you may more willingly free my spirit 126

of this glaze of frozen tears that shrouds my face,
I will tell you this: when a soul betrays as I did,
it falls from flesh, and a demon takes its place, 129

ruling the body till its time is spent.
The ruined soul rains down into this cistern.
So, I believe, there is still evident 132

in the world above, all that is fair and mortal
of this black shade who winters here behind me.
If you have only recently crossed the portal 135

from that sweet world, you surely must have known
his body: Branca D'Oria is its name,
and many years have passed since he rained down." 138

"I think you are trying to take me in," I said,
"Ser Branca D'Oria is a living man;
he eats, he drinks, he fills his clothes and his bed." 141

"Michel Zanche had not yet reached the ditch
of the Black Talons," the frozen wraith replied,
"there where the sinners thicken in hot pitch, 144

when this one left his body to a devil,
as did his nephew and second in treachery,
and plumbed like lead through space
to this dead level. 147

But now reach out your hand, and let me cry."
And I did not keep the promise I had made,
for to be rude to him was courtesy. 150

Ah, men of Genoa! souls of little worth,
    corrupted from all custom of righteousness,
    why have you not been driven from the   153
    earth?

For there beside the blackest soul of all
    Romagna's evil plain, lies one of yours
    bathing his filthy soul in the eternal   156

glacier of Cocytus for his foul crime,
    while he seems yet alive in world and time!

NOTES

1–90. *Ugolino and Ruggieri:* (Oog-oh-LEE-noe: Roo-DJAIR-ee) Ugolino, Count of Donoratico and a member of the Guelph family della Gherardesca. He and his nephew, Nino de' Visconti, led the two Guelph factions of Pisa. In 1288 Ugolino intrigued with Archbishop Ruggieri degli Ubaldini, leader of the Ghibellines, to get rid of Visconti and to take over the command of all the Pisan Guelphs. The plan worked, but in the consequent weakening of the Guelphs, Ruggieri saw his chance and betrayed Ugolino, throwing him into prison with his sons and his grandsons. In the following year the prison was sealed up and they were left to starve to death. The law of retribution is cleary evident: in life Ruggieri sinned against Ugolino by denying him food; in Hell he himself becomes food for his victim.

18. *you will know already:* News of Ugolino's imprisonment and death would certainly have reached Florence, *what you cannot know:* No living man could know what happened after Ugolino and his sons were sealed in the prison and abandoned.

22. *coop:* Dante uses the word *muda,* in Italian signifying a stone tower in which falcons were kept in the dark to moult. From the time of Ugolino's death it became known as The Tower of Hunger.

25. *several waning moons:* Ugolino was jailed late in 1288. He was sealed in to starve early in 1289.

28. *This beast:* Ruggieri.

29–30. *the mountain that hides Lucca from Pisa:* These two cities would be in view of one another were it not for Monte San Giuliano.

32. *Gualandi and Sismondi and Lanfranchi:* (Gwah-LAHN-dee . . . Lahn-FRAHN-kee) Three Pisan nobles, Ghibellines and friends of the Archbishop.

51–71. UGOLINO'S "SONS": Actually two of the boys were grandsons and all were considerably older than one would gather from Dante's account. Anselm, the younger grandson, was fifteen. The others were really young men and were certainly old enough for guilt despite Dante's charge in line 90.

75. *Then fasting overcame my grief and me:* i.e., He died. Some interpret the line to mean that Ugolino's hunger drove him to cannibalism. Ugolino's present occupation in Hell would certainly support that interpretation but the fact is that cannibalism is the one major sin Dante does not assign a place to in Hell. So monstrous would it have seemed to him that he must certainly have established a special punishment for it. Certainly he could hardly have relegated it to an ambiguity. Moreover, it would be a sin of bestiality rather than of fraud, and as such it would be punished in the Seventh Circle.

79–80. *the land where "si" sound sweet and clear:* Italy.

82. *Caprara and Gorgona:* These two islands near the mouth of the Arno were Pisan possessions in 1300.

86. *betrayed your castles:* In 1284, Ugolino gave up certain castles to Lucca and Florence. He was at war with Genoa at the time and it is quite likely that he ceded the castles to buy the neutrality of these two cities, for they were technically allied with Genoa. Dante, however, must certainly consider the action as treasonable, for otherwise Ugolino would be in Caïna for his treachery to Visconti.

88. *you modern Thebes:* Thebes, as a number of the foregoing notes will already have made clear, was the site of some of the most hideous crimes of antiquity.

91. *we passed on further:* Marks the passage into Ptolomea.

105. *is not all heat extinguished:* Dante believed (rather accurately, by chance) that all winds resulted from "exhalations of heat." Cocytus, however, is conceived as wholly devoid of heat, a metaphysical absolute zero. The source of the wind, as we discover in the next Canto, is Satan himself.

117. *may I descend to the last rim of the ice:* Dante is not taking any chances; he has to go on to the last rim in any case. The sinner, however, believes him to be another damned soul and would interpret the oath quite otherwise than as Dante meant it.

118. *Friar Alberigo:* (Ahl-beh-REE-ghoe) Of the Manfredi of Faenza. He was another Jovial Friar. In 1284 his brother Manfred struck him in the course of an argument. Alberigo pretended to let it pass, but in 1285 he invited Manfred and his son to a banquet and had them murdered. The signal to the assassins was the words: "Bring in the fruit." "Friar Alberigo's bad fruit," became a proverbial saying.

125. *Atropos:* The Fate who cuts the thread of life.

137. *Branca d'Oria:* (DAW-ree-yah) A Genoese Ghilbelline. His sin is identical in kind to that of Friar Alberigo. In 1275 he invited his father-in-law, Michel Zanche, to a banquet and had him and his companions cut to pieces. He was assisted in the butchery by his nephew.

Canto XXXIV
Circle Nine: Cocytus
Compound Fraud
Round Four: Judecca
The Treacherous to Their Masters
The Center
Satan

"On march the banners of the King," Virgil begins as the Poets face the last depth. He is quoting a medieval hymn, and to it he adds the distortion and perversion of all that lies about him. "On march the banners of the King—of Hell." And there before them, in an infernal parody of Godhead, they see Satan in the distance, his great wings beating like a windmill. It is their beating that is the source of the icy wind of Cocytus, the exhalation of all evil.

All about him in the ice are strewn the sinners of the last round, *Judecca,* named for Judas Iscariot. These are the *Treacherous to Their Masters.* They lie completely sealed in the ice, twisted and distorted into every conceivable posture. It is impossible to speak to them, and the Poets move on to observe Satan.

He is fixed into the ice at the center to which flow all the rivers of guilt; and as he beats his great wings

as if to escape, their icy wind only freezes him more
surely into the polluted ice. In a grotesque parody of the
Trinity, he has three faces, each a different color, and in
each mouth he clamps a sinner whom he rips eternally
with his teeth. *Judas Iscariot* in the central mouth: *Brutus*
and *Cassius* in the mouths on either side.

Having seen all, the Poets now climb through the
center, grappling hand over hand down the hairy flank
of Satan himself—a last supremely symbolic action—and
at last, when they have passed the center of all gravity,
they emerge from Hell. A long climb from the earth's
center to the Mount of Purgatory awaits them, and they
push on without rest, ascending along the sides of the
river Lethe, till they emerge once more to see the stars
of Heaven, just before dawn on Easter Sunday.

"On march the banners of the King of Hell,"
  my Master said. "Toward us. Look straight
    ahead:
    can you make him out at the core   3
    of the frozen shell?"
Like a whirling windmill seen afar at twilight,
  or when a mist has risen from the ground—
    just such an engine rose upon my sight   6

stirring up such a wild and bitter wind
  I cowered for shelter at my Master's back,
    there being no other windbreak I could find.   9

I stood now where the souls of the last class
  (with fear my verses tell it) were covered
    wholly;
    they shone below the ice like straws in glass.   12

Some lie stretched out; others are fixed in place
  upright, some on their heads, some on their
    soles;
    another, like a bow, bends foot to face.   15

When we had gone so far across the ice
  that it pleased my Guide to show me the foul
    creature
    that once had worn the grace of Paradise,   18

he made me stop, and, stepping aside, he said:
  "Now see the face of Dis! This is the place
    where you must arm your soul against all   21
    dread."

Do not ask, Reader, how my blood ran cold
  and my voice choked up with fear. I cannot
    write it:
    this is a terror that cannot be told.   24

I did not die, and yet I lost life's breath:
  imagine for yourself what I became,
    deprived at once of both my life and death.   27

The Emperor of the Universe of Pain
  jutted his upper chest above the ice;
    and I am closer in size to the great mountain   30

the Titans make around the central pit,
  than they to his arms. Now, starting from
    this part,
    imagine the whole that corresponds to it!   33

If he was once as beautiful as now
  he is hideous, and still turned on his Maker,
    well may he be the source of every woe!   36

With what a sense of awe I saw his head
  towering above me! for it had three faces:
    one was in front, and it was fiery red;   39

the other two, as weirdly wonderful,
  merged with it from the middle of each
    shoulder
    to the point where all converged   42
    at the top of the skull;

the right was something between white and
    bile;
  the left was about the color one observes
    on those who live along the banks of the   45
    Nile.

Under each head two wings rose terribly,
  their span proportioned to so gross a bird:
    I never saw such sails upon the sea.   48

They were not feathers—their texture and their
    form
  were like a bat's wings—and he beat them so
    that three winds blew from him in one   51
    great storm:

it is these winds that freeze all Cocytus.
  He wept from his six eyes, and down three
    chins
    the tears ran mixed with bloody froth and   54
    pus.

In every mouth he worked a broken sinner
  between his rake-like teeth. Thus he kept
    three
    in eternal pain at his eternal dinner.   57

For the one in front the biting seemed to play
  no part at all compared to the ripping: at
    times
    the whole skin of his back was flayed away.   60

"That soul that suffers most," explained my
    Guide,
  "is Judas Iscariot, he who kicks his legs
    on the fiery chin and has his head inside.   63

Of the other two, who have their heads thrust
    forward,
  the one who dangles down from the black
    face
    is Brutus: note how he writhes without a   66
    word,

And there, with the huge and sinewy arms, is the soul
   of Cassius.—But the night is coming on
   and we must go, for we have seen the whole."   69

Then as he bade, I clasped his neck, and he,
   watching for a moment when the wings
   were opened wide, reached over dexterously   72

and seized the shaggy coat of the king demon;
   then grappling matted hair and frozen crusts
   from one tuft to another, clambered down.   75

When we had reached the joint where the great thigh
   merges into the swelling of the haunch,
   my Guide and Master, straining terribly,   78

turned his head to where his feet had been
   and began to grip the hair as if he were climbing;
   so that I thought we moved toward Hell again.   81

"Hold fast!" my Guide said, and his breath came shrill
   with labor and exhaustion. "There is no way
   but by such stairs to rise above such evil."   84

At last he climbed out through an opening
   in the central rock, and he seated me on the rim;
   then joined me with a nimble backward spring.   87

I looked up, thinking to see Lucifer
   as I had left him, and I saw instead
   his legs projecting high into the air.   90

Now let all those whose dull minds are still vexed
   by failure to understand what point it was
   I had passed through, judge if I was perplexed.   93

"Get up. Up on your feet," my Master said.
   "The sun already mounts to middle tierce,
   and a long road and hard climbing lie ahead."   96

It was no hall of state we had found there,
   but a natural animal pit hollowed from rock
   with a broken floor and a close and sunless air.   99

"Before I tear myself from the Abyss,"
   I said when I had risen, "O my Master,
   explain to me my error in all this: 102

where is the ice? and Lucifer—how has he
   been turned from top to bottom: and how can the sun
   have gone from night to day so suddenly?"   105

And he to me: "You imagine you are still
   on the other side of the center where I grasped
   the shaggy flank of the Great Worm of Evil   108

which bores through the world—you *were*
   while I climbed down,
   but when I turned myself about, you passed
   the point to which all gravities are drawn.   111

You are under the other hemisphere where you stand;
   the sky above us is the half opposed
   to that which canopies the great dry land.   114

Under the midpoint of that other sky
   the Man who was born sinless and who lived
   beyond all blemish, came to suffer and die.   117

You have your feet upon a little sphere
   which forms the other face of the Judecca.
   There it is evening when it is morning here.   120

And this gross Fiend and Image of all Evil
   who made a stairway for us with his hide
   is pinched and prisoned in the ice-pack still.   123

On this side he plunged down from heaven's height,
   and the land that spread here once hid in the sea
   and fled North to our hemisphere for fright;   126

and it may be that moved by that same fear,
   the one peak that still rises on this side
   fled upward leaving this great cavern here."   129

Down there, beginning at the further bound
   of Beelzebub's dim tomb, there is a space
   not known by sight, but only by the sound   132

of a little stream descending through the hollow
   it has eroded from the massive stone
   in its endlessly entwining lazy flow.   135

My Guide and I crossed over and began
   to mount that little known and lightless road
   to ascend into the shining world again.   138

He first, I second, without thought of rest
   we climbed the dark until we reached the point
   where a round opening brought in sight the blest   141

and beauteous shining of the Heavenly cars.
And we walked out once more beneath the Stars.

NOTES

1. *On march the banners of the King:* The hymn (*Vexilla regis prodeunt*) was written in the sixth century by Venantius Fortunatus, Bishop of Poitiers. The original celebrates the Holy Cross, and is

part of the service for Good Friday to be sung at the moment of uncovering the cross.

17. *the foul creature:* Satan.

38. *three faces:* Numerous interpretations of these three faces exist. What is essential to all explanation is that they be seen as perversions of the qualities of the Trinity.

54. *bloody froth and pus:* The gore of the sinners he chews which is mixed with his slaver.

62. *Judas:* Note how closely his punishment is patterned on that of the Simoniacs.

67. *huge and sinewy arms:* The Cassius who betrayed Caesar was more generally described in terms of Shakespeare's "lean and hungry look." Another Cassius is described by Cicero (*Catiline* III) as huge and sinewy. Dante probably confused the two.

68. *the night is coming on:* It is now Saturday evening.

95. *middle tierce:* In the canonical day tierce is the period from about six to nine A.M. Middle tierce, therefore, is seven-thirty. In going through the center point, they have gone from night to day. They have moved ahead twelve hours.

128. *the one peak:* The Mount of Purgatory.

129. *this great cavern:* The natural animal pit of line 98. It is also "Beelzebub's dim tomb," line 131.

133. *a little stream:* Lethe. In classical mythology, the river of forgetfulness, from which souls drank before being born. In Dante's symbolism it flows down from the top of Purgatory, where it washes away the memory of sin from the souls that have achieved purity. That memory it delivers to Hell, which draws all sin to itself.

143. *Stars:* As part of his total symbolism Dante ends each of the three divisions of the *Commedia* with this word. Every conclusion of the upward soul is toward the stars, God's shining symbols of hope and virtue. It is just before dawn of Easter Sunday that the Poets emerge—a further symbolism.

Purgatory

Canto I

Ante-Purgatory: the Shore of the Island
Cato of Utica

The Poets emerge from Hell just before dawn of Easter Sunday (April 10, 1300), and Dante revels in the sight of the rediscovered heavens. As he looks eagerly about at the stars, he sees nearby an old man of impressive bearing. The ancient is *Cato of Utica,* guardian of the shores of Purgatory. Cato challenges the Poets as fugitives from Hell, but Virgil, after first instructing Dante to kneel in reverence, explains Dante's mission and Beatrice's command. Cato then gives them instructions for proceeding.

The Poets have emerged at a point a short way up the slope of Purgatory. It is essential, therefore, that they descend to the lowest point and begin from there, an allegory of Humility. Cato, accordingly, orders Virgil to lead Dante to the shore, to wet his hands in the dew of the new morning, and to wash the stains of Hell from Dante's face and the film of Hell's vapors from Dante's eyes. Virgil is then to bind about Dante's waist one of the pliant reeds (symbolizing Humility) that grow in the soft mud of the shore.

Having so commanded, Cato disappears. Dante arises in silence and stands waiting, eager to begin. His look is all the communication that is necessary. Virgil leads him to the shore and performs all that Cato has commanded. Dante's first purification is marked by a miracle: when Virgil breaks off a reed, the stalk immediately regenerates a new reed, restoring itself exactly as it had been.

For better waters now the little bark
    of my indwelling powers raises her sails,
    and leaves behind that sea so cruel and dark.   3

Now shall I sing that second kingdom given
    the soul of man wherein to purge its guilt
    and so grow worthy to ascend to Heaven.   6

Yours am I, sacred Muses! To you I pray.
    Here let dead poetry rise once more to life,
    and here let sweet Calliope rise and play   9

some far accompaniment in that high strain
    whose power the wretched Pierides once felt
    so terribly they dared not hope again.   12

Sweet azure of the sapphire of the east
    was gathering on the serene horizon
    its pure and perfect radiance—a feast   15

to my glad eyes, reborn to their delight,
    as soon as I had passed from the dead air
    which had oppressed my soul and
        dimmed my sight.   18

The planet whose sweet influence strengthens love
    was making all the east laugh with her rays,
    veiling the Fishes, which she swam above.   21

I turned then to my right and set my mind
    on the other pole, and there I saw four stars
    unseen by mortals since the first mankind.   24

The heavens seemed to revel in their light.
    O widowed Northern Hemisphere, bereft
    forever of the glory of that sight!   27

As I broke off my gazing, my eyes veered
    a little to the left, to the other pole
    from which, by then, the Wain had   30
        disappeared.

I saw, nearby, an ancient man, alone.
    His bearing filled me with such reverence,
    no father had had more from any son.   33

His beard was long and touched with strands of white,
    as was his hair, of which two tresses fell
    over his breast. Rays of the holy light   36

that fell from the four stars made his face glow
    with such a radiance that he looked to me
    as if he faced the sun. And standing so,   39

he moved his venerable plumes and said:
    "Who are you two who climb by the dark
        stream
    to escape the eternal prison of the dead?   42

Who led you? or what served you as a light
    in your dark flight from the eternal valley,
    which lies forever blind in darkest night?   45

Are the laws of the pit so broken? Or is new
        counsel
    published in Heaven that the damned may
        wander
    onto my rocks from the abyss of Hell?"   48

At that my Master laid his hands upon me,
    instructing me by word and touch and
        gesture
    to show my reverence in brow and knee,   51

then answered him: "I do not come this way
    of my own will or powers. A Heavenly Lady
    sent me to this man's aid in his dark day.   54

But since your will is to know more, my will
    cannot deny you; I will tell you truly
    why we have come and how. This man has   57
        still

to see his final hour, though in the burning
    of his own madness he had drawn so near it
    his time was perilously short for turning.   60

As I have told you, I was sent to show
    the way his soul must take for its salvation;
    and there is none but this by which I go.   63

I have shown him the guilty people. Now I
        mean
    to lead him through the spirits in your keep-
        ing,
    to show him those whose suffering makes   66
        them clean.

By what means I have led him to this strand
    to see and hear you, takes too long to tell:
    from Heaven is the power and the command.   69

Now may his coming please you, for he goes
    to win his freedom; and how dear that is
    the man who gives his life for it best knows.   72

You know it, who in that cause found death
        sweet
    in Utica where you put off that flesh
    which shall rise radiant at the Judgment Seat.   75

We do not break the Laws: this man lives yet,
    and I am of that Round not ruled by Minos,
    with your own Marcia, whose chaste eyes   78
        seem set

in endless prayers to you. O blessed breast

to hold her yet your own! for love of her
    grant us permission to pursue our quest   81

across your seven kingdoms. When I go
    back to her side I shall bear thanks of you,
    if you will let me speak your name below."   84

"Marcia was so pleasing in my eyes
    there on the other side," he answered then
    "that all she asked, I did. Now that she lies   87

beyond the evil river, no word or prayer
    of hers may move me. Such was the Decree
    pronounced upon us when I rose from there.   90

But if, as you have said, a Heavenly Dame
    orders your way, there is no need to flatter:
    you need but ask it of me in her name.   93

Go then, and lead this man, but first see to it
    you bind a smooth green reed about his
        waist
    and clean his face of all trace of the pit.   96

For it would not be right that one with eyes
    still filmed by mist should go before the
        angel
    who guards the gate: he is from Paradise.   99

All round the wave-wracked shore-line, there
        below,
    reeds grow in the soft mud. Along that edge
    no foliate nor woody plant could grow.   102

for what lives in that buffeting must bend.
    Do not come back this way: the rising sun
    will light an easier way you may ascend."   105

With that he disappeared; and silently
    I rose and moved back till I faced my Guide,
    my eyes upon him, waiting. He said to me: 108

"Follow my steps and let us turn again:
    along this side there is a gentle slope
    that leads to the low boundaries of the   111
        plain."

The dawn, in triumph, made the day-breeze flee
    before its coming, so that from afar
    I recognized the trembling of the sea.   114

We strode across that lonely plain like men
    who seek the road they strayed from and
        who count
    the time lost till they find it once again.   117

When we had reached a place along the way
    where the cool morning breeze shielded the
        dew
    against the first heat of the gathering day,   120

with gentle graces my Sweet Master bent
    and laid both outspread palms upon the
        grass.

Then I, being well aware of his intent,   123

lifted my tear-stained cheeks to him, and there
he made me clean, revealing my true color
under the residues of Hell's black air.   126

We moved on then to the deserted strand
which never yet has seen upon its waters
a man who found his way back to dry land.   129

There, as it pleased another, he girded me.
Wonder of wonders! when he plucked a reed
another took its place there instantly,   132

arising from the humble stalk he tore
so that it grew exactly as before.

NOTES

4. *that second kingdom:* Purgatory.

5. *to purge its guilt:* (See also line 66: *those whose suffering makes them clean.*) There is suffering in Purgatory but no torment. The torment of the damned is endless, produces no change in the soul that endures it, and is imposed from without. The suffering of the souls in Purgatory, on the other hand, is temporary, is a means of purification, and is eagerly embraced as an act of the soul's own will. Demons guard the damned to inflict punishment and to prevent escape. In Purgatory, the sinners are free to leave off their sufferings: nothing but their own desire to be made clean moves them to accept their pains, and nothing more is needed. In fact, it is left to the suffering soul itself (no doubt informed by Divine Illumination) to decide at what point it has achieved purification and is ready to move on.

8. *dead poetry:* The verses that sang of Hell. Dante may equally have meant that poetry as an art has long been surpassed by history as the medium for great subjects. Here poetry will return to its classic state.

7–12. THE INVOCATION. Dante invokes all the Muses, as he did in *Inferno*, II, 7, but there the exhortation was to his own powers, to High Genius, and to Memory. Here he addresses his specific exhortation to Calliope, who, as the Muse of Epic Poetry, is foremost of the Nine. In *Paradiso* (I, 13) he exhorts Apollo himself to come to the aid of the poem.

Dante exhorts Calliope to fill him with the strains of the music she played in the defeat of the Pierides, the nine daughters of Pierius, King of Thessaly. They presumed to challenge the Muses to a contest of song. After their defeat they were changed into magpies for their presumption. Ovid (*Metamorphoses*, V, 294–340 and 662–678) retells the myth in detail.

Note that Dante not only calls upon Calliope to fill him with the strains of highest song, but that he calls for that very song that overthrew the arrogant pretensions of the Pierides, the strains that humbled false pride. The invocation is especially apt, therefore, as a first sounding of the theme of Humility.

17. *the dead air:* Of Hell.

19–21. *The planet whose sweet influence strengthens love:* Venus. Here, as morning star, Venus is described as rising in Pisces, the Fishes, the zodiacal sign immediately preceding Aries. In Canto I of the *Inferno* Dante has made it clear that the Sun is in Aries. Hence it is about to rise.

Allegorically, the fact that Venus represents love is, of course, indispensable to the mood of the *Purgatory*. At no time in April of 1300 was Venus the morning star. Rather, it rose after the sun.

Dante's description of the first dawn in Canto I of the *Inferno* similarly violates the exact detail of things. But Dante is no bookkeeper of the literal. In the *Inferno* he violated fact in order to compile a perfect symbol of rebirth. Here, he similarly violates the literal in order to describe an ideal sunrise, and simultaneously to make the allegorical point that Love (Venus) leads the way and that Divine Illumination (the Sun) follows upon it.

23. *four stars:* Modern readers are always tempted to identify these four stars as the Southern Cross, but it is almost certain that Dante did not know about that formation. In VIII, 89, Dante mentions three other stars as emphatically as he does these four and no one has been tempted to identify them on the star-chart. Both constellations are best taken as allegorical. The four stars represent the Four Cardinal Virtues: Prudence, Justice, Fortitude, and Temperance. Dante will encounter them again in the form of nymphs when he achieves the Earthly Paradise.

24. *the first mankind:* Adam and Eve. In Dante's geography, the Garden of Eden (the Earthly Paradise) was at the top of the Mount of Purgatory, which was the only land in the Southern Hemisphere. All of what were called "the southern continents" were believed to lie north of the equator. When Adam and Eve were driven from the Garden, therefore, they were driven into the Northern Hemisphere, and no living soul since had been far enough south to see those stars.

Ulysses and his men had come within sight of the Mount of Purgatory, but Ulysses mentioned nothing of having seen these stars.

29. *the other pole:* The North Pole. The Wain (Ursa Major, *i.e.,* the Big Dipper) is below the horizon.

31 ff. CATO OF UTICA. Marcus Porcius Cato the Younger, 95–46 B.C. In the name of freedom, Cato opposed the policies of both Caesar and Pompey, but because he saw Caesar as the greater evil joined forces with Pompey. After the defeat of his cause at the Battle of Thapsus, Cato killed himself with his own sword rather than lose his freedom. Virgil lauds him in the *Aeneid* as a symbol of perfect devotion to liberty, and all writers of Roman antiquity have given Cato a similar high place. Dante spends the highest praises on him both in *De Monarchia* and *Il Convivio*.

Why Cato should be so signally chosen by God as the special guardian of Purgatory has been much disputed. Despite his suicide (and certainly one could argue that he had less excuse for it than had Pier delle Vigne—see *Inferno*, XIII—for his) he was sent to Limbo as a Virtuous Pagan. From Limbo he was especially summoned to his present office. It is clear, moreover, that he will find a special triumph on Judgment Day, though he will probably not be received into Heaven.

The key to Dante's intent seems to lie in the four stars, the Four Cardinal Virtues, that shine so brightly on Cato's face when Dante first sees him. Once Cato is forgiven his suicide (and a partisan could argue that it was a positive act, a death for freedom), he may certainly be taken as a figure of Prudence, Justice, Fortitude, and Temperance. He does very well, moreover, as a symbol of the natural love of freedom; and Purgatory, it must be remembered, is the road to Ultimate Freedom. Cato may be taken, therefore, as representative of supreme virtue short of godliness. He has accomplished everything but the purifying total surrender of his will to God. As such he serves as an apt transitional symbol, being the highest rung on the ladder of natural virtue, but the lowest on the ladder of those godly virtues to which Purgatory is the ascent. Above all, the fact that he took Marcia (see line 78, note) back to his love makes him an especially apt symbol of God's forgiveness in allowing the strayed soul to return to him through Purgatory.

53. *A Heavenly Lady:* Beatrice.

77. *Minos:* The Judge of the Damned. The round in Hell not ruled by Minos is Limbo, the final resting place of the Virtuous Pagans. Minos (see *Inferno,* V) is stationed at the entrance to the second circle of Hell. The souls in Limbo (the first circle) have never had to pass before him to be judged.

78. *Marcia.* The story of Marcia and of Cato is an extraordinary one. She was the daughter of the consul Philippus and became Cato's second wife, bearing his three children. In 56 B.C., in an unusual transaction approved by her father, Cato released her in order that she might marry his friend Hortensius. (Hence line 87: "that all she asked I did.") After the death of Hortensius, Cato took her back.

In *Il Convivio,* IV, 28, Dante presents the newly widowed Marcia praying to be taken back in order that she may die the wife of Cato, and that it may be said of her that she was not cast forth from his love. Dante treats that return as an allegory of the return of the strayed soul to God (that it may die "married" to God, and that God's love for it be made manifest to all time). Virgil describes Marcia as still praying to Cato.

89. *the Decree:* May be taken as that law that makes an absolute separation between the damned and the saved. Cato cannot be referring here to *Mark,* xii, 25 ("when they shall rise from the dead, they neither marry, nor are given in marriage") for that "decree" was not pronounced upon his ascent from Limbo.

98. *filmed by mist:* Of Hell.

100. ff. THE REED. The pliant reed clearly symbolizes humility, but other allegorical meanings suggest themselves at once. First, the Reed takes the place of the Cord that Dante took from about his waist in order to signal Geryon. The Cord had been intended to snare and defeat the Leopard with the Gaudy Pelt, a direct assault upon sin. It is now superseded by the Reed of submission to God's will. Second, the reeds are eternal and undiminishable. As such they must immediately suggest the redemption purchased by Christ's sufferings (ever-abounding grace), for the quantity of grace available to mankind through Christ's passion is, in Christian creed, also eternal and undiminishable. The importance of the fact that the reeds grow at the lowest point of the Island and that the Poets must descend to them before they can begin, has already been mentioned. Curiously, the reed is never again mentioned, though it must remain around Dante's waist. See also *Matthew,* xxvii, 29.

119. *breeze shielded the dew:* The dew is a natural symbol of God's grace. The morning breeze shields it in the sense that, being cool, it retards evaporation.

Even more naturally, being bathed in the dew may be taken to signify baptism. The structure of Purgatory certainly suggests a parable of the soul's stages of sacred development: the dew, baptism; the gate of Purgatory, above, first communion; Virgil's certification of Dante as lord of himself (XXVII, 143), confirmation; and Dante's swoon and awakening as extreme unction and the reception into the company of the blessed.

Canto IX
The Gate of Purgatory
The Angel Guardian

Dawn is approaching. Dante has a dream of A GOLDEN EAGLE that descends from the height of Heaven and carries him up to the Sphere of Fire. He wakes to find he has been transported in his sleep, that it was LUCIA [Divine Light] who bore him, laying him down beside an enormous wall, through an opening in which he and Virgil may approach THE GATE OF PURGATORY.

Having explained these matters, Virgil leads Dante to the Gate and its ANGEL GUARDIAN. The Angel is seated on the topmost of THREE STEPS that symbolize the three parts of a perfect ACT OF CONFESSION. Dante prostrates himself at the feet of the Angel, who cuts SEVEN P's in Dante's forehead with the point of a blazing sword. He then allows the Poets to enter. As the Gates open with a sound of thunder, the mountain resounds with a great HYMN OF PRAISE.

Now pale upon the balcony of the East
    ancient Tithonus' concubine appeared,
    but lately from her lover's arms released.   3

Across her brow, their radiance like a veil,
    a scroll of gems was set, worked in the shape
    of the cold beast whose sting is in his tail.   6

And now already, where we were, the night
    had taken two steps upward, while the third
    thrust down its wings in the first stroke of   9
    flight;

when I, by Adam's weight of flesh defeated,
    was overcome by sleep, and sank to rest
    across the grass on which we five were   12
    seated.

At that new hour when the first dawn light
    grows
    and the little swallow starts her mournful cry,
    perhaps in memory of her former woes;   15

and when the mind, escaped from its
    submission
    to flesh and to the chains of waking thought,
    becomes almost prophetic in its vision;   18

in a dream I saw a soaring eagle hold
    the shining height of heaven, poised to strike,
    yet motionless on widespread wings of gold.   21

He seemed to hover where old history
    records that Ganymede rose from his friends,
    borne off to the supreme consistory.   24

I thought to myself: "Perhaps his habit is
    to strike at this one spot; perhaps he scorns
    to take his prey from any place but this."   27

Then from his easy wheel in Heaven's spire,
    terrible as a lightning bolt, he struck
    and snatched me up high as the Sphere of   30
    Fire. [266]

It seemed that we were swept in a great blaze,
    and the imaginary fire so scorched me
    my sleep broke and I wakened in a daze.   33

266 Gustave Doré. *The Eagle*. 1868. Wood engraving, 10 × 8″ (25 × 20 cm). Prints Division, New York Public Library. Probably the most successful illustrator of the 19th century was the Frenchman Gustave Doré (1832–1883). He made 135 wood engravings of scenes from the *Divine Comedy*. Here Doré shows Dante with his head thrown back as he sleeps.

Achilles must have roused exactly thus—
  glancing about with unadjusted eyes,
  now here, now there, not knowing   36
    where he was—

when Thetis stole him sleeping, still a boy,
  and fled with him from Chiron's care to
    Scyros,
  whence the Greeks later lured him off to   39
    Troy.

I sat up with a start; and as sleep fled
  out of my face, I turned the deathly white
  of one whose blood is turned to ice by dread. 42

There at my side my comfort sat—alone.
  The sun stood two hours high, and more. I sat
  facing the sea. The flowering glen was gone. 45

"Don't be afraid," he said. "From here our
    course
  leads us to joy, you may be sure. Now,
    therefore,
  hold nothing back, but strive with all your 48
    force.

You are now at Purgatory. See the great
  encircling rampart there ahead. And see
  that opening—it contains the Golden Gate. 51

A while back, in the dawn before the day,
  while still your soul was locked in sleep
    inside you,
  across the flowers that made the valley gay, 54

a Lady came. 'I am Lucia,' she said.
  'Let me take up this sleeping man and bear him
  that he may wake to see his hope ahead.' 57

Sordello and the others stayed. She bent
  and took you up. And as the light grew full,
  she led, I followed, up the sweet ascent. 60

Here she put you down. Then with a sweep
  of her sweet eyes she marked that open
    entrance.
  Then she was gone; and with her went your 63
    sleep."

As one who finds his doubt dispelled, sheds fear
  and feels it change into new confidence
  as bit by bit he sees the truth shine clear— 66

so did I change; and seeing my face brim
  with happiness, my Guide set off at once
  to climb the slope, and I moved after him. 69

Reader, you know to what exalted height
  I raised my theme. Small wonder if I now
  summon still greater art to what I write. 72

As we drew near the height, we reached a place
  from which—inside what I had first believed
  to be an open breach in the rock face— 75

I saw a great gate fixed in place above
  three steps, each its own color; and a guard
  who did not say a word and did not move. 78

Slow bit by bit, raising my lids with care,
  I made him out seated on the top step,
  his face more radiant than my eyes could 81
    bear.

He held a drawn sword, and the eye of day
  beat such a fire back from it, that each time
  I tried to look, I had to look away. 84

I heard him call: "What is your business here?
  Answer from where you stand. Where is
    your Guide?
  Take care you do not find your coming 87
    dear."

"A little while ago," my Teacher said,
  "A Heavenly Lady, well versed in these
    matters,
  told us 'Go there. That is the Gate ahead.'" 90

"And may she still assist you, once inside,

to your soul's good! Come forward to our
   three steps,"
the courteous keeper of the gate replied.   93

We came to the first step: white marble
   gleaming
so polished and so smooth that in its mirror
I saw my true reflection past all seeming.   96

The second was stained darker than blue-black
   and of a rough-grained and a fire-flaked
   stone,
   its length and breadth crisscrossed   99
   by many a crack.

The third and topmost was of porphyry,
   or so it seemed, but of a red as flaming
as blood that spurts out of an artery.   102

The Angel of the Lord had both feet on
   this final step and sat upon the sill
which seemed made of some adamantine   105
   stone.

With great good will my Master guided me
   up the three steps and whispered in my ear;
   "Now beg him humbly that he turn the   108
   key."

Devoutly prostrate at his holy feet,
   I begged in mercy's name to be let in,
but first three times upon my breast I beat.   111

Seven *P*'s, the seven scars of sin,
   his sword point cut into my brow. He said:
   "Scrub off these wounds when you have   114
   passed within."

Color of ashes, of parched earth one sees
   deep in an excavation, were his vestments,
   and from beneath them he drew out two   117
   keys.

One was of gold, one silver. He applied
   the white one to the gate first, then the
   yellow,
and did with them what left me satisfied.   120

"Whenever either of these keys is put
   improperly in the lock and fails to turn it,"
the Angel said to us, "the door stays shut.   123

One is more precious. The other is so wrought
   as to require the greater skill and genius,
for it is that one which unties the knot.   126

They are from Peter, and he bade me be
   more eager to let in than to keep out
whoever cast himself prostrate before me."   129

Then opening the sacred portals wide:
   "Enter. But first be warned: do not look
   back
or you will find yourself once more outside."   132

The Tarpeian rock-face, in that fatal hour
   that robbed it of Metellus, and then the
   treasure,
   did not give off so loud and harsh a roar   135

as did the pivots of the holy gate—
   which were of resonant and hard-forged
   metal—
   when they turned under their enormous   138
   weight.

At the first thunderous roll I turned half-round,
   for it seemed to me I heard a chorus singing
   Te deum laudamus mixed with that sweet   141
   sound.

I stood there and the strains that reached my
   ears
   left on my soul exactly that impression
a man receives who goes to church and hears   144

the choir and organ ringing out their chords
and now does, now does not, make out the
   words.

NOTES

1–9. There is no wholly satisfactory explanation of this complex opening description. Dante seems to be saying that the third hour of darkness is beginning (hence, if sunset occurred at 6:00 it is now a bit after 8:00 P.M.) and that the aurora of the rising moon is appearing above the horizon.

He describes the moon as the concubine of Tithonus. Tithonus, however, married the daughter of the sun, Aurora (dawn), and it was she who begged Jove to give her husband immortality while forgetting to ask perpetual youth for him. Thus Tithonus lived but grew older and older beside his ageless bride. (In one legend he was later changed into a grasshopper.) Despite his advanced years, however, he seems here to be philandering with the moon as his concubine. Dante describes the moon as rising from Tithonus' bed and standing on the balcony of the East (the horizon) with the constellation Scorpio gemmed on her forehead, that "cold [blooded] beast whose sting is in his tail" being the scorpion.

Having given Tithonus a double life, Dante now adds a mixed metaphor in which the "steps" of the night have "wings." Two of the steps (hours) have flown, and the third has just completed the first downstroke of its wings (i.e., has just begun its flight).

15. *former woes:* Tereus, the husband of Procne, raped her sister Philomela, and cut out her tongue so that she could not accuse him. Philomela managed to communicate the truth to Procne by means of her weaving. The two sisters thereupon took revenge by killing Itys, son of Procne and Tereus, and serving up his flesh to his father. Tereus, learning the truth, was about to kill the sisters when all were turned into birds. Ovid (*Metamorphoses,* VI, 424 ff.) has Tereus changed into a hoopoe, and probably (though the text leaves some doubt) Procne into a swallow and Philomela into a nightingale. Dante clearly takes the swallow to be Philomela.

18. *prophetic in its vision:* It was an ancient belief that the dreams that came toward dawn were prophetic.

19–33. DANTE'S DREAM. Each of Dante's three nights on the Mount of Purgatory ends with a dream that comes just before dawn. The present dream is relatively simple in its symbolism, and as we learn shortly after Dante's awakening, it parallels his ascent of the mountain in the arms of Lucia. The dream is told, however, with such complexities of allusion that every reference must be carefully weighed.

To summarize the symbolism in the simplest terms, the Golden Eagle may best be rendered in its attributes. It comes from highest Heaven (from God), its feathers are pure gold (Love? God's splendor?), its wings are outspread (the open arms of Divine Love?), and it appears poised to descend in an instant (as is Divine Grace). The Eagle snatches Dante up to the Sphere of Fire (the presence of God? the beginning of Purgatorial purification? both?), and both are so consumed by the fire that Dante, in his unpurified state, cannot bear it.

On another level, of course, the Eagle is Lucia (Divine Light), who has descended from Heaven, and who bears the sleeping Dante from the Flowering Valley to the beginning of the true Purgatory. Note that Lucia is an anagram for *acuila,* "eagle."

On a third level, the dream simultaneously connects with the earlier reference to Ganymede, also snatched up by the eagle of God, but the two experiences are contrasted as much as they are compared. Ganymede was carried up by Jove's eagle, Dante by Lucia. Ganymede was out hunting in the company of his worldly associates; Dante was laboring for grace, had renounced worldliness, and was in the company of great souls who were themselves awaiting purification. Ganymede was carried to Olympus; Dante to the beginning of a purification which, though he was still too unworthy to endure it, would in time make him a perfect servant of the true God. Thus, his experience is in the same pattern as Ganymede's, but surpasses it as Faith surpasses Human Reason, and as Beatrice surpasses Virgil.

23. *Ganymede:* Son of Tros, the mythical founder of Troy, was reputedly the most beautiful of mortals, so beautiful that Jove sent an eagle (or perhaps went himself in the form of an eagle) to snatch up the boy and bring him to Heaven, where he became cupbearer to the gods. The fact that Dante himself is about to begin the ascent of Purgatory proper (and hence to Heaven) inevitably suggests an allegory of the soul in the history of Ganymede. God calls to Himself what is most beautiful in man.

The fact that Dante always thought of the Trojans as an especially chosen people is also relevant. Ganymede was the son of the founder of Troy; Troy, in Dante's Virgilian view, founded Rome. And through the Church of Rome men's souls were enabled to mount to Heaven.

24. *consistory:* Here, the council of the gods on Olympus. Dante uses the same term to describe Paradise.

30. *Sphere of Fire:* The four elemental substances are earth, water, fire, and air. In Dante's cosmography, the Sphere of Fire was located above the Sphere of Air and just under the Sphere of the Moon. Hence the eagle bore him to the top of the atmosphere. The Sphere of Fire, however, may also be taken as another symbol for God.

34–39. ACHILLES' WAKING. It had been prophesied that Achilles would be killed at Troy. Upon the outbreak of the Trojan War, his mother, Thetis, stole him while he was sleeping, from the care of the centaur Chiron who was his tutor and fled with him to Scyros, where she hid him disguised as a girl. He was found there and lured away by Ulysses and Diomede, who burn for that sin (among others) in Malebolge. Thus Achilles, like Dante, was borne off in his sleep and awoke to find himself in a strange place.

51. *that opening:* The Gate, as the Poets will find, is closed and guarded. Dante (here and in line 62, below) can only mean "the

opening in which the gate was set" and not "an open entrance." At this distance, they do not see the Gate itself but only the gap in the otherwise solid wall.

55. *Lucia* (Loo-TCHEE-ya): Symbolizes Divine Light, Divine Grace.

77. *three steps:* (See also lines 94–102, below.) The entrance into Purgatory involves the ritual of the Roman Catholic confessional with the Angel serving as the confessor. The three steps are the three acts of the perfect confession: candid confession (mirroring the whole man), mournful contrition, and burning gratitude for God's mercy. The Angel Guardian, as the priestly confessor, does not move or speak as the Poets approach, because he can admit to purification only those who ask for admission.

86. *Where is your Guide?* It must follow from the Angel's question that souls ready to enter Purgatory are led up the mountain by another Angel. Dante and Virgil are arriving in an irregular way, as they did to the shore below, where they were asked essentially the same question by Cato. Note, too, that Virgil answers for the Poets, as he did to Cato. The allegory may be that right thinking answers for a man, at least to start with, though the actual entrance into the state of Grace requires an act of Faith and of Submission.

90. *told us:* Lucia spoke only with her eyes, and what Virgil is quoting is her look. What he is quoting is, in essence, correct, but it does seem he could have been a bit more accurate in his first actual conversation with an Angel.

94–96. *the first step:* Contrition of the heart. White for purity, shining for hope, and flawless for perfection. It is not only the mirror of the soul, but it is that mirror in which the soul sees itself as it truly is and not in its outward seeming.

97–99. *the second:* Contrition of the mouth, i.e., confession. The color of a bruise for the shame that envelops the soul as it confesses, rough-grained and fire-flaked for the pain the confessant must endure, and cracked for the imperfection (sin) the soul confesses.

100–102. *the third:* Satisfaction by works. Red for the ardor that leads to good works. Porphyry is, of course, a purple stone, but Dante does not say the stone was porphyry; only that it resembled it, though red in color.

"Artery" here is, of course, an anachronism, the circulation of the blood having yet to be discovered in Dante's time. Dante uses the word *vena* (vein), but it seems to me the anachronism will be less confusing to a modern reader than would be the idea of bright red and spurting venous blood.

103–105. The Angel, as noted, represents the confessor, and, more exactly, the Church Confessant. Thus the Church is founded on adamant and rests its feet on Good Works.

112. *Seven P's:* P is for the Latin *peccatum.* Thus there is one *P* for each of the Seven Deadly Sins for which the sinners suffer on the seven ledges above: Pride, Envy, Wrath, Acedia (Sloth), Avarice (Hoarding and Prodigality), Gluttony, and Lust.

Dante has just completed the act of confession and the Angel confessor marks him to indicate that even in a shriven soul there remain traces of the seven sins which can be removed only by suffering.

115–117. *Color of ashes, of parched earth:* The colors of humility which befit the office of the confessor. *two keys:* (Cf. the Papal Seal, which is a crown above two crossed keys.) The keys symbolize the power of the confessor (the Church, and hence the Pope) to grant or to withhold absolution. In the present context they may further be interpreted as the two parts of the confessor's office of admission: the gold key may be taken to represent his ordained authority, the silver key as the learning and reflection with which he must weigh the guilt before assigning penance and offering absolution.

126. *unties the knot:* Another mixed metaphor. The soul-searched judgment of the confessor (the silver key) decides who may and who may not receive absolution, and in resolving that problem the door is opened, provided that the gold key of ordained authority has already been turned.

133–138. *The Tarpeian rock-face:* The public treasury of Rome was kept in the great scarp of Tarpeia on the Campidoglio. The tribune Metellus was its custodian when Caesar, returned to Rome after crossing the Rubicon, moved to seize the treasury. Metellus opposed him but was driven away and the great gates were opened. Lucan (*Pharsalia,* III, 154–156 and 165–168) describes the scene and the roar that echoed from the rock face as the gates were forced open.

139–141. The thunder of the opening of the Gates notifies the souls within that a new soul has entered, and they burst into the hymn "We Praise Thee, O God." (Contrast these first sounds of Purgatory with the first sounds of Hell—*Inferno,* III, 22–24.) Despite the thunderous roar right next to him, Dante seems to hear with his "allegorical ear" what certainly could not have registered upon his physical ear.

This seeming incongruity has long troubled me. I owe Professor MacAllister a glad thanks for what is certainly the essential clarification. The whole *Purgatorio,* he points out, is built upon the structure of a Mass. The Mass moreover is happening not on the mountain but in church with Dante devoutly following its well-known steps. I have not yet had time to digest Professor MacAllister's suggestion, but it strikes me immediately as a true insight and promises another illuminating way of reading the *Purgatorio.*

Canto XXVII
The Seventh Cornice
The Angel of Chastity
The Wall of Fire
The Earthly Paradise
The Angel Guardian

A little before sunset of the third day on the Mountain the Poets come to the further limit of the Seventh Cornice and are greeted by THE ANGEL OF CHASTITY, who tells them they must pass through the wall of fire. Dante recoils in terror, but Virgil persuades him to enter in Beatrice's name.

They are guided through the fire by a chant they hear coming from the other side. Emerging, they find it is sung by THE ANGEL GUARDIAN of the Earthly Paradise, who stands in a light so brilliant that Dante cannot see him. (It is probably here that THE LAST P is stricken from Dante's brow. Or perhaps it was consumed by the fire. [The other six P's have been removed in preceding cantos.])

The Angel hurries them toward the ascent, but night overtakes them, and the Poets lie down to sleep, each on the step on which he finds himself. (For Statius [a pagan poet, encountered in Canto XXI, who in Canto XXII attributes his conversion to Christianity to Virgil's sup-

posed prediction of Christ's coming in one of his Bucolics] it will be the last sleep, since there is no night in Heaven.) There, just before dawn, Dante has a prophetic DREAM OF LEAH AND RACHEL, which foreshadows the appearance, above, of Matilda and Beatrice.

Day arrives; the Poets rise and race up the rest of the ascent until they come in sight of THE EARTHLY PARADISE. Here VIRGIL SPEAKS HIS LAST WORDS, for the Poets have now come to the limit of Reason, and Dante is now free to follow his every impulse, since all motion of sin in him has been purged away.

As the day stands when the Sun begins to glow
   over the land where his Maker's blood was
      shed,
   and the scales of Libra ride above the Ebro,   3

while Ganges' waters steam in the noonday
      glare—
   so it stood, the light being nearly faded,
   when we met God's glad Angel standing   6
      there

on the rocky ledge beyond the reach of the fire,
   and caroling *"Beati mundo corde"*
   in a voice to which no mortal could aspire.   9

Then: "Blessed ones, till by flame purified
   no soul may pass this point. Enter the fire
   and heed the singing from the other side."   12

These were his words to us when we had come
   near as we could, and hearing them, I froze
   as motionless as one laid in his tomb.   15

I lean forward over my clasped hands and stare
   into the fire, thinking of human bodies
   I once saw burned, and once more   18
      see them there.

My kindly escorts heard me catch my breath
   and turned, and Virgil said: "Within that
      flame
   there may be torment, but there is no death.   21

Think well, my son, what dark ways we have
      trod . . .
   I guided you unharmed on Geryon:
   shall I do less now we are nearer God?   24

Believe this past all doubt: were you to stay
   within that womb of flame a thousand years,
   it would not burn a single hair away.   27

And if you still doubt my sincerity,
   but reach the hem of your robe into the
      flame:
   your hands and eyes will be your guarantee.   30

My son, my son, turn here with whole
      assurance.

Put by your fears and enter to your peace."
And I stood fixed, at war with my own   33
  conscience.

And seeing me still stubborn, rooted fast,
  he said, a little troubled: "Think, my son,
  you shall see Beatrice when this wall is past."   36

As Pyramus, but one breath from the dead,
  opened his eyes when he heard Thisbe's
    name,
  and looked at her, when the mulberry   39
    turned red—

just so my hard paralysis melted from me,
  and I turned to my Leader at that name
  which wells forever in my memory;   42

at which he wagged his head, as at a child
  won over by an apple. Then he said:
  "Well, then, what are we waiting for?"   45
  and smiled.

He turned then and went first into the fire,
  requesting Statius, who for some time now
  had walked between us, to bring up the rear.   48

Once in the flame, I gladly would have cast
  my body into boiling glass to cool it
  against the measureless fury of the blast.   51

My gentle father, ever kind and wise,
  strengthened me in my dread with talk of
    Beatrice,
  saying: "I seem already to see her eyes."   54

From the other side, to guide us, rose a paean,
  and moving toward it, mindless of all else,
  we emerged at last where the ascent began.   57

There I beheld a light that burned so brightly
  I had to look away; and from it rang:
  "Venite benedicti patris mei."   60

"Night falls," it added, "the sun sinks to rest;
  do not delay but hurry toward the height
  while the last brightness lingers in the west."   63

Straight up through the great rock-wall lay the
    way
  on such a line that, as I followed it,
  my body blocked the sun's last level ray.   66

We had only climbed the first few stairs as yet
  when I and my two sages saw my shadow
  fade from me; and we knew the sun had set.   69

Before the vast sweep of the limned horizon
  could fade into one hue and night win all
  the immeasurable air to its dominion,   72

each made the step on which he stood his bed,
  for the nature of the Mount not only
    stopped us

but killed our wish to climb, once day had   75
  fled.

As goats on a rocky hill will dance and leap,
  nimble and gay, till they find grass, and then,
  while they are grazing, growing as tame as   78
    sheep

at ease in the green shade when the sun is high
  and the shepherd stands by, leaning on his
    staff,
  and at his ease covers them with his eye—   81

and as the herdsman beds down on the ground,
  keeping his quiet night watch by his flock
  lest it be scattered by a wolf or hound;   84

just so we lay there, each on his stone block,
  I as the goat, they as my guardians,
  shut in on either side by walls of rock.   87

I could see little ahead—rock blocked the
    way—
  but through that little I saw the stars grow
    larger,
  brighter than mankind sees them. And as I   90
    lay,

staring and lost in thought, a sleep came on
    me—
  the sleep that oftentimes presents the fact
  before the event, a sleep of prophecy.   93

At the hour, I think, when Venus, first
    returning
  out of the east, shone down upon the
    mountain—
  she who with fires of love comes ever-   96
    burning—

I dreamed I saw a maiden innocent
  and beautiful, who walked a sunny field
  gathering flowers, and caroling as she went: 99

"Say I am Leah if any ask my name,
  and my white hands weave garlands wreath
    on wreath
  to please me when I stand before the frame   102

of my bright glass. For this my fingers play
  among these blooms. But my sweet sister
    Rachel
  sits at her mirror motionless all day.   105

To stare into her own eyes endlessly
  is all her joy, as mine is in my weaving.
  She looks, I do. Thus live we joyously."   108

Now eastward the new day rayed Heaven's
    dome
  (the sweeter to the returning wanderer
  who wakes from each night's lodging   111
    nearer home),

and the shadows fled on every side as I
    stirred from my sleep and leaped upon my
      feet,
    seeing my Lords already standing by.   114

"This is the day your hungry soul shall be
    fed on the golden apples men have sought
    on many different boughs so ardently."   117

These were the very words which, at the start,
    my Virgil spoke to me, and there have never
    been gifts as dear as these were to my heart.   120

Such waves of yearning to achieve the height
    swept through my soul, that at each step I
      took
    I felt my feathers growing for the flight.   123

When we had climbed the stairway to the rise
    of the topmost step, there with a father's love
    Virgil turned and fixed me with his eyes.   126

"My son," he said, "you now have seen the
      torment
    of the temporal and the eternal fires;
    here, now, is the limit of my discernment.   129

I have led you here by grace of mind and art;
    now let your own good pleasure be your
      guide;
    you are past the steep ways, past the narrow   132
      part.

See there the sun that shines upon your brow,
    the sweet new grass, the flowers, the fruited
      vines
    which spring up without need of seed or   135
      plow.

Until those eyes come gladdened which in pain
    moved me to come to you and lead your way,
    sit there at ease or wander through the plain. 138

Expect no more of me in word or deed:
    here your will is upright, free, and whole,
    and you would be in error not to heed   141

whatever your own impulse prompts you to:
lord of yourself I crown and mitre you."

NOTES

1–4. *As the day stands:* Meaning of this passage: It is shortly before sunset of the third day on the Mountain. Dante's details here are the reverse of those given at the opening of II. *the land where his Maker's blood was shed:* Jerusalem. *the Ebro:* For Spain.

6. *God's glad Angel:* The Angel of Chastity. He is standing on the narrow rocky path outside the wall of fire.

8. *Beati mundo corde:* "Blessed are the pure in heart [for they shall see God]." (*Matthew,* v, 8.)

10–12. THE WALL OF FLAMES. It is, of course, the fire in which the Lustful are purified. It is also the legendary wall of fire that surrounded the Earthly Paradise. Note that all souls must pass

through that fire. The readiest interpretation of that fact is that every soul must endure some purification before it can approach God (theoretically, a soul could climb Purgatory and endure no pain but this). Since no man's soul is perfect in its love, moreover, it must endure the fire that purifies impure love. Additionally, the allegorical intent may be that no man is entirely free of Lust. Having reached the Earthly Paradise, the soul has reached the Perfection of the Active Life. Below, its motion has been *toward* perfection. Now, after a few final rituals, the soul *becomes* perfect, and therefore changeless.

16. *I lean forward over my clasped hands:* Dante's hands must be clasped a bit below the waist. It is an odd posture, but it is also oddly Dantean.

17–18. *bodies I once saw burned:* Dante must mean as a witness at an execution. Burnings at the stake generally took place in public squares. They were a rather common spectacle. Dante's sentence of exile, it is relevant to note, decreed that he was to be burned if taken on Florentine territory.

23. *Geryon:* The Monster of Fraud. See *Inferno,* XVII, 1 ff., note.

37–39. *Pyramus . . . Thisbe:* Famous tragic lovers of Babylon. Ovid (*Metamorphoses,* IV, 55–166) tells their story. At a tryst by a mulberry (which in those days bore white fruit) Thisbe was frightened by a lion and ran off, dropping her veil. The lion, his jaws bloody from a recent kill, tore at the veil, staining it with blood. Pyramus, arriving later, saw the stained veil, concluded that Thisbe was dead, and stabbed himself. Thisbe, returning, found him and cried to him to open his eyes for his Thisbe. At that name Pyramus opened his eyes, looked at her, and died. Thisbe, invoking the tree to darken in their memory, thereupon stabbed herself. (*Cf.* Shakespeare's *Romeo and Juliet.*) The mulberry roots drank their blood and the fruit turned red ever after.

40. *my hard paralysis melted:* Note how Dante describes his emotions throughout this passage. He is afraid, to be sure. But the fear is of his human body and habit. His soul yearns forward, but his body will not obey until Reason has overcome mortal habit.

58. *a light:* This is the Angel Guardian of the Earthly Paradise. He corresponds to the Angel guarding the Gate. At every other ascent in Purgatory, Dante has met one angel. Here, he meets two, one on either side of the fire. It is the song of this Angel that has guided the Poets through the flames. In all probability, too, it is this Angel that strikes away the final *P* from Dante's brow (or perhaps it was consumed in the fire). It is unlikely that the final *P* was removed by the Angel of Chastity, since the Poets had not yet been through the fire, i.e., had not really crossed all of the Cornice.

60. *Venite benedicti patris mei:* "Come ye blessèd of my Father." (*Matthew,* XXV, 34.)

68. *my shadow:* Virgil and Statius, of course, cast none.

94. *At the hour . . . when Venus, first returning:* Venus is in the sign of Pisces, which immediately precedes Aries, in which sign the sun now is. It is, therefore, Venus Morningstar. Thus it is the hour before dawn, in which the truth is dreamed.

97–108. DANTE'S DREAM. Leah and Rachel were, respectively, the first- and second-born daughters of Laban and the first and second wives of Jacob. Many authors before Dante had interpreted them as representing the Active and the Contemplative Life of the Soul. Leah's white hands (*le belle mani*) symbolize the Active Life, as Rachel's eyes (lines 104–108) symbolize the Contemplative Life.

Since it is the truth Dante is dreaming, these figures must foreshadow others, as the eagle of his earlier dream (IX, 19 ff.) represented Lucia. Thus Leah prefigures Matilda, who will appear soon, and Rachel prefigures Beatrice, who will appear soon thereafter. But just as the eagle is not to be confused with Lucia, so Leah and Rachel are not to be narrowly identified with Matilda and Beatrice except as allegorical dream equivalents, for Matilda and Beatrice may very well be taken, as part of their total allegory, to represent the Active and the Contemplative Life of the Soul.

127 ff. *"My son," he said:* These are Virgil's last words, for the Poets have now reached the extreme limit of Reason's (and Art's) competence. Virgil continues awhile with Dante into the Earthly Paradise (walking, one should note, behind rather than ahead of Dante) but he has no more to say. A little later in fact (XXIX, 55–57) when Dante turns to Virgil out of old habit as if for an explanation of the strange and marvelous sights he comes on, he receives in answer only a look as full of awe as his own. And later yet (XXX, 43 ff.), when Dante turns from Beatrice to look for him, Virgil has vanished.

For Virgil has now performed all that he had promised at their first meeting (*Inferno,* I, 88 ff.), and Dante's soul is now free to obey its every impulse, for it now contains nothing but Good.

143. *I crown and mitre you:* Crown as king of your physical self and mitre (as a bishop) as lord of your soul. Dante has not, by much, achieved the full lordship of his soul, but he has achieved as much as Virgil (Reason) can confer upon him. A bishop's mitre, though it confers great authority, does not confer final authority. And a king, for that matter, may still be subject to an emperor, as he certainly would be, in Dante's view, to God.

Paradise

Canto I

The Earthly Paradise
The Invocation
Ascent to Heaven
The Sphere of Fire • The Music of the Spheres

Dante states his supreme theme as Paradise itself and invokes the aid not only of the Muses but of Apollo.

Dante and Beatrice are in *The Earthly Paradise,* the Sun is at the Vernal Equinox, it is noon at Purgatory and midnight at Jerusalem when Dante sees Beatrice turn her eyes to stare straight into the sun and reflexively imitates her gesture. At once it is as if a second sun had been created, its light dazzling his senses, and Dante feels the ineffable change of his mortal soul into Godliness.

These phenomena are more than his senses can grasp, and Beatrice must explain to him what he himself has not realized: that he and Beatrice are soaring toward the height of Heaven at an incalculable speed.

Thus Dante climaxes the master metaphor in which purification is equated to weightlessness. Having purged all dross from his soul he mounts effortlessly, without even being aware of it at first, to his natural goal in the Godhead. So they pass through *The Sphere of Fire,* and so Dante first hears *The Music of the Spheres.*

The glory of Him who moves all things rays
    forth
through all the universe, and is reflected
    from each thing in proportion to its worth.   3

I have been in that Heaven of His most light,
    and what I saw, those who descend from
      there
    lack both the knowledge and the power to   6
      write.

For as our intellect draws near its goal
    it opens to such depths of understanding
    as memory cannot plumb within the soul.   9

Nevertheless, whatever portion time
    still leaves me of the treasure of that
      kingdom
    shall now become the subject of my rhyme.   12

O good Apollo, for this last task, I pray
    you make me such a vessel of your powers
    as you deem worthy to be crowned with   15
      bay.

One peak of cleft Parnassus heretofore
    has served my need, now must I summon
      both
    on entering the arena one time more.   18

Enter my breast, I pray you, and there breathe
    as high a strain as conquered Marsyas
    that time you drew his body from its sheath.   21

O power divine, but lend to my high strain
    so much as will make clear even the shadow
    of that High Kingdom stamped upon my   24
      brain,

and you shall see me come to your dear grove
    to crown myself with those green leaves
      which you
    and my high theme shall make me   27
      worthy of.

So seldom are they gathered, Holy Sire,
    to crown an emperor's or a poet's triumph
    (oh fault and shame of mortal man's desire!)   30

that the glad Delphic god must surely find
    increase of joy in the Peneian frond
    when any man thirsts for it in his mind.   33

Great flames are kindled where the small
      sparks fly.
    So after me, perhaps, a better voice
    shall raise such prayers that Cyrrha will   36
      reply.

The lamp of the world rises to mortal view
    from various stations, but that point which
      joins
    four circles with three crosses, it soars   39
      through

to a happier course in happier conjunction
   wherein it warms and seals the wax of the
      world
   closer to its own nature and high function.   42

That glad conjunction had made it evening here
   and morning there; the south was all alight,
   while darkness rode the northern hemisphere;   45

when I saw Beatrice had turned left to raise
   her eyes up to the sun; no eagle ever
   stared at its shining with so fixed a gaze.   48

And as a ray descending from the sky
   gives rise to another, which climbs back
      again,
   as a pilgrim yearns for home;   51
      so through my eye

her action, like a ray into my mind,
   gave rise to mine: I stared into the sun
   so hard that here it would have left me blind;   54

but much is granted to our senses there,
   in that garden made to be man's proper
      place,
   that is not granted us when we are here.   57

I had to look away soon, and yet not
   so soon but what I saw him spark and blaze
   like new-tapped iron when it pours   60
      white-hot.

And suddenly, as it appeared to me,
   day was added to day, as if He who can
   had added a new sun to Heaven's glory.   63

Beatrice stared at the eternal spheres
   entranced, unmoving; and I looked away
   from the sun's height to fix my eyes on hers.   66

And as I looked, I felt begin within me
   what Glaucus felt eating the herb that made
      him
   a god among the others in the sea.   69

How speak trans-human change to human
      sense?
   Let the example speak until God's grace
   grants the pure spirit the experience.   72

Whether I rose in only the last created
   part of my being, O Love that rulest Heaven
   Thous knowest, by whose lamp I was   75
      translated.

When the Great Wheel that spins eternally
   in longing for Thee, captured my attention
   by that harmony attuned and heard by Thee,   78

I saw ablaze with sun from side to side
   a reach of Heaven: not all the rains and rivers
   of all of time could make a sea so wide.   81

That radiance and that new-heard melody

fired me with such a yearning for their Cause
   as I had never felt before. And she   84

who saw my every thought as well as I,
   saw my perplexity; before I asked
   my question she had started her reply.   87

Thus she began: "You dull your own
      perceptions
   with false imaginings and do not grasp
   what would be clear but for your   90
      preconceptions.

You think you are still on earth: the lightning's
      spear
   never fled downward from its natural place
   as rapidly as you are rising there." [267]   93

I grasped her brief and smiling words and shed
   my first perplexity, but found myself
   entangled in another, and I said: 96

"My mind, already recovered from the surprise
   of the great marvel you have just explained,
   is now amazed anew: how can I rise   99

in my gross body through such aery
      substance?"
   She sighed in pity and turned as might a
      mother
   to a delirious child. "The elements   102

of all things," she began, "whatever their mode,
   observe an inner order. It is this form
   that makes the universe resemble God.   105

In this the higher creatures see the hand
   of the Eternal Worth, which is the goal
   to which these norms conduce, being so   108
      planned.

All Being within this order, by the laws
   of its own nature is impelled to find
   its proper station round its Primal Cause.   111

Thus every nature moves across the tide
   of the great sea of being to its own port,
   each with its given instinct as its guide.   114

This instinct draws the fire about the moon.
   It is the mover in the mortal heart.
   It draws the earth together and makes it one.   117

Not only the brute creatures, but all those
   possessed of intellect and love, this instinct
   drives to their mark as a bow shoots forth   120
      its arrows.

The Providence that makes all hunger here
   satisfies forever with its light
   the heaven within which whirls the fastest   123
      sphere.

And to it now, as to a place foretold,

267 Sandro Botticelli. *Dante and Beatrice*. c. 1495. Silverpoint with pen and ink on vellum, 12 ½ × 18¼″ (32 × 47 cm). Department of Prints and Drawings, State Museums, East Berlin. Beatrice, leading the way, has just told Dante that he has risen from the ground. She is shown larger than the poet to emphasize that she is his guide and instructor. The great Renaissance Italian Sandro Botticelli (c. 1444–1510) made a famous series of drawings of scenes from the *Divine Comedy,* of which 93 survive.

are we two soaring, driven by that bow
   whose every arrow finds a mark of gold.   126

It is true that oftentimes the form of a thing
   does not respond to the intent of the art,
   the matter being deaf to summoning—   129

just so, the creature sometimes travels wide
   of this true course, for even when so driven
   it still retains the power to turn aside   132

(exactly as we may see the heavens' fire
   plunge from a cloud) and its first impulse may
   be twisted earthward by a false desire.   135

You should not, as I see it, marvel more
   at your ascent than at a river's fall
   from a high mountain to the valley floor.   138

If you, free as you are of every dross,
   had settled and had come to rest below,
   that would indeed have been as marvelous   141

as a still flame there in the mortal plain.''
So saying, she turned her eyes to Heaven again.

NOTES

1. *of Him who moves all things:* God as the unmoved mover. Since any change from perfection would have to be toward a lessening, God is changeless in Dante's conception. Himself changeless (unmoved), therefore, he imparts the creating motion to all things.

2–3. *reflected . . . in proportion to its worth:* The more perfect the thing, the more perfectly it will reflect God's perfect shining. The more clouded the glass, so to speak, the less its ability to reflect the light.

4. *that Heaven of His most light:* "that heaven that takes (i.e., "receives" and, by implication, "reflects again") the most of His light." The Empyrean.

5–12. *those who descend . . . lack:* Dante was not a mystic in the pure sense of the word, but all mystics have stressed the ineffability of the mystical experience. How does one convey any rapturous experience once the rapture is over? William James in his *Varieties of Religious Experience* offers a fine introductory discussion of this question. *as our intellect draws near its goal:* The goal of intellect is God.

13–36. THE INVOCATION. Herefore, Dante has invoked the Muses. Now he invokes Apollo himself as the God of Poetry, and as the father of the Muses. Note, too, that Apollo is identified with the Sun and that Dante has consistently used the Sun as a symbol for God.

15. *crowned with bay:* The laurel wreath awarded to poets and conquerors. See also line 29.

16. *one peak of cleft Parnassus:* Parnassus has two peaks: Nisa, which was sacred to the Muses; and Cyrrha, which was sacred to Apollo. Heretofore Nisa has been enough for Dante's need, but for this last canticle he must summon aid from both peaks (i.e., from all the Muses and from Apollo as well).

20–21. *Marsyas:* The satyr Marsyas challenged Apollo to a singing contest and was defeated. Ovid (*Metamorphoses,* VI, 382–400) recounts in gory detail how Apollo thereupon punished him by pulling him out of his skin leaving all the uncovered organs still functioning.

Note that in this godly sport the skin was not pulled off Marsyas but that Marsyas was pulled out of his skin. In citing this incident Dante may be praying that he himself, in a sense, be pulled out of himself (i.e., be made to outdo himself), however painfully. *its sheath:* its skin.

23–27. *make clear even the shadow:* Sense: "Lend me enough power to make clear so much as the shadow of the ineffable light, and your power and my lofty theme will win me a laurel crown." *your dear grove:* The grove in which grows the sacred laurel, or bay.

31. *the glad Delphic god:* Apollo.

32. *Peneian frond:* The laurel or bay, so called for Daphne, daughter of the river god Peneus. Cupid, to avenge a taunt, fired an arrow of love into Apollo and an arrow of aversion into Daphne. Fleeing from the inflamed Apollo, Daphne prayed to her father and was changed into a laurel tree.

36. *Cyrrha will reply:* Cyrrha, Apollo's sacred peak, is here taken for Apollo himself. If Apollo does not heed his prayer, Dante will at least show the way, and perhaps a better poet will come after him and have his prayer answered by Apollo, whereby Paradise will at last be well portrayed.

37–42. THE POSITION OF THE SUN AT THE VERNAL EQUINOX. Short of pages of diagrams, there is no way of explaining Dante's astronomical figure in detail. A quick gloss must do. *the lamp:* The Sun. *various stations:* various points on the celestial horizon from which the sun rises at various times of the year. *four circles with three crosses:* The four circles here intended are: (1) the celestial horizon, (2) the celestial equator, (3) the ecliptic, and (4) equinoxial colure. The equinoxial colure is the great circle drawn through both poles and the two equinoxial points (the solsticial colure, similarly, passes through both poles and the two solsticial points). Since the equinox occurs when the sun crosses the celestial equator, both equinoxial points must lie on the equator and the equinoxial colure must be at right angles to the celestial equator. The celestial equator is the infinite extension of the plane of the earth's equator into the celestial sphere.

When the sun is in [a certain] position the time is sunrise of the vernal equinox and all four circles meet, each of the other three forming a cross with the celestial horizon. Astrologers took this to be a particularly auspicious conjunction. Its *happier course* (line 40) brings the brighter and longer days of summer. Its *happier conjunction* (line 40) with the stars of Aries bring it back to the sign of the first creation (*see Inferno,* I, 38–39, note). And certainly the fact that the diagram forms three crosses would weigh it with the good omens of both the cross and trinity. All would once more be in God's shaping hand. So the *wax of the world* (line 41) is warmed and sealed, in a first sense by the warmth of approaching summer, and

in a clearly implicit spiritual sense by the favor of God's will upon His creation.

This complicated figure could hardly have failed to suggest, further, some reference to the Four Cardinal Virtues, the Three Theological Virtues, and to the approaching Sun as Divine Illumination, now drawing to the full summer of mankind—for bear in mind that the southern hemisphere, in Dante's geography, was all water: there would be no mankind for the Sun to shine upon in its southern summer.

43–44. *evening here and morning there:* At the time Dante returned from drinking the waters of Eunöe. It is now noon, for only at noon could the entire southern hemisphere be alight and the north dark—or so Dante must clearly intend, though I do not understand how that could be.

46. *had turned left:* Beatrice had been facing east with Eunöe before her. She now turns her eyes north to the sun.

47. *no eagle ever:* In the Middle Ages men believed that the eagle was able to stare directly into the sun.

49–54. *and as a ray:* Just as a descending ray of light strikes a reflecting surface and sends a reflected ray back upward, and at the same angle at which it struck the surface, so Beatrice's action in looking at the sun descends upon Dante like a ray from on high that enters through his eyes and strikes upward to his mind giving rise to a "reflected" action.

62. *day was added to day:* Dante perceives the increased brilliance of the light as if God had added a second sun to the sky, and he wonders at it. He does not yet know that the light has grown so much more brilliant because he is soaring through space toward the sun. He believes himself to be still in the Terrestrial Paradise.

Dante's device here, in showing himself as soaring toward God at enormous speed without, at first, realizing that he is soaring, is a superbly conceived climax to the whole theme of Purification as Gradual Weightlessness. In Hell all is gross and heavy. At the start of the Ascent of Purgatory, Dante almost drops from exhaustion. As he mounts and sin is stricken from him, he climbs ever more lightly. Now purified and perfected, he need not even think about mounting on high. His new nature draws effortlessly to God.

68. *Glaucus:* The fisherman Glaucus, noting how his catch revived and leaped into the sea after being laid upon a certain herb, ate some of it and was transformed into a god (Ovid, *Metamorphoses,* XIII, 898–968). Staring at Beatrice, Dante feels the beginning inside himself of that change that will make him, too, immortal.

73–75. *the last created part of my being:* The soul, which is created after the body. *O Love that rulest Heaven:* God. *whose lamp:* Beatrice as the reflector of God's love.

76–78. *The Great Wheel etc.:* Dante says, literally: "The wheel that Thou, in being desired [i.e., loved] by it, makest eternal." The Great Wheel is the Primum Mobile, its motion deriving from the love of God. *captured my attention:* Indicates that Dante turned his eyes from Beatrice to look up again. *that harmony:* The Music of the Spheres.

80. *ablaze with sun:* Dante believed that the earth's atmosphere extended as high as the Sphere of the Moon. Beyond the Moon is another atmosphere of fire. This sphere of fire was believed to cause lightning. (See also line 115, "the fire about the moon".)

92. *natural place:* The Sphere of Fire. It summons all fire to itself. Conflicting forces of nature force the lightning downward, but the fiery elements dislocated under stress find their way back to their natural place. Dante still has not realized that he and Beatrice are soaring toward Heaven at an incalculable speed.

93. *there:* To the Sphere of Fire.

104. *an inner order:* In relation to one another, and each in its relation to the total and to its final end, as fire to fire (see line 115). The end of man is God; therefore, the purified soul ascends naturally and inevitably to Him.

106. *the higher creatures:* The rational beings of creation: angels, heavenly spirits, and men.

108. *these norms:* The mode and form of lines 103–104.

123–124. *the heaven:* The Empyrean. *the fastest sphere:* The Primum Mobile. The Empyrean does not move and it is beyond space. It is eternal and perfect Love (therefore unchangeable) and holds within its constancy all of space, including the outermost and greatest sphere, the Primum Mobile.

125. *that bow:* The innate impulse of all creatures to seek their place in God.

127–135. The free will of creatures allows them, despite the innate order of all things, to yield to false pleasures and so to resist God's plan as the matter in which the artist works, being base and imperfect, may resist his intent to give it ideal form. One might argue against this figure that the artist in this case, being God, is omnipotent and could, at will, work in perfect matter. But to enter into such an argument would only be to bump heads on the question of fallible free will within an omnipotent creation—a question that has vexed Christian theology for millennia.

141. *that would indeed have been . . . marvelous:* Because then it would be going against the order of the universe. What is purified must ascend to God as inevitably as earthly waters must flow downhill.

Canto XI

The Fourth Sphere: the Sun
Doctors of the Church
The First Garland of Souls: Aquinas • Praise of St. Francis • Degeneracy of Dominicans

Aquinas reads Dante's mind and speaks to make clear several points about which Dante was in doubt. He explains that Providence sent two equal princes to guide the Church, St. Dominic, the wise law-giver, being one, and St. Francis, the ardent soul, being the other. Aquinas was himself a Dominican. To demonstrate the harmony of Heaven's gift and the unity of the Dominicans and Franciscans, Aquinas proceeds to pronounce a *Praise of the Life of St. Francis.* His account finished, he returns to the theme of the unity of the Dominicans and Franciscans, and proceeds to illustrate it further by himself lamenting the *Degeneracy of the Dominican Order.*

O senseless strivings of the mortal round!
  how worthless is that exercise of reason
  that makes you beat your wings into the
    ground! 3

One man was giving himself to law, and one
  to aphorisms; one sought sinecures,
  and one to rule by force or sly persuasion; 6

one planned his business, one his robberies;
  one, tangled in the pleasure of the flesh,
  wore himself out, and one lounged at his 9
    ease;

while I, of all such vanities relieved
  and high in Heaven with my Beatrice,
  arose to glory, gloriously received. 12

—When each had danced his circuit and come
    back
  to the same point of the circle, all stood still,
  like votive candles glowing in a rack. 15

And I saw the splendor of the blazing ray
  that had already spoken to me, smile,
  and smiling, quicken; and I heard it say: 18

"Just as I take my shining from on high,
  so, as I look into the Primal Source,
  I see which way your thoughts have turned, 21
    and why.

You are uncertain, and would have me find
  open and level words in which to speak
  what I expressed too steeply for your mind 24

when I said 'leads to where all plenty is,'
  and 'no mortal ever rose to equal this one.'
  And it is well to be exact in this. 27

The Providence that governs all mankind
  with wisdom so profound that any creature
  who seeks to plumb it might as well be 30
    blind,

in order that the Bride seek her glad good
  in the Sweet Groom who, crying from on
    high,
  took her in marriage with His blessed blood, 33

sent her two Princes, one on either side
  that she might be secure within herself,
  and thereby be more faithfully His Bride. 36

One, in his love, shone like the seraphim.
  The other, in his wisdom, walked the earth
  bathed in the splendor of the cherubim. 39

I shall speak of only one, though to extol
  one or the other is to speak of both
  in that their works led to a single goal. 42

Between the Tupino and the little race
  sprung from the hill blessed Ubaldo chose,
  a fertile slope spreads up the mountain's face. 45

Perugia breathes its heat and cold from there
  through Porta Sole, and Nocera and Gualdo
  behind it mourn the heavy yoke they bear. 48

From it, at that point where the mountainside
  grows least abrupt, a sun rose to the world
  as this one does at times from Ganges' tide. 51

Therefore, let no man speaking of that place
  call it *Ascesi*—'I have risen'—but rather,
  Oriente—so to speak with proper grace. 54

Nor was he yet far distant from his birth

when the first comfort of his glorious powers
   began to make its warmth felt on the earth: 57

a boy yet, for that lady who, like death
   knocks on no door that opens to her gladly,
   he had to battle his own father's wrath.   60

With all his soul he married her before
   the diocesan court *et coram patre;*
   and day by day he grew to love her more.   63

Bereft of her First Groom, she had had to stand
   more than eleven centuries, scorned, obscure;
   and, till he came, no man had asked her
      hand: 66

none, at the news that she had stood beside
   the bed of Amyclas and heard, unruffled,
   the voice by which the world was terrified;   69

and none, at word of her fierce constancy,
   so great, that even when Mary stayed below,
   she climbed the Cross to share Christ's
      agony.   72

But lest I seem obscure, speaking this way,
   take Francis and Poverty to be those lovers.
   That, in plain words, is what I meant to say.   75

Their harmony and tender exultation
   gave rise in love, and awe, and tender glances
   to holy thoughts in blissful meditation.   78

The venerable Bernard, seeing them so,
   kicked off his shoes, and toward so great a
      peace
   ran, and running, seemed to go too slow.   81

O wealth unknown! O plentitude untried!
   Egidius went unshod. Unshod, Sylvester
   followed the groom. For so it pleased the   84
      bride!

Thenceforth this father and this happy lord
   moved with his wife and with his family,
   already bound round by the humble cord.   87

He did not grieve because he had been born
   the son of Bernardone; he did not care
   that he went in rags, a figure of passing   90
      scorn.

He went with regal dignity to reveal
   his stern intentions to Pope Innocent,
   from whom his order first received the seal.   93

There as more souls began to follow him
   in poverty—whose wonder-working life
   were better sung among the seraphim—   96

Honorius, moved by the Eternal Breath,
   placed on the holy will of this chief shepherd
   a second crown and everflowering wreath.   99

Then, with a martyr's passion, he went forth

and in the presence of the haughty Sultan
   he preached Christ and his brotherhood on   102
      earth;

but when he found none there would take
      Christ's pardon,
   rather than waste his labors, he turned back
   to pick the fruit of the Italian garden.   105

On the crag between Tiber and Arno then, in
      tears
   of love and joy, he took Christ's final seal,
   the holy wounds of which he wore two   108
      years.

When God, whose loving will had sent him
      forward
   to work such good, was pleased to call him
      back
   to where the humble soul has its reward,   111

he, to his brothers, as to rightful heirs
   commended his dearest Lady and he bade
      them
   to love her faithfully for all their years.   114

Then from her bosom, that dear soul of grace
   willed its return to its own blessed kingdom;
   and wished its flesh no other resting place.   117

Think now what manner of man was fit to be
   his fellow helmsman, holding Peter's ship
   straight to its course across the dangerous   120
      sea.

Such was our patriarch. Hence, all who rise
   and follow his command will fill the hold,
   as you can see, with fruits of paradise.   123

But his flock has grown so greedy for the taste
   of new food that it cannot help but be
   far scattered as it wanders through the waste.   126

The more his vagabond and distant sheep
   wander from him, the less milk they bring
      back
   when they return to the fold. A few do keep   129

close to the shepherd, knowing what wolf
      howls
   in the dark around them, but they are so few
   it would take little cloth to make their cowls.   132

Now, if my words have not seemed choked and
      blind,
   if you have listened to me and taken heed,
   and if you will recall them to your mind,   135

your wish will have been satisfied in part,
   for you will see how the good plant is broken,
   and what rebuke my words meant to impart   138

when I referred, a while back in our talk,
   to 'where all plenty is' and to 'bare rock.'"

NOTES

15. *rack:* Dante says "candellier," which may be taken to mean candlestick, but equally to mean the candle-racks that hold votive candles in churches. The image of the souls as twelve votive candles in a circular rack is certainly apter than that of twelve candles in separate candlesticks.

25–26. *lead to . . . all plenty:* X, 95. *no mortal ever:* X, 114.

28–42. INTRODUCTION TO THE LIFE OF ST. FRANCIS. Compare the words of Bonaventura in introducing the life of St. Dominic, XII, 31–45.

31. *the Bride:* The Church.

32. *crying from on high: Matthew,* XXVII. 46, 50; *Mark* XV, 34, 37; *Luke,* XXIII, 46; and *John,* XIX, 26–30; all record Christ's dying cries upon the cross.

34. *two Princes, one on either side:* St. Dominic and St. Francis. Dominic, on one side (line 39 equates his wisdom with the cherubic), by his wisdom and doctrinal clarity made the church secure within itself by helping to defend it against error and heresy. Francis, on the other hand (line 37 ascribes to him seraphic ardor of love), set the example that made her more faithfully the bride of Christ.

43–51. ASSISI AND THE BIRTH OF ST. FRANCIS. The passage, in passage, in Dante's characteristic topophiliac style, is full of local allusions, not all of them relevant to St. Francis, but all describing the situation of Assisi, his birthplace. Perugia stands to the east of the upper Tiber. The Tiber at this point runs approximately north to south. Mt. Subasio, a long and many spurred crest, runs roughly parallel to the Tiber on the west. Assisi is on the side of Subasio, and it was from Assisi that the sun of St. Francis rose to the world, as "this one" (the actual sun in which Dante and Aquinas are standing) rises from the Ganges. The upper Ganges crosses the Tropic of Cancer, the line of the summer solstice. When the sun rises from the Ganges, therefore, it is at its brightest.

the Tupino: Skirts Mt. Subasio on the south and flows roughly west into the Tiber. *the little race:* The Chiascio [KYAH-show] flows south along the length of Subasio and empties into the Tupino below Assisi. *blessèd Ubaldo:* St. Ubaldo (1084–1160), Bishop of Gubbio from 1129. He chose a hill near Gubbio as a hermitage in which to end his days, but died before he could retire there. *Porta Sole:* Perugia's west gate. It faces Mt. Subasio. In summer its slopes reflect the sun's ray through Porta Sole; in winter, covered with snow, they send the cold wind. *Nocera* [NAW-tcheh-ra], *Gualdo* [GWAHL-doe]: Towns on the other side of (behind) Subasio. Their heavy yoke may be their subjugation by Perugia, or Dante may have meant by it the taxes imposed by Robert of Naples and his Spanish brigands.

51–54. It is such passages that certify the failures of all translation. *Ascesi,* which can mean "I have risen," was a common name for Assisi in Dante's day. *Oriente,* of course, is the point at which the sun rises. Let no man, therefore, call Assisi "I have risen" (i.e., a man has risen), but let him call it, rather, the dawning east of the world (a sun has risen).

55 ff. *yet far distant:* While he was still young. The phrasing continues the figure of the new-risen sun.

Francis, born Bernardone, was the son of a relatively prosperous merchant and, early in life, assisted his father. In a skirmish between Assisi and Perugia he was taken prisoner and later released. On his return to Assisi (he was then twenty-four) he abandoned all worldly affairs and gave himself entirely to religious works.

a boy yet: Here, as in line 55, Aquinas is overdoing it a bit: twenty-four is a bit old for being a boy yet. *that lady:* Poverty. *his*

own father's wrath: In 1207 (Francis was then twenty-five) he sold one of his father's horses along with a load of bread and gave the money to a church. In a rage, his father forced the church to return the money, called Francis before the Bishop of Assisi, and there demanded that he renounce his right to inherit. Francis not only agreed gladly but removed his clothes and gave them back to his father saying, "Until this hour I called you my father on earth; from this hour I can say in full truth 'our Father which art in Heaven.'"

he married: In his "Hymn to Poverty" Francis himself celebrated his union to Poverty as a marriage. He had married her before the diocesan court of Assisi, *et coram patre* (before the court, i.e., in the legal presence of, his father). The marriage was solemnized by his renunciation of all possessions.

64–66. *her First Groom:* Christ. *he:* St. Francis.

68. *Amyclas:* Lucan reported (see also *Convivio,* IV, 13) how the fisherman Amyclas lay at his ease on a bed of seaweed before Caesar himself, being so poor that he had nothing to fear from any man. Not even this report of the serenity Mistress Poverty could bring to a man, and not even the fact that she outdid even Mary in constancy, climbing the very cross with Christ, had moved any man to seek her in marriage.

79. *Bernard:* Bernard di Quintavalle, a wealthy neighbor, became the first disciple of Francis, kicking off his shoes to go barefoot in imitation of the master.

82–84. *unknown:* To men. Holy Poverty is the wealth none recognize, the plenitude none try. *Egidius . . . Sylvester:* The third and fourth disciples of Francis. Peter, the second disciple, seems not to have been known to Dante. *the groom:* Francis. *the bride:* Poverty.

87. *the humble cord:* Now a symbol of the Franciscans but then in general use by the poor as a makeshift belt.

88. *grieve:* At his humble origins.

93. *his order first received the seal:* In 1210. But Innocent III thought the proposed rule of the order so harsh that he granted only provisional approval.

96. *among the seraphim:* In the Empyrean, rather than in this Fourth Heaven.

97–99. *Honorius . . . second crown:* In 1223, Pope Honorius III gave his fully solemnized approval of the Franciscan Order.

100–105. In 1219, St. Francis and eleven of his followers made missionary pilgrimage to Greece and Egypt. Dante, whose facts are not entirely accurate, may have meant that pilgrimage; or he may have meant Francis's projected journey to convert the Moors (1214–1215) when Francis fell ill in southern Spain and had to give up his plans.

106–108. In 1224, on a crag of Mt. Alverna (on the summit of which the Franciscans have reared a commemorative chapel), St. Francis received the stigmata in a rapturous vision of Christ. He wore the wound two years before his death in 1226, at the age of (probably) forty-four.

109–117. The central reference here is to Dame Poverty. *her bosom:* The bare ground of Poverty. *no other resting place:* Than in the bare ground.

119. *his fellow helmsman:* St. Dominic. *Peter's ship:* The Church.

121–132. THE DEGENERACY OF THE DOMINICANS IN DANTE'S TIME. Aquinas was a Dominican. As a master touch to symbolize the harmony of Heaven and the unity of Franciscans and Dominicans, Dante puts into the mouth of a Dominican the praise of the life of St. Francis. That praise ended, he chooses the Dominican to lament the degeneracy of the order. In XII, Dante will have the Franciscan, St. Bonaventure, praise the life of St. Dominic and lament the degeneracy of the Franciscans.

122. *his command:* The rule of the Dominicans. *will fill his hold:* With the treasures of Paradise. Dante is carrying forward the helmsman metaphor of lines 118–120, though the ship is now commanded by a patriarch. Typically, the figure changes at once to a shepherd-and-flock metaphor.

136. *in part:* In X, 95–96, in identifying himself as a Dominican, Aquinas said the Dominican rule "leads to where all plenty is" unless the lamb itself stray to "bare rock." In lines 25–26, above, he refers to these words and also to his earlier statements (X, 114) about Solomon's wisdom (that "no mortal ever rose to equal this one"). What he has now finished saying about the degeneracy of the Dominicans will satisfy part of Dante's wish (about "plenty" and "bare rock"). The other part of his wish (about "no mortal ever rose to equal this one") will be satisfied later.

137. *the good plant:* Of the Dominican rule strictly observed.

Canto XXXIII

The Empyrean

St. Bernard • Prayer to the Virgin • The Vision of God

St. Bernard offers a lofty *Prayer to the Virgin,* asking her to intercede in Dante's behalf, and in answer Dante feels his soul swell with new power and grow calm in rapture as his eyes are permitted the Direct Vision of God.

There can be no measure of how long the vision endures. It passes, and Dante is once more mortal and fallible. Raised by God's presence, he had looked into the Mystery and had begun to understand its power and majesty. Returned to himself, there is no power in him capable of speaking the truth of what he saw. Yet the impress of the truth is stamped upon his soul, which he now knows will return to be one with God's Love.

"Virgin Mother, daughter of thy son;
    humble beyond all creatures and more
        exalted;
    predestined turning point to God's intention;   3

thy merit so ennobled human nature
    that its divine Creator did not scorn
    to make Himself the creature of His creature.   6

The Love that was rekindled in Thy womb
    sends forth the warmth of the eternal peace
    within whose ray this flower has come to   9
        bloom.

Here, to us, thou art the noon and scope
    of Love revealed; and among mortal men,
    the living fountain of eternal hope.   12

Lady, thou art so near God's reckonings
    that who seeks grace and does not first seek
        thee
    would have his wish fly upward without   15
        wings.

Not only does thy sweet benignity
    flow out to all who beg, but oftentimes
    thy charity arrives before the plea.   18

In thee is pity, in thee munificence,
    in thee the tenderest heart, in thee unites
    all that creation knows of excellence!   21

Now comes this man who from the final pit
    of the universe up to this height has seen,
    one by one, the three lives of the spirit.   24

He prays to thee in fervent supplication
    for grace and strength, that he may raise his
        eyes
    to the all-healing final revelation.   27

And I, who never more desired to see
    the vision myself than I do that he may see
        It,
    add my own prayer, and pray that it may be   30

enough to move you to dispel the trace
    of every mortal shadow by thy prayers
    and let him see revealed the Sum of Grace.   33

I pray thee further, all-persuading Queen,
    keep whole the natural bent of his affections
    and of his powers after his eyes have seen.   36

Protect him from the stirrings of man's clay;
    see how Beatrice and the blessèd host
    clasp reverent hands to join me as I pray."   39

The eyes that God reveres and loves the best
    glowed on the speaker, making clear the joy
    with which true prayer is heard by the most   42
        blest.

Those eyes turned then to the Eternal Ray,
    through which, we must indeed believe, the
        eyes
    of others do not find such ready way.   45

And I, who neared the goal of all my nature,
    felt my soul, at the climax of its yearning,
    suddenly, as it ought, grow calm with   48
        rapture.

Bernard then, smiling sweetly, gestured to me
    to look up, but I had already become
    within myself all he would have me be.   51

Little by little as my vision grew
    it penetrated further through the aura
    of the high lamp which in Itself is true.   54

What then I saw is more than tongue can say.
    Our human speech is dark before the vision.
    The ravished memory swoons and falls   57
        away.

As one who sees in dreams and wakes to find
    the emotional impression of his vision

still powerful while its parts fade from his mind— 60

just such am I, having lost nearly all
the vision itself, while in my heart I feel
the sweetness of it yet distill and fall. 63

So, in the sun, the footprints fade from snow.
On the wild wind that bore the tumbling leaves
the Sybil's oracles were scattered so. 66

O Light Supreme who doth Thyself withdraw
so far above man's mortal understanding,
lend me again some glimpse of what I saw; 69

make Thou my tongue so eloquent it may
of all Thy glory speak a single clue
to those who follow me in the world's day; 72

for by returning to my memory
somewhat, and somewhat sounding in these verses,
Thou shalt show man more of Thy victory. 75

So dazzling was the splendor of that Ray,
that I must certainly have lost my senses
had I, but for an instant, turned away. 78

And so it was, as I recall, I could
the better bear to look, until at last
my vision made one with the Eternal Good. 81

Oh grace abounding that had made me fit
to fix my eyes on the eternal light
until my vision was consumed in it! 84

I saw within Its depth how It conceives
all things in a single volume bound by Love,
of which the universe is the scattered leaves; 87

substance, accident, and their relation
so fused that all I say could do no more
than yield a glimpse of that bright revelation. 90

I think I saw the universal form
that binds these things, for as I speak these words
I feel my joy swell and my spirits warm. 93

Twenty-five centuries since Neptune saw
the Argo's keel have not moved all mankind,
recalling that adventure, to such awe 96

as I felt in an instant. My tranced being
stared fixed and motionless upon that vision,
ever more fervent to see in the act of seeing. 99

Experiencing that Radiance, the spirit
is so indrawn it is impossible
even to think of ever turning from It. 102

For the good which is the will's ultimate object
is all subsumed in It; and, being removed,
all is defective which in It is perfect. 105

Now in my recollection of the rest
I have less power to speak than any infant
wetting its tongue yet at its mother's breast; 108

and not because that Living Radiance bore
more than one semblance, for It is unchanging
and is forever as it was before; 111

rather, as I grew worthier to see,
the more I looked, the more unchanging semblance
appeared to change with every change in me. 114

Within the depthless deep and clear existence
of that abyss of light three circles shown—
three in color, one in circumference: 117

the second from the first, rainbow from rainbow;
the third, an exhalation of pure fire
equally breathed forth by the other two. 120

But oh how much my words miss my conception,
which is itself so far from what I saw
that to call it feeble would be rank deception! 123

O Light Eternal fixed in Itself alone,
by Itself alone understood, which from Itself
loves and glows, self-knowing and self-known; 126

that second aureole which shone forth in Thee,
conceived as a reflection of the first—
or which appeared so to my scrutiny— 129

seemed in Itself of Its own coloration
to be painted with man's image. I fixed my eyes
on that alone in rapturous contemplation. 132

Like a geometer wholly dedicated
to squaring the circle, but who cannot find,
think as he may, the principle indicated— 135

so did I study the supernal face.
I yearned to know just how our image merges
into that circle, and how it there finds place; 138

but mine were not the wings for such a flight.
Yet, as I wished, the truth I wished for came
cleaving my mind in a great flash of light. 141

Here my powers rest from their high fantasy,
but already I could feel my being turned—
instinct and intellect balanced equally 144

as in a wheel whose motion nothing jars—
by the Love that moves the Sun and the other stars

NOTES

1–39. ST. BERNARD'S PRAYER TO THE VIRGIN MARY. No reader who has come this far will need a lengthy gloss of Bernard's prayer. It can certainly be taken as a summarizing statement of the special place of Mary in Catholic faith. For the rest only a few turns of phrase need underlining. 3. *predestined turning point of God's intention:* All-forseeing God built his whole scheme for mankind with Mary as its pivot, for through her He would become man. 7. *The Love that was rekindled in thy womb:* God. In a sense he withdrew from man when Adam and Eve sinned. In Mary He returned and Himself became man. 35. *keep whole the natural bent of his affections:* Bernard is asking Mary to protect Dante lest the intensity of the vision overpower his faculties. 37. *Protect him from the stirrings of man's clay:* Protect him from the stirrings of base human impulse, especially from pride, for Dante is about to receive a grace never before granted to any man and the thought of such glory might well move a mere mortal to an hybris that would turn glory to sinfullness.

40. *the eyes:* Of Mary.

50. *but I had already become:* i.e., "But I had already fixed my entire attention upon the vision of God." But if so, how could Dante have seen Bernard's smile and gesture? Eager students like to believe they catch Dante in a contradiction here. Let them bear in mind that Dante is looking directly at God, as do the souls of Heaven, who thereby acquire—insofar as they are able to contain it—God's own knowledge. As a first stirring of that heavenly power, therefore, Dante is sharing God's knowledge of St. Bernard.

54. *which in Itself is true:* The light of God is the one light whose source is Itself. All others are a reflection of this.

65–66. *tumbling leaves . . . oracles:* The Cumean Sybil (Virgil describes her in *Aeneid,* III, 441 ff.) wrote her oracles on leaves, one letter to a leaf, then sent her message scattering on the wind. Presumably, the truth was all contained in that strew, could one only gather all the leaves and put the letters in the right order.

76–81. How can a light be so dazzling that the beholder would swoon if he looked away for an instant? Would it not be, rather, in looking at, not away from, the overpowering vision that the viewer's senses would be overcome? So it would be on earth. But now Dante, with the help of all heaven's prayers, is in the presence of God and strengthened by all he sees. It is by being so strengthened that he can see yet more. So the passage becomes a parable of grace. Stylistically it once more illustrates Dante's genius: even at this height of concept, the poet can still summon and invent new perceptions, subtlety exfoliating from subtlety.

The simultaneous metaphoric statement, of course, is that no man can lose his good in the vision of God, but only in looking away from it.

85–87. The idea here is Platonic: the essence of all things (form) exists in the mind of God. All other things exist as exempla.

88. *substance:* Matter, all that exists in itself. *accident:* All that exists as a phase of matter.

92. *these things:* Substance and accident.

109–114. In the presence of God the soul grows ever more capable of perceiving God. Thus, the worthy soul's experience of God is a constant expansion of awareness. God appears to change as He is better seen. Being perfect, He is changeless within himself, for any change would be away from perfection.

130–144. The central metaphor of the entire *Comedy* is the image of God and the final triumphant in Godding of the elected soul returning to its Maker. On the mystery of that image, the metaphoric symphony of the *Comedy* comes to rest.

In the second aspect of Trinal-unity, in the circle reflected from the first, Dante thinks he sees the image of mankind woven into the very substance and coloration of God. He turns the entire attention of his soul to that mystery, as a geometer might seek to shut out every other thought and dedicate himself to squaring the circle. In *Il Convivio,* II, 14, Dante asserted that the circle could not be squared, but that impossibility had not yet been firmly demonstrated in Dante's time and mathematicians still worked at the problem. Note, however, that Dante assumes the impossibility of squaring the circle as a weak mortal example of mortal impossibility. How much more impossible, he implies, to resolve the mystery of God, study as man will.

The mystery remains beyond Dante's mortal power. Yet, there in Heaven, in a moment of grace, God revealed the truth to him in a flash of light—revealed it, that is, to the God-enlarged power of Dante's emparadised soul. On Dante's return to the mortal life, the details of that revelation vanished from his mind but the force of the revelation survives in its power on Dante's feelings.

So ends the vision of the *Comedy,* and yet the vision endures, for ever since that revelation, Dante tells us, he feels his soul turning ever as one with the perfect motion of God's love.

Further Reading

Adams, Henry. *Mont-Saint-Michel and Chartres.* Garden City, NY: Doubleday Anchor, 1959. A brilliant, albeit eccentric, work on the culture of the Gothic world. While its scholarship has been superseded in this century, it is still an aesthetic classic.

Aubert, Marcel. *Gothic Cathedrals of France and Their Treasures.* London: Nicholas Kaye, 1959. A handy encyclopedia of Gothic architecture by a noted French scholar of the era.

Cobban, A. B. *The Medieval University: Their Development and Organization.* London: Methuen, 1975. A work of solid scholarship that summarizes and adds to the ongoing research of the last hundred years. Excellent bibliographies.

Daly, Lowrie. *The Medieval University: 1200–1400.* New York: Sheed & Ward, 1961. Less scholarly than Cobban's work but a handy and readable introduction.

Gilson, Étienne. *Reason and Revelation in the Middle Ages.* New York: Scribner, 1966. A brief but excellent survey of the intellectual milieu of the period by one of the foremost authorities of our century.

Gimpel, Jean. *The Medieval Machine: The Industrial Revolution of the Middle Ages.* New York: Penguin, 1977. A wonderful introduction to technology in medieval times.

Golding, William. *The Spire.* New York: Harcourt, 1964. A brilliant fictional evocation of medieval cathedral building.

Holmes, Urban T. *Daily Living in the Twelfth Century.* Madison: University of Wisconsin, 1966. An extremely readable account of ordinary life in medieval London and Paris drawn from documentary evidence.

Knowles, David. *The Evolution of Medieval Thought*. New York: Vintage, 1962. A classic study of medieval thought from Augustine to the eve of the Reformation.

Macauley, David. *Cathedral: The Story of Its Construction*. Boston: Houghton Mifflin, 1973. A book for young and old readers on the construction of a cathedral, with pen-and-ink drawings by the author. A fascinating and lovely work that is simple but richly informative.

Panofsky, Erwin. *Abbot Suger*. Princeton, NJ: Princeton University Press, 1946. A translation of Suger's booklets on Saint Denis with an important introduction and full notes. Indispensable for the period.

Simson, Otto von. *The Gothic Cathedral*. New York: Harper, 1964. A classic work on the aesthetics of the Gothic era in the Île de France. The work is quite valuable for its study of Saint Denis and Chartres.

Singleton, Charles. *The Divine Comedy of Dante Alighieri*, 6 vols. Princeton, NJ: Princeton University Press, 1972. The commentary in English by the foremost authority on Dante in America. There are separate volumes of the poem in English with companion volumes of commentary. Excellent and indispensable.

Weisheipl, James. *Friar Thomas D'Aquino: His Life, Thought, and Work*. Garden City, NY: Doubleday, 1974. Reflects the current state of Thomistic studies; scholarly, with good notes and bibliography.

Suggestions for Listening

The Musical Heritage Society has made available a rich historical anthology of music for study and enjoyment in its *History of Western Music*. Volume I, "The Music of the Early Middle Ages" (two discs: OR 349, OR 350), provides a fine and wide-ranging selection of medieval music from chants and simple organum to conductus and motet. For a sense of the strong devotion to the Virgin prevalent in the Middle Ages the student might sample some music and verse dedicated to the Virgin from 11th- and 12th-century Spain. The music, derived from the court of Alfonso X, is available on the following recording: *Las Cantigas de Santa Maria* (VSD 71175). For secular music the Vanguard recording (VCS 10049) called "The Jolly Minstrels" is worthwhile, espe-cially for its attention to the musical instruments of the High Middle Ages. One of the finest recordings of the Carl Orff *Carmina Burana* is the Deutsche Grammophon (139362) version performed by the Berlin Opera Company (the Latin and German text comes with translations).

Questions for Further Discussion

1. We have suggested that the Gothic cathedral had more than a religious significance for the population of a medieval town; it had a social, economic, technological, and cultural value as well. Think about such influences in terms of some contemporary architectural works. What, for example, might a future scholar say about the 20th-century shopping mall?

2. One basic idea of medieval culture was the notion that the reality of this world pointed to or was a symbol of the reality of the world of God, an idea that is hardly part of the modern consciousness. What leading ideas, philosophies, and ideologies of today's intellectual world most strongly deny or undermine the medieval position?

3. Our description of the medieval university points out its continuity with the universities of the present day. The university is a sign of the conservative nature of culture—culture as a protector of certain institutions and ideas. What other civil, social, or religious institutions have been conserved for a long period in the history of Western culture?

4. We have all known pain, suffering, guilt, and the burden of striving. In that sense, at least, Dante could write from some sense of experience about hell and purgatory. What, however, are the special problems involved in the writing of a poem like the *Paradiso*?

5. Compare the symbolism of light as it is used by Suger with the symbolism of Dante in the *Paradiso*. As a dramatic contrast with medieval light symbolism read a bit about Albert Speer's use of light for the Nazi rallies at Nuremburg in the 1930s. What were his sources and intentions as he used massive spotlights to create what he called "cathedrals of light"?

6. After reading the selections from Dante, explain what a writer who uses the adjective *Dantesque* might mean.

INTERLUDE

Abelard and Heloise

In the true story of Peter Abelard and Heloise we are confronted by two preeminent individualists from the 12th century. Their quite remarkable lives make it difficult to accept without examination the well-established notion that individualism is a characteristic only of the postmedieval world. To contrast the strong individualities of the Renaissance with the somewhat submerged personalities of the medieval era has been usual since the publication of Jacob Burckhardt's *Civilization of the Renaissance in Italy* in 1860. Burckhardt held that the Renaissance encouraged the emergence of the strong individual who sought fame and personal expression in this world instead of repressing the ego toward a reward in the hereafter—which it did.

But well before the first real stirrings of the Renaissance there lived and loved Peter Abelard and Heloise, about whom Etienne Gilson wrote: "This story of flesh and blood, carried along by a passion at once brutal and ardent to its celebrated conclusion, we know from within, as, indeed, we know few others. Its heroes observe themselves, analyze themselves as only Christian consciences fallen prey can do it. Nor do they merely analyze themselves, but they talk about themselves as well. What Renaissance autobiographies can be compared with the correspondence of Abelard and Heloise?"

Beyond the forceful portraits of their personalities reflected in their letters to each other, the story of Heloise and Abelard is significant for the times in which they lived, the myth their story generated, and the people with whom they had contact during their stormy careers. Peter Abelard (1079–1142) can be described as the single most important personality in establishing 12th-century Paris as the university center of Europe. Among his many books, his *Sic et Non* (*Yes and No*) marks the beginning of the application of dialects to theology, permitting the rise of the whole scholastic movement in philosophy and theology. Both Heloise and Abelard crossed paths (and, on occasion, intellectual swords) with some of the most notable figures of the time. Abelard had a noteworthy antagonist in Bernard of Clairvaux, the most influential churchman and theologian of the century. For a time Abelard was a monk at the famous abbey of Saint Denis in Paris when its fortunes were being guided by the celebrated Abbot Suger, the founder of Gothic architecture. Both Heloise and Abelard had been friendly with Peter the Venerable; Abelard, in fact, was sheltered at Peter's abbey of Cluny at the end of his life. When Abelard died it was Peter who sent the body to Heloise for burial. Subsequent centuries would look back on their

268 "Portraits" of Abelard and Heloise. 19th-century engravings by Grevedon. Bibliothèque Nationale, Paris. An excellent illustration of the sentimental regard the Romantics had for the medieval couple. Abelard—35 when he met Heloise—is depicted as a youth and Heloise is presented as a demure nun living as a "prisoner of love."

story and create from it a whole fabric legend that would inevitably color our understanding and change our perception of what the 12th century was all about. Today scholars are beginning better to understand Abelard and his place in medieval intellectual life, but for two hundred years people of many diverse backgrounds have been far more interested in the complexities of the couple's "star-crossed" love for each other [268].

In 1113 Abelard, then nearly 35 years old, began teaching in Paris. His early, stormy career had been marked by clashes with his own teachers and masters, a succession of schools he founded in various towns outside Paris, and a physical breakdown triggered by his own overwrought activity. Shortly after Abelard began his Paris career he was the most sought-after and lionized teacher in the city. This brilliant and handsome figure, with his masterful style of lecturing and his easy command of critical analysis, heard of a young girl named Heloise who lived with her uncle, the Canon Fulbert, in the same city. Heloise was distinguished not only for her beauty but for her learning. For a young girl to have a reputation for scholarly attainment was quite rare given the limited opportunities for female education in the period. Although certain noblewomen and a few cloistered nuns could make claim to an education, it was virtually unheard of for a girl still in her teens to have an arts education. In a letter to Heloise many years later Peter the Venerable (himself a student in Paris during Abelard's period there) would remember this about her: "When wisdom has difficulty in finding a haven—I will not say among the female sex, from where it is utterly banished, but even in the minds of men—your burning zeal has raised you above all women, and there are few men whom you have not surpassed."

Abelard's interest in Heloise could hardly be called strictly academic, although it was her reputation as an intellectual that had first piqued his rather egocentric curiosity. With some calculation, Abelard took rooms at Canon Fulbert's house. It was an easy thing to do; the canon was greedy for more income and hopeful that a noted scholar would consent to tutor his precocious niece. With the handsome professor and the beautiful young girl under the same roof, the outcome was predictable. Abelard, never reticent in these matters, describes it:

> We were first together in one house and then one in mind. Under the pretext of work we made ourselves entirely free for love and the pursuit of her studies provided the secret privacy which love desired. We opened our books but more words of love than of the lessons asserted themselves. There was more kissing than teaching; my hands found themselves at her breasts more often than on the book. Love brought us to gaze into each other's eyes more than reading kept them on the text. . . . No sign of love was omitted by us in our ardor and whatever unusual love could devise, that was added too. And the more such delights were new to us, the more ardently we indulged in them, and the less did we experience satiety.

Heloise became pregnant and Abelard sent her to his family home, where she bore him a son whom they named Peter Astralabe. Heloise's uncle, wild with grief and shame over the affair, demanded satisfaction. Abelard brought Heloise back to Paris and proposed marriage in order to placate the irate canon. Heloise refused the offer with a long philosophical argument studded with citations from Holy Scripture, Saint Jerome, and Saint Augustine, as well as Seneca and Socrates. Her reasoning, basically, was that the married life was incompatible with the scholarly life: "What," Heloise asked, "could be in common between scholars and wet nurses, writing desks and cradles, books, writing tablets, and distaffs, styles, pens, and spindles? Or who is there who is bent on sacred or philosophical reflections who could bear the wailing of babies, the silly lullabies of nurses to quiet them, the noisy herd of servants, both male and female; who could endure the constant degrading defilement of infants?" (Though her tone was vastly different, another Frenchwoman, but of our century, Simone de Beauvoir, used the same argument to the philosopher Jean-Paul Sartre when he suggested marriage: "I saw," Beauvoir wrote in her autobiography, "what it was costing Sartre to say goodbye to travel and freedom and youth in order to become a provincial schoolmaster and finally and conclusively, an adult. Joining the ranks of the married would have been a further renunciation.")

Despite the intellectual resistance of Heloise, the two were married in Paris in the presence of the uncle and his friends. Fulbert made the news of the marriage public—something the couple did not want—and, as a consequence, Abelard persuaded Heloise to seek the security of a nearby convent. Abelard, betrayed by a servant, was ambushed by the cohorts of the indignant uncle who, as an act of fearful revenge for the seeming repudiation of his niece, assaulted and castrated him.

After this horrendous incident Heloise entered permanently into the monastic life of the convent. She finally settled in a religious house as its superior—a house Abelard had originally founded as a hostel for students. She remained as superior of this convent until her death. In her mature years Heloise wrote Abelard telling him of the sacrifice that life in the convent had brought her, frank confession that more than any other incident in their story created the later romantic legend about the couple. The letters between Heloise and Abelard reveal a bitterly human exchange of accusation ("Tell me if you can why after the two of us embraced the religious life—a decision which was yours alone—I had neither your presence to fortify me nor even a letter to console me in my loneliness?" asks Heloise), guilt ("Shall I remind you," asks Abelard, "of our early defilements, of the shameful licentiousness which preceded our marriage, the base treachery I inflicted on your uncle by so brazenly seducing you at a time when I was his guest and table companion?"), and unabashed lust ("The sensual delights which we enjoyed together were so dear to me that I cannot help loving the memory of them and am quite unable to erase them from my mind. . . . I ought to groan at the sins which I have perpetrated yet I sigh for those which I am unable to commit.").

Abelard's subsequent life was marked by restlessness and turmoil. After Heloise became a nun, he entered the famous Parisian monastery of Saint Denis, but left when the monks threatened him because of his suggestion—correct, as it turns out—that their patron saint was not the Saint Denis who wrote the famous mystical treatises so much revered in the medieval period. He founded the hostel of the Paraclete in 1125 after having been censured as a heretic by a cabal of his enemies at Soissons in 1121. From the Paraclete he went to Brittany, where he served as abbot of a monastery. His return to teaching brought him into conflict with the famous Saint Bernard of Clairvaux, who was responsible for Abelard's condemnation at the Council of Sens in 1141. Abelard, appealing the condemnation to the pope, found temporary refuge at the famous abbey of Cluny under the patronage of its abbot, Peter the Venerable. A year later Abelard died. In an exquisite gesture of friendship, Peter sent his body back to Heloise, who had it interred at the Paraclete. When she herself died at this religious center in 1164, the nuns wrote in their book of necrology that their late lamented foundress had been "renowned for her learning and piety, having given us the hope of her life. . . ."

Despite the high drama of their life, the story of Heloise and Abelard held few attractions for the people of the later Middle Ages. Jean de Meun did tell the story of the two lovers in *The Romance of the Rose,* an immensely popular 13th-century love poem [269], but his purpose was to use the story as an example of the dangers of marriage. Chaucer's wife of Bath makes a passing reference to Heloise in *The Can-*

269 Abelard teaching Heloise, from the *Roman de la Rose* by Jean de Meun. 13th century. Manuscript illumination. Musée Condé, Chantilly.

terbury Tales, and Petrarch had a copy of their letters, but by and large their story was obscured as the Renaissance turned away from the happenings of the medieval world. It was inevitable that the more sophisticated world of the 18th-century Enlightenment would see Abelard as a champion of intellectual freedom and Heloise as a romantic lover as well as a victim of circumstance.

The idealization of the life of Heloise and Abelard may be clearly seen in Alexander Pope's long poem *Eloise to Abelard,* published in England in 1717 [270]. The particular focus of Pope's poem is the separated lovers. Heloise lives in the austere retirement of the Paraclete, still much in love with the absent Abelard. Pope's poem is almost entirely concerned with the psychological state of separated lovers. The very sense of separation and unrequited love is echoed by the melancholy and austere setting of Heloise's convent: "In these deep solitudes and awful cells, / Where heavenly-pensive, contemplation dwells, / And ever-musing melancholy reigns, / What means this tumult in a vestal's veins?" The "tumult in a vestal's veins" is, for Pope, the struggle between Heloise's desire to lead a God-centered real life and her desire for the physical love of Abelard. At the poem's end, Heloise recognizes that only in death will she be rejoined to the love of her life. Pope closes the poem with his own sentiments of his imagined Heloise. Many scholars have seen the ending as an oblique reference to Pope's own love for a woman who was not available to him; the words of Heloise and the poet blend into one:

Alexander Pope
from ELOISE TO ABELARD

And sure, if some future bard shall join
In sad similitude of griefs to mine,
Condemned whole years in absence to deplore,

270 "Eloisa." Engraving of Heloise from the second edition of Alexander Pope's *Eloise to Abelard.* 1720. Princeton University Library (Sinclair Hamilton Collection of American Illustrated Books). Pope's poem had a great influence on the development of the legend of the two lovers.

271 *Left:* Jean Gigoux. *A Visit to the Tomb of Abelard and Heloise.* 1839. Engraving. Bibliothèque Nationale, Paris. Note the floral offering in the young woman's hand. *Right:* The tomb of Heloise and Abelard in the Père Lachaise Cemetery, Paris.

> And image charms he must behold no more;
> Such if there be, who loves so long, so well;
> Let him our sad, our tender story tell;
> The well-sung woes will soothe my pensive ghost;
> He best can paint 'em who shall feel 'em most.

Pope's *Eloise to Abelard* had been inspired by an English translation of the letters of Heloise and Abelard which Pope had read. His poem, in turn, was translated into French by a forgotten poet, Colardeau. Colardeau's translation, now resting in the obscurity it deserves, was eminent in his own time. The story of Heloise and Abelard kindled an intense curiosity combined with a wave of sentimental enthusiasm for these now-famous lovers. The graves of the pair—still at the Paraclete in this period—became a tourist attraction of some repute in late-18th-century travels. In 1802 the remains of the lovers were transferred to Paris and housed in a rather strange "Museum of French Monuments" built to preserve cultural monuments threatened by the egalitarian zeal of the French Revolution. The monument to Heloise and Abelard, constructed by the founder of the museum, Alexander Lenoir, consisted of an elaborate tomb housed in a small chapel with a rather dramatic inscription carved in Greek over the chapel doors: "Forever United."

In 1815 the remains of the pair were again moved, this time to that most curious of European cemeteries, Père Lachaise in Paris. The burial chapel became a required pilgrimage spot for admirers and romantics of the 19th century, just as admirers go today to Père Lachaise to leave a rose at the grave of Jim Morrison of the rock group The Doors or the tomb of Edith Piaf the singer. The decidedly unromantic American humorist and novelist Mark Twain could write in *Innocents Abroad* (1869) that "Go when you will, you find somebody snuffling over that tomb. Go when you will, you find it furnished with those bouquets and *immortèles*" [271].

The legend of Heloise and Abelard has been kept alive in this century through the agency of both novel and drama. George Moore's *Heloise and Abelard* (1921) was in keeping with the Celtic romanticism of the author himself. Moore depicted Abelard as a thinker, musician, lover, and victim—all characteristics the author attributed to himself. Heloise was depicted as a semipagan given to a wild capacity for love and nature, nurtured more on the classics than on the constrictive tradition of the medieval Church. Helen Waddell's *Peter Abelard* (1933) is a much more satisfactory novel [272]. The author, an eminent medievalist, had a better grasp of the milieu of the Middle Ages. Her eye for detail gives the picture of an era which is more faithful to the original than Moore's. For all of that, the novel has been written not from the presuppositions of the 12th century, but against the background of two hundred years of a sentimental legend about the lovers as well as the Freudianism of our time. This novel has been influential in our perception of Abelard and Heloise. That Heloise should exalt a moment of passion that transcends the boundaries of time—that provides an "eternity"—is a sentiment about ecstasy with which the modern temper can identify; it is not a very convincing evocation of the medieval understanding of the nature of reality.

The dramatic story of Heloise and Abelard lifts the medieval story from the abstractions that so often characterize the period. It permits us a rare look into the real lives of women and men and is, in a sense, an antidote to our standard feelings about the period. It is particularly useful to remind ourselves that the Middle Ages, which tended to idealize women to an almost ethereal degree (either by emphasis on courtly love or the cult of the Virgin) or caricature them as sources of lust and temptation, also could produce a Heloise—a woman of strong passion, keen intelligence, deep learning, and rigorous self-confidence. For that alone her story, and that of Abelard, is important. It serves as a corrective and, as subsequent history has shown, an almost mythic example of how people attempt to transcend the conditions cultures impose upon them.

272 Diana Rigg as Heloise and Keith Michell as Abelard in Ronald Millar's stage adaptation of the novel by Helen Waddell. Los Angeles, 1971.

Bibliography

Besides the novels mentioned in the text, the following are useful surveys:

Gilson, Etienne. *Heloise and Abelard*. Translated by L. K. Shook. Ann Arbor: University of Michigan, 1961. A work that defends the authenticity of the couple's letters, it is also one of the classic studies of Heloise and Abelard.

Muckle, J. T. (trans.). *The Story of Abelard's Adversities*. Toronto: Pontifical Institute of Medieval Studies, 1954. A translation of Abelard's "autobiography" with an excellent introduction. The other letters of the couple are also to appear in this series. They are currently available in Muckle's edition in *Medieval Studies* (1950, 1953, 1955).

Pernoud, Regine. *Heloise and Abelard*. Translated by Peter Wiles. New York: Stein & Day, 1973. A very readable study of the couple written for a nonscholarly audience. There is a bibliography but the translator did not revise it for an English audience.

Robertson, D. W. *Abelard and Heloise*. New York: Dial, 1972. The best book on the pair from the humanistic perspective. Robertson traces their story from its origin down to the present age. Indispensable.

Sikes, J. G. *Peter Abailard*. New York: Oxford, 1938. A classic study; the scholarship is somewhat out of date.

	GENERAL EVENTS	LITERATURE & PHILOSOPHY	ART

1280

13th cent. Dependence on Byzantine models in Italian painting

c. 1280–1290 Cimabue, *Madonna Enthroned; Crucifix,* Arezzo

1300 Pope Boniface VIII proclaims first Jubilee Year ("Holy Year")

1303 Philip the Fair of France humiliates Pope Boniface VIII

c. 1303–1321 Dante, *Divine Comedy*

c. 1300 New naturalism in Italian painting appears with work of Giotto

1305–1306 Giotto, Arena Chapel frescoes

c. 1308–1311 Duccio, *Maestà* altarpiece, Siena

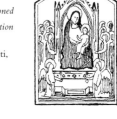

1309

1309 "Babylonian Captivity" of the papacy at Avignon begins

c. 1310 G. Pisano completes Pisa Cathedral pulpit; Giotto, *Madonna Enthroned*

1326 Earliest known use of cannon

1333 Martini, *Annunciation*

1337–1453 "Hundred Years' War" between France and England

1338–1339 A. Lorenzetti, *Good Government* fresco, Siena

1346–1378 Reign of Charles IV, Holy Roman emperor

1346 English defeat French at Crécy

c. 1347–1360 Prague, as residence of Charles IV, becomes major art center

1348 Bubonic plague depopulates Europe

1348–1352 Boccaccio, *Decameron,* collection of tales

c. 1350–1360 Unknown Bohemian Master, *Death of the Virgin*

1356 English defeat French at Poitiers

after 1350 Petrarch compiles *Canzoniere,* collection of poems

1358 Revolt of lower classes (*Jacquerie*) in France

c. 1370 Saint Catherine of Siena urges end of "Babylonian Captivity"

c. 1363 Court of dukes of Burgundy at Dijon becomes important center of International Style

1363–1404 Reign of Philip the Bold, duke of Burgundy

1376 Popes return to Rome from Avignon

1373 Petrarch, *Letter to Posterity,* autobiography

1377

1377–1399 Reign of Richard II in England

c. 1377 Wycliff active in English church reform; translates Bible into English

c. 1377–1413 *Wilton Diptych*

1378 "Great Schism" begins

1381 Peasant riots ("Wat Tyler Rebellion") in England

c. 1385–1400 Chaucer, *The Canterbury Tales,* collection of tales

1395–1399 Broederlam, *Presentation in the Temple and Flight into Egypt*

1399–1413 Reign of Henry IV in England

1395–1406 Sluter, *Well of Moses*

1413 English defeat French at Agincourt

1417 Council of Constance ends "Great Schism" with election of Pope Martin V

1413–1416 Limbourg Brothers, illustrations for *Très Riches Heures du Duc de Berry*

1417

"Babylonian Captivity" of the Papacy

The Great Schism

1288–1309 Palazzo
Pubblico, Siena

1295 Santa Croce, Florence,
begun

1296 Florence Cathedral
(Duomo) begun

1298 Palazzo Vecchio,
Florence, begun

14th cent. Secular
music flourishes

1325 Vitry, *Ars Nova Musicae,*
treatise describing new
system of musical notation

1332–1357 Gloucester Cathedral choir
("Perpendicular" style)

after 1337 Machaut, *Messe de
Notre Dame,* polyphonic setting
of the Ordinary of the Mass

c. 1345–1438 Doge's Palace, Venice

c. 1350 Landini famous in
Florence as performer and
composer of madrigals
and ballads

9

The 14th Century: A Time of Transition

1386 Duomo of Milan begun

Calamity, Decay, and Violence

The 14th century (often called the *Trecento,* Italian for "thirteen hundred") is usually described by historians as the age that marks the end of the medieval period and the beginning of the Renaissance in Western Europe. If we accept this rather neat description of the period we should expect to see strong elements of the medieval sensibility as well as some stirrings of the "new birth" (*Renaissance*) of culture that was the hallmark of 15th-century European life. We must be cautious, however, about expecting the break between "medieval" and "Renaissance" to be clean, dramatic, and easily noted. History does not usually work with the precision employed by the historians. Nor should we expect to see cultural history moving upward in a straight line toward greater modernity or greater perfection. In fact, the 14th century was a period of unparalleled natural calamity, institutional decay, and cruel violence.

The Black Death

Midway through the century, in 1348, bubonic plague swept through Europe in a virulent epidemic that killed untold numbers of people and upset trade, culture, and daily life in ways hard for us to imagine. It has been estimated that some cities in Italy lost as much as two-thirds of their population in that year.

One prominent figure who lived through that devastation was the Italian writer Giovanni Boccaccio (1312–1353). His great collection of stories, the *Decameron,* has a plague setting. A group of young men and women flee Florence to avoid the plague; during their ten days' sojourn in the country (*Decameron* is Greek for "ten days") they amuse each other by the telling of stories [273]. Each of the ten young people tells two stories on each of the ten days. The resulting two hundred stories constitute a brilliant collection of folk tales, *fabliaux* (ribald fables), *exempla* (moral stories), and romances Boccaccio culled from the oral and written traditions of Europe. Because of their romantic elements, earthiness, and somewhat shocking bawdiness the *Decameron* has often been called the "Human Comedy" to contrast it with the lofty moral tone of Dante's epic work of an earlier generation.

However delightful and pleasing those stories are to read, they stand in sharp contrast to the horrific picture Boccaccio draws of the plague in his introduction to the *Decameron.* Boccaccio's account has the ring of authenticity. He had been an eyewitness to the events he describes. His vivid prose gives some small sense of what the plague must have been like for a people who possessed only the most rudimentary knowledge of medicine and no knowledge at all about the source of illness and disease.

Giovanni Boccaccio
from DECAMERON
Preface to the Ladies

How many times, most gracious ladies, have I considered in my innermost thoughts how full of pity you all are by nature. As often as I have thought this, I recognized that this present work will have in your judgment a depressing and unpleasant beginning. For it bears in its initial pages a disheartening remembrance of the past mortal pestilence, which was irksome and painful to all who saw it or otherwise knew it. But I do not wish that this should frighten you from going further, as if your reading will continuously carry you through sighs and tears. Let this horrid beginning be to you not otherwise than a rugged and steep mountain to travelers, next to which lies a lovely and delightful plain. The plain is all the more pleasing to them, in proportion to the great difficulties of climbing and descending. For just as sorrow dims out extreme happiness, so miseries are ended by supervening joy. To this brief unpleasantness (I say brief since it is contained in few words) there shall at once follow sweetness and delight. I have promised it to you in advance; for it might not have been expected from such a beginning, if it hadn't been told you. In truth, if I could have in honesty led you where I want by a way other than a path as rough as this, I would willingly have done so. But without this recollection I could not have shown you the reason why the things took place, of which you soon will be reading. Thus even, strained, as if by necessity, I brought myself to write of them.

I say, then, that it was the year of the bountiful Incarnation of the Son of God, 1348. The mortal pestilence then arrived in the excellent city of Florence, which surpasses every other Italian city in nobility. Whether through the operations of the heavenly bodies, or sent upon us mortals through our wicked deeds by the just wrath of God for our correction, the plague had begun some years before in Eastern countries. It carried off uncounted numbers of inhabitants, and kept moving without cease from place to place. It spread in piteous fashion towards the West. No wisdom of human foresight worked against it. The city had been cleaned of much filth by officials delegated to the task. Sick persons were for-

273 The ten young people gathered to tell stories, manuscript illumination illustrating the Prologue to the *Decameron*. 15th century. Bibliothèque Nationale, Paris. The gravediggers at left are a reminder of the plague raging in Florence.

bidden entrance, and many laws were passed for the safeguarding of health. Devout persons made to God not just modest supplications and not just once, but many, both in ordered processions and in other ways. Almost at the beginning of the spring of that year, the plague horribly began to reveal, in astounding fashion, its painful effects.

It did not work as it had in the East, where anyone who bled from the nose had a manifest sign of inevitable death. But in its early stages both men, and women too, acquired certain swellings either in the groin or under the armpits. Some of these swellings reached the size of a common apple, and others were as big as an egg, some more and some less. The common people called them plague-boils. From these two parts of the body, the deadly swellings began in a short time to appear and to reach indifferently every part of the body. Then, the appearance of the disease began to change into black or livid blotches, which showed up in many on the arms or thighs and in every other part of the body. On some they were large and few, on others small and numerous. And just as the swellings had been at first and still were an infallible indication of approaching death, so also were these blotches to whomever they touched. In the cure of these illnesses, neither the advice of a doctor nor the power of any medicine appeared to help and to do any good. Perhaps the nature of the malady

did not allow it; perhaps the ignorance of the physicians (of whom, besides those trained, the number had grown very large both of women and of men who were completely without medical instruction) did not know whence it arose, and consequently did not take required action against it. Not only did very few recover, but almost everyone died within the third day from the appearance of these symptoms, some sooner and some later, and most without any fever or other complication. This plague was of greater virulence, because by contact with those sick from it, it infected the healthy, not otherwise than fire does, when it is brought very close to dry or oily material.

The evil was still greater than this. Not only conversation and contact with the sick carried the illness to the healthy and was cause of their common death. But even to handle the clothing or other things touched or used by the sick seemed to carry with it that same disease for those who came into contact with them. You will be amazed to hear what I now must tell you. If the eyes of many, including my own, had not seen it, I would hardly dare to believe it, much less to write it, even if I had heard it from a person worthy of faith. I say that the character of the pestilence we describe was of such virulence in spreading from one person to another, that not only did it go from man to man, but many times it also apparently did the following, which is even more remarkable. If an animal outside the human species contacted the belongings of a man sick or dead of this illness, it not only caught the disease, but within a brief time was killed by it. My own eyes, as I said a little while ago, saw one day (and other times besides) this occurrence. The rags of a poor man dead from this disease had been thrown in a public street. Two pigs came to them and they, in their accustomed manner, first rooted among them with their snouts, and then seized them with their teeth and tossed them about with their jaws. A short hour later, after some staggering, as if the poison was taking effect, both of them fell dead to earth upon the rags which they had unhappily dragged.

Such events and many others similar to them or even worse conjured up in those who remained healthy diverse fears and imaginings. Almost all were inclined to a very cruel purpose, that is, to shun and to flee the sick and their belongings. By so behaving, each believed that he would gain safety for himself. Some persons advised that a moderate manner of living, and the avoidance of all excesses, greatly strengthened resistance to this danger. Seeking out companions, such persons lived apart from other men. They closed and locked themselves in those houses where no sick person was found. To live better, they consumed in modest quantities the most delicate foods and the best wines, and avoided all sexual activity. They did not let themselves speak to anyone, nor did they wish to hear any news from the outside, concerning death or the sick. They lived amid music and those pleasures which they were able to obtain.

Others were of a contrary opinion. They affirmed that heavy drinking and enjoyment, making the rounds with singing and good cheer, the satisfaction of the appetite with everything one could and the laughing and joking which derived from this, were the most effective medicine for this great evil. As they recommended, so they put into practice, according to their ability. Night and day, they went now to that tavern and now to another, drinking without moderation or measure. They did even more in the houses of others; they had only to discern there things which were to their liking or pleasure. This they could easily do, since everyone, as if he was destined to live no more, had abandoned all care of his possessions and of himself. Thus, most houses had become open to all, and strangers used them as they happened upon them, as their proper owner might have done. With this inhuman intent, they continuously avoided the sick with all their power.

In this great affliction and misery of our city, the revered authority of both divine and human laws was left to fall and decay by those who administered and executed them. They too, just as other men, were all either dead or sick or so destitute of their families, that they were unable to fulfill any office. As a result everyone could do just as he pleased.

Many others held a middle course between the two mentioned above. Not restraining themselves in their diet as much as the first group, nor letting themselves go in drinking and other excesses as the second, they satisfied their appetites sufficiently. They did not go into seclusion but went about carrying flowers, fragrant herbs and various spices which they often held to their noses, believing a good to comfort the brain with such odors since the air was heavy with the stench of dead bodies, illness and pungent medicines. Others had harsher but perhaps safer ideas. They said that against plagues no medicine was better than or even equal to simple flight. Moved by this reasoning and giving heed to nothing but themselves, many men and women abandoned their own city, their houses and homes, their relatives and belongings in search of their own country places or those of others. Just as if the wrath of God, in order to punish the iniquity of men with the plague, could not pursue them, but would only oppress those within city walls! They were apparently convinced that no one should remain in the city, and that its last hour had struck.

Although these people of various opinions did not all die, neither did they all live. In fact many in each group and in every place became ill, but having given example to those who were still well, they in turn were abandoned and left to perish.

We have said enough of these facts: that one townsman shuns another; that almost no one cares for his neighbor; that relatives rarely or never exchange visits, and never do they get too close. The calamity had instilled such terror in the hearts of men and women that brother abandoned brother, uncle nephew, brother sister, and often wives left their husbands. Even more extraordinary, unbelievable even, fathers and mothers shunned their children, neither visiting them nor helping them, as though they were not their very own.

Consequently, for the enormous number of men and women who became ill, there was no aid except the charity of friends, who were few indeed, or the avarice of servants attracted by huge and exorbitant stipends. Even so, there weren't many servants, and those few men and women were of unrefined capabilities, doing little more than to hand the sick the articles they requested and to mark their death. Serving in such a capacity, many perished along with their earnings. From this abandonment of the sick by neighbors, relatives and friends and from the scarcity of servants arose an almost unheard-of custom. Once she became ill, no woman, however attractive, lovely or well-born, minded having as her servant a man, young or old. To him without any shame she exhibited any part of her body as sickness required, as if to another woman. This explains why those who were cured were less modest than formerly. A further consequence is that many died for want of help who might still be living. The fact that the ill could not avail themselves of services as well as the virulence of the plague account for the multitude who died in the city by day and by night. It was dreadful to hear tell of it, and likewise to see it. Out of necessity, therefore, there were born among the survivors customs contrary to the old ways of the townspeople.

It used to be the custom, as it is today, for the female relative and neighbors of the dead man to gather together with those close to him in order to mourn. Outside the house of the dead man his friends, neighbors and many others would assemble. Then, according to the status of the deceased, a priest would come with the funeral pomp of candles and chants, while the dead man was borne on the shoulders of his peers to the church chosen before death. As the ferocity of the plague increased, such customs ceased either totally or in part, and new ones took their place. Instead of dying amidst a crowd of women, many left this life without a single witness. Indeed, few were conceded the mournful wails and bitter tears of loved ones. Instead, quips and merry-making were common and even normally compas-

sionate women had learned well such habits for the sake of their health. Few bodies had more than ten or twelve neighbors to accompany them to church, and even those were not upright citizens, but a species of vulture sprung from the lowly who called themselves "grave-diggers," and sold their services. They shouldered the bier and with hurried steps went not to the church designated by the deceased, but more often than not to the nearest church. Ahead were four or six clerics with little light or sometimes none, who with the help of the grave-diggers placed the dead in the nearest open grave without straining themselves with too long or solemn a service.

Much more wretched was the condition of the poor people and even perhaps of the middle class in large part. Because of hope or poverty, these people were confined to their houses. Thus keeping to their quarters, thousands fell ill daily and died without aid or help of any kind, almost without exception. Many perished on the public streets by day or by night, and many more ended their days at home, where the stench of their rotting bodies first notified their neighbors of their death. With these and others dying all about, the city was full of corpses. Now a general procedure was followed more out of fear of contagion than because of pity felt for the dead. Alone or with the help of whatever bearers they could find, they dragged the corpses from their houses and piled them in front so, particularly in the morning, anyone abroad could see countless bodies. Biers were sent for and when they were lacking, ordinary planks carried

274 Pisan School. *The Triumph of Death,* detail. c. 1350 (partially destroyed 1944). Fresco. Camposanto, Pisa. This fresco in the monumental cemetery of Pisa sums up a number of themes from the Black Death: the horror of the dead, the monks who demand repentance, the various classes the plague cut down. The scene of seven women and three men in the cherry grove at the right side of the fresco is undoubtedly a reference to Boccaccio's *Decameron.* Note the figure of Death, symbolized as a great blonde woman with a scythe, to the left of the garden group.

the bodies. It was not an isolated bier which carried two or three together. This happened not just once, but many biers could be counted which held in fact a wife and husband, two or three brothers, or father and son. Countless times, it happened that two priests going forth with a cross to bury someone were joined by three or four biers carried behind by bearers, so that whereas the priests thought they had one corpse to bury, they found themselves with six, eight or even more. Nor were these dead honored with tears, candles or mourners. It had come to such a pass that men who died were shown no more concern than dead goats today.

All of this clearly demonstrated that although the natural course of events with its small and occasional stings had failed to impress the wise to bear such trials with patience, the very magnitude of this now had forced even the simple people to become indifferent to them. Every hour of every day there was such a rush to carry the huge number of corpses that there was not enough blessed burial ground, especially with the usual custom of giving each body its own place. So when the ground was filled, they made huge trenches in every churchyard, in which they stacked hundreds of bodies in layers like goods stowed in the hold of a ship, covering them with a bit of earth until the bodies reached the very top.

And so I won't go on searching out every detail of our city's miseries, but while such hard times prevailed, the surrounding countryside was spared nothing. There, in the scattered villages (not to speak of the castles which were like miniature cities) and across the fields, the wretched and impoverished peasants and their families died without any medical aid or help from servants, not like men but like beasts, on the roads, on their farms, and about the houses by day and by night. For this reason, just like the townspeople, they became lax in their ways and neglected their chores as if they expected death that very day. They became positively ingenious, not in producing future yields of crops and beasts, but in ways of consuming what they already possessed. Thus, the oxen, the asses, sheep, goats, pigs and fowl and even the dogs so faithful to man, were driven from the houses, and roamed through the fields where the abandoned wheat grew uncut and unharvested. Almost as if they were rational, many animals having eaten well by day returned filled at night to their houses without any shepherding.

To leave the countryside and to return to the city, what more could be said? Such was heaven's cruelty (and perhaps also man's) that between March and the following July, the raging plague and the absence of help given the sick by the fearful healthy ones took from this life more than one hundred thousand human beings within the walls of Florence. Who would have thought before this deadly calamity that the city had held so many inhabitants? Oh, how many great palaces, how many lovely houses, how many rich mansions once filled with families of lords and ladies remained empty even to the lowliest servant! Alas! How many memorable families, how many ample heritages, how many famous fortunes remained without a lawful heir! What number of brave and beautiful ladies, lively youths, whom not only others, but Galen, Hippocrates, and Aesculapius themselves would have pronounced in the best of health, breakfasted in the morning with their relatives, companions and friends, only to dine that very night with their ancestors in the other world! ◖

The Great Schism

Nature was not the only scourge to affect the stability of Europe. The medieval Christian church, that most powerful and permanent large institution in medieval life, underwent convulsive changes in the 14th century, changes that were distant warning signals of the Reformation at the beginning of the 16th century.

A quick look at some dates indicate clearly the nature of these changes. In 1300 Pope Boniface VIII celebrated the great jubilee year at Rome which brought pilgrims and visitors from all over the Christian West to pay homage to the papacy and the church it represented and headed. This event was one of the final symbolic moments of papal supremacy over European life and culture. Within the next three years Philip the Fair of France imprisoned and abused the same pope at the papal palace of Anagni. The pope died as a result of his humiliating encounters with royal power; even Dante's implacable hatred of Boniface could not restrain his outrage at the humiliation of the office of the pope. By 1309 the papacy, under severe pressure from the French, had been removed to Avignon in southern France, where it was to remain for nearly 70 years. In 1378 the papacy was further weakened by the Great Schism, which saw European Christianity divided into hostile camps each of which pledged allegiance to a rival claimant to the papacy. Not until 1417 was this breach in church unity healed; a church council had to depose three papal pretenders to accomplish the reunification of the church.

The general disarray of the church in this period spawned ever more insistent demands for church reforms. Popular literature (as both Boccaccio and, in England, Geoffrey Chaucer, clearly demonstrate) unmercifully satirized the decadence of the church. Great saints like the mystic Catherine of Siena (1347–1380) wrote impassioned letters to the popes at Avignon in their "Babylonian Captivity" demanding that they return to Rome free from the political ties of the French monarchy. In England, John Wyclif's cries against the immorality of the higher clergy and the corruption of the church fueled indignation at all levels. The famous Peasant Revolt of 1381 was greatly aided by the activism of people aroused by the ideas of Wyclif and his followers.

The 1381 revolt in England was only the last in a series of lower-class revolutions that occurred in the 14th century. The frequency and magnitude of these revolts (like that of the French peasants beginning in 1356) highlight the profound dissatisfactions with the church and the nobility in the period. It is not accidental that the story of Robin Hood, with its theme of violence toward the wealthy and care for the poor, began in the 14th century.

The Hundred Years' War

The terrible violence of the 14th century was caused not only by the alienation of the peasants but also by the Hundred Years' War between France and England. While the famous battles of the period—Poitiers, Crécy, Agincourt—now seem romantic and distant, it is undeniable that they brought unrelieved misery to France for long periods. Between battles roaming bands of mercenaries pillaged the landscape

275 Idealized portrait of Petrarch, from a manuscript of his works. 15th century. Vatican Library, Rome.

to make up for their lack of pay. The various battles were terrible in themselves. One example must suffice. According to Jean Froissart's *Chronicles,* the English King Edward III sent a group of his men to examine the battlefield after the battle of Crécy (1346)—in which the English longbowmen slaughtered the more traditionally armed French and mercenary armies: "They passed the whole day upon the field and made a careful report of all they saw. According to their report it appeared that 80 banners, the bodies of 11 princes, 1200 knights, and 30,000 common men were found dead on the field." It is no wonder that Barbara Tuchman's splendid history of life in 14th-century France, *A Distant Mirror* (1978), should have been subtitled "The Calamitous Fourteenth Century."

Literature in Italy and England

Amid the natural and institutional disasters of the 14th century there were signs of intense human creativity in all the arts, especially in literature. In Italy, Dante's literary eminence was secure at the time of his death (1321) and the reputation of Italian letters was further enhanced by two other outstanding Tuscan writers: Francesco Petrarca and Giovanni Boccaccio, famed for the *Decameron.* In England, one of the greatest authors in the history of English letters was active: Geoffrey Chaucer. His life spanned the second half of the 14th century; he died, almost symbolically, in 1400.

Francesco Petrarca

It is appropriate to begin a discussion of 14th-century culture with Petrarch [275]. His life spanned the better part of the century (1304–1374) and in that life we can see the conflict between the medieval and early Renaissance ideals being played out.

Francesco Petrarca (called Petrarch in English) was born in Arezzo, a small town in Tuscany south of Florence. As a young man, in obedience to parental wishes, he studied law for a year in France and for three years at the law faculty in Bologna. He abandoned his legal studies immediately after the death of his father to pursue a literary career. To support himself he accepted some minor church offices but was never ordained to the priesthood.

Petrarch made his home at Avignon (and later at a much more isolated spot near that papal city, Vaucluse), but for the greater part of his life he wandered from place to place. He never could settle down; his restlessness prevented him from accepting lucrative positions that would have made him a permanent resident of any one place. He received invitations to serve as secretary to various popes in Avignon and, through the intercession of his close friend Boccaccio, was offered a professorship in Florence. He took none of these positions.

Petrarch was insatiably curious. He fed his love for the ancient classics by searching out and copying ancient manuscripts that had remained hidden and unread in the various monasteries of Europe. It is said that at his death he had one of the finest private libraries in Europe. He wrote volumes of poetry and prose, carried on a vast correspondence, advised the rulers of the age, took a keen interest in horticulture, and kept a wide circle of literary and artistic friends. At his death we know that he possessed pictures by both Simone Martini and Giotto, two of the most influential artists of the time. In 1348 he was crowned poet laureate of Rome, the first artist so honored since the ancient days of Rome.

One true mark of the Renaissance sensibility was a keen interest in the self and an increased thirst for personal glory and fame. Petrarch surely is a 14th-century harbinger of that spirit. Dante's *Divine Comedy* was totally oriented to the next life; the apex of Dante's vision is that of the soul rapt in the vision of God in eternity. Petrarch, profoundly religious, never denied that such a vision was the ultimate goal of life. At the same time his work exhibits a tension between that goal and his thirst for earthly success and fame. In his famous prose work *Secretum (My Secret),* written in 1343, the artist imagines himself in conversation with Saint Augustine. In a dialogue extraordinary for its sense of self-confession and self-scrutiny Petrarch discusses his moral and intellectual failings, his besetting sins, and his tendency to fall into fits of depression. He agrees with his great hero Augustine that he should be less concerned with his intellectual labors and the fame that derives from them and concern himself more with salvation and the spiritual perfection of his life. However, Petrarch's argument has a note of ambivalence: "I will be true to myself as far as it is possible. I will pull myself together and collect my scattered wits, and make a great endeavor to possess my soul in patience. But even while we speak, a crowd of important affairs, though only of this world, is waiting for my attention."

The inspiration for the *Secretum* was Augustine's *Confessions,* a book Petrarch loved so much that he carried it with him everywhere. It may well have been the model for Petrarch's *Letter to Posterity,* one of the few examples of autobiography we possess after the time of Augustine. That Petrarch would have written an autobiography is testimony to his strong interest in himself as a person. The *Letter* was probably composed in 1373, a year before his death. Petrarch reviews his life up until 1351, where the text abruptly breaks off. The unfinished work is clear testimony to Petrarch's thirst for learning, fame, and self-awareness. At the same time, it is noteworthy for omitting any mention of the Black Death of 1348, which carried off the woman he loved. The letter is an important primary document of the sensibility of the 14th-century "proto-Renaissance."

Francesco Petrarch
LETTER TO POSTERITY

Greeting.—It is possible that some word of me may have come to you, though even this is doubtful, since an insignificant and obscure name will scarcely penetrate far in either time or space. If, however, you should have heard of me, you may desire to know what manner of man I was, or what was the outcome of my labours, especially those of which some description or, at any rate, the bare titles may have reached you.

To begin with myself, then, the utterances of men concerning me will differ widely, since in passing judgment almost every one is influenced not so much by truth as by preference, and good and evil report alike know no bounds. I was, in truth, a poor mortal like yourself, neither very exalted in my origin, nor, on the other hand, of the most humble birth, but belonging, as Augustus Caesar says of himself, to an ancient family. As to my disposition, I was not naturally perverse or wanting in modesty, however the contagion of evil associations may have corrupted me. My youth was gone before I realised it; I was carried away by the strength of manhood; but a riper age brought me to my senses and taught me by experience the truth I had long before read in books, that youth and pleasure are vanity—nay, that the Author of all ages and times permits us miserable mortals, puffed up with emptiness, thus to wander about, until finally, coming to a tardy consciousness of our sins, we shall learn to know ourselves. In my prime I was blessed with a quick and active body although not exceptionally strong; and while I do not lay claim to remarkable personal beauty, I was comely enough in my best days. I was possessed of a clear complexion, between light and dark, lively eyes, and for long years a keen vision, which however deserted me, contrary to my hopes, after I reached my sixtieth birthday, and forced me, to my great annoyance, to resort to glasses. Although I had previously enjoyed perfect health, old age brought with it the usual array of discomforts.

My parents were honourable folk, Florentine in their origin, of medium fortune, or, I may as well admit it, in a condition verging upon poverty. They had been expelled from their native city, and consequently I was born in exile, at Arezzo, in the year 1304 of this latter age which begins with Christ's birth, July the twentieth, on a Monday, at dawn. I have always possessed an extreme contempt for wealth; not that riches are not desirable in themselves, but because I hate the anxiety and care which are invariably associated with them. I certainly do not long to be able to give gorgeous banquets. I have, on the contrary, led a happier existence with plain living and ordinary fare than all the followers of Apicius, with their elaborate dainties. So-called "convivia," which are but vulgar bouts, sinning against sobriety and good manners, have always been repugnant to me. I have ever felt that it was irksome and profitless to invite others to such affairs, and not less so to be bidden to them myself. On the other hand, the pleasure of dining with one's friends is so great that nothing has ever given me more delight than their unexpected arrival, nor have I ever willingly sat down to table without a companion. Nothing displeases me more than display, for not only is it bad in itself, and opposed to humility, but it is troublesome and distracting.

I struggled in my younger days with a keen but constant and pure attachment, and would have struggled with it longer had not the sinking flame been extinguished by death—premature and bitter, but salutary. I should be glad to be able to say that I had always been entirely free from irregular desires, but I should lie if I did so. I can, however, conscientiously claim that, although I may have been carried away by the fire of youth or by my ardent temperament, I have always abhorred such sins from the depths of my soul. As I approached the age of forty, while my powers were unimpaired and my passions were still strong, I not only abruptly threw off my bad habits, but even the very recollection of them, as if I had never looked upon a woman. This I mention as among the greatest of my blessings, and I render thanks to God, who freed me, while still sound and vigorous, from a disgusting slavery . . . hateful to me. But let us turn to other matters.

I have taken pride in others, never in myself, and however insignificant I may have been, I have always been still less important in my own judgment. My anger has very often injured myself, but never others. I have always been most desirous of honourable friendships, and have faithfully cherished them. I make this boast without fear, since I am confident that I speak truly. While I am very prone to take offence, I am equally quick to forget injuries, and have a memory tenacious of benefits. In my familiar associations with kings and princes, and in my friendship with noble personages, my good fortune has been such as to excite envy. But it is the cruel fate of those who are growing old that they can commonly only weep for friends who have passed away. The greatest kings of this age have loved and courted me. They may know why; I certainly do not. With some of them I was on such terms that they seemed in a certain sense my guests rather than I theirs; their lofty position in no way embarrassing me, but, on the contrary, bringing with it many advantages. I fled, however, from many of those to whom I was greatly attached; and such was my innate longing for liberty, that I studiously avoided those whose very name seemed incompatible with the freedom that I loved.

I possessed a well-balanced rather than a keen intellect, one prone to all kinds of good and wholesome study, but especially inclined to moral philosophy and the art of poetry. The latter, indeed, I neglected as time went on and took delight in sacred literature. Finding in that a hidden sweetness which I had once esteemed but lightly, I came to regard the works of the poets as only amenities. Among the many subjects which interested me, I dwelt especially upon antiquity, for our own age has always repelled me, so that, had it not been for the love of those dear to me, I should have preferred to have been born in any other period than our own. In order to forget my own time, I have constantly striven to place myself in spirit in other ages, and consequently, I delighted in history; not that the conflicting statements did not offend me, but when in doubt I accepted what appeared to me most probable, or yielded to the authority of the writer.

My style, as many claimed, was clear and forcible: but to me it seemed weak and obscure. In ordinary conversation with friends, or with those about me, I never gave any thought to my language, and I have always wondered that Augustus Caesar should have taken such pains in this respect. When, however, the subject itself, or the place or listener, seemed to demand it, I gave some attention to style, with what success I cannot pretend to say; let them judge in whose presence I spoke. If only I have lived well, it matters little to me how I talked. Mere elegance of language can produce at best but an empty renown.

My life up to the present has, either through fate or my own choice, fallen into the following divisions. A part only of my first year was spent at Arezzo, where I first saw the light. The six following years were, owing to the recall of my mother from exile, spent upon my father's estate at Ancisa, about fourteen miles above Florence. I passed my eighth year at Pisa, the ninth and following years in Father Gaul, at Avignon, on the left bank of the Rhone, where the Roman Pontiff holds and has long held the Church of Christ in shameful exile. It seemed a few years ago as if Urban V[1] was on the point of restoring the Church to its ancient seat, but it is clear that nothing is coming of this effort, and, what is to me the worst of all, the Pope seems to have repented him of his good work, for failure came while he was still living. Had he lived but a little longer, he would certainly have learned how I regarded his retreat. My pen was in my hand when he abruptly surrendered at once his exalted office and his life. Unhappy man, who might have died before the altar of Saint Peter and in his own habitation! Had his successors remained in their capital he would have been looked upon as the cause of this benign change, while, had they left Rome, his virtue would have been all the more conspicuous in contrast with their fault.

But such laments are somewhat remote from my subject. On the windy banks of the river Rhone I spent my boyhood, guided by my parents, and then, guided by my own fancies, the whole of my youth. Yet there were long intervals spent elsewhere, for I first passed four years at the little town of Carpentras, somewhat to the east of Avignon: in these two places I learned as much of grammar, logic, and rhetoric as my age permitted, or rather, as much as it is customary to teach in school: how little that is, dear reader, thou knowest. I then set out for Montpellier to study law, and spent four years there, then three at Bologna. I heard the whole body of the civil law, and would, as many thought, have distinguished myself later, had I but continued my studies. I gave up the subject altogether, however, so soon as it was no longer necessary to consult the wishes of my parents. My reason was that, although the dignity of the law, which is doubtless very great, and especially the numerous references it contains to Roman antiquity, did not fail to delight me, I felt it to be habitually degraded by those who practise it. It went against me painfully to acquire an art which I would not practise dishonestly, and could hardly hope to exercise otherwise. Had I made the latter attempt, my scrupulousness would doubtless have been ascribed to simplicity.

So at the age of two and twenty I returned home. I call my place of exile home, Avignon, where I had been since childhood; for habit has almost the po-

[1] Urban V died in 1370.

tency of nature itself. I had already begun to be known there, and my friendship was sought by prominent men; wherefore I cannot say. I confess this is now a source of surprise to me, although it seemed natural enough at an age when we are used to regard ourselves as worthy of the highest respect. I was courted first and foremost by that very distinguished and noble family, the Colonnesi, who, at that period, adorned the Roman Curia with their presence. However it might be now, I was at that time certainly quite unworthy of the esteem in which I was held by them. I was especially honoured by the incomparable Giacomo Colonna, then Bishop of Lombez, whose peer I know not whether I have ever seen or ever shall see, and was taken by him to Gascony; there I spent such a divine summer among the foot-hills of the Pyrenees, in happy intercourse with my master and the members of our company, that I can never recall the experience without a sigh of regret.

Returning thence, I passed many years in the house of Giacomo's brother, Cardinal Giovanni Colonna, not as if he were my lord and master, but rather my father, or better, a most affectionate brother—nay, it was as if I were in my own home. About this time, a youthful desire impelled me to visit France and Germany. While I invented certain reasons to satisfy my elders of the propriety of the journey, the real explanation was a great inclination and longing to see new sights. I first visited Paris, as I was anxious to discover what was true and what fabulous in the accounts I had heard of that city. On my return from this journey I went to Rome, which I had since my infancy ardently desired to visit. There I soon came to venerate Stephano, the noble head of the family of the Colonnesi, like some ancient hero, and was in turn treated by him in every respect like a son. The love and good-will of this excellent man toward me remained constant to the end of his life, and lives in me still, nor will it cease until I myself pass away.

On my return, since I experienced a deep-seated and innate repugnance to town life, especially in that disgusting city of Avignon which I heartily abhorred, I sought some means of escape. I fortunately discovered, about fifteen miles from Avignon, a delightful valley, narrow and secluded, called Vaucluse, where the Sorgue, the prince of streams, takes its rise. Captivated by the charms of the place, I transferred thither myself and my books. Were I to describe what I did there during many years, it would prove a long story. Indeed, almost every bit of writing which I have put forth was either accomplished or begun, or at least conceived, there, and my undertakings have been so numerous that they still continue to vex and weary me. My mind, like my body, is characterised by a certain versatility and readiness, rather than by strength, so that many tasks that were easy of conception have been given up by reason of the difficulty of their execution. The character of my surroundings suggested the composition of a sylvan or bucolic song. I also dedicated a work in two books upon *The Life of Solitude,* to Philip, now exalted to the Cardinal-bishopric of Sabina. Although always a great man, he was, at the time of which I speak, only the humble Bishop of Cavaillon. He is the only one of my old friends who is still left to me, and he has always loved and treated me not as a bishop (as Ambrose did Augustine), but as a brother.

While I was wandering in those mountains upon a Friday in Holy Week, the strong desire seized me to write an epic in an heroic strain, taking as my theme Scipio Africanus the Great, who had, strange to say, been dear to me from my childhood. But although I began the execution of this project with enthusiasm, I straightway abandoned it, owing to a variety of distractions. The poem was, however, christened *Africa,* from the name of its hero, and, whether from his fortunes or mine, it did not fail to arouse the interest of many before they had seen it.

While leading a leisurely existence in this region, I received, remarkable as it may seem, upon one and the same day, letters from the Senate at Rome and the Chancellor of the University of Paris, pressing me to appear in Rome and Paris, respectively, to receive the poet's crown of laurel. In my youthful elation I convinced myself that I was quite worthy of this honour; the recognition came from eminent judges, and I accepted their verdict rather than that of my own better judgment. I hesitated for a time which I should give ear to, and sent a letter to Cardinal Giovanni Colonna, of whom I have already spoken, asking his opinion. He was so near that, although I wrote late in the day, I received his reply before the third hour on the morrow. I followed his advice, and recognised the claims of Rome as superior to all others. My acceptance of his counsel is shown by my twofold letter to him on that occasion, which I still keep. I set off accordingly; but although, after the fashion of youth, I was a most indulgent judge of my own work, I still blushed to accept in my own case the verdict even of such men as those who summoned me, despite the fact that they would certainly not have honoured me in this way, had they not believed me worthy.

So I decided, first to visit Naples, and that celebrated king and philosopher, Robert, who was not more distinguished as a ruler than as a man of culture. He was, indeed, the only monarch of our age who was the friend at once of learning and of virtue, and I trusted that he might correct such things as he found to criticise in my work. The way in which he received and welcomed me is a source of astonishment

to me now, and, I doubt not, to the reader also, if he happens to know anything of the matter. Having learned the reason of my coming, the King seemed mightily pleased. He was gratified, doubtless, by my youthful faith in him, and felt, perhaps, that he shared in a way the glory of my coronation, since I had chosen him from all others as the only suitable critic. After talking over a great many things, I showed him my *Africa,* which so delighted him that he asked that it might be dedicated to him in consideration of a handsome reward. This was a request that I could not well refuse, nor, indeed, would I have wished to refuse it, had it been in my power. He then fixed a day upon which we could consider the object of my visit. This occupied us from noon until evening, and the time proving too short, on account of the many matters which arose for discussion, we passed the two following days in the same manner. Having thus tested my poor attainments for three days, the King at last pronounced me worthy of the laurel. He offered to bestow that honour upon me at Naples, and urged me to consent to receive it there, but my veneration for Rome prevailed over the insistence of even so great a monarch as Robert. At length, seeing that I was inflexible in my purpose, he sent me on my way accompanied by royal messengers and letters to the Roman Senate, in which he gave enthusiastic expression to his flattering opinion of me. This royal estimate was, indeed, quite in accord with that of many others, and especially with my own, but to-day I cannot approve either his or my own verdict. In his case, affection and the natural partiality to youth were stronger than his devotion to truth.

On arriving at Rome, I continued, in spite of my unworthiness, to rely upon the judgment of so eminent a critic, and, to the great delight of the Romans who were present, I who had been hitherto a simple student received the laurel crown. This occasion is described elsewhere in my letters, both in prose and verse. The laurel, however, in no way increased my wisdom, although it did arouse some jealousy—but this is too long a story to be told here.

On leaving Rome, I went to Parma, and spent some time with the members of the house of Correggio, who, while they were most kind and generous towards me, agreed but ill among themselves. They governed Parma, however, in a way unknown to that city within the memory of man, and the like of which it will hardly again enjoy in this present age.

I was conscious of the honour which I had but just received, and fearful lest it might seem to have been granted to one unworthy of the distinction; consequently, as I was walking one day in the mountains, and chanced to cross the river Enza to a place called Selva Piana, in the territory of Reggio, struck by the beauty of the spot, I began to write again upon the *Africa*, which I had laid aside. In my enthusiasm, which had seemed quite dead, I wrote some lines that very day, and some each day until I returned to Parma. Here I happened upon a quiet and retired house, which I afterwards bought, and which still belongs to me. I continued my task with such ardour, and completed the work in so short a space of time, that I cannot but marvel now at my despatch. I had already passed my thirty-fourth year when I returned thence to the Fountain of the Sorgue, and to my Transalpine solitude. I had made a long stay both in Parma and Verona, and everywhere I had, I am thankful to say, been treated with much greater esteem than I merited.

Some time after this, my growing reputation procured for me the good-will of a most excellent man, Giacomo the Younger, of Carrara, whose equal I do not know among the rulers of his time. For years he wearied me with messengers and letters when I was beyond the Alps, and with his petitions whenever I happened to be in Italy, urging me to accept his friendship. At last, although I anticipated little satisfaction from the venture, I determined to go to him and see what this insistence on the part of a person so eminent, and at the same time a stranger to me, might really mean. I appeared, though tardily, at Padua, where I was received by him of illustrious memory, not as a mortal, but as the blessed are greeted in heaven—with such delight and such unspeakable affection and esteem, that I cannot adequately describe my welcome in words, and must, therefore, be silent. Among other things, learning that I had led a clerical life from boyhood, he had me made a canon of Padua, in order to bind me the closer to himself and his city. In fine, had his life been spared, I should have found there an end to all my wanderings. But alas! nothing mortal is enduring, and there is nothing sweet which does not presently end in bitterness. Scarcely two years was he spared to me, to his country, and to the world. God, who had given him to us, took him again. Without being blinded by my love for him, I feel that neither I, nor his country, nor the world was worthy of him. Although his son, who succeeded him, was in every way a prudent and distinguished man, who, following his father's example, always loved and honoured me, I could not remain after the death of him with whom, by reason especially of the similarity of our ages, I had been much more closely united.

I returned to Gaul, not so much from a desire to see again what I had already beheld a thousand times, as from the hope, common to the afflicted, of coming to terms with my misfortunes by a change of scene. . . .

Petrarch regarded as his most important works the Latin writings over which he labored with devotion and in conscious imitation of his most admired classical masters: Ovid, Cicero, and Vergil. Today, however, only the literary specialist or the antiquarian is likely to read his long epic poem in Latin called *Africa* (written in imitation of Vergil's *Aeneid*), or his prose work in praise of the past masters of the world *(De Viris Illustris),* or his meditations on the benefits of contemplative life *(De Vita Solitaria).* What has assured the literary reputation of Petrarch is his incomparable vernacular poetry, which he considered somewhat trifling but collected carefully into his *Canzoniere (Songbook).* The *Canzoniere* contains more than three hundred sonnets and forty-nine *canzoni* (songs) written in Italian during the span of his adult career [276].

The subject of a great deal of Petrarch's poetry is his love for Laura, a woman with whom he fell immediately in love in 1327 after seeing her at church in Avignon. Laura died in the plague of 1348. The poems in her honor are divided into those written in her lifetime and those which mourn her untimely death. Petrarch poured out his love for Laura in over three hundred *sonnets,* fourteen-line poems he typically broke into an octave and a sestet. Although they were never actually lovers (Petrarch says in the *Secretum* that this was due more to her honor than to his; Laura was a married woman), his Laura was no mere literary abstraction. She was a flesh-and-blood woman whom Petrarch genuinely loved. One of the characteristics of his poetry, in fact, is the palpable reality of Laura as a person; she never becomes (as Beatrice does for Dante) a symbol without earthly reality.

The interest in Petrarch's sonnets did not end with his death. Petrarchism, by which is meant the Petrarchan form of the sonnet and particularly the poet's attitude to his subject matter—praise of a woman as the perfection of human beauty and the object of the highest expression of love—was introduced into other parts of Europe before the century was over. In England, Petrarch's sonnets were first imitated in form and subject by Sir Thomas Wyatt in the early 16th century. Although the Elizabethan poets eventually developed their own English form of the sonnet, the Renaissance English tradition of poetry owes a particularly large debt to Petrarch, as the poetry of Sir Philip Sidney (1554–1586), Edmund Spenser (1552–1599), and William Shakespeare (1564–1616) shows. Their sonnet sequences follow

276 The Chest Master. *Triumph of Love, Chastity, Death*. 15th century. Front panel of a dowry chest. Victoria and Albert Museum, London. This panel illustrates one of Petrarch's *canzoni*. Petrarch wrote "triumphs" as poetic equivalents of the arches of victorious Roman generals. The "triumph of death" at right was inspired by the plague of 1348.

the example of Petrarch in linking together a series of sonnets in such a way as to indicate a development in the relationship of the poet to his love.

One measure of the importance of Petrarch's poetry can be seen in the number of his sonnets and songs that have been translated into English at different times. The selection below is only a small sampling. Chaucer's translation, made in the 14th century, is actually a paraphrase of Sonnet 132 in the standard edition of Petrarch's *Rime*. It was originally incorporated into a lengthy narrative poem with its own rhyme scheme, which probably explains why it is not in the form of a Petrarchan sonnet. It was published as a separate poem in 1483 by the printer Caxton:

Geoffrey Chaucer
PETRARCH'S SONNET 132

If no love is, O God, what fele I so
And if love is, what thing and whiche is he?
If love be good, from whennes comth my wo?
If it be wikke, a wonder thinketh me,
When every torment and adversitee
That cometh of him, may to me savory[1] think;
For ay thurst, I more that I it drinke.

And if that at myn owene lust I brenne[2]
Fro whennes cometh my wailing and my
      pleynte[3]?

---
[1] savory: pleasing   [2] brenne: burn   [3] pleynte: lament

If harm agree me, where-to-pleyne I thenne?   10
I noot, ne why unwery I feynte.
O quike deeth, o swete harm to queynte,
How may of thee in swich quantitee,
But-if that I consente that it be?

An if that I consente, I wrongfully
Compleyne, y-wis;[4] thus possed to and from
Al sterless[5] with-inne a boot[6] am I
Amid the see, by twixen windes two,
That in contrarie stonden ever mo.
Allas! what is this wonder[7] maladye?   20
For hete of cold, for cold of hete, I dye.

Thomas Wyatt's translation of Petrarch's Sonnet 19 was published in 1557 in *Tottel's Miscellany,* a collection of lyric poetry that was a major factor in introducing the sonnet form to English letters.

Thomas Wyatt
PETRARCH'S SONNET 19

Some fowles there be, that haue so perfit sight
Against the sunne their eies for to defend;
And some, because the light doth them offend,
Neuer appere, but in the darke, or night.
Other rejoice that see the fire bright
And wene to play in it, as they pretend;
But find contrary of it, that they intend.
Alas, of that sort may I be, by right.
For to withstand her loke, I am not able;

---
[4] y-wis: truly   [5] sterless: rudderless   [6] boot: boat
[7] wonder: strange

Yet can I not hide me in no dark place;   10
So foloweth me remembrance of that face,
That with my teary eyn, swolne, and unstable,
My desteny to beholde her doth me lead:
And yet I knowe, I runneth into the glead.[1]

Petrarch composed the *canzone* translated by Leigh
Hunt (1784–1859) after seeing Laura seated by the
banks of a river, probably in 1343.

Leigh Hunt
PETRARCH'S CANZONE 126

Clear, fresh, and dulcet streams
Which the fair shape, who seems
To me sole woman, haunted at noontide;
Fair bough, so gently fit,
(I sigh to think of it,)
Which lent a pillar to her lovely side;
And turf, and flowers bright-eyed,
O'er which her folded gown
Flow'd like an angel's down;
And you, oh holy air, and hush'd,   10
Where first my heart at her sweet glances gush'd;
Give ear, give ear, with one consenting,
To my last words, my last and my lamenting.

It is my fate below
And heaven will have it so,
That Love must close those dying eyes in tears,
May my poor dust be laid
In middle of your shade,
While my soul, naked, mounts to its own spheres.
The thought would calm my fears,   20
When taking, out of breath,
The doubtful step of death;
For never would my spirit find
A stiller port after the stormy wind;
Nor in more calm, abstracted bourne,
Slip from my travail'd flesh, and from my bones
    outworn.

Perhaps, some future hour
To her accustom'd bower
Might come the untamed, and yet the gentle she;
And where she saw me first,   30
Might turn with eyes athirst
And kinder joy to look again for me;
Then, oh, the charity,
Seeing amidst the stones
The earth that held my bones,
A sigh for very love at last
Might ask of heaven to pardon me the past;
And heaven itself could not say nay,
As with her gentle veil she wiped the tears away.

How well I call to mind,   40

[1]glead: light

When from those boughs the wind
Shook down upon her bosom flower on flower;
And there she sat, meek-eyed,
In midst of all that pride,
Sprinkled and blushing through an amorous
    shower.
Some to her hair paid dower,
And seemed to dress the curls,
Queenlike, with gold and pearls;
Some, snowing, on her drapery stopp'd,
Some on the earth, some on the water dropp'd;
While others, fluttering from above,   51
Seem'd wheeling, round in pomp, and saying,
    "Here reigns Love."

How often then I said,
Inward, and filled with dread,
"Doubtless this creature comes from Paradise!"
For at her look the while,
Her voice, and her sweet smile,
And heavenly air, truth parted from mine eyes;
So that, with long sighs,
I said, as far from men,   60
"How came I here and when?"
I had forgotten; and alas!
Fancied myself in heaven, not where I was;
And from that time till this, I bear
Such love for the green bower, I can not rest
    elsewhere.
If thou dids't apparel as thou hast good will,
Thou couldst have boldly broke
Out from the woods, and gone amidst the folk.

The last of the translations reprinted here is by the
Victorian literary critic and essayist on the Italian
Renaissance John Addington Symonds (1840–1893).
Petrarch may have written this sonnet while journey-
ing to Rome in 1336.

John Addington Symonds
PETRARCH'S SONNET 15

Backwards at every weary step and slow
These limbs I turn which with great pain I bear;
Then take I comfort from the fragrant air
That breathes from thee, and sighing onward go.
But when I think how joy is turned to woe,
Remembering my short life and whence I fare,
I stay my feet for anguish and despair,
And cast my tearful eyes on earth below.
At times amid the storm of misery
This doubt assails me: how frail limbs and poor
Can severed from their spirit hope to live.   11
Then answers Love: Hast thou no memory
How I to lovers this great guerdon give,
Free from all human bondage to endure?

Geoffrey Chaucer

While it is possible to see the beginning of the Renaissance spirit in Petrarch and other Italian writers of the 14th century, the greatest English writer of the century, Geoffrey Chaucer (1340–1400), still reflects the culture of his immediate past. The new spirit of individualism discernible in Petrarch is missing in Chaucer. He is still very much a medieval man. Only in the later part of the 15th century, largely under the influence of Italian models, can we speak of the Renaissance in England. This underscores the valuable lesson about history that movements do not necessarily happen immediately and everywhere.

Scholars have been able to reconstruct Chaucer's life with only partial success. We know that his family had been fairly prosperous wine merchants and vintners and that he entered royal service early in his life, eventually becoming a squire to King Edward III. After 1373 he undertook various diplomatic tasks for the king, including at least two trips to Italy to negotiate commercial contracts. During these Italian journeys Chaucer came into contact with the writings of Dante, Petrarch, and Boccaccio. There has been some speculation that he actually met Petrarch, but the evidence is tenuous. Toward the end of his life Chaucer served as the customs agent for the port of London on the river Thames. He was thus never a leisured "man of letters"; his writing had to be done amid the hectic round of public affairs that engaged his attention as a highly placed civil servant.

Like many other successful writers of the late medieval period, Chaucer could claim a widespread acquaintance with the learning and culture of his time. This was still an age when it was possible to read most of the available books. Chaucer spoke and wrote French fluently, and his poems show the influence of many French allegories and "dream visions." That he also knew Italian literature is clear from his borrowings from Dante and Petrarch and from his use of stories and tales in Boccaccio's *Decameron* (although it is not clear that he knew that work directly). Chaucer also had a deep knowledge of Latin literature, both classical and ecclesiastical. Furthermore, his literary output was not limited to the composition of original works of poetry. He made a translation from Latin (with an eye on an earlier French version) of Boethius' *Consolation of Philosophy* as well as a translation from French of the 13th-century allegorical erotic fantasy *The Romance of the Rose*. He also composed a short treatise on the astrolabe and its relationship to the study of astronomy and astrology (two disciplines not clearly distinguished at that time).

The impressive range of Chaucer's learning pales in comparison with his most memorable and noteworthy talents: his profound feeling for the role of the English language as a vehicle for literature; his efforts to extend the range of the language (the richness of Chaucer's vocabulary was not exceeded until Shakespeare); and his incomparable skill in the art of human observation. Chaucer's characters are so finely realized that they have become standard types in English literature: his pardoner is an unforgettable villain, his knight the essence of courtesy, his wife of Bath a paradigm of rollicking bawdiness.

These characters, and others, are from Chaucer's masterpiece, *The Canterbury Tales,* begun sometime after 1385. To unify this vast work, a collection of miscellaneous tales, Chaucer used a typical literary device: a narrative frame, in this case a journey during which people tell each other tales. As noted, Boccaccio had used a similar device in the *Decameron.*

Chaucer's plan was to have a group of 30 pilgrims travel from London to the shrine of Thomas à Becket at Canterbury and back. After a general introduction, each pilgrim would tell two tales on the way and two on the return trip in order to pass the long hours of travel more pleasantly. Between tales they might engage in perfunctory conversation or prologues of their own to cement the tales further into a unified whole.

Chaucer never finished this ambitious project; he died before half of it was complete. The version we possess has a General Prologue in which the narrator, Geoffrey Chaucer, describes the individual pilgrims, his meeting with them at the Tabard Inn in London, and the start of the journey. Only 23 of the 30 pilgrims tell their tales (none tells two tales) and the group has not yet reached Canterbury. There is even some internal evidence that the material we possess was not meant for publication in its present form.

Although *The Canterbury Tales* is only a draft of what was intended to be Chaucer's masterwork, it is of incomparable literary and social value. A close reading of the General Prologue, for instance—with its representative, although limited, cross section of medieval society (no person lower in rank than a plowman or higher in rank than a knight appears)—affords an effortless entry into the complex world of

277 Sir Edward Burne-Jones. Illustration for the beginning of the Tale of the Wife of Bath. 1896. Edition of Chaucer's works designed and printed by William Morris, Kelmscott Press, Middlesex, England. New York Public Library (Spencer Collection). The prologue to this tale is one of the most interesting pieces in the *Tales*. The Wife of Bath, arguing that an active sexual life is just as legitimate as a life of chastity, describes her own five marriages with great gusto. She also bitterly criticizes the anti-feminism and misogyny of her culture. Her tale concerns a clever woman who outwits a man and then lives happily ever after with him. William Morris (1834–1896) was an Englishman of great talent in literature and the decorative arts. Toward the end of his life he turned to book design; his edition of Chaucer's works was his crowning achievement.

late-medieval England. With quick, deft strokes Chaucer not only creates verbal portraits of people who at the same time seem both typical and uniquely real but also introduces us to a world of slowly dying knightly values, a world filled with such contrasts as clerical foibles, the desire for knowledge, the ribald taste of the lower social classes, and an appetite for philosophical conversation.

After the General Prologue, the various members of the pilgrim company begin to introduce themselves and proceed to tell their tales [277]. Between the tales, they may engage in small talk or indulge in lengthy prologues of their own. In the tales that he

completed, we see that Chaucer drew on the vast treasury of literature, both written and oral, that was the common patrimony of medieval culture. The Knight's Tale is a courtly romance; the miller and reeve tell stories that spring from the ribald *fabliaux* tradition of the time; the pardoner tells an *exemplum* such as any medieval preacher might employ; the prioress draws from the legends of the saints; the nun's priest uses an animal fable, while the parson characteristically enough provides a somewhat tedious example of a medieval prose sermon.

Reprinted here in a modern English version by J. U. Nicolson is the entire General Prologue.

Here begins the Book of the Tales of Canterbury

When April with his showers sweet with fruit
The drought of March has pierced unto the root
And bathed each vein with liquor that has power
To generate therein and sire the flower;
When Zephyr also has, with his sweet breath,
Quickened again, in every holt and heath,
The tender shoots and buds, and the young sun
Into the Ram one half his course has run,
And many little birds make melody
That sleep through all the night with open eye   10
(So Nature pricks them on to ramp and rage)
Then do folk long to go on pilgrimage,
And palmers to go seeking out strange strands,
To distant shrines well known in sundry lands.
And specially from every shire's end
Of England they to Canterbury wend,
The holy blessed martyr there to seek
Who helped them when they lay so ill and weak.
   Befall that, in that season, on a day
In Southwark, at the Tabard, as I lay   20
Ready to start upon my pilgrimage
To Canterbury, full of devout homage,
There came at nightfall to that hostelry
Some nine and twenty in a company
Of sundry persons who had chanced to fall
In fellowship, and pilgrims were they all
That toward Canterbury town would ride.
The rooms and stables spacious were and wide,
And well we there were eased, and of the best.
And briefly, when the sun had gone to rest,   30
So had I spoken with them, every one,
That I was of their fellowship anon,
And made agreement that we'd early rise
To take the road, as you I will apprise.
   But none the less, whilst I have time and space,
Before yet farther in this tale I pace,
It seems to me accordant with reason
To inform you of the state of every one
Of all of these, as it appeared to me,
And who they were, and what was their degree,   40
And even how arrayed there at the inn;
And with a knight thus will I first begin.
   A *knight* there was, and he a worthy man,
Who, from the moment that he first began
To ride about the world, loved chivalry,
Truth, honour, freedom and all courtesy.
Full worthy was he in his liege-lord's war,
And therein had he ridden (none more far)
As well in Christendom as heathenesse,
And honoured everywhere for worthiness.   50

At Alexandria, he, when it was won;
Full oft the table's roster he'd begun
Above all nations' knights in Prussia.
In Latvia raided he, and Russia,
No christened man so oft of his degree.
In far Granada at the siege was he
Of Algeciras, and in Belmarie.[1]
At Ayas was he and at Satalye[2]
When they were won; and on the Middle Sea
At many a noble meeting chanced to be.   60
Of mortal battles he had fought fifteen,
And he'd fought for our faith at Tramissene[3]
Three times in lists, and each time slain his foe.
This self-same worthy knight had been also
At one time with the lord of Palatye[4]
Against another heathen in Turkey:
And always won he sovereign fame for prize.
Though so illustrious, he was very wise
And bore himself as meekly as a maid.
He never yet had any vileness said,   70
In all his life, to whatsoever wight.
He was a truly perfect, gentle knight.
But now, to tell you all of his array,
His steeds were good, but yet he was not gay.
Of simple fustian wore he a jupon
Sadly discoloured by his habergeon;
For he had lately come from his voyage
And now was going on this pilgrimage.
   With him there was his son, a youthful
      squire,
A lover and a lusty bachelor,   80
With locks well curled, as if they'd laid in press.
Some twenty years of age he was, I guess.
In stature he was of an average length,
Wondrously active, aye, and great of strength.
He'd ridden sometime with the cavalry
In Flanders, in Artois, and Picardy,
And borne him well within that little space
In hope to win thereby his lady's grace.
Prinked out he was, as if he were a mead,
All full of fresh-cut flowers white and red.   90
Singing he was, or fluting, all the day;
He was as fresh as is the month of May.
Short was his gown, with sleeves both long and
      wide.
Well could he sit on horse, and fairly ride.
He could make songs and words thereto indite,
Joust, and dance too, as well as sketch and write.
So hot he loved that, while night told her tale,
He slept no more than does a nightingale.
Courteous he, and humble, willing and able,

---

[1] Benimarim (the name of a tribe), in Morocco.
[2] Modern Adalia, in Asia Minor.
[3] Modern Tlemçen, in Algeria.
[4] Modern Balat.

And carved before his father at the table.   100
A *yeoman* had he,[5] nor more servants, no,
At that time, for he chose to travel so;
And he was clad in coat and hood of green.
A sheaf of peacock arrows bright and keen
Under his belt he bore right carefully
(Well could he keep his tackle yeomanly:
His arrows had no draggled feathers low),
And in his hand he bore a mighty bow.
A cropped head had he and a sun-browned face.
Of woodcraft knew he all the useful ways.   110
Upon his arm he bore a bracer gay,
And at one side a sword and buckler, yea,
And at the other side a dagger bright,
Well sheathed and sharp as spear point in the light;
On breast a Christopher[6] of silver sheen.
He bore a horn in baldric all of green;
A forester he truly was, I guess.
　　There was also a nun, a *prioress,*
Who, in her smiling, modest was and coy;
Her greatest oath was but "By Saint Eloy!"   120
And she was known as Madam Eglantine.
Full well she sang the services divine,
Intoning through her nose, becomingly;
And fair she spoke her French, and fluently,
After the school of Stratford-at-the-Bow,
For French of Paris was not hers to know.
At table she had been well taught withal,
And never from her lips let morsels fall,
Nor dipped her fingers deep in sauce, but ate
With so much care the food upon her plate   130
That never driblet fell upon her breast.
In courtesy she had delight and zest.
Her upper lip was always wiped so clean
That in her cup was no iota seen
Of grease, when she had drunk her draught of
　　wine.
Becomingly she reached for meat to dine.
And certainly delighting in good sport,
She was right pleasant, amiable—in short.
She was at pains to counterfeit the look
Of courtliness, and stately manners took,   140
And would be held worthy of reverence.
　　But, to say something of her moral sense,
She was so charitable and piteous
That she would weep if she but saw a mouse
Caught in a trap, though it were dead or bled.
She had some little dogs, too, that she fed
On roasted flesh, or milk and fine white bread.
But sore she'd weep if one of them were dead,
Or if men smote it with a rod to smart:
For pity ruled her, and her tender heart.   150

Right decorous her pleated wimple was;
Her nose was fine; her eyes were blue as glass;
Her mouth was small and therewith soft and red;
But certainly she had a fair forehead;
It was almost a full span broad, I own,
For, truth to tell, she was not undergrown.
Neat was her cloak, and I was well aware.
Of coral small about her arm she'd bear
A string of beads and gauded[7] all with green;
And therefrom hung a brooch of golden sheen   160
Whereon there was first written a crowned "A,"
And under, *Amor vincit omnia.*
　　Another little *nun* with her had she,
Who was her chaplain; and of *priests* she'd three.
　　A *monk* there was, one made for mastery,
An outrider,[8] who loved his venery;
A manly man, to be an abbot able.
Full many a blooded horse had he in stable:
And when he rode men might his bridle hear
A-jingling in the whistling wind as clear,   170
Aye, and as loud as does the chapel bell
Where this brave monk was master of the cell.[9]
The rule of Maurus or Saint Benedict,
By reason it was old and somewhat strict,
This said monk let such old things slowly pace
And followed new-world manners in their place.
He cared not for that text a clean-plucked hen
Which holds that hunters are not holy men;
Nor that a monk, when he is cloisterless,
Is like unto a fish that's waterless;   180
That is to say, a monk out of his cloister.
But this same text he held not worth an oyster;
And I said his opinion was right good.
What? Should he study as a madman would
Upon a book in cloister cell? Or yet
Go labour with his hands and swink and sweat,
As Austin[10] bids? How shall the world be
　　served?
Let Austin have his toil to him reserved.
Therefore he was a rider day and night;
Greyhounds he had, as swift as bird in flight.   190
Since riding and the hunting of the hare
Were all his love, for no cost would he spare.
I saw his sleeves were purfled at the hand
With fur of grey, the finest in the land;
Also, to fasten hood beneath his chin,
He had of good wrought gold a curious pin:
A love-knot in the larger end there was.
His head was bald and shone like any glass,
And smooth as one anointed was his face.

[7] In a rosary the beads marking divisions are called gauds
[8] Outrider: a monk privileged to ride abroad on the business of
his order.
[9] Cell: as here used, a small priory.
[10] Austin: Saint Augustine.

[5] That is, the Knight.
[6] That is, an image of Saint Christopher.

278 Portrait of Chaucer from the Ellesmere manuscript of *The Canterbury Tales.* c. 1410. Manuscript illumination. Henry E. Huntington Library and Art Gallery, San Marino, California. The pilgrim on horseback, Chaucer himself, tells the Tale of Melibee, a prose discussion of governance that concludes that a ruler succeeds better with love and arbitration than with force.

Fat was this lord, he stood in goodly case. 200
His bulging eyes he rolled about, and hot
They gleamed and red, like fire beneath a pot;
His boots were soft; his horse of great estate.
Now certainly he was a fine prelate:
He was not pale as some poor wasted ghost.
A fat swan loved he best of any roast.
His palfrey was as brown as is a berry.
 A *friar* there was, a wanton and a merry,
A limiter,[11] a very festive man.
In all the Orders Four is none that can 210
Equal his gossip and his fair language.
He had arranged full many a marriage
Of women young, and this at his own cost.
Unto his order he was a noble post.[12]

[11] Limiter: a friar licensed to beg within a certain district—within limits.
[12] That is, a pillar.

Well liked by all and intimate was he
With franklins everywhere in his country,
And with the worthy women of the town:
For at confessing he'd more power in gown
(As he himself said) than a good curate,
For of his order he was licentiate. 220
He heard confession gently, it was said,
Gently absolved too, leaving naught of dread.
He was an easy man to give penance
When knowing he should gain a good pittance;
For to a begging friar, money given
Is sign that any man has been well shriven.
For if one gave (he dared to boast of this),
He took the man's repentance not amiss.
For many a man there is so hard of heart
He cannot weep however pains may smart. 230
Therefore, instead of weeping and of prayer,
Men should give silver to poor friars all bare.
His tippet was stuck always full of knives
And pins, to give to young and pleasing wives.
And certainly he kept a merry note:
Well could he sing and play upon the rote.
At balladry he bore the prize away.
His throat was white as lily of the May;
Yet strong he was as ever champion.
In towns he knew the taverns, every one, 240
And every good host and each barmaid too—
Better than begging lepers, these he knew.
For unto no such solid man as he
Accorded it, as far as he could see,
To have sick lepers for acquaintances.
There is no honest advantageousness
In dealing with such poverty-stricken curs;
It's with the rich and with big victuallers.
And so, wherever profit might arise,
Courteous he was and humble in men's eyes. 250
There was no other man so virtuous.
He was the finest beggar of his house;
A certain district being farmed to him,
None of his brethren dared approach its rim;
For though a widow had no shoes to show,
So pleasant was his *In principio,*
He always got a farthing ere he went.
He lived by pickings, it is evident.
And he could romp as well as any whelp.
On love days[13] could he be of mickle help. 260
For there he was not like a cloisterer,
With threadbare cope as is the poor scholar,
But he was like a lord or like a pope.
Of double worsted was his semi-cope,
That rounded like a bell, as you may guess.
He lisped a little, out of wantonness,
To make his English soft upon his tongue;

[13] Love days: days appointed for the settling of disputes by arbitration.

And in his harping, after he had sung,
His two eyes twinkled in his head as bright
As do the stars within the frosty night.   270
This worthy limiter was named Hubert.
   There was a *merchant* with forked beard, and
     girt
In motley gown, and high on horse he sat,
Upon his head a Flemish beaver hat;
His boots were fastened rather elegantly.
He spoke his notions out right pompously,
Stressing the times when he had won, not lost.
He would the sea were held at any cost
Across from Middleburgh to Orwell town.
At money-changing he could make a crown.   280
This worthy man kept all his wits well set;
There was no one could say he was in debt,
So well he governed all his trade affairs
With bargains and with borrowings and with
     shares.
Indeed, he was a worthy man withal,
But, sooth to say, his name I can't recall.
   A *clerk* from Oxford was with us also,
Who'd turned to getting knowledge, long ago.
As meagre was his horse as is a rake,
Nor he himself too fat, I'll undertake,   290
But he looked hollow and went soberly.
Right threadbare was his overcoat; for he
Had got him yet no churchly benefice,
Nor was so worldly as to gain office.
For he would rather have at his bed's head
Some twenty books, all bound in black and red,
Of Aristotle and his philosophy
Than rich robes, fiddle, or gay psaltery.
Yet, and for all he was philosopher,
He had but little gold within his coffer;   300
But all that he might borrow from a friend
On books and learning he would swiftly spend,
And then he'd pray right busily for the souls
Of those who gave him wherewithal for
     schools.
Of study took he utmost care and heed.
Not one word spoke he more than was his
     need;
And that was said in fullest reverence
And short and quick and full of high good
     sense.
Pregnant of moral virtue was his speech;
And gladly would he learn and gladly teach.   310
   A *sergeant*[14] *of the law,* wary and wise,
Who'd often gone to Paul's walk to advise,
There was also, compact of excellence.
Discreet he was, and of great reverence;
At least he seemed so, his words were so wise.
Often he sat as justice in assize,

[14]Sergeant: in English law, a barrister of the highest rank.

By patent or commission from the crown;
Because of learning and his high renown,
He took large fees and many robes could own.
So great a purchaser[15] was never known.   320
All was fee simple to him, in effect,
Wherefore his claims could never be suspect.
Nowhere a man so busy of his class,
And yet he seemed much busier than he was.
All cases and all judgments could he cite
That from King William's[16] time were apposite.
And he could draw a contract so explicit
Not any man could fault therefrom elicit;
And every statute he'd verbatim quote.
He rode but badly in a medley coat,   330
Belted in a silken sash, with little bars,
But of his dress no more particulars.
   There was a *franklin* in his company;
White was his beard as is the white daisy.
Of sanguine temperament by every sign,
He loved right well his morning sop in wine.
Delightful living was the goal he'd won,
For he was Epicurus' very son,
That held opinion that a full delight
Was true felicity, perfect and right.   340
A householder, and that a great, was he;
Saint Julian[17] he was in his own country.
His bread and ale were always right well done;
A man with better cellars there was none.
Baked meat was never wanting in his house,
Of fish and flesh, and that so plenteous
It seemed to snow therein both food and drink
Of every dainty that a man could think.
According to the season of the year
He changed his diet and his means of cheer.   350
Full many a fattened partridge did he mew,
And many a bream and pike in fish-pond too.
Woe to his cook, except the sauces were
Poignant and sharp, and ready all his gear.
His table, waiting in his hall alway,
Stood ready covered through the livelong day.
At county sessions was he lord and sire,
And often acted as a knight of shire.
A dagger and a trinket-bag of silk
Hung from his girdle, white as morning milk.   360
He had been sheriff and been auditor;
And nowhere was a worthier vavasor.[18]
   A *haberdasher* and a *carpenter,*
An *arras-maker, dyer,* and *weaver*
Were with us, clothed in similar livery.
All of one sober, great fraternity.

[15]Purchaser: one who acquires lands by means other than descent or inheritance.
[16]King William I.
[17]The patron saint of hospitality.
[18]A subvassal, next in rank below a baron.

Their gear was new and well adorned it was;
Their weapons were not cheaply trimmed with
    brass,
But all with silver; chastely made and well.
Their girdles and their pouches too, I tell.   370
Each man of them appeared a proper burgess
To sit in guildhall on a high dais.
And each of them, for wisdom he could span,
Was fitted to have been an alderman;
For chattels they'd enough, and, too, of rent;
To which their goodwives gave a free assent,
Or else for certain they had been to blame.
It's good to hear "Madam" before one's name,
And go to church when all the world may see,
Having one's mantle borne right royally.   380
    A *cook* they had with them, just for the
        nonce,
To boil the chickens with the marrow-bones,
And flavour tartly and with galingale.
Well could he tell a draught of London ale.
And he could roast and seethe and broil and fry,
And make a good thick soup, and bake a pie.
But very ill it was, it seemed to me,
That on his shin a deadly sore had he;
For sweet blanc-mange,[19] he made it with the
    best.
    There was a *sailor,* living far out west;   390
For aught I know, he was of Dartmouth town.
He sadly rode a hackney, in a gown,
Of thick rough cloth falling to the knee.
A dagger hanging on a cord had he
About his neck, and under arm, and down.
The summer's heat had burned his visage
    brown;
And certainly he was a good fellow.
Full many a draught of wine he'd drawn, I
    trow,
Of Bordeaux vintage, while the trader[20] slept.
Nice conscience was a thing he never kept.   400
If that he fought and got the upper hand,
By water he sent them home to every land.
But as for craft, to reckon well his tides,
His currents and the dangerous watersides,
His harbours, and his moon, his pilotage,
There was none such from Hull to far Carthage.
Hardy, and wise in all things undertaken,
By many a tempest had his beard been shaken.
He knew well all the havens, as they were,
From Gottland to the Cape of Finisterre,   410
And every creek in Brittany and Spain;
His vessel had been christened *Madeleine.*
    With us there was a *doctor of physic;*

In all this world was none like him to pick
For talk of medicine and surgery;
For he was grounded in astronomy.[21]
He often kept a patient from the pall
By horoscopes and magic natural.
Well could he tell the fortune ascendent
Within the houses for his sick patient.   420
He knew the cause of every malady,
Were it of hot or cold, of moist or dry,
And where engendered, and of what humour;
He was a very good practitioner.
The cause being known, down to the deepest
    root,
Anon he gave to the sick man his boot.[22]
Ready he was, with his apothecaries,
To send him drugs and all electuaries;
By mutual aid much gold they'd always won—
Their friendship was a thing not new begun.   430
Well read was he in Esculapius,
And Deiscorides, and in Rufus,
Hippocrates, and Hali, and Galen,
Serapion, Rhazes, and Avicen,
Averrhoës, Gilbert, and Constantine,
Bernard, and Gatisden, and John Damascene.
In diet he was measured as could be,
Including naught of superfluity,
But nourishing and easy. It's no libel
To say he read but little in the Bible.   440
In blue and scarlet he went clad, withal,
Lined with a taffeta and with sendal;
And yet he was right chary of expense;
He kept the gold he gained from pestilence.
For gold in physic is a fine cordial,
And therefore loved he gold exceeding all.
    There was a *housewife* come from *Bath,* or
        near,
Who—sad to say—was deaf in either ear.
At making cloth she had so great a bent
She bettered those of Ypres and even of Ghent.   450
In all the parish there was no goodwife
Should offering make before her, on my life;
And if one did, indeed, so wroth was she
It put her out of all her charity.
Her kerchiefs were of finest weave and ground;
I dare swear that they weighed a full ten pound
Which, of a Sunday, she wore on her head.
Her hose were of the choicest scarlet red,
Close gartered, and her shoes were soft and new.
Bold was her face, and fair, and red of hue.   460
She'd been respectable throughout her life,
With five churched husbands bringing joy and
    strife,

[19]Not akin to the modern dish, but a compound of minced
capon, with cream, sugar and flour.
  [20]That is, his passenger.

[21]Astronomy: Chaucer means the "science" we would now
call astrology.
  [22]Boot: remedy, relief.

279 William Blake. *The Canterbury Pilgrims.* 1810. Engraving, 12¼ × 37⅝″ (31 × 96 cm). Henry E. Huntington Library and Art Gallery, San Marino, California. As Chaucer and the pilgrims leave the Tabard Inn, the squire and the knight lead the way. The host is in the center. In the rear, Chaucer, the clerk, and the reeve emerge from the gateway. In front of them are the cook (quaffing a draught of London ale) and the wife of Bath (with her broad hat). Blake wrote: "Every age is a Canterbury Pilgrimage; we all pass on, each sustaining one of these characters; nor can a child be born who is not one or another of these characters of Chaucer."

Not counting other company in youth;
But thereof there's no need to speak, in truth.
Three times she'd journeyed to Jerusalem;
And many a foreign stream she'd had to stem;
At Rome she'd been, and she'd been in
     Boulogne,
In Spain at Santiago, and at Cologne.
She could tell much of wandering by the way:
Gap-toothed was she, it is no lie to say.   470
Upon an ambler easily she sat,
Well wimpled, aye, and over all a hat
As broad as is a buckler or a targe;
A rug was tucked around her buttocks large,
And on her feet a pair of sharpened spurs.
In company well could she laugh her slurs.
The remedies of love she knew, perchance,
For of that art she'd learned the old, old dance.
   There was a good man of religion, too,
A country *parson,* poor, I warrant you;   480
But rich he was in holy thought and work.
He was a learned man also, a clerk,
Who Christ's own gospel truly sought to
     preach;
Devoutly his parishioners would he teach.
Benign he was and wondrous diligent,
Patient in adverse times and well content,
As he was ofttimes proven; always blithe,
He was right loath to curse to get a tithe,

But rather would he give, in case of doubt,
Unto those poor parishioners about,   490
Part of his income, even of his goods.
Enough with little, coloured all his moods.
Wide was his parish, houses far asunder,
But never did he fail, for rain or thunder,
In sickness, or in sin, or any state,
To visit to the farthest, small and great,
Going afoot, and in his hand a stave.
This fine example to his flock he gave,
That first he wrought and afterwards he taught;
Out of the gospel then that text he caught,   500
And this figure he added thereunto—
That, if gold rust, what shall poor iron do?
For if the priest be foul, in whom we trust,
What wonder if a layman yield to lust?
And shame it is, if priest take thought for keep,
A shitty shepherd, shepherding clean sheep.
Well ought a priest example good to give,
By his own cleanness, how his flock should
     live.
He never let his benefice for hire,
Leaving his flock to flounder in the mire,   510
And ran to London, up to old Saint Paul's
To get himself a chantry there for souls,
Nor in some brotherhood did he withhold;
But dwelt at home and kept so well the fold
That never wolf could make his plans miscarry;

He was a shepherd and not mercenary.
And holy though he was, and virtuous,
To sinners he was not impiteous,
Nor haughty in his speech, nor too divine,
But in all teaching prudent and benign.   520
To lead folk into Heaven but by stress
Of good example was his busyness.
But if some sinful one proved obstinate,
Be who it might, of high or low estate,
Him he reproved, and sharply, as I know.
There is nowhere a better priest, I trow.
He had no thirst for pomp or reverence,
Nor made himself a special, spiced conscience,
But Christ's own lore, and His apostles' twelve
He taught, but first he followed it himself.[23] 530
    With him there was a *plowman,* was his
        brother,
That many a load of dung, and many another
Had scattered, for a good true toiler, he,
Living in peace and perfect charity.
He loved God most, and that with his whole
        heart,
At all times, though he played or plied his art,
And next, his neighbour, even as himself.
He'd thresh and dig, with never thought of pelf,
For Christ's own sake, for every poor wight,

All without pay, if it lay in his might.   540
He paid his taxes, fully, fairly, well,
Both by his own toil and by stuff he'd sell.
In a tabard he rode upon a mare.
    There were also a *reeve*[24] and *miller* there;
A *summoner, manciple*[25] and *pardoner,*
And these, beside myself, made all there were.
    The *miller* was a stout churl, be it known,
Hardy and big of brawn and big of bone;
Which was well proved, for when he went on
        lam
At wrestling, never failed he of the ram.[26]   550
He was a chunky fellow, broad of build;
He'd heave a door from hinges if he willed,
Or break it through, by running, with his head.
His beard, as any sow or fox, was red.
And broad it was as if it were a spade.
Upon the coping of his nose he had
A wart, and thereon stood a tuft of hairs,
Red as the bristles in an old sow's ears;
His nostrils they were black and very wide.
A sword and buckler bore he by his side.   560
His mouth was like a furnace door for size.
He was a jester and could poetize,

[23] An old form of himself.

[24] Reeve: a steward or bailiff of an estate.
[25] Manciple: an officer who purchases victuals for a college.
[26] Ram: a usual prize in wrestling.

But mostly all of sin and ribaldries.
He could steal corn and full thrice charge his
    fees;
And yet he had a thumb of gold, begad.
A white coat and blue hood he wore, this lad.
A bagpipe he could blow well, be it known,
And with that same he brought us out of town.
    There was a *manciple* from an inn of court,
To whom all buyers might quite well resort   570
To learn the art of buying food and drink;
For whether he paid cash or not, I think
That he so knew the markets, when to buy,
He never found himself left high and dry.
Now is it not of God a full fair grace
That such a vulgar man has wit to pace
The wisdom of a crowd of learned men?
Of masters had he more than three times ten,
Who were in law expert and curious;
Whereof there were a dozen in that house   580
Fit to be stewards of both rent and land
Of any lord in England who would stand
Upon his own and live in manner good,
In honour, debtless (save his head were wood)
Or live as frugally as he might desire;
These men were able to have helped a shire
In any case that ever might befall;
And yet this manciple outguessed them all.
    The *reeve* he was a slender, choleric man,
Who shaved his beard as close as razor can.   590
His hair was cut round even with his ears;
His top was tonsured like a pulpiteer's.
Long were his legs, and they were very lean,
And like a staff, with no calf to be seen.
Well could he manage granary and bin;
No auditor could ever on him win.
He could foretell, by drought and by the rain,
The yielding of his seed and of his grain.
His lord's sheep and his oxen and his dairy,
His swine and horses, all his stores, his poultry,   600
Were wholly in this steward's managing;
And, by agreement, he'd made reckoning
Since his young lord of age was twenty years;
Yet no man ever found him in arrears.
There was no agent, hind, or herd who'd cheat
But he knew well his cunning and deceit;
They were afraid of him as of the death.
His cottage was a good one, on a heath;
By green trees shaded with this dwelling-place.
Much better than his lord could he purchase.   610
Right rich he was in his own private right,
Seeing he'd pleased his lord, by day and night,
By giving him, or lending, of his goods,
And so got thanked—but yet got coats and
    hoods.
In youth he'd learned a good trade, and had been

A carpenter, as fine as could be seen.
This steward sat a horse that well could trot,
And was all dapple-grey, and was named Scot.
A long surcoat of blue did he parade,
And at his side he bore a rusty blade.   620
Of Norfolk was this reeve of whom I tell,
From near a town that men call Badeswell.
Bundled he was like friar from chin to croup,
And ever he rode hindmost of our troop.
    A *summoner* was with us in that place,
Who had a fiery-red, cherubic face,
For eczema he had; his eyes were narrow.
As hot he was, and lecherous, as a sparrow;
With black and scabby brows and scanty beard;
He had a face that little children feared.   630
There was no mercury, sulphur, or litharge,
No borax, ceruse, tartar, could discharge,
Nor ointment that could cleanse enough, or
    bite,
To free him of his boils and pimples white,
Nor of the bosses resting on his cheeks.
Well loved he garlic, onions, aye and leeks,
And drinking of strong wine as red as blood.
Then would he talk and shout as madman
    would.
And when a deal of wine he'd poured within,
Then would he utter no word save Latin.   640
Some phrases had he learned, say two or three,
Which he had garnered out of some decree;
No wonder, for he'd heard it all the day;
And all you know right well that even a jay
Can call out "Wat" as well as can the pope.
But when, for aught else, into him you'd grope,
'Twas found he'd spent his whole philosophy;
Just *"Questio quid juris"* would he cry.
He was a noble rascal, and a kind;
A better comrade 'twould be hard to find.   650
Why, he would suffer, for a quart of wine,
Some good fellow to have his concubine
A twelve-month, and excuse him to the full
(Between ourselves, though, he could pluck a
    gull)
And if he chanced upon a good fellow,
He would instruct him never to have awe,
In such a case, of the archdeacon's curse,
Except a man's soul lie within his purse;
For in his purse the man should punished be.
"The purse is the archdeacon's Hell," said he.   660
But well I know he lied in what he said;
A curse ought every guilty man to dread
(For curse can kill, as absolution save),
And 'ware *significavit* to the grave.
In his own power had he, and at ease,
The boys and girls of all the diocese,
And knew their secrets, and by counsel led.

Plate 23 Giotto. *The Meeting of Joachim and Anna*. c. 1305. Fresco. Arena Chapel, Padua.

left: **Plate 24** Simone Martini. *Annunciation*. 1333. Tempera on panel, 8′8″ × 10′ (2.64 × 3.05 m). Uffizi, Florence. The courtly elegance of the figures is in strong contrast to the massive realism of Giotto's Madonna (see figure **287,** page 458).

below: **Plate 25** Doge's Palace, Venice. 1345–1438. Unlike the heavily fortified Palazzo Pubblico at Siena (see figure **299,** page 465), this palace of the rulers of Venice, with its light, open arches, reflects the stability and security of the Venetian Republic.

A garland had he set upon his head,
Large as a tavern's wine-bush on a stake;
A buckler had he made of bread they bake.   670
   With him there rode a gentle *pardoner*
Of Rouncival, his friend and his compeer;
Straight from the court of Rome had journeyed
       he.
Loudly he sang "Come hither, love, to me,"
The summoner joining with a burden round;
Was never horn of half so great a sound.
This pardoner had hair as yellow as wax,
But lank it hung as does a strike of flax;
In wisps hung down such locks as he'd on head,
And with them he his shoulders overspread;   680
But thin they dropped, and stringy, one by one.
But as to hood, for sport of it, he'd none,
Though it was packed in wallet all the while
It seemed to him he went in latest style,
Dishevelled, save for cap, his head all bare.
As shiny eyes he had as has a hare.
He had a fine veronica sewed to cap.
His wallet lay before him in his lap,
Stuffed full of pardons brought from Rome all
       hot.
A voice he had that bleated like a goat.   690
No beard had he, nor ever should he have,
For smooth his face as he'd just had a shave;
I think he was a gelding or a marc.
But in his craft, from Berwick unto Ware,
Was no such pardoner in any place.
For in his bag he had a pillowcase
The which, he said, was Our True Lady's veil:
He said he had a piece of the very sail
That good Saint Peter had, what time he went
Upon the sea, till Jesus changed his bent.   700
He had a latten cross set full of stones,
And in a bottle had he some pig's bones.
But with these relics, when he came upon
Some simple parson, then this paragon
In that one day more money stood to gain
Than the poor dupe in two months could attain.
And thus, with flattery and suchlike japes,
He made the parson and the rest his apes.
But yet, to tell the whole truth at the last,
He was, in church, a fine ecclesiast.   710
Well could he read a lesson or a story,
But best of all he sang an offertory;
For well he knew that when that song was
       sung,
Then might he preach, and all with polished
       tongue,
To win some silver, as he right well could;
Therefore he sang so merrily and so loud.

   Now have I told you briefly, in a clause,
The state, the array, the number, and the cause

Of the assembling of this company
In Southwark, at this noble hostelry   720
Known as the Tabard Inn, hard by the Bell.
But now the time is come wherein to tell
How all we bore ourselves that very night
When at the hostelry we did alight.
And afterward the story I engage
To tell you of our common pilgrimage.
But first, I pray you, of your courtesy,
You'll not ascribe it to vulgarity
Though I speak plainly of this matter here,
Retailing you their words and means of cheer;   730
Nor though I use their very terms, nor lie.
For this thing do you know as well as I:
When one repeats a tale told by a man,
He must report, as nearly as he can,
Every least word, if he remember it.
However rude it be, or how unfit;
Or else he may be telling what's untrue,
Embellishing and fictionizing too.
He may not spare, although it were his brother;
He must as well say one word as another.   740
Christ spoke right broadly out, in holy writ,
And, you know well, there's nothing low in it.
And Plato says, to those able to read:
"The word should be the cousin to the deed."
Also, I pray that you'll forgive it me
If I have not set folk, in their degree
Here in this tale, by rank as they should stand.
My wits are not the best, you'll understand.

   Great cheer our host gave to us, every one,
And to the supper set us all anon;   750
And served us then with victuals of the best.
Strong was the wine and pleasant to each guest.
A seemly man our good host was, withal,
Fit to have been a marshal in some hall;
He was a large man, with protruding eyes,
As fine a burgher as in Cheapside lies;
Bold in his speech, and wise, and right well
       taught,
And as to manhood, lacking there in naught.
Also, he was a very merry man,
And after meat, at playing he began,   760
Speaking of mirth among some other things,
When all of us had paid our reckonings;
And saying thus: "Now masters, verily
You are all welcome here, and heartily:
For by my truth, and telling you no lie,
I have not seen, this year, a company
Here in this inn, fitter for sport than now.
Fain would I make you happy, knew I how.
And of a game have I this moment thought
To give you joy, and it shall cost you naught.   770
   "You go to Canterbury; may God speed
And the blest martyr soon requite your meed.

And well I know, as you go on your way,
You'll tell good tales and shape yourselves to
 play;
For truly there's no mirth nor comfort, none,
Riding the roads as dumb as is a stone;
And therefore will I furnish you a sport,
As I just said, to give you some comfort.
And if you like it, all, by one assent,
And will be ruled by me, of my judgment,   780
And will so do as I'll proceed to say,
Tomorrow, when you ride upon your way,
Then, by my father's spirit, who is dead,
If you're not gay, I'll give you up my head.
Hold up your hands, nor more about it speak.''
    Our full assenting was not far to seek;
We thought there was no reason to think twice,
And granted him his way without advice,
And bade him tell his verdict just and wise,
    "Masters," quoth he, "here now is my
        advice;   790
But take it not, I pray you, in disdain;
This is the point, to put it short and plain,
That each of you, beguiling the long day,
Shall tell two stories as you wend your way
To Canterbury town; and each of you
On coming home, shall tell another two,
All of adventures he has known befall.
And he who plays his part the best of all,
That is to say, who tells upon the road
Tales of best sense, in most amusing mode,   800
Shall have a supper at the others' cost
Here in this room and sitting by this post,
When we come back again from Canterbury.
And now, the more to warrant you'll be merry,
I will myself, and gladly, with you ride
At my own cost, and I will be your guide.
But whosoever shall my rule gainsay
Shall pay for all that's bought along the way.
And if you are agreed that it be so,
Tell me at once, or if not, tell me no,   810
And I will act accordingly. No more.''
    This thing was granted, and our oaths we
        swore,
With right glad hearts, and prayed of him, also,
That he would take the office, nor forgo
The place of governor of all of us,
Judging our tales; and by his wisdom thus
Arrange that supper at a certain price,
We to be ruled, each one, by his advice
In things both great and small; by one assent,
We stood committed to his government.   820
And thereupon, the wine was fetched anon;
We drank, and then to rest went every one,
And that without a longer tarrying.
    Next morning, when the day began to spring,

Up rose our host, and acting as our cock,
He gathered us together in a flock,
And forth we rode, a jog-trot being the pace,
Until we reached Saint Thomas' watering-place.
And there our host pulled horse up to a walk,
And said: "Now, masters, listen while I talk.   830
You know what you agreed at set of sun.
If even-song and morning-song are one,
Let's here decide who first shall tell a tale.
And as I hope to drink more wine and ale,
Whoso proves rebel to my government
Shall pay for all that by the way is spent.
Come now, draw cuts, before we farther win,
And he that draws the shortest shall begin.
Sir knight,'' said he, "my master and my lord,
You shall draw first as you have pledged your
        word.   840
Come near," quoth he, "my lady prioress:
And you, sir clerk, put by your bashfulness,
Nor ponder more; out hands, now, every
        man!''
    At once to draw a cut each one began,
And, to make short the matter, as it was,
Whether by chance or whatsoever cause,
The truth is, that the cut fell to the knight,
At which right happy then was every wight.
Thus that his story first of all he'd tell.
According to the compact, it befell,   850
As you have heard. Why argue to and fro?
And when this good man saw that it was so,
Being a wise man and obedient
To plighted word, given by free assent,
He said: "Since I must then begin the game,
Why, welcome be the cut, and in God's name!
Now let us ride, and hearken what I say.''
    And at that word we rode forth on our way;
And he began to speak, with right good cheer,
His tale anon, as it is written here.   900

HERE ENDS THE PROLOGUE OF THIS BOOK.

Art in Italy

Giorgio Vasari's *Lives of the Artists* (1550), the earliest
account of the rebirth of Italian art in the Renaissance,
treats first of all the great Florentine painter Giotto di
Bondone (1266 or 1267–1337). In his *Life of Giotto*
Vasari pays tribute to Giotto's work and also gives
him credit for setting painting once again onto the
right path, from which it had strayed.
    Later generations have accepted Vasari's assess-
ment and have seen Giotto as a revolutionary figure
not for the 14th century alone but for the entire his-

tory of European art, marking a major break with the art of the Middle Ages. Like all revolutionary figures, Giotto was more intimately linked with his past than his contemporaries and immediate successors realized, and to understand the magnitude of his achievements we must first see something of their context.

The Italo–Byzantine Background

Throughout the later Middle Ages art in Italy showed little of the richness and inventiveness of the great centers of northern Europe. Not only in France, where the University of Paris formed the intellectual capital of the Western world, but also in England and Germany, construction of the great Gothic cathedrals provided opportunities for artists to refine and develop their techniques. Sculptured decorations like *The Death of the Virgin* from Strasbourg Cathedral [280] are stylistically far more advanced than contemporary work in Italy. One of the reasons for this is that northern Gothic artists were beginning to return

for inspiration not to their immediate predecessors but to classical art, with its realistic portrayal of the body and drapery. In Italy, however, artists were still rooted in the Byzantine tradition. Italian churches were generally decorated not with lifelike sculptural groups like the one from Strasbourg but with solemn and stylized frescoes and mosaics, a style called Italo-Byzantine.

There are notable exceptions to the generally conservative character of Italian art in the 13th century. Nicola Pisano (1220/1225–1284?) and his son Giovanni (1245/1250–1314) have been described as the creators of modern sculpture. Nicola's first major work was a marble pulpit for the Baptistery in Pisa completed in 1260, clearly influenced by the Roman sarcophagi the sculptor could see around him in Pisa. By crowding in his figures and filling the scene with lively detail Nicola recaptured much of the vitality and realism of late Roman art while retaining the expressive qualities of Gothic sculpture. The work of his son Giovanni was less influenced by classical

280 *The Death of the Virgin,* tympanum of the south transept portal, Strasbourg Cathedral. c. 1220. The expressive faces and elaborate drapery show the influence of classical sculpture.

281 Nicola Pisano. *Annunciation and Nativity,* detail of pulpit. 1259–1260. Marble. Baptistery, Pisa. By crowding his figures together Nicola was able to combine the scene of the Nativity with the Annunciation and the shepherds in the fields.

282 Giovanni Pisano. *Nativity and Annunciation to the Shepherds,* detail of pulpit. 1302–1310. Marble. Cathedral, Pisa. The slender figures and sense of space create an effect very different from that of the work of the artist's father in figure **281**.

models than by his contemporaries in northern Europe—so much so that some scholars believe he must have spent some time in France. In his pulpit for the cathedral at Pisa, finished in 1310, the figures are more elegant and less crowded than those of his father, and show an intensity of feeling typical of northern late Gothic art [281,282]. Both of these great sculptors foreshadowed major characteristics in the art of the Renaissance, Nicola by his emphasis on classical models and Giovanni by the naturalism and emotionalism of his figures and by his use of space.

While some Italian sculptors were responding to influences from outside, painting in Italy remained firmly grounded in the Byzantine tradition. It was precisely this strongly conservative dependence on Byzantine models that permitted Giotto to make his revolutionary break with the past. Byzantine art was, after all, originally derived from classical art. Although its static and solemn characteristics seem a long way away from Greek or Roman styles, Byzantine painters and mosaicists inherited the late Hellenistic and Roman artists' ability to give their figures a three-dimensional quality and to represent foreshortening. With these techniques available to him, Giotto was better able to break away from the stereotyped forms of Italo-Byzantine art and bring to painting the same naturalism and emotional power that appear in Giovanni Pisano's sculptures.

Giotto's predecessor as the leading painter in Florence, and perhaps also his teacher, was Cimabue

283 Cimabue. *Crucifixion.* c. 1268–1271. Painted and gilded wood, 10'11" × 8'8⅛" (3.36 × 2.67 m). San Domenico, Arezzo.

(1240?–1302?). Not enough of his work has survived for us to have a clear impression of how much Giotto owed to Cimabue's influence, but the crucifix he painted for the church of San Domenico in Arezzo shows a remarkable realism and sophistication in the depiction of Christ's body [283]. Cimabue shows a genuine if incomplete understanding of the anatomy of the figure and, more important, uses it to enhance the emotional impact of his painting by emphasizing the sense of strain and weight. At the same time the draped loincloth is not merely painted as a decorative design but as naturalistically soft folds through which the limbs beneath are visible. If in other works, like the immense Santa Trinità *Madonna* [284], Cimabue is more directly in the Italo-Byzantine tradition, here at least he seems directly to prefigure the impact of Giotto's art.

The works of Cimabue's contemporary Duccio di Buoninsegna (1255/1260–1318/1319) are more directly Byzantine in inspiration, but here too the new spirit of the times can be felt. His greatest achievement was the huge *Maestà,* painted between 1308 and 1311, for the high altar of the cathedral of Siena, his native city. The majestic Madonna who gives the work its name faced the congregation [285], while both the front and back of the altarpiece were cov-

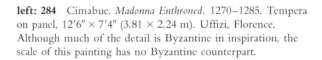

left: **284** Cimabue. *Madonna Enthroned.* 1270–1285. Tempera on panel, 12′6″ × 7′4″ (3.81 × 2.24 m). Uffizi, Florence. Although much of the detail is Byzantine in inspiration, the scale of this painting has no Byzantine counterpart.

below: **285** Duccio. *Madonna Enthroned,* detail of front panel of *Maestà* Altar. c. 1308–1311. Tempera on panel, height 6′10½″ (2.1 m). Cathedral Museum, Siena. Notice the greater gentleness of the faces and the softer, flowing robe of the Virgin here than in Cimabue's painting.

ered with small compartments filled with scenes from the lives of Christ and the Virgin. As Giotto was to do a few years later, Duccio developed the art of storytelling. The episodes themselves are familiar from earlier painters, but the range of emotional expression is new and astonishing, as Duccio reveals to us not only the physical appearance of each of his subjects but their emotional states as well. In a number of the scenes the action takes place within an architectural setting that conveys a greater sense of space than we find in any earlier paintings, including those from the ancient world [286].

Giotto's Break with the Past

Great as was Duccio's contribution to the development of painting, it was achieved without any decisive break with the tradition in which he worked. Giotto, in the eyes of his contemporaries, represented a new era in the history of art. Even if we can now see the roots of some of his achievements in the works of Cimabue, the boldness of Giotto's vision, and the certainty with which he communicates it to us, represent one of the supreme achievements of Western art.

Giotto's preeminent characteristic was his realism. The Byzantine style had aimed for a rich, glowing surface, with elaborate linear designs. Now for the first time figures were painted with a sense of depth, their volume represented by a careful use of light and dark, so that they took on the same strength and presence as works of sculpture. Instead of being confronted with an image, spectators saw the living and breathing figures before them. In his great altarpiece of the Madonna enthroned, painted in 1310, Giotto brings us into the presence of the Virgin herself [287]. We see the majestic solidity of her form, an impression enhanced by the realistic throne on which she sits. This is achieved not only by the three-dimensional modeling of the figures but also by the sense of space that surrounds the Virgin and Child and separates them from the worshiping angels.

But Giotto's greatness lay not so much in his ability to create realistic images—to "imitate Nature," as his contemporaries called it—as in using these images for dramatic effect. Rather than confining himself to single subjects in individual panel paintings, like that of the Madonna enthroned, he preferred to work on a more complex and monumental scale. His chief claim

above: 286 Duccio. *The Annunciation of the Death of the Virgin,* from the *Maestà* Altar. c. 1308–1311. Tempera on panel. Cathedral Museum, Siena. One of the episodes from the *Maestà* altarpiece, this scene demonstrates Duccio's ability to create a convincing architectural space around his figures.

right: 287 Giotto. *Madonna Enthroned.* c. 1310. Tempera on panel, 10′8″ × 6′8″ (3.25 × 2.03 m). Uffizi, Florence. Although contemporary with Duccio's Madonna from the *Maestà* altarpiece, Giotto's painting has a much greater sense of weight and volume.

288 Giotto. *Pietà (Lamentation)*. 1305–1306. Fresco, 7'7" × 7'9" (2.31 × 2.36 m). Arena Chapel, Padua.

to fame is the great cycle of frescoes that fills the walls of the Arena Chapel in Padua. In these panels, which illustrate the lives of the Virgin and of Christ, Giotto used the new naturalistic style he had developed to express an almost inexhaustible range of emotions and dramatic situations. In the scene depicting the meeting of Joachim and Anna, the parents of the Virgin, the couple's deep affection is communicated to us with simplicity and humanity [Plate 23, page 451]. The quiet restraint of this episode is in strong contrast to the cosmic drama of the lamentation over the dead body of Christ [288]. Angels wheel overhead, screaming in grief, while below Mary supports her dead son and stares fiercely into his face. Around her are the other mourners, each a fully characterized individual. If the disciple John is the most passionate in the expression of his sorrow, as he flings his arms out, no less moving are the silent hunched figures in the foreground.

Painting in Siena

Giotto's appeal was direct and immediate, and at Florence his pupils and followers continued to work under his influence for most of the rest of the 14th century, content to explore the implications of the master's ideas rather than devise new styles. As a result, the scene of the most interesting new developments in the generation after Giotto was Siena, where Duccio's influence (although considerable) was much less overpowering. Among Duccio's pupils was Simone Martini (c. 1285–1344), a close friend of Petrarch, who worked for a time at Naples for the French king Robert of Anjou and spent the last years of his life at the papal court at Avignon. In Martini's work we find the first signs of the last great development of Gothic art, the so-called International Style. The elegant courts of France and the French kingdoms of Italy had developed a taste for magnificent colors, fashionable costumes, and rich designs. Although Simone's Sienese background preserved him from the more extreme effects, his *Annunciation* has an insubstantial grace and sophistication that are in strong contrast to the solid realism of Giotto [Plate 24, page 452]. The resplendent robe and mantle of the angel Gabriel and the deep blue dress of the Virgin, edged in gold, produce an impression of great splendor, while their willowy figures approach the ideal of courtly elegance.

If Simone Martini was willing to sacrifice naturalism to surface brilliance, two of his contemporaries in Siena were more interested in applying Giotto's dis-

above: 289 Ambrogio Lorenzetti. *Effects of Good Government* (scenes in the city). 1337–1339. Fresco. Sala dei Nove, Palazzo Pubblico, Siena. Note the skillful use of perspective.

left: 290 Ambrogio Lorenzetti. *Effects of Good Government,* detail (scenes in the countryside). 1337–1339. Fresco. Sala dei Nove, Palazzo Pubblico, Siena.

rounding countryside [289]. The streets and buildings, filled with scenes of daily life, are painted with elaborate perspective. The richly dressed merchants with their wives, the craftsmen at work, and the graceful girls who dance in the street preserve for us a vivid picture of a life style that was to be abruptly ended by the Black Death. The scenes in the country, on the other hand, show a world that survives even today in rural Tuscany: peasants at work on farms and in orchards and vineyards [290].

Art in Northern Europe

coveries to their own work. Pietro Lorenzetti was born around 1280, his brother Ambrogio around 1285; both probably died in 1348, the year of the Black Death. The younger brother's best-known work is a huge fresco that decorates an entire wall in Siena's city hall, the Palazzo Pubblico; it was painted between 1338 and 1339 and illustrates the effects of good government on the city of Siena and the sur-

By the middle of the 14th century the gulf between artists in Italy and those north of the Alps had been reduced considerably. Painters like Simone Martini carried the latest developments in Sienese art to France, were in turn influenced by styles they found there, and subsequently brought them back to Italy. The growing tendency toward a unity of artistic style throughout Western Europe was further increased by

political developments. When, for example, in 1347 the city of Prague became the residence of the Emperor Charles IV, it became a major art center rivaling even Paris in importance. Around 1360 an unknown Bohemian master working there painted a panel showing the death of the Virgin that combines the rich colors and careful architecture of Sienese painting with the strong emotional impact of northern Gothic art [291]. By the end of the century it was no longer possible to identify an artist's origins from the work. The *Wilton Diptych* was painted in England sometime after 1377 [292]. One of the two panels shows the young king Richard II accompanied by his patron saints, while on the other the Virgin and Child appear before the praying king, accompanied by eleven angels. They probably commemorate Richard's coronation in 1377, since he was eleven years old at the time. The wonderfully delicate yet rich colors and the careful use of shading have no parallel in English art of the period. The artist seems to have been familiar with the work of painters like Duccio and Simone Martini, but the elegance of style and technique are neither simply Italian nor French. The painter of the *Wilton Diptych* was working in a style that can only be called International.

One of the first great centers of the International Style was the court of the Duke of Burgundy at Dijon, where sculptors like the Dutchman Claus Sluter and painters like the Flemish Melchior Broederlam served Duke Philip the Bold, who ruled there from 1364 to 1404, and his brother John, Duke

above: 291 Unknown Bohemian Master. *Death of the Virgin.* 1350–1360. Tempera (?) on panel, 39 × 27¾″ (99 × 70 cm). Museum of Fine Arts, Boston (purchased, income of William Francis Warden Fund by exchange).

right: 292 French School. *Richard II Presented to the Virgin and Child by His Patron Saints ("Wilton Diptych").* c. 1395. Oak panels, each 18 × 11½″ (46 × 29 cm). National Gallery, London (reproduced by courtesy of the Trustees).

of Berry. Sluter (active about 1380–1406) was commissioned to provide sculpture for a monastery founded near Dijon by Duke Philip, the Chartreuse de Champmol. His most impressive work there is the so-called Moses Well designed for the monastery's cloister [293]. Not really a well at all, it consists of an elaborate base surrounded by statues of Moses and five other Old Testament prophets on which originally stood a crucifixion, now missing. At first glance the style of the figures is reminiscent of earlier Gothic statues, like those at Strasbourg, but a more careful look shows a host of carefully depicted details. In the figure of Moses the textures of the heavy drapery, the soft beard, and the wrinkled face are skillfully differentiated, and the expression has the vividness of a portrait. Equally realistic is the sense of weight and mass of the body beneath the drapery.

Contemporary with these statues is a painting by Broederlam (active 1385–1409), produced for an altar in the same monastery, that combines the *Presentation in the Temple* and the *Flight into Egypt* into a single scene [294]. Here too the convincingly rounded bodies are clad in the heavy, loose drapery worn by Sluter's figures. Furthermore, the elegance and precision inherited from Italian painting are used to produce one of the International Style's most characteristic features, the careful and realistic depiction of details, like the charmingly painted donkey and the flowers and foliage that are so delicately and precisely rendered.

But for the most attractive details in all of late Gothic art we must turn to the *Très Riches Heures du Duc de Berry,* an illustrated prayerbook commissioned by Philip the Bold's brother and completed in

below left: 293 Claus Sluter. The Moses Well. 1395–1406. Marble, height of figures about 6′ (1.83 m). Chartreuse de Champmol, Dijon. The horns mean rays of light (a usage based on a Bible mistranslation).

below right: 294 Melchior Broederlam. *Presentation in the Temple and Flight into Egypt.* 1394–1399. Panel, 5′5¾ ″ × 4′1¼″ (1.67 × 1.25 m). Musée des Beaux-Arts, Dijon. The two episodes are combined into a single painting that contrasts the architectural setting of the Presentation with the beautifully painted landscape scene of the Flight into Egypt.

above left: 295 Limbourg Brothers. February page from the *Très Riches Heures du Duc de Berry*. 1416. Manuscript illumination, 8⅞ × 5⅜″ (22 × 14 cm). Musée Conde, Chantilly. The chart above the painting represents the signs of the zodiac for the month of February.

above right: 296 Limbourg Brothers. May page from the *Très Riches Heures du Duc de Berry*. 1416. Manuscript illumination, 8⅞ × 5⅜″ (22 × 14 cm). Musée Condé, Chantilly. The hunters blow their horns, but the courtiers are more interested in the ladies.

1416. It was painted by the Limbourg brothers—Pol, Hennequin, and Herman. They were Flemish in origin, may have spent some time in Italy, and finally settled in France. Twelve illuminated pages are included in the book, which illustrate the twelve months of the year. These pages are filled with an almost inexhaustable range of details that combine to depict the changing seasons of the year with poetry and humanity. On the page representing February the farm workers warming themselves inside the cottage and the sheep huddling together outside attract

our attention immediately, but the whole painting is filled with marvelously painted details, from the steamy breath of the girl on the far right, stumbling back through the snow toward a warm fireside, to the snow-laden roofs of the frozen village in the far distance [295]. In May we move from the world of peasants to that of the aristocracy as a gorgeously dressed procession of lords and ladies rides out in the midst of the fresh greenery of springtime with the roof and turrets of a great castle in the background [296]. The sense of idleness and the delightful con-

297 Duomo, Florence. 1296–1436.

298 Duomo, Milan. Begun 1368. The classical moldings over the windows and doorways of the façade serve as a reminder that the Duomo was not completed until the Renaissance.

ceits of chivalry seem to evoke the world of Chaucer, while stylistically the sense of perspective and elegance of the figures is still another reminder of the influence of Sienese art.

Late Gothic Architecture

As in the case of painting and sculpture, the generally unified style of northern Gothic architecture never really crossed the Alps in Italy. Although some of the most important Italian buildings of the 14th century are generally labeled Gothic, their style is very different from their northern counterparts. Two of the century's greatest churches illustrate this, both begun at Florence at the end of the 13th century—Santa Croce around 1295 and the cathedral (better known by the Italian word for cathedral, *duomo*) in 1296. Neither has buttresses and in both most of the wall surface is solid rather than pierced with the typical Gothic windows. The Duomo's most outstanding feature does not even date to the 14th century: its magnificent dome was built by the great early Renaissance architect Filippo Brunelleschi between 1420 and 1436 [297].

More self-consciously Gothic is the Duomo in Milan, begun in 1386, which perhaps makes one feel relieved that Italian architects in general avoided the chief features of northern Gothic style. The immensely elaborate facade, bristling with spires, and the crowded piers of the sides seem to be stuck on rather than integrated into the design. The presence of classical elements in the decorations is a reminder that by the time the Milan Duomo was completed the Renaissance had dawned [298].

Far more attractive are the secular public buildings of the age. The town halls of Florence and Siena, the Palazzo Vecchio (begun 1298) and the Palazzo Pubblico (begun 1288), convey the sense of strong government and civic pride that characterized life in these cities during the Trecento [299]. The towers served the double purpose of providing a lookout over the city and surrounding countryside while they expressed the determination of the city rulers to resist attack. The most beautiful of all government centers is probably the Doge's Palace in Venice, a city where more than anywhere else Gothic architecture took on an almost magical quality of lightness and delicacy. The Doge's Palace (begun about 1345) is composed of a heavy upper story that seems to float on two arcades, the lower a short and sturdy colonnade and the upper composed of tall, slender columns. The effect is enhanced by the way in which the whole building seems suspended in space between sky and sea [Plate 25, page 452].

For a final look at late Gothic architecture at its most typical we must turn to England, where the style of this period is generally known as Perpendicular. The choir of Gloucester Cathedral, built between 1332 and 1357, illustrates the reason for the label [300]. The vertical line is emphasized, and our eyes are carried up to the roof, where a complex web of ribs decorates the vault. Unlike the ribs in earlier buildings, these serve no structural purpose but have

right: 299   Palazzo Pubblico, Siena. 1288–1309. The slits around the base of the gallery at the top of the tower were used for firing through on attackers below.

below: 300   Choir, Gloucester Cathedral. 1332–1357. The strong vertical lines show why the style of such buildings is called Perpendicular.

become purely decorative. Their delicacy seems an apt reflection in stone of the graceful precision of the *Wilton Diptych* and the *Très Riches Heures*.

Music: *Ars Nova*

While Giotto was laying the foundations of a new naturalistic style of painting and writers like Petrarch and Chaucer were breathing fresh life into literary forms, composers in France and Italy were changing the style of music. To some extent this was the result of social changes: musicians had begun to break away from their traditional role as servants of the church and to establish themselves as independent creative figures; most of the music that survives from the 14th

301 A knight playing and singing to a lady, manuscript illumination illustrating the *Roman de la Rose*. Flemish. 14 × 10″ (36 × 25 cm). British Library, London. The romantic interlude is enhanced by the idyllic surroundings: a walled garden with a fountain playing.

century is secular. Much of it was written for singers and instrumentalists to perform at home for their own pleasure [301], or for the entertainment of aristocratic audiences like those depicted in the *Très Riches Heures*. The texts composers set to music were increasingly varied; ballads, love songs, even descriptions of contemporary events, in contrast to the religious settings of the preceding century.

As the number of people who enjoyed listening to music and performing it began to grow, so did the range of musical expression. The term generally used to describe the sophisticated musical style of the 14th century is *Ars Nova,* derived from the title of a treatise written by the French composer Philippe de Vitry (1291–1361) around 1325. The work was written in Latin and called *Ars Nova Musicae (The New*

Art of Music). Although it is really concerned only with one aspect of composition and describes a new system of rhythmic notation, the term *ars nova* has taken on a wider use and is applied to the new musical style that began to develop in France in the early 14th century and soon spread to Italy.

Its chief characteristic is a much greater richness and complexity of sound than before. This was partly achieved by the use of richer harmonies; thirds and sixths were increasingly employed and the austere sound of parallel fifths, unisons, and octaves was generally avoided. Elaborate rhythmic devices were also introduced, including the method of construction called *isorhythm* (from the Greek word *isos,* which means equal). Isorhythm consisted of allotting to one of the voices in a polyphonic composition a repeated single melody. The voice was also assigned a repeating rhythmical pattern. Since the rhythmical pattern was of a different length from the melody, different notes would be stressed on each repetition. The purpose of this device was twofold: it both created a richness and variety of texture and imparted an element of unity to the piece.

The most famous French composer of this period was Guillaume de Machaut (1304?–1377), whose career spanned the worlds of traditional music and of the *Ars Nova*. He was trained as a priest and took holy orders, but much of his time was spent traveling throughout Europe in the service of the kings of Bohemia, Navarre, and France. Toward the end of his life he retired to Rheims, where he spent his last years as a canon. His most famous composition, and the most famous piece of music from the 14th century, is the *Messe de Notre Dame*. A four-part setting of the Ordinary of the Mass, it is remarkable chiefly for the way in which Machaut gives unity to the five sections that make up the work by creating a similarity of mood and even using a single musical motive that recurs throughout:

Machaut's *Messe de Notre Dame* is the first great example of the entire Ordinary of the Mass set to polyphonic music without recourse to the standard Gregorian melodies. The Ordinary of the Mass refers to those parts of the Roman Catholic liturgy that do not change from day to day in contrast to the Propers (the readings from the Gospel or Epistle), which change daily. The parts of the Ordinary are:

1. The *Kyrie Eleison:* the repeated Greek phrases which mean "Lord have mercy on us!" and "Christ have mercy on us!"
2. The *Gloria:* a hymn of praise sung at all masses except funerals and masses during Lent and Advent
3. The *Credo:* the Profession of Faith sung after the Gospel
4. The *Sanctus* and *Benedictus:* a short hymn based on the angelic praise found in Isaiah 6, sung at the beginning of the eucharistic prayer
5. The *Agnus Dei:* the prayer that begins "Lamb of God," sung before Communion

Machaut's *Messe de Notre Dame,* then, stands at the head of a long tradition of musical composition in which composers use the Ordinary of the Mass to express in their own cultural idiom the timeless truths of the liturgy. Machaut, in that sense, is the ancestor of the Renaissance compositions of Palestrina in the 16th century, the Baroque masses of Johann Sebastian Bach in the 18th century, and the frenetically eclectic contemporary *Mass* of Leonard Bernstein.

Machaut also contributed to another great musical tradition, that of secular song. With the increasing use of polyphony, composers began to turn their attentions to the old troubadour songs and write new settings that combined several different voices. Machaut's polyphonic secular songs took a number of forms. His *ballades* were written for two or three voices, the top voice carrying the melody while the others provided the accompaniment. These lower voices were probably sometimes played by instruments rather than sung. As in the ballades of earlier times the poems consisted of three stanzas, each of seven or eight lines, the last one or two lines being identical in all the stanzas to provide a refrain.

Many of these secular songs, both by Machaut and by other composers, deal with amorous topics, and often are addressed to the singer's beloved. The themes are predictable—the sorrow of parting, as in Machaut's *Au departir de vous*—reproaches for infidelity, protestations of love, and so on, but the freshness of the melodies and Machaut's constant inventiveness prevent them from seeming artificial.

The other important composer of the 14th century was the Italian Francesco Landini (1325–1397), who lived and worked in Florence. Blinded in his youth by smallpox, he was famous in his day as a virtuoso performer on the organ, lute, and flute. Among his surviving works are a number of *madrigals,* a form of composition involving two or three verses set to the same music and separated by a refrain set to different music. In addition he wrote a large number of *ballate* (ballads) including many for solo voice and two accompanying instruments. The vocal lines are often elaborate, and Landini makes use of rich, sonorous harmonies. But in the case of these and other works of the period, there is no specification of the instruments intended, or, indeed, of the general performance style Landini would have expected [302]. We know from contemporary accounts that in some cases performers would have changed the written notes by sharping or flatting them, following the convention of the day. This practice of making sounds other than those on the page was called *musica ficta* (fictitious music), but no systematic description

302 Music and musicians, manuscript illumination illustrating a treatise, *De Musica*. 14th century. Biblioteca Nazionale, Naples. Some of the instruments of the time are shown. The goddess Music is at center, playing a small organ. Grouped around her are musicians with stringed instruments, percussion, and wind instruments. The inset shows David, founder of church music, plucking a psaltery.

of the rules followed has been handed down to us. As a result, modern editors and performers often have only their own historical research and instincts to guide them. Although the *Ars Nova* of the 14th century marks a major development in the history of music, our knowledge of it is far from complete.

The 14th century was a time of stark contrast between the horrors of natural and social disasters and the flowering of artistic and cultural movements that were the harbingers of the 15th-century Renaissance in Italy. Chaucer, as we have seen, died in 1400, the year that may be taken as the close of the medieval period. By that time, some of the prime figures of the Italian Renaissance—Donatello, Fra Angelico, and Ghiberti—were already in their teens. The great outburst of cultural activity that was to mark Florence in the 15th century was near, even though it would not make a definite impact on England until the end of the century. The calamitous 14th century was a costly seedbed for rebirth and human renewal.

Further Reading

Ayrton, Michael. *Giovanni Pisano, Sculptor*. New York: Weybright and Talley, 1969. A useful collection of illustrations of Pisano's work with an informative commentary.

Gardner, John. *The Life and Times of Chaucer*. New York: Knopf, 1976. A readable biography by a contemporary American novelist, critic, and literary scholar.

Lerner, Robert. *The Age of Adversity: The Fourteenth Century*. Ithaca, NY: Cornell, 1968. A brief but readable survey of the period covering both historical and cultural events of the century.

Martindale, Andrew. *The Complete Paintings of Giotto*. New York: Abrams, 1966. After a brief introduction the book consists of a fully illustrated catalogue of Giotto's paintings with some excellent detailed photographs.

Meiss, Millard. *French Painting in the Time of Jean de Berry*. London: Phaidon, 1967. A two-volume work, one of text and one of plates. Although technical in places, it provides a masterly survey of painting and patronage in the late 14th century.

Meiss, Millard. *Painting in Florence and Siena after the Black Death*. New York: Harper Torchbooks, 1964. A brilliant work of scholarship that treats "The arts, religion and society in the mid-Fourteenth Century."

Pope-Hennessy, John. *Italian Gothic Sculpture*. London: Phaidon, 1972. An excellent illustrated survey. The comprehensive bibliography is especially valuable.

Stubblebine, James (ed.). *The Arena Chapel Frescoes*. New York: Norton, 1969. A collection of essays on Giotto's frescoes, illustrated.

Tuchman, Barbara. *A Distant Mirror: The Calamitous Fourteenth Century*. New York: Knopf, 1978. A brilliant work by one of our best popular writers on history. The book focuses almost exclusively on France and as a result lacks some balance. A joy to read and very revealing nevertheless.

White, John. *Art and Architecture in Italy 1250–1400*. Baltimore: Pelican, 1966. A useful single-volume survey, comprehensive yet detailed. Highly recommended.

Wilkins, Ernest H. *Life of Petrarch*. Chicago: University of Chicago, 1961. An exemplary biography valuable for its discussion of Italy in the 14th century and Petrarch's relationship with such figures as Boccacio, Giotto, Simone Martini, and Chaucer.

Suggestions for Listening

Machaut's music has been recorded many times. The Seraphim label (S–6092) has a collection of his ballads and other shorter pieces. Deutsche Grammaphon (D. KG. ARC 2533054) has recorded the *Messe de Notre Dame,* which should be the focus for listening in this chapter. The Haydn Society's useful *Masterpieces of Music before 1750* has selections from Machaut and Landini on their recording subtitled "Gregorian Music to the Sixteenth Century" (HS 9038). The records in the *Masterpieces of Music* series generally are most useful.

Questions for Further Discussion

1. The plague as a literary subject has a long history. Compare Boccaccio's treatment of the plague with that of Daniel Defoe *(Journal of the Plague Year),* Samuel Pepys (in his *Diaries*), and Albert Camus *(La Peste—The Plague).*

2. Petrarch's *Letter to Posterity* is, after Augustine's *Confessions,* one of the finest pieces of autobiographical writing. Discuss the different approaches, motives, and style of the two writers. Remember that Petrarch admired Augustine.

3. Chaucer's pilgrimage group was, to a great extent, meant to be representative of medieval society. If one were to write a contemporary *Prologue,* who might be the representative personages who would replace such medieval folk as the summoner, pardoner, nun's priest, and so on?

4. While there were some continuing links, Italian painting after Giotto begins to differ noticeably from painting in the North. What are the most apparent differences in style and technique?

5. Compare the architecture of Chartres Cathedral (figure 251, page 361) and a 14th-century public building like Siena's Palazzo Pubblico. What differences in function can you detect just by looking at them from the outside?

Glossary

Terms *italicized* within the definitions are themselves defined in the Glossary.

a cappella Music sung without instrumental accompaniment.

abacus (1) The slab that forms the upper part of a *capital*. (2) A computing device using movable counters.

acropolis Literally, the high point of a Greek city, frequently serving as refuge in time of war. The best known is the Acropolis of Athens.

allegory A dramatic or artistic device in which the superficial sense parallels or represents a deeper or more profound sense.

ambulatory Covered walkway around the *apse* of a church.

amphora Greek wine jar.

apse Eastern end of a church, generally semicircular; houses the altar.

architrave The lowest division of an *entablature*. See figure 85.

archivolt The molding that frames an arch.

Ars Nova Latin for "the New Art." Describes the more complex new music of the 14th century, marked by richer harmonies and elaborate rhythmic devices.

atelier A workshop.

atrium An open court in front of a Christian church or in a Roman home.

aulos Greek wind instrument, similar to an oboe but consisting of two pipes.

ballad A narrative poem or song with simple stanzas and a refrain which is usually repeated at the end of each stanza.

basilica Originally a large hall used in Roman times for public meetings, law courts, etc.; later applied to a specific type of early Christian church.

bas-relief Low relief; see *relief*.

black figure A technique used in Greek vase painting which involved painting figures in black paint in silhouette and incising details with a sharp point. It was used throughout the Archaic period. Compare *red figure*.

Bronze Age The period during which bronze (an alloy of copper and tin) was the chief material used for tools and weapons. It began in Europe around 3000 B.C. and ended around 1000 B.C. with the introduction of iron.

buttress An exterior architectural support.

caliph An Arabic term for leader or ruler.

canon From the Greek meaning a "rule" or "standard." In architecture it is a standard of proportion. In literature it is the authentic list of an author's works. In music it is the melodic line sung by overlapping voices. In religious terms it represents the authentic books in the Bible or the authoritative prayer of the Eucharist in the Mass or the authoritative law of the church promulgated by church authority.

canzoniere The Italian word for a songbook.

capital The head, or crowning part, of a column, taking the weight of the *entablature*. See figure 85.

capitulary A collection of rules or regulations sent out by a legislative body.

catharsis Literally "purgation." Technical term used by Aristotle to describe the effect of a tragic drama on the spectator.

cathedra The bishop's throne. From that word comes the word cathedral, i.e., a church where a bishop officiates.

cella Inner shrine of a Greek or Roman temple.

chancel The part of a church that is east of the *nave* and includes *choir* and *sanctuary*.

chansons de geste Songs of deeds. Epic poems and tales disseminated by poets and *jongleurs*.

chapter The body of priests who advise a bishop and conduct services at the cathedral.

chevet The eastern end (altar end) of a church.

choir The part of a church *chancel* between *nave* and *sanctuary;* where the monks sang the Office.

cithara An elaborate seven-string *lyre* used in Greek and Roman music.

clerestory A row of windows in a wall above an adjoining roof.

cloister The enclosed garden of a monastery, surrounded by a covered walkway; by extension, the monastery itself. Also, a covered walkway alone.

codex A manuscript volume.

coffer Indented panels in a roof or ceiling.

consul One of two Roman officials elected annually to serve as the highest state officials in the Republic.

Corinthian An order of architecture that was popular in Rome, marked by elaborately decorated *capitals*. See figure 154. Compare *Doric; Ionic*.

cornice The upper part of an *entablature*. See figure 85.

counterpoint Two or more distinct melodic lines sung or played simultaneously in a single unified composition.

cruciform Arranged or shaped like a cross.

cuneiform A system of writing, common in the ancient Near and Middle East, using characters made up of wedge shapes. Compare *hieroglyphics*.

dialectics A logical process of arriving at the truth by putting in juxtaposition contrary propositions; a term often used in medieval philosophy and theology.

dithyramb Choral hymn to the Greek god Dionysus, often wild and violent in character. Later any violent song, speech, or writing. Compare *paean*.

Doric One of the Greek orders of architecture, simple and austere in style. See figure 85. Compare *Corinthian; Ionic*.

echinus The lower part of a *capital.*

encaustic A painting technique using molten wax colored by pigments.

entablature The part of a Greek or Roman temple above the columns, normally consisting of *architrave, frieze,* and *cornice.* See figure 85.

entasis The characteristic swelling of a Greek column at a point about a third from its base.

epic A long narrative poem celebrating the exploits of a heroic character.

Epicurean A follower of the Greek philosopher Epicurus, who held that pleasure was the chief aim in life.

epithet Adjective used to describe the special characteristics of a person or object.

flutes Architectural term for the vertical grooves on Greek (and later) columns.

foreshortening The artistic technique by which a sense of depth and three-dimensionality is obtained by the use of receding lines.

forum The central area of a Roman town or city, containing the chief administrative and religious buildings.

fresco A painting technique that employs the use of pigments on wet plaster.

friar A member of one of the religious orders of begging brothers found in the Middle Ages.

frieze The middle section of an *entablature.* A band of painted or carved decoration, often found running around the outside of a Greek or Roman temple. See figure 85.

Gregorian chant *Monophonic* religious music usually sung without accompaniment. Called plainsong. Compare *melisma; neum; trope.*

guilloche A decorative band made up of interlocking lines of design.

hamartia Literally "failure" or "error." Term used by Aristotle to describe the character flaw which would cause the tragic end of an otherwise noble hero.

hieroglyphics A system of writing in which the characters consist of realistic or stylized pictures of actual objects, animals, or human beings (whole or part). The Egyptian hieroglyphic script is the best known,

but by no means the only one. Compare *cuneiform.*

hippodrome A race course for horses and chariots. Compare *spina.*

Homo sapiens The zoological term for the human species.

homophony Music in which a single melody is supported by a harmonious accompaniment. Compare *monophonic.*

hubris The Greek word for "insolence" or "excessive pride."

icon Greek word for "image." Panel paintings used in the Orthodox church as representation of divine realities.

iconography The set of symbols and allusions that give meaning to a complex work of art.

intercolumniation The horizontal distance between the central points of adjacent columns in a Greek or Roman temple.

interval Musical term for the difference in pitch between two musical notes.

Ionic One of the Greek orders of architecture, elaborate and graceful in style. See figure 85. Compare *Corinthian; Doric.*

Iron Age The period beginning in Europe around 1000 B.C. during which iron was the chief material used for tools and weapons. The term is generally applied only to the two or three centuries that followed the introduction of iron, although its use as a prime material in fact continued until the 19th century.

jamb Upright piece of a window or a door frame, often decorated in medieval churches.

jongleur Wandering minstrel. A professional musician, actor, or mime who went from place to place, offering entertainment.

keystone Central stone of an arch. See figure 152.

kore Type of standing female statue produced in Greece in the Archaic period.

kouros Type of standing male statue, generally nude, produced in Greece in the Archaic period.

lancet A pointed window frame of a medieval Gothic cathedral.

lekythos Small Greek vase for oil or perfume, often used during funeral ceremonies.

lintel The piece which spans two upright posts.

liturgy The rites used in public and official worship.

lunette Semicircular space in wall for window or decoration.

lyre Small stringed instrument used in Greek and Roman music. Compare *cithara.*

Madonna Italian for "My Lady." Used as a generic title for the Virgin Mary.

madrigal *Polyphonic* song for three or more voices, with verses set to the same music and a refrain set to different music.

mandorla Almond-shaped light area surrounding a sacred personage in a work of art.

matroneum Gallery for women in churches, especially churches in the Byzantine tradition.

mausoleum Burial chapel or shrine.

meander Decorative pattern of Greek Geometric art in the form of a maze.

melisma In *Gregorian chant,* singing an intricate chain of notes on one syllable. Compare *trope.*

metopes Square slabs often decorated with sculpture which alternated with *triglyphs* to form the *frieze* of a *Doric* temple. See figure 85.

minnesingers German medieval musicians of the aristocratic class who composed songs of love and chivalry. Compare *troubadours.*

mode (1) In ancient and medieval music an arrangement of notes forming a scale which, by the character of intervals, determines the nature of the composition. Compare *tetrachord.* (2) In modern music one of the two classes, major or minor, into which musical scales are divided.

monophonic From the Greek meaning "one voice." Describes music consisting of a single melodic line. Compare *polyphonic.*

mullions The lines dividing windows into separate units.

mural Wall paintings or mosaics attached to a wall.

narthex The porch or vestibule of a church.

nave From the Latin meaning "ship." The central space of a church.

Neanderthal Early stage in the development of the human species, lasting from before 100,000 B.C. to around 35,000 B.C.

Neolithic Last part of the Stone Age, when agricultural skills had been developed but stone was still the principal material for tools and weapons. It began in the Near East around 8000 B.C. and in Europe around 6000 B.C.

neum The basic symbol used in the notation of *Gregorian chant.*

Opus Dei Latin for "work of God." Used to describe the choral offices of monks which are sung during the hours of the day.

oral composition The composition and transmission of works of literature by word of mouth, as in the case of the Homeric epics.

organum An early form of *polyphonic* music in which one or more melody lines were sung along with the song line of plainsong. Compare *Gregorian chant.*

Orientalizing Label used to describe Greek art that was influenced by new Eastern styles.

paean A Greek hymn to Apollo and other gods, either praying for help or giving thanks for help already received. Later generally applied to any song of praise or triumph. Compare *dithyramb.*

Paleolithic The Old Stone Age, during which human beings appeared and manufactured tools for the first time. It began around two and a half million years ago.

Pantocrator From the Greek meaning "one who rules or dominates all." Used for those figures of God and/or Christ found in the *apses* of Byzantine churches.

parallelism A literary device, common in the Psalms, of either repeating or imaging one line of poetry with another which uses different words but expresses the same thought.

pediment The triangular space formed by the roof *cornices* on a

Greek or Roman temple. See figure 85.

pendentives Triangular architectural devices used to support a dome of a structure; the dome may rest directly on the pendentives. See figure 174. Compare *squinches.*

Peripatetic Greek for "walking around." Specifically applied to followers of the philosopher Aristotle.

peristyle An arcade (usually of columns) around the outside of a building. The term is often used of temple architecture.

plainsong See *Gregorian chant.*

polis The Greek word for "city," used to designate the independent city-states of ancient Greece.

polyphonic From the Greek meaning "many voices." Describes a musical composition built from the simultaneous interweaving of different melodic lines into a single whole. Compare *monophonic.*

portal A door, usually of a church or cathedral.

Presocratic Collective term for all Greek philosophers before the time of Socrates.

prophet From the Greek meaning "one who speaks for another." In the Hebrew and Christian tradition it is one who speaks with the authority of God. In a secondary meaning, it is one who speaks about the future with authority.

Psalter Another name for the Book of Psalms from the Bible.

red figure A technique used in Greek vase painting which involved painting red figures on a black background and adding details with a brush. Compare *black figure.*

relief Sculptural technique whereby figures are carved out of a block of stone, part of which is left behind to form a background. Depending on the degree to which the figures project, the relief is described as either high or low.

sanctuary In religion, a sacred place. The part of a church where the altar is placed.

sarcophagus From the Greek meaning "flesh eater." A stone (usually limestone) coffin.

satyr Greek mythological figure usu-

ally shown with an animal's ears and tail.

skolion Greek drinking song, generally sung at banquets.

sonnet A fourteen-line poem, either eight lines (octave) and six lines (sestet) or three quatrains of four lines and an ending couplet. Often attributed to Petrarch, the form—keeping the basic fourteen lines—was modified by such poets as Spencer, Shakespeare, and Milton.

spina A monument at the center of a stadium or *hippodrome,* usually in the form of a triangular obelisk. The obelisk in Saint Peter's Square was originally the spina for Nero's race course in his nearby circus.

squinches Either columns or *lintels* used in corners of a room to carry the weight of a superimposed mass. Their use is not unlike that of *pendentives.*

stele Upright stone slab decorated with relief carving, frequently used as a grave marker.

Stoic School of Greek philosophy, later popular in Rome, which taught that the universe is governed by Reason and that Virtue is the only good in life.

tenor The highest range of the masculine voice. In medieval *organum* it is the voice which holds (Latin tenere, "to hold") the melody of the plainsong. Compare *Gregorian chant.*

tesserae The small pieces of colored stone used for the creation of a mosaic.

tetrachord Musical term for a series of four notes. Two tetrachords formed a *mode.*

tholos Term in Greek architecture for a round building.

toga Flowing woolen garment worn by Roman citizens.

transept In a *cruciform* church, the entire part set at right angles to the *nave.*

triglyphs Rectangular slabs divided by two vertical grooves into three vertical bands; these alternated with *metopes* to form the *frieze* of a *Doric* temple. See figure 85.

trompe l'oeil From the French meaning "to fool the eye." A painting technique by which the viewer seems to see real subjects or objects instead of their artistic representation. The most famous example of antiquity was the painting of a fly on a bowl of fruit which was so cunning that viewers would attempt to brush it away.

trope   In *Gregorian chant,* words added to a long *melisma.*

troubadours   Aristocratic southern French musicians of the Middle Ages who composed secular songs with themes of love and chivalry; called trouvères in northern France. Compare *minnesingers.*

trumeau   A supporting pillar for a church *portal,* common in medieval churches.

tympanum   The space, usually decorated, above a *portal,* between a *lintel* and an arch.

vault   A roof composed of arches of masonry construction. See figure 152.

volutes   Spirals that form an *Ionic capital.* See figure 85.

voussoirs   Wedge-shaped blocks in an arch. See figure 152.

ziggurat   An Assyrian or Babylonian stepped pyramid.

Index

References are to page numbers. **Boldface** numbers indicate illustrations and literary selections. Works are listed under the names of their creators, when known; otherwise under their titles. Architectural works and the art associated with them are listed under the cities where they are located. Unless repeated in the text, events cited in the chapter-opening chronologies are not indexed. Many technical terms are included in the Index, with references to their text definitions. For a more complete list of terms, consult the Glossary.

(continued from page iv)
227–228 Pliny the Younger, Book VI, Letter 20, translated by John Paul Hieronimus, in *Classics in Translation,* Vol. II, pp. 365–366. Madison: The University of Wisconsin Press; copyright © 1952 by the Regents of the University of Wisconsin. **235–236** From *The Satires of Juvenal,* translated by Rolfe Humphries. Copyright © 1958 by Indiana University Press. Reprinted by permission of the publisher. **248–249** From the *Aeneid* by Vergil, translated by C. Day Lewis. Copyright © 1952 by C. Day Lewis. Reprinted by permission of Literistic, Ltd. **249** Constantine Cavafy, "Antony's Ending," translated by Edmund Keeley, from *The "New" Poems of Cavafy,* in *Modern Greek Writers,* ed. by Edmund Keeley and Peter Bien, p. 138. Copyright © 1972 by Princeton University Press. Reprinted by permission of Princeton University Press. **254** Bible selection from the Revised Standard Version of the Bible, copyright 1946, 1952, © 1971, 1973. Reprinted by permission of the National Council of the Churches of Christ. **259–263** From Saint Augustine, *Confessions,* translated by R. S. Pine-Coffin (Penguin Classics, 1961), pp. 172–179, 196–200. Copyright © 1961 by R. S. Pine-Coffin. Reprinted by permission of Penguin Books, Ltd. **269–272** Chapter 24 from the *History* by Procopius, pp. 58–64 in *The Great Histories Series: Procopius,* ed. by Averil Cameron. Copyright 1967 by Twayne Publishers, Inc., and reprinted by permission of Twayne Publishers, a division of G. K. Hall & Co., Boston. **273–275** From Boethius, *The Consolation of Philosophy,* translated by S. J. Tester. Cambridge, Mass.: Harvard University Press, copyright © 1973 by the President and Fellows of Harvard College. Reprinted by permission of the publishers and The Loeb Classical Library. **307–309** Excerpts from *The Rule of Saint Benedict,* translated by Anthony C. Meisel and M. L. del Mastro. Translation, introduction, and notes copyright © 1975 by Anthony C.

Meisel and M. L. del Mastro. Reprinted by permission of Doubleday & Company, Inc. **315–317** Two tropes and "Peregrini," translated by Joseph Quincy Adams, from *Chief Pre-Shakespearean Dramas,* ed. by Joseph Quincy Adams. Copyright © 1924, renewed 1952 by Houghton Mifflin Company. Reprinted by permission of the publishers. **318–331** *Everyman,* text edited by A. C. Cawley (1956), in *Everyman and Medieval Miracle Plays,* Everyman's Library Series. Reprinted by permission of J. M. Dent & Sons, Ltd. **334–343** From *Song of Roland,* translated from the Old French and with an intro. by Robert Harrison. Copyright © 1970 by Robert Harrison. Reprinted by arrangement with The New American Library, Inc., New York, N.Y. **356** From *Abbot Suger: On the Abbey Church of Saint-Denis and Its Art Treasures,* edited, translated, and annotated by Erwin Panofsky; 2nd ed. by Gerda Panofsky-Soergel (copyright 1946, © 1973, 2nd ed. © 1979 by Princeton University Press), p. 23. Reprinted by permission of Princeton University Press. **376–416** Reprinted from The John Ciardi Translation of *The Divine Comedy,* Dante Alighieri, with the permission of the translator and the publisher, W. W. Norton & Company, Inc. Copyright © 1954, 1957, 1959, 1960, 1961, 1965, 1967, 1970 by John Ciardi. **428–432** From Giovanni Boccaccio, *Decameron,* translated by David and Patricia Herlihy, from *Medieval Culture and Society,* ed. by David Herlihy, pp. 351–358. New York: Harper & Row, 1968. Reprinted by permission of the publisher. **434–438** From Francesco Petrarch, *Letter to Posterity,* translated by James H. Robinson and Henry W. Rolfe. New York and London: Knickerbocker Press, 1898. **443–454** From Geoffrey Chaucer, *The Canterbury Tales,* translated from the Middle English by J. U. Nicolson. Copyright © 1934 by Covici Friede, Inc. Courtesy of Crown Publishers, Inc.

Photographic credits The authors and publisher wish to thank the custodians of the works of art for supplying photographs and granting permission to use them.

Photographs have been obtained from sources listed in the captions, unless listed below.

A/EPA: Alinari/Editorial Photocolor Archives, New York
AF: Alison Frantz, Princeton
AFK: A. F. Kersting, London
AH: André Held, Ecublens/Lausanne
AM: Ann Münchow, Aachen
A/Ma: Alinari/Mansell, London
BM: British Museum, London
BN: Bibliothèque Nationale, Paris
BPK: Bildarchiv Preussischer Kulturbesitz, West Berlin
CAISSE: Caisse Nationale des Monuments Historiques et des Sites, Paris, © ARCH. PHOT., Paris/SPADEM/VAGA, New York, 1981
FU: Fototeca Unione, Rome
G: Giraudon, Paris
GAI: German Archaeological Institute
H: Hirmer, Munich
HH: Photocolor Hans Hinz, Allschwill
HRV: H. Roger Violett, Paris
JR: Jean Roubier, Paris
LVM: Leonard Von Matt, Buochs
M: Marburg, Marburg/Lahn
MA/EA: Mikael Audrain/Editions Arthaud, Paris/fapc
MPA: Reproduced through the courtesy of the Michigan-Princeton-Alexandria Expedition to Mount Sinai
NYPL: New York Public Library
OI: Oriental Institute of the University of Chicago
PR: Photo Researchers, New York
S: Sovfoto, New York
S/EPA: Scala/Editorial Photocolor Archives, New York
SG: Soprintendenza alle Gallerie, Florence
WS: Wim Swann, New York

References are to **boldface** figure numbers.

Color **Plate 1:** HH. **Plate 2:** BPK. **Plate 3:** Dmitri Kessel, Paris. **Plate 4:** S/EPA. **Plate 7:** H. **Plate 8:** John Lewis Stage/Image Bank, NYC. **Plate 9:** H. **Plate 10:** Katherine Young, NYC. **Plates 11, 12:** Emile Serafis, Athens. **Plate 13:** S/EPA. **Plate 14:** LVM. **Plate 15:** S/EPA. **Plate 16:** WS. **Plate 17:** LVM. **Plate 18:** MPA. **Plate 19:** AM. **Plate 20:** Pierre Belzeaux/PR. **Plate 21:** Loomis Dean, LIFE Magazine, © 1950, Time Inc. **Plate 22:** WS. **Plate 23, 24:** S/EPA. **Plate 25:** G. Barone/Shostal, NYC.

Chapter 1 **2:** H. **3:** Georg Gerster/PR. **4:** Kodansha, Ltd., Tokyo. **5:** H. **6:** G. **7:** H. **8:** BPK. **9:** H. **10:** Photography by Egyptian Expedition. The Metropolitan Museum of Art. **11:** George Holton/PR. **12:** center and bottom: H. **13:** H. **14:** G. **16, 17:** H. **18:** top: BM; bottom: H. **19:** H. **20:** G. **24:** H. **26:** AF. **27:** After S. Marinatos, *Kreta und das Mykenische Hellas*, Hirmer Verlag, München, 1959, fig. 4/NYPL. **28, 29:** H. **30:** Bettmann Archive, NYC. **31:** H. **32:** Painting by Alton S. Tobey in the *Mycenae Guide*, by courtesy of Mrs. A. J. B. Wace/photo: Thames & Hudson, London. **33:** GAI, Athens/German Hafner, Mainz.

Chapter 2 **34:** A/Ma. **35, 36:** OI. **38:** A/EPA. **39, 40, 41:** Courtesy Lee C. Ellenberger for the American Schools of Oriental Research, Ann Arbor. **42:** Under the direction of Bernhard W. Anderson, this sketch was made by Charles S. Winters, assisted by Janet Michalson Clasper; photographed by James Stewart. **43:** OI. **44:** Mansell. **45, 46:** A/EPA. **47:** Consulate General of Israel in New York. **48:** Inger McCabe/PR. **55:** CAISSE. **56:** A/EPA. **58:** Wide World, NYC. **59:** Louis Goldman/PR.

Interlude: Judith and Holofernes **60, 62, 63:** A/EPA. **65:** Martha Swope, NYC.

Chapter 3 **66:** S/EPA. **68, 70:** G. **71, 72:** GAI, Athens. **73, 74, 75:** H. **76:** GAI, Athens. **78, 79:** H. **80:** A/EPA. **81, 82, 84, 86, 88:** H. **89:** GAI, Athens.

Chapter 4 **91:** AF. **92:** A/EPA. **93:** Rev. Raymond V. Schoder, SJ, Loyola University, Chicago. **96:** David

Seymour/Magnum, NYC. **97:** John Vickers/MPG Collection, NYC. **98:** F. Kaufmann, Munich. **99:** Soprintendenza alle Antichità della Campania, Naples. **100:** H. **101:** reconstruction drawing: From Helmut Berve und Gottfried Gruben, *Griechische Tempel und Heiligtumer*, Hirmer Verlag, München, 1964, fig. 10/NYPL. **102:** AF. **104:** top: AF; bottom: After Isobel Grinnell, *Greek Temples*, Metropolitan Museum of Art, 1943, p. 34/NYPL. **105, 106, 107, 109:** H. **110:** From James Morton Paton, *The Erechtheum*, Harvard University Press, reconstruction drawings by G. P. Stevens, 1927, Plate XIII top/NYPL. **111:** AF. **113:** From *Great Dialogues of Plato* translated by W. H. D. Rouse and edited by Philip G. Rouse and Eric H. Warmington. Copyright © 1956, 1961 by John Clive Graves Rouse. Reprinted by arrangement with the New American Library, Inc., NYC. **115:** Courtesy Professor Manolis Andronikos. **116:** A/EPA. **119, 121:** H. **122:** From Hermann Thiersch, *Pharos Antike Islam und Occident*, B. G. Teubner, Leipzig, 1909, opp. title page/NYPL. **123:** BPK.

Chapter 5 **129:** A/EPA. **130:** GAI, Rome. **131:** A/EPA. **132:** FU. **133, 134, 135:** A/EPA. **136:** After H. Kähler, "Das Fortunaheiligtum von Palestrina Praeneste," in *Annales Universitatis Saraviensis*, Vol. VII, p. 198 Saarbrüken, 1958/NYPL. **137:** A/EPA. **138:** AH. **141:** A/EPA. **142:** FU. **143:** A/EPA. **144:** FU. **145, 146, 147:** A/EPA. **150:** FU. **151:** Servizio Editoriale Fotografico/EPA. **156, 157, 158, 159:** FU. **160, 161, 162:** A/EPA.

Interlude: Antony and Cleopatra **163:** left: Culver Pictures, NYC; right: Angus McBean/Harvard Theatre Collection. **164:** far right: BN. **167:** A/Ma. **168:** (Ms. Fr. 1240, fol. 129v). **169:** A/EPA.

Chapter 6 **170:** AH. **173:** From Kenneth John Conant, *Early Mediaeval Church Architecture*, The Johns Hopkins Press, Baltimore, 1942, Plate VIb/NYPL. **175:** Dumbarton Oaks, Washington. **176:** Ara Güler, Constantinople. **177:** (Ms. Grec. 1208, fol. 3v). **178:** A/EPA. **179:** H. **180:** Raymond Bial, Urbana. **181:** WS. **182:** H. **183:** LVM. **184:** A/EPA. **185:** H. **186:** LVM. **187:** right: A/EPA. **189, 190:** LVM. **191:** H. **192, 193, 194:** A/EPA. **195, 196:** Fotocielo, Rome. **197, 198:** A/EPA. **199:** S/EPA. **200:** H. **201, 202, 203:** MPA. **204:** Ann Odom, Washington. **205, 206:** A/EPA. **207:** B. Trepetov/S.

Chapter 7 **208:** G (Ms. 722, fol. 105). **209:** S/EPA. **210:** G. **212, 214, 215:** AM. **216:** (Ms. Lat. 1572, fol. 79). **217:** AM (Karol. Evangeliar, fol. 14v). **218:** (Ms. 32, fol. 83r). **219:** AM **220:** (Cod. 1861, fol. 25). **221:** G. **222:** left: (Ms. Laud, Misc. 126, fol. 260r); right: (M.1, fol. 29v). **224:** LVM. **225:** (Ms. Cotton Claud, E. IV, Part I, 124r). **226:** both: (Ms. 170: S. Gregorius, Moralia in Job, fols. 59 and 75v). **227:** After Walter Horn and Ernest Born, *The Plan of Saint Gall*, University of California Press, 1979, Vol. II, p. xii/Univ. of Cal. Press. **228:** After Kenneth John Conant, *Carolingian and Romanesque Architecture* (The Pelican History of Art, Second integrated editions, revised 1978), p. 159, fig. 113/4, copyright © Kenneth John Conant, 1978/NYPL. **229:** HRV. **230:** M. **232:** CAISSE. **233:** Bulloz. **234:** W. Rabanus/Press Bureau, Salzburg Festival. **235, 236:** AM.

Chapter 8 **237:** G. **238:** (Ms. Fr. 2091, fol. 125). **239:** (Ms. Lat. 962, fol. 264r). **240:** top: After Prof. Sumner McK. Crosby, Yale University; bottom: M. **241:** MA/EA. **242:** JR/PR. **243:** (Cod. 2549, fol. 164r). **244:** After Sir Banister Fletcher, *A History of Architecture on the Comparative Method*, Charles Scribner's Sons, 1963, p. 531. **246:** AFK. **247:** CAISSE. **248:** A/EPA. **249:** MA/EA. **250:** © Vu du Ciel par Alain Perceval®, Paris. **251:** left: JR. **252, 253:** G. **254, 255, 256:** (Ms. Fr. 19093, fols. 5, 22v, 20). **257:** Yan, Toulouse. **258:** James Austin, Cambridge, Eng. **259:** BPK. **260:** G. **261:** A/EPA. **262:** HH. **263:** S/EPA. **264:** A/EPA. **267:** BPK.

Interlude: Abelard and Heloise **269:** G. **271:** right: HRV. **272:** Theatre World Collection, NYC.

Chapter 9 **273:** (Ms. Fr. 129, fol. 1). **274:** A/EPA. **280:** CAISSE. **282, 283:** A/EPA. **284:** SG. **285, 286:** A/EPA. **287:** SG. **288, 289, 290:** A/EPA. **293:** CAISSE. **295, 296:** G. **297, 298, 299:** A/EPA. **300:** AFK. **301:** (Ms. Harl. 4425, fol. 12v). **302:** (Ms. V.A. 14, C. 47)/S/EPA.